Clear Answers & Smart Advice for Your Baby's First Year

Dr. Ari Brown and Denise Fields

Copyright Page and Low-Impact Pilates Workout

Saxophone, lead guitar by Denise Fields
Drums, rhythm guitar and interior layout by Alan Fields
Cover/interior design and keyboard solo by Epicenter Creative
Catering by Mark Brown and the Salt Lick
Backing harmony vocals and keyboards by Andy and Julia Brown
Percussion and additional guitar by Ben and Jack Fields
Index by New West Indexing
Band photography by Tracy Trahar

To order this book, order online at Baby411.com or call 1-800-888-0385. Questions or comments? Please call the authors at (303) 442-8792. Or fax them a note at (303) 442-3744. Or write to them at Windsor Peak Press, 436 Pine Street, Boulder, CO 80302. E-mail us at authors @baby411.com. Baby 411 is a trademark of Windsor Peak Press.

The latest info on this book is online at www.Baby411.com

Distributed to the book trade by Ingram Publisher Services, (866) 400-5351

Library Cataloging in Publication Data

Brown, Ari, M.D.
Fields, Denise
Baby 411: Clear Answers & Smart Advice for Your Baby's First Year/ Ari Brown, M.D. and Denise Fields
608 pages.
Includes index.
ISBN 978-1-889392-45-5

1. Infants. 2. Child rearing. 3. Infants–Care.

Child Care–Handbooks, manuals, etc. 2. Infants' supplies–Purchasing–United States, Canada, Directories. 3. Children's paraphernalia–Purchasing–Handbooks, manuals. 4. Product Safety–Handbooks, manuals. 5. Consumer education.
649'.122'0296–dc20. 2015.

Version 6.1

Do you have an old copy of this book? Check our web site at Baby411.com to make sure you have the most current version (click About, then Which Version?).

Baby 411 Medical Advisory Board

Steven Adair, DDS, MS
Pediatric Dentist
Professor and Chair, Pediatric Dentistry
Medical College of Georgia

Mark T. Brown, MD, FACS
Ear, Nose, and Throat, Sleep Medicine Specialist
Great Hills ENT
Austin, TX

Jose C. Cortez, MD
Pediatric Urologist
Dell Children's Medical Center
Austin, TX

Lewis First, MD, FAAP
Professor and Chair
University of Vermont Department of Pediatrics
Burlington, VT

Corinne Frank, Esq.
Professional Mother

Linda Hill, RN, IBCLC
Certified Lactation Consultant
Midland, TX

Thomas Hughes, MD, FAAP
Pediatrician
Capital Pediatric Group
Austin, TX

Joyce Jordan, LVN
Pediatric Triage Nurse
Capital Pediatric Group
Austin, TX

Randy Kunik, DDS
Orthodontist and Cosmetic Dentist
Austin, TX

Arlinda Michael, RN, CIMI, IBCLC
Certified Lactation Consultant
Infant Massage Instructor
Minneapolis, MN

Paul Offit, MD, FAAP
Director, Vaccine Education Center
Children's Hospital of Philadelphia
Philadelphia, PA

Edward Peters, MD, FAAAI
Allergist, Pulmonologist
Allergy & Asthma Assoc. of Austin
Austin, TX

Sidney Seidman, MD, FAAP
Pediatrician
Baltimore, MD

Gabriella Shaughnessy, RNC, BS, IBCLC
Manager, OB Education
Hoag Memorial Hospital
Newport Beach, CA

Shelley Solka, MS, CCC-SLP
Speech Language Pathologist
Austin, TX

Karen L. Wright, MD
Pediatric Cardiologist
Children's Cardiology Associates
Austin, TX

Mark Zamutt, RPh.
Outpatient Pharmacy Manager
University Medical Center, Brackenridge Hospital
Austin, TX

R. Jeff Zwiener, MD
Medical Director, Pediatric Gastroenterology
Dell Children's Medical Center
Austin, TX

ACKNOWLEDGEMENTS

So how'd a pediatrician like me end up writing three books and being on national TV? I ponder that myself every once in a while!

As we put the finishing touches on the sixth edition of *Baby 411*, it makes me look back on the past twelve years. Boy, time flies. I was perfectly content with life as I knew it prior to June 2002. I had a great pediatric practice with the nicest families I could ever dream of. And I found child advocacy for my local and state medical societies to be very rewarding.

Then I had a conversation that changed my life. Alan and Denise Fields were long-time friends and bestselling authors of *Baby Bargains*. Based on our collective experiences, we came to the following conclusion: despite the surplus of parenting books, today's parents needed help.

The Information Age led parents to more questions than answers. The Fields were experts in writing books but did not go to medical school (maybe a wise decision!). I could answer all the questions, but I didn't have the time (or so I thought) or the skill (I learned along the way) to write a book. But I had a passion to educate parents—just like I did in my office every day.

"Write a couple chapters and send them to us," said my friends.

So I did.

"We like it," said my friends/future co-author/editors/publishers. "Give us 15 chapters by Thanksgiving."

"But that's a chapter a week!" I protested.

"Yep. Welcome to the book business."

Jotting down ideas between seeing patients, pulling an all-nighter to write the sleep chapter, and missing a few bedtime stories with my own kids . . . *Baby 411* was born. *Toddler 411* and *Expecting 411* followed to complete the trilogy.

Since the first edition was published, many aspects of pediatric healthcare have changed: New recommendations to prevent SIDS . . . new studies shedding light on colic . . . completely new recommendations on feeding babies solid foods. And that's just to name a few. It's no wonder parents are confused about what to do!

It's sad but true: any parenting book written before 2013 is already outdated. So, in retrospect, writing the first edition of *Baby 411* was the easy part. Revising the book to keep up with the pace of medicine has been the challenge. (Note to self: next time, write a book on a topic that doesn't change but every ten years.)

Life as an author, speaker, and full-time pediatrician is a bit chaotic at times, but it has taken my mission of child advocacy to a larger stage. And I wouldn't change a thing. Well, more sleep would be nice. The wonderful notes from our readers keep me energized. Keep 'em coming—we love hearing from you!

I owe many thanks to the Fields for believing in me and in this project.

Biggest thanks go to my husband, Mark, for walking down this road with me. I never could have done it without you. I also thank my sister and brothers for their grassroots marketing efforts, giving books to everyone they know, and approaching random pregnant women in Costco parking lots across the country. (I swear I had nothing to do with this idea.)

To my patients and their parents. You are my inspiration. Thank you for sharing your experiences to help other families. You teach me everyday!

I thank the citizens of Austin and the Austin medical community for their extraordinary encouragement. I am so proud to call you my friends, neighbors, and colleagues. I vow to Keep Austin Weird.

Other special folks, friends, and spiritual advisors include: the stellar communications department of the American Academy of Pediatrics, Texas Medical Association and Texas Pediatric Society, the staff at Parents Magazine and Parents.com.

And finally, I dedicate this book to Andy and Julia. I love you so much and am so very proud to be your mom. *– Ari Brown, M.D.*

Overview

SECTION ONE: 3-2-1 BABY! PREPARING FOR THE NEW ONE 1

What decisions do you have to make before your baby is born? This section explores finding a pediatrician, the latest news on newborn screening and other timely topics. Next, let's talk about your baby's doctor—what are the insider tips to scheduling appointments and what to do on weekends and holidays. Finally, it's Labor Day. Your baby is here! We'll talk about your baby's first few days . . . plus how to survive the first two weeks.

SECTION TWO: CARE & FEEDING...73

How do you care for your newborn? The first part of this section explores cleaning your newborn, diaper rash and other hygiene issues. Next, let's talk nutrition and growth—what do growth charts mean? What nutrition does your baby need for the first year? We've got the low-down on your baby's nutrition, including tips on vitamin supplements, avoiding obesity and getting enough calcium, fiber and iron. Finally, we'll break down nutrition into separate chapters that focus on liquids and solids. We'll discuss breastfeeding, formula and other liquids like cow's milk. Next, we'll discuss how to tell when your baby is ready for solid foods, including advice on avoiding food allergies. The last chapter in this section is titled "The other end"—everything you wanted to know about baby poop and more!

SECTION THREE: SLEEP, DEVELOPMENT & DISCIPLINE 207

Let's talk sleep—this section will give you the scoop on your baby's sleep (or lack thereof). We'll talk about setting up good habits and look at the different sleep "gurus" that haunt the bookstore aisles. Next, we'll look at how your baby will develop, including milestones and social/emotional growth. Finally, it's a topic every parent must deal with: discipline. We'll give you advice on how to soothe a newborn, how to develop a good discipline style and dealing with temper tantrums.

SECTION FOUR: SICKNESS & HOW TO AVOID IT! 297

Here, we'll discuss vaccinations—what's required and what's optional. We'll hit the vaccines controversies head on, including the autism debate and thimerosal. This section also covers the most common infections and diseases, with separate chapters devoted to such topics as the common cold, bacterial infections and more.

SECTION FIVE: FIRST AID—TOP 12 PROBLEMS & SOLUTIONS...............411

What should you do when your baby gets sick? This section will give you advice on taking your baby's vital signs and what to have in a first aid kit. We'll hit the Top 12 problems and solutions for newborns, including fever, rashes, trauma and more.

SECTION SIX: THE REFERENCE LIBRARY...465

This section includes detailed information on medicines, alternative therapies, lab tests, the glossary, references and footnotes.

Table of Contents

Introduction xiii

SECTION ONE: 3-2-1 BABY! PREPARING FOR THE NEW ONE

Chapter 1

DECISIONS

Picking A Parenting Style 4
Selecting A Medical Provider For Your Baby 6
Behind The Scenes: Why Is My Doctor So Late? 8
Circumcision Pros And Cons 14
Optional Newborn Metabolic Screening 18
Cord Blood Banking 20
Childcare 24
Six Commandments For Balancing Work & Baby 25
Juggling Family & Career: 15 Tips 26
The 5 Options For Childcare 28
Adoption 33

Chapter 2

YOU & YOUR BABY'S DOC: INSIDER TIPS & ADVICE

The Schedule Of Well Baby Checkups 36
10 Screening Tests 36
Who Is The AAP? 37
The Difference Between A Sick Visit And A Consultation 38
Insider Tip: The Best Time To Schedule An Appointment. 39
What To Do: Evening and Weekends 42

Chapter 3

BIRTH DAY

Your Baby's First Physical Exam 43
Screening Tests, Vitamin K, And Eye Ointment 49
Group B Strep 51
Getting To Know You: Your Baby's 1st Days 53
Does My Baby Need To Study For His APGARs? 53
What's THAT In My Baby's Diaper? 53
Why Is My Baby Turning Yellow? 55
When Do I Have To Use A Car Seat? 57
Preemie Primer 58
Special Section: The Two-Week Survival Guide. 64
New Dad 411: Tips & Advice 68
The Baby Blues 69
The Handy Feeding And Elimination Table 72

Section Two: Care & Feeding

Chapter 4

HYGIENE: THE SPA TREATMENT

The First Manicure....75
When Can I Use Diaper Wipes?....76
How Often Do I Clean The Belly Button?....76
Diaper Rash: 5 Tips & Tricks....77
Bathing Baby....78
Cradle Cap....80
Eczema: Advice And Tips....81
Sun Block And Insect Repellent....81
The Boy Parts....83
The Girl Parts....85
Mouth care: Thrush, Dental Care, and Drool....86

Chapter 5

NUTRITION & GROWTH

What Growth Charts Mean....89
How Infants Grow (Height, Head Size, Weight)....90
Flat Heads & Tummy Time....92
Calories & Nutrition For The First Year....94
The Big Picture: Nutrition For The First Year....96
Feeding Schedules, Or Lack Thereof....97
Special Concerns: Dropping Down The Growth Chart....99
Does My Baby Need A Vitamin Supplement?....100
Fluoride: Does Baby Need A Supplement?....103
Overeating, Obesity, And The Body Mass Index....105
New Parent 411: How To Avoid Obesity....105
Feedback From The Real World: Avoiding The 4C's....106
Calcium, Fiber, Zinc And Iron....109
Happy Birthday! You're One!....111

Chapter 6

LIQUIDS

Breast Milk....114
- The Advantages Of Breast Milk....114
- Why Women Stop....115
- Day-By-Day Guide....118
- New Parent 411: Anxiety At Checkout....120
- Top 10 Tips To Survive The First Two Weeks....121
- Is It Ok to Supplement With Formula?....125
- Top 8 Breastfeeding Problems and Solutions....130
- Troubleshooting: When Breastfeeding Goes Wrong....133
- Sore Nipples: 6 Tips For Relief....137
- Expressing Milk: Breast Pumps....140
- Mom Concerns: Work, Diet, Medications....143

Special Situations: Adoptions, Twins, Preemies....148
Weaning: The Guide....152
The Big Picture: Breastfeeding For The First Year....153
Formula....155
Coke Vs. Diet Coke: The Types Of Formula....155
Soy Formula....158
The Gourmet Formulas....159
Powder Vs. Liquid: Which Formula is Best?....162
Bottles: Which Are Best?....163
The Big Picture: Formula Feeding For The First Year....164
Other Liquids: Water, Juice, Milk....165

Chapter 7

SOLIDS

The Five Types Of Solid Foods....169
How To Tell When Your Baby Is Ready?....170
What Is Rice Cereal And Other Stage One Foods?....172
How Do I Know If Baby Has A Food Allergy?....177
Six Months & Beyond: Textures, Feeding Oneself, Fish....184
The Big Picture For Liquid And Solid Nutrition....186

Chapter 8

THE OTHER END

What Is Normal Newborn Poop?....188
The Top 5 Worrisome Poops....189
5 Trade Secrets For Constipation Relief....190
Older Babies: Solid Foods = Solid Poop....191
Fun Fiber Foods....192
Spit Up, Regurgitation, And Vomit....194
What Is Gastroesophageal Reflux (GER)?....194
Tricks Of The Trade: Treating GER....196
Quiz: Does Your Baby Have GERD?....198
Top 5 Worries About Vomit....200
Urine And Bladder Infections....202
Burping, Hiccups, And Gas....205

SECTION THREE: SLEEP, DEVELOPMENT & DISCIPLINE

Chapter 9

SLEEP

The Science Of Sleep....210
How Long Should Newborns Sleep?....211
Sleep Safety Tips: SIDS And Other Dangers....216
Deciding On Your Family's Sleep Routine....221
Family Bed: Pros & Cons....221
Solitary Sleep: Pros & Cons....222
Setting Up Good Habits....222

Top 10 Commandments For Establishing A Sleep Routine....224
Undoing Bad Habits....227
Top 10 Mistakes Parents Make With Infant Sleep....229
The Sleep Gurus: 6 Approaches Explained....231
Progressive Waiting or Rapid Extinction?....235
Naps....241
Special Situations: Multiples And Preemies....243

Chapter 10

DEVELOPMENT

What Does Development Mean?....246
How Do I Know My Baby Is Developing Normally?....247
Bookmark this page! Our Development Checklist....248
Failing Milestones: What To Do....252
What Is Autism And When Do I Worry?....253
Developmental Differences....258
How Your Baby Learns....261
Your Baby's Social And Emotional Growth....262
Development By Age....263
- Birth to Two Months....263
- Two to Four Months....265
- Four to Six Months....266
- Six to Nine Months....268
- Nine to 12 Months....270

Watching TV: When And How Much Is Appropriate?....273
Good Toys And Books....277
New Parent 411: Top 14 Safety Tips....277

Chapter 11

DISCIPLINE & TEMPERAMENT

Getting To Know Your Baby's Temperament....280
The 3 Rules Of Cry Management....283
10 Tips For Soothing The Savage Beast: Newborns....283
The Great Binky Debate....284
What Is Colic And What Can I Do About It?....287
A Miracle Cure for Colic?....288
Planting The Seeds Of Discipline....290
11 Tips For Developing A Discipline Style....293
Special Situations: Separation Anxiety, Thumb Sucking....294

SECTION FOUR: SICKNESS & HOW TO AVOID IT!

Chapter 12

VACCINATIONS

Vaccines: A Bit Of History....299
The 5 Biggest Misconceptions....302
The Top 15 Vaccine Questions....303
7 Truths About Vaccines....303

Vaccines And The Diseases They Stop....312
The Vaccination Schedule....312
Vaccine Controversies: MMR/Autism, Thimerosal & More....323
Thimerosal 411....327
Vaccine Additives: What are They?....329
Alternative Vaccine Schedules....330
Vaccine Shortages....331
Aluminum 411....332

Chapter 13

COMMON INFECTIONS

What Are Viruses?....336
The Common Cold....340
Humidifiers & Vaporizers....342
What Are Bacteria?....343
What's The Difference? Bacterial Infection Vs. Virus....344
Antibiotic Resistance....345
When Your Child Can Return To Childcare Or Playgroup....347
Viral Infections: Flu, Croup, Chickenpox....348
Bacterial Infections: Food Poisoning, Pneumonia and more....354
Things That Make You Itch....358
Special Feature: Ear Infections....361
7 Risk Factors For Ear Infections....362
The Infection Hit Parade....369

Chapter 14

COMMON DISEASES

Eyes: Lazy Eye....371
Lungs: Asthma, Bronchiolitis....372
Heart: Murmurs....375
Blood: Anemia, Sickle Cell Disease, Iron Deficiency, Lead Exposure....377
Skin: Eczema....380
Muscles/Bones: Intoeing, Bow-Legged, Flat Feet....382
Endocrine: Diabetes....384
Allergies: Seasonal, Environmental....385
Genitals....387
What's That Smell? Unusual Odors....388

Chapter 15

THE ENVIRONMENT AND YOUR BABY

Why Are Children More Vulnerable?....390
The Top Eco Hazards....392
Food: Additives, Contaminants, Facts & Fables....393
    Formula, Breastmilk....393
    6 Ways To Reduce Pesticide Exposure....395
    RBGH, Nitrates, High Fructose Corn Syrup....397
    Artificial Sweeteners, Food Coloring, Grilling....398

Home: Water, BPA, Phthalates, Lead 401
Formaldehyde, Cleaning Products, Carpeting, Pesticides 403
Air: Indoors/Outdoors 407
28 Tips for Reducing Eco Hazards 408

SECTION FIVE: FIRST AID—TOP 12 PROBLEMS & SOLUTIONS

Chapter 16

FIRST AID

9 Hints: Making The Most Of A Call To Your Doc 413
Your First Aid Kit 415
How To Take Your Baby's Vital Signs 415
Making A Diagnosis Over The Phone? 416
The Top Problems & Solutions 417
Abdominal Pain 417
Allergic Reaction 418
Bleeding And Bruising 420
How To Avoid Food-Poisoning 424
Burns 424
Breathing Problems (Respiratory Distress) 425
Everything You Wanted To Know About Croup 427
Choking Emergencies: 4 Tips 428
Cough & Congestion 429
Diarrhea 431
How To Tell If Your Baby Is Dehydrated 433
Vomiting 435
Eye Problems: Pink Eye, Blocked Tear Ducts 437
Fever: A Special Section 439
How To Take Your Baby's Temperature 443
10 Commandments To Treating A Fever 445
Poisoning 449
The Most Dangerous Household Products 449
Rashes 450
Seizures 455
Does It Need Stitches? 456
Trauma: Injuries To The Head, Neck, Back, Eyes 459

SECTION SIX: THE REFERENCE LIBRARY

Appendix A: Medications 467
Appendix B: Alternative Medicines 495
Appendix C: Lab Work & Tests 505
Appendix D: Glossary 515
Appendix E: References 539
Appendix F: Footnotes 549
Index 558
How To Reach The Authors, Baby411.com 589
Our Other Books: Toddler 411, Expecting 411 590

Icons

Helpful Hint

Reality Check

Bottom Line

Red Flags

Feedback from the Real World

Old Wives Tale

Insider Secrets

New Parent 411

WHY READ THIS BOOK?

Intro

WHAT'S IN THIS CHAPTER

- ◆ MEET THE AUTHORS
- ◆ HOW TO USE THIS BOOK
- ◆ NO ADS! NO PLUGS!
- ◆ SHOW US THE SCIENCE
- ◆ THE 6 GROUND RULES FOR BEING A PARENT

Welcome to the world of parenthood. Yes, having a baby is both exciting . . . and terrifying.

Soon, you'll be responsible for taking care of this little urchin 24/7, with no time off for good behavior. We've been there—and know what it feels to stand on the edge of the new parent abyss wondering just what the heck we were doing.

Once your baby is born, your thoughts will be swimming with dozens of questions . . . from the mundane (what's THAT in my baby's diaper?) to the serious (Why won't my baby stop crying? Does he have a fever? Should I call the doctor?).

That's why we are here. Think of us as your sherpa guide as you climb Mt. Everest Baby. You need detailed, up-to-date info about taking care of your baby—we've got it. You want straight answers on hot topics like vaccines, circumcision and toxic baby cereal—again, we're there.

Yes, we realize there are many other baby books out there, all promising to reveal the secrets to taking care of your baby. So, does the world really need another baby book? Let's put that into bold type.

Does the World Need Another Baby Book?

Well, darn it, we think so. Yes, if you stand in the parenting aisle of your local bookstore, you'll be assaulted by an ava-

lanche of baby books with titles like ***Your Baby's First Year: Second by Second*** . . . and our personal fave, ***We Know More Than You: What Celebrities & Supermodel Can Teach You About Being a Parent.***

All that is well and good, but we found that MOST baby books miss the mark when it comes to nuts and bolts issues–like how do you clean a baby? And feed it? And what happens when something goes wrong, like God forbid, your baby gets sick?

And let's not forget about the new addition to your family–no, not your baby. We're talking about your baby's *doctor*. How do you pick a pediatrician? And how do you get along with this person? Can you call your doc at 2am and ask a question about diaper rash? (Short answer: yes, but don't expect the doc to be real cheery on the phone).

When it comes to offering advice about medical issues with newborns, most baby books fail because, well, they aren't written by someone who's actually been to medical school. Yes, there are guidebooks written by "girlfriends" and other so-called experts . . . but for actual medical advice, we'd prefer someone who knows more about medicine than you can learn from watching *Grey's Anatomy*.

Okay, to be honest, there are a few baby books written by doctors and nurses. But we found many so boring and dry, they are listed as FDA-approved cures for insomnia. (Not that new parents will ever have that problem, of course).

And other good books on babies by respected docs haven't been updated since the Reagan administration. Sorry, the world of baby care moves at Internet speed these days, so a book published ten years ago isn't going to cut it when it comes to a topic like cord blood banking. We're proud that this book contains the very latest recommendations and controversies swirling around the world of babies. And we are one of the few baby books with a detailed web site with bonus material (including our world famous rash-o-rama section) along with detailed updates and breaking news on infant health via our Facebook page (facebook.com/expecting411) and Twitter (@baby411)

Finally, let's talk about our biggest pet peeve when it comes to baby books: generic advice. Too many books on babies are marred by a lack of specifics and detail.

We get the feeling that authors water down their advice and opinions so as not to offend any reader. While that's nice, it doesn't help when you want a specific answer to a question you have at 3am with your baby. As new parents, we wanted detailed, specific answers to our questions about our newborn–not bland generic platitudes.

Yes, despite all the resources available to new parents (books, magazines, the web), it is amazing how we all end up asking all the same questions as new parents: will we ever sleep through the night again? How come this breastfeeding thing is so difficult? How do I take my baby's temperature? And another 337 questions like that.

That's why we wrote this book–think of it as an FAQ for new parents.

Meet the New Authors, Same as the Old Authors

This book was created by the same team that brought you Baby Bargains–Denise & Alan Fields. This time, we've added a twist: a co-author, Dr. Ari Brown.

Actually, Dr. Brown has written the majority of this book . . . especially the detailed medical advice. An award-winning pediatrician in private practice in Austin, TX, Dr. Brown graduated from the Baylor College of Medicine. She did her pediatric residency at the renowned Children's Hospital in Boston, and serves as a spokesperson for the American Academy of Pediatrics. In short, Dr. Brown knows her stuff.

Denise Fields brings her 20 years of experience as a consumer advocate to *Baby 411*—as the co-author of *Baby Bargains*, Fields has been featured on Oprah and in the *Wall Street Journal*. For *Baby 411*, Denise adds in her experience as both a mom and author—many of the questions we get on our message boards hit the same hot button issues you'll see here.

As always, the secret sauce to our books is reader feedback. First, you'll notice readers of our previous books contributed to this book—you'll see their "Real World Feedback" when it comes to topics like child care, feeding and more. Second, look at the questions we list in each chapter. These are the frequent questions asked by patients of Dr. Brown and the readers of *Baby Bargains* . . . and the same questions that most first-time parents ponder.

Yes, both of the authors of this book are also mommies. They have four children between them. Best of all, the authors are from your generation—we know you want detailed info, the latest research and trends, plus handy web resources. We know you want to go online to get the latest updates, so we've created a special web site for this book (Baby411.com). There you can read any breaking news on our blog, swap stories with other parents on our message boards and sign up for a free newsletter. Fan our facebook page (facebook.com/expecting411) or follow us on Twitter (twitter.com/baby411). And download our free iPhone app (Baby 411) for news updates, video links and more.

How to Use this Book

Instructions: Open cover. Start reading.

Just kidding! We realize you know how to read a book, but let's go over a few details on how to get the most out of *Baby 411*.

First, let's talk about BIG UGLY LATIN WORDS. You can't discuss baby's health without whipping out the Latin. To keep the jargon from overwhelming you, we have a handy glossary at the end of this book. When you see a **LATIN WORD** in bold small caps, turn to the back to get a quick definition.

Second, if you flip through the chapters, you'll note boxes with Dr. B's opinion. As it sounds, these are her *opinions* on several hot button issues. Feel free to disagree with these thoughts, but they are based on years of seeing real-world patients and talking with parents. Unlike some other parenting books, we think readers deserve to know where the line is drawn between fact and opinion. You can then decide what works for you and your family.

Finally, let's talk footnotes—we've footnoted the sources used throughout this book. These references are in Appendix F in the back of the book.

No Ads? No Plugs?

Yes, that's true—as with all our books, this guide contains ZERO ads, spam and commercial plugs. No pharmaceutical or formula company has paid the authors to plug their products in this book. Dr. Brown does NOT go on all-

expense paid junkets to Aruba to learn about the latest drug or medical research (although she could use a beach vacation after writing this book). The opinions in this book are those of Denise Fields and Dr. Brown–in the latter case, based on her training and experience practicing pediatric medicine.

Unlike other doctor-authors, we don't sell our own line of fish oil supplements or baby slings. You won't find us doing ads for homeopathic nasal sprays. We do this to remain objective–this makes sure the info you get here is based on the best scientific research, not who pays us a commission, ad fee or royalty.

Full disclosure: Windsor Peak Press does offer a "custom publishing" program that allows companies or organizations to purchase bulk copies of our books to give away to their customers, clients or employees. These books are often specially printed with a company logo and (sometimes) a customized title page. Such arrangements do NOT imply an endorsement or recommendation of the company or its products by Windsor Peak Press, this book or its authors.

Show us the Science!

The goal of *Baby 411* is to provide you with the most up-to-date medical info on your baby. We're talking state-of-the-art when it comes to your baby's health and nutrition.

So, in the age of Internet rumors and 24/7 cable news, let's take a moment to talk SCIENCE.

When it comes to your baby's health, our mantra is SHOW US THE SCIENCE! Before we recommend a particular treatment, parenting method or medicine, we expect there to be good science behind it.

What is good science? Good scientific research is conducted by reputable researchers and published in a major medical journal, like the *New England Journal of Medicine*. Good science is based on a large enough sample to be statistically significant–and verified by peers before it is published.

Contrast this to junk science. Much of what you see online is, unfortunately, junk science–"research" done by questionable individuals who are usually trying to sell a miracle cure along with their theories. Junk science is often based on flawed studies that use too-small samples to be relevant. Just because four of your friends have babies with blue eyes does not mean there is an epidemic of blue-eyed babies on your block.

Much of the junk science you see online or read in the media is there to push a political agenda. Sure, these zealots are well meaning, but they harm their cause by hyping some obscure study from a doctor in Fiji as medical "truth."

Of course, this isn't always so black and white–sometimes good science is "spun" or hyped by groups who want to push their cause. And, sometimes bad science is too tempting for the media to ignore.

To put this in perspective, let's look at this example: a 2008 study from Cornell University compared the rates of autism and the amount of rainfall in a community. Researchers took a weak hypothesis (that spending excessive time indoors would increase the chances of having autism), performed mathematical acrobatics and presto! Rain = autism. If you live in a community with lots of rain, your child has an increased chance of autism, the study declared.

Bottom line: this was a flawed study that never should have been published in the first place.

Of course, that didn't matter to the media. Outlets like *USA Today* and MSNBC reported that rainfall and autism were linked. And some autism advocacy groups used this study as proof that indoor environmental toxins were surely the reason for their children's diagnoses. None of which is true.

This is just one example of how "science" gets distorted and warped as it winds its way through the meat grinder of the web and media these days.

Here's the take-home message: as your guides in Baby Health Land, we hope to steer you toward the *good* science when making decisions for your baby.

What's New In This Edition?

As usual, we just can't leave well enough alone! This updated and expanded version of *Baby 411* covers the latest, breaking health news on babies. Here's a quick look at what's new:

Sleep safety continues to be in the headlines, as leading experts take a firm position against bed sharing with infants. We'll go over the safest ways for your baby to sleep. And speaking of sleep, how do you convince your baby to sleep through the night? Our revamped sleep chapter has the answers you are looking for.

After the recent whooping cough outbreaks made national headlines, we've got the updated guidelines on how to protect your child from this potentially deadly infectious disease.

And what about technology and babies? Even though your baby might be able to navigate an iPad better than you, is it a good idea to let him? We'll give you some straight talk on screen time, as one of the authors of this book (Dr. Brown) wrote the national policy statement for the American Academy of Pediatrics on media use and young children.

And, like every new edition, you can be sure you are reading the most recent research and data on every child health topic.

Now that you know what's new, let's go over some ground rules.

Baby411.com: Advice, How-To Videos & More—All Free!

Wish you could have all the info in Baby 411 on your tablet, laptop and mobile phone? Our newly expanded web site, Baby411.com does all that and more–all the advice from all three of the best-selling 411 books (Expecting 411, Baby 411, and Toddler 411) is online to read.

And here's the best part: it's free! Pop a question into the search engine. Browse a topic with detailed questions and answers. Watch how-to videos on everything from soothing a fussy baby to potty training. Check it out at Baby411.com.

The Six Ground Rules for Being a Good Parent

1 **THERE ARE NO GROUND RULES.** Well, what we mean is there are no absolute truths. Thanks to that quirky thing called DNA, every baby

is different. Yes, there are "general" guidelines that will help you be a good parent (and we'll spend the next 500+ pages giving you those guidelines), but there are no absolute truths. Your baby will consistently amaze, surprise, frustrate and confound you. Did we mention surprise?

2 **CHECK YOUR PRIORITIES AT THE DOOR.** Make a list of all things that are important in your life–your friends, house, etc. Now, crunch that list up into a little ball and throw it out the window. Your baby is now priorities #1 through #17. Example: your house. Don't expect it to be clean again until 2026.

3 **GO WITH YOUR GUT.** Well-meaning people–friends, your parents, book authors, complete strangers–are going to try to advise you as to what's best for you and your baby. That's nice, but after a while you are just going to have figure out this parent thing on your own. Think of it like flying a plane . . . you can sit in a flight simulator all you want, but taking the controls in a 747 zipping along at 500 MPH at 30,000 feet is more like what it feels like to be a real parent.

4 **SCHEDULE TIME FOR YOURSELF.** Want to take a shower after your baby is born? You've got to schedule that 15 minutes. After the first couple of months (or sooner), take time OFF from being mommy and daddy. Have a friend or babysitter watch the baby and go out to dinner and a movie. Give your spouse a break once a week for an hour of "hobby time."

5 **CALLING ALL FAVORS.** Don't be afraid to ask for help–and feel free to lean on your friends and relatives, at least through the first few weeks.

6 **BELIEVE IN YOUR CHOICES.** No matter what you decide for your family (breastfeeding, work, child care, etc), you're going to hear sniping from others. Often, guilt-driven folks feel defensive about what they decided for their own kids . . . so, they take it out on you. Nice, eh? The best advice: surround yourself with supportive friends who can counter any negativism.

Major Legal Disclaimer

No medical book about babies is complete without that ubiquitous legal disclaimer . . . so here's ours:

The information we provide in this book is intended to help families understand their baby's medical issues. It is NOT intended to replace the advice of your doctor. Before you start any medical treatment, always check in with your baby's doctor who can counsel you on the specific needs of your baby.

We have made a tremendous effort to give you the most up-to-date medical info available. However, medical research is constantly providing new insight into pediatric healthcare. That's why we have an accompanying website at Baby411.com to give you the latest breaking updates (and why you should also discuss your baby's medical care with your baby's doc).

Okay, enough of the introductions–let's get rolling. First up: preparing for your new baby. You've got decisions to make . . . we'll discuss this first.

Section 1

3-2-1 Baby!

Preparing for the New One

Decisions

Chapter 1

"When choosing between two evils, always choose the one you haven't tried yet."
~ Mae West

What's in this Chapter

- Picking a parenting style
- Selecting a medical provider for your baby
- Circumcision pros & cons
- Optional newborn metabolic screening
- Cord blood banking
- Childcare options
- Adoption options

Yes, your job as a parent begins the moment your baby is conceived. You will find yourself instinctively making decisions from a parent's viewpoint. Maybe it's the hormones. Or, maybe for the first time in your life, you have a sense of responsibility to a helpless little urchin inside of you. Yes, YOU are now a GROWN-UP.

This sense of responsibility will cause you to ponder the questions that all parents ponder.

1. **Will I be a good parent?** (Babysitting and pet ownership are helpful job experiences.)
2. **Can I be as good a parent as my parents were?** (Yes. You've learned from their mistakes!)
3. **Will I handle discipline dilemmas better than my friends do?** (Maybe. It's very easy to be critical when you aren't yet a parent.)
4. **Will I make the right decisions for my child's health?** (That's why we're here–to help point the way to the best choices for you and your child).

Hopefully you will get a chance to read this chapter before your baby is born because it addresses decisions you will need to make before D-day (delivery day). But even if you pick up this book after labor and delivery is over, we can still help. First, we'll discuss parenting styles–yep, you should pick one BEFORE any other decisions are made. That's because your style will impact all those other choices. Then let's talk about finding the baby's doctor. Unlike most experiences you've had with doctors, this one you actually pick before you need her. Next, it's on to some controversial topics like circumcision, optional newborn metabolic screening, and banking your newborn's cord blood. Yes, your parents never had to deal with all these issues.

Finally, let's talk about that endless debate: childcare. Is it better to stay at home with your baby or can you work outside the home and be guilt-free? We'll discuss the latest research and give our perspective as real-life moms. What are the options for childcare? We'll discuss the choices. Our advice: you must at least mull over this issue before baby is born—that's because other expectant parents are already putting their names on waiting lists for the hottest day care options in your community now.

If you are adopting a baby, we'll discuss the decisions you'll face in this chapter as well.

With all these decisions that need to be made, let's get rolling. In order to make some sense of this, let's start with a timeline of what you should decide and when (see below). If you are joining us after reading *Expecting 411,* you will see that the parenthood prep topics overlap with this chapter in *Baby 411*. However, you'll get more detail on these topics here.

Once you have reached your seventh month of pregnancy, it's time to make some decisions. No, we're not talking about choosing names or wallpaper designs. Now you'll have to make choices that will affect how you raise your child together as a team (that includes moms, dads, grandparents, etc.). First and foremost is determining your team's parenting style.

Picking a Parenting Style

Q. How do I pick a parenting style?

Remember Dorothy in the Wizard of Oz? She always wore the shoes she needed to take her home, but didn't realize it. You, New Parent, are wearing the shoes. You have the skills and instincts to be a great parent.

Baby 411 Decision Timeline

DECISION	WHEN IT NEEDS TO HAPPEN
Childbirth classes	28-34 weeks (of pregnancy)
Breastfeeding class	32-38 weeks
Infant CPR class	Ideally, before delivery
Recommended tests	First 20 weeks
Cord blood banking	Anytime before delivery
Circumcision decision	32-36 weeks
Expanded newborn screen	Before delivery
Hire a doula	Start interviews at 28 weeks
Select a pediatrician	28-34 weeks
Find lactation consultant	Ideally, before delivery
Work/childcare options	Ideally, before delivery
Make a will	Now

TRUST YOURSELF.

Your style reflects your approach to certain situations. This includes food (breast vs. formula), sleep (family bed vs. crib), and discipline of your newest family member.

Every generation of parents faces "trendy" choices, but honestly, there are really just a few child-rearing philosophies and the pendulum has been swinging back and forth for years. The styles differ in parents' responsiveness and expectations of their kids.

Here are the four basic schools of thought:

1 **POSITIVE PARENTING.** This household is run like a democracy. Positive parents set up rules and expect their children to follow them. These rules and limits guide children's behavior. Although there are clear expectations, positive parents are willing to listen to their children's perspective and problem-solve together. The hallmarks of positive parenting are fairness, consistency, and parent-child relationships based on mutual respect. Positive parents are inclined to establish sleep and feeding routines for their babies. Kids who grow up in these households turn out to be pretty independent and have high self-esteem.

2 **AUTHORITARIAN PARENTING.** This is a dictatorship. Mom and Dad know best. Authoritarian parents have firm rules and high expectations and do not want to hear the child's opinion. Because these households are more parent-centered than child-centered, authoritarian parents try to establish rigid sleep and feeding routines very early in infancy. They tend to use negative forms of discipline, like spanking. Children who grow up in these households are more likely to have poor self-esteem and rebel later in life. This parenting style is less popular today, but some families still choose it based on their personal values.

3 **PERMISSIVE PARENTING.** Welcome to anarchy. Permissive parents are very responsive to their children, but they don't set up limits, rules, or expectations. In these households, parents are friends with their kids, but not leaders or advisors. As you might expect, the result is usually chaos.

4 **ATTACHMENT PARENTING.** Sorry, we don't have a government analogy for this one. Attachment parents are highly responsive to their child, 24/7. The Attachment Parenting movement of today pays homage to 1950's research that showed children who form a tight parent-child bond are more confident and secure. That seems obvious, right? Well, this was ground breaking at the time, as other experts were warning that parents who were too affectionate to their kids made children weak or clingy. Attachment parents respond to their child's needs day and night—hence, sleep training that involves crying is discouraged. The emphasis is on human touch, breastfeeding, baby-wearing, non-physical forms of discipline, and parents being the primary caregiver.

You will find that some parents (and experts) can be very passionate about these camps. Don't let friends, family, or random bloggers dictate how you raise your child.

The take-home message: often what works for families is a blend of parenting styles. But it is up to you to decide as a family what works for you.

You and your partner will need to discuss these issues and come to terms that are agreeable to both. Remember when you had to agree on a china pattern for your wedding registry? (Hopefully there will be fewer arguments). You *both* need to be happy about your strategy. This can be modified once you really have a baby to care for, but it helps to have some of the ground rules in place..

Be flexible–sometimes the best parenting style is a combination of approaches, mixing a bit of this and some of that. Your style may change over time as well. And yes, your parenting style will change out of sheer necessity when you have more than one child. You will be more confident in your skills, and you won't have time to sweat the small stuff. That's why children have certain personality traits based on their birth order.

Remember, you are giving your child roots and wings–a solid foundation that fosters her independence.

Finally, federal law requires us to warn you of the following: you may not agree with some parts of this book. . . especially if you feel strongly about one parenting school of thought. We don't mean to be flip, but we didn't write this book to advance a political agenda. Instead, our goal is to be pro-science. We want to arm you with the best and latest research and medical information. Then you decide how to raise your baby.

Yep, we realize folks feel passionately about certain parenting issues (just take a look at the debate on circumcision, coming later in this chapter). But we ask you to look at our book as a whole . . . take the parts of this book that work for you and combine them with other parenting advice (from friends, other books) to create your own parenting style.

Selecting a Doctor

Q. Do I need to select a pediatrician before the baby is born? If so, why?

Yes. It's helpful to meet a pediatrician (at a prenatal consultation) before the baby is born. Here are three reasons:

1. **It gives the pediatrician a chance to review any medical problems** during your pregnancy or with your family members that could affect the baby. (The doctor appreciates being prepared.)
2. **You can get advice** regarding medical decisions you'll be making in the first few days of your baby's life. (You'll appreciate being prepared.)
3. **You will be more relaxed** knowing who is examining and advising you in the hospital–yes, your pediatrician will come to visit both you and baby right there in the maternity ward. (More details in the Birth Day chapter.)

Q. So, how do I pick a pediatrician?

Ask your OB-GYN for a recommendation or consult with friends, relatives or other parents. Then, schedule a "prenatal consultation" with each candidate (keep the list short to maintain your sanity). While doctors consider this meeting a consultation, it's really a job interview–you are considering hiring this doctor to take care of your baby, from birth to college. Consider your prenatal consultation as parent-doctor bonding time.

Q. When should I schedule a prenatal consultation?

Schedule a consult as you begin your third trimester. Don't wait any later than your 36th week. Why so early? Two reasons: first, to get some help making the medical decisions you need to make about your newborn. Second, because your pregnancy and due date are unpredictable–your baby could be early. You don't want to be shopping for a pediatrician while you are recovering from labor!

Q. Do pediatricians charge a fee for prenatal consultations?

Some do, some don't.

Pediatricians are about the only physician specialists who routinely schedule "meet the doctor" visits. Such visits aren't just for the parent's benefit–it helps give the doctor a heads up about any potential medical problems the baby may have. Don't be offended if you get a bill–it is perfectly kosher. Pediatricians are offering their time to answer parenting questions–and some parents come in with *lots* of questions! A smart move: when you schedule the appointment, ask if there is a charge for the prenatal visit.

Q. What general questions should I ask at a prenatal consultation?

If you've read any pregnancy book, you've seen a list of questions to ask at your prenatal visit. Here is some advice: ignore those cookie-cutter lists and make your own, based on the issues that are important to you. This could include:

1. **Ask questions about topics you are wondering about.** You may be so overwhelmed, you can't come up with specifics and that's okay–just pick the topic and we can fill in the details. Example: allergies. You might discuss how to avoid food allergies or the history of allergies in your family.
2. **Ask open-ended questions.** You definitely want to get a feel for how you and the doc communicate. Questions with "yes" or "no" responses don't lead to conversation.
3. **Ask questions about how the practice flows.** There is more to your office experience than your doctor. You need to be an informed consumer. Medical care has changed dramatically since you were a kid. We'll discuss more details on this next.

BOTTOM LINE: You don't have to ask *every* question that you have in your first meeting with your pediatrician.

Q. Okay, what smart questions SHOULD parents ask of a pediatrician?

Let us walk you through a typical prenatal visit and tell you what parents USUALLY ask . . . and what questions parents SHOULD ask instead. (Note: at the end of this section, we'll organize all these questions you should ask in one handy list).

Parent asks: What is your training?
A better question: How did you decide on pediatrics?

All pediatricians have about the same training. Just look on the wall. We spent a lot of time and money to get all those degrees. Our parents would kill us if we didn't get them framed and hung up in our office. Pediatricians complete four years of medical school and then three more years of a residency program focused only on children's medical care. Family Practitioners complete four years of medical school and then three to four years of residency that includes child and adult health care. Regardless of where a doctor trained, we will take a Board Certification Exam to prove we learned our stuff. Look for the letters F.A.A.P. or F.A.A.F.P. after our names. The "F" stands for Fellow, a distinguished title doctors get for passing our boards in either pediatrics or family practice. All pediatricians take continuing medical education courses annually and recertification exams every ten years to make sure we are keeping up with current trends in medicine.

Ask why the doctor chose pediatrics for a career, instead of say, urology. It's a more open-ended question. You'll likely hear her credentials in the answer, but you'll get a better idea of whom this person is.

Parent asks: Do you divide the sick and well waiting rooms?

BEHIND THE SCENES: WHY IS MY DOCTOR SO LATE?

Do you ever wonder why your doctor is late? I'll let you in on the secrets behind the waiting room door. Let's look at a typical morning at my practice:

- "Dr. Brown, your 8 am well child appointment is stuck in traffic, can you see them at 8:20 am?" (Answer—"Yes.") That patient actually arrives at 8:25 am and is brought to an exam room at 8:30 am.
- My 8:15 am well-child appointment is brought back to a room at 8:35 am because they had new insurance that needed to be verified first (this takes my business office about 20 minutes).
- My 8:30 am sick child with the flu also has asthma and needs a breathing treatment. I need to go back and examine him a second time after my nurse administers a treatment.
- "Dr. Brown, your 8:45 am sick visit has a sister who is sick, too. Do you have time to see her?" (Answer—"Yes," . . . but now I am double booked at 8:45 am.)

So, at 8:35 am, I have five patients in four exam rooms that all need to be seen. By 9 am, I'm already 20 minutes behind and will need

A better question: How long will I be sitting in your waiting room?

Even if the practice's waiting room is divided into sick and well areas, the *patient/exam* rooms are not. Don't expect the entire doctor's office to be germ free. View your trip to the doctor like a trip anywhere else–where there are kids, there will be germs. One tip: bring your own toys and wash your hands after the visit.

I'd rather know how long I have to entertain my child before the doctor sees us. You'll get an idea by how late the doctor is for the prenatal visit. We all try to be as punctual as possible, but unexpected things happen. A practice that flows well should get you and the doctor face to face within 30 minutes of your scheduled appointment.

Insider Secrets

Real world mom advice: first, call BEFORE you leave home and make sure the doctor is on schedule. If your doctor is running behind, you can prepare. Bring extra entertainment for you and your child and even snacks. Another tip: if you are sitting in the office and are not called within 20 minutes of your appointment time, it's time to find out what's going on–ask the front desk for an update on the doctor's situation. Finally, don't add to your stress–never schedule another appointment or meeting immediately after your doctor appointment. Doing so (and then running late) will only add to the frustration.

Let's talk about acceptable wait times to see your baby's doctor. On the message board for our books, when discussing how to select a pediatrician, we were shocked that some parents were left waiting for up to three hours!

to play catch up. It's about this time I'm dreaming of sitting on a beach somewhere with a drink adorned with a cute umbrella.

All hope is not lost. Some sick visits are simple and will take less time than the appointment slot (i.e. rashes, ear infection rechecks). Some days, there are only sick kids that are "sicker than billed" and parents that need extra handholding. I will be behind all morning.

Reality check: doctors are notoriously behind schedule because we try to address the needs of each patient, no matter how long it takes. It helps if we can anticipate those needs. If you want to discuss your child's school problems during an appointment for a sore throat, tell the appointments person. Otherwise, it's likely your doctor will ask you to schedule another appointment so there is more time to talk.

For more tips on when is the best time to schedule your baby's check ups, see Chapter 2, You And Your Baby's Doc. Finally, another point to remember: some doctors now have amazing office hours. More practices are offering evening and weekend office hours to compete with the after-hours and urgent care clinics popping up everywhere. Yes, these are typically larger practices in bigger cities, but they do exist. And if a practice has longer "operating hours" and more doctors, odds are the waits will be less. Again, the key is to shop around and see what is available in your community.

Obviously, that was the extreme . . . we found "average" wait times to be all over the board. Some parents wait as little as ten or 15 minutes while others reported average wait times of an hour or more. In our opinion, acceptable average wait times should be about ten to 15 minutes during non-flu season. When doctors get slammed with sick patients at the height of flu season, it is understandable that wait times can slip to 30 minutes or more. Bottom line, waiting longer than an hour to see your doctor for a scheduled visit is not acceptable–you need to shop for another pediatrician.

So, what are doctors doing back there while you cool your heels in the waiting room? Are they watching CNN? Shooting the breeze over a latte with other doctors? No, there are several things that usually conspire to make a doctor run late. See the box,"Behind the Scenes" for more on this.

Parent asks: How do I schedule well child visits/sick visits?
A better question: How does your daily schedule flow? How much time is allotted for visits?

Most practices schedule well child checks in advance. A smart tip: in a busy practice, schedule the *next* well child visit when you are in the office having one. The doctor's nurse or secretary will always advise you when another well child visit is needed.

Sick visits are usually scheduled on the same day you call. Obviously, you can't predict when your child will get sick and you won't settle for waiting until tomorrow to be seen. This is probably different than what you are used to with your own doctor. I once tried to see my doctor for a sick visit and was told I could have an appointment a week later. I told the receptionist, "Thank you. I could be dead by then." But I digress.

What you really want to know is how much time you will spend with the pediatrician. Every practice varies, but well checks usually get more time than sick visits. A typical well check may be a 15-minute appointment. A sick visit may be ten minutes. If there is a chronic problem (e.g. headaches, constipation, school problem, behavior problem), we may schedule consultation appointments which are 30 minutes or longer. You'll note these time guidelines are never published or posted in a doctor's office. Why? Because doctors will take as long as needed to address the issues at hand–even if this means making other patients wait (which leads us back to the earlier discussion of why it takes so long to see a doctor). Remember appointment slots are just a framework for a doctor's day.

NEW PARENT 411: WELL-CHILD VERSUS SICK VISITS

Doctors divide their visits with your baby into two categories: well-child and sick visits. Well-child visits are what you might think of as a routine check-up–these are scheduled at regular intervals to check your child's general health, do vaccinations, etc. Sick child visits are when your child is, well, sick. FYI: Each of these visits is scheduled differently by most doctors. We'll discuss this in Chapter 2, You and Your Baby's Doc.

BOTTOM LINE

Sick visits are "problem oriented." Be prepared to ask all your questions up front. If you have numerous issues or chronic issues to discuss, schedule a separate consultation. Doctors expect your list of burning questions at *well check* appointments, not sick visits. You can always call too.

Parent asks: What is your philosophy? (This one must be in some parenting book because everyone asks it.)
Better questions to ask: How do you approach the doctor-parent relationship? How do you feel about complementary/alternative therapies? How do you feel about vaccinations?

Doctor-parent relationships have changed since you were a child. When you went to the doctor, he told your mother what she needed to do to make you feel better. Your mother said "thank you" and did what she was told. There was no debate . . . and no "alternative therapies" mom could look up on the Internet. Doctors still wistfully reminisce about these days like a retired hall-of-famer recalls the '64 World Series.

When some parents ask about "philosophy," they really want to know about what type of medicine the doctor practices. An M.D. (medical doctor) educated in the United States is almost exclusively trained in traditional medicine. She is a scientist who learns how the body works and malfunctions and how to fix the body with medicine or surgery. Doctors also learn how scientific research is done and how to read medical studies critically. As a rule, doctors are skeptical of new therapies unless they see data and good science to support the treatment.

If you want to integrate complementary or alternative therapies into your child's healthcare, consider medical provider who is on the same page so you will have a good fit. And if you have significant vaccination concerns, now is the time to speak up. It's good to get honest, reliable advice from your baby's potential doc *before* it's time for all those shots. (See Chapter 12, Vaccines to read up on this subject)

Parent asks: Do you accept our health insurance?
A better question: Do you have a list of health insurance plans you accept?

Both big and small businesses switch insurance plans as frequently as the weather changes. The result: doctors lose patients when they change insurance. There is a reasonable chance that the doctor you select now may not perform your baby's college physical. Watching your child grow is one of the most rewarding parts of any pediatrician's job. So, losing a family to another practice due to insurance change is something most doctors try hard to avoid. A good practice will have a smart office administrator at the helm that negotiates reasonable contracts with *many* insurance plans.

Parent asks: What hospitals do you have privileges at?
Better questions to ask: Do you have privileges at the hospital where I am delivering? Who cares for my child in an emergency hospital visit, or hospitalization?

The answers to these questions will vary significantly depending on where you live. Gone are the days of the "Do It All Doctor" unless you live in a rural area.

Although continuity of patient care is important, doctors are starting to realize they only have so many hours in a day. The current trend in medicine is to divide outpatient care (office-based practice) and in-patient care (hospital-based practice). Our patients get more specialized care and our spouses are happier with us. So, this is how some practices work:

1. **An office-based pediatrician may or may not go to the hospital to examine newborns.** If your pediatrician does not make hospital rounds, a hospital-based pediatrician will care for your newborn until he goes home. And, if there is a problem with the baby at the time of delivery, there is likely to be a hospital-based pediatrician or neonatologist to handle emergencies.
2. **An office-based pediatrician is available by phone in emergency situations.** But if an emergency room visit is warranted, an emergency room physician may evaluate and treat your child. That doctor will call your doctor to discuss a plan.
3. **An office-based pediatrician will coordinate a child's admission to the hospital.** But a hospital-based pediatrician ("hospitalist") may be responsible for your child's care while he stays in the hospital overnight (an admission). That doctor will call your doctor to make discharge and follow up plans.

BOTTOM LINE: You may not see your own doctor if you have an emergency or a hospital stay.

Parent asks: How are phone calls handled?
Better questions to ask:
1. Who answers your patient calls during the day?
2. Who answers emergency calls at night?
3. What is the expected waiting time for a phone call to be returned?

Phone calls during office hours are handled in a variety of ways. On one extreme, a nurse will screen and answer all phone calls. On the other extreme, the doctor will answer all calls (a rarity now, as most doctors are busy seeing patients). Most practices fall somewhere in the middle. Some practices offer a "call in hour" each day where patients can speak directly to the doctor. I'm not fond of this approach. I'd compare it to calling a radio station to win tickets for something. If you don't have auto-redial, forget it. Some progressive practices offer health privacy compliant patient e-mail portals where, yes, you can actually email your doctor. But in general, most practices will have a nurse who can answer routine calls efficiently and hand the more complicated calls over to the doctor.

After office hours, practices usually have an answering service that dispatches emergency calls to the physician "on-call." The on-call doctor is usually (but not always) an associate in the practice. You will likely see or speak to all of your doctor's partners at some point in your child's life. Some practices utilize a nurse call center after hours to handle routine calls. Call centers use strict protocols to manage every type of emergency imaginable. Even with a call center, the on call doctor is still available for questions.

Here are more questions to ask about phone calls:

1. ***What is the name of the nurse who handles phone calls?*** You two will be on a first name basis soon, so ask now.
2. ***If you want to speak to the doctor, can you?*** You should never feel that there is a fortress built around your doctor. You have every right to talk to your doctor directly. If it's not an urgent call, it may take until the end of the business day to get back with you . . . but it should be an option.
3. ***How long does it take for the nurse or doctor to return calls?*** You'll want to know how long to sit by the phone (you can also leave a cell phone number). If you don't hear from us in a "reasonable" amount of time you should call us back.
4. ***Do you charge for phone call consultations?*** Many (but not all) doctors charge a nominal fee for phone call consultations or calls that occur after regular office hours. It's wise to know this up front!

BOTTOM LINE: THE 12 QUESTIONS YOU SHOULD ASK Okay, let's sum it up again. Here are the 12 questions we suggest you ask any potential pediatrician. (See earlier in this chapter for an explanation of why we think these questions are important–and some good answers you should hear from the doctor).

1. How did you decide on pediatrics?
2. How long will I be sitting in your waiting room?
3. How does your daily schedule flow?
4. How much time is allotted for visits?
5. How do you approach the doctor-parent relationship?
6. How do you feel about complementary/alternative therapies? Vaccines?
7. Do you have a list of health insurance plans you accept?
8. Do you have privileges at the hospital where I am delivering?
9. Who cares for my child in an emergency hospital visit, or hospitalization?
10. Who answers your patient calls during the day?
11. Who answers emergency calls at night?
12. What is the expected waiting time for a phone call to be returned?

BEHIND THE SCENES: CALLING YOUR DOC AT 3AM

When doctors are on call at night, we are not sitting by the phone in our offices waiting for your call. We go to sleep at home with our cell phones at our bedside table. So if you talk to us at 3 am and we sound sleepy . . . we are. In our residency training (the medical equivalent of boot camp), doctors become experts at answering questions while sleep deprived. I'm not gonna lie. Don't expect us to have any information from your child's chart, schedule appointments, or be excited about discussing diaper rash creams at 3 am. Be a friend and save those calls for office hours.

Q. How do I decide which doctor is right for my child?

Go with your gut instincts. Think to yourself, "Will I feel comfortable asking this person some really embarrassing questions?" If the answer is yes, go for it.

Pediatricians develop a relationship with you and your child. Doctors enjoy being a part of your family and watching your child grow with you. Unless you move or change insurance, your doctor will see your child until he moves out of your house. That means you will probably see him more than any other medical provider until you get your AARP card and senior discounts at the movies.

So now that you have discussed how you will parent with your partner and chosen your child's doctor it's time to move onto some more controversial topics. If you're having (or think you're having) a son, congratulations!

With three boys between us, we authors are pretty on top of the boy thing. And one of your first decisions when you have a boy will be: circumcision or not?

Circumcision

Before we delve into this hot topic, we have a major disclaimer. Discussing circumcision is like a "friendly" discussion on abortion—this is a topic that provokes very strong reactions in some people.

We realize no matter how "fair and balanced" we are, some readers will NOT be happy (believe us, we've tried). Even a discussion of "pros and cons" of circumcision is considered blasphemy—anti-circumcision groups believe circumcision should not be an option at all. They also complain that the studies showing medical benefits of circumcision are flawed and biased.

Our goal for this section is to let parents hear both sides of the argument so you can make an informed decision on your own. Honestly, we don't have an agenda here (beyond providing a balanced look at the subject)—what you decide to do with your son's penis is your decision.

Q. What is a circumcision anyway?

Circumcision is the surgical removal of the foreskin of the penis. It's been done as a religious ritual for centuries.

The practice of circumcision (surgical removal of foreskin) became common in the United States in the late 1800's for hygienic reasons as well as a proposed way to reduce masturbation (ha—didn't work, did it?). It has continued to be a popular choice for most American boys . . . and the subject of much controversy.

Q. When do I need to make this decision?

Before your son is born, you should decide whether or not you want to have him circumcised. That's because doctors typically perform the procedure before a baby goes home from the hospital, or within the first week or two of life in the doctor's office. When a circumcision is part of a Jewish religious ceremony (a "Brit milah" or "bris" for short), it is done at eight days of life.

Alternatively, you could wait and let him decide on his own, but it is a much bigger ordeal to go through circumcision as an adult (wasn't that a Seinfeld episode?). If you feel weird thinking about the future of your son's penis, join the club.

Q. What are the arguments FOR circumcision?

In a nutshell, fewer hygiene problems, sexually transmitted infections, and risk of cancer.

1. **Better hygiene.** The foreskin of an uncircumcised penis can harbor germs (see **HUMAN PAPILLOMAVIRUS–HPV**). Compared with a circumcised penis, it is harder to keep the uncircumcised penis clean. The foreskin can get infected and swell (see **BALANITIS**). Although balanitis doesn't occur often, it really hurts. The foreskin can also get stuck in a pulled back position (see **PARAPHIMOSIS**)–OUCH!
2. **Fewer bladder infections.** Bladder infections (see **URINARY TRACT INFECTION-UTI**) occur more frequently in girls. However, boys who are uncircumcised have a three to 12 times greater risk of infection than their circumcised friends. This again is due to hygiene reasons. In general, boys have about a 1% risk of getting a bladder infection.
3. **Less risk of penile cancer.** Cancer of the penis is rare. A man's lifetime risk of getting penile cancer is 1 in 100,000. Compared to breast cancer (1 in 8 women) and skin cancer (1 in 75 people), it's almost not worth worrying about. But yes, you guessed it, it's three to six times more common in uncircumcised men.
4. **Reduced risk of HIV.** Uncircumcised men are more likely to have the HIV virus and infect their partners. Why? Because the area under the foreskin makes a nice spot for the virus to set up housekeeping. A landmark study in South Africa found that circumcised men were 60% less likely to be infected with HIV compared to their uncircumcised peers. (*Quinn*) Based on this study, many African men are choosing to undergo circumcision.
5. **Reduced risk of sexually transmitted infections.** Besides HIV, circumcised men are also less likely to become infected with nasty little germs like trichomonas or herpes (HSV-2). (*Tobian*)
6. **Reduction in cervical cancer.** This is where our gynecology colleagues get involved. A study published in the *New England Journal of Medicine* is intriguing. (*Castellsague*) It showed that women involved with uncircumcised "high risk" partners (more than six previous sexual partners) had a five-times greater risk of getting cancer of the cervix compared to women whose sex partners were circumcised. The reason? **HUMAN PAPILLOMAVIRUS–HPV** (a sexually transmitted virus) loves to live under the foreskin. HPV is a known cause of cervical cancer. So, your decision to circumcise your son may affect your daughter-in-law's health someday.

Reality Check

Since the HPV vaccine is now approved for both young women and men, your daughter may have a lower risk of cervical cancer anyway–making that last argument for circumcision less relevant.

Q. What are the arguments AGAINST circumcision?

Like any surgical procedure, circumcision has risks:

1. **The risk of surgery.** Circumcision involves cutting the foreskin away from the head of the penis. As with any surgical procedure, there is a small chance of bleeding (1 in 3000 risk) or infection (1 in 1000 risk).
2. **Penile adhesions.** Occasionally, the skin between the shaft and the head of the penis will get stuck together due to a collection of sticky, cream cheesy stuff called smegma. The penis will look like it is uncircumcised. Minor adhesions will resolve on their own. But if the adhesions are really tight, they may need to be treated by using steroid cream, having a doctor pull the skin back, or having another surgical procedure ("circumcision revision"). For more details, see Chapter 4, Hygiene, and **PENILE ADHESIONS**).
3. **The hidden penis.** It sounds like a concealed weapon, doesn't it? Chubby baby boys have a fat roll above their genitals. It causes the circumcised penis to get sucked inwards. The penis looks normal as the boys grow up, but it's always concerning to parents.
4. **Reduced sexual pleasure.** Some concerns have been raised about the removal of sensitive nerve fibers in the foreskin when a male is circumcised. Anti-circumcision groups contend that circumcision is genital mutilation. So what's the latest science on this subject? Studies that address this question report conflicting results. Some studies show a decrease in sexual pleasure; others show no difference. The data is based on men who were circumcised as adults who subjectively rated their sexual pleasure before and after circumcision. (*Collins, Masood, Kim*)

Q. What do the experts say about circumcision?

What's the right thing to do? Let's see how the experts weigh in.

Based on the findings of the significant 2007 study done in Africa, the World Health Organization supports circumcision in countries with high HIV rates to reduce the risk of HIV in men. The 2012 American Academy of Pediatrics policy statement also acknowledges that the health benefits outweigh the risks of circumcision. Should families choose it, they say the benefits justify doing the procedure. *(AAP)*. In a more neutral stance, the American College of Obstetricians and Gynecologists (ACOG) said in 2011 that there is insufficient evidence to support routine circumcision.

Perhaps the most surprising of all, the American Urological Association has no official policy on circumcision—and they are the penis doctors!

Ultimately, *you* have to make the call.

Q. Who performs the circumcision?

Most often, your obstetrician performs the circumcision procedure just before your baby leaves the hospital. But family practitioners or pediatricians may also do it. As long as the person has been trained to do the procedure, it does not matter what the doctor's specialty is.

Why the obstetrician? Many pediatricians, like me, do not perform any surgical procedures–for good reason. You wouldn't want to see the way I slice my Thanksgiving turkey! Obstetricians have surgical training and are already at the hospital taking care of Mommy. Ask your OB first what the usual protocol is. Urologists can also perform a circumcision on your baby. This requires special arrangements, however. Urologists do not generally come to the hospital to perform routine circumcisions. You'll need to do some homework if you choose this option.

What if you decide to circumcise your son after he leaves the hospital? That's fine, but there is one caveat: some insurance providers will NOT cover the cost of the procedure once baby leaves the hospital.

Circumcision is performed as a religious ritual for some families. The person performing the procedure is called a mohel. Families pay out of pocket for this service.

Q. Is any pain medication used during the circumcision?

Most of the time, yes. Every doctor has her own approach. You can ask your doctor what she feels comfortable doing. Here are the options:

1. Injecting numbing medicine directly into the area (nerve block).
2. Applying topical numbing cream one hour before the procedure.
3. Giving the baby sugar water just prior to the procedure.

Q. How do I care for the area once the procedure is done?

You will need two things to make a dressing for the wound: gauze pads (2″x2″ or preferably 3″x3″) and a big tube of petroleum jelly (Vaseline).

The goal: keep the scab on the wound from sticking to a diaper and pulling off with each diaper change (that sounds excruciating and we don't even have male parts!). And one cautionary note: the yellowish stuff stuck to the penis is the scab, NOT pus. Do not try to brush or scrub it off!

At all poopie diaper changes and whenever else the need arises, remove the dressing and gently clean the penis with gauze soaked in warm water. Because urine is sterile, you don't have to change the dressing just for a wet diaper. Once the penis is completely healed, you can use diaper wipes.

Put a big glob of petroleum jelly in the center of the gauze pad and place it over the penis. Fold the gauze in half over the penis so it looks like

DR B'S OPINION: CIRCUMCISION

While there are some medical benefits to circumcision (and the HIV research is certainly intriguing), the benefits are not clear enough for every medical group to advocate for the procedure. One might argue that if everyone engaged in safe sexual behavior, there would be fewer sexually transmitted infections, including HIV. I think it is a very personal decision, without a right or wrong answer. And while it is hard to assess how circumcision affects sexual pleasure, I don't think either group of men is complaining.

an envelope. You will "seal" the ends of the gauze with all that petroleum jelly squishing out. Voila.

Continue to apply a dressing until the skin of the penis is covered with new skin. That's usually three to five days after the procedure.

If your doctor used a "plastibell" for the procedure, that bell falls off around one week later.

Once the penis is completely healed (usually seven to 14 days later), make sure you can always see the head (glans) of the penis distinctly from the shaft. It should look like a helmet with a rim. Pull back at the base of the penis at your son's diaper changes so you can specifically clean that area. If you don't, your son will end up with a circumcised penis that develops adhesions and looks somewhere between circumcised and uncircumcised. Avoid this, obviously!

We realize this care sounds a bit daunting, if you are a first-time parent. Ask your baby's doc for more advice or if you need help.

Check out Chapter 4, Hygiene, for more details on circumcision care after the initial healing is over.

Red Flags: Circumcision Complications

- Excessive bleeding.
- Pus draining from circumcision site.
- Fever of 100.4 F or above.
- Extreme lethargy more than four hours after procedure

BOTTOM LINE: The whole procedure is relatively brief. Yes, it hurts—but using pain medication has become the standard of care. Most babies will go to sleep afterwards as a stress response and wake up happy to see you.

Optional Newborn Metabolic Screening: What To Know

Once your baby is born, you'll notice that he is whisked away to get cleaned up and, some at point later, tested. No, not an IQ test, a blood test. Your state requires some tests and others are optional. Recently parents have become more interested in the optional tests available. Here's an idea of what's out there and how newborn screening works.

Q. What is the newborn screening test?

The first newborn screening test dates to 1961, when Dr. Robert Guthrie discovered he could diagnose a newborn with a genetic metabolic disorder called phenylketonuria (PKU) using a little dried blood on some filter paper.

This was a huge deal because babies with PKU weren't ordinarily diagnosed until at least six months of age . . . after they were permanently neurologically impaired.

Newborn screening has come a long way since then. Every state in the U.S. now requires an extensive panel of blood tests on every newborn—done with just a few drops of blood on filter paper.

Most of the tests detect "inborn errors of metabolism." Translation: these

BEHIND THE SCENES: MORE ON OPTIONAL SCREENS

Although most metabolic diseases are rare, early detection is critical to the health of an affected baby. Many states have expanded the number of government-subsidized tests. However, some states still only offer a bare bones minimum. If your state is one of those, you can pay for additional testing on your own. FYI: If you choose to bank your baby's cord blood (see more below), you may get a "free" supplemental newborn screen to go with it. For more information, here are some groups you can contact:

1. **Baylor Medical Center.** Web: baylorhealth.edu (800)-422-9567
2. **Mayo Clinic.** Web: mayomedicallaboratories.com (800)-533-1710
3. **University of Colorado** (303) 724-3826.

To see which states require what screens, visit the National Newborn Screening and Genetics Resource Center (web: genes-r-us.uthscsa.edu). We also have a state by state list of required screens on our web site at Baby411.com (click on "bonus material").

are diseases caused by a failure of the body to break down (metabolize) certain products. If these products are not broken down, they start to build up in the body and create problems—heart enlargement, intellectual disability, and even death. Other tests screen for hormone abnormalities, blood disorders, and cystic fibrosis.

Q. Do all babies get tested for metabolic diseases?

Yes. Every state in the U.S. performs a panel of blood tests on every newborn. All states test for at least 26 standard or "core" disorders.

There are also tests for 25 *additional* disorders. Whether or not you are required to do these tests varies by state. These 25 other diseases are very rare and there's no treatment, even if a diagnosis is made in the first weeks of life. That's why some states don't require these tests. To find information on required screenings in your state, go to the National Newborn Screening & Genetics Resource Center (genes-r-us.uthscsa.edu). Or simply click on the link on our website at Baby411.com.

Q. Are there more screening tests available other than those required by the state?

Yes. If you live in a state that only tests for core disorders, you can get your baby tested for many more disorders on your own dime. Private laboratories and academic institutions offer a low-cost expanded test that screens for up to 60 metabolic disorders. Most of the tests target metabolic diseases. What is that? Metabolic diseases are disorders in which the body fails to break down (metabolize) certain products. If these products are not broken down, they start to get stored up in the body and that creates problems, including heart enlargement, intellectual disability, and even death.

When blood is drawn for the state-mandated screening test (shortly after birth or at the two week well check), additional blood can be used for these optional tests. You can get more information from either your obstetrician or pediatrician or check out genes-r-us.uthscsa.edu/resources/newborn/commercial.htm for a list of non-profit and commercial labs that perform expanded screening. The cost varies, but it is usually about $35. You probably spent twice as much on a diaper bag.

Keep in mind that disorders tested for in the optional screen are quite rare (about 1 in 56,000), which is why some states weigh the cost of testing, the low yield of abnormal results, and lack of treatments and opt to test only for the more common disorders.

Our opinion: in an ideal world, there would be one NATIONAL standard for newborn screenings. But that just isn't reality today.

BOTTOM LINE: Although most metabolic diseases are rare, early detection is very important.

Another amazing option available to parents today: cord blood banking. Yes, parents can "bank" their baby's cord blood in case of an emergency illness in the future. So here's one more decision for parents to make.

Cord Blood Banking

Q. What exactly is cord blood banking anyway?

The era of modern medicine has given us the opportunity to collect and store the blood and tissue from your baby's umbilical cord.

Why is this a cool idea? Well, that blood is loaded with the "seeds" (hematopoietic stem cells) that later grow into white and red blood cells. These very special cells are also found in the bone marrow of all humans.

As a result, the umbilical cord blood/tissue can be used like a bone marrow transplant. These cells are currently used to treat some genetic and blood disorders and certain types of cancer. One of the advantages of using a cord blood transplant as opposed to bone marrow transplant is that you don't have to have a perfect genetic match to the recipient and there may be less transplant rejection.

Q. Does cord blood contain "embryonic stem cells"?

No.

The cells in cord blood come from your baby's blood after birth, not from an embryo. The only similarity here is that both cord blood cells and embryonic cells are considered "stem" cells because they can develop into mature cells. Stem cells from cord blood are considered "hematopoietic" (blood) stem cells because they can become white and red blood cells and other specialized types of cells. To make things even more confusing, umbilical cord *tissue* contains "mesenchymal" stem cells that have the ability to grow into other cell types, raising the possibility of additional medical uses. The placenta is also rich in stem cells, which is why some private cord blood banks offer placental storage options.

Q. What can cord blood be used for?

Cord blood transplants are now used for several diseases, and there are more potential therapeutic uses in the pipeline.

Note: your baby may not be able to use his own stem cells for certain diseases, though. For example, if your baby ends up having leukemia, his frozen stem cells cannot be used to treat it. Those stem cells may already have pre-cancerous changes in them.

But here is the good news: your healthy baby's stem cells could be used for another family member (sibling, parent, etc.) who has a disease treatable with cord blood.

Q. Are there options for storing the cord blood?

Yes. There are basically two options for banking your baby's cord blood: private and public.

With a private, or "family" bank, you pay a company to store your baby's cord blood for potential personal use. If you bank your blood privately, only your family or loved ones who need it and are an acceptable match can use it.

Public banks are donation programs, where families contribute cord blood for use by the general public. If you donate cord blood to the public bank, anyone who needs it can use it. Every day, 6000 patients worldwide are looking for a match in the national donor registry to treat their leukemia, lymphoma, or other disease with a bone marrow or cord blood transplant.

Unfortunately, a public cord blood donation program is only in an infancy stage as of this writing. There are 200 participating hospital programs in the U.S–a tiny fraction of the nation's 5700+ hospitals. You can find out if your hospital is one of them by going to the National Marrow Donor website at marrow.org.

ParentsGuideCordBlood.com is a fabulous site, run by an astrophysicist who lost her own daughter to leukemia. It includes a terrific sample questionnaire for parents to use when they interview cord blood banks.

If your delivery hospital doesn't participate, Cryobanks International (800-869-8608 or cryo-intl.com) accepts donations anywhere in the continental U.S. and sends them to the national donor bank.

If you want your baby's cord blood to go to the public donor program, you just need to pass some screening questions before the program accepts the donation. You should contact these folks before 34 weeks gestation if you want to donate. We'll discuss private cord blood banking next.

Insider Secret

If you have twins (or more) you cannot donate to the National Donor Program. The reason? With two or more umbilical cords, there is a potential to mix up the blood, making it too risky.

Q. Is it worth the money to privately store cord blood?

And you thought selecting a crib was a major decision...

Here's some information to help you decide if you want to open an account at the local blood bank: *(AAP, Pasquini)*

What are the odds your or a family member will need to use the cord blood? The estimates vary from 1 in 400 to 1 in 200,000. *(AAP, Pasquini)* The odds are a bit of a moving target because no one can look into a crystal ball and predict the potential uses of umbilical cord blood in the future. If you already have a family member with a disease known to be treatable with cord blood, obviously the likelihood of ever needing it goes way up.

Bottom line: cord blood isn't a panacea for every problem. There are some cases when a sick child can't use his own cord blood–for example, cord blood stem cells may already have pre-cancerous changes, so a child who later develops leukemia cannot use his own stored cord blood to treat it. However, the stored cord blood of a *healthy child* could be used for another family member who has a disease treatable with that cord blood. *(AAP Section on Hematology/Oncology)*

The stem cells may have great potential to treat many diseases, but many of the treatments are experimental at this point. The chance you'll use it will depend on a variety of factors, like scientific advances and if the blood specimen is still viable when you are 70. At this moment, these potential uses are being tested in the research labs of academic medical centers and pharmaceutical companies. If your family has a genetic disorder, banking might be worth it for you.

Here are the costs: there is an initial enrollment fee ranging from about $1700 to $2200. Then there is a storage fee of $130 to $200 per year. Those fees are just for cord blood; there are additional fees to store umbilical cord and placenta tissue, both of which have promise to treat medical disorders in the future.

Here is sample pricing from the Cord Blood Registry, one of the large players in this market. As of press time, CBR charges a total of $1995–that includes $1695 in collection in processing, $130 first year storage and $170 shipping. Annual storage fee is $130 after year one. If you also want to store the tissue from the cord and placenta, the total is $2895 plus $260 for annual storage after the first year.

Some banks charge a one-time, lump sum fee to store the cord blood "forever." (With current technology, banks can freeze and utilize cord blood for at least 20 years.)

BEHIND THE SCENES: DONATING CORD BLOOD

The American Academy of Pediatrics supports donating umbilical cord blood to a public donation bank. While we support this policy, realize that donating cord blood isn't always easy. As of this writing, the ability to donate to the national donor program is limited. If you want to donate your baby's cord blood, find out if your hospital participates in the national donor program at marrow.org (click on Donor Resources).

Reality Check

◆ Be sure to use a company that processes and stores cord blood in their own facility. Why does that matter? Because some companies subcontract the storage to another company.

◆ If a company you're interested in does other lab work besides cord blood banking, make sure their storage facilities are intended for long-term use. Special cryogenic techniques are required to make sure the blood is stored properly.

◆ Ask about the bank's storage method. Studies show that cord blood can be preserved and used for at least 20 years. Virtually all American cord blood banks store the blood in multi-compartmental bags to prevent contamination.

◆ Be sure your obstetrician is experienced in cord blood collection. It is imperative that the blood be collected quickly (within ten minutes) and that enough blood is collected. Obviously, if you don't get enough cord blood, the specimen cannot be stored. Multiple births and low birth weight reduce the chance of getting enough blood. Most companies offer training resources for doctors. Obstetricians will charge a fee ($100 or more) to collect the cord blood even if it is for donation. Be sure to find out this cost in advance.

Q. If I want to privately bank my baby's cord blood, which company should I choose?

There isn't one company we recommend over all others—instead, see the cord blood chart nearby for a list of reputable companies. These are the largest private cord blood banks; all have been accredited by the American Association of Blood Banks (AABB.org). Make sure the bank you select follows the standards set by the Foundation for the Accreditation of Cellular Therapy (factwebsite.org).

An excellent non-profit web site with advice on evaluating cord banks is ParentsGuideCordBlood.com. The site is run by an astrophysicist who lost her daughter to leukemia.

DR B'S OPINION

"Don't let potentially life-saving cells go to waste. Donate them or bank them privately."

Q. What happens to cord blood if it isn't saved or banked?

It clots in the umbilical cord and gets sent to the pathology lab with the placenta. Ultimately, it gets disposed of in a biohazard bag. If you don't authorize it to be publicly or privately banked, the blood is discarded.

Okay, we realize you're a bit overwhelmed with all these decisions, but here's just one more to consider before your child is born: staying at home or going back to work. And if you go back to work, what are your child-care options? Let's look at this topic next.

Childcare

It's probably safe to assume that if you are a woman without children, you are working outside the home while you are pregnant. And no doubt, there is an office pool going on behind your back about the odds of you returning after your baby is born.

Raising a family is one of life's major crossroads that makes you ponder which path to take. Should you drop your current career and make raising your child your new career? Can you carve out some creative combination of working part-time and staying at home with your little one? Or, will you return to the daily grind and make the most of your family time when you are able? These decisions weigh heavily on the minds of today's working moms, and for some, choosing to stay at home is not an option because their salary is paying the bills.

For those who have a choice whether or not to work, this decision can be very stressful and laden with guilt. Perhaps you've heard of the "Mommy Wars." There is no doubt: you will feel pressured about your decision from a variety of sources—your spouse, your mother, even your best girlfriends.

Our advice? Make your decision and then make the best of it. You can always re-assess down the road and change your mind.

We give you this advice based on scientific data. Research shows that *quality* time is more important than the sheer number of hours you spend with your child. Kids do best when their moms *focus* their attention, engage, and respond to them. (*Huston*)

Q. When do I need to start thinking about childcare?

Now.

I know you don't even have a baby yet, but this is something you need to think about now. Why? Because all of your buddies in your baby care class already have. Yes, it IS that competitive. The best daycares and preschools in town will have your baby's due date (instead of birth date) listed on the waiting list application.

Q. Why is my selection for childcare so important?

That seems like an obvious one—your baby is the most precious gift in the world to you. And you want to give your baby the best childcare you can find. Here are some things you should think about:

Studies have consistently shown that the first three years of life are critical times in your child's development. This is when your baby learns to trust others, function independently, problem solve, and learn the boundaries of acceptable behavior. The person/people you choose to care for your baby are incredibly important. Of course, there are economic decisions as well. Consider what your family can afford.

Reality Check

Your child's illness may cost you a lost workday, and the price of co-payments and deductibles when you visit the doctor.

We'll discuss the types of child care in a second; first let's talk about juggling work, family and your sanity.

Feedback from the Real World

If you plan on returning to work after your baby is born, be prepared for a fine balancing act. I suggest you strongly consider how your life will "work."

Just getting out the door in the morning may be more stressful than any board meeting you've attended. Getting yourself ready is the easy part. If you use out-of-the-home childcare, you will have to get your baby ready and fed, plus pack up his food for the day. This can take awhile because your baby has no idea what your schedule is, nor does he care. He also won't care if he spits up on your silk blouse or suit jacket.

Another point: be prepared for that phone call from childcare telling you that your baby is sick and needs to be sent home.

Balancing Act: Juggling work and family

How do you balance family, career—and your sanity? While the ideal situation would be to be at home for your baby 24/7, some parents find they want to work outside the home at least some of the time. For others, it is a necessity.

So, let's take a look at how moms and dads do the seemingly impossible—juggling baby, career, marriage and more. How do they do it all? To get the answers, we asked the readers of our books to share their wisdom. First, check out our Six Commandments for Balancing Work & Baby. Next, we'll look at this issue day to day, with 15 tips and tricks for juggling family and a career.

Six Commandments for Balancing Work & Baby

1 **FORGET BALANCE.** When we say "balance" work and family, this implies some kind of happy equilibrium. Forget it—the best you can hope for is OCCASIONAL peaceful coexistence between your family and job. Something will always be working to upset the balance, however . . . a childcare situation, sickness, job demands, etc.

2 **DO THE MATH.** Sit down with a piece of paper and do a serious cost/benefit analysis before returning to work. Kelly Anderson of San Diego, CA emailed her advice to moms: "Most people would be shocked to see how all the hidden costs of working outside the home add up (dry

cleaning, taxes, eating out, gas, plus the fact that someone else will be essentially raising your child for you). For many people, the benefits just don't outweigh the costs." Good point: even if you have a good job with excellent pay, the cost of childcare and other hidden expenses may wipe out a good part of the earnings.

3 **DUAL CAREERS, DUAL SACRIFICE.** Both you and your spouse must make sacrifices for this to work. While nothing in life or marriage is always 50/50, both parents must help to make the schedule work.

4 **MEET THE NEW BOSS—YOUR BABY.** That means your old boss at work must adjust to your new life. "You don't want to work for a boss who does not put family first," says reader Tricia Gagnon. She's right—if your boss doesn't understand why you need to take a day off to care for a sick child, you need to find a new job.

5 **AVOID THE GUILT TRIPS.** Whatever you decide for your baby, get ready for second-guessing from friends, relatives and complete strangers. E. Moeller, Boulder, CO, wrote in to stress this important point: A happy mommy (and daddy) makes for a happy baby. "If you are fulfilled and enjoying your work and have made good childcare choices, your baby will thrive."

6 **WILL IT MATTER NEXT MONTH? OR NEXT YEAR?** When you have to decide whether to work late or another weekend, ask yourself: "How important is my job as a ________ compared to my job as a father or mother. Will this project matter next month, year or in five years?" Your child will.

Day-to-Day: Tips & Tricks for Juggling Family & Career

Sometimes it is the small details that make the difference—here are our readers' tips and tricks for balancing work and family in their daily routines:

◆ ***The routine is KING.*** Reader Wendy Stough emailed: "Create one that works for you and do your best to stick to it, to some degree. It cuts down on the chaos of little things like lost keys and forgotten diaper bags and allows us, as parents, to take advantage of those special moments when our children need us most. Even when chaos reigns, you'll still know where the keys are!"

◆ ***Make up snacks in advance.*** Reader MK Krum of Toledo, Ohio makes up snacks and even sippy cups for snack-time a week in advance. "In the morning, just grab what you need and stick it in the diaper bag and go!"

◆ ***Organize your baby's closet.*** One reader uses a hanging organizer marked with the days of the week. "On Sunday, we load it up with the clothes for each day and any diaper bag refills." Of course, as your baby gets older, she may want a say in what she wears, but that's a story for the next book in this series, *Toddler 411*.

◆ ***Don't be afraid to ask for help.*** When you feel overwhelmed, ask friends and relatives to pitch in.

◆ ***Look for a local "Mom's Day Out" program*** to get a break once in a while. Laurie Galbreath of San Antonio emailed us this tip: "Many churches offer this and you don't have to be a member! It is also very reasonable."

◆ ***Create shortcuts to make your life easier.*** Example: use white boards in each room of your house to write down needed supplies. This tip was sent in by Debby Moro of Cumming, GA. She emailed: "I stuck a small write on/wipe off board on the back of every door in the house. When I was in a particular room and noticed I was getting low on some supply, I jotted it down then and there. Before I hit the store, I walked through the house, made out the list, and avoided forgetting something."

◆ ***Use the web.*** You have one advantage that previous generations of parents didn't–the Internet. The web is your friend . . . use it to shop for everything. Reader Area Madaras uses the web to order groceries. "It's cheaper for me to pay $10 for Albertsons.com or Vons.com to deliver my groceries than it is for me to pay a babysitter." And always consider the value of your time–it may be better to shop online and save a car trip.

◆ ***Pack the car the night before.*** Avoid forgetting something during morning rush by packing that diaper bag, wallet and cell in the car the night before (assuming you have a secure garage).

◆ ***When you cook, double the quantity***–then freeze the extra portion for a quick meal later in the week.

◆ ***Get up a bit earlier.*** This will give you a jump-start on the day–many moms and dads find they can get some chores done in the 30 minutes or so before baby wakes up.

◆ ***Have a "two stop" rule.*** We found our children would get very cranky/hungry/(fill in blank) when we tried to do more than two errand stops. While it is tempting to try to sync errands together by stopping at X, Y and Z after work, we found there was a limit to our children's patience–usually more than two stops would make life less than pleasant for all.

◆ ***Know your employer's sick leave policy.*** The Family Medical Leave Act (FMLA) allows parents to stay at home with a sick child without penalty (except for lost wages).

◆ ***Schedule fun time.*** One mom takes ten minutes out of every morning to jump on the bed or read stories with her toddler. A few stolen moments like that can make the difference.

◆ ***Cook on the weekend for the rest of the week.*** "That way we always have home-cooked meals that are healthy and tasty ready to pack for lunches or to re-heat at dinner time," emailed Lori Lankey of Woodbury MN. "It saves time and energy during the week, not to mention calories and money if we ended up eating out instead."

◆ ***Have a backup sitter plan.*** And then get a backup for the backup. That way, if an emergency strikes, you have a plan B. And plan C.

So, let's sum it up. Here are the Top Tips to Balancing Work & Family:

1. Be organized.
2. Trust your instincts.
3. Prioritize.
4. Stick to the routine.
5. But be flexible too.
6. Ask for help when you need it.
7. Lower your expectations.
8. Control freaks need not apply.
9. Laugh! Keeping a sense of humor about EVERYTHING is key.

Q. So what are my options for childcare?

Your baby stays at home with someone, goes to someone else's home, or goes to a licensed childcare facility. Let's go over these options so you can get moving on this one.

1 PARENT AT HOME. This is not just an option for moms anymore. More dads are staying at home these days. Your childcare cost is the loss of one parent's salary—which may be significant unless you already have a single-earner household. Think of your parenting job as a career change. Full time parenting is hard work, and an admirable profession. (I have great respect for stay at home parents! My job at work is much easier than my job at home.)

"If you decide to be a stay-at-home parent, enjoy your new identity and don't look back. You will never regret being there to watch your baby grow."

Reality Check

First babies in the household rarely get sick from birth to one year. They spend their days playing on the living room floor with their own toys. When playgroups get together (a good sanity break), the infants play independently of each other. When children start playing with each other and sharing toys (12 to 24 months), they start sharing germs. Firstborn babies who stay at home don't get sick that often.

However, your second child will get *much* sicker in his first year of life. Why? Big brother or sister brings illnesses home from preschool, the drop-off childcare at your gym, Gymboree, etc. Second babies also get dragged around to more family activities. It's almost guaranteed that you'll have more trips to the doctor with each subsequent child.

2 FAMILY CARETAKER. This is when a grandparent or some other willing family member cares for your baby while you go to work.

It is a great alternative if you have someone who is able and willing. It lets you pay the bills while your baby is at home with someone you can trust. Not only is family childcare free, but your child develops a special relationship with a family member.

Your child's frequency of illness is the same as if a parent stays at home.

Reality Check

Be sure you have a healthy grandparent! Infants require lots of lifting and time on the floor to play.

DR B'S OPINION

"You won't be able to call all the shots on childrearing. It's difficult to tell your mother-in-law what to do! Set up a consistent parenting plan with your caretaker before differences in parenting styles arise. Otherwise, it could get ugly!"

3 **NANNY/AU PAIR.** You hire someone to parent your child in your home. This may be a professional, or someone who just enjoys taking care of kids.

This is a great way to have a consistent caregiver. Your child will have a special relationship with another caring adult. Because you are paying her and she isn't your mother-in-law, you can set up the parenting guidelines you have in mind. If your child gets sick, you don't need to miss work. You'll only have a problem if your provider gets sick, needs to take a vacation or (yes, it happens) quits.

And it is the most expensive form of childcare. Some parents fear that they cannot trust someone (other than a family member) alone with their child. This option requires good instincts of both the parents and the provider.

Reality Check

You won't need a home surveillance system (a.k.a. a nanny cam) to check on your nanny or manny. An infant will tell you if he is uncomfortable with someone–he won't be happy to see that person. Obviously, you need to do an extensive background check on a nanny BEFORE you hire them. See our other book, *Baby Bargains* (see the back of this book for details), for tips and advice on how to do a background check on potential nannies.

Tips for finding a nanny

There are various ways to find a childcare provider who will come to your home. If you put an ad in the paper or on a bulletin board in the education building of your local college, you'll need to rely on your first impression to make a decision. If you go through a nanny or au pair place-

COSTS: CHILD CARE OPTIONS

CHILD CARE	COST	MORE INFO
Au Pair	$7295 annual program fee plus $200 per week	AuPairAmerica.com or AuPairCare.com
Nanny	$36,000 per year or $700 per week	Nanny.org
Day Care	$15,000 to $24,000 per year or $300 to $600 per week	Naeyc.org

ment service, you can pay huge sums of money to them to screen candidates for you. (They will do a police, credit, and reference background check.) Our advice: we'd recommend a trial day with your prospective provider to see how it goes before hiring her/him.

4 **IN HOME DAY CARE.** A parent has a license to care for a few children (in addition to their own kids) in her home.

This is a way to hire a mother for your child. It can be great. Your child will be around different ages of children. Often, older kids enjoy playing with the little ones. Your child may get lots of love and attention. He may also see these kids as role models. Sick child policies with in-home daycare tend to be less rigid than those in licensed daycare facilities. So, you can go to work occasionally, even if your child is ill. The cost is moderate but if your child gets sick, you may need to take off work.

Reality Check

As discussed in the stay-at-home scenario, second kids always get more illnesses. You will be adding your child to an existing household of children, so expect the same result. Also, those older kids may not be great role models. You might want to interview both the provider *and* the children she cares for before you make any decisions.

Tips for finding in-home daycare

To find these hidden gems, you'll need to start asking friends, neighbors, and co-workers for possible leads of in-home daycare providers. It's definitely a word-of-mouth kind of option.

5 **LICENSED DAY CARE FACILITY (CENTER CARE).** This is a popular option for many parents. So, I'll spend a bit more time talking about it. If you plan to have your child in daycare, you should already have done some homework. If not, put this book down right now and start!

Tips for finding a good daycare facility

Here are some quick tips on finding a good center care facility:

◆ *Look for a program that is NAEYC (National Association for the Education of Young Children; web: www.naeyc.org) approved.* This organization sets high standards for childcare facilities. If a program has been accredited, you are more likely to be in good hands. You'll be able to do a search on their site based on your zip code.

◆ *Look up your potential program's last inspection.* Thirty-three states now post childcare facility inspections, citations, and complaint investigations online. Unfortunately, the amount of info can vary dramatically from

GOOD NEWS FOR WORKING PARENTS: QUALITY TIME IS KEY

You can have a nurtured, well-adjusted child even if you and your partner both work outside the home. A recent study in the journal *Child Development* proved that "quality time" is more important than the sheer number of hours parents spend with their young children.

state to state. And some inspections only happen once every three years—so the information may not be totally up to date.

◆ ***Talk to parents whose kids are in the program.***

◆ ***Find out how approachable the teachers and director are.*** Are modifications made if there is a problem?

◆ ***Spend some time observing in the classroom.***

◆ ***How do the teachers manage discipline?***

◆ ***Do the teachers get down on the floor and play with the kids?***

◆ ***Are both the children and the adults having fun?***

◆ ***What are the program's policies regarding infection control (sick child policy)?*** Some programs are so strict that they require a doctor's note for your child to get back in.

Center care is the most popular form of childcare in the United States. Parents have a sense of security knowing that the providers are licensed professionals. You can always check up on them. Also, good news—many daycares are trending towards a "preschool" format. Translated, they emphasize a more structured environment and learning through play.

Center daycare is relatively inexpensive as far as childcare goes. But there are hidden costs: you will have to factor in several missed workdays and doctor bills into the price tag.

Reality Check

Hopefully, you are sitting down for the following statistic: *young children have an average of eight to ten viral infections per year.* (Celedon) Infants are at highest risk of getting respiratory infections in the first several months of daycare attendance. In fact, six-month-olds who are day-care attendees have a 79% greater risk of being admitted to the hospital for an acute respiratory infection than their stay-at-home friends (who don't have siblings). (*Kamper-Jorgensen*) Your child will be asked to leave daycare every time he gets sick and asked not to return until he is fever free for 24 hours. With each illness, expect your child to be contagious for the first two to four days of the illness.

The Monster Virus from Venus

As parents (we, the Fields) of a new baby, we got a quick lesson on daycare sickness—and it wasn't pretty. Our oldest son, Ben, was about two years old when he started a part-time program at a local daycare center. When the MONSTER VIRUS FROM VENUS struck, we didn't see it coming.

See, as parents who worked at home, the most human contact we had was with the UPS guy. And as long as he wasn't coughing on us when he made a package delivery, we were fine. Then our son started at the day care center. About a month into the adventure, he came home with a new friend—we called it the monster virus. Sure, he had a slight fever and stuffy nose–one day later, he was fine. But not Mom and Dad. Somehow, this little virus mutated and by the time it hit us it had become a cross between Ebola and the Black Plague. We were so sick, we couldn't get out of bed for three days and had to call in the emergency parent response team (that is, grandma).

The lesson: be prepared to be struck by all sorts of bizarre diseases if your baby starts daycare. And it won't only be your baby that will suffer . . . everyone in your family is going to have to deal with this!

Feedback from the Real World

There's nothing more vexing than searching for the right childcare for your child. And the "answer" is always a moving target–your childcare needs will change as your child grows. We asked our readers how they made sense of all the childcare options out there. Here are their tips on finding the best childcare:

◆ ***Look for a referral service.*** MK Krum of Ohio points out that many local YMCAs "offer a free or low-cost referral service. You tell them what kind of daycare you are interested in (center, provider's home, your home, etc) and they match it up to you by zip code." Each year the providers are required to resubmit their info along with letters of recommendation. "It gave us several options both close to work and home."

◆ ***Evaluate your commute.*** You may find it makes more sense to use a day care close to your home or work, depending on the circumstance.

◆ ***Look for red flags when you visit a childcare facility.*** Do children seem unattached to their caregivers? Or vice versa?

◆ ***Consider going slow to ease the transition.*** Instead of dropping your child in to a new childcare situation cold turkey, take it slow. "Bring her for a few hours one day while you're with her," said one mom we interviewed. Or do a new program part-time for a week or more to ease the transition.

◆ ***Don't make any firm decisions about childcare until AFTER your baby is born.*** Now that sounds like a contradiction with the previous tip, but it isn't–getting on a waiting list for a popular childcare alternative in your town does NOT mean you have to take the spot. Meanwhile, many parents advise waiting until after baby is born before you make your decision about whether to go back to work. Deb Steenhagen, Muskegon, MI emailed her advice: "You may feel completely differently once the baby is born. Give yourself as much time for maternity leave as possible, it helps to

BEHIND THE SCENES: IS DAYCARE SICKNESS GOOD?

From a health standpoint, it's not all bad that your child gets exposed to infections. A recent study showed that children who were in daycare/center care from birth to at least one year of age had fewer allergies at age two than their "sterile" stay-at-home peers. It's called the "Hygiene Hypothesis."

bond with the baby strongly before you go back to work and then you'll have those memories to hold onto after you do go back."

◆ ***"If you can find one, go with an in-home provider,"*** emailed E. White of Maple Grove, MN. "They are much cheaper. The different centers I looked at cost twice as much as in-home daycares."

◆ ***"Talk to friends and co-workers about what they did.*** You might stumble upon a great nanny referral or a nanny share option. My co-worker turned me on to a great service (non-profit organization) in our area that links parents to home daycare providers. While I was leery of home daycare providers (because they have no standards governing their behavior), these particular providers are subject to rules and regulations set by the non-profit organization. Now our son is being watched after by a wonderful woman and we could not be happier!" T. Ross, Arlington, Virginia.

◆ ***"In Texas, some of the best center care to be found is provided by churches, which don't advertise heavily like private day care centers***. Ask around, visit lots of places, and ask the tough questions." L. Alvarado, Houston.

◆ ***Consider an au pair.*** Au pairs are authorized cultural exchanges—a young woman in her 20's comes to live with you to do childcare. Pros: you have one person who takes care of your baby in your home and the au pair becomes part of your family instead of just hired help. Downsides: you have to have a separate bedroom because you have a new family member and they must leave after two years. For more info, go to AuPairAmerica.com.

◆ ***Accept the fact that your babysitter or nanny will do things differently than you do.*** As long as your child is content and healthy, that is just fine. Don't try to micromanage day care.

◆ Laura L. of Hot Springs, AR says ***getting some help cleaning your house was critical to her sanity***: "Hiring a housekeeper, even one that comes every two weeks, is worth every penny you pay. Amazing how much more time it gives you with your baby and family to have that help, even if your budget is already strained!"

Adoption

Having a child is quite an exciting experience, no less so for parents who choose to adopt. In their case, there's more to it than just picking up their new baby and heading on home. Here are some topics for adoptive parents to consider while you're waiting to adopt.

Q. I plan on adopting a baby. Is there anything special I should know?

It depends on the age of the baby at the time of adoption, and from whom you are adopting the baby (for example, international adoption). Here are some considerations:

1. If you are adopting the baby in infancy, adoptive mothers can try to stimulate their breast milk production with a prescription medication. If this is something you are interested in, contact your doctor.

2. It is helpful to know the medical history of the birth parents (if possible). Parental drug use and high-risk sexual activity are important to find out. For all babies, screening tests for HIV, Hepatitis B and syphilis are encouraged.

3. For infants adopted internationally, additional testing is suggested including the following:

- Stool culture for intestinal parasites (especially adoptions from Russia, Eastern Europe, China).
- Complete blood count.
- Hepatitis A screening.
- Hepatitis C screening (especially adoptions from Russia, Eastern Europe, Southeast Asia, China).
- TB (tuberculosis) screening test.
- Tests routinely done in U.S. on state metabolic screens (thyroid, phenylketonuria, sickle cell disease, etc.). You can also opt for the expanded metabolic screening.

4. Vision, hearing, nutrition status, anemia testing, and developmental milestones can be assessed when your baby meets the pediatrician.

5. If the baby's immunization status is unknown, he is presumed NOT to be immunized and will start the series at the beginning. (*AAP, Centers for Disease Control*) If there is any doubt about the quality of the country's vaccine supply, it is better to err on the side of repeating the entire vaccination series.

Q. Are there special doctors who care for children who are adopted?

Because adoption is an increasingly common choice for families, most pediatricians and family practice doctors feel comfortable taking care of these children.

However, there are some physicians who have an additional level of expertise in the field. For a listing of these physicians and general info on adoptions, check out the AAP website (aap.org/section/adoption). Another good site is the National Adoption Information Clearinghouse, calib.com/naic.

Wow, that was quite a few decisions! Now that you've navigated the new parent decision tree, let's talk about that new relationship in your life: your baby's doctor.

You & Your Baby's Doc

Insider Tips & Advice

Chapter 2

"There is no such thing as fun for the whole family."

~ Jerry Seinfeld

What's in this Chapter

- The schedule of well baby checkups
- How and why to schedule a sick visit appointment
- The difference between a sick visit and a consultation
- Insider tips for booking appointments
- What to do in the evening and on weekends
- Getting in touch: phone calls, voicemail, email, etc

Welcome to your baby's second home—the doctor's office. Now that you've picked the person you want to be your baby's doctor, it's important to understand how their office works—and the insider tips and tricks to making your time here as smooth as possible. Let's take a walk around.

Q. Does my baby need to be seen by a doctor regularly?

Yes. These appointments are called well-child visits or well baby checkups.

Bringing your child in at regular intervals is an important part of his health care. These visits let your doctor evaluate your child's health, growth, and development. It lets you address issues that concern you. Smart advice: make a list of questions to discuss at each appointment. At the first few visits, your list may be quite lengthy (up to several pages!). But by the one-year well check, your list will probably fit on a sticky note. That's when you know you have graduated to professional parenthood.

Q. Is there a standard well child visit?

Yes. Most pediatric practices follow the guidelines of the American Academy of Pediatrics (AAP) for routine well child checks. At every visit, we examine your child head to toe. Some visits involve screening tests and immunizations. Below is a standard well child visit schedule up to age five. Note: the immunization schedule has some variability, but this gives you a rough idea of what to expect.

AGE AT VISIT	SCREENING TESTS	IMMUNIZATIONS*
Birth	**Metabolic screen, hearing**	Hep B
2 weeks	**Metabolic screen**	
2 months		DTaP, IPV, Hep B, HIB, Prevnar, Rotavirus
4 months		DTaP, IPV, HIB, Prevnar, Rotavirus
6 months		DTaP, IPV, Hep B, HIB, Prevnar, Rotavirus
9 months	**Hematocrit, Lead screen**	
12 months	**First dental visit**	MMR, Varicella, Prevnar, Hep A
15 months		DTaP, HIB
18 months	**Lead screen, Developmental/Autism screen**	Hep A
2 years	**Body Mass Index (BMI), Cholesterol screen Developmental/Autism screen**	
2.5 years	**Developmental/Autism screen, BMI**	
3 years	**Blood pressure, BMI**	
4-5 years	**Hearing, vision, BMI Cholesterol screen, TB screen**	DTaP, IPV, MMR, Varicella

* What the heck is a DTaP? IPV? HIB? Yes, the world of immunizations has a language all its own. We'll explore the topic of immunizations (and decipher these codes) in Chapter 12, "Vaccines."

Screening Tests

◆ ***Metabolic Screen.*** This is a blood test performed at 24 hours of life and repeated at two weeks of age. The number of tests varies by state, but at the minimum includes screens for (big words alert) phenylketonuria, congenital hypothyroidism, galactosemia, sickle cell disease, and adrenal gland insufficiency. (See Chapter 3, Birth Day and the glossary.)

◆ ***Hearing Screen.*** The AAP recommends all newborns have a hearing test before leaving the hospital. This simple test identifies children with congenital deafness (Again, see Chapter 3, Birth Day and BAERS in glossary). A hearing screen is often repeated before starting kindergarten.

◆ ***Hematocrit.*** This is a blood test performed at nine months or one year of age to determine if your child is anemic. This test may be repeated as necessary.

◆ ***Body Mass Index.*** This calculation (which compares the height and the weight) measures the risk of health-related consequences due to overweight and obesity. It is measured annually at each well child visit, starting at two years of age.

◆ ***Urinalysis***. A urine sample is no longer done as a routine screening test. It may be done as needed to evaluate for infection, diabetes, or kidney function.

◆ *TB (Tuberculosis) screen*. Routine testing is no longer performed. If a child

has had potential exposure to someone with TB or possible symptoms, a skin test called a PPD can be done to confirm or rule out exposure to tuberculosis.

◆ ***Vision screen.*** A formal vision test is performed at age four to five and may be repeated as necessary. If your school district screens annually, this may be omitted from your child's physical exam. Some practices offer a high-tech device to assess lazy eye and refractive errors as young as one year of age, but many insurance plans do not cover the cost of this cutting edge screening test (yet).

◆ ***Lead Screen.*** This blood test demonstrates exposure to lead. High levels can cause anemia and neurological problems. A child is screened for potential exposure with a series of questions asked at nine, 12, and 18 months old. Routine testing is performed in high-risk areas. If you live in a house built before 1978 that has peeling paint or has been renovated, notify your baby's doctor. If you have other concerns about potential lead exposure (remember the Toxic Toy Scare of 2007?), your child can have a blood lead level tested at any time.

◆ ***Developmental/Autism Screen.*** Parents fill out a standardized questionnaire at the 18 month and two year well check to assess for autism.

◆ ***Cholesterol screen.*** A doctor routinely screens for potentially elevated cholesterol by asking parents if someone in their family has had problems with high cholesterol, or heart problems before the age of 55. Routine blood testing is recommended for school-aged children. And, kids who have risk factors or children whose Body Mass Index (BMI) is over the 85th percentile should also have a blood test for high cholesterol. The blood test identifies children who have elevated levels of fat that can lead to heart disease.

BEHIND THE SCENES: WHO IS THE AMERICAN ACADEMY OF PEDIATRICS (AAP)?

Just who is the AAP? And why are their "policy statements" so important? The AAP is an organization of 60,000+ pediatricians who are "dedicated to the health, safety, and well being of infants, children and adolescents in North, Central, and South America."

This active group makes recommendations (called policy statements) that allow doctors to maintain the highest standard of care for their patients. The policies are reviewed and updated frequently. You can check the AAP's policy statements online at aap.org.

Doctors who bear the letters, F.A.A.P. after their names are pediatricians who are Fellows of the American Academy of Pediatrics. Fellowship is granted after passing a standardized board certification exam and learning the secret handshake (just kidding on that last one). Fellows must take recertification exams every ten years to remain board certified. Look for the FAAP designation from your pediatrician. This means your doctor is not only trained in her specialty, but also has proof of her competency.

◆ *Immunizations*. This is a whole chapter unto itself, literally. (See Chapter 12, "Vaccines.")

Q. What kind of appointment do I make if my baby is sick?

A sick visit. This is a problem-focused appointment. Your child has a problem (fever, ear ache, rash) that needs to be evaluated. Your doctor will focus on the issue and likely do a physical exam limited to the problem. We point this out so you can appreciate the difference in appointments.

Reality Check

Your baby can get his vaccinations at his well child visit even if he is sick. Many families cancel a well child visit if their baby wakes up ill on the day of his appointment. This causes delays in getting the baby immunized. Unless your baby has a fever of 102 degrees or greater, he can still get his shots. There are also lots of other things to do at a well baby check besides shots. Bottom line: keep your well child appointments!

Q. What kind of appointment do I schedule if I have several/chronic issues I want to discuss?

See if your doctor schedules consultations.

Many doctors offer longer office visits for patients with chronic medical problems or several involved issues. Typically these concerns are behavioral issues, sleep problems, school problems, or medical problems that have been occurring for more than three or four weeks. If the appointment is scheduled this way, your doctor can provide ample time to assess these problems.

Insider Tips: How To Make Friends With The Office Staff

Bringing cookies is helpful. Just kidding! Seriously, here are five tips to make a nice impression in the doctor's office:

1. **Bring your insurance card.** Most doctors' staffs verify proof of insurance at *every* office visit.
2. **When you come for your first office visit, arrive 30 minutes before your appointment time.** You'll need to fill out a

New Parent 411: When does my child stop going to the pediatrician?

It depends on the child. Some teenagers wouldn't be caught dead in their pediatrician's waiting room. Other teenagers never want to leave the nest. Most pediatricians feel comfortable seeing their patients until the age of 18-21 years, if they still want to see us. (My pediatrician kicked me out after he performed my physical examination for medical school.)

Family practice physicians are comfortable seeing teenagers. Internal medicine physicians (internists) are not. They often limit their practice to age 18 and up.

DR B'S OPINION: WELL CHECKS

Don't try to squeeze in a well-child visit when you come in for a sick visit. Busy families frequently bring their baby in for a sick visit and ask, "So, can't you do a well check today since we are here?" I usually say no, unless my schedule is light. I need time to do a complete exam and evaluation. Doing a quick once-over isn't doing justice to the importance of a well-child visit.

lot of paperwork and the office staff need to verify your insurance (that often takes 20 minutes on the phone with your insurance company). The same is true if you have changed insurance plans. If the practice posts their new patient forms online, take advantage of the convenience. Fill them out ahead of time!

3. **If you are an established patient, come a few minutes early for well child visits.** You will soon understand why. You will need to completely undress your baby to take his measurements. This itself can be an event. Then, inevitably, the baby will either poop or pee on the measuring scale, which then further delays the measurements being taken. Multiply this experience by two if you have twins.
4. **If you have more than one child that needs to be evaluated by the doctor, schedule an appointment for each of them.** It shows that you respect your doctor's time. If everyone would follow this mantra, there's no doubt that wait times to see your doctor would decline.
5. **If you are running late for an appointment, call your doctor.** Most medical offices can modify their schedule if they know when you are coming.

Insider Tips: The Best Time To Schedule Appointments

Let's make an analogy to an airport. Your baby's doctor's office is a bit like La Guardia. When is the best time to fly? In the early morning, before delays pile up.

When is the worst time to fly? Monday mornings, Friday afternoons, and national holidays.

Now let's look at some trends in the doctor's office. Because many doctors' offices are closed on the weekends, parents tend to bring their sick kids in either before the weekend or after enduring a long weekend with them. Translation: *peak volume days are Mondays and Fridays.*

Seasons also cause volume trends. Cold and flu season (October through April) is the highest patient volume all year. Christmas Eve is always busy because no good parent will allow his or her child to be ill on Christmas. National holidays are popular times to visit because many parents have the day off from work.

In the summer (June through August), our older patients keep us busy with well child visits because they don't have to miss school. They also need camp or sports physicals. May and September are the slowest months of the year (that's when I usually take a vacation!)

If you want to visit your doctor when the office is quieter (or running less behind) here are some tips:

1. *Schedule well checks on Tuesdays, Wednesdays, or Thursdays.*
2. *Try to get the first appointment of the morning or afternoon to avoid delays.*
3. ***Schedule well baby visits that occur in the winter months far in advance.*** There are often fewer well child visits offered to make room for the sick visits.
4. *If you want to avoid the rush for school or camp physicals, consider booking in May or September.*
5. *See if your doctor offers weekend hours. Then you can avoid the Monday/Friday crunch.*

Insider Tips: How To Save Money

With medical care costs soaring, how can you save on your baby's healthcare? Follow these tips to save hundreds of dollars:

Insurance

◆ ***If you don't have insurance for your kids, apply for CHIP*** (Children's Health Insurance Program). Administered by your local state health department, CHIP is intended for working parents or those between jobs. More folks can qualify for CHIP than Medicaid because the income requirements are not as strict.

◆ If you don't have health insurance or have a restrictive plan that doesn't cover the cost of shots, ***consider the Vaccines For Children program (VFC).*** While the program includes all public health clinics, many private practices also participate. The government supplies doctors with free vaccines. Ask your doctor about it. There should be no reason that your baby gets behind on his shots.

Medications

◆ ***Ask your doctor or pharmacist for a generic medication***, if one is available. Good news: almost all routine oral antibiotics for kids are now available in generic form.

◆ ***If the prescription is a brand name medication, ask your doctor if he has any coupons.*** Many pharmaceutical companies provide coupons to medical offices that defray or eliminate the co-pay of a medication. If your doc is like me, she may forget about the pile of papers (and coupons) the sample fairies leave behind. So as a patient, it pays to speak up.

◆ ***Ask for samples.*** Again, don't be shy. As a doc, I try to give samples out as much as possible. I'm happy to give them to families—especially those who are uninsured or paying out of pocket.

◆ ***Make your own.*** Two obvious examples: saline and Pedialyte. Saline is just salt water that can be made at home (1/2 tsp salt in 8 oz water). Pedialyte is 4 cups water, 1/2 tsp salt, 2 Tbsp sugar, 1/2 tsp instant Jello powder for flavor.

BEHIND THE SCENES: CONFIDING IN YOUR BABY'S DOC

If you found yourself struggling with depression after your baby is born, who would you turn to for help? A doctor? Friends? The 'net?

A recent study looked at mothers of young children and whether or not they felt comfortable discussing their "emotional health" with their pediatrician. Although pediatricians could be a resource for help, many moms said that discussing stress with their pediatrician would be admitting failure. (Hello? Isn't stress part of the job description?) Moms relied on breastfeeding groups, postpartum groups, playgroups, and the Internet as sources of support. Yet, over 50% of pediatricians feel it is their responsibility to recognize postpartum depression.

Bottom line: it's okay to confide in your baby's doctor. She might just steer you in the right direction.

Avoid unnecessary appointments

◆ If you are on the fence about whether your child really needs to be seen for that cough or cold, call the nurse/doctor before booking your appointment. You may be able to wait it out a day or two and if so, things may clear up without an appointment.

◆ *Avoid going to the emergency room*. Some visits are impossible to avoid, but you may be able to make it until morning for others (like an earache, which is not an emergency). Consider using an after-hours or urgent care center instead of the ER. Find out your doctor's office hours–some offer extended and weekend hours. And if she isn't open, ask if there is another practice in town that offers appointments to non-patients.

◆ *If your child has PE tubes and has an ear infection that is just draining (no fever), he only needs ear drops* (which usually doesn't require an appointment). Find out what your doctor specifically does, so you don't have to pay a co-pay. The same sometimes goes for allergy med refills/asthma meds, etc.

◆ *Get a home nebulizer if your child has asthma.* This will save you office visits, ER visits, and maybe even a hospitalization. Insurance companies know this and some cover the cost of purchasing the machine.

◆ *Use this book and our website's rash-o-rama.* We give a guarantee that we'll save you at least one co-pay if you take the time to read about your child's symptoms. What's worrisome? And what's not–you'll find all the answers here. Common rashes like yeast diaper rash do not require an appointment (and can usually be treated over-the-counter).

Q. Who will I meet in the doctor's office?

Let me introduce you to the office staff. Practices vary a great deal, but these are the usual folks that you will encounter.

◆ *The medical provider or "primary care provider:"* This is the person responsible for your child's medical care. This may be a pediatrician or family practice doctor, depending on whom you select. Their initial medical school

training is through a certified medical school (M.D.) or a school of osteopathic medicine (D.O.). Their specialty training is either in children's healthcare (pediatrics) or a combination of both adult and children's healthcare (family practice). When all is said and done, either type of provider will have at least seven years of training beyond college before they have their own office.

◆ ***Mid-level providers:*** These people have been popular additions to busy offices. Nurse practitioners (NP's) and physician assistants (PA's) help with straightforward sick visits and well child visits. They can evaluate patients, make decisions, and treat patients with the supervision of a medical provider. Nurse practitioners have at least two years of training beyond their bachelor's degree in nursing (B.S.N.). Physician assistants complete a two-year master's program after completing college.

◆ ***Nursing staff:*** The staff may have a variety of degrees. The head nurse may have either a R.N. (registered nurse) or L.V.N. (licensed vocational nurse) degree. Many pediatric offices utilize medical assistants who are trained to administer shots and perform screening tests.

Q. What do I do if my baby gets sick in the evening or on the weekend?

It is Murphy's Law: your baby will only get sick when the office is closed.

Be prepared for this and have a game plan. Some offices offer limited evening and weekend hours. Find out the specifics for your doctor's office.

If the office is closed, the next option is a minor care center or an emergency department of your local hospital. Ask your office for their recommendation. The most convenient location may not be the best place to go. Look for some practical tips on navigating the ER in Chapter 15, First Aid.

BOTTOM LINE: Always call your doctor first before you go running anywhere. What may seem like an emergency to you may not be. Your phone call might save you a trip in the middle of the night.

Q. What is the best way to contact my doctor's office?

Ah, the age of technology. So many options—email, text message, etc.

Despite the digital age, the most effective way to contact the office is by picking up the phone. Doctors' offices anticipate numerous calls during office hours and have systems in place to answer the calls efficiently.

Some progressive offices answer questions online via a health privacy secure patient portal. However, most offices still rely on the telephone to communicate with patients. Why are docs resistant to change? Thank your federal government. The law protecting medical information (HIPAA) is rather onerous, with stiff fines for knowingly or unknowingly violating a patient's privacy. As a result, medical offices cannot transmit medical records via fax, unencrypted email or text message—or leave medically sensitive information on answering machines or voicemail. Although this may seem like a hassle, these restrictions are meant to protect you.

Reality Check

If you find yourself lying to your baby's doc to avoid an unwanted discussion, you probably need to find a doctor that is a better fit!

What's in this Chapter

- The details of your baby's first physical examination
- Screening tests, Vitamin K, and eye ointment
- The significance of Group B Strep
- Why is your baby shrinking?
- What you will see in your baby's diaper
- Jaundice
- Car seats
- Preemie Primer
- Special Section: The Two-Week Survival Guide

Birth Day is finally here—the most incredible day of your life. You have prepared the nursery and taken the birthing class, breastfeeding class, and baby care class. You've bought too many childcare and parenting books. Hopefully, you've also met with your pediatrician (see Chapter 1, "Decisions"). So you're ready, right?

There is no way anyone can prepare you for this, but this chapter will guide you through your baby's first days of life.

Let's leave the giving birth part to the pregnancy books (see our other book, *Expecting 411*) . . . Instead, we'll focus on what happens once your baby is born. Many people are not aware of this, but pediatricians and family practitioners examine their patients for the first time in the hospital. Why, you may ask? Because entering the world is a big transition. Babies who are still inside the womb may have certain medical problems that do not show themselves until they take their first breath of fresh air. It is very helpful in the world of modern day medicine to have ultrasounds, lab tests, and amniocentesis to get a glimpse of potential problems in your baby—but they don't cover every problem.

Q. When is my baby examined for the first time?

If you deliver at a hospital, the nurses who staff the newborn nursery do a general assessment shortly after delivery. Then the staff notifies your doctor about the birth. The doctor will examine the baby and visit with mom and dad (that's you—has a nice ring to it) within 24 hours of the birth and then daily until you are discharged home. If your personal pediatrician does not make hospital rounds, a pediatrician on the hospital staff will take care of these initial exams. If you deliver at a birthing center or at home, the midwife/practitioner does the initial and follow up examinations of your baby; the pediatrician meets your baby at two weeks of age. (Alternatively, your pediatrician may enter the scene at two months of age if the midwife handles the two week visit).

If there is an emergency at delivery, or urgent problems with your newborn, the hospital may ask a neonatologist (newborn intensive care specialist) or a staff pediatrician in the hospital to care for your baby immediately. All C-sections should have a pediatric nurse practitioner or a pediatrician in attendance in the operating room. In smaller towns, your pediatrician may be the person who attends routine C-section deliveries. In larger cities and hospitals, the hospital staffs a pediatric specialist to perform these duties.

If you deliver at a birthing center or at home and there is a problem, your baby would need to be transported to the nearest medical facility via ambulance.

Q. Tell me about the baby's first exam. What are you looking for?

Bear with us—this stuff is a little dry, but we think it will help you to understand what your doctor is doing. It will also make you appreciate how fortunate you are to have a baby who makes an A+ on his first exam!

Vital Signs

This includes heart rate (pulse), breathing rate (respiratory rate), body temperature, and weight. Abnormalities can indicate infection, dehydration, and heart/lung abnormalities. These are checked at least every eight hours. Babies are weighed daily. Input (length of breastfeeding/amount of formula) and output (number of pees and poops) are also documented.

The Head

- Shape of the head. (Your baby will not be a permanent member of the Conehead family—it rounds out after a few weeks). The skull bones often overlap right after delivery (that's what allows the baby's head to leave the birth canal) so there may be a firm ridge present. Those ridges go away in the first week of life.
- Bruises from the trauma of delivery caused by forceps, vacuum, or pushing on your pelvic bones for two-plus hours. Big bruises can take six to eight weeks to resolve (see **CEPHALHEMATOMA**)
- Soft spot. The soft spot (**ANTERIOR FONTANELLE**) in the middle of the skull is open with room for the brain to grow (see **CRANIOSYNOSTOSIS**). There is also a very small soft spot on the back of the skull called the posterior fontanelle, which is sometimes large enough to feel at birth.

The Eyes

- Red reflex. Doctors use a special light to see the baby's red reflex (the "red eye" you see in flash photography pictures). **CATARACTS** and eye tumors (see **RETINOBLASTOMA**) are two problems doctors

are trying to catch here.

- Broken blood vessel. **SUBCONJUNCTIVAL HEMORRHAGES** are broken blood vessels in one or both eyes that can happen when the baby is pushed through the birth canal. These are common and go away in a few weeks.
- Tear ducts. Many newborns get clogged tear ducts (see **NASOLACRIMAL DUCT OBSTRUCTION**). The ducts are narrow and cause the tears to get goopy and make the eye look infected. This can come and go for your baby's entire first year of life. We'll cover this issue later in Chapter 15, "First Aid" in the eye problems section.

Reality Check

Newborns can only see 8 to 12 inches in front of them. They can see you if you bring their face up close to yours. They frequently look cross-eyed for the first two months. Most newborns are born with blue eyes—we can't predict their true eye color until about six months of life.

The Ears

- Eardrums are checked, as well as abnormal formations of the outer part of the ears (see **PREAURICULAR PITS**, **SKIN TAGS**).
- A hearing test should be performed on all newborns. No, we don't ask them to raise their hand when they hear the beep. The baby wears headphones and we measure the electrical activity of the brain when a noise is made. (See **BAER**).

Reality Check

The American Academy of Pediatrics recommends hearing screening for *all* newborns. Thirty-six states require the testing by law. However, only 17 states enforce their legislation by requiring insurance companies to foot the bill for the test. Even if a hearing test is not a covered benefit, however, you should have the test done. Congenital hearing loss occurs in 3 per 1000 newborns. Early detection can make a considerable difference for a child's language development. (*AAP*) For more information on state laws and testing see ncsl.org/issues-research/ health/newborn-hearing-screening-state-laws.aspx.

The Nose

- Can baby breathe through his nose (see **CHOANAL ATRESIA**)? By the way, all babies have stuffy noses at birth and continue to have nasal congestion for the next four to six weeks (see **NEWBORN NASAL CONGESTION**).

The Mouth

- Formation of the mouth. A doctor will check to make sure the roof of the mouth (palate) has formed and the funny thing hanging in the back of the mouth (uvula) is there (see **CLEFT LIP** and **CLEFT PALATE**). Some babies are born with white pimples on the roof of their mouths (see **EPSTEIN'S PEARLS**) that go away on their own.
- Tongue. Your baby's tongue is checked for a forked tip or any trouble in moving it. This is called a tongue tie or a tight frenulum (see **ANKYLOGLOSSIA**).

- Gums. Many babies have white pimples on the gums that go away on their own. These are not teeth–the first tooth usually comes out between six to 12 months of age. However, every once in a blue moon (I've never had a patient with one in 18 years), a baby is born with a tooth. These are called **NATAL TEETH.** They usually fall out on their own, but occasionally need to be pulled.

The Throat

- Breathing. Occasionally, babies make unusual noises when breathing. Some babies are born with floppy breathing tubes (see **LARYNGOMALACIA**) that they will outgrow. This sound concerns parents, but is usually of no consequence.

The Neck and Shoulders

- These areas are checked for any unusual lumps, bumps, or cysts (see **BRANCHIAL CLEFT CYST**).
- If birth was difficult (big baby, small mommy), the collarbone can break (see **CLAVICLE FRACTURE, SHOULDER DYSTOCIA**).
- Can your baby turn its head to each side? Some babies will have a stiff neck muscle that limits head motion (see **TORTICOLLIS**).

The Chest

- Doctors look for any signs of labored breathing (see **RESPIRATORY DISTRESS**). Adults breathe 12 times per minute at an even rate. Newborns breathe 30 to 40 times per minute and have episodes of **PERIODIC BREATHING**. So, your baby will breathe rapidly several times, p-a-u-s-e, then breathe again. That pause will seem like an eternity to you. It is normal. Signs of respiratory distress are:

1. A pause between two breaths that lasts 15-20 seconds (see **APNEA**).
2. Baby is consistently breathing over 60 times per minute. (see **TACHYPNEA OF NEWBORN**)
3. Baby's ribs are sucking in at each breath, nostrils are flaring, grunting noises are heard (see **RETRACTIONS, RESPIRATORY DISTRESS**)

The Heart and Circulation

- Murmurs (unusual noises), irregular heartbeats, fast or slow heart rate, unusual discoloration (pale or dusky blue). Many heart problems, especially severe defects (see **CONGENITAL HEART DISEASE**) are now detected on fetal ultrasounds. However, doctors listen carefully with their good old stethoscopes to pick up abnormalities.
- Baby's pulses are carefully checked, particularly those in the groin area (femoral pulses). The main blood vessel (aorta) supplying oxygen rich blood to the body can have kinks and narrowings (see **COARCTATION OF AORTA**) causing a weakened pulse in the groin. Many hospitals now routinely assess for potential heart defects by checking a newborn's oxygen supply with a non-invasive monitoring device.
- A normal, benign murmur is often heard in the first 24 hours of life, as the newborn's circulation transitions from that of the fetus. This murmur, often called a **TRANSITIONAL MURMUR** resolves within the first few days and does *not* represent a problem.

- Purple hands and feet (see **ACROCYANOSIS**) are due to newborn circulation. Your baby is merely attempting to adapt to life outside the womb. This is normal and can last from weeks to sometimes months, especially after exposure to cold, or following a bath.

The Abdomen

- Your baby's doctor will feel her belly to check the size of her liver and spleen. The belly should be soft and not hurt to touch. Abnormally large body organ size can be caused by problems metabolizing foods (see **METABOLIC STORAGE DISEASE**) or poor heart function (see **CONGESTIVE HEART FAILURE**). Abnormal fullness or distention alerts doctors to look for **ABDOMINAL TUMORS**.
- Firm or full bellies may be a sign of abnormal intestine formation (see **MALROTATION**, **DUODENAL ATRESIA**). An abnormal exam and problems feeding—that is, vomiting, especially bile, will be a tip off to investigate things further.
- A baby is expected to pass one stool called **MECONIUM** in the first 24 hours of life. If a baby doesn't poop on Day 1, we evaluate for abnormal anus formation (see **HIRSCHSPRUNG'S DISEASE**, **ANAL ATRESIA**) or poor stool formation that can be seen in cystic fibrosis (see **MECONIUM PLUG**, **CYSTIC FIBROSIS**).
- Sometimes the belly button (umbilicus) pops out. This is the extreme form of an "outty" (see **UMBILICAL HERNIA**) and often resolves on its own.

Factoid: Your doc will check the umbilical cord stump to make sure the cord had two umbilical arteries and one vein. In rare cases, cords have only one umbilical artery—this can be a sign of kidney malformation. Your doctor may order an ultrasound of your baby's kidneys to rule that out.

Old Wives Tale

Placing a coin or a Band-Aid on the belly button will help the "outty" belly button go in. FALSE. Time is the best therapy.

The Genitals

Boys

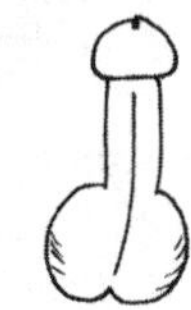
Normal penis

Hypospadias

- For boys, the baby's doctor makes sure both testes are in the scrotum. Occasionally, one or both testes will not make the pilgrimage south (see **UNDESCENDED TESTES**).
- For boys, the fullness of the scrotum is also checked. Many boys are born with extra fluid in the scrotum that goes away over the first six months of life. (see **HYDROCELE**) The other thing that causes fullness is a hernia—part of the intestine that has pushed into the scrotum (see **INGUINAL HERNIA**). Cool doctor trick: we can tell the difference by shining a light on the scrotum. Fluid (hydrocele) is light and intestine (hernia) is dark.
- For boys, the baby's doctor will make sure the opening (urethra) is at the tip of the penis. The opening can abnormally develop on the undersurface of the penis shaft (see **HYPOSPADIAS,** see picture at right) or on topside

(see **EPISPADIAS**). Boys with this problem are not routinely circumcised because the foreskin is needed to surgically correct it around six months of age.

GIRLS

- For girls, the vagina and urethra (the holes tucked inside the lips) are checked. The lips (labia minora) can be stuck together (see **LABIAL ADHESION**). Usually, you see some white mucousy fluid (see **VAGINAL DISCHARGE**). This is normal. Occasionally, newborn girls also have some vaginal bleeding (see What's That in My Baby's Diaper? question in the "Getting to Know You" section later in this chapter). Dads—you need to learn how to clean this area well. (See Chapter 4, "Hygiene" in the "Girl Parts" section for details.)

BOTH SEXES

- When the clitoris looks too large, or the penis looks too small, your doctor will evaluate for problems with the baby's hormones or chromosomes. (see **AMBIGUOUS GENITALIA**)
- **Breast or nipple enlargement:** For both sexes, the breasts can be swollen due to Mom's hormones passing through to baby. It is temporary and they shrink back down on their own. And just to really freak you out, a baby's breast will also occasionally secrete milk (called Witch's Milk) in the first weeks of life.
- **Accessory (or SUPRANUMERARY) nipples**: About one in 40 babies will have extra nipples (more common in African-American babies). They are usually brown and flat and just look like a birthmark. They're not functional and don't cause any problems.

The Kidneys and Bladder

- Expect the baby to pee (urinate) once in the first 24 hours of life. We start investigating if this does not occur.
- Abnormal formation of the passageway from the kidneys to the bladder (see **VESICOURETERAL REFLUX**, **POSTERIOR URETHRAL VALVES**) can occur in rare occasions. An evaluation for this is done if a baby develops a bladder or kidney infection. (see **URINARY TRACT INFECTION**, **PYELONEPHRITIS**)

The Spine and Nervous System

- Your baby's doctor will look for dimples or tufts of hair near the buttocks. Abnormalities on the skin can be a clue to a spine abnormality underneath the skin (see **SACRAL DIMPLE**, **NEURAL TUBE DEFECT**, **SPINA BIFIDA**).
- Also checked: the newborn's unique reflexes that fade over the first six months of life. It tells us their brain and nerves are coordinated. (see **CEREBRAL PALSY**) These reflexes include: *Rooting* (turning the head when the cheek is rubbed), *Sucking* (automatically sucking on objects placed in the mouth), *Palmar Grasp* (closing fingers on object placed on the palm), and *Moro* (body startles when head is dropped back).

The Arms and Legs (Extremities)

- Do both arms move? A weakness of the nerves causes a limp arm.

(see **ERB'S PALSY**)

- Many people are familiar with purebred dogs with hip problems. Humans can have similar problems. We check the hips by rotating them in and out. If there is a concern, we'll order an ultrasound to look at the hips. Breech babies have a slightly increased risk of this disorder. (see **HIP DYSPLASIA**)
- Rarely, babies will have extra fingers and toes, and some that are fused together (see **POLYDACTYLY**, **SYNDACTYLY**).
- A severe deformity (see **CLUB FOOT**) makes the bottoms of the feet face each other and requires casting. This occurs in about 1 in 1000 births.

The Skin

- Brown birthmarks: Moles (see **CONGENITAL NEVUS**) and light brown oval shaped areas (see **CAFÉ AU LAIT SPOTS**) are permanent markings and rarely are related to other medical problems.
- Purple birthmarks: These marks (see **PORT WINE STAINS**) are permanent and can be quite large. If they are located on the face, your baby's doctor will look for other medical problems (see **STURGE-WEBER SYNDROME**).
- Red birthmarks: These marks (see **STRAWBERRY HEMANGIOMA**) may be seen at birth, or by the first month of life. They start out flat, grow much larger and become raised. These particular marks shrink and go away by the age of ten.
- More red birthmarks: Red marks known as stork bites and angel kisses (see **NEVUS FLAMMEUS, FLAT ANGIOMATA**) are on the back of the neck or eyelids and fade over the first few months of life. When your baby gets mad at you, you will see them turn even redder.
- Blue, bruise-like marks: These spots (see **MONGOLIAN SPOTS**) are found on the buttocks of dark skinned babies. They fade over several years.
- Yellow skin: This is a whole topic in itself–see **JAUNDICE** in the "Getting to Know You" section later in this chapter.

Go to our web site Baby411.com for pictures of all of these common birthmarks. Click on "Bonus Material".

Reality Check

Newborns are really rashy. Most rashes will come and go. You'll have a window of "photo opportunity" from two to three weeks of age when their skin is clearer. Then more rashes crop up at four to eight weeks of age. These are all due to fluctuating hormone levels. No matter what you do, they will go away. A good thing to remember is your baby could care less. The names are listed below. For details, refer to the glossary. (see **ERYTHEMA TOXICUM, MILIA, MILIARIA, NEONATAL ACNE, PUSTULAR MELANOSIS**). For pictures of these rashes, check out our web site Baby411.com (click on "Bonus Material.")

Q. What is the PKU/Newborn Screen and why does my baby need to be tested?

This is a test required by all 50 states to check for serious diseases that

would otherwise go undetected in the first several weeks to months of life. The number of screening tests varies from state to state but all include: **HYPOTHYROIDISM**, **PHENYLKETONURIA (PKU)**, **GALACTOSEMIA**, **SICKLE CELL ANEMIA** and **ADRENAL GLAND INSUFFICIENCY** (see glossary for details of diseases). These tests are done once at the hospital, and again at two weeks of age.

Although the risk of any of these diseases is quite low, the benefit of making an early diagnosis is tremendous. Children with undetected hypothyroidism were permanently intellectually disabled prior to the era of state newborn screening programs.

FYI: We've posted a list of which states require what screens on our web site Baby411.com (again, click on "Bonus Material").

Q. Why do all babies get a shot of Vitamin K?

Vitamin K is essential for blood clotting. Babies who are born with a Vitamin K deficiency can have significant bleeding into vital organs (such as the brain, see **HEMORRHAGIC DISEASE OF THE NEWBORN**). Since time is of the essence, it makes more sense to give all babies the Vitamin K than to test them all and find out too late who needed it.

Q. Why do all babies get eye ointment?

Having a baby is messy. Some mothers carry bacteria that can lead to serious eye infections in the baby. Again, it makes more sense to treat every baby immediately than to test every mother at delivery and figure out which baby needs it. Antibiotic ointment has low risk with great benefit.

Q. Will my baby's blood type be tested?

Sometimes. Blood types are not routinely tested in the hospital. This might worry some parents, who are concerned that not knowing their baby's blood type immediately is dangerous. You should know that any person with a medical emergency (such as a car accident) that requires a blood transfusion gets type O negative blood regardless of his or her blood type. O negative blood is compatible with ALL blood types. For less urgent situations that require a blood transfusion, a person's blood type is tested to find a donor blood match.

Your baby's blood type will be tested if Mommy has O blood type because blood type incompatibility (i.e. baby is A or B) can lead to problems with jaundice. See Jaundice (**ABO INCOMPATIBILITY**) information in the "Getting to Know You" section later in this chapter.

NEW PARENT 411: WHY DO ALL THESE TESTS?

Some parents feel uncomfortable with all the poking and prodding their newborn endures. Trust us—there is a method to the madness. Your doctor wants to make sure you are taking home a healthy baby! Remember the key rule to all these tests: if it weren't important, we wouldn't be doing it!

Group B Strep: All You Ever Wanted to Know & More!

Q. What is the significance of the Group B Strep or Beta Strep test?

Mothers are routinely screened at the 35th to 37th week of their pregnancy for the presence of a bacteria that lives harmlessly in the genitals and intestines of some healthy women. This bacteria, called Group B Strep, can infect a newborn as he passes through the birth canal.

If Mom is a carrier for Group B Strep, she is given intravenous (IV) antibiotics during labor to suppress the growth of this bacteria. If Mom goes into labor before 37 weeks, has her water broken for more than 18 hours or has a fever greater than 100.4 degrees, she also gets IV antibiotics because of the risk of Group B Strep infection. (Women who have a C-section before going into labor don't have to worry about this stuff).

Doctors get worked up about Group B Strep because it can cause blood infection (bacteremia), pneumonia, and meningitis in newborns. All newborns are watched closely, but those babies with moms who test positive for Group B Strep are watched even more closely.

It is standard protocol to get a complete blood count and blood culture on a newborn *if:*

- Mom is Group B Strep positive and she didn't get pretreated with at least one dose of antibiotics at least four hours prior to delivery
- Mom appears to have a womb infection (chorioamnionitis)
- Or if a baby starts misbehaving (temperature instability, labored breathing, etc.). (*CDC*)

Reality Check
Don't be too alarmed if you carry Group B Strep. This does not mean you are Typhoid Mary. Most babies with Group B Strep positive mothers do not get sick—they are just at a slightly higher risk.

Q. Are there any other tests on mom done during pregnancy that the pediatrician needs to know about?

Yes! It is a standard of prenatal care to obtain blood tests looking for previous infections in the mother. This panel of tests includes Hepatitis B exposure (see **TORCH INFECTIONS**). If Mom received prenatal care, her lab work should be on the baby's chart at the hospital. But, it is always wise to have a copy of your medical record in your own hands.

This wasn't in the birth plan!

While most full-term deliveries and post-partum days go smoothly, your newborn may throw you a curve ball. While we don't mean to freak you out, here are some of the more common complications that might happen:

- *Group B Strep.* As we discussed in the section above, your baby may

have blood tests done in certain situations to look for infection.

◆ ***Blood sugar testing.*** If your baby is very large (over eight pounds), very small (under five pounds), feeding poorly, jittery, cold, or very sleepy, he will have his blood sugar tested to be sure that his level is high enough (usually that magic number is 40 mg/dl during the first 24 hours of life). Blood sugar is also routinely tested in babies whose mothers have diabetes or gestational diabetes. Be aware that some hospitals will test at-risk babies several times in the first couple of days. If your baby's blood sugar is low, you may need to supplement with formula for a day or two, even if breast-feeding is your long-term plan.

◆ ***Meconium.*** Babies who are stressed prior to or at delivery may pass their first poop before they leave the womb. That poop can be seen in the amniotic fluid. If the meconium enters the baby's lungs, it can cause inflammation and problems breathing. So, it's important to clear the baby's airway before he takes his first breath. If your water breaks and your OB sees the meconium, a neonatal team is called to attend the delivery. Yes, even more people get to see you naked—you won't care at that point, trust us.

◆ ***Labored breathing.*** Babies who are delivered by C-section don't get their fetal fluid squeezed out of their lungs because they don't squeeze through the birth canal. As a result, some babies may have temporary labored breathing for the first few hours after delivery (called Transient Tachypnea of the Newborn, or TTN). Occasionally, babies delivered vaginally will have this too. If your baby has TTN, the medical staff monitors him for a little while in the nursery before he gets his first snuggles with you.

◆ ***Fever.*** Your baby's body temperature will be watched closely during the first two days. If your baby runs a fever of 100.4 (taken rectally), he will have lab tests done to rule out infection. Occasionally, a baby will have an elevated body temperature (in the 100 to 100.3 range) if he is dehydrated. If your breastfed baby has lost close to 10% of his birth weight and his body temperature is rising, you may need to supplement with formula to avoid extensive testing for infection.

◆ ***Jaundice:*** See the next section in this chapter for details.

NEW PARENT 411: WHY IS MY BABY SHRINKING?

The shrinking baby phenomenon! No, it's not a headline ripped from the tabloids. Babies travel out of the womb with extra baggage. They have about 10% more fluid than their bodies need. Over the first few days of life, they will lose 10% of their birth weight, then quickly gain about an ounce a day once they start eating (about their third day of life). This is sure to cause you anxiety, particularly if you are breastfeeding. For details, see the "infant calorie and nutrition needs" section in Chapter 5, "Nutrition and Growth."

Getting to Know You: Your Baby's First Few Days

After your baby passes his first exam, the fun is just beginning–it's time for you the parent to get to know your little guy or gal. Let's talk about what you'll experience for the first few hours . . . and days. This section will cover Apgar tests, changing those first diapers and more.

Q. Are there any vaccinations given to the baby at the hospital?

The Hepatitis B vaccine is recommended for all newborns as part of the universal immunization series. Infants usually get the first of three doses between birth and two months of age. It is ESSENTIAL to get the first dose at birth if Mom tests positive for Hepatitis B to prevent infection in the newborn. For more information see Chapter 12, "Vaccines."

Q. Does my baby need to study for the Apgar test?

No. He probably won't score a perfect "10" either–those foreign judges are so critical of the dismount. Just kidding. The Apgar test determines which babies need extra help adjusting to life outside the womb. They are given a score from zero to ten. Your baby's **A**ppearance (color), **P**ulse (heart rate), **G**rimace (reaction to stimulation), **A**ctivity (tone), and **R**espiration rate are assessed at one minute of life and again at five minutes. Babies who endure difficult deliveries often have low (less than five) Apgar scores at one minute then perk up (greater than seven) at five minutes. The babies that don't rise in their scores may need observation and assistance by medical staff. Rest assured, low Apgar scores do NOT correlate with low SAT scores and future intelligence.

Q. What's THAT in my baby's diaper?

We've got an entire chapter (Chapter 8 "The Other End") with accompanying pictures on our website dedicated to poop (exciting, no?), but let's give you a brief primer on what you'll be seeing in those first few diapers.

◆ *Black tar poop.* The official name is **MECONIUM.** Doctors expect one of these poops in the first day of life. If you see more, congratulations–you're

NEW PARENT 411: BIRTH TRAUMA

This is what happens when your baby is larger than your pelvis can handle or just simply doesn't want to leave the womb. Your newborn's head may be pressed against your pelvic bones for 2 hours or he may have had forceps or a vacuum applied to his head. The result: a huge bruise on his head caused by bleeding just under the skin that clots and looks rather dramatic. (see baby411.com for a great picture).

Because the skin is also injured, a scab will form and peel off (like a sunburn). The blood clot will get hard and leave a lump for up to eight weeks. Not to worry, none of this is permanent.

on your way to being a diaper changing pro. See Chapter 8, "The Other End," Newborn Poop section for details.

◆ *Brick dust.* Babies should urinate (pee) at least once in the first day as well. If your baby is hovering around that 10% weight loss (see box in this section, Why is My Baby Shrinking?), you may see a red-orange brick dust spot in the diaper (see **URIC ACID CRYSTALS**). You'll think it is blood, but take a closer look. Blood gets absorbed into the diaper since it's a liquid. The crystal powder sits on the surface. It just means your baby needs to drink. For a great picture of this, go to Baby411.com/bonus and click on the Visual Library.

◆ *Blood*. Baby girls will have a "period" thanks to Mom's hormones. Don't worry, they don't get the PMS to go with it! This should only happen in the first month of life and not again until puberty.

◆ *Gel balls.* This did not come out of your baby. It is your super absorbent diaper. When the volume of urine (pee) exceeds the diaper absorbency, the gels rise to the surface. Your baby is not an alien and it is not a health hazard.

Q. Should I "room-in" with my baby at the hospital?

Yes. The American Academy of Pediatrics recommends rooming in to help make breastfeeding successful. This will allow you to learn your baby's hunger cues and nurse before your baby is screaming and demanding to be fed.

However, we should warn you that babies are very noisy sleepers. Try not to obsess over every squeak your baby makes. You need sleep to recover from the delivery and produce milk.

If you are formula feeding, it is your call. We recommend rooming-in to bond and get to know your baby. But, the nursery staff is happy to babysit for a few hours while you get some shut-eye.

Yellow Baby 411: Jaundice

Although most newborns turn a little bit yellow, pediatricians monitor all babies closely for a rare, but preventable form of brain damage (see **KERNICTERUS**) caused by excessive bilirubin levels. Levels of bilirubin (see **JAUNDICE**) start to rise just as babies go home from the hospital at 48 hours of life. The levels usually peak between 3-5 days of life. Breastfeeding can be a risk factor for jaundice if the baby is not feeding at least eight times a day or there is a delay in mother's milk coming in.

The American Academy of Pediatrics wants to improve identification of any babies at risk for brain damage. The AAP recommends that parents ROUTINELY schedule an appointment with their baby's medical provider at three to five days of life—even if that means an appointment on a weekend! And if your baby starts to look like a pumpkin, don't wait to call your doctor.

Q. My baby sleeps all the time. Were my prayers answered?

Wait until the baby gets home . . . you will find out then! All babies sleep through their first two days of life. They have been through the same experience as their Mom. They realize they have left the womb about the exact moment you take them home. It is not the magic of the nursery nurse's touch (although you will feel inadequate when faced with a screaming baby). Newborns don't have the skills to pull it together and settle down. You will need to figure out what soothes your baby. We answer all of your sleep questions for birth to the first birthday in Chapter 9, "Sleep."

Q. Why is my baby turning yellow? What is jaundice?

Here's the 411 on jaundice. While it sounds scary, there are two types of jaundice when it comes to newborns: NORMAL jaundice and ABNORMAL jaundice. Yes, you read it right–there is a form of jaundice that is NORMAL in newborns.

So what is jaundice? Short answer: it's body garbage that hasn't been eliminated yet. Long answer: humans make body garbage called bilirubin. Bilirubin breaks down in our livers and comes out in our poop. The problem: a newborn's liver is not working at full speed yet, nor are his intestines.

So, for most newborns, the body garbage (bilirubin) will start to collect in the skin. This is normal jaundice. Bilirubin has a yellow pigment, causing the whites of the eyes and skin to yellow. The level of yellow (jaundice) correlates with how far down the yellow gets on the body (increasing from head to toe.) The level will continue to rise until baby is eating and pooping regularly (day four to five). You will notice that the poop changes from black to a yellow/green/brown color at that time.

Again, by day four or five of life, bilirubin *normally* comes out in the poop and no longer collects in the skin. For **LATE PRETERM INFANTS** (born at 34 to 36 6/7 weeks gestation; see more on this in the "Preemie Primer" section later in this chapter), it is no longer an issue by day five to seven of life.

What about abnormal jaundice? See the following red flags.

RED FLAGS: Abnormal Jaundice.

These are signs for ABNORMAL jaundice (see the previous discussion of normal versus abnormal jaundice):

- Jaundice is seen in the first 24 hours of life
- Jaundice persists more than five days of life
- Level of jaundice descends below the belly button

Q. What happens if my baby has ABNORMAL jaundice?

In most cases of jaundice, doctors check bilirubin levels with a blood test on a daily basis until the level plateaus or drops, and the baby is eating and pooping well.

There is a graph based on gestational age and number of days old (called a *nomogram;* see below) that doctors use to predict how high the bilirubin level is likely to rise. So, for instance, your doc might be concerned about a full-term baby who has a bilirubin level of ten at two days of life, but not concerned at all if it is 10 at five days of life. That's because on day

Jaundice: which babies are at highest risk?

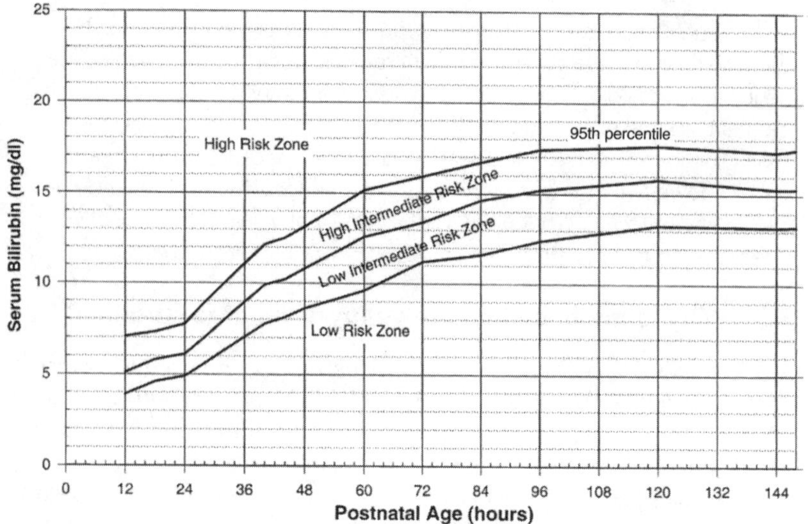

two, that baby's bilirubin level is just beginning to rise. On day five, it's unlikely that the bilirubin will go anywhere but down as the baby's body metabolizes and eliminates it properly.

If the blood bilirubin level continues to rise and could potentially reach a point that might result in **KERNICTERUS** doctors intervene and help the baby break down the bilirubin until he is capable of doing it himself.

Some babies either have a delay in eliminating bilirubin, or produce higher levels than their bodies can eliminate effectively. Those reasons include: being a late-preterm infant, having a traumatic delivery (see **CEPHALHEMATOMA**), or having a blood type incompatibility with mom (see ABO incompatibility below). These babies are more likely to need help for a few days to get rid of the bilirubin.

Bottom line: Your baby may need his blood drawn every day to monitor his bilirubin level until his doctor gives him the "all clear." If the level is significantly high, he may need treatment to bring it down.

Factoid: ABO Incompatibility: What is it? When mom and baby's blood types are different (mom is O and baby is A or B). Mom's blood can potentially mount a response that destroys some of baby's red blood cells. This leaves the baby with even more bilirubin to break down than your average newborn. If Mom's blood type is O, a blood test called a **COOMBS TEST** is done to see if mom mounted a response to her baby's blood. If the Coombs test is positive, the baby routinely gets a bilirubin level check at 24 hours of life since we know that baby is at risk to have abnormal jaundice.

Q. How is jaundice treated?

One or more of the following interventions are used to reduce the bilirubin load:

1. Supplementation with formula until Mom's milk comes in. Remember the more your baby eats, the more he will poop, and the more

he will get rid of his bilirubin. If your mature milk isn't in yet, this is a justifiable health reason to supplement with formula.

2. Phototherapy. This technique uses blue light to breakdown the bilirubin. Babies either rest with a lighted blanket around them or under a bank of lights similar to a tanning booth. If your baby is jaundiced while at the hospital, either method may be used. If your baby needs treatment after you've been discharged home, you can rent a "bili blanket" or a "bili bed" from a home health agency or medical supply company. Warning: many insurance companies do not cover the cost of these appliances, but they are worth it even if you have to pay out of pocket for a couple of days. That's because these devices will save you and your baby another hospital stay!

3. Intravenous fluid. Dehydrated babies have more trouble with jaundice. In rare cases, a baby might need an IV to get fluid and nutrients.

BOTTOM LINE: If you are nursing, the first line of treatment is to supplement with expressed breast milk and formula. If your baby needs more aggressive intervention and you are already at home, a phototherapy blanket/bed can be rented temporarily. Your doctor will check bilirubin levels everyday and continue therapy until the levels drop significantly. Another warning: that drop could take a day or two or it could take up to a week! Be patient.

If the bilirubin level is extremely high, or it's not dropping enough with home phototherapy, or your baby is severely dehydrated, he may need to be readmitted to the hospital for additional treatment.

FYI: It is NOT recommended that you lay out poolside with your newborn, or place him by a sunny window to treat jaundice. It's not that effective and can overheat him. Yes, everyone will tell you to try this, but it's not a good idea.

Q. I am getting a lot of different advice from nurses and lactation specialists—who is right?

Everyone, sort of. You will meet many health care professionals in your baby's first few days. They will all have different approaches to the same child health issues. To avoid frustration and confusion, realize that there are many ways, for example, to position a baby to nurse. Just take it all in, then figure out what works for you and your child. P.S. If you feel like you have NEW PARENT stamped on your forehead, you do!

Q. When will I need to use a car seat?

Every time you take your baby with you in the car! This includes your trip home from the hospital. It's the law, folks. Here's what you need to know:

- All 50 states require that infants under one year of age be restrained in an approved car seat. Laws vary from state to state beyond a year of age. However, the American Academy of Pediatrics advises that children be in a safety restraint (convertible car seat and then a booster seat) until they are 4'9" tall.
- Infants should ride rear-facing until they are at least two years of age, as long as they do not exceed the seat's height and weight limits.

- Kids under age 13 should be in the back seat of your vehicle. Front air bags deploy right at the level of a child's head, which can be fatal.
- So what do you need to buy now? Newborns can sit in either an infant car seat (birth to 30+ pounds) or a convertible car seat (birth to 40 or 65 pounds). To save money, you can conceivably use only a convertible car seat from birth. But most parents choose the more expensive option of getting the infant car seat (knowing they'll have to get the convertible car seat after their baby outgrows the infant seat) because it's more portable. When your baby falls asleep in the car, you'll find it's worth the investment.
- Practice using the car seat *before* game day so you don't feel foolish. You may need an engineering degree to figure out how your particular car seat works, especially if you bought a fancy Swedish one. The hospital nurses will help you get the baby strapped in, but you'll need to do the rest. Our advice: get your seat safety-checked BEFORE the baby is born to make sure it is correctly installed.
- Where to get help: The National Highway Transportation Safety Administration is the government entity that regulates car seat restraints. They have a helpful web site at nhtsa.gov including info on finding someone to check for proper car seat installation (click on "car seat inspections"). Check out chop.edu/carseat for a virtual car seat demonstration sponsored by Children's Hospital of Philadelphia. The American Academy of Pediatrics also offers a car seat check app for $1.99.
- Car seat test: hospitals test premature and small babies in their car seats to be sure they can breathe properly while restrained. Ask your healthcare provider about this simple test if your baby is born before 37 weeks or weighs under six pounds.

Special Section: The Preemie Primer

Premature babies (before 37 weeks gestation) make up 12.5% of all babies born in the United States each year. (*Hovert*) While this is certainly not in the master plan for any pregnancy, it could become reality with little notice.

Instead of that special bonding time with your newborn post-delivery, your baby may be whisked away to a neonatal intensive care unit (NICU). Scary? Yep. What a way to be initiated as a new parent! Keep your chin up—most parents graduate from the NICU with healthy babies . . . it just may take a while.

Key point: Babies born between 34 weeks and 36 6/7 weeks are considered premature. They are called **LATE PRETERM INFANTS (LPI).** In fact, late-preterm infants make up 70% of all preemies. These little peanuts account for most of the surge in preterm deliveries in the past decade. Although they don't have many of the major medical complications that more premature babies do, they still need to be treated more care than their full-term friends. Here's some more advice on LPI's.

Q. My baby is a late preterm infant. Is there anything special I need to look out for?

Yes. Just like babies are not little adults, late preterm infants are not little versions of full-term babies. Your baby is immature. Here is a list of his unique issues:

◆ **Neurologic:** About one-third of a baby's brain volume grows in the last eight weeks of gestation, so it's no surprise that your newborn will be neurologically immature. What does that really mean? Well, he'll probably be very sleepy and need to be awakened for feedings. He may have a poor ability to suck, which can make feedings (especially breastfeeding) a real challenge. He may be cranky, startle or get over-stimulated easily, and have difficulty being soothed (don't get too discouraged). He may also not be great at regulating his body temperature yet (in addition to having very little body fat to retain heat). All of these things resolve, they just take a little time until your baby's brain and body matures.

And because long-term studies show that late preterm infants are at risk for mild learning disabilities in the school years, you should watch your little one extra carefully for developmental delays.

◆ **Respiratory**: Your baby is being born just about the time his lungs are fully mature. If you baby is on the younger end of the spectrum of LPI's (34-35 weeks), it's still possible that he will have respiratory distress and need temporary breathing support because of immature lungs. Due to neurologic immaturity, your baby is also at risk for forgetting to breathe (also known as **APNEA OF PREMATURITY** or AOP). Obviously, your baby won't be allowed to go home from the hospital until he proves that he does remember to breathe! You also need to take extra care when holding your newborn upright, as he has very poor head control and can collapse his airway.

◆ **Infectious Diseases:** Being born early is considered a risk factor for newborn bloodstream infection (sepsis). So although the chance of this is very small, your baby may have lab work and tests to rule it out.

◆ **Gastrointestinal:** Your baby will be a pokey eater (more on that below) and as such, he also won't be pooping very much. That, and an immature liver, make your baby more at risk of developing jaundice than his full-term peers. And while term newborns may encounter jaundice for the first four to five days of life, late preterm infants may have jaundice issues for the first five to seven days.

◆ **Growth/Nutrition:** This is a major issue with late preterm infants. They are notoriously difficult feeders. They are sleepy. They don't wake up on their own for feedings. They tire easily and fall asleep feeding. And their sucking ability, to put it bluntly, sucks. So your baby is at risk for excessive weight loss or poor weight gain—both of which can lead to dehydration. To complicate matters even further, your baby is also at risk for low blood sugar in the first 24 hours of life—which would prevent just about anyone from having the energy to eat. Don't worry—we have lots of tips below to help with all these problems.

So, here are some top tips to navigate your baby's special challenges. More feeding tips are covered in the breastfeeding section in Chapter 6:

◆ **Temperature regulation:** Swaddle your baby with two or three receiving blankets and have him wear a hat for those first days after birth.

◆ **Feedings:** Aim for eight feedings a day. Wake your baby up if he doesn't wake on his own. Maximum feeding time should be 40 minutes because your baby will tire easily. If you are breastfeeding, use a nipple shield if your baby has a poor latch. (See more details on this in the breastfeeding section in Chapter 6, Liquids). Don't be discouraged. Your baby may also temporarily need formula supplements if his blood sugar is low.

◆ **Late discharge:** Your baby is not ready for primetime. Don't head out the door for home until he is ready to go. That means 48 hours in the hospital at the very least! Here are the criteria established by the American Academy of Pediatrics for Late Preterm Infant discharge: stable vital signs (body temperature, blood pressure, heart rate, and respiratory rate) for at least twelve hours before discharge, 24 hours of successful feedings with coordinated sucking/swallowing/breathing, formal breastfeeding assessment by a trained caregiver, at least one spontaneous poop, dehydration assessment if baby loses over 3% of his birth weight per day or more than 7% during hospitalization, jaundice assessment, and a plan for follow up with pediatrician in 24 to 48 hours. (*AAP Clinical Report*)

◆ **Car seat test:** Your baby should have a formal car seat test done by the hospital staff before you go home (see details in this chapter). But here are some specific tips: Your car seat should have a weight limit of less than five pounds. It should have a five-point harness, with multiple shoulder slots with the lowest slot less than ten inches from the seat bottom, and multiple crotch slots with the closest slot less than 5.5 inches from the seat back.

◆ **Jaundice:** Remember that your baby's peak jaundice issues will occur between five to seven days of life. If your baby looks yellow at home, take him back to your baby's doctor to check him out.

◆ **Watch development:** While your baby does not necessarily need a special evaluation with a developmental specialist, keep your eyes out for any delays in developmental milestones and mention them to your baby's doc. Be sure to give your baby lots of tummy time when he is awake. With his floppy head and increased sleep needs, he's more at risk for developing a flat head. (*AAP*)

Q. My baby was born before 34 weeks. What should I be prepared for?

Well, that really is a book in and of itself. But the basic concept is this: your baby needs to mature outside the womb and will not go home until he is ready to face the world. Discharge Day usually equates to near or at his actual due date. Hopefully, that path to maturity goes smoothly, but there can be some unpredictable bumps along the road.

While we don't have enough room in this book to go over all the medical issues you may face with a premature baby, there are two books we'd recommend for further reading: *Preemies: The Essential Guide for Parents of Premature Babies*, by Dana Linden and *The Preemie Primer*, by Dr Jennifer Gunter.

Once you are ready to head home with your preemie graduate, here are some key issues. You'll also find more preemie advice scattered throughout the rest of this book. (*Sturgeon*)

Neurologic/Developmental

Intraventricular hemorrhage

If your baby was born before 34 weeks gestation, he's probably had at least one ultrasound to rule out bleeding in the brain (**INTRAVENTRICULAR HEMORRHAGE** or **IVH**). If an abnormality was detected, you will need to follow up with a pediatric neurologist.

Eye exams

If your baby was born before 32 weeks gestation or weighed less than three pounds, a pediatric ophthalmologist has already seen him at the hospital, looking for immaturity of the eyes (**RETINOPATHY OF PREMATURITY OR ROP**). Premature babies are also at risk for **AMBLYOPIA, STRABISMUS,** and **REFRACTIVE ERRORS** (see Chapter 14, "Diseases" in the eye section for details). Your baby will need to have his vision checked periodically by the eye doctor once you go home.

Hearing tests

A routine hearing screen is done on all newborns. Babies who are born prematurely have a ten to 20 times greater risk of hearing loss than full term babies. If an abnormality is detected or concerns arise later, you should follow up with an ear, nose, and throat specialist and an audiologist.

Developmental assessment and therapy

Babies who are born prematurely are developmentally delayed compared to their peers who are the same age. To know where your child's milestones should be tracking, subtract the number of months missed in pregnancy from the baby's current age to determine the "adjusted age." For example, your four-month-old baby who was born two months early will be expected to have the milestones of a two-month-old. Preemies should catch up on their milestones by two years of age. However, very low birth weight babies (under three pounds), are at risk for the following delays: communication (including autism), large and small muscle group, and learning. All premature babies should be assessed by developmental assessment program (often referred to as "Early Childhood Intervention") in your community.

Respiratory

Apnea of prematurity

If your baby has trouble remembering to breathe (**APNEA OF PREMATURITY OR AOP**), your doctor may prescribe medication (caffeine) and a breathing monitor. Parents will need to download data from the monitor periodically and review those findings with a lung specialist.

Chronic lung disease

If your baby has chronic lung disease (**BRONCHOPULMONARY DYSPLASIA OR BPD**), you will also need to consult with a lung specialist.

Infectious Diseases

After being a NICU veteran, you have learned the art and science of good hand washing. Keep up the good work at home. No doubt the NICU nurses have instilled the fear of God in you when it comes to infections (especially **RSV**—see below).

RSV/Synagis injections

Depending on the time of year and the age of your baby, she will probably get an injection of Synagis, a medication that contains antibodies to a virus called **RESPIRATORY SYNCYTIAL VIRUS** or **RSV**. Your baby will need to continue to get Synagis injections on a monthly basis during the peak time RSV hits your community (usually the fall/winter/early spring). You may need a referral to a community resource that administers this injection—many pediatric offices do not routinely stock it. For more information on Synagis, see the Medications section in the Appendix A.

Flu vaccine

If you are bringing baby home during flu season, be sure your entire household has received a flu vaccine.

Other vaccinations

Babies who weigh under 4.5 pounds under one month of age do not routinely get their first Hepatitis B vaccine because they do not mount an adequate immune response. This first dose may be given at one month of age, as long as the baby is medically stable. If your baby spends his two-month birthday in the NICU, he can get his other first shots there before heading home.

Gastrointestinal

Gastroesophageal reflux

If your premature baby has **GASTROESOPHAGEAL REFLUX (GERD)**, he may be on a prescription medicine even after you come home. The therapeutic dose of that medication is based on his weight. Since he'll be growing like a weed, be sure to ask your pediatrician to re-calculate his dose based on his weight each time you visit the doctor.

Growth/Nutrition

Catch up growth

Your baby will be doing catch up growth for several months. Full-term newborns gain 3/4 to one ounce a day. Ideally, your baby should grow *at least* one ounce a day for the first four months of life. Consider buying or renting an infant scale to weigh your baby once a week for at least the first four to six weeks. Alternatively, you can pop in and borrow your doctor's scale. For information about preemie growth, see the special growth chart for premature babies at the back of this book.

Breastfeeding a preemie

Many preemie grads go home on a diet of both breast milk and high-calorie premature formula (which has 22 calories per ounce).

If you are breastfeeding, you'll probably find that your little one gets tired out long before he fills his tummy. And since your baby is small or weak, he may not be able to rev up your breast milk supply with his demand. Therefore, it's a good idea to pump after nursing sessions to improve your milk production. You may be doing a combination of feeding at the breast, and supplementing with expressed breast milk from a bottle. Our advice: it's wise to meet with a lactation consultant to make sure breastfeeding is successful. If you are exclusively breastfeeding, your baby may need "human milk fortifier" added to expressed milk to increase his calcium, phosphorous, and caloric intake. We have several more tips on breastfeeding a preemie in Chapter 6, Liquids.

Babies who were less than 3 lbs. at birth (very low birth weight or VLBW) and those who had poor growth in the NICU should probably get at least two bottles of high-calorie premature formula a day. This should continue until the baby is nine months old (adjusted age) to improve bone growth. (*Abrams*)

Premature formula

Whether you are breastfeeding and adding human milk fortifier, breastfeeding and supplementing with high-calorie premature formula, or exclusively formula feeding with high-calorie formula, there is no magic age or weight at which you can discontinue fortifying or switch to the regular (and cheaper) formula. As we discussed above, very low birth-weight babies (under three pounds at birth) should probably remain on the premature formula until nine months adjusted age. For bigger preemie grads, there's less consensus on when to make the switch. (*Shaheed*)

Vitamin supplements

Premature babies may benefit from a daily multivitamin and iron supplement, depending on what they are eating (breast milk/formula). If your baby is sent home from the NICU on these supplements, you can continue them for the first year of life.

Feeding schedules

Your baby was probably on a rigid feeding schedule of every three hours in the NICU. Once you are home, if your baby sticks with that routine, great. Depending on how old your baby is when he leaves the NICU and how he is growing, you may be able to relax that schedule a bit, and even let him sleep at night if he wants to—be sure you have the green light to do this from your doc, however.

Dental

Premature babies are at increased risk of poor development of tooth enamel (**ENAMEL HYPOPLASIA**) as well as cavities. Be aware of these potential problems. You should visit a dentist at your baby's first birthday.

Sleep

You may still need to wake your baby up at night for feedings, depending on his age and growth.

But even if your doc gives you her blessing to let him sleep through the night, your baby may have his own ideas. As you will see in our chapter on sleep, the ability to sleep through the night is based on a baby's neurological maturity. So, if your baby is six months old, but was born three months early, he's really only three months old (brain-wise) ... don't expect miracles.

Safety

You may not be able to use a standard infant car seat to transport your child home from the hospital. Why? Infant car seats do not fully recline so you may find your baby's head plops forward when placed in the car seat causing a blocked airway. For situations like this, you can purchase a car bed, a seat that allows your child to lay flat but still be protected in case of a crash. FYI: your child will be given a car seat test before leaving the NICU to be sure you have the appropriate safety seat.

Another tip: parents and caretakers should all take an infant CPR course before going home.

So, let's sum up your to-do list with a preemie:

- Follow-up eye exam.
- Assessment by developmental assessment program (often called Early Childhood Intervention).
- Monthly Synagis injections.
- Flu shots for the entire household.
- Rent/buy infant scale or weigh regularly with pediatrician.
- Get help with breastfeeding. Use human milk fortifier.
- Feed or supplement with high-calorie formula made for premature babies.
- Continue multivitamin and iron supplement, if prescribed.
- Do car seat test before checkout.
- CPR Class for Mom and Dad.

The Baby 411 Two-Week Survival Guide a.k.a. What Do I do NOW?

Okay, now you are ready to take your baby home. Without the luxury of the nursery nurses right down the hall, you are probably scared to death.

Hopefully, this book will be helpful in answering all those questions you have. But remember, your pediatrician or family practitioner is only a phone call away. We've covered the basics in this section, but each chapter in this book has information pertinent to newborns. We'll refer you to those sections for more details.

Q. When can I take my baby outside?

It is perfectly fine to go outside with your baby at any age. Dress him in the same layers you would wear.

However, I recommend avoiding crowded restaurants, grocery stores, and airplanes in the wintertime until your baby is four weeks old (if possible). This minimizes exposure to cold and flu viruses that are spread from respiratory droplets (coughs and sneezes). For details, see Chapter 13, "Common Infections."

Next: our detailed two-week survival guide. We've divided this advice into five areas: breathing, feeding, elimination, sleep and skin. Let's go:

1 **BREATHING.** As adults, we breathe about 12 times per minute at an even rate. As we discussed earlier in this chapter, newborns breathe 30 to 40 times per minute and have episodes of *periodic breathing*. This means that your baby may breathe rapidly several times, p-a-u-s-e, then breathe again. This pause can last several seconds (less than ten seconds). This is normal, but is bound to freak you out.

Nasal congestion is normal in the first several weeks of life. Use saline nose drops to flush the secretions.

RED FLAGS: Breathing

- When a pause between breaths lasts 15 to 20 seconds.
- If your baby is panting, or breathing over 50 to 60 times per minute.
- If your baby's rib cage sucks in (*retractions*), nostrils flare, or he makes grunting noises.

OLD WIVES TALE

My baby will catch pneumonia if he gets cold.

Pneumonia is an infectious disease. It does not infect people who are cold; pneumonia infects people who *have* a cold. Here are two

NEW PARENT 411: GERM-O-PHOBIA

Many new parents (especially parents of premature babies) have a mortal fear of germs. And we can understand that. As a doctor, I recommend avoiding crowd scenes and airplane travel for the first four weeks of your baby's life. Why? If your baby catches a bug and develops a fever of 100.4 or more during his first 28 days of life, he must be admitted to a hospital. Yes, even if it is just a cold.

Of course, that doesn't mean you must live in fear and never have contact with the outside world! Here is a Q&A with some practical suggestions to limit your newborn's exposure to germs . . . without going overboard.

- *Can your newborn go for a stroll around the neighborhood?* Yes.
- *Can a few family members and friends come over to your house and hold the newborn?* Yes. But, ask them to wash hands first and not visit if they are sick.
- *Can you hold your newborn if you are sick?* Yes, but wash hands, don't touch your face, and try not to breathe on her! If your spouse can take over the baby chores, go for it. Yes, you can and should continue breastfeeding.
- *Can your newborn be around other children?* Yes, as long as they are not sick. You can have a rule that the children can touch baby's head or feet, but not her hands or mouth.

more old wives tales:

- ***Baby will catch pneumonia if he is out in cold weather.*** FALSE!
- ***Baby will get an ear infection if the wind blows in his ears.*** FALSE! Wind blows into the outer ear canal. Ear infections are due to pus behind the eardrum, where the wind cannot reach anyway.

Q. My baby has a snotty nose. What can I do about it?

All newborns have nasal congestion for four to six weeks after birth. It's not a cold.

Some congested babies are extraordinarily loud. They may snort, snore, cough, and sneeze. That's all normal. If the congestion interferes with feedings or sleep, use saline nose drops to clear the mucous.

Saline is just salt water (1/2 tsp salt to 8oz water). You can make it or buy it. It is impossible to overdose and can be used any time your baby has thick mucus or congestion. Shoot several drops in each nostril before feedings. *You don't need to suck it out with a bulb syringe*.

The saline will either make your baby sneeze or loosen the mucous enough for the baby to swallow it.

BOTTOM LINE

Leave the bulb syringe at the hospital!

Bulb syringes can irritate a baby's nostrils to the point of nosebleeds. And if you don't evacuate the air in the bulb before sucking out the snot, you may get some unpleasant results. One family I know tried this...the baby was shocked and held its breath. The parents were shocked and called 911. Saline drops are a more effective and less traumatic way to deal with baby snot.

2 **FEEDING.** Whether you breast or bottle-feed, your newborn will be very sleepy for the first few days. The result? He may fall asleep during a feeding, sometimes after only a few minutes. Encourage your baby to stay awake by rubbing his head, playing with his feet, or unwrapping him and placing him away from your warm body.

How often does a newborn eat?

- A breast-fed baby usually eats every two to three hours (at least eight times in 24 hours).
- A formula-fed baby eats about two to three ounces every three

NEW PARENT 411: THE NEWBORN HOLD

If you have never held a newborn, keep reading. Newborns have poor control of their neck muscles, and thus, cannot hold their relatively large heads up. If possible, hold your newborn with two hands, one supporting the body, and one supporting the head. If you don't have two free hands, cradle her head in the crook of your arm (kind of like a football, dads). With a little practice, you'll be an old pro in no time.

NEW PARENT 411: DR. BROWN'S STOOL RULES

1. Once your baby starts to eat, his poop will change colors and texture.
2. Breastfed babies often have yellow, watery, seedy poop.
3. Formula fed babies often have green, pasty strained-peas poop.
4. Any shade of yellow, green, or brown is normal.
5. Stool frequency can vary from once every feeding to once a week. The frequency is not an indication of constipation–the texture is.
6. All babies (not just yours!) turn red and grunt when they poop.

2 week survival guide

to four hours (six to eight times in 24 hours).

Either way, your baby should wake up spontaneously and eat frequently. In the first two weeks of life, *do not let your newborn go more than FOUR hours without eating*. You need to wake him up to feed him if this occurs. (Note: after two weeks of age, if your baby wants to sleep longer and is gaining weight appropriately–let him!)

Mom's breast milk usually arrives on the baby's third to fourth day of life. Until then, the baby gets antibody rich (but lower-calorie) colostrum when he nurses. This is all your baby needs right now.

Spitting up some milk is normal. It can look fresh or curdled. Both are normal. Vomiting up large volumes at every feeding is not normal.

RED FLAGS: Feeding

- ◆ You consistently have to awaken your baby to eat.
- ◆ Your baby is consistently vomiting large volumes of milk (i.e. the whole feeding)
- ◆ If nursing, your milk has not come in after three or four days.

For more information on this topic, check out Chapter 5, Nutrition and Growth, Chapter 6, Liquids and Chapter 8, The Other End. See the end of this section for a handy guide to keep track of feedings.

3 **ELIMINATION**. Your newborn's body is just learning how things work initially. In the first 24 hours of life, he may pee (urinate) and poop (stool) only once. When he really begins to take food in, things should start to come out. This is a good way to tell if your infant is eating enough, particularly if you are nursing. Your hospital may give you a diary to keep track of intake and output.

Urine: By the third day of life, your baby should pee at least four times a day. By one week of age, six to 12 wet diapers a day is normal.

Stool: The first few poops are called **MECONIUM** and are black and ***tarry*** looking.

RED FLAGS: Elimination

- ◆ Your baby is not urinating at least every six hours.
- ◆ Your baby's poop looks red, mucousy, or does not change

from the black meconium.

◆ Your baby's poop looks like yours.

For more information, check out Chapter 8, The Other End as well as our website at Baby411.com for pictures!

4 **SLEEP.** Your baby sleeps 17 to 20 hours a day, but rarely more than four to five hours at a time. He may be very hard to console initially and force you to walk with him or rock him to sleep. *You can't spoil a newborn*. Do what it takes to get him to sleep. Bad habits happen AFTER two months of age.

Yes, you can swaddle your newborn with a light receiving blanket (see details on the "baby burrito wrap" in Chapter 9, Sleep). Just be sure to wrap the legs loosely so your baby can move his hips around.

NEW DAD 411: 4 TIPS FOR NEW FATHERS

Hello Dads! Yes, we know you read baby books too—so let's go over a few specific new dad tips to help out in those first days.

1. BYOW. That is, Bring Your Own Wipes. Surprise! You, Daddy-o, will be doing most of the diaper changes at the hospital—especially if your partner had a C-section. But as we discussed earlier, those first poops will not be pretty (meconium, that black, tar-like stuff). Now, the hospital will probably give you gauze pads and water for this task . . . and that frankly won't be up to the job. Our advice: bring in your own baby wipes. If for some reason your baby's skin is super sensitive, you can go back to the gauze if necessary.

2. Pay attention to the lactation consultant (LC). If your spouse is breastfeeding, you will need to watch how the baby latches on to the breast (that's where a LC works her magic). After the LC departs, you may need to help position the baby's mouth on mom's nipple (it sometimes takes four hands to maneuver this in the early days). *You* will be the lactation consultant at home, so take notes!

3. Sleep when you can. The first few days of your baby's life is so exciting. Well-wishers are calling and visiting you throughout the day. Guess what—that's when your baby is sleeping! You will then be up all night with the little rugrat. So, take advantage of daylight hours to catch a nap and encourage your spouse to do the same. Turn off all electronic devices for the duration of the nap!

4. Smile, nod and be supportive. Your partner will be on a hormonal roller coaster after delivery. That will equate to laughter one moment and tears another. Be on the lookout for something above and beyond normal emotions. (See the discussion on baby blues and postpartum depression on the next page.)

RED FLAGS: Sleep

◆ Your baby consistently needs to be awakened to eat.

◆ Your baby is completely inconsolable for over three hours straight. *For more information, check out Chapter 9, Sleep.*

5 **SKIN.** Your newborn may have a few bruises from delivery that will fade with time. He may also have a few rashes—also normal.

◆ ***Jaundice***, is often normal, but is something that should be followed. Your baby's liver is just starting its job of breaking down a body waste called bilirubin. Until this happens, the skin on the face may be a little yellow as a result of the bilirubin's pigment. That's okay. What is NOT normal:

BABY BLUES

Here is a newsflash for you...your life will never be the same. I know, everyone has told you this during your entire pregnancy. But by now reality has hit you like a sledgehammer. Becoming a parent is the most amazing experience of your life—so why are you crying right now?!!

Let's see. Your physical body feels like it was run over by a truck. Your hormone levels are off the charts. You haven't had a good night's sleep since the baby was born. You understand why sleep deprivation is used as a form of torture in POW camps. You find it difficult to make rational decisions, or any decisions for that matter.

Here's another newsflash for you . . . you are normal. No matter how wonderful it is to become a parent, it takes time for your body and mind to adjust to it.

RED FLAGS: When Mom has Postpartum Depression

The Baby Blues are short-term feelings of sadness that subside after a few much needed breaks provided by supportive family and friends. Postpartum depression doesn't go away that easily. Here are the clues that professional help is needed:

1. Frequent episodes of crying or weepiness.
2. Lack of enthusiasm for living (big clue: Mom doesn't smile anymore).
3. Lack of interest in the family or the baby.
4. Loss of appetite.
5. Difficulty sleeping. (This is a big clue since new moms sleep whenever they can!)

Mothers who experience postpartum depression often don't recognize the clues. If a family member expresses concerns about you, be smart and let them get you some help!

if you see this in the first 24 hours of life, or if the yellow color descends below your baby's waistline.

◆ ***The umbilical cord*** takes one to four weeks to fall off. Until then, the stump is gooey. This is normal. If the skin around the cord is getting infected (see **OMPHALITIS**), the area is red, tender, and foul smelling.

RED FLAGS: Skin

◆ Jaundice occurs in the first 24 hours of life or below the waistline once you get home.

◆ Redness of the skin around the umbilical cord, or pus draining from it. *See Chapter 4, "Hygiene" and the glossary for more information.*

6 **FEVERS.** We'll discuss fevers in-depth in Chapter 15, "First Aid." For now, read the red flags below for the basics.

FEEDBACK FROM THE REAL WORLD: TWINS!

Meet Agustina, mom of twins, who'll give you some great real world tips throughout this book:

"My twins, Malena and Gael, were born 18 month ago and as a new mom I wanted everything to be perfect. It is natural for expectant moms to over-prepare (i.e., overspend) to meet the challenges and demands of raising infant twins. Hopefully some of my tips and strategies, which I learned from experience, will save you time and money.

Tired, dazed and confused summarizes my first six months of motherhood with twins. Call on family and friends for support, or hire night nanny—well worth the money if it is within your means.

My head was spinning between pumping milk, feeding babies, changing diapers and cleaning all the equipment every two or three hours. Once the cycle was complete, it was time to go at it again. I found feeding logs from the hospital very helpful to keep track of feeding times and amounts, diaper changes and medicines.

One of our twins was born with a congenital heart defect while the other one was born at a low birth weight, so keeping track of their calorie consumption and medicine was very important. With little sleep, it was hard for me to see through the fog. At times I couldn't remember whose diaper I had changed or who I had fed! The log sheet was also a great way of communicating with my night nanny. At one glance, I could see a quick overview of the night.

The log sheet also helped me understand my twins' natural tendencies of awake/sleep time and the amount of calories consumed during the day. I came to realize that their calorie consumption during the day was a good predictor of how the night would go. The logs were a systematic and organized way of keeping track and also proved pivotal in putting them on a schedule."

RED FLAGS: Fever

From birth to three months of age, *any* fever can be a sign of a serious infection. You need to call your doctor immediately if your baby has a temperature greater than 100.3 F taken *rectally*. (See the section how to take a rectal temp in Chapter 15, "First Aid").

Ear thermometers tend to be unreliable and since a fever in an infant is so concerning, these are not recommended for use. Fever medications should not be used for infants under three months of age unless recommended by your doctor (for example, when your baby is vaccinated).

Q. My mother/mother-in-law will be helping me for the first couple of weeks at home. Do you have any suggestions to keep my sanity?

Some people get along with their parents and in-laws better than others. But even if you have a terrific relationship, a newborn makes things more stressful. New moms are sleep deprived, healing from childbirth, and off-the-charts hormonally. Throw in a well-meaning grandmother who wants to share her sage advice–which often is interpreted as criticism–and it takes you over the edge.

So, before the fireworks start, think about *how* you and your mother (or mother-in-law) will spend time together. A few suggestions:

◆ ***Baby chores.*** If you are breastfeeding, put grandma in charge of everything else baby: diaper changes, rocking, bathing. It will be her pleasure.

◆ ***Household chores.*** Don't be a control freak. Let her cook, clean, or even run a few errands.

◆ ***Ask for advice on small matters.*** "How did you swaddle your babies?" It will make her feel important–and that her opinion is valued.

◆ ***Avoid conflict.*** If you run into conflicting parenting approaches, feel free to quote your pediatrician's advice (feel free to blame any controversial decision on your baby's doc).

On the next page, we have a chart to help you track your newborn's pee and poop for the first seven days. After day eight, you'll be an old pro. Of course, there are also iPhone and Android apps that do this as well! Reader favorites include Baby Connect and Total Baby.

Handy Feeding & Elimination Table: The First 7 Days

Instructions: Circle the hour your baby nurses.
Circle W for wet diaper (urine). Circle S for soiled diaper (poop).

Day 1 *Goal 6-8 feedings*
Diapers: 1 wet, 1 soiled

12am 1 2 3 4 5 6 7 8 9 10 11 12pm 1 2 3 4 5 6 7 8 9 10 11

W S (black, tarry)

Day 2 *Goal 8-12 feedings*
2 wet 2 soiled

12m 1a 2 3 4 5 6 7 8 9 10 11 12pm 1 2 3 4 5 6 7 8 9 10 11

W W S S (black/brown)

Day 3 *Goal 8-12 feedings*
2 wet 2 soiled

12m 1a 2 3 4 5 6 7 8 9 10 11 12pm 1 2 3 4 5 6 7 8 9 10 11

W W S S (green, yellow)

Day 4 *Goal 8-12 feedings*
4 wet 3 soiled

12m 1a 2 3 4 5 6 7 8 9 10 11 12pm 1 2 3 4 5 6 7 8 9 10 11

W W W W S S S (yellow)

Day 5 *Goal 8-12 feedings*
5 wet 3 soiled

12m 1a 2 3 4 5 6 7 8 9 10 11 12pm 1 2 3 4 5 6 7 8 9 10 11

W W W W W S S S (yellow)

Day 6 *Goal 8-12 feedings*
6 wet 4 soiled

12m 1a 2 3 4 5 6 7 8 9 10 11 12pm 1 2 3 4 5 6 7 8 9 10 11

W W W W W W S S S S

Day 7 *Goal 8-12 feedings*
6 wet 4 soiled

12m 1a 2 3 4 5 6 7 8 9 10 11 12pm 1 2 3 4 5 6 7 8 9 10 11

W W W W W W S S S S

Section 2

Care & Feeding

Hygiene

The Spa Treatment

Chapter 4

"Ray! You take that diaper off your head, you put it back onto your sister!"
~ Raising Arizona

What's in this Chapter

- ◆ The first manicure
- ◆ Yes, it's okay to use diaper wipes
- ◆ How many layers of clothing your baby really needs
- ◆ What to do about diaper rashes
- ◆ Belly button/cord care
- ◆ Soaps, cremes, and detergents
- ◆ Cradle cap
- ◆ Eczema
- ◆ Sunblock and insect repellents
- ◆ The Boy parts
- ◆ The Girl parts
- ◆ Thrush, dental care, and drool

You survived nine months of pregnancy, Birth Day and the hospital food after your baby was born. Now the fun begins–it's time to take baby home.

Due to budget cutbacks at the federal government, babies are no longer sent home with personal butlers or detailed care instructions on cleaning and hygiene. Just kidding! They never used to do that. You are expected to know about this stuff on your own. Consider this chapter your baby care primer.

Warning: we'll talk candidly about diaper rash. No it isn't pretty, but there are several steps you can take to stop it. Next, it's on to belly button care. Also, we'll discuss the topic of dressing your baby as well as tips on cradle cap, sun block, dental care and more. And let's talk about your baby's private parts–you've got questions and we've got the answers!

Q. When can I clip my newborn's nails?

Around three to four weeks of life.

The fingertip and nail are stuck together for the first few weeks. Attempts to use a nail clipper will result in drawing blood. For now, you can use a nail file and give your baby a manicure.

Helpful Hint

You can place socks on your baby's hands if he is scratching his face and you want nice pictures.

Q. When can I use diaper wipes?

Now.

Most hospital nurseries use gauze pads soaked in water for diaper cleanups. This is done to prevent potential skin irritation. The truth is that most babies have no problem with typical diaper wipes.

DR B'S OPINION

"Bring your own diaper wipes to the hospital. If your baby's skin gets irritated, then you can use water and gauze pads. After your first diaper change cleaning meconium, you will understand why I recommend using diaper wipes."

Helpful Hint

Some parents like to keep alcohol-based hand sanitizer at the changing table (for mom and dad's hands). It's not a bad idea, since you need to keep your hands and your eyes on your baby.

Q. How many layers of clothing should my baby wear?

As many as you do.

Babies live at the same body temperature as we all do. They will be comfortable in the same number of clothes as you are. It is true that your baby loses heat a little more quickly than you, so keep an eye on him in cooler weather.

If you have a late preterm newborn (34 to 36 6/7 weeks gestation), you'll want to wrap her up in an extra receiving blanket or two in the first several days of life. But once she's got her temperature regulation under control and a little meat on her bones, the same rules apply as with full-term newborns.

Reality Check

Parents often dress their babies for an arctic freeze in July. Then they wonder why their baby has a heat rash.

Q. How often do I clean the belly button?

While the idea of cleaning your baby's belly button may seem a no-brainer, there is actually quite a bit of debate about it. According to the American Academy of Pediatrics, "no single method of umbilical cord care has proved to be superior in preventing...disease (that is, infection of the belly button)." (*AAP*). Hence, there is some variability in what hospital nurseries do. Some apply antibiotic solutions, "triple-dye" (an antiseptic) or alcohol to the cord. The current trend among hospitals, however, is moving AWAY from these treatments. Why? Some research suggests the stump may heal faster if simply left alone. (*Palazzi*) Your doctor will probably have his or her own preference.

So what do you do with the umbilical cord stump once you get home? Well you can't just pretend it's not there and ignore it! Check on it at diaper changes, and clean it at least once a day. Keep an eye out for infection too. Infection clues: redness and swelling around the cord, continued bleeding, yellowish pus and/or foul smelling discharge from the area.

How should you clean the belly button? You have two choices: sterile water or rubbing alcohol. The time-honored method is alcohol. But we now know that using rubbing alcohol does not prevent infection or make

Treating Diaper Rash: 5 Tips & Tricks

There are basically two kinds of diaper rashes:

Irritated skin. Flat red rash caused when poop and pee break down the skin, causing redness and irritation.

Yeast infection. Raised, pimply rash surrounds an area that looks like raw meat. (Yeast likes the diaper area because it is dark, warm, and moist.)

Curious to see exactly what these different rashes look like? Check out our web site at Baby411.com (click on Bonus Material). For basic skin irritation, creating a barrier to protect the skin from further insults is key. Here are our tips:

1. **Use petroleum jelly** (Vaseline) **or zinc oxide** (store brand: Balmex, Desitin) at every diaper change. Avoid powders—baby can inhale the powder into his lungs when it is poured out. Creams are a better bet.
2. **Let your baby "air dry."** If you are feeling brave, let your baby go bare bottomed for a while. For the less ambitious types, use a blow dryer on a cool setting and dry the diaper area after cleaning.
3. **For more severe rashes,** try Dr. Smith's Diaper Ointment, Triple Paste, or Boudreaux's Butt Paste. These products are a little thicker and more protective. Although they are available over-the-counter, you may have to ask your pharmacist to order some for you.
4. **Use pure lanolin.** Many women use this for cracked nipples caused by breastfeeding. It's very expensive to recommend as a first line of defense against diaper rash, but if you have it in the house, use it. If you want to buy it in bulk and save some cash, look into Corona Ointment (coronaproducts.com). Yes, it's designed for horses—but the active ingredient, lanolin, is the same! A 14 ounce jar is $14.50. Compare that to Lansinoh at $8.33 for just two ounces!
5. **If the rash looks like yeast, try an over-the-counter antifungal** (e.g. Lotrimin AF or Triple Paste AF)—the package will say it's for jock itch and athlete's foot. Don't be alarmed. Apply twice daily for a week.

If none of these tricks work, check in with your doctor. Most docs have additional tips for stopping diaper rash.

the cord fall off any faster. The only benefit to using alcohol on the cord stump is to keep the belly button from getting stinky. Alcohol should be applied to the BASE of the belly button, where the gooey stuff is—exactly where you are afraid to go. (*Zupan*)

The alternative: you can spot clean the cord with sterile water on a gauze pad if it gets dirty. Whichever method you choose, just make sure the cord stump stays clean.

RED FLAG: Belly Buttons

A foul smelling belly button with pus draining from it and surrounded by red skin indicates infection (see **OMPHALITIS**). You need to call your doctor immediately.

Q. When will my newborn get his first bath?

Your baby will get cleaned up shortly after delivery. Most hospitals will sponge bathe newborns and recommend parents do the same at home until the umbilical cord falls off. Babies don't get that dirty and sponge bathing minimizes heat loss.

Sponge-bathing also keeps the umbilical cord dry until it falls off. You can sponge bath your baby with soap, water, and a washcloth every few days. Once the cord falls off, you can give him his first real bath.

Q. I heard in my childbirth class that it's better NOT to bathe your newborn in the first 24 hours of life. Is this true?

Let's go over the usual hospital protocol first. After you give birth in a delivery room, you spend about the next hour getting to know your newborn and having your first nursing session. (That's assuming you are nursing, your baby is full term, and he has no immediate medical issues to deal with.)

Then, you get cleaned up and transferred to your postpartum room, and your baby heads to the nursery to be examined, monitored, and bathed. While this is the norm, it does have a couple of disadvantages. Occasionally, the baby gets cold after his bath and then has to stick around the nursery under warming lights until his body temperature rises. This delays getting the baby back to you.

The other issue with the first bath is that it usually washes off the baby's **VERNIX** (that white cheesy stuff that protects the fetus' skin from getting pruny in the amniotic fluid). Vernix also fights off germs so it's not a bad idea to let it stay a little while longer. In fact, the World Health Organization recommends waiting on that first bath until six hours after birth. (*World Health Organization*)

But here's a little reality check and the downside to delaying a bath: your baby isn't just covered with vernix. He's also covered in your blood and vaginal secretions after delivery. If you choose to wait and give baby his first bath after 24 hours (or even later, at home), anyone handling your newborn (healthcare providers, grandparents, other well wishers) will need to wear protective gear and gloves. This avoids any handling of bodily fluids that are caked all over your baby's skin.

Bottom line: If you deliver at a birthing center, or at home and no one is going to be handling your baby but you, do whatever you like. If you deliver at a hospital, get a good nursing session in and some skin-to-skin bonding time—then let him get cleaned up. Waiting beyond six hours of life makes handling baby a hassle and doesn't have any major health advantages.

Feedback from the Real World

Some hospitals have changed their bath procedures for newborns. For example, Hoag Hospital in Newport Beach, CA has abandoned the age-old tradition of sponge-bathing and are now immersing their newborns in a full bath. The Association of Women's Health Obstetric and Neonatal Nurses supports this practice, so you may see it popping up in a hospital near you in the future. We should point out that while your hospital may do an immersion bath, we advise a sponge bath until the umbilical cord stump falls off.

Q. How often should I bathe my baby?

As often as you wish.

You can bathe your baby every day if you like. Many parents and babies enjoy the time together. On the other hand, your baby does not make body odor or play in the sandbox yet. You can bathe him as infrequently as two to three times per week.

Q. What soap products should I use on my baby?

We like Dove or Cetaphil soap, because they are perfume and dye free. Plus, they contain a moisturizer (particularly good for babies with eczema). Johnson's hypoallergenic baby shampoo or the generic off-brand is fine for most babies (although most of them are slightly scented). Aquaphor 2-in-1 Baby Gentle Wash and Shampoo is an option for supersensitive babies (although we should note this product contains chamomile, which is a scent).

Helpful Hint

A good rule for baby products—if it smells good or has a color, don't use it on your baby.

Q. Can I put lotion on my baby's dry skin?

Sure. Just be sure it is perfume-free and dye-free.

Most newborns have dry skin from swimming around in water (technical term: amniotic fluid) for nine months and they are just exfoliating. But, if you really feel compelled to do something, we personally recommend

Bathing Baby 411: The 10 Step Method

Never bathed a baby before? Relax. Here is your 10 step how-to guide for a sponge bath:

1. **Get everything ready first.** Have two baby towels, washcloth, a bowl of warm soapy water and a bowl of warm water for rinsing, baby comb, shampoo, fresh diaper, and clean outfit.
2. **Place a towel in the infant tub** (you won't be filling the tub with water).
3. **Put naked baby onto the towel in the tub.** Cover all body parts not being cleaned at the moment.
4. **Expose one body part at a time (starting head to toe) and wash with soapy water except eye areas.** Rinse.
5. **Take the other towel and dry the area that has been cleaned.**
6. **Be sure to get into the creases,** especially under the chin/neck.
7. **Shampoo hair, rinse, and dry quickly.**
8. **Move baby from the towel he is sitting in and dry him completely with the other towel.**
9. **Diaper and dress.**
10. **Clean up mess later.**

hydrated petroleum jelly (Creamy Vaseline or Cerave are examples of brand name products). When it comes to dry skin, the greasier the better. One warning: there are products claiming to be "hypoallergenic" or "natural" that contain food products which are highly ALLERGENIC. Avoid products that contain milk, almond, or peanuts (or arachis oil) in their ingredients. If you don't already read labels, get used to it now. You should be careful about anything that goes in your baby's mouth or on her skin.

Q. My baby has acne. Should I buy some Oxy 10?

No. Do nothing and it goes away by eight weeks of life.

Acne develops from your baby's rapidly changing body hormones. It is the worst from age four to eight weeks. Putting creams and lotions on the skin only makes it worse. Most importantly, your baby is not bothered by it.

Q. What laundry detergent do I use to clean baby's clothes? Do I really need to wash everything before I use it?

It depends on the baby.

Stick with the perfume-free and dye-free rule, especially for babies with sensitive skin. But, that does NOT necessarily mean that your baby's laundry needs to be washed separately with his own expensive detergent. The whole family's laundry can be done with a product like ALL Free and Clear or Tide Free.

For the baby with sensitive skin, pre-wash items that will be touching him. It may also be helpful to double rinse the laundry. And remember to avoid dryer sheets (they all contain perfume).

Helpful Hint

Have a spray bottle of stain remover next to baby's laundry basket. You'll probably need it for the shoulders on all of your shirts, too. Another seasoned parent tip: if you've been thinking about getting a new washing machine, now is the time. Newer, front-loading washers really do clean clothes better. Considering the time you and your washer will be spending together, it is probably worth the investment.

Q. What is the scaly stuff in my baby's hair?

For twenty points, Alex, what is cradle cap?

Cradle cap (see **SEBORRHEA**) is caused by baby's hormonal changes and possibly yeast. It causes dry, flaking patches on the scalp, eyebrow and behind the ear. It can last for several months and sometimes, even years.

Because it is similar to dandruff, it can be treated the same way. Anti-dandruff shampoos (Head and Shoulders, Selsun Blue, Sebulex) work well if used two or three times a week. You can also massage vegetable oil into the areas and lift the scales up with an old toothbrush. You can use an anti-yeast product like Nizoral AD shampoo (over the counter) for resilient cases.

Eyebrows can be treated with 1% Hydrocortisone cream (over the counter) twice daily for a week.

Reality Check: Cradle cap may bother you, but it doesn't bother baby.

Q. Does my baby need a waxing? She has hair on her ears and on her back.

Nope. We know it is cosmetically undesirable (especially for those baby girls), but it's not permanent. What's not normal: pubic hair or armpit hair–time to call your doctor if you see this before puberty.

Q. When can my baby start using sunblock?

Now. Sunblock can be applied to newborns, although staying out of the sun (especially during peak hours of 10am to 4pm) is a better choice to avoid sun damage and sunburn.

The AAP *previously* recommended that sunblock be used only in infants over six months of age (because of the potential for skin irritation). However, the risk of skin cancer (1 in 75 over a lifetime) has outweighed concerns over potential skin irritation. Sunblock is critical because sun damage and sunburn at an early age is correlated with a higher risk of skin cancer later in life. Translation: use the sunblock on that baby.

Select a sunblock with a SPF of 30 or higher. FYI: Avoid sunblocks with

ECZEMA: ADVICE ON DEALING WITH DRY SKIN

Some babies develop dry, scaly patches on the skin (see **eczema**). It gets worse when the skin is dry. The key to keeping it in check is using a moisturizing soap and frequent applications of moisturizing cream. For some reason our family (the Fields) has been unlucky enough to be plagued by eczema. Perhaps it's thanks to the ultra-dry climate here in Colorado, where the relative humidity is often measured in single digits. Mom, Dad and both boys have had it, including one child with severe, chronic eczema. Here are our tips for living with this itchy-scratchy skin condition:

1. **Baths:** Avoid bubble baths, oils, perfumes, dyes, and detergents. Try Dove bar soap (not the liquid), Cetaphil, Aveeno, or Cal-Ben's Seafoam liquid soap (available online or at natural food stores). Consider adding a half-cup of bleach to a full bathtub of water for bath time twice a week to reduce skin germs known to worsen eczema. (*Huang*)
2. **Moisturize constantly.** As a side benefit, this is a great way to bond with your baby when you massage lotions or creams into his skin frequently. A room humidifier will help introduce moisture as well.
3. **Avoid detergents.** If your baby has severe eczema, this family commitment may be worth the effort. Detergents may break down already sensitive skin. Avoid all detergents in the home–yes that means dishwashing, laundry, and personal hygiene products. Try Cal-Ben's products: Seafoam Dish Glow, Gold Star Shampoo, and Seafoam liquid soap (CalBenPureSoap.com). Another option: soap-flakes.com.
4. **Observe** whether eczema shows up when you start adding new foods to baby's diet. Eliminating the offending food will obviously help. And if it happens frequently, you should consider seeing a food allergy specialist.
5. **Don't be afraid** to get a referral to a dermatologist if your baby's eczema gets really bad. Dermatologists are skin experts with knowledge of the newest treatments.

the chemical PABA—sunblocks with PABA are more likely to cause skin irritation than PABA-free sunblock.

Other tips: try to keep baby out of the sun, especially from 10am to 4pm every day, apply sunblock liberally (at least a half ounce each time) and reapply frequently (every two hours and after swimming or sweating).

Both UVA and UVB sunrays can cause skin damage and cancer. The SPF factor refers to UVB protection only. But, obviously, it is best to cover for both UVA and UVB rays. Look for products that contain titanium dioxide, zinc oxide, oxybenzone, or Parsol 1789 to be certain of UVA protection.

What sunblock is best? *Consumer Reports* has a report on sunblock on their web site (consumerreports.com) that includes product tests and ratings.

The key to preventing sunburn is to RE-APPLY the sunblock frequently—don't buy the combo sunblock and bug repellent (we'll explain why next).

Old Wives Tale

Dark skinned people do not need to wear sunblock.

All humans who have skin need to wear sunblock. While it is true that darker-pigmented people have less risk of skin cancer, there is still a risk and prevention is easy.

Q. My spouse and I are both African-American and our newborn looks white! Is this normal?

Yes. The skin pigmentation, called melanin, develops as the baby grows. Babies born with light skin may get significantly darker with time.

Q. When should I apply insect repellent on my baby?

Apply it when your baby (of any age) is hanging out in the great outdoors, especially at dawn or dusk in the summer months.

Mosquitoes and ticks are known carriers of illness. The most notable diseases in the United States spread by these bugs are West Nile Virus (mosquitoes) and Lyme Disease (deer ticks). The safest option to avoid mosquitoes is to stay inside at dawn and at dusk, when they are out in greatest numbers. If you go out and about, have your baby wear light colored clothing, long sleeves, and long pants. And you can get insect netting to cover little ones who are just sitting in their infant carriers or strollers.

As far as insect repellents go, the most effective products contain DEET, picaridin (sold as Cutter Advanced or Off Skintastic), or Oil of Lemon Eucalyptus. But the age of your child limits your options. Picaridin based products are the only ones approved for use in babies from birth to two months of age. DEET based products are considered safe for babies *over* two months of age. And Oil of Lemon Eucalyptus is only recommended for kids over three years of age (because even small doses in young children have led to serious side effects—like coma and seizures).

Many parents want to avoid using harsh chemicals on their child's skin and have turned to citronella-based repellents. However, products containing citronella repel mosquitoes for a mere 9.6 minutes, while 23% DEET will repel mosquitoes for five *hours*. (*Fradin*)

The problem with DEET is that it can be absorbed into the body via the skin and cause "neurotoxic effects" like dizziness (and rare, more serious adverse effects in massive doses). Therefore, you should wash the DEET repellent off once returning indoors. Here are some additional safety tips for using insect repellents on your baby: (*Wall Street Journal*)

1. **Young children should not apply repellent themselves**–that's mom and dad's job.
2. **Don't apply repellent under clothing or to wounds. It goes on exposed skin**–yes, that means ALL exposed skin areas, not just the arms or legs.
3. **Don't put any repellent near children's mouths or eyes**–and avoid getting it on their hands.
4. **Insect repellents come in several forms**–the liquids, sprays, washcloths, and lotions are effective. Exception: The DEET wrist-bands don't work.
5. **When you come back inside, WASH your baby's skin.**
6. **DEET products with a concentration of 30% are as safe as those with 10%.** 30% DEET lasts for five hours, 10% just two hours.
7. **How much DEET should you use?** That depends on how long you plan to be outdoors–10% is fine for less than two hours, etc.
8. **DEET should only be applied once a day.** Picaridin based products should be re-applied every 3–4 hours.

hygiene

The Boy Parts

Q. When can I stop using gauze around my newborn's circumcision?

Once a scab starts to form (around four days after circumcision).

This question usually comes up at the two-week well baby check–but you can stop long before that! The nurses at the hospital will show you how to apply a gauze dressing and petroleum jelly (Vaseline). I tell parents to place a big dollop of jelly in the center of the gauze, position the penis right where the jelly is, fold over the gauze, and seal it like an envelope (the petroleum jelly will allow it to stick together).

You'll want to change that dressing at least three times a day and every time your son has poop in his diaper. Since urine is sterile (germ-free), you don't necessarily have to change the dressing if he has only peed.

The skin starts to heal around three or four days after a circumcision procedure is done. It starts to look gross with a yellowish scab. You will think it looks infected, but it's not. When it looks like that, it no longer needs gauze to protect it.

Helpful Hint

A parent remarked to me, "You need to tell me the endpoint for certain things. Otherwise I'll think I'm just supposed to keep doing it." If you are still putting gauze on your six month old, you have gone above and beyond the call of duty! Bottom Line: If you don't know when to stop, ask your doctor. It will save you a lot of time and labor.

Q. How do I care for my son's circumcised penis in the long term?

Make sure you always see a definite separation between the head (technical term: glans) and the shaft of the penis. In the first week after the circumcision, you won't see this separation due to swelling from the healing process. But once it is completely healed, you should see what we are talking about—the head of the penis should look like a helmet, with a defined rim.

When you change your baby's diaper, gently pull down at the base of the penis and clean the area where the head meets the shaft. This area collects dead skin (this is called smegma; memo to Seattle-area musicians, this would be a great band name). If the smegma remains there, it can cause the head and shaft to adhere together (see **PENILE ADHESION;** second memo to Seattle bands—this is NOT a good name).

Be sure to follow these instructions and ask your baby's doc for help if you are uncertain. Over the past decade, there has been a steady rise in the number of re-do circumcisions to remove adhesions.

Q. My son's circumcised penis is stuck and I can't see the head. Now what do I do?

There are a few options to "Free Willy" (a patient's father gets the credit for coining this term). If the skin on the shaft is stuck to the head of the penis (see **PENILE ADHESION**), it can be unstuck. The options: applying a prescription steroid cream, manually pulling it apart, or having a surgical procedure to correct it. Check in with your doctor to decide on the best plan. If the adhesion is minor, it may even un-stick on its own.

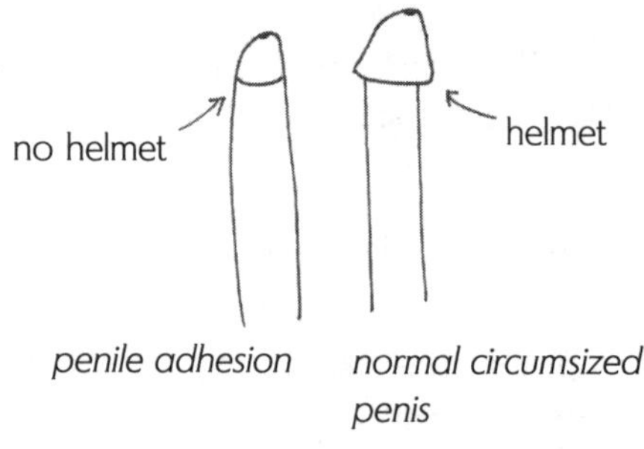

Reality Check

Often, a boy with a penile adhesion is also one with a hidden penis (we also discuss this in the circumcision section of Chapter 3, Birth Day). These thriving little boys have fat rolls above their genital area, which allows the penis to naturally sit in a sucked in, or concealed position. Bring that penis out (by pulling down at the base) for a cleaning at diaper changes, or you'll be dealing with a penile adhesion later. No, you won't still be doing this when your son is a teenager. It's usually not an issue after your son is about two years old.

Q. How do I care for my son's uncircumcised penis?

Here are four rules:

1. Do NOT forcefully pull the foreskin back to clean the penis.
2. Dead skin (smegma) collects under the foreskin and will come out on its own.
3. Once the foreskin pulls back on its own (usually by age five years), clean under the foreskin one or two times per week with water. Always push the foreskin back down after pulling it up to clean it.
4. Teenagers need to clean under the foreskin daily.

The foreskin is attached to the shaft of the penis with tight tissue called

adhesions. Most of the time, these adhesions loosen up by the age of five. Some boys, however, may have adhesions into their teen years and this is still okay (but check it out with your doctor).

Rarely, the foreskin remains tight and hard to pull back (see **PHIMOSIS**). The foreskin can also get pulled back and unable to be manually brought back down (see **PARAPHIMOSIS**).

BOTTOM LINE

If your son has a red, swollen penis, or an abnormal stream of urine, call your doctor.

The Girl Parts

Q. How do I clean my daughter's private parts?

Front to back, and in every crease. Dads–time to pay attention.

Poop has bugs in it (bacteria). Pee (urine) does not. If the poop ends up in the opening to the bladder (urethra), the bacteria will climb in and grow there (see **BLADDER INFECTION/UTI**). This is a bad thing.

Look at your daughter's private parts. Gently separate the lips (labia). You will see two holes. The top hole is the urethra; the bottom hole is the vagina. These areas, including the lips, need to be poop-free zones. Wipe from the top of the genitals, down to the anus. Never go backwards and use several wipes if you need to.

BOTTOM LINE

Don't ever hesitate to change your daughter's poopy diaper, even if it isn't your turn. Delay can lead to a bladder infection.

Q. When can I get my daughter's ears pierced?

Although ear piercing is a safe procedure for your infant, there is no consensus on the right time to do it. Here are some things to consider:

- ***Infection***: Inserting a needle through the skin carries a small risk of infection. You might want to wait until your baby is at least 4 mos. old.
- ***Allergy***: Some people are allergic or sensitive to the metal in the posts or backing. Use either surgical steel or 14k gold products.
- ***Scarring***: Some people have poor wound healing where a thickened area of skin forms at the break in the skin. If a family member has this problem, you might want to wait and let your baby decide if she wants to take this risk.
- ***Cosmetic result***: Babies can be moving targets. Be sure the person performing the procedure is comfortable with infants or you could end up with uneven results!

Mouth Care

Q. Why is my baby's mouth coated in white? Is that milk?

It is either milk or thrush (a yeast infection in the mouth).

When babies are toothless, their mouths don't have many bacteria (germs) living there. Teeth provide a home for bacteria (that's what plaque is). Remember the yeast diaper rash? Yeast likes dark, warm, wet places that don't have other germs around. A newborn's mouth is a perfect locale.

How do you tell the difference between milk and thrush? Milk wipes off and is only on the tongue. Thrush collects on the gums and inner cheeks and can't be wiped off. Thrush requires a prescription anti-fungal mouthwash to be treated. Call your doctor.

Helpful Hint

If your baby gets thrush, you need to sterilize any products that go in baby's mouth (rubber nipples, pacifiers), as yeast will continue to grow on these items. Breastfeeding moms frequently develop a yeast infection on their nipples when their baby has thrush. See Chapter 6, "Liquids," in the breastfeeding troubleshooting section for top tips to treat yeast infections with nursing moms.

Q. When do baby's teeth come in?

Around six to 12 months old. There are some kids whose teeth come in earlier or later, though. Universally, the first tooth to erupt is a bottom, middle one. The rest come in randomly. See the chart on the next page for more info on which teeth come in when.

Q. How many teeth should my baby have at his one-year birthday?

When it comes to one-year olds, teething varies widely.

Some babies have several teeth at their one-year birthdays, others may just have one. Don't worry if your child only has one tooth at his first birthday and his other friends have more than that.

Your baby's doc is looking for at least one tooth that is in the midst of eruption or has already erupted by the first birthday. That means your baby's tooth development is okay.

If there are more teeth than that, terrific. If not, no worries.

Reality Check

Drool is not a reliable indicator of teething. All four-month-olds are drooling and usually toothless. Why? The salivary glands are getting revved up at this age to start digesting solid foods. Yes, a baby may drool more when he is teething, but he may just drool a lot with or without a tooth coming in.

Q. How can I tell if my baby is teething?

Babies who are teething have a lower coping threshold and trouble settling down. But, they usually forget the pain of throbbing gums when they are busy playing.

As a doc, I think I have heard it all when it comes to symptoms blamed on teething–from runny nose, diarrhea, and fever, to sleep disruption. *Teething pretty much gets blamed for everything and is usually responsible for nothing.* Your baby is allowed to have a cold virus AND teething . . . or acid reflux AND teething. It's a good idea to check things out and not

just blame every problem on teething.

First-year molars come in somewhere between 12 to18 months, even if the more central teeth are not in yet. And yes, these do hurt more than the others when they start to erupt. Don't be fooled when your baby starts pulling on his ears–it's most likely not an ear infection. Look in his mouth. It's often the jaw pain from the molars that causes the ear pulling. It will save you a trip to the doctor.

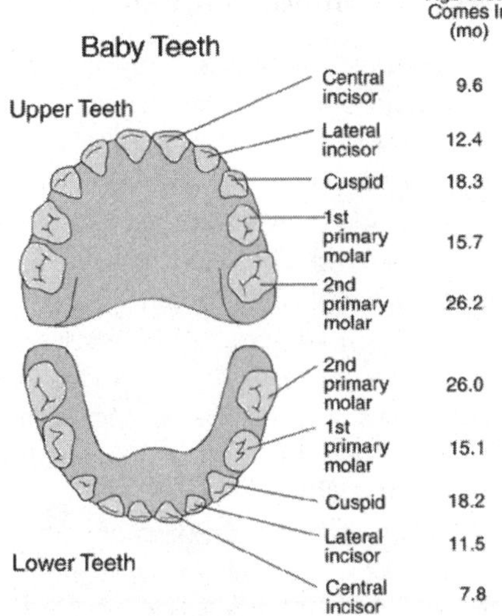

Old Wives Tales:

Teething causes a fever. False. Teething causes diarrhea. False. Teething causes a runny nose. False.

Q. There's something purple in my one year old's mouth. Is this an emergency?

Nope, it's just a one-year molar trying to break through.

When teeth are trying to erupt through the gums, they sometimes form a bruise or blood blister in the surrounding gum area. It looks swollen and purple or blue. This is particularly true for molars, but can happen with other teeth as well. It's called an **ERUPTION HEMATOMA.** No worries. It doesn't hurt and it goes away on its own once the tooth erupts. If you see the hematoma, the tooth will be coming through in about two or three weeks.

Feedback from the Real World

Seth Silber, a seven-month-old from Austin, TX likes to gnaw on frozen celery when he is teething. His dad claims it works like magic.

Helpful Hint

Acetaminophen (Tylenol) is the safest and most effective medication choice for teething pain at bedtime. Ibuprofen (Motrin, Advil) is also fine for babies who are at least six months of age. For daytime, try frozen mini-bagels or a cold teething ring to gnaw on. Teething gels (Numzit, Orange) can have adverse health effects and the FDA warns against using them.

Homeopathic teething tablets, which contain trace amounts of belladonna (a toxin) and caffeine, were taken off the market in 2010 after the FDA issued a safety warning. Teething tablets have since returned to the market, but we don't recommend them.

Another product to avoid: amber teething necklaces. Sellers claim these necklaces offer a "natural" remedy of succinic acid that gets absorbed through the skin while wearing this nifty accessory. But makers also warn that the product is NOT intended for children under three years of age or children who are sleeping. Hmmm. That pretty much eliminates the target market for teething!

Q. When do I start cleaning baby's teeth?

You should wipe your baby's mouth with a soft cloth after every feeding even before he has teeth, according to Steven Adair, DDS, MS, Professor and Chair of Pediatric Dentistry at the Medical College of Georgia.

Start regular tooth care when your baby's first tooth comes in. Use a wet washcloth or soft bristle brush with a pea-size amount of fluoride toothpaste when brushing, at least twice daily. It is ok if your baby swallows a small amount of toothpaste.

Here is a key point: you absolutely need to clean your baby's teeth AFTER the last feeding of the night, before your baby goes to sleep. Yes, that means you may be waking up a baby who has fallen asleep while feeding. But if you don't do this, you will be asking for cavities (also known as **NURSING CARIES**).

Parents fall into the routine of feeding/nursing their babies to sleep (and back to sleep throughout the night)—and then don't know when to stop doing it. If your baby is old enough to have teeth, I guarantee he is old enough to fall asleep on his own and sleep through the night without a feeding. The alternative is poor sleep habits, reliance upon sucking/eating to fall asleep, and high dental bills. Remember, we'll cover the sleep routine issues in depth in Chapter 9, Sleep.

As for tooth cleansers, fluoride-containing toothpaste is best. I do not recommend using fluoride-free tooth gels or baby toothpaste. Why? Because babies like to suck on them . . . and that interferes with your ability to get into their mouths and finish cleaning. Plus they are expensive.

Fluoride is a whole topic unto itself. You'll find that in Chapter 5, "Nutrition and Growth" in the vitamin supplements section.

Q. When is the first trip to the dentist?

Both the American Academy of Pediatrics and the American Academy of Pediatric Dentistry recommend a first dental visit at one year of age.

Which babies are at greatest risk for tooth problems? Those include kids:

- Whose mothers have cavities.
- With special medical needs.
- With teeth, who fall asleep with a formula bottle/sleep with a formula bottle. Or with teeth who breastfeed throughout the night (and don't brush after each nursing).
- With plaque buildup on their teeth.

However, even if your baby doesn't fall into a high-risk category, it is a good idea for ALL kids to have an initial dental visit around their first birthday so you can establish a "dental home." You'll then have a point person if you have questions or a dental emergency. Your child can visit the dentist every six months after that. While a professional cleaning may not happen until your child is two years old, these early visits can provide guidance and direction.

FYI: Tooth decay is contagious. Plaque is bacteria that can be passed from person to person. So it is NOT recommended that parents share food utensils or clean pacifiers by using their saliva (that's gross if you think about it, anyway)! (*AAP*)

What's in this Chapter

- What growth charts mean
- How infants grow (height, head size, weight)
- Teeth
- Calories & nutrition for the first year
- Feeding schedules, or lack thereof
- Vitamin supplements
- Overeating, obesity, and the Body Mass Index
- Calcium, fiber, and iron
- Once your child turns one

Welcome to the world of food. This section of *Baby 411* is dedicated to growth and nutrition—first, we'll look at the general questions you might have about your baby's growth, like what those ominous-looking growth charts really mean. We'll also discuss HOW your baby will grow (height, head size, weight), as well as the needed calorie and nutrition for the first year. Should you put your baby on a feeding schedule? We'll hit that hot-button issue here, as well as discuss vitamin supplements, obesity and your baby's needs for calcium, fiber and iron.

The next two chapters (six and seven) will get into the nuts and bolts of nutrition, as we discuss liquids (breast milk, formula, juice) and solids (baby and table foods). But first things first—let's dive into Baby Nutrition 101.

Infant Growth

Q. At my baby's well checks, my doctor charts her growth on a chart. What's this for?

Growth charts help your doctor follow the trends of your child's growth.

Your baby's height, weight, and head size are checked at every well child visit. (Weight is usually checked at sick visits too, to assess the severity of an illness—for example, dehydration—and in case medication needs to be prescribed). Many

doctors still compare your child's statistics to standard charts created by the Centers for Disease Control (CDC) over a decade ago. The percentiles on the charts compare your child to other children the same age and gender in America. (For example, a boy in the 75th percentile for height is taller than 75% of boys his age.)

While not nearly as popular, doctors should be using the newer World Health Organization (WHO) growth charts for children under two years of age. That's the advice of both the American Academy of Pediatrics and the CDC.

Why? Because the WHO charts are based on how a *breastfed* baby should grow, regardless of what country she lives in. Breastfed babies gain slightly less weight than their formula-fed counterparts from four to six months of life—and therefore may look like they are not thriving on the CDC's charts. Breastfed babies also weigh less than formula-fed babies at their first birthdays. (*Kim*) The WHO also used more children's growth data to create their percentiles, which makes them more accurate. See Appendix E to find the WHO growth charts.

The key issue: is your baby's growth consistent? In other words, if your child is at the 50th percentile for height at three months, he should roughly be at the 50th percentile at six months. What if your child's height and weight percentiles are significantly different? We'll address the issue with a discussion of the Body Mass Index (BMI) later in this chapter in the section on overeating, obesity, and the BMI. Also later: what if you child's head size is growing too fast or too slow? We'll cover that too.

Q. How much weight can I expect my baby to gain in his first year?

Here are some general guidelines. Babies double their birth weight by four to five months of age. They triple their birth weight by one year, and quadruple their birth weight by age 2. After age 2, kids gain about four pounds a year until they hit puberty.

For example: A seven-pound newborn should weigh about 14 pounds at five months and 21 pounds at one year. (*Behrman*)

Q. How tall will my baby grow in his first year?

Your baby will grow ten inches in his first year (about an inch a month for the first six months and 1/2 inch per month from seven to twelve

PREEMIES & CATCH-UP GROWTH

Babies born prematurely experience a phenomenon called catch-up growth. Most preemies catch up to their peers by the age of two, but some continue to play catch up until age seven. Your baby's measurements can be plotted on the full term baby growth chart both by *chronological age* (determined by birth date) and by *adjusted age* (determined by due date).

The head catches up the fastest, followed by weight, then height. (*Bernbaum*) That's why doctors continue to adjust for their age for 18 months for head size, 24 months for weight, and 40 months for height.

months). He'll grow another four inches from age one to two. After that, he'll grow three inches a year from ages three to five, then two inches a year until he hits his growth spurt at puberty (rule of thumb is 10-4-3-3-2 inches per year). For example: A 20-inch tall newborn should be about 30 inches tall at one year.

Q. Can you predict how tall my baby will be?

For boys: Add five inches to Mom's height and average that number with Dad's height.

For girls: Subtract five inches from Dad's height and average that number with Mom's height.

This number is your baby's growth potential. Of course, some people exceed their potentials and some people never reach their potentials.

The first fairly accurate height predictor is the measurement taken at age two years. Kids have established their growth curves by then. A good rule of thumb is that kids are half of their adult height at 24 to 30 months old.

Q. Why do you measure my baby's head size?

Because your baby's brain is also growing at a tremendous rate. Most of this growth occurs in the first two years of life. His brain weight doubles, just in the first six months. We want to make sure this is happening, and that the skull is providing enough room for this to happen (see **CRANIOSYNOSTOSIS**).

Some babies have huge heads (see **MACROCEPHALY**) and some babies have tiny heads (see **MICROCEPHALY**). Most of the time, this is thanks to their gene pool. The apple doesn't fall far from the tree. A baby's head size percentile may be completely different than his height or weight percentiles—and that's okay.

The average newborn head size is 35 cm. It grows 12 cm in the first year, and then only 10 cm more for an entire lifetime!

Q. My baby has a flat head. Will he need to wear a helmet?

Unlikely.

Changes in infant sleep position recommendations have done wonders to reduce the risk of sudden infant death syndrome (SIDS) by 50%. (See Chapter 9, "Sleep" in the sleep safety tips section for more discussion of SIDS.) However, many babies have flat heads (official name: **POSITIONAL PLAGIOCEPHALY**) as a result of being placed to sleep on their backs. In most cases, the head shape improves once kids begin to move and reposition themselves during sleep. Helmets are recommended as one of a few treatment options for *severe* flattening, and effective if used only between four and 12 months of age. (*AAP*) See the nearby section later in this chapter for more on flat heads and tummy time.

Q. When does the soft spot (anterior fontanelle) close?

Anywhere between nine to 18 months. The anterior fontanelle gives the brain the growing room it needs.

Pediatricians rely on that soft spot to provide clues for fluid status (dehydration), infection (meningitis), and problems inside the skull (brain tumors, hydrocephalus).

Q. When will my baby's teeth come in?

Anytime between six and 12 months.

Teeth may erupt as early as two months, but that is a rare event. As discussed in Chapter 4, teething is variable. A baby might have several teeth at his one-year birthday, another may just have one. Don't worry either way.

As a rule, the first teeth to erupt are the bottom middle teeth (medial incisors). After that, it's anyone's guess. There is no order to further eruptions. Frequently, a baby's one-year molars will come in before the middle or eye teeth (incisors/canines).

By the way, once the teeth arrive, you need to clean them! See Chapter 4, "Hygiene" section on dental care for teeth cleaning tips and a handy visual aid to explain which teeth are which.

Flat heads and tummy time!

Why do some babies wear helmets? Why is it important for babies to have tummy time? And what the heck is tummy time, anyway?

Before we answer that, here's a quick 411 on your baby's skull: newborns have skull bones with soft tissue between them (sutures) and a couple of bigger gaps or soft spots (anterior and posterior fontanelles). This skull structure allows the baby's head to squeeze through the birth canal and the brain to grow rapidly in the first two years of life.

By the time the child is two years old, her skull has hardened and those gaps and sutures have closed.

A newborn's malleable skull can put her head at risk for some really odd shapes after delivery. Later if a baby spends much time on her back (or in one position), the skull may flatten. While most newborn heads will eventually round out and look normal, here are some things to be watching for:

◆ ***Molding***. Some newborns look like they have a "cone head" because the skull compresses as it goes through the birth canal (more common in vaginal deliveries than C-sections). Babies who have had vacuum- or forceps-assisted deliveries may have pretty dramatic molding or even a large bruise (**CEPHALHEMATOMA**) that can harden and leave a lump on the skull for several weeks. These irregular head shapes are present at birth and resolve by six to eight weeks of life.

◆ ***Positional Plagiocephaly.*** Yes, we know this is a mouthful–it literally means "oblique (flat) head." A baby who spends significant time lying on his back or leaning his head back (sleeping, sitting in a car seat or in an infant swing) is at risk for a flat head. This odd head shape becomes noticeable after eight weeks of life. In most cases, the flattening is mild or moderate, and rounds out over the first year. You can try to avoid this problem by following the tips at the end of this section.

◆ ***Torticollis***. A tightening, shortening, or bruising of a neck muscle when baby's head favors in one position for a long time. This becomes a vicious cycle, because the baby then develops a preference for turning his head to one particular side. The result? The skull flattens on one side and the facial structure starts to look asymmetric. **TORTICOLLIS** can be present at birth or begin during infancy. Aggressive neck stretching exercises are required to fix this problem.

◆ *Craniosynostosis*. This is a premature closure of one of the suture lines that sits between the skull bones. Unlike some of these other problems, **CRANIOSYNOSTOSIS** is not something that is preventable–it's an uncommon disorder that just happens to some kids. Early closure not only causes a funny looking head shape, but also interferes with the brain's ability to grow. If untreated, these babies can be at risk for vision defects and increased pressure within the skull. Surgery is required to fix this problem.

Now you know how your newborn's skull will change and what problems to look for. But let's look at the most common cause for head-shape problems: sleep position.

Ever since safety advocates recommended infants sleep on their backs, babies have spent an increasing amount of time in that position. Add in time spent in car seats and swings–and you can understand why positional plagiocephaly (flat head) is an increasing concern. Of course, there is a simple answer: tummy time.

So, what is tummy time? Simply put, tummy time is an opportunity for your baby to lie on his belly while awake and practice lifting up his head. This will develop neck and other muscles for head control and rolling over. Tummy time also keeps the pressure OFF the back of baby's head by altering his position.

Here are some simple guidelines for tummy time. For babies age birth to eight weight weeks, offer at least five minutes of tummy time a day. For older babies (two months and up), do tummy time five minutes or more *at least three times a day*.

What if your baby hates tummy time? One idea: have him lie on your chest and he will work to lift up his head. Or get on the floor with baby so it doesn't seem so lonely down there. To help baby lift up his head, you can use a rolled-up receiving blanket under the chest.

What else can you do to prevent a flat head?

- Alternate which direction you do diaper changes so your baby has to turn his head both ways to look at you.
- Alternate turning your baby's head from left to right on his back when he is sleeping.
- Play "airplane" with your baby and let him lift his head to look at you.

What to do once your baby has a flat head or torticollis:

1. Aggressively work on **neck stretching exercises** at home. See Chapter 14, "Common Diseases," in the muscles/bones section for specific advice on exercises you can do.
2. Hire a personal trainer (okay, really it's a **physical therapist**) to help with neck exercises.
3. **Encourage your baby to spend more time holding his head up**–see the tummy time tips above.
4. **Check in with your doctor** every month so she can monitor

your baby's progress.

5. If the head is significantly misshapen and not improving with exercise, **consult with a neurosurgeon or a craniofacial surgeon** and consider a helmet. Again, your doctor should be able to give some guidance. (*Nield, Persing*)

Infant Calorie and Nutrition Needs

Q. How quickly will my newborn grow on a day-to-day basis?

Faster than you want him to.

After you look at the following stats, you will never buy newborn clothes as baby gifts again. You can also understand why babies need to eat all the time. It takes a lot of caloric energy to grow that much.

On a day-to-day basis, here is what you can expect:

- *Birth to four days old:* A weight LOSS of 5-10%. As we discussed earlier, babies are born with extra baggage for the trip out into the world.
- *Four days to three months:* A weight GAIN of about 2/3 to one ounce a day (1/2 lb a week). Note: newborns should be back to birth weight by their second week doctor visit.
- *Three months to six months:* A weight gain of about 1/2 to 2/3 ounce a day (1/2 lb every 2 weeks).
- *Six months to 12 months:* A weight gain of about 1/4 to 1/2 ounce a day (3/4 to 1 lb per month).

Q. How many calories does my baby need to eat?

It depends on her age. Another factor: babies born very small . . . or very big.

The calculations are listed on the next page, but please don't get too

COMMON CONVERSIONS

For the mathematically challenged (that is, us writers) and for those who have forgotten the metric system, here are the common conversions you'll need to digest this chapter:

cc (cubic centimeter) or ml (milliliter) are ways of measuring fluid volumes.
1cc = 1ml
5cc or 5ml = 1 teaspoon
15cc or 15 ml = 1 tablespoon
3 teaspoons = 1 tablespoon
There are 30cc per ounce, or 2 tablespoons per ounce (oz).
There are 16 ounces (oz) in 1 pound (lb).
There are 2.2 pounds in 1 kilogram (kg).

There will be a quiz on this next Tuesday.

wound up about these numbers. Do NOT do calorie counts on your baby. As you can see, your baby's calorie needs will increase as she grows.

Real mom tip: baby's appetite can vary from day to day. This advice also applies to older children. Focus on what your child eats over the space of a week, not every meal. Let's put this in bold: ***Obsessing over every ounce of milk/formula or spoonful of rice cereal isn't healthy for you or your baby.***

That said, here's how many calories a baby typically needs to eat per day (given your baby's weight in kilograms):

- Babies birth to two months consume 90-110 calories per kilogram in 24 hours.
- Babies three to eight months consume 80-100 calories per kg in 24 hours.
- Babies nine to 12 months need 80–90 calories per kg in 24 hours.

Don't know your baby's weight in kilos? To convert pounds to kilograms, divide the weight in pounds by 2.2. For example, a baby weighing seven pounds would weigh 3.2 kilograms.

Now that we have all the formulas, let's figure out how many calories your average seven pound newborn will need each day to grow normally. Realize this is a ballpark figure because each person has individual energy (calorie) needs. Your little 3.2 kg bundle of joy needs between 288–384 calories per day (3.2 x 90 or 120). Breast milk and formula have 20 calories per ounce. So divide 288 or 384 by 20 calories per ounce and you'll find that your baby needs to consume about 15 to 19 ounces a day. But, once again, obsessing over every ounce will only give you an overwhelming need for Zantac.

A word on preemies: Premature babies have higher calorie needs to catch up on their growth. Some babies go home from the Neonatal Intensive Care Unit (NICU) with a higher calorie diet requirement. This is achieved with either a higher-calorie formula or a special human-milk fortifier that is added to expressed (pumped) breast milk.

A word on big babies: The calorie calculations we've made here are accurate for average sized babies. All babies gradually increase their daily breast milk/formula intake and eventually max out at *about 40 oz. a day.* Average-sized babies get to that point at four to six months of age. A ten-pound newborn may reach that 40 oz. a day maximum before his friends do and will just stick to that daily volume. We point this out so you don't try to give him 50 or 60 oz. at six months of age.

Q. Can you show me how a baby's calorie needs change for the first year of life?

Okay, here is an example . . . but remember these are *ballpark figures*. Fair warning: we get many emails from worried readers who think their babies aren't reaching these numbers. Again, there is no reason to obsess over these figures.

So here are the numbers for a 7 lb. newborn: (*AAP Committee on Nutrition*)

AGE	WEIGHT (LBS)	WEIGHT (KG)	CALORIES PER DAY	BREAST MILK OR FORMULA PER DAY
Newborn	7 lbs	3.2 kg	288-384	15-19 oz
1 month	8 lbs 4 oz	3.75 kg	338-450	17-23 oz
2 months	10 lbs 2 oz	4.6 kg	414-552	21-28 oz
3 months	12 lbs	5.5 kg	440-550	22-28 oz
4 months	13 lbs 14 oz	6.3 kg	504-630	25-32 oz liquid + solid food (0-4 oz)
6 months	16 lbs 8 oz	7.5 kg	600-750	30-38 oz liquid + solid food (0-4 oz)
9 months	19 lbs 8 oz	8.9 kg	712-810	liquid (~28-36 oz) + solid food (6-14 oz)
1 year	21 lbs	9.5 kg	760-855	liquid (~20-30 oz) + solid food (10-18 oz)

BOTTOM LINE

Do NOT calculate your baby's dietary needs at every moment. You will drive yourself, your spouse (and your doctor) nuts. This is especially challenging to do if you are breastfeeding and can't see the volume. It's just helpful information to help you gauge things.

The Big Picture: Nutrition For The First Year

The details will become clearer to you as you read through the next couple of chapters, but here is the big picture:

1. **Babies need either formula or breast milk exclusively for the first four to six months of life.**
2. **Some babies are ready to eat solid food (a.k.a. "complementary food") at four months old, and others aren't.** The right time to start offering solid foods mostly depends on when a baby knows what to do with food in his mouth. However, allergists, nutritionists, and pediatricians all agree that there is no need to start before four months of age. Breast milk and formula are the *main source* of nutrition and solid food is complementary. (For details see Chapter 7, "Solids").
3. **From six to nine months of age,** a baby drinks less liquid nutrition (breast milk or formula) as he eats more solid food nutrition.
4. **From nine to twelve months of age, a baby usually eats three solid meals a day** and takes 20 to 30 oz of breast milk or formula.
5. **After a year of age, a toddler can drink breast milk or whole or 2% milk,** with a goal of 16 oz. or dairy serving equivalent a day. Formula is no longer needed. The norm: three solid meals and one to two snacks per day. Toddlers can continue breastfeeding, but they need additional sources of nutrition.

NEW PARENT 411: GROWTH SPURTS

Babies will have growth spurts and their appetites may seem insatiable at times. These episodes usually occur at three weeks, six weeks, and occasionally later in the first year. They may last a couple of days or a week. If you are breastfeeding, do not be alarmed that you can't satisfy your baby. His appetite will ramp up your milk supply.

Reality Check

When it's your first baby, you can't wait to start solid food. When it's your second or third child, you'll avoid it as long as possible! Why? Solid food becomes yet one more chore you have to do–and it's really not that much fun.

We'll go into further detail on how liquid and solid nutrition divide up in Chapter 6, Liquids and Chapter 7, Solids. But, below is the big picture. Remember, these are average ranges. There's no need to panic if your baby isn't right on the curve:

AGE	BREAST MILK/FORMULA	SOLID FOODS
0 to 2 weeks	15–24 oz	none
2 weeks to 2 mos	17–32 oz	none
2 to 4 months	21–40 oz	none
4 to 6 months	25–40 oz	0–4 oz
6 to 9 months	28–36 oz*	6–14 oz
9 to 12 months	20–30 oz*	10–18 oz
12 months +	16 oz whole or 2% milk	3 solid meals plus 2 snacks

**Liquid volumes decrease as solid volumes increase.*

See later in this chapter for information on calcium and dairy requirements at one year of age. For a more detailed chart of liquids and solids, see Chapter 7 in the section titled "The Big Picture on Liquids and Solids."

Reality Check

Babies have "off" days and growth spurts. So, your baby may not be as predictable as you would like when it comes to meals. Occasionally, he will be less interested in feedings. And sometimes, he will seem like he hasn't eaten in days.

Feeding Schedules

Q. I've heard about putting my newborn on a feeding schedule. How do I do it?

You don't. Your baby does it for you.

The phrase "newborn feeding schedule" is an oxymoron. Newborns are learning how life works outside the womb. Before birth, they were on a 24/7 feeding schedule. Now, your newborn will have to rely on her innate sense of being hungry when her body needs energy. However, she will not have a neat and tidy schedule.

Newborns need to eat about eight to 12 times in a 24-hour day. This may be every 1 1/2 hours for a few cycles, then four hours later, then two hours, etc. Somehow, in 24 hours, they do it. This is called "ad lib" or feeding on demand. Ideally, parents (and their doctors) would like their baby to have ""cluster feeding"" of every 1 1/2 hours during the day and a nice four hour stretch at night. But, short of divine intervention, there is little that can be done to *make* this happen.

For parents of preemies: Premature babies *really* need those feedings frequently. Their smaller tummies, and need for catch-up growth often require feedings every two to three hours until they are at least four months old. (That is, four months from the original due date, not the actual birth—their so-called adjusted age).

BOTTOM LINE

Although newborns can't be put on a schedule, by four months of age, your baby WILL BE capable of regular feeding and sleeping patterns. Some lucky moms and dads will have a baby that falls into a predictable feeding/sleeping pattern by two months of age.

Q. My six-week-old seemed to have somewhat of a feeding schedule . . . but now seems insatiable. Is my milk drying up?

No. Babies often have growth spurts at three weeks and six weeks of age. They will have feeding frenzies during those periods of time. As your baby's demands increase, so will your milk supply. (We have a comprehensive breastfeeding chapter ahead in Chapter 6, "Liquids".) If your baby continues to act this way, it's time to check in with your doc and make sure you are making enough milk and your baby is appropriately gaining weight.

Old Wives Tale

Adding rice cereal to formula or expressed breast milk will make your baby sleep through the night.

The truth: Only if your baby has heartburn. Let's think about this in a scientific way. Formula has 20 calories per ounce. If your baby is taking a six oz bottle, he gets 120 calories. A teaspoon of rice cereal flakes has about five calories. It's not providing any calories to fill them up. But it is heavier. If your baby has acid reflux, he will be happier but he still won't sleep through the night!

DR B'S OPINION: FEEDING SCHEDULES?

The AAP advises parents that "newborns should be nursed whenever they show signs of hunger, such as increased alertness or activity, mouthing, or rooting... newborns should be nursed approximately eight to 12 times every 24 hours until satiety." This is termed "ad lib" or "on demand" feedings. And that's pretty much the way it should be for the first eight weeks with your newborn.

Here's the take-home message: lower your expectations. Yes, your baby IS in charge of your house right now. That'll change in about 18 years. Or 26.

Special Concerns

Q. My 6 month old has dropped his weight percentiles from 75% to 25% since his four-month visit. What happened?

Did he start solid food? Solid foods contain *significantly* fewer calories than formula or breast milk. When babies are given solid foods *before* their milk, it reduces the amount of formula or breast milk they drink. Don't get carried away with feeding your baby solid foods until he can take one or two jars (two to four oz. of solids) at a sitting. What many parents don't realize is that your baby will tell you when he or she wants more. If your little one is finished, you'll know it. And until she's asking for more, don't push the solid food. (We cover solid foods in-depth in Chapter 7.)

If your baby is exclusively breastfed, check out the World Health Organization's growth charts. Remember, your baby's doctor may still use the CDC's growth charts, which may not reflect a breastfed baby's growth curve from four to six months. If your baby is tracking fine on WHO's curves, that's all the reassurance you need (see Appendix E).

Q. My nine month old seems to be dropping on his growth percentiles. Is he malnourished?

Probably not.

Babies these days are born much bigger than they used to be (good for them, bad for Mom's pelvis)–thanks to good prenatal care. But not all babies turn out to be sumo wrestlers. Their genetic makeup (i.e. Mom and Dad) determines their ultimate size. Big babies that have more average sized parents start to plateau, showing their truer growth curves as they approach a year of age.

Your doctor will check for iron deficiency anemia at this age, as this can also be a cause of poor growth (a drop in growth percentiles). If your baby is dropping off the growth charts, your doctor should perform a thorough evaluation to figure out what's going on.

Q. My baby has dropped off the growth charts for his weight. What is wrong with him?

No, your baby hasn't begun the South Beach Diet behind your back. The official term for this problem is **FAILURE TO THRIVE.**

Babies whose weight percentiles start off fine, then plateau or fall below the third percentile need to be evaluated. The causes are various and include: poor feeding routines, incorrect formula preparation, gastroesophageal reflux, malabsorption of food from intestinal problems, kidney disease, metabolic disease, hypothyroidism, and anemia.

An extensive medical evaluation is usually performed, unless a cause is found easily. If no cause is identified, a higher calorie diet is initiated and baby's weight is checked frequently.

Vitamin Supplements

Q. Does my baby need a Vitamin D supplement?

Probably. But bear with us–the answer is confusing.

Babies from 0-1 years of age need 400 IU (International Units) of Vitamin D a day to prevent **RICKETS**, a bone malformation (see glossary). Vitamin D may have other health benefits as well but the data on this is less conclusive.

While Vitamin D is present in some foods (cod liver oil, salmon, sardines, fortified milk), we get most of our Vitamin D from the sun's rays. Mother Nature planned on children producing Vitamin D in their skin after sun exposure. She did not plan on the creation of sun block that blocks UVB rays–an essential component of Vitamin D synthesis. (*Gartner, Taylor*)

Because it is impossible to determine the amount of sunlight every baby needs to make enough Vitamin D (skin color, sun block, and the your home's latitude complicate the equation), the American Academy of Pediatrics and the National Institutes of Health recommend Vitamin D supplements for all babies. (*AAP Committee on Nutrition*)

Before we list the specific guidelines, here are few comments:

- Breast milk is perfect nutrition with one caveat. Frequently, there is not enough Vitamin D in breast milk for your baby's growth (primarily because most mothers are deficient in Vitamin D themselves).

- One formula, Enfamil Premium "Newborn" formula (it has a big "N" on the label) contains higher concentrations of Vitamin D, allowing a 0-3 month old to get 400 IU of Vitamin D by drinking 27 oz/day.

Here are the Vitamin D supplement guidelines from the AAP. Vitamin D supplements of 400 IU per day are recommended beginning after birth for:

1. Babies who are exclusively breastfed.
2. Babies who are breastfed and receive less than 1000ml (32oz) of supplemental formula daily (or 27 oz daily of Enfamil Premium Newborn formula).
3. Babies who are formula fed but eat less than 1000ml (32oz) of formula daily–this covers most babies under two months of age. (Or, babies who drink less than 27 oz/day of Enfamil Premium Newborn formula).

DR B'S OPINION: SUPPLEMENTS

I recommend D-Vi-Sol (which contains Vitamin D only). Use one, 1 ml dropper-full for the baby, once a day. Yes, super-concentrated Vitamin D drops are also available, but those are not recommended since it is easy to overdose. D-Vi-Sol is available over the counter or from web sites like DrugStore.com. I also suggest that Mom stay on her prenatal vitamins.

4. After twelve months of age, children and adults need 600 IU of Vitamin D daily. Since that would require drinking SIX cups of milk or consuming other Vitamin D rich foods (salmon, or a daily dose of cod liver oil) on a daily basis, most people need to take a Vitamin D supplement. Yes, that means you, too.

FYI: Babies who are at the greatest risk of Vitamin D deficiency rickets are those with darkly pigmented skin living above latitude 40 degrees (that's Iowa and north). However, breastfed babies in Texas and Georgia have been found to have rickets too.

Factoid: The peak incidence of rickets is between 3 and 18 months of age. However, adequate daily Vitamin D intake may also play a role in preventing autoimmune disease, some cancers, and Type 2 Diabetes later in life, although the jury is still out on those health benefits. (*Institute of Medicine*)

Q. Does my baby need an iron supplement?

There are a few kids who will need this.

Here's the 411 on iron. Our bodies need iron to carry oxygen on red blood cells. Iron deficiency causes **ANEMIA** (see glossary). Anemia causes fatigue, poor weight gain, and poor intellectual functioning.

Newborns have a large iron bank, thanks to Mom. They fill up that bank while in the womb during in the third trimester (which is one reason why babies born prematurely are more prone to iron deficiency). As withdrawals are made from the bank, the supply needs to be replenished via baby's nutritional intake. By six to nine months, the original iron stores are gone and baby is on his own. So, it becomes important for baby to get iron in the diet.

Formula-fed babies get an appropriate amount of iron in their iron-fortified formula. According to a recent AAP report, exclusively breastfed babies need an additional source of iron after four months of age until they start to eat iron-containing solid foods. (*Baker*) (Note: some nutrition and breastfeeding experts argue that breastfed babies do not need an additional source of iron until six months of age– saying the AAP recommendation is based on a very small study of just 77 babies. We point this out because you may see or hear some conflicting advice on this topic).

Here are the latest AAP guidelines on iron:

◆ Babies who are born full term and are fed with an iron-containing formula do NOT need iron vitamin supplements. Babies should eat iron-rich foods when they start solid foods. (See the list later in this chapter in the "Calcium, Fiber, Zinc, and Iron" section for food ideas!)

◆ Babies who are exclusively breastfed or those who are primarily breastfed (supplemented with only a small percentage of formula) DO need an iron supplement from four to six months of age until they start eating iron-containing solid food. Your baby's doctor can recommend an iron supplement that is the right dose for your baby.

◆ Babies who are born prematurely (under 37 weeks) DO need an iron supplement (2mg/kg of weight–your baby's doc can give you the dosing) starting by one month of age. Breastfed preemies need that iron supplement until they are weaned to formula or they begin eating iron-containing solid foods . . . although some docs may recommend an iron supplement be continued until age one.

◆ Babies from 6-12 months of age should get about 11 mg per day of iron in their diets. The AAP Nutrition Committee recommends red meat, high-iron containing vegetables, and iron-fortified cereals to get those dietary needs met. In general, babies should start eating red meat sooner than later.

◆ Toddlers from 1-3 years of age need 7 mg per day of iron in their diets. (If you have a toddler who definitely does not eat iron-containing foods—we know, toddlers can be picky—talk to your child's doc about an iron vitamin supplement. See our sister book, Toddler 411, for more about this issue.)

◆ All children should be screened for iron deficiency anemia at 12 months of age. (Note: this is not a new recommendation. Many docs screen their patients at either the nine-month or one-year-old well child visit.) A child needs an iron supplement if he is anemic.

BOTTOM LINE

Many babies get the iron they need, but make a concerted effort to offer iron rich foods once your baby starts eating solid foods. And if you have a preemie or you are exclusively breastfeeding, be sure to ask your child's doc about iron supplements.

Now you can see one of the key reasons to start solid food at four to six months of age: to get more iron into your baby's diet. (*Baker*)

Helpful Hint

If your doctor prescribes an iron supplement for your baby, do not give it with a dairy product (e.g. breast milk, formula, whole milk). The calcium and iron compete for absorption in the digestive tract and will decrease the amount of iron that the body gets.

Q. Does my baby need a multivitamin?

Babies do NOT need multivitamin *if* they born at full-term, are growing appropriately on breast milk or formula and have a relatively "balanced" diet once they start eating solid foods. So, no, we don't routinely recommend iron or multivitamins for all babies.

Q. Does my baby need DHA/fish oil supplements?

Docohexaenoic acid (DHA) is an Omega-3 fatty acid used in our bodies to make nerve tissue, hormones, and cell membranes. Found in fish oil among other foods, DHA promotes brain and vision development in infancy. But are there lifelong health benefits to daily DHA intake?

Here's a reality check: there is no long-term data that shows DHA has a significant health impact. The most compelling studies, however, show some protection against heart disease and high cholesterol.

Foods that contain DHA naturally are human breast milk, fatty fish

(salmon, herring, tuna, rainbow trout, whitefish), and organ meats. Most commercial infant formulas contain DHA. Some foods, including commercial baby foods, are now "fortified with DHA."

But here's the rub: the fortified foods do NOT have nearly the same amount of DHA that you can find in fish. Example: a three-ounce serving of Atlantic salmon has 1825 mg of DHA. An eight ounce cup of Horizon Organic milk fortified with DHA has 30 mg.

While there is no official recommendation about adding fish oil supplements to your child's diet, the AAP does recommend that nursing moms have 200-300 mg of daily DHA. (*AAP*) FYI: Adults with heart disease should have 1000mg of DHA per day. There are no such nutritional guidelines for kids.

Bottom line: if you want your child to get DHA in his diet (beyond what he gets in breast milk or formula), offer fish on a regular basis.

nutrition

Q. I've heard about fluoride supplements. Does my baby need this?

The answer is a riddle . . . wrapped in an enigma.

Fluoride prevents tooth decay. The process of adding fluoride to water supplies that do not contain it naturally is one of the top public health achievements of the twentieth century. Despite the overwhelming evidence of benefit, there are a few vocal skeptics who think this is a government conspiracy to hurt children. I'll respectfully disagree on that one.

However, kids need the *right amount* of fluoride. Too little, and you risk tooth decay. Too much, and you risk fluorosis (a permanent stain on tooth enamel). Fluorosis occurs only in teeth that are developing under the gums–the teeth are not at risk once they have erupted. So, the greatest risk of fluorosis is in kids under three years of age.

So, how much fluoride the right amount? Fluoride is measured in parts per million or "ppm." As of 2011, the U.S. government recommends that the maximum fluoride level in drinking water should be 0.7ppm. Be aware that some communities (particularly in Texas, Oklahoma, South Carolina and Virginia) have water supplies with high levels of naturally occurring fluoride–above 2 ppm. Some towns have 4ppm or more of fluoride in their water, which is clearly a concern. You can contact your local water department or public works agency to find out the fluoride level in your local tap water.

Here's the key point: babies *under* six months don't need fluoride, babies *over* six months do. Both breast and formula-fed babies should drink fluoride-containing water on a daily basis starting at six months of life. They need 0.25 mg fluoride a day. (Note: the dose for fluoride is in milligrams; fluoride content of water is measured in ppm or parts per million).

So, exactly how much water should baby drink to get the recommended 0.25mg dose? Well, there's no easy answer. That's because your child gets fluoride from sources other than drinking water. Fluoride is not only found in your tap water, but also in foods you prepare with water, and commercially produced beverages, etc. Since the American Dental Association (ADA) doesn't specify volumes, I'll conservatively suggest four to six ounces of fluoridated water a day.

Because striking the right balance for fluoride intake is key in babies, the American Dental Association (ADA) has some very specific advice:

◆ ***Breastfed babies.*** Babies who are breastfed for the first year of life should drink fluoride-containing water (tap or bottled water that has 0.7 ppm fluoride) on a daily basis starting at six months of life.

◆ ***Formula-fed babies.*** For the entire first year, use ready-to-feed formula (no water added) or prepare formula with "low fluoride" water (less than 0.3 ppm is probably okay). The ADA further advises to offer drinking water with fluoride (0.7ppm) once your baby is six months old. Yes, you read that correctly. Always prepare formula with low-fluoride water, but offer additional fluoride-containing water starting at six months of age.

As you'll read in the next chapter, there are three general types of baby formula: ready-to-feed, powder and liquid concentrate. For powder or liquid concentrate (which you mix with water), the ADA recommends either using "low fluoride" tap water or bottled water specifically labeled "purified, demineralized, deionized, distilled or reverse osmosis filtered." (*ADA*) You can also use a home water treatment system (reverse osmosis filter) that removes fluoride from your tap water. Those little carbon filters that attach to faucets do not remove fluoride.

FYI: Just to make your life difficult, bottled water companies are *not* required by the government to label fluoride content. Most bottled water (like Ozarka, etc) contains less than 0.9ppm of fluoride, but it may or may not be less than 0.3ppm or "low fluoride." That's why it's easier to go with the bottled water the ADA recommends (as described in the previous paragraph).

◆***All babies from 6 to 12 months old:*** Babies *over six months* of age need 0.25 mg fluoride a day (about four to six ounces a day of water that has 0.7ppm of fluoride) to get their daily recommended fluoride intake.

So, let's sum this up for babies ***over six months*** of age:

1. **First: Call your local water supplier and find out how much fluoride is in your water.**
2. **If you are breastfeeding or using ready-to-feed formula**, your baby should also drink fluoridated water daily. Again, the safe level is 0.7 ppm. There is no official recommendation from the AAP or ADA on the amount of water a baby should drink. Our rough guess: aim for four to six ounces a day. If your tap water has the right amount, go for it. If not buy nursery water or talk to your doctor about a fluoride supplement.
3. **If you use powder/liquid concentrate formula:** continue mixing it with low/no fluoride water for the entire year.
4. **Which children need a fluoride supplement?** If your baby is over six months of age, and is drinking water that contains LESS than 0.6ppm fluoride for whatever reason (reverse osmosis filtered tap water, well water, etc), your doctor or dentist can prescribe a fluoride supplement. Be sure to ask about it! For yet more details on fluoride supplements, see Appendix A, "Medications." And we'll tackle other formula preparation details in Chapter 6, Liquids.

Overeating, Obesity, And The Body Mass Index

Q. I am concerned that I am overfeeding my baby. Is that possible?

It is unlikely, but it can happen in rare cases.

Let's look at this rationally. Most infants do not think, "I'm full, but that dessert looks pretty good." That is a *learned* behavior in our society. Most

NEW PARENT 411: AVOIDING OBESITY

Set up the right routines while your baby is an infant and toddler. Here are our tips:

1. Keep your child physically active.
2. Make restaurant food a treat. McDonald's should be a once a month treat–not a weekly outing.
3. Offer appropriate serving sizes. Start with two tablespoons per serving. Most older babies eat about 4-6 oz, three times a day until their first birthdays. Offer seconds on fruit and vegetables.
4. Banish the "Clean Plate Club." Don't force your child to eat. Yes, there are starving children in India, but they won't be eating your leftovers.
5. Make juice a low-priority item.
6. Keep the four C's out of your pantry: cola, chips, cookies, and candy. If you have to go out of the house to get these items, they will truly be a treat.
7. Be a good role model. Your child is watching what you are eating.
8. No TV while food is being served. Watching the tube while you eat encourages overeating. Don't watch the news during dinner–set the DVR and watch it after the kids go to bed.

One of the realities of being a parent is that you often end up eating what your kids eat. That's how you end up at the end of baby's first year still wearing those prenatal pounds. What to do? Change your eating habits now and everyone in the family will benefit.

Next, buy healthy, yet good snacks: think portable fresh fruit, veggie spreads/dips, yogurt, and whole grain cereals and bread products. And if you are going to buy juice, stick with 100% juice products. Read the package labels. You may be stunned at what you discover. And be a good example to your kids. Don't drink soda in front of them day and night. Instead opt for milk or here's a crazy thought: water!

In the end, an outright ban on cookies, soda, chips and candy can backfire. As we said earlier, these can be occasional treats. Otherwise, you're going to have a kid who sneaks out to a neighbors' to indulge or spends his allowance on the sly to buy candy bars.

infants self-regulate. In other words, they will eat until their tummies are full and stop. If they do overindulge, they usually just throw up.

But, it is a good idea to learn your child's cues. Some new parents think their baby needs to eat every time he cries. This becomes a set up for obesity.

Bottom line: your baby gets weighed in at every well child visit with his doctor. That's when you will see if your baby is eating enough or too much.

FEEDBACK FROM THE REAL WORLD: AVOIDING THE 4 C'S

You've seen the statistics and you're worried. You don't want your child to be one of them. We're talking about overweight and obese children. They are a statistic on the rise and if they start out overweight, most likely they'll be overweight adults. You've also seen the incredible array of snack foods on the shelf at your local grocery store. So it's time to ask our experienced moms for tips on keeping your baby off the junk and excited about healthy snacks.

1. **It takes a family.** Julie DeCamp Palmer of Seattle, WA spoke for most of our readers when she said, "It takes the whole family eating a healthy diet." So lead by example and don't stock the four C's (cola, chips, cookies, candy) in your home. For those of us who want a little of the forbidden items ourselves, eat them when your child is not around or when you're out and about without him.

2. **Presentation is important.** Healthy snacks can still be exciting to a child when they are presented with enthusiasm. One reader Tiffany Johnson from Vancouver, WA, who is also a daycare provider noted that "children like anything that isn't called what it is...i.e. celery sticks with cream cheese and raisins becomes much more appealing when you call it ants on a log. Cottage cheese with raw fruit or veggies is a hit when you make it into a face and call it clown food."

3. **Moderation.** Yes, an occasional cookie as a treat is just fine. In fact, S. Von Lengerke had a great story about her own childhood where the four C's were completely banned: "I believe everything in moderation is OK. I was raised in one of those families where we could never have soda or sweets, so my brother and I chose our friends based on their snacks. We were chubby kids. I think having some access to sweets, rather than forbidding them, makes them less of an allure to kids and the children, in turn, will have a healthy regard for snacks."

4. **Go with the flow.** "One item I think many parents forget is that kids' eating often ebbs and flows. Kids will be starving and eat more than Dad at one meal and turn up their noses at even

Q. Is it possible for my baby to be overweight? His weight percentile is off the charts!

Yes, but that does not mean he needs to join Weight Watchers.

A landmark study found that 32% of American babies were already overweight at ***nine months*** of age and 44% of those babies were still overweight at age two. Boys and those of Latino heritage are most at risk. FYI: overweight is defined as a Body Mass Index of at least 85th percentile

favorite foods the next. It's not easy, but we offer a variety of healthy and favorite foods at meal- and snack-time and let the kids decide if they are going to eat or not. We don't take it personally and trust that our children will eat when they are hungry. Not always easy, but usually very successful." –Wendy Stough

Not only did our readers have great tips on avoiding the four C's, they also offered food recommendations on what snacks work best in their households. Here are a few suggestions:

1. **Veggie Booty and Pirate Booty.** Manufactured by Robert's American Gourmet (web: robscape.com), the veggie variety of this puffed rice snack food is sprinkled with a blend of spinach, kale, cabbage, carrots and broccoli. Pirate Booty is a cheddar version of the snack and there is a fruit version as well. Readers report their kids love them.

2. Another reader recommended dehydrated vegetables from a company called **Just Tomatoes** (web: justtomatoes.com). Crunchy and salt- and fat-free they don't spoil like fresh food so they're great to pop into your diaper bag.

3. Other readers recommend **rice cakes, whole grain crackers,** or organic products from Hain (web: hain-celestial.com), including their all-natural animal cookies.

4. **Yogurt pops:** Several brands come in those easy to transport squeeze tubes (hint: pick the brands with the least sugar). One mom recommended freezing the tubes for a popsicle treat!

5. **Fresh fruits and veggies are the ultimate snacks.** Bananas, peaches, avocados, or pears are easy to pack and then cut up at snack time. Cooked peas or soft-cooked carrots are also easy to transport and make for great finger foods.

When you find a great product, check to see if they have a web site. We discovered that they are full of nutritional information, fun games and even e-coupons for their products.

or more.

If your baby fits into this category, your baby's healthcare provider may chat with you about appropriate baby-sized serving sizes of solid foods, daily intake of breast milk/formula, and discontinuing night-feedings if he was born full-term and is over four to five months of age.

Q. Is there anything I can do while my baby is an infant to prevent obesity later in life?

Yes. Here are three things you can do.

1 **START A HEALTHY DIET AND LIFESTYLE FOR YOU AND YOUR CHILD FROM DAY 1.** Before parenthood, maybe you didn't work out as much as you should have . . . or ate too much take-out food. It's time to change those habits. Your baby looks to you as a role model–so be a good one. He also looks to you to put his food on the table for the next 18 years–so make it good, healthy food.

2 **BREASTFEED FOR AT LEAST FOUR MONTHS.** Breastfeeding for at least the first four months lowers the odds of childhood obesity. Breastfed babies (no matter when they begin eating solid food) have only a one in 14 chance of being obese as a preschooler.

3 **START SOLID FOODS AT FOUR MONTHS OF LIFE OR LATER.** Introducing solid food at four to six months of life seems to reduce childhood obesity rates. One study showed that formula-fed babies who started solid food *before* four months of age had a one in four chance of being obese at three years of age. Those who indulged in solid food at four to five months of age had only one in 20 odds. (*Huh*)

Reality Check

Could a viral infection lead to obesity? A recent study found that children who had a previous infection with adenovirus strain 36 were often heavier than those who had no antibodies to this virus. Unfortunately, there is currently no way to prevent becoming infected with this virus. (*Gabbert*)

See below for some astounding facts on the childhood obesity epidemic and ways to prevent it.

The Rise In Childhood Obesity

The United States is super-sized, to paraphrase an article in *U.S. News and World Report*. A startling fact: the number of overweight school-aged children has *doubled* in the past 20 years.

Why? Here are some of the key reasons:

1. **Lack of activity.** Children are spending more time (about three hours a day) watching TV and playing on computers and other screens than ever before. Whatever happened to the good old days of playing outside?

2. **Eating out and take-out food.** 34% of our calories are eaten outside of the home. Restaurant food has more fat, salt, and sugar than home prepared meals.
3. **Larger serving sizes.** Super-size servings have become the norm at all types of restaurants, not just fast food outlets. This trend toward giant portions has even crept onto our own dinner tables.
4. **Too many sugar drinks.** Although juice has some nutritional benefits, they are also full of sugar. This adds extra calories to your baby's daily intake. (More on this in the Other Liquids section of Chapter 6 "Liquids".) Don't let your child become a juice-a-holic. Kids graduate from juice to soft drinks. Believe it or not, the average teenage boy drinks *three* sodas a day.

Q. How can I find out if my child is overweight?

There is a calculation called the **BODY MASS INDEX (BMI)** that compares your child's height to his weight. The formula is applicable to children ages 2-20 years of age. The ranges vary for gender and age (because the BMI varies as kids grow).

Here's the formula:

$$\frac{\text{Weight in lbs.}}{(\text{height in inches}) \times (\text{height in inches})} \times 703 = \text{BMI}$$

For children, the risk for obesity is a BMI of 85-95%. An overweight child has a BMI of 95% or higher. To check your child's BMI, go to www.KeepKidsHealthy.com (click on "Useful Tools" and then the "BMI Calculator").

The BMI range for ADULTS is based on the number derived from the calculation above:

Healthy BMI	18–25
Overweight BMI	25– 30
Obese BMI	Greater than 30

For more information on body mass indexes for both children and adults, check out the Centers for Disease Control's website at: cdc.gov/nccdphp/dnpa/growthcharts/bmi_tools.htm

Calcium, Fiber, Zinc, And Iron

Q. Are there any nutrients that children eat too little of?

Calcium, fiber, zinc, and iron. Let's take a look at each.

1 **CALCIUM.** Calcium is a key nutrient for healthy bones. The requirements change as children grow. Babies from birth to 12 months get enough calcium from breast milk or formula. For ages one to three years, children need 500 milligrams per day (mg/day). Kids ages four to six need 800 mg/day. Kids ages seven to 14 need a whopping 1300 mg/day. If your child has a milk intolerance or allergy, try calcium fortified orange juice,

broccoli, rhubarb, or tofu as alternative calcium sources. If you are looking for a vitamin supplement that contains calcium, get one with Vitamin D added (it helps the body absorb calcium better).

Calcium Content Of Foods

Food	Calcium content (mg)
8 oz cup of milk	250 mg
1 slice of cheese	200 mg
1 cup of ice cream	175 mg
4 oz cup of yogurt	200 mg
3 oz salmon	200 mg
1/2 cup tofu	200 mg
1/2 cup white beans	80 mg
1/2 cup broccoli	30 mg
1/2 cup collards	130 mg
8 oz cup calcium fortified OJ	300 mg

Note: As you can see, milk is the most efficient way of getting calcium. But don't lose sleep if your child has a milk allergy. Calcium fortified beverages have comparable absorption to dairy products and the calcium in green leafy vegetables is absorbed better than milk (that is, if you can get your kid to eat kale or collards).

2 **FIBER**. Not only does fiber make your child a regular guy or gal, it also has potential benefits to reducing heart disease. So, make it a little family project to increase everyone's fiber intake.

The fiber requirement for children is calculated by: Age in years + 5 = Number of fiber grams/day. Example: a two-year old needs seven grams of fiber day. However, there are no established guidelines for children under one year of age. So, you and your baby's healthcare provider will have to tinker with how much fiber to offer if your baby gets constipated! Adults need 25–30 grams of fiber per day. The average American diet doesn't come anywhere close to our daily needs.

So, how do you get a baby to eat high fiber foods? Try whole grain cereals and breads, prunes and other fruits, beans, and green leafy vegetables. If you are laughing at the prospect of convincing your baby to eat kale, see the section Solid Food Equals Solid Poop in Chapter 8, "The Other End" for our tricks.

Reality Check

Many parents don't realize that the source of fiber in many fruits is the skin, which usually gets peeled off before a child gets to the fruit.

3 **ZINC**. Zinc is necessary for immune function, cell growth and repair. Research shows kids who have high zinc levels also have fewer serious respiratory infections. Babies from birth to six months need 2 mg per day and babies from seven months to age three need 3 mg per day of zinc.

Zinc is in both breast milk and formula. However, babies need an addi-

tional source of zinc in their food, starting around six months of age. This is especially important for babies who were born prematurely and are growing faster than their peers.

The best and most practical source for zinc is meat. Lentils are another great option. Fortified cereals for infants also contain zinc, but this is less effective (it is harder for the body to absorb this type of zinc). Less baby friendly sources of zinc include oysters, beef liver, and crab.

4 **IRON.** We have already chatted about this one. It's important for babies six to 12 months old to have a daily intake (11 mg/day) for growth and brain function.

Here are some good sources of iron:

Meat, poultry, fish, bread, enriched pasta, dark green vegetables (spinach, broccoli, kale), legumes (dried beans, soybeans, lentils), eggs, nuts/seeds, peanut sauce and butter, dried fruits (raisins, etc)*, cereals (infant as well as grown up breakfast cereals are iron fortified). *Note: Eating iron in combination with Vitamin C (orange juice, etc), helps the body absorb iron.*

**Because of risk of choking, hold off on these foods until after three years of age.*

Happy Birthday, You're Turning One!

Yes, your child is turning one! How exciting, no? No doubt you've heard about the revised food pyramids launched by the federal government. Unfortunately, there aren't any cool food pyramids for one year olds. The following servings should help you determine the proper diet for your child. You can check out choosemyplate.gov for food guidelines for kids ages two and older.

Food Guidelines for a One Year Old

The serving size is listed beside the food item.
The average calorie intake for a one year old is 900 calories. Two to three year olds consume 1000-1400 calories a day

Breads/Grains	**4-6 servings/day**
Whole wheat bread	1/2 slice
Cooked cereal, rice, pasta	1/4 cup
Cold cereal	1/2 cup
Fruits/Vegetables	**4 servings/day (1 Vitamin A/ 1 Vitamin C)**
Vitamin C	
Citrus, berries, melons, Tomatoes, broccoli, potatoes, cauliflower	1/4 cup

Vitamin A	
Peaches, carrots, peas,	2 Tbsp
Green beans, melons, apricots	
Other	2 Tbsp
Milk/Dairy	**4 servings/day**
Whole or 2% milk	1/2 cup
Cheese slice	1 slice (1 oz)
Yogurt	4 oz
Ice Cream	1/2 cup
Meat/Protein	**2 servings/day**
Beef, chicken fish, pork	2 Tbsp
Egg	1 egg
Beans	1/4 cup
Fats	**3 servings/day**
Butter, mayo, ranch dressing	1 tsp

Q. My one year old is on a hunger strike. Help!

Very few one year olds have a world cause they support that passionately!

The *toddler diet* appears as your baby approaches one year old. The typical toddler eats well once every three days or eats one good meal in 24 hours. The food that is loved for seven straight days will be refused shortly thereafter. A good strategy is to offer three food choices in a meal. Pick one that is sure to be a hit—the others are trial offerings. If your child refuses everything, *do not make another meal for him*. Mealtime is over. Don't worry, your child will eat at the next opportunity.

All humans have both a hunger and thirst drive that compels us to fulfill our calorie and fluid needs. Your toddler is regulating his food needs. Embrace it.

Now that you have the low down on your baby's nutrition, let's get specific: next up is a discussion of both liquids (breast milk, formula, milk) and solid foods. We'll start with the liquids.

LIQUIDS

Chapter 6

"In short, breastfeeding occurs above the eyebrows as much as or more than it occurs in the mammary glands."

~ Judithe A. Thompson

WHAT'S IN THIS CHAPTER

BREAST MILK
- THE ADVANTAGES OF BREAST MILK
- HOW LONG TO DO IT
- WHY WOMEN STOP
- GETTING STARTED
- TROUBLESHOOTING
- WHERE TO GET HELP
- HOW TO PUMP AND STORE BREAST MILK
- CONSIDERATIONS FOR MOM (DIET, GOING BACK TO WORK, ETC.)
- INTRODUCING A BOTTLE
- SPECIAL SITUATIONS
- WEANING

FORMULA
- FORMULA OPTIONS
- BOTTLE MANAGEMENT

OTHER LIQUIDS
- WATER, JUICE, MILK

For the first four to six months of your baby's life, you only have one decision to make about her nutrition: breast milk or formula. You can guarantee that decision won't occur in a vacuum: friends, neighbors, relatives and complete strangers at the grocery store will want to weigh in on what's "best." But you are the only one who can make that decision for your baby.

This chapter will offer you the pros and cons of both breast milk and formula. We promise we won't make judgments about your choice. But like every medical organization on this planet, we agree that human breast milk is the perfect nutrition for human babies. No matter how much formula companies tinker with their products, formula will only be a close approximation to the real thing. Breast milk has living ingredients (including all those antibodies you've been making your entire life)...and you just can't package this stuff and sell it in the grocery store.

So, we will do our best to convince you to breastfeed and to stick with it—with lots of tips and handholding along the way. However, we won't make you feel guilty if you decide on formula or can't make a go of breastfeeding. We just hope you give breastfeeding your best effort, because any breast milk you feed your baby is a gift to her or him.

If you decide to go with infant formula or need to supplement your breast milk supply, this chapter explains what you what you need to know about formula options.

Besides breast milk and formula, you'll be addressing the question of what other liquids to serve your child. These include water, juice and cow's milk. We'll discuss these other liquids in this chapter as well.

Breast Milk

Q. I have heard that breastfeeding is best for babies, but what are the real advantages?

There are advantages for both baby and mom. Let's take a look at each:

Breastfeeding Advantages for Baby:
Mother's milk:

1. **Has the ideal ingredients for a human body.** Formula is an approximation of the real thing. Breast milk is living food.
2. **Carries the mother's antibodies to protect baby** from various infections.
3. **Reduces the severity of certain infections**, like stomach viruses and the common cold.
4. **Is hypoallergenic.** It is rare to be allergic to human milk.
5. **Is brain food.** Breast milk naturally contains nutrients (called DHA and ARA) known to stimulate brain and vision development. Interestingly, boys who have nursed for at least six months score higher on standardized tests! (*Oddy*)
6. **Reduces risk of obesity, diabetes, inflammatory bowel disease, asthma, and some forms of cancer later in life.**
7. **Reduces a baby's risk of Sudden Infant Death Syndrome (SIDS).** (*Vennemann*)

Breastfeeding Advantages for Mom:

1. **It may be the easiest way to lose those pregnancy pounds** and still eat like you are a professional wrestler.
2. **It is always ready to serve, at the perfect temperature.**
3. **It's free. Formula can cost $1200 or more for the entire first year of life.**
4. **It reduces a woman's risk of breast cancer.** Any amount or duration of breastfeeding lowers your risk of developing breast cancer before menopause. Currently, one in eight women will get breast cancer.
5. **It may reduce a woman's risk of ovarian and endometrial cancer.**
6. **It may lower a woman's risk** of osteoporosis, diabetes, high blood pressure, heart disease, and rheumatoid arthritis. You can lower your risk of many of these disorders by nursing for at least a year of your life (not necessarily with just one baby). You can lower your risk of having a heart attack or stroke after menopause by 10% if you nurse for at least one month.
7. **It can be a form of birth control, but don't rely on it exclusively** (unless you want a toddler and a newborn in the house!)

ENCOURAGING BREASTFEEDING

How can both doctors and parents ensure that breastfeeding is successful? Here are the AAP's guidelines:

- Encourage "rooming-in" with your newborn at the hospital to learn baby's cues.
- Trained caregivers should formally evaluate breastfeeding (latch, position, etc) at least twice daily while newborns are at the hospital. (If that doesn't happen, speak up!)
- Supplements (water, sugar water, formula) should not be given to a breastfed newborn unless ordered by the baby's doctor for a medical reason.
- Pacifiers are discouraged until breastfeeding is going well.
- Breastfed babies should see their healthcare provider at three to five days of life and again at two weeks of age to assess breastfeeding.
- "Complementary foods" (solid food) should be introduced from four to six months of life. (Good luck convincing your mother about this one!)
- Babies should sleep in close proximity to their moms to encourage breastfeeding. (Note the word choices here—the AAP is not recommending a family bed).

BOTTOM LINE: Breastfeeding is worth the effort it takes to learn how to do it.

Q. How long should I breastfeed my baby?

The American Academy of Pediatrics recommends breastfeeding for at least the first year of life. The latest statistics show that 77% of American babies go home from the hospital breastfed. But only 47% are still breastfed at six months of life. The numbers are even lower for babies who are breastfed until one year of age.

Q. If breast milk is recommended for the first year of life, why do most American families stop before then?

That's a great question. We'll give you the big picture here and then more details throughout this chapter.

Most women stop nursing because breastfeeding can be a real pain (literally and figuratively) for the first couple of weeks. Some lack support to overcome the initial challenges. Others stop when they return to work, when they find it nearly impossible to balance their work-life and nursing-life.

Here are the five key reasons why moms stop nursing before their baby's first birthday and our solutions:

1 **IT HURTS.** *The Problem*: Breastfeeding is a learned process. It's not as natural as you might think. Babies know how to suck, and Mom's body knows how to make milk. But the technique of getting the baby

DR B'S OPINION: GRANDPARENTS & BREASTFEEDING

There are some things about babies that will never change. But there are many things we have learned in the past 20 or 30 years that are different than what our parents were taught (like using car seats, for instance). Learn grandparents' trade secrets for soothing your crying baby because they have been there and done that. Learn the 411 on current pediatric trends in this book.

latched on correctly requires a great deal of patience and sometimes *four* hands. Throw in a hormonal roller coaster after delivery and you'll understand why many women give up. Then comes **ENGORGEMENT**. This is what happens when the milk actually comes in. Your breasts may be more impressive than your neighbor's boob job. Your spouse will want to take pictures. *You* will wish that it is a bad dream and hope that your old breasts will be back when you wake up—engorgement often means tenderness, pain, sore nipples and more.

The Solution: Get professional help to learn how to get the baby latched on appropriately. Know that engorgement will pass. And check out our troubleshooting guide later in this section.

2 **YOU'RE EXHAUSTED AND LACK SUPPORT.** *The Problem:* You are the only one who can feed your baby for the first few weeks while you establish your milk supply to meet your baby's demands. That means you never get a stretch of sleep longer than three hours at a time . . . at the same time you are recovering from childbirth. Sometimes newly minted grandmothers arrive on the scene in the first few weeks of your baby's life. Since many of them fed their babies formula, they will watch you struggle with breastfeeding and throw in little zingers like, "It's so much easier to formula feed—I never had this trouble."

The Solution: Sleep when your baby sleeps (don't try to do laundry or catch up on Facebook). After a few weeks, you can start pumping (expressing) your breast milk. Then your partner (and anyone else who is willing) can take a turn feeding your baby with a bottle of expressed breast milk. Put Grandma to work cooking dinner, changing diapers, and soothing your baby. She is an expert in those categories. And this will give you the freedom to concentrate on breastfeeding your baby.

3 **YOU DON'T HAVE ENOUGH MILK.** *The Problem:* It doesn't happen that often, but some women cannot produce enough milk to meet the demands of their baby. Trying to rev up mom's supply takes a lot of effort, medication, and persistence. And even then, the milk might not come in for some moms. The reasons: advanced maternal age (over 35), some types of breast surgery, or hormonal issues. Watching a hungry baby scream at the breast 24/7 can make any mom want to throw in the towel.

The Solution: You may be able to increase your milk supply by nursing often, pumping between nursing sessions, and taking medication to increase milk production. And remember, every ounce of breast milk counts—even if you don't breastfeed exclusively. Your baby still reaps the benefits from breast milk. See our troubleshooting guide to follow for details.

THE FACTS OF LIFE—A.K.A. SCIENCE OF BREASTFEEDING

Keep in mind these four tips on the "science" of nursing your baby:

- Breast milk production is a supply and demand phenomenon. You should have no trouble making enough milk if the demand is there. Nursing at least eight times in 24 hours promotes a good supply.
- Colostrum, the first milk, is all your baby needs for the first few days of life. Mature milk, the high fat stuff, arrives when your baby needs it–around the fourth day of life.
- ALL babies are exhausted by the birth process and are not very interested in eating for the first 48 hours. They latch on, get cozy...and fall asleep after five minutes. This behavior will change (at almost the same moment you leave the hospital!)
- Babies are born with 10% extra baggage to carry them through the first few days of life. They will lose 5-10% of their birth weight–expect that. Do not think you are failing at breastfeeding because your baby is losing weight.

breastfeeding

4 **YOU RETURN TO WORK.** *The Problem:* Working moms, in general, have trouble finding time to pump. To completely keep up with your baby's demands, you need to pump every three hours (nearly impossible, right?). But remember, pumping *some* breast milk is better than none at all. This is not an "all or nothing" situation.

The Solution: Figure out what works for you. Some moms can only pump once while at work, and continue to nurse while at home. Your body can adjust to many different feeding patterns . . . which means you can continue some level of breastfeeding even after you head back to work.

5 **YOUR BABY HAS A PROBLEM THAT MAKES BREASTFEEDING DIFFICULT.** *The Problem:* If your baby was born prematurely (before 37 weeks), has acid reflux (GERD), or a significant food allergy, it may be even more challenging to breastfeed successfully.

The Solution: Get professional help from a lactation consultant and your baby's doctor regarding pumping, supplementing, or eliminating foods in your own diet to accommodate for your baby's dietary issues. See the section on "Special Situations" later in this chapter for our tips.

DR B'S OPINION

"Despite all these challenges, it is well worth the effort to make breastfeeding successful. Breastfeeding is like running a race, with the hardest hurdles up front. Many moms don't realize that they will be coasting the rest of the way if they just make it past the first mile."

Denise's Opinion: Sometimes, the criticism you get about your decision to breastfeed comes from unlikely sources. Exhibit 1: grandparents. Parents from previous generations seldom breastfed their babies—it just wasn't fashionable. And the idea of baring your breast in

BREASTFEEDING MOJO: LINDA'S TIPS

Before we delve into our breastfeeding tips, we'd like to give a special shout out to a special expert here at Baby 411: Linda Hill. Linda is a registered nurse and a certified lactation consultant (IBCLC). Linda and Dr. Brown have worked together for over a decade. We appreciate her sharing her thoughts and advice. Look for "Linda's Tips" throughout this chapter.

front of them (especially grandfathers) makes them squeamish to say the least. Here are some suggestions for how to deal with their objections.

1. **When in your own home, you have a right to nurse in your living room**. It's your house, your rules. But your dad will probably appreciate it if you either cover yourself with a shawl or warn him before you whip out your breast.
2. **At their house, be discreet.** Try nursing in a bedroom if you know it makes them uncomfortable.
3. **When they ask,** "Why can't we just give baby a bottle so we can participate in feedings," promise that they can when your baby's nursing is well established and you can pump a bottle or two.

When they ask you why you're still nursing your baby at ten months, calmly inform them that the American Academy of Pediatrics recommends that babies breastfeed for at least a year of age.

Q. If I have trouble breastfeeding, whom should I turn to for help?

A poignant comment from one mom we interviewed: "If everyone would just leave the baby and I alone, we could figure it out!" Truer words were never spoken. However, if you are at wit's end, utilize your pediatrician and a lactation consultant. Lactation specialists (IBCLC's) are medical personnel certified to handle breastfeeding challenges. We suggest you ask your obstetrician or pediatrician for a recommendation. Lactation consultants who have an established relationship with your doctor are best. It is helpful to have everyone working towards the same goal: your success!

Q. What do I need to know about my baby's first few days of breastfeeding?

Let's break this down, day by day...

First Day of Life (0–24 hours old):

1. Nurse your baby for the first time within an hour or so of his birth. He will be awake, alert, and interested.
2. At two hours of life, he will be exhausted and hard to arouse for several (three to four) hours. Don't get too worked up about trying to nurse right now. Take a nap yourself. Or, place your newborn skin to skin with you and relax together.
3. Frequency goal: six to eight feedings in the first 24 hours of life.

4. Your baby will probably fall asleep at the breast after a few minutes of nursing. An acceptable feeding session for today is five to ten minutes per breast.

Second Day of Life (24–48 hours old):

1. Today's goal is working on your technique. It may take a second set of hands to position the baby while you hold your breast. You

NEW PARENT 411: BREASTFEEDING LINGO

Breastfeeding has a language all its own. Here is a quick overview:

- ***Colostrum.*** The first milk that your breasts produce. Some women start making (and leaking) it before the baby is even born. It is a high-protein drink, filled with mom's antibodies that boost the immunity of a newborn. It has fewer calories than mature milk because of a lower fat content.
- ***Mature Milk.*** The milk that arrives on the third or fourth day after birth. It is about 50% fat.
- ***Foremilk.*** The milk that comes out in the first several minutes of feeding. In general, it contains slightly less fat. Babies who "snack" end up getting mostly foremilk, leading to more frequent feedings (and possibly, fussiness).
- ***Hindmilk.*** The milk that comes out in the later part of a feeding. It is slightly higher in fat than foremilk. Babies who drain a whole breast in a feeding tend to be more satisfied, for good reason.
- ***Let down.*** When your milk rushes into the milk ducts as your baby suckles or as you pump. Most women feel this "let-down."
- ***Engorgement.*** In the first days when you make mature milk, your breasts may feel full, tender, lumpy, and hard.
- ***Plugged ducts.*** An area of the breast has obstructed milk flow, creating a hard, tender lumpy area. These areas are at risk of getting infected (mastitis–ouch!). See tips below for more info.
- ***Inverted nipples.*** Your nipples have an indentation in the center. It can make it more difficult for your baby to latch on.
- ***Flat nipples.*** Your nipples are flush against your breast tissue. Like inverted nipples, flat nipples can make it difficult for baby to latch.
- ***Breast shells.*** Plastic devices that pull out inverted nipples. They can also be worn to protect sore nipples from rubbing against your bra.
- ***Nipple shields.*** Plastic devices that protect sore or cracked nipples. These are also used for moms with flat or inverted nipples. Unfortunately, they can sometimes limit the amount of milk that flows to the baby's mouth.
- ***Lanolin.*** A thick emollient that helps heal cracked nipples. Brand names: Lansinoh, Pur-lan. Available at breastfeeding boutiques and even Wal-Mart.

will fly solo eventually. See tips to survive the first two weeks later in this chapter.

2. Frequency goal: eight feedings in 24 hours. Do not let your baby sleep more than three hours during the day or four hours at night or you will have trouble meeting this goal.
3. Length of feedings goal: at least five to ten minutes per breast. Do not take baby off the breast at ten minutes if he is still actively sucking.
4. If your nipples are cracked and bleeding, you need help with your technique.

Third Day of Life (48–72 hours old):

1. Your baby is suddenly awake and sometimes, insatiable. As long as your baby has lost less than 10% of his birth weight (and has no other risk factors–see below), keep your chin up and resist the temptation to supplement with formula. Your baby's demand is precisely what your body needs to create the supply of milk.
2. Make sure your technique is okay and you are comfortable when your baby latches on.
3. Frequency goal: eight feedings in 24 hours (it should be an easy goal to reach today!)
4. Length of feedings goal: at least ten minutes per breast.
5. You may feel that your baby is on your breast non-stop. If that is the case and your nipples are sore, take a break if you have nursed for more than 45 minutes. Let someone else have a chance to soothe your baby. (Letting baby suck on someone's finger may be helpful.)

Fourth Day of Life (72–96 hours old):

1. Hello milk! There is usually little question of whether or not your milk has arrived. How will you know? Your breasts will be much larger, heavier, and tender. You should feel full before you nurse, and soft-

NEW PARENT 411: ANXIETY AT CHECK OUT

You will go home from the hospital with a shrinking baby and no "mature" milk in your breasts. Understandably, this often creates great anxiety for new parents. Your baby will do just fine with colostrum as long as your breast milk comes in around the fourth day. The circumstances that interfere with this perfect plan are:

1. Jaundice (elevated bilirubin).
2. Prematurity or small gestational age (small for dates).
3. Loss of more than 10% of birth weight.
4. Delay in milk's arrival.

The AAP recommends follow-up appointments for babies at the third to fifth day of life to make sure things are heading in the right direction.

It's a good idea to keep a breastfeeding diary (see our handy two week survival guide earlier in Chapter 3) that tracks both feeding and elimination for the first two weeks. Or try an app like Baby Connect (baby-connect.com) for iPhone or iPad. If the milk is going in, it will come out the other end. If you are still uncertain of how things are going, schedule an appointment!

er after you nurse. You should also see milk when you burp your baby (and sometimes when you shower). The change in your baby's poop will also tell you the milkman has arrived. See the section Newborn Poop in Chapter 8 "The Other End" for more.

2. If your breasts are rock hard and your areola (the darker colored ring around your nipple) are flattened against them, you are officially engorged. This lasts for a day or two. See troubleshooting tips below.
3. Frequency goal: eight feedings in 24 hours. Do not let your baby sleep for more than 3.5 hours during the day or a four hour stretch at night.

Top 10 Survival Tips for The First Two Weeks

And now, from the home office here in Austin, TX, our top 10 list of advice for breastfeeding success in the first two weeks:

1. Make sure your baby is latched on to your areola and not just the tip of your nipple.
2. If it hurts for more than a few seconds, take your baby off your breast and reposition him. Do not be a martyr.
3. If the position you are using is not working, try another one. See more tips on positions in this chapter.
4. Have a spouse or willing volunteer get the baby's open mouth to your breast while you hold your breast. Have this person pull down your baby's chin gently with their finger.
5. Ask for a nipple shield (a plastic covering with a hole) if your nipples are too tender or cracked to nurse comfortably. This is a controversial option because the volume of fluid coming to baby is reduced. But it may make the difference for some women if used for a day or two. If you choose this option, schedule a follow-up appointment with a lactation consultant.
6. One word: LANOLIN. Various brands of this ointment (such as Lansinoh) are available. Any product with this active ingredient provides comfort to healing nipples. (It's also great for baby's bad diaper rashes.) If your nipples are really in dire straits, you can buy Elastogel (a wound dressing) at your local hospital pharmacy or from a lactation consultant. Your doctor can also prescribe an antibiotic cream if necessary.
7. Use both breasts during each feeding to stimulate milk production. Once your milk supply is established at four weeks, it is fine to nurse on one breast per feeding if your baby consistently refuses the second breast and is gaining weight. One exception: veteran moms may have plenty of milk to accomplish this sooner.
8. Sleep when your baby sleeps. Your baby should not sleep more than a four-hour stretch in the first two weeks.
9. Don't be afraid to ask for help.
10. Don't give up. The first two weeks can be rough, but then it will all be worth it!

4. Length of feedings goal: at least ten to 15 minutes per breast. Once your milk supply is well established (around four weeks of life), some women prefer to nurse with one breast per feeding. For now, use both at each feeding as it stimulates your milk production.

You should be on your way now. Your baby should be gaining about an ounce a day.

Days 5–14

1. Breastfed newborns eat about every 2-3 hours (or 8-12 times) in a 24-hour day. They may cluster feed as often as every 90 minutes (that's from the beginning of one feeding to the beginning of the next). They usually eat about 2-3 ounces at each feeding.
2. Babies who try to nurse more frequently than every 90 minutes are either nursing for comfort or not getting enough milk. So, if it has been less than 90 minutes since the beginning of the last feeding, try using your finger to let her suck. Your breasts will thank you.
3. If your baby is truly nursing non-stop, go get your baby weighed. Make sure you have enough milk supply to meet your baby's demand.
4. On the other hand, do not let your baby go for more than 3.5 hours during the day or more than 4 hours at night without nursing. Frequent feedings improve your milk production and give your baby what he needs to grow.

Two Weeks

If your full term baby is at or above birth weight at his check up, you have my blessing to let your baby sleep as long as he wants at night.

The One Month Mark

Your baby should be more efficient at feeding sessions. And nursing is (hopefully!) on auto-pilot.

See the section called The Big Picture: Breastfeeding for the First Year, later in this chapter for a nice summary of what lies ahead this year.

Helpful Hints

◆ When you are told that babies feed every two to three hours, time is measured from the BEGINNING of one feeding until the beginning of the next. If the feeding session itself lasts 45 minutes or an hour, that may leave less than an hour before it's time to nurse again.

◆ Your goal is to nurse at least EIGHT TIMES a day. This may be every two to three hours or it may be a series of cluster feedings every 90 minutes, followed by a four-hour stretch. As long as the number of feedings add up to eight in a 24-hour period, it is fine.

Old Wives Tale

"My doctor told me I didn't have enough milk."

The truth: Thirty years ago, doctors thought breast milk was supposed to come in immediately after birth—and hence when it didn't appear in day one or two, panic bells went off. We now know that it is Nature's Way to have colostrum first and mature milk later. This is one of the reasons why our mothers did not breastfeed us.

BOTTOM LINE: Be prepared for the 72 hour Colostrum Zone. Your mature milk will arrive soon enough.

RED FLAGS

Check in with your baby's doctor if:

1. You don't have a dramatic change in your breasts by the fifth day of life.
2. You don't hear your baby swallowing ("cuh" sound) when he is at the breast.
3. Your baby's poops have not changed from black tar (meconium) to a greenish-yellowish color by the fourth day.
4. Your baby does not have at least four wet diapers on the fourth day.
5. Your baby is sleepy and hard to arouse for feedings.
6. Your baby is nursing non-stop.

Q. Is it okay for me to take pain medication when I am nursing?

Yes.

The medications that your OB prescribes for discomfort after delivery are safe to take while you are breastfeeding. It's true that a tiny amount of these medicines end up in your breast milk, so it's important to watch your baby for extreme lethargy (for example, not waking up for feedings).

Whether you are nursing or not, you should wean off of narcotic pain medications (Vicodin, Tylenol #3 with codeine) as soon as you feel better.

Breastfeeding positions

◆ ***Cradle hold:*** Baby's head rests on Mom's forearm with his belly next to Mom's (that is, left arm holding baby for feeding at the left breast).

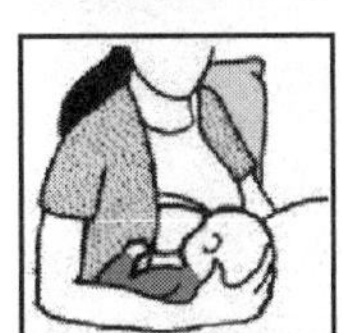

◆ ***Football hold:*** Baby's head rests on Mom's hand with his body coming underneath Mom's armpit. (Good for after a C-section, large breasted moms, preemies, and twins.)

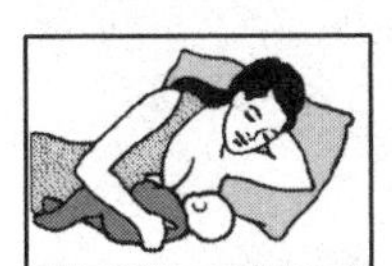

◆ ***Side-lying:*** Baby and Mom lie on their sides and face each other, tummy to tummy. (Popular at night feedings) (*Danner*)

◆ ***Cross cradle hold (not pictured):*** The baby's neck and upper back are supported by the opposing hand (that is, left hand cradles the baby's head to the right breast and right hand holds right breast). This is a good position to start with as it gives you more control. When the latch is comfortable, you can switch to the cradle hold.

breastfeeding

Linda's Tips: Positioning

- Mom should be comfortable with her arms and back supported.
- Mom should not lean over the baby. Instead, use a breastfeeding pillow—a firm pillow that wraps around Mom's waist and allows baby to rest supported. Linda's favorite brand is called (don't laugh at the name) My Brest Friend because it provides more support than the competing brands on the market.
- Baby should directly face the breast without having to turn his head.
- Baby's stomach should be pulled in close to Mom, tummy to tummy.
- Baby's ear, shoulder, and hip should be in a straight line.

The other critical issue is making sure your baby's bottom lip latches onto the pigmented area (areola) and not at the base of the nipple.

Linda's Tips for a comfortable latch

- Position your baby at the breast so that his nose is directly across from your nipple.
- Aim your nipple up with your thumb so that it is pointing to the roof of his mouth when opened.
- Touch his lips with your breast and he will look up to the nipple as he opens his mouth.
- Have his bottom lip latch onto the pigmented tissue (areola) beneath the nipple. Push your nipple into his mouth as you pull him into you.
- If it hurts more than 10-20 seconds beyond the initial latch, break the suction seal (see below), reposition, and try again. DO NOT NURSE IF IT HURTS BEYOND THE INITIAL LATCH. It's normal to feel a tugging sensation. It's not normal to feel pinching, burning, or stinging. You are not doing yourself or your baby a favor by suffering. Pain means you don't have a good latch—or you are paying for previous damage you've already done.
- You should hear gulping ("cuh") noises. Take your baby off if you hear a clicking sound.
- Signs of a bad latch: Your nipple looks like a tube of lipstick or you see a white line across the nipple that eventually leads to cracks, bleeds, and scabs.

Helpful Hint

To take your baby off of your nipple without causing excruciating pain, place one of your fingers into the corner of his mouth and break the suction seal. If the seal doesn't break, slip your finger deeper into his mouth to relax his jaw.

Infant Feeding Behaviors

Newborns can be divided into five types of feeding styles. Identifying what type your baby is may help you understand how to help him feed better. The types listed below were characterized by a study done in the 1950's, but are still relevant today:

1. **The Barracuda.** This little guy attacks the breast and gets down

to business. Mom's nipples sometimes pay the price for this style in the beginning weeks.

2. **The Excited Ineffective.** Yes, this is the baby who is so excited to eat that he loses his latch. Calming, then reattempting to latch helps until baby figures out the routine.
3. **The Procrastinator.** The baby who waits until the milk lets down to bother with eating. There is no rush. Be patient and keep trying.
4. **The Gourmet.** She must mouth the nipple, have a taste test, then begin the meal. Again, there is no need to rush. Let her do her thing.
5. **The Rester** (similar to a cow who grazes). He takes his own sweet time. He eats for a few minutes, rests, then continues. He will eventually finish the meal and eat well but you can encourage him by rubbing his back or head. (*Barnes*)

Q. Is it okay to supplement with formula until my mature milk comes in?

Yes, it's okay, but it's usually not necessary.

Mother Nature has an elaborate plan for babies and breast milk. Newborns arrive with some extra nutritional baggage to carry them through the first few days of life. That's good because they'd rather sleep than eat. It's also good because your body is making early milk (**COLOSTRUM**) that is antibody-rich, but calorie-poor (it has fewer calories in it than mature milk, which shows up around day three or four).

In fact, we pediatricians expect most newborns to *lose* about 10% of their birth weight by the third or fourth day. That's supposed to happen.

At about 48 hours of life (at precisely the moment most of you are heading home from the hospital), your baby suddenly says, "Hey, I'm starving, what have you got to eat around here?!"

He'll act completely differently than his first two days and want to nurse non-stop. That demand drives your milk supply up. Although that can be pretty nerve-wracking for about 24 hours or so, it's what gets your milk production going.

BOTTOM LINE: You don't need to tinker with Mother Nature's grand scheme by offering formula. Unless there is a medical reason to give formula (see box below), let nature take its course.

Top 6 reasons why you SHOULD supplement with formula

Women who are certain they want to breastfeed are often devastated if they need to temporarily supplement with formula.

The key point to remember: you are not a failure. And it isn't the end of the world. There are some key medical reasons why it's necessary. And offering formula for a short time won't sabotage breastfeeding success.

1 PREMATURE NEWBORN. If your baby is born between 24 to 34 weeks gestation, he probably won't be able to breastfeed initially. Depending on how premature your baby is, he might not even eat by mouth at first. You'll need to start pumping to stimulate your milk production. When your baby can get his nutrition by mouth, he can either drink your pumped (expressed) breast milk through a feeding tube or take it from a bottle. Most likely, he'll also need some formula made especially for premature babies to fulfill his nutritional needs.

2 **LATE PRETERM NEWBORN.** Babies born between 34 to 36 6/7 weeks gestation tend to be very sleepy, lazy, and inept at efficient suckling at the breast. So, until your baby gets the hang of it, you may need to offer the breast and then some pumped breast milk in a bottle after each nursing session to fulfill his nutritional needs. If you don't have enough milk, formula will work. You can nurse exclusively once his skill and energy level improves, he is gaining weight appropriately and you are making at least 3 oz. of milk combined from both breasts for each feeding. This is usually for a week or two, or until your baby reaches the day he was *supposed* to deliver.

Linda's Tip: In the first month, be sure to pump for ten minutes every time you "top your baby off with a bottle." This rule applies even if you already breastfed and even if nothing is coming out. It's very important for the stimulation to equal the baby's demand when you are establishing your milk supply.

3 **LOW BLOOD SUGAR (HYPOGLYCEMIA).** Some newborns have trouble maintaining an adequate blood sugar level. Low blood sugar can become a vicious cycle. Babies with low blood sugars lack the energy to eat, which leads to persistently low blood sugar. Besides its negative impact on feeding, sustained low blood sugars can lead to brain injury and seizures. Hence, the temporary solution is to offer supplemental formula in addition to nursing until your baby maintains normal blood sugar levels. For a full term baby, born between 37 to 40 weeks, this may be for a feeding or two, or a day or two at most.

4 **EXCESSIVE WEIGHT LOSS.** A newborn that loses more than 10% of his birth weight usually needs both breast milk and formula until he starts to gain weight. As we mentioned earlier, it is normal and expected for your baby to lose 10% of his weight at birth. But more than 10% means that your baby is dehydrated. Dehydrated babies are not happy babies. They lack energy to eat (another vicious cycle) and so they lose more weight, end up with low blood sugar, and develop jaundice (more on this next). Don't let your baby become a martyr in the name of breastfeeding. If he is dehydrated and your mature milk hasn't arrived yet, supplement with formula. It prevents him from having other medical issues. Remember, this is temporary until your baby gains weight and your mature milk is plentiful enough to feed him.

5 **SIGNIFICANT JAUNDICE.** Let's talk about poop for a minute. Humans clear out a waste product (called **BILIRUBIN**) in their poop. Bilirubin has a yellow pigment to it. In the first few days of life, a newborn doesn't clear out much bilirubin because her liver (which breaks it down) doesn't function at 100% and she isn't pooping very much (since she isn't eating much). As a result, all newborns temporarily collect some bilirubin in their skin, causing a yellowish glow (called *physiologic jaundice*). This resolves on its own around three to five days of life once they eat a lot, poop a lot,

and have fully functioning livers.

For a variety of reasons, some newborns get significantly jaundiced. If there is more bilirubin than the skin can handle, it collects in the brain and can cause permanent brain damage (called *kernicterus*). It goes without saying that everyone wants to avoid this! There are several ways to prevent kernicterus, but the first and simplest thing to do is to get a newborn to eat and poop more. The more he eats, the more he poops, the more he gets rid of his bilirubin load. For a breastfed baby, that means supplementing with formula for a few days.

Once you see the poop turn from black to dark green to yellow (that yellow pigmented bilirubin makes it change color) and your mature breast milk is in, the bilirubin levels will drop and you'll be able to resume nursing exclusively.

6 **MATERNAL REASON.** Sometimes a mom intends to nurse, but encounters a medical problem of her own that prevents her from doing so at first. Those problems include: postpartum bleeding, high blood pressure, etc. If this happens to you, don't let it get you down. Nurse as much as your OB doctor allows and let your baby have some formula until you have recuperated. Your baby will be fine. You need to be healthy to be able to make milk. If you can, pump to protect your milk supply.

THE LOW DOWN ON BREAST PUMPS

You can rent a hospital grade pump, purchase an electric pump, or purchase a manual pump.

A smart move: rent a pump when you go home from the hospital. Renting lets you figure out whether you need a pump long term, without making a serious financial commitment. Most hospitals offer rentals or at least provide a list of medical supply companies in the area that rent pumps.

Moms who are returning to work but still want to pump have two options: rent a pump for an extended period of time or buy a pump. Either way recommend a professional-grade dual electric pump. You can control the speed and pressure, which less expensive models don't allow. For working moms, efficiency is key. You can pump both breasts simultaneously in 15 minutes. A Medela rental pump will cost $45-75 per month to rent. It pumps 50 cycles per minute (baby sucks about 60 times/minute) at a comfortable pressure.

You can purchase a professional grade equivalent pump (example: Medela "Pump In Style") for $250 to $300. Another good brand: Ameda Purely Yours for $200. Both are decent double pumps.

You might get a manual pump as a shower gift. This is convenient for emergencies or travel. The mechanism is similar to operating a bike pump. Your arm may get tired out long before your breasts have emptied.

FYI: For an in-depth discussion on buying a breast pump (including brand name reviews) as well as the best milk storage options, check out our other book *Baby Bargains* (see back of this book for details).

Top 3 reasons why women end up supplementing (but don't need to)

◆ *Exhaustion.* Delivering a baby is an exhausting experience. After many hours of labor, you'll just want someone to tuck you in for a long night's sleep. No such luck for a breastfeeding mom. You might get about four to five hours of sleep after delivery (the "honeymoon" period while your exhausted newborn sleeps too). Then, the party is over. You'll need to feed your baby EIGHT times every 24 hours—yes, that's every three hours on average.

To get your milk production up to speed, you shouldn't go any longer than four hours between feedings. With that pace, it's no wonder women ask to let their baby camp out in the nursery and get a bottle of formula while mom gets some shut-eye. If this is the deal breaker for whether or not you will continue breastfeeding, okay, take a break. But we don't recommend it. Once you start on this road, you're more likely to give up nursing altogether. If you can get through these early days, we promise it gets easier!

◆ *Pain.* If you start off with poor technique, each breastfeeding session is incredibly painful. The thought of bringing the baby to the breast can bring some women to tears. Hopefully, our tips will prevent this situation from happening. But if you find yourself in this place and need to take a break from nursing for a few feedings or 24 hours until your nipples can heal, so be it. You need to continue removing milk from your breasts for every feeding, though. Pump and offer that expressed milk to your little one. You can also temporarily use nipple shields while nursing. You are more likely to continue nursing if you can forge ahead (with proper technique going forward, of course).

◆ *Fear.* Women mistakenly fear that their baby is not getting enough to eat when they are producing early milk (**COLOSTRUM**). They see their baby losing weight and get worried. Don't worry! If your baby has no medical issues and your pediatrician does not feel you need to supplement with formula, you don't need to supplement with formula! If you start supplementing when you don't need to, your baby will fill up. You need his hunger drive to get your breast milk production going. Don't mess with Mother Nature.

Nursing: Two Weeks and Beyond

At this point, nursing should be fairly routine and comfortable (if not, read the next section on troubleshooting). Take a look at the Big Picture summary at the end of this section to see how your baby begins to take larger quantities of breast milk at each feeding. But in general, expect that your baby will continue to eat about every two to three hours during the day and start eating less often (and sleeping more) at night after the first two months of life.

Here are some common concerns that arise after two weeks and beyond:

Q. Can my baby use a pacifier if I am nursing?

Yes. Babies are soothed by sucking. In the first two months of life, sucking on a pacifier may be the only thing that reliably settles your baby. Despite what you may hear, binkies and breastfeeding can mix.

Experts used to believe that pacifiers shortened the length of time that moms continued to nurse. So, it was almost taboo to offer a binky to a breastfed baby. Research suggests otherwise. Pacifiers don't make a baby or mom stop breastfeeding. Parents who use a binky choose to discontinue nursing for a variety of other reasons. (*O'Connor*)

In our opinion, breastfeeding and pacifiers are not mutually exclusive—pacifiers are NOT evil. But it is wise to wait on introducing a pacifier until your baby is a confident breastfeeder (between one and four weeks old) because babies suck pacifiers differently than the breast. And we recommend the "Soothie" brand (green with a long nipple; web: soothie-pacifier.com) as it is more similar to the human nipple than other brands. A reasonable alternative to the pacifier is a parent's finger. The other obvious alternative is to offer your breast for comfort nursing. This may or may not be for you.

Note: as we'll discuss in the section on Sleep Safety Tips in Chapter 9, Sleep, pacifiers have been shown to reduce the risk of SIDS in babies under six months.

BOTTOM LINE

If you opt to use a pacifier, we suggest getting it out of your baby's life by six months of age when he no longer needs to be soothed by sucking. For more information, see the section on Soothing a New Baby in Chapter 11, "Discipline."

Q. My baby prefers one of my breasts to the other. Is that ok?

Yes. Why does this happen? One of your breasts may produce more milk than the other, flow differently or be easier to latch onto. And your baby will figure that out and may develop a preference for the better-producing breast. Some babies will even refuse the breast that has slower flow or less volume.

If your baby doesn't get too frustrated, offer the slower flow breast first because he will nurse more aggressively at the beginning and that helps increase your supply. When he becomes frustrated, switch to the other breast. And try pumping the lower-producing breast after nursing to improve production.

No worries if your baby completely refuses one breast. It's possible to make enough milk from one breast to completely satisfy your baby. (I've even had a patient whose mom had a mastectomy and successfully nursed on the remaining breast!)

Nutrition is not the issue. You will just start to look rather lopsided if you nurse on only one side!

Q. My baby fills up after taking just one breast. Can I nurse alternate breasts at each nursing session?

Yes. Once breastfeeding is well established and your milk supply is stable, it's fine to alternate breasts for each feeding. For first time moms, that's about 3-4 weeks after delivery. For seasoned moms, their milk supply is fairly stable after two weeks.

Insider tip: some moms place a safety pin on the bra cup of the breast they used at the last feeding. (Sleep deprivation takes a toll on the memory!)

INSIDER SECRETS: TOP 8 BREASTFEEDING PROBLEMS . . .

Sure, you know that breastfeeding is best for your baby . . . but if something goes wrong? Don't give up! Here are the top eight breastfeeding problems and how to solve them.

PROBLEM	SOLUTIONS
#1 Underproduction ◆ *Newborn*: less than three poops a day by Day 3 of life, poop not yellow/seedy by Day 5 of life, less than six wet diapers a day by Day 4 of life, no weight gain by Day 5 of life, birth weight not regained by Day 14. ◆ *Day 5-4 Months:* weight gain less than 5 oz/week. ◆ *4 Months-1 Year*: weight gain less than 3 oz/week.	◆ *Continue nursing and pump with hospital-grade pump after each feeding* ◆ *After nursing, feed baby with expressed breast milk or formula* ◆ *Check baby's ability to get milk at the breast and discuss options to increase milk production with a certified lactation consultant.*
#2 Overproduction ◆ *Baby*: coughs or chokes while nursing, excessive weight gain, green frothy poops. ◆ *Mom*: always feels full, milk shoots out forcefully.	◆ *Nurse on one breast per feeding and return to that same breast if baby wants to nurse within two hours.* ◆ *Manually express or pump off for a minute before having the baby latch on (don't overdo it, or you will have even more milk production!)* ◆ *Lean back while nursing to reduce the flow.*
#3 Engorgement ◆ *Baby*: has trouble latching on. ◆ *Mom*: has severe fullness and pain, nipples are flattened.	◆ *Increase milk removal by nursing more often or pumping.* ◆ *Cold packs for 10-15 minutes after feedings.* ◆ *Ibuprofen.* ◆ *Should get better in 1-2 days, if not, visit a lactation consultant.*
#4 Nipple Pain ◆ *Mom*: nipples/areola are red, cracked or bleeding, look like a tube of lipstick after nursing, look blanched after nursing, or have blebs (white cysts).	◆ *Check baby's mouth and chin (tongue tie or a recessed chin can cause a latch problem).* ◆ *Have a lactation professional assess how baby is latching on.* ◆ *Have a lactation professional assess mom for a nipple infection.*

. . . AND SOLUTIONS!

#5 Nipple Bacterial Infection

◆ *Mom:* nipples are cracked, painful during latching, draining pus or has golden crust.

◆ *Mom's doctor can prescribe an antibiotic cream until nipples are healed.*

#6 Plugged Duct

◆ *Mom*: localized area of a breast is painful, red, and tender usually before nursing, decreased milk production, fever free or temperature below 101.3F.

◆ *Breastfeed frequently, always starting on the affected breast.*

◆ *Position baby with chin pointing towards the affected area.*

◆ *Massage the area while nursing or pumping. Apply heat before and ice after feedings.*

◆ *See a lactation consultant for more help.*

#7 Mastitis

◆ *Mom*: Fever, body aches, redness or red streak on breast(s), decreased milk production

◆ *Milk is safe to use. Nurse frequently on the affected breast.*

◆ *Use a hot pack on the breast for four minutes before each feeding (if breast is not feeling hot).*

◆ *Alternatively, if the breast feels hot, use ice pack before and after feedings.*

◆ *Mom's doctor can prescribe an oral antibiotic that's ok to use while nursing.*

◆ *Mom can take probiotics while taking antibiotics to prevent a yeast infection.*

#8 Yeast infection

◆ *Baby*: may be symptom free, or may have white adherent plaques on the tongue, inside of cheek, inner lip, and gum line.

◆ *Mom*: may be symptom free or may have sharp/shooting/burning pain while nursing, shiny/red areola, cracked/ easily bleeding nipples, painful or itchy nipples/breasts throughout the day.

◆ *Mom and baby should be treated for infection, even if only one party has symptoms.*

◆ *Baby: doctor can prescribe oral antifungal medication.*

◆ *Mom: can use over-the-counter antifungal cream on nipples or doctor can prescribe oral antifungal if pain is deep. Take probiotic supplement.*

◆ *Sterilize all pacifiers, teething toys, pump parts, breast shells, bottle nipples daily.*

◆ *Good hand washing before and after breastfeeding. (West)*

This chart is adapted with permission from Physician's Breastfeeding Triage Tool Kit, developed by Diana West, IBCLC, for International Lactation Consultant Association, Copyright 2007.

Q. I am exhausted after several weeks of every-two-hour nursing sessions 24/7. Will I get more sleep if I supplement with formula?

Nope. A recent study compared a mother's level of sleep deprivation (and ability to function) after living with a newborn (between 2–12 weeks old) to what the baby ate—exclusively breast milk, exclusively formula, or a combination of breast milk and formula. The answer? There was absolutely no statistical difference . . . all the mothers were walking zombies! (*Montgomery-Downs*)

DR B'S OPINION

"Babies will get what they need from breast milk, at the expense of Mom's body. I recommend continuing your prenatal vitamins if you are nursing."

Although what you feed your baby doesn't make a bit of difference, you are certainly entitled to a few hours of uninterrupted shut-eye for your physical and mental health. After 2–4 weeks, you can pump (express) some breast milk and let your partner take a turn doing an evening feeding. Getting a four or five hour stretch of sleep will feel like an amazing night's sleep!

Q. My four month old still nurses every two to three hours at night. Is this really necessary or is it just a habit?

Four-month old babies who were born full-term, don't have acid reflux (GERD), and are gaining weight appropriately should be able to sleep at least *six* hours without needing to eat. Five-month olds can go at least *nine* hours. And six-month olds can go up to *twelve* hours!

Bottom line: your baby should have at least one, long sleep stretch a night. Then it may be mealtime every two to three hours after that. If he awakens after six hours, asks to eat and actually EATS, then assume he is hungry and continue to follow his cues.

But if he fusses and falls asleep at the breast without actually eating much, that is your clue that he doesn't really need to be fed. Next time just try patting him back to sleep. That will help begin the process of lengthening that "long stretch" of sleep.

However, even if your baby is sleeping longer, you may have to get up

DR B'S OPINION: MEDICATIONS AND BREASTFEEDING

Mothers frequently call me about medications they are taking and if they are okay to use while breastfeeding. Although I sound smart knowing all the answers on the phone, I find the answers in a book called *Medications and Mother's Milk* by Thomas Hale, Ph.D. If you are planning on nursing for the long haul, or have a chronic medical condition, it might be worth having this gem on your bookshelf at home. (Find it at iBreastfeeding.com or 800-378-1317.)

DIETARY RESTRICTIONS FOR CERTAIN CIRCUMSTANCES

Two and a half percent of all newborns have a hypersensitivity to cow's milk. Occasionally, babies with a milk allergy can have problems if their breastfeeding moms have milk products in their diet (see "I Give Up" story below). For more information on food allergies, see Chapter 7, "Solid Nutrition." (*Sampson*)

and pump. Some moms need to pump after six hours, otherwise their milk supply vanishes. Moms who struggle to make enough milk often have to follow this rule: *aim for at least six to eight stimulations a day (whether pumping or breastfeeding) and take no longer than one six hour break of no stimulation.*

If your healthy, thriving baby is over six months of age and nursing every two to three hours at night, he is officially a trained night feeder. This is not good! Read Chapter 9, Sleep so you can all get more sleep!

Reality Check

Babies continue to eat about every two to three hours during the day for a very long time. Even preschoolers eat three meals and two snacks a day (eating about every three hours). Do not try to increase the time interval between meals during the day—just aim for spacing them out at night.

Q. I need to leave my baby for a few days. Do you have any tips?

Leaving your nursing baby can be anxiety producing for both mom and baby. Some ideas to make life easier are:

- Start stockpiling expressed breast milk in the freezer a few weeks before the trip.
- Take an electric breast pump and a hand held one if you have a long flight.
- Offer breast milk in a bottle once daily before your travel begins.
- Take a picture of baby with you to inspire you to let down.
- Leave your slept-in nightie or another clothing item with your scent on it for your baby.
- Know that your baby will be just fine while you are away and happy to see you when you return.

Linda's tip: Fresh breast milk is always better for your baby than frozen. Freezing/warming destroys certain properties in your milk like some vitamins and antibodies. So, while this thawed breast milk is still better for your baby than formula, it is better to pump for the next day's supply and only have an emergency stash of frozen milk in the freezer. If you are going to be away from your baby for a few days, then stockpiling in the freezer is the way to go!

Trouble Shooting

When breastfeeding goes wrong, these are the usual suspects:

- **Underproduction or insufficient transfer of milk to the baby.**
- **Overproduction.**
- **Engorgement.**
- **Nipple pain.**
- **Nipple bacterial infection.**
- **Plugged duct.**
- **Mastitis.**
- **Yeast overgrowth/infection.**

Here is our discussion on these problems and solutions in full detail. See the handy summary table of survival tips earlier in this chapter.

1 UNDERPRODUCTION OR INSUFFICIENT TRANSFER OF MILK TO THE BABY.

Q. My milk supply is low. Can I do anything to improve my production?

Milk supply is based on demand. So if your baby is not stimulating you enough (premature babies and late preterm infants are often at fault for this), use a breast pump to rev up the supply. Pump a few minutes after each feeding session.

And yes, some women do not make enough breast milk to feed their baby. Here are some suggestions to pump up the volume:

1. Try pumping with a high-efficiency breast pump AFTER nursing sessions. An empty breast signals the body to make more milk.
2. Try herbal supplements. Fenugreek (three pills, three times daily) and blessed thistle (three pills, three times daily) or a tincture called More Milk Plus appear to be safe and may improve milk supply.
3. Try Reglan (metoclopramide). This medication requires a prescription from your doctor and may have some undesirable side effects.
4. Eat and sleep more. Your milk production depends on you taking good care of yourself.
5. Try eating a combo carbohydrate/protein snack just before or during nursing. This increases your prolactin hormone level, which in turn, increases milk supply.

FYI: Sometimes the problem lies with the baby, and not with the mother. A mom may make plenty of breast milk, but the baby does not effectively get it from the breast. This is called ***insufficient milk transfer***. This may happen with late preterm babies, babies with medical issues (for example: heart, neurologic problems, etc.), and babies with mouth abnormalities like a tongue-tie (see more on this below).

2 OVERPRODUCTION.

Q. Holy cow! I have to change my shirt before I start nursing! I have so much milk, what do I do?

Some women naturally make an overabundance of milk. We're not

talking just in the first couple of weeks, when your supply and your baby's demand are trying to sync. We are talking several weeks down the road, you still look like Dolly Parton, and your milk shoots out across the room. If this describes your situation, your baby may be unhappy (and even upset). He may feel like he's treading water in the ocean with the excessive flow. And as a result, he may choke, cough, and arch while nursing.

If you have this issue, try nursing at just one breast per feeding. Lean back or lie flat while you nurse to slow down the velocity of that milk stream!

Linda's tip: Remove your baby from your breast after the first several gulps and squeeze out the overflowing (or spraying) milk into a burp cloth. Then put the baby back to the breast. Repeat with each let down or gulping phase.

3 ENGORGEMENT.

Q. My breasts look like I have had implants and my baby can't get latched on. Help!

Welcome to engorgement. Don't worry, this is only a two or three day experience at most.

When your body first starts making milk, it sometimes gets carried away. This also happens if your baby takes less volume or suddenly starts sleeping through the night. Here are some ways to feel better:

1. **Pump or manually express for a few minutes before getting baby latched on.** Your nipple will stand more upright, be soft, and compressible.
2. **Pump or manually express only to soften the breast.** Pump off after feedings only if your baby is unsuccessful in nursing. Otherwise it can create an even greater supply of milk.
3. **Wear a bra 24 hours a day for support.** No underwires, ladies.
4. **Take a hot shower and massage breasts to encourage let down.**
5. **Cabbage leaves.** Yes, they can help. Try this: wear washed, chilled, crushed cabbage leaves in your bra. Replace wilted leaves every fifteen minutes for a total 45 minute experience, three times daily. Reality check: your baby may refuse the breast due to the cabbage flavor, so try to keep the cabbage away from your nipples.
6. **Put a bag of frozen vegetables** on your breasts for ten to 20 minutes before nursing if your breasts are hard and not leaking. Some women feel better using ice packs after nursing, too.
7. **Encourage your baby to nurse at least ten minutes on each breast.** This is the time women usually get desperate and wake their babies up to relieve their own discomfort.
8. **Take some ibuprofen (Motrin).** Yes, it's safe to use while breastfeeding. (*Huggins*)

4 NIPPLE PAIN.

Q. Ouch! My nipples hurt! Any suggestions?

There are several reasons why your nipples may hurt during or after nursing. Solving this mystery, and fixing the problem will make breastfeeding much more pleasant and enjoyable. And in turn, it will enable you to successfully continue nursing!

◆ **Poor position.** There are several positions that keep you and your baby comfortable. If one is not working, try another one. See the recommendations below and the graphics earlier in this chapter.

◆ **Poor latch.** You should hear your baby swallowing/gulping. Clicking is NOT a sound you should hear. Get your baby to open wide, with lips curled out. Make sure his nose and chin are next to your breast. Don't let go of your breast until your baby is securely latched on. Poor latch leads to problem sore nipples. If your nipple looks like a new tube of lipstick after nursing, you have a problem (see picture). When your nipple returns from the lipstick shape to the normal shape after a few minutes, you may see a bruised line (called a ***compression stripe***) down the center of your nipple. With continued shallow latches, that bruise will turn into a more significant injury, where the skin will start to split, bleed and scab. If all of this describes your nipples, seek professional help, try different positions so that the nipple isn't always being injured in the same place, and start "moist wound healing" to prevent scabbing (use lanolin and gel pads on your nipples). Bottom line: cracks and open wounds are a dead giveaway for a latch issue (ouch!)

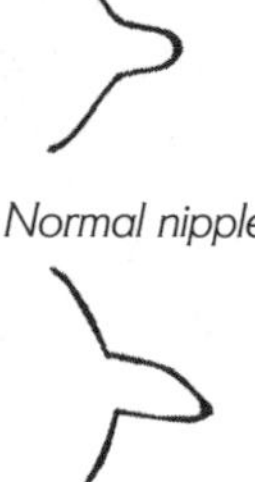
Normal nipple

Lipstick nipple

◆ **Houston, we have a nipple problem.** Flat and inverted nipples pose a challenge. The football hold may help get baby latched on.

FLAT AND INVERTED NIPPLES

When a woman gets physically cold, it's normal for her nipples to harden and stick out. If this doesn't happen to you, you might have flat or inverted nipples.

Flat nipples: Is your breast perfectly smooth? Try pinching the pigmented area (**AREOLA**) just beneath the nipple to help your baby find it. Avoid baby bottles and pacifiers in the beginning, as your baby will prefer them since they are easier to latch on to.

Inverted nipples: Do you see an indentation in the center of your nipple? Try pinching your nipple. Does it stick out or go in? If it goes in, pull your nipple out before offering it to your baby. If it "hides," then you may want to wear *nipple shells* during your pregnancy. You can also use a breast pump after you deliver to help bring out your nipple. *Nipple shields* are useful if the baby can pull the nipple into the shield.

Stimulating inverted nipples to stand out prior to nursing may help. Breast shells (see Breastfeeding Lingo box earlier in this chapter) also help inverted nipples. Lactation consultants are very helpful for this situation.

◆ **Mouth problem.** Babies with tongue thrusting and tongue-tie can have poor technique. See more about tongue-tie below. Babies who thrust their tongues forward while nursing can be taught how to suck correctly (with a lot of patience and professional help).

◆ **Tongue-tie.** Sometimes a baby has a poor sucking technique because he has a tongue-tie (**ANKYLOGLOSSIA**). This leads to cracked, painful nipples in Mom and poor intake because baby has trouble compressing the nipple.

There are four types of tongue-tie. Two types (1 and 2) are usually detected on the newborn exam because the tip of the tongue is forked and the tongue cannot extend out. The other two types (3 and 4) are more often missed on exam because the tongue moves outward normally. However, the tongue cannot reach the roof of the mouth. This is not only an issue with breastfeeding, but also with speech later in life.

If you think this may be a problem, let your pediatrician know about it. The thin piece of tissue causing the problem can be easily clipped before you leave the hospital or in an office setting in the first couple of weeks of life. This procedure is called a **FRENULECTOMY**.

Consider using a nipple shield for your own protection until the tongue-tie can be clipped. Getting the procedure done sooner rather than later prevents your baby from developing bad sucking habits.

Factoid: Tongue-tie often runs in families.

Q. My nipples are already cracked and it's only my second day of nursing! My nurse offered me some nipple shields. Are these okay to use?

Yes, temporarily.

As we've discussed, a nipple shield is a piece of thin plastic that you place on top of your nipple and surrounding tissue (**AREOLA**) while you nurse. It has four holes that allow most of your breast milk to pass to your baby. They can be a real lifesaver for you if your nipples/areolas are raw, cracked, or bleeding because they keep your baby from being able to do any more damage and give you some time to heal.

Another suggestion: Soothies by Lansinoh ($12 at Walgreens) are reusable gel pads that provide a cooling sensation—a lifesaver for sore nipples!

Of course, these are only temporary solutions. The long-term goal is to have good nursing technique so you don't have repeated injuries!

Q. My nipples are really sore. What can I do to get some relief?

Linda has several tips to help your nipples heal:

◆ *Get out some shot glasses.* While you might consider doing some tequila shots to ease your pain, we have something else in mind. Place a mixture of one teaspoon of Epsom salts to one cup water in the glasses and soak your nipples in them twice daily for two to five minutes.

- *Go topless.* Let your nipples air dry for a few minutes twice a day. You can also expose them to sunlight through a sunny window for additional comfort.
- *Lube up.* Before you nurse or pump, apply a tiny amount of pure lanolin ointment or olive oil to the wound(s). The lubrication will protect the tender skin from further insults.
- *Get rid of germs.* After you nurse or pump, apply antibiotic cream—either over the counter polysporin or prescription mupiricin (Bactroban)—to the wound(s).
- *One word—Elastogel.* These are basically bandaids for boobs. You can buy these gel pads at your pharmacy. Place the gel pad over the wounded area (and over the antibiotic cream if you are using it) *after* you have nursed or pumped.
- *Pump it up (and out).* If you are in complete agony, try pumping and offering your milk through a bottle occasionally. But to maintain your milk supply, you'll need to pump each time your baby gets a bottle. If you do bottle feed your nursing baby, keep the bottle in a horizontal position so she has to work to get the milk like she does at the breast.

Linda's Tip: Cracked Nipples. Your body can heal itself. Squeeze out some breast milk and place it on your nipples after every feeding. And if your nipples are painful from pumping, try putting some olive oil on them beforehand.

5 **NIPPLE BACTERIAL INFECTION.** If your nipples are already cracked and bleeding, you are at risk for getting a bacterial infection. If you notice redness, draining pus, or golden crust, call your OB doc for a prescription antibiotic cream.

6 **PLUGGED DUCT.** Equate this to a clogged pipe. The milk backs up and causes a hard, lumpy, tender area. Massage these areas while you nurse. Use moist heat before feedings and ice afterwards. Nurse or pump frequently (at least every three hours). Beware of any redness on the skin or fever. Plugged ducts are the precursor for a breast infection called mastitis (see later in the chapter for more info).

Linda's Tip: Try nursing your baby with his chin pointing to the plugged duct—the suckling motion will massage the area and perhaps help unplug the duct. You can also try using a homemade "castor oil pack." Apply castor oil to a clean dry cloth to make it saturated, but not dripping. Fold the cloth to the size that will cover the plugged area. Apply plastic wrap over the area, place a heating pad on low setting over the plastic wrap, and leave for 20 minutes. Repeat every 1-2 hours as needed. It is very helpful to nurse or pump immediately after applying the castor oil pack. Just be sure to wash the area thoroughly before nursing.

7 **MASTITIS.**

Q. So, what is mastitis?

A breast infection due to raw nipples and germs from your baby's mouth.

New mothers often have trouble with their baby's latch initially, leading to raw and cracked nipples. This lets baby's mouth germs enter Mom's breast. Symptoms include fever, chills (like you have the flu), pain/swelling/redness of the breast. Women are usually afflicted with this one to four weeks after delivery.

Treatment requires antibiotics (you need to call your OB for this) and continued elimination of breast milk from the breasts. Yes, you either need to continue nursing or pumping through this unpleasant experience. Your baby will not be harmed–it's *his* germs that did this to you!

If you take antibiotics, we suggest you also take probiotics (also known as acidophilus or lactobacillus). These are good germs (found naturally in yogurt) that will help prevent you from getting a yeast infection on top of everything else!

What causes mastitis?

1. Cracked nipples (mostly from poor latch technique)
2. Plugged milk ducts (from incomplete emptying at a feeding, tight clothes)
3. Missed feedings (lack of nursing or pumping for several hours)
4. Stress and exhaustion
5. Rapid weaning (lack of nursing)

If you notice that you have a tender, painful area on your breast–do something about it ASAP. Massage the area while you nurse or pump to unclog the duct. Apply a warm compress to the area. Try the castor oil pack as discussed earlier. Nurse or pump every two to three hours. And get some sleep! (*Lawrence*) If your symptoms persist or worsen, call your OB.

8 YEAST OVERGROWTH/INFECTION

Q. My nipples are burning every time I nurse. Why?

This is likely to be a yeast infection.

Pediatricians try to stay out of Mom's medical care, but parents often ask their opinion. Yeast infections also come from your little one's mouth. Babies (who are toothless) have some bacteria in their mouths, but not nearly as much as we do (because plaque goes along with teeth). Yeast likes dark, warm, moist, low bacteria places. So, newborns often get yeast or **THRUSH** infections in their mouths. It looks like curdled milk that can't be wiped off the gums, cheek lining, and roof of their mouth.

If your nipples burn or itch and you experience shooting pains every time your baby nurses, check your baby's mouth, and check with both your obstetrician and pediatrician. A family practitioner should be able to handle both of these problems.

Your baby can get an antifungal mouthwash and you can get an antifungal cream or oral medication.

There is evidence to show that the yeast clears more quickly if both mother and baby are treated, even if only one party is showing symptoms of infection. And some yeast infections get passed back and forth for what seems like forever. If that is your situation, see below.

Linda's Tips: Top 10 Tips to Beat Yeast

- Wash hands with hot, soapy water and dry with paper towels before and after nursing, toileting, and changing baby's diaper.
- Wash laundry in hottest water possible. Add a cup of white distilled vinegar to final rinse.
- If you have intercourse, use condoms to prevent cross-infection.
- Sterilize all pacifiers, bottle nipples, pump flanges daily.
- Do not freeze breast milk while being treated. But it is OK to nurse and pump for daily use.
- Change bra pads as soon as they become moist.
- Wear a clean bra each day.
- Eat yogurt/take probiotics daily.
- Decrease your consumption of refined sugars. Increase your veggie and garlic intake.
- Wash nipples with a mixture of vinegar and water (1/4 cup vinegar to 1 cup water) after each feeding. Apply over-the-counter antifungal cream (like clotrimazole) to your nipples afterwards. Gently wipe off any excess prior to the next feeding.

Whew! That's a lot of things that can go wrong! We sum up the Top 8 breastfeeding problems and solutions with the chart earlier in the chapter.

Breastfeeding Books

Among the best is *The Nursing Mother's Companion* by Kathleen Huggins, R.N. It will hold your hand and give you 25 different ways to relieve engorgement. Also good: *The Womanly Art of Breastfeeding* by La Leche League.

Expressing Milk

Q. Why do some women express their breast milk (that is, pump)?

Many mothers pump to survive engorgement. You can pump off the excess milk to get more comfortable and baby can have an easier time getting latched on. For working moms, it's essential to pump to maintain breast milk supply. For stay-at-home moms, it allows you to escape your house for a little while.

Q. How do I pump and store my milk?

Here's what you need to know:

- Wash your hands.
- Clean all breast pump apparatus thoroughly.
- Freshly pumped breast milk will last eight hours at room temperature and 24 hours in a cooler with blue ice.
- Use sterilized opaque plastic bottles (polypropylene) or polyethylene disposable bags for collection of milk. See the Reality Check below for a discussion of disposable bottle bags.
- Fresh breast milk retains more of the antibodies and vitamins than

breast milk that has been frozen and then thawed/warmed. So limit the amount of breast milk that is frozen and stored.

- Remember to put a collection date on the bottles or bags! Use the oldest milk first.
- Yes, you can combine expressed milk from different pumping sessions together in one container. Just keep it going for a full day, then divide the milk up into individual servings.
- Start with three oz servings of milk to freeze. Store four to six oz servings when your baby is three months old. Leave room in the container; fluids expand when frozen.
- Newly expressed breast milk can sit out at room temperature for up to six to eight hours. So you can take freshly pumped milk with you when you are out and about without keeping it on ice. (*Human Milk Banking Association of North America*)

See the handy chart later in this section for details on how long expressed milk can safely be refrigerated or frozen.

Reality Check

There is no perfect container in which to store breast milk. Plastic disposable bottle bags are very convenient. You can pour the milk directly into them and freeze. For use, immerse the bag in a bowl of warm water to thaw it out. But many of those great antibodies in Mom's milk stick to the bags and don't get to baby's mouth. The bags are also more likely to spill or tear.

Glass bottles are eco-friendly, but can potentially break.

Most lactation professionals prefer the soft polypropylene bottles (frosted or colored plastic) for breast milk storage because the antibodies in the breast milk won't stick to these bottles as much—but know that some of the rich fatty milk does get stuck. (*Riordan*)

Another reality check: Breast milk can be different colors (white, yellow, blue, brown, black) and that's okay. Once it is frozen, it can smell kind of like soap. If it smells rancid, it has spoiled and needs to be tossed. If you notice this rancid smell with freshly expressed milk, scald (not boil) your freshly expressed milk, then quickly cool it and put it in the freezer. This will prevent it from spoiling.

Q. How do I serve my expressed breast milk?

Warmed and gently shaken. Some tips:

1. Thaw frozen milk in the refrigerator overnight.
2. Warm it up by placing the bottle into warm water.
3. Do not microwave it! It may lead to hot spots that can burn baby's mouth.
4. The milk will separate into water and fat. Mix the bottle up before serving.
5. Once the milk has been thawed, it will last in the refrigerator for up to 24 hours.
6. Thawed (defrosted) milk is good for one hour at room temperature.

An unfinished (fresh, not defrosted) breast milk bottle can be placed back in the refrigerator and used within four hours. It's okay to reheat it.

To maintain the most nutritional value of expressed breast milk and offer it safely, here is a chart with the optimal time frames for use. If a baby drinks all breast milk from a bottle or if he is premature or immune deficient, use milk within the "optimal" time frame. If your baby gets most of his nutrition directly from the breast, then the longer time frame is considered "acceptable".

TIMEFRAMES FOR USE:	OPTIMAL	ACCEPTABLE
Freshly expressed, at room temp (up to 77 F) *never frozen*	4 hours	6-8 hours
Feeding begun, *refrigerate leftover**	4 hours	
Refrigerator (39 F)	3 days	5-8 days
Standard Freezer (0 F)	3 months	6 months
Deep Freezer (-4 F)	6 months	12 months
Previously frozen, *thawed in refrigerator but not warmed**	4 hours	24 hours
Previously frozen, *brought to room temperature**	1 hour, then discard	
Infant has started feeding *Fresh milk, never frozen*	4 hours refrigerated	

*Do not refreeze
(*Source*: *Human Milk Banking Association of North America*)

Reality Check

In the past, few insurance companies will cover the cost of a breast pump or a private lactation consultation. The good news: Affordable Care Act legislation requires insurance plans to cover lactation services, although as we went to press, most insurance plans were still working out the details. Also: breast pumps and breastfeeding supplies are currently tax deductible. Stay tuned for updates from the U.S. Department of Health and Human Services at hrsa.gov/womensguidelines/.

Q. When can I introduce a bottle?

Ideally, introduce one bottle a day of expressed (pumped) breast milk at two to four weeks of age. Why?

- Dad gets involved.
- Mom can go out to get her hair cut (remember you are nursing every 2-3 hours).
- Baby learns that food comes in different packages.

A common mistake is waiting until the end of maternity leave or when you want a date with your spouse to try a bottle. Once a baby is in the breast-only mode, he is less flexible about change.

Linda's Tip: Introducing a Bottle. Keep the bottle more horizontal, keeping the nipple half full of milk when you are bottle feeding a breast-

fed baby. Using a "vented" bottle also helps. That way, the baby has to actively remove milk from the bottle, just like at the breast. Don't let him chug it or he may not want to work at the breast. A key tip: it is very important to maintain a bottle a day in your baby's routine, so that he doesn't "forget" how to take a bottle. Many parents get their babies to take a bottle but then don't offer one for a couple of weeks. Then, surprise, baby won't accept a bottle anymore!

DR B'S OPINION

"It is very healthy for your marriage to leave your baby at home with a loving family member or friend! I frequently prescribe this form of mental health therapy to my families. Dinner or a movie (you won't have time for both) is much cheaper than marital counseling."

Q. My baby is refusing to take a bottle. Help!

Babies are smarter than you give them credit for. They can see and smell Mom if she is anywhere in sight. Get out of the house and let someone else feed your baby the bottle.

Babies have thirst and hunger drives. No matter how stubborn your baby is, he will eventually accept a bottle of your breast milk if he is not given an option.

This is not cruel or unusual punishment. It's also a good excuse for you to spend a day at the spa.

Considerations for Mom

Q. I have small breasts. Will I make enough milk?

Probably. Size doesn't matter. It's what's inside that counts.

You should have enough milk if you have normal breast tissue (milk ducts, nipples), make hormones that trigger milk production, and have enough stimulation from your baby suckling or using a breast pump.

Q. I have very large breasts/nipples. Is this good for nursing?

Sometimes yes, sometimes no.

If you have large, pendulous breasts, you may have more difficulty getting your baby correctly latched. You may want to try the "football hold" or lying on your side while nursing so you don't have to hold up the weight of your breast. Or, you can try a nursing pillow that supports both your breast and your baby.

If the entire dark pigmented area (**AREOLA**) including the nipple is so large that your baby cannot latch on, you may need to pump until he and his mouth get bigger.

Q. I've had a breast reduction. Will this be a problem?

Possibly.

Certain types of breast reduction surgery disrupt the milk duct super-highway. This may mean you do not have enough milk to breastfeed exclusively. You may not even make more than a drop or two at each nursing session. In this scenario, formula feeding is the most reasonable choice for your baby.

However, no one can predict whether you will be able to nurse or not before you try. And even if you cannot nurse for the long haul, it's great to offer your first milk (**COLOSTRUM**) to your newborn. Work with a lactation consultant to get help with your situation.

Q. I have implants. Can I still nurse?

Yes.

However, certain types of reconstructive surgery may interfere with your ability to breastfeed exclusively. Get professional help from a lactation consultant.

Q. I've heard I need to restrict my diet while I am breastfeeding. Is this true?

Not really.

Human milk is remarkably uniform despite differences in women's diets. It is always a good idea to eat healthfully for both you and your baby, though. There are actually very few restrictions. Here are the recommendations, according to the Institute of Medicine:

1. Avoid diets that promise rapid weight loss.
2. Eat a wide variety of foods including breads/grains, fruits, vegetables, dairy products, meats or meat alternatives daily.
3. At least three servings of milk (dairy) products daily.* But see below for details on milk protein allergies in babies.
4. Specifically eat Vitamin A rich foods: carrots, spinach, greens, sweet potatoes, cantaloupe.
5. Drink water when you are thirsty.
6. Caffeine-containing products (cola, coffee) are suggested in moderation (300mg or less per day). A standard 12 oz cup of coffee has about 200mg of caffeine. The caffeine enters the breast milk—so nurse first, and then have your coffee. Preterm babies and newborns may metabolize caffeine at a slower pace and be a bit more sensitive to it—so take that into consideration.
7. Avoid eating shark, swordfish, king mackerel, and tilefish because they may contain high levels of methyl mercury which can interfere with neurological development. (*Suitor*)
8. It's okay to eat 12 ounces or less of shellfish, canned fish, small ocean fish, or farm-raised fish (and less than six ounces of canned tuna) per week. (*Suitor*)

*If you drink cow's milk or eat dairy products, some of the cow milk protein ends up in your human breast milk. And some babies who are sensitive to this protein end up extremely gassy and fussy. Does that mean baby is allergic to cow's milk? Not necessarily. Babies with true milk protein allergies who are consistently exposed to cow's milk protein end up having blood-streaked or mucousy/stringy poop, or diarrhea.

If your baby has a true milk protein allergy, you'll have to cut out ALL milk and dairy products from your diet (more on this below). If your baby just seems sensitive, you can try eating dairy products that have been cooked or fermented (yogurt, cheese) and avoiding milk for the first six months of breastfeeding. Why? Milk contains unprocessed cow milk protein, which seems to be more problematic for allergic babies than protein that's been processed in other dairy products.

For more details on food allergies in general, flip over to the section on food allergies in Chapter 7, Solids.

Feedback from the Real World: "I Give Up"

One of our readers sent us a note, in desperation, regarding her baby's problems. The mom had been exclusively breastfeeding her baby. She wrote, "it breaks my heart to hear her scream all the time... to have your child be so obviously unhappy and/or in pain all the time is the worst feeling in the world...I think it's time for me to give up (breastfeeding) because nothing else I've tried seems to work." A milk protein allergy was ultimately diagnosed.

Our response: You are not alone. Babies who suffer from this problem leave both baby and parents in misery. But do not fear–your child will not be like this forever. Some babies outgrow this problem by six months of age, and over 80% outgrow it by age five. Babies who are breastfed and have a milk protein allergy can still have problems because mom's milk/dairy intake can end up in the breast milk. If you want to continue breastfeeding, you need to avoid ALL products containing milk or dairy. There are often hidden dairy sources, so it's not only the obvious dairy products you need to avoid. Check out the web site FoodAllergy.org for more information.

When your doctor gives you the green light to reintroduce dairy into your diet how will you accomplish this? After all, you don't want to start drinking a half-gallon of milk a day with extra-cheese pizzas and such. Here is a reasonable approach to introducing dairy gradually:

- Step 1: Start with small amounts of hard cheeses (cheddar, Swiss) or yogurt for the first week.
- Step 2: If baby does well, try soft cheeses (gouda, cottage, cream, American) for week two.
- Step 3: If baby does well, try butter, ice cream, and cooked dairy products for week three.
- Step 4: If baby does well, have a glass of milk.

Of course, if your baby shows allergy symptoms again, it's back to the dairy free diet for you.

Insider Tip: One promising treatment for breastfed babies with food allergies–a nursing mom may take a prescription digestive aid (called Pancrease) with meals and snacks that helps break down the offending food in her diet before it passes into her breast milk. Talk to your doctor about this possible treatment option. (*Schach*)

Old Wives Tale

You need to drink excessive amounts of water when you are nursing.

The Truth: Your body will increase its thirst drive to accommodate for your fluid needs. You don't need to go overboard.

FYI: Your daily caloric needs will be higher if you are breastfeeding. The average recommended daily allowance for non-pregnant women is 2100 calories. With breastfeeding, the recommendation is 2700 calories. (*Lawrence*) Don't bother counting calories, though, unless you are losing too much weight or having a problem producing enough milk.

Old Wives Tale

You need to avoid gassy foods like beans because they will make the baby gassy.

The truth: You may want to avoid gassy foods because other people might not want to be around you. Your baby is unaffected by this food choice.

Q. Is there any truth that some foods in my diet will make my baby fussy?

Yes, but there is no reason to restrict your diet unless you identify a problem. Foods that *might* cause a problem: cabbage, turnips, broccoli, rhubarb, apricots, prunes, melons, and peaches. (*Lawrence*)

Linda's Tip: Funky food, fussy baby? Is your baby fussy because of something you ate before nursing? Remember it takes anywhere from four to 24 hours to notice the effect. So if your baby is acting unusually fussy, think about what you ate in the past day. Since the oils from the foods you eat transfer into breast milk, your baby may not like the "taste" of something you ate.

Factoid: If you are nursing, don't smoke. (We don't recommend it for formula-fed babies either, by the way). Besides the health reasons, you won't get much sleep. Nicotine passes into breast milk and nicotine exposed babies sleep about 30% less than their non-exposed friends. If you want more sleep, quit smoking! That's just one of the many good reasons to kick the habit.

Q. Should I take DHA (Omega 3 fatty acids) supplements while I am nursing?

Yes. DHA is an essential fatty acid found in fish oils. DHA is found in breast milk, but the amount varies depending on the nursing mother's diet. DHA is known to promote brain and vision development in infants. Because the FDA has issued warnings about limiting fish consumption (tuna, mackerel, shark, swordfish, tilefish), nursing moms may be getting less fish oil in their diet. The American Academy of Pediatrics currently recommends that nursing moms take 200–300 mg a day of DHA supplements.

Q. Can I eat sushi while I am nursing?

Yes. Just be aware that consumption of raw fish (whether you are nursing or not) carries a slight risk of food-borne infection. And the FDA rec-

ommends that you eat less than 6 oz a week of tuna. So, order less toro and more unagi.

Q. Can I eat peanuts and peanut butter while I am nursing?

Yes! With the increase in people with peanut allergies, there has been quite a bit of research on this subject. A landmark study in the *New England Journal of Medicine (NEJM)* looked at the diets of breastfeeding women and later development of food allergies in infants. The results: there was no association or prevention of peanut allergy even if mom avoided these foods in her diet. And more recent studies have found the same results. (*Sicherer*)

Q. Can I drink any alcoholic beverages while I am nursing?

breastfeeding

Yes, in limited amounts.

Alcohol enters the bloodstream and the breast milk anywhere from 30-90 minutes after ingestion. The levels in the milk drop quickly. Each individual's metabolism is slightly different. So, a good rule of thumb is to avoid nursing for at least two hours after drinking. And don't nurse if you feel tipsy!

I'd suggest you limit your intake to one alcoholic beverage, sporadically, if you are nursing.

Old Wives Tale

Drinking alcohol improves your milk supply.

The truth: Drinking alcohol may help relax an over-stressed mother, but it does not improve breast milk volumes or let-down reflexes.

Q. Are there any medications to avoid while I am nursing?

Yes, lots of them.

The short answer to this question is, always inform your doctor that you are breastfeeding. That way, a medication choice for you can be made safely. You can always call your child's doctor, or your pharmacist to double check.

See Appendix A, "Medications" for more information.

Q. I love exercising. Any problems with that while I am breastfeeding?

If you exercise vigorously then nurse, your milk may have a sour taste that your baby may not like. Exercise produces lactic acid in your body, which goes into your breast milk. It's not harmful, it just tastes funny. There have also been anecdotal reports of infant fussiness up to six hours after Mom's exercise/nursing session. Here are some suggestions:

- Pump or express for a minute or two before nursing.
- If your baby gives you a strange look, use some stored breast milk for that feeding!

Reality Check

While we are on the subject of sour tasting milk…your breast milk may change flavors during your period (if you have one). And it may not be a flavor your baby likes, according to lactation expert Dr. Ruth Lawrence.

Q. I am going back to work after my maternity leave. How am I going to make this breastfeeding thing work?

Setting aside time, having a progressive workplace, and being committed.

Some women are able to go back to work AND provide breast milk to feed their babies. It may take some trial and error to figure out what works for you, but here are some ideas.

1. Leave for work a little early and pump BEFORE you start working. Or, nurse before childcare/work.
2. Invest in a high-powered, double pump. You can successfully pump in 15 minutes with one of these models.
3. Let your boss/co-workers know of your intentions. You may be surprised at how understanding people are.
4. Think about where you will be able to pump and how often.
5. Think about where you will *store* your expressed milk until you get home. It can sit in a cooler with ice packs if you don't have access to a refrigerator.
6. Start stockpiling expressed milk BEFORE maternity leave is over. See "Linda's tip" regarding stockpiling earlier in this chapter.
7. Be prepared for being exhausted the first few weeks. It does get better.

If you don't have enough breast milk for the whole time you are away, supplementing with formula is okay. Your baby will benefit from any milk you can provide. Every ounce counts!

Reality Check

The percentage of fat, protein, and sugar in breast milk not only varies from the beginning let down (foremilk) to the latter part (hindmilk) of the nursing session, but also in the time of day.

If you notice your baby seems more satisfied with your evening nursing sessions more than morning ones, it may be because your breast milk has more fat in it during that time of day!

Q. I have a fever, can I still nurse?

Absolutely!

Your body is producing antibodies to whatever infection your body is fighting. Those antibodies are going directly to your baby. If you have a cold or upper respiratory infection, not breathing on your baby would be helpful!

Contact your doctor (obstetrician, preferably) if you have a fever shortly after the birth of your baby. You could have a bladder infection, womb infection, or mastitis.

Special situations

Q. I am adopting a baby. I have heard that I can take a medicine to stimulate my milk supply. Is this true?

Yes. There is a medication called metoclopramide (the brand name is Reglan) that helps some women produce milk. This is also used for women who have trouble producing enough milk for their babies. While there are natural remedies to stimulate milk production, there is no scientific data on how effective these are. A good web source for info on this topic is AskLenore.info.

Q. I am unable to breastfeed, but I want my baby to receive breast milk. Can I buy breast milk?

Yes. There are several programs across the country called Mother's Milk Banks that sell breast milk, primarily to ill, premature babies. The donors are rigorously tested to be certain they are free of infectious diseases like Hepatitis B and HIV. And the breast milk is pasteurized. If a bank has excess supply, they will sell it to healthy newborns. It's quite pricey ($4.25 per oz). Check with your area hospital's lactation services or visit the Human Milk Banking Association of North America's website at hmbana.org.

On the flip side, if you have more milk than your freezer can handle, consider making a donation!

breastfeeding

Reality Check

Certified milk banks check donors and their milk rigorously for infection before the milk is sold. It is becoming trendy for moms to purchase breast milk from neighbors, friends, and even wet nurses via the Internet. Let the buyer beware—this is probably not the safest idea for your baby.

Q. I have twins and want to breastfeed. How do I make it work?

The key is getting both babies fed at the same time. Otherwise, it will be a challenge to get any sleep. Start this routine from day one and you will have more success.

When it comes to multiples, you will do a little more scheduling and a little less feeding "on demand." If you are able to get some hired or volunteered help around the house, things may be less chaotic for you.

The football hold and/or the cradle hold work well for simultaneous feeding sessions. It's probably wise not to have one breast exclusively designated for one baby. That way, they will accept either breast in the long run. And, just in case one breast produces more milk than the other, one baby won't get short-changed.

Q. I have a baby who was born prematurely. Anything special I need to know about breastfeeding?

Yes—it's even more important to breastfeed these little ones. Here are some special considerations:

1. Many premature babies get tired easily while nursing. If you no longer hear your baby swallowing, take him off the breast and burp him. Then return to feeding.
2. Many premature babies have poor technique (sucking, latching). Get professional help (from a lactation consultant) if you are having trouble.
3. You may be supplementing with formula or expressed breast milk for a while. Don't give up.

4. Rent a hospital grade pump for the first month because you will need to pump eight times daily to protect your milk supply until your baby is feeding well at the breast. A rental pump is the fastest, easiest option when pumping this often.
5. Weigh your baby once or twice weekly to make sure he is gaining, ideally, an ounce a day. Eventually you can stop doing this—check with your doctor. You can usually stop the weekly weight checks when you reach your baby's actual due date.
6. The football hold works well for little preemies. That way you have better control of positioning and latch.
7. Give baby skin to skin time. This stimulates your milk production (and promotes bonding!)
8. Most babies born 37 weeks gestation or younger do better at the breast with a nipple shield, as this helps stimulate their sucking reflex.
9. Because it is often difficult to tell if your baby is actually eating at the breast versus pacifying, it is helpful to do the following:

    - Limit breastfeeding to about ten minutes per side in the beginning weeks when your baby is falling asleep at the breast.
    - Pump for ten minutes after all daytime feedings and at least once during the night
    - Supplement the baby with 15-30 ml (1/2 to 1 ounce) of expressed breast milk after breastfeeding to guarantee he is getting enough calories.

10. When you are supplementing, you may notice that your baby is getting lazier at the breast in anticipation of taking the easier bottle. If that is the case, then supplement BEFORE offering the breast.

As your premature baby gets closer to his real due date, he will have more energy and be able to stay awake longer. At that point, you can start experimenting with getting him off of the nipple shield and taking away the supplemental feedings and pumpings.

Q. My baby was born at 35 1/2 weeks gestation. Should I treat him like a full-term baby when it comes to breastfeeding?

No. You have a "late preterm infant" who may have more difficulty with nursing because he may not have the skills or the energy to suck effectively. Here are some specific tips to make breastfeeding successful:

- Aim for at least eight feedings a day.
- Wake your baby up if: he doesn't wake on his own, it has been more than three hours between feedings during the day, or four hours at night until he reaches his real due date.
- Feeding time should be 40 minutes, tops. After that, your baby will be exhausted.
- Use a nipple shield if your baby has a poor latch—most late preterm infants do!
- Use a "supplemental nursing system" to offer expressed milk or formula while your baby is at your breast. You can use a tube with

a bottle reservoir that attaches to either your nipple or your finger. Offer 5-10 ml (1-2 tsp) per feed on Day 1, 10-20 ml (1/2 oz) per feed on Day 2, and 20-30 ml (up to one oz) per feed on Day 3. The nurses or lactation consultant at the hospital can show you how to use these supplemental nursing systems.

- Pump after each feeding to stimulate your milk production, because your newborn won't.
- Have a lactation consultant check to make sure your milk is successfully being transferred to your baby when he is at the breast.

Don't be discouraged. Do weight checks every week until your baby reaches his actual due date.

Reality Check

American Red Cross makes an infant scale that is accurate, user friendly, and moderately priced at Walmart or Amazon.com for about $50.

Q. I have a baby with acid reflux (GERD). Is there anything differently I should do when I am nursing?

We'll tackle gastroesophageal reflux (GERD) in depth in Chapter 8, The Other End. But yes, nursing a reflux baby presents special challenges.

First problem: Positioning. Reflux babies do better when they are more upright with feedings. Unless you are a Cirque de Soleil performer, it's physically impossible to nurse your baby upright. However, if you keep him at a 45-degree angle with his bottom down more towards your lap, he may fare better. Also, avoid the side-lying position.

Next problem: what do you do when you've just completed a nursing session, your baby spits it all back at you, and then wants to eat again? You won't have much milk left at your breast to offer. But you can still put him back to the breast. Why? Breast milk is made as your baby sucks. And that richer, heavier hindmilk he's drinking is more likely to stay down.

If that doesn't work, you may have to offer a bottle stashed away in your freezer. Breastfeeding moms quickly realize they need to have a stash of expressed milk, just in case the entire feeding comes back up.

Other breastfeeding moms offer expressed milk in a bottle (instead of direct nursing at the breast) for one or more feedings. This enables you to feed your baby in an upright position as well as to thicken up your breast milk. (Thicker, heavier milk may be beneficial in keeping the milk down in the stomach where it belongs.) One idea: it's okay to add rice cereal to your expressed milk, but it loses its thickness quickly. Why? Live enzymes in breast milk will break the cereal down before your baby has a chance to to finish drinking it.

Here are the take-home tips for nursing a baby with acid reflux:

- Read your baby's cues and adjust his feedings accordingly.
- Burp him more frequently.
- Don't sit him up to burp as that creates too much pressure on his tummy.

- Let him rest between breasts.
- Keep him upright for 30 minutes after feedings.
- Make sure your "let down" of milk isn't too fast, causing him to gulp down a lot of air as he nurses.

Weaning

Q. When should I wean my baby off of breast milk?

When one or both of you is ready.

The American Academy of Pediatrics recommends breastfeeding for at least a year, with the addition of "complementary" solid food by six months. Hopefully, both you and your baby will enjoy nursing for at least that long. Some nursing teams (mother and baby) opt to continue even after one year.

So, the right time to wean is when one or both of you thinks it is time to stop. That time may be when your baby refuses the breast, when you decide you want your body to yourself, or when your ten-year-old asks for your breast by name. It is really a personal decision.

Reality Check

Americans tend to nurse their babies for less time than many other cultures. In some cultures, women nurse one child until the next one arrives. These same women have lower rates of breast cancer. Food for thought.

Q. I am planning to wean my baby. How do I do it?

Slowly and methodically.

If you stop breastfeeding abruptly, your body will be unhappy with you. Milk ducts get clogged (and infected). With that said, here is a typical strategy:

1. Create a timetable for the projected target date of nursing completion.
2. Eliminate one nursing session every three to four days, two to three weeks before your target date. The length of time for the entire weaning process depends on how many times a day you are currently nursing.
3. If you are weaning prior to one year of age, replace that feeding with either previously expressed breast milk or formula.
4. Eliminate the first morning and last evening feeding at the end of the weaning process.
5. Once you have completely stopped nursing, you may continue to leak milk for a week or two.
6. Wear an old bra (non-nursing), even though it is a little binding.
7. If your breasts feel so full that they are going to explode, pump or manually express just enough milk to get comfortable.
8. Taking pseudoephedrine (Sudafed) during the day, diphenhydramine (Benadryl) at night, and/or drinking three cups/day of sage tea may also help.

Q. I want to continue breastfeeding, but my nine-month old seems to be weaning himself. Is that okay?

Yes, but you may gently encourage him to continue. Babies go on strike (from formula or bottles, too) for various reasons.

- Some babies get distracted during feeding sessions when they realize the world is pretty interesting. Nurse in a boring, dark, quiet place. Or nurse while he is sleeping.
- Some babies don't want to suck if they are teething. Try using acetaminophen to relieve teething discomfort.
- Ear infections and nasal congestion can also discourage a baby from nursing. Check in with your doctor.

If none of the advice above helps, transition to formula in a bottle or a cup (depending on your baby's age and skills). Transition to whole milk if your baby is over a year of age. (*Lawrence*)

Linda's tip: You will need to protect your milk supply during this time of breast refusal by pumping and offering your milk in a bottle or cup. Try to get your baby back to the breast by offering it when she is asleep or drowsy. Don't let the breast become a battleground. These strikes can last up to a week sometimes. Be patient. Skin-to-skin time in the bathtub together can often work wonders!

Q. If I stop breastfeeding before my baby is one year old, what do I offer him instead?

Commercial-brand formula is the acceptable substitute for breast milk in the first year of life.

Note: cow's milk, soymilk, goat's milk, and rice milk are NOT substitutes for breast milk in the first year of life.

The Big Picture: Breastfeeding for the First Year

Okay, let's sum up this breastfeeding section with an overview of nursing for your baby's first year:

Birth to 2 weeks: (15-24 ounces/day)

Breastfed newborns tend to eat every two or three hours. That adds up to eight to 12 times in a 24-hour day. They may cluster feed as frequently as every 1 1/2 hours (that's from the beginning of one feeding to the beginning of the next). If you are expressing breast milk and feeding via a bottle, your baby will probably take two or three ounces at a feeding.

Babies who try to nurse more frequently than every 90 minutes are usually nursing for comfort.

Babies have no other way of consoling themselves. They can't just pull it together and settle down. Sucking is extremely soothing. So, if it has been less than 90 minutes since the beginning of the last feeding, try using your finger to let him suck. Your breasts will thank you. ***Note: If your baby is truly nursing non-stop, have your baby weighed to ensure proper weight gain. Make sure you have enough milk supply.***

On the flip side, your baby may take a four-hour stretch before feeding again. In the first two weeks of life, do not let your baby go more than four hours without feeding. Why?

- Breast milk is a supply and demand phenomenon. To get your supply established, the demand must be there.
- Your breasts will feel like they are going to explode. If that four-hour stretch is during daylight hours, you are in for a long night of cluster feedings.

2 weeks to 2 months: (17—32 ounces/day)

Once your baby is two weeks old, you can relax a bit. Your milk supply will be better established and your baby will have regained his birth weight. If he sleeps through the night, let him! You may need to pump to get comfortable during the night, but don't wake a sleeping baby. By the way, this is unlikely to happen. If it does, don't tell your friends about it. They will hate you.

This feeding "pattern" goes on for at least the first two months of life. While this seems a bit erratic, it is normal for a newborn to be irregular with her feeding (and sleep patterns).

2 to 4 months: (21—40 ounces/day)

Your baby will start to have some regularity! He will have more predictable wakeful periods and sleep periods. Hopefully, you will be down to one or two night feedings. If you are returning to work and pumping, plan on four ounces per feeding at two months of age and up to eight ounces per feeding at four months. ***Babies usually max out at 40 oz per day at four months of age.***

4 to 6 months: (25—40 ounces/day)

You can look forward to five or six breast feedings a day. You should be able to get an evening stretch of six hours without nursing. Six hours is considered "sleeping through the night", although this is probably not your definition.

You may begin offering complementary solid food between 4-6 months of age. While there are some differing opinions, the American Academy of Pediatrics recommends your exclusively breastfed baby receive an iron supplement from 4-6 months if you wait to offer infant iron-fortified cereal until six months of age.

Initially, solid food is dessert. Your baby needs the same volume of breast milk until he takes large volumes of solid foods.

6 to 9 months: (28—36 ounces/day)

Your baby will nurse four or five times per day. You should be done with night feedings. If you are not, do some problem solving with your doctor. You may enjoy those cuddly moments nursing in the middle of the night, but these are not a necessity. Your baby is comforted and used to feeding at night. Frequently, so is Mommy. If both of you are enjoying this situation, keep doing it. If one of you (Mom) is not enjoying it and wants more sleep, read Chapter 9, Sleep.

Solid foods should be in full swing at this point (see the next chapter on solid nutrition). You'll probably see your baby eat more and drink less between 7—9 months of age.

9 to 12 months: (20-30 ounces/day)

Babies are well into solid foods and start to wean—that is, their volume and frequency of nursing decline. Your baby may nurse three or four times per day.

By one year of age, babies wean to 16 to 24 oz per day. At this point, you deserve a gold medal of honor. If you and baby are ready, you can stop breastfeeding.

We recommend switching to whole or 2% milk with Vitamin D added at one year of age. The goal is two cups of milk per day (or dairy serving equivalents). Remember, breast milk is low in Vitamin D and iron. So, if you want to go beyond a year of nursing, find other nutritional sources for these nutrients.

Now that you've learned all you wanted to know about breastfeeding, let's talk about formula.

Formula

Q. Is it okay to feed formula to my newborn?

Yes.

Although it is wonderful to breastfeed, it is also acceptable to feed your baby infant formula for the first year of life. Here are the key advantages to formula:

- It's about as close as it gets to human milk. Formulas are specially prepared to contain the appropriate amount of fat, protein, carbohydrates, and other nutrients that growing babies need.
- It's convenient. You can take a formula bottle anywhere you go. Just keep it cool and then find a place to warm it when it is time to use. (It's less convenient at 2am when your baby is screaming while you frantically have to warm up a bottle.)
- It isn't mom-dependent. Yes, any willing and able-bodied person can feed a baby a bottle of formula anytime during the day or night.
- There are options. While not all babies can tolerate cow's milk-based formula, there are several alternatives for babies with food allergies.
- But formula is also very expensive. Expect to pay $550+ for a year if your baby tolerates the least expensive cow's milk based powered formula (that's a generic brand formula bought in bulk from a warehouse club). Name brand powered formula is about $1200 a year. Hypoallergenic formula could run $2000 to $6000 or more.

Q. I have chosen to feed my baby formula. What formula do you recommend?

The cheapest cow's milk based formula with iron you can find. Get a warehouse club membership now, if you don't have one already. In general, the cheapest formula is the generic or store brand sold at discount stores like Wal-Mart, Target, Costco or Sam's Club. Buy in bulk (the bigger the container, the better) to get the maximum savings.

Here is an overview of these products. Dr. Lewis First, Chief of Pediatrics at the University of Vermont, deserves credit for the explanations below. He classifies formula into three categories: Coke, Diet Coke, and Caffeine Free Diet Coke. We'll also provide you the brand names for each type in the following list:

◆ **Coke =** Cow's Milk Based Formula with iron. This is the formula tolerated by most babies and recommended first by most doctors.

Name brands include: Enfamil Premium (Newborn and Infant), Similac Early Shield Advance, Gerber Good Start (Gentle or Protect Plus), Earth's Best. There are also generic or store brand cow's milk formula found at Wal-Mart, Target, and your grocery store.

◆ **Diet Coke =** Soy Protein Formula with iron. Some doctors recommend soy protein formula for babies who seem intolerant to cow's milk formula. (Note: this intolerance is NOT an allergy to milk protein, which is addressed with the formula type discussed next). "Intolerance" is a vague term for extremely gassy babies, or those who throw up more formula than they keep down. About 25% of American babies are fed soy formula. Soy formula is also an option for parents looking for a vegetarian-based alternative to cow's milk-based formula.

Name brands include: Enfamil Prosobee, Similac Soy (Isomil), Gerber Good Start Soy Plus. As you might guess, there are also generic/store brand soy formulas sold at Target and Wal-Mart as well.

◆ **Caffeine Free Diet Coke =** Extensively hydrolyzed casein protein formula with iron. The Dom Perignon of formulas, these are for babies with a **MILK PROTEIN ALLERGY**, not merely an intolerance to regular milk-based formula. Babies who are allergic to cow's milk protein have diarrhea with blood and/or mucous in their poop. Occasionally, babies with milk protein allergy

THE HISTORY OF BABY FORMULA

1700's: "Wet nurses" were paid to breastfeed infants who could not be fed by their mother.

1800's: Milk from other animals was used as a substitute.

1700's

1800's

1838: The ingredients of animal milk and human milk were analyzed. We learned that cow's milk had a higher protein and lower sugar content which could cause problems for infants trying to digest it. This led to the first chemical "formula" that was added to cow's milk.

1870's: Nestle made the first infant formula that only required water to be added. It was very expensive and therefore quite unpopular.

The inventions of evaporated milk (1883), pasteurization (1890), and the refrigerator (1910) allowed parents to make infant formula in the comfort of their own home.

also have a soy protein allergy. Some babies need this formula for the entire first year—but, based on a family history of food allergies and the severity of the baby's reaction to milk protein, your doctor may attempt a trial of soy formula before one year.

Name brands include: Enfamil Nutramigen, Similac Alimentum.

DR B'S OPINION

"Although we encourage you to breastfeed your baby for obvious benefits, your baby will be fine if he is formula fed."

FYI: Babies with the most severe cow's milk protein allergy may not even tolerate the hydrolyzed casein protein formulas. They need amino acid-based formulas that are completely milk protein free and of course, even more expensive! Name brands include Neocate Infant, Elecare infant, or Enfamil Puramino. (All are sold online or can be special ordered.)

Special formulas are expensive. Some insurance companies will partially cover the cost for "medical foods," so be sure to inquire about it.

Helpful Hint

Do not switch formulas without asking your doctor. Most babies who are gassy and fussy will be gassy and fussy for the first three months of life no matter what they are eating.

BOTTOM LINE

All marketed formulas are tested extensively and required by law (Infant Formula Act 1986) to contain minimum levels of 29 different nutrients.

1940-1960: Parents made infant formula out of evaporated milk, water, and corn syrup or sugar. The elaborate process of making formula daily provides much of the basis for the Old Wives Tales you hear about formula today.

1900'S — **PRESENT DAY**

1960's: Commercial formulas become popular due to a reduction in cost and ease of preparation. Breastfeeding rates drop sharply.

1970's: Only 25% of newborns left the hospital breastfeeding. As a result, the parents of this generation are the most formula fed babies in recorded history.

1980's and 90's: New studies tout the benefits of breastfeeding, spur renaissance in nursing.

2013: 77% of babies go home from the hospital breastfeeding, but only 47% are still breastfeeding at six months of life. And only 16% were *exclusively* breastfed through six months of life.

Soy Formula

DR B'S OPINION

"If you think Coke and Pepsi have an intense rivalry, check out the competition between formula companies. Despite the hype and spin, the products are basically equivalent in each category."

Considering soy formula? The American Academy of Pediatrics (AAP) recommends soy formula for the following reasons:

- Full term babies who are not breastfeeding and whose parents want a vegetarian alternative to cow's milk-based formula. Soy formula is considered a safe alternative.
- Full term babies with galactosemia or hereditary lactase deficiency.
- Full term babies with documented (diagnosed) transient lactase deficiency.
- Babies with documented (diagnosed) IgE-mediated allergy to cow's milk.

The AAP does NOT recommend soy formula for:

- Preterm infants with birth weights less than 1800g (4 lbs).
- Prevention of colic or allergy.
- Infants with cow's milk protein-induced enterocolitis/enteropathy (i.e. food allergy causing blood in stool). *(AAP Committee on Nutrition)*

Q. What are "comfort proteins" and "gentle formulas"? Should I believe claims that some formulas are easier to digest?

The cynic in us says: beware of marketing ploys! But there *are* some minor differences among formula brands. The Infant Formula Act requires a standard AMOUNT of protein in formula, but the TYPE of protein (the whey to casein ratio) can vary a great deal. Whey and casein are two types of protein found in milk. (Whey is acid soluble, casein is not).

Human milk has a whey to casein ratio of 60:40. Cow's milk has a ratio of 18:82. Because of the casein, cow's milk is much harder for a human baby to digest. Cow's milk based formula makers alter the ratios so the product is more easily digested. Enfamil and generic products have a 60:40 ratio. Similac has a 48:52 ratio. Gerber Good Start Gentle Plus, however, is 100% whey, and the whey is pre-digested (partially hydrolyzed).

Enfamil's "Gentlease" and Wal-Mart's Parent's Choice "Gentle" formulas contain partially digested whey protein in the 60:40 ratio with reduced levels of lactose (milk sugar). Similac Total Comfort also touts partially broken down milk protein for easier digestion.

Do any of these formulas actually make babies happier? Maybe or maybe not—there is no good scientific data to prove that these are superior products.

Q. So which is better, cow's milk formula or soy formula?

The consensus here: cow's milk. Why? Cow's milk-based formula is a better source of protein than soy, according to research studies. But nei-

WHAT ARE DHA AND ARA? LIPIDS?

DHA stands for Docosahexaenoic Acid. ARA stands for Arachidonic Acid. DHA and ARA are also called "lipids." Walk into your grocery store and you'll see lots of formula cans hyping their added lipids. So, what is this stuff? Lipids (DHA/ARA) are polyunsaturated fats that occur naturally in breast milk. They are also found in fish oils, egg yolks, and algae/fungal oil.

There has been a fair amount of research done on these fatty acids because they are present in nerve tissue and the eyes. Some studies show improved vision and scoring on infant developmental testing when babies have DHA and ARA in their diets. (*Chandran*)

Both the major brand-name formulas and generic versions have lipids. That's a good thing because a baby's formula should be as close to breast milk as possible.

ther is without controversy . . . see Chapter 15, The Environment and Your Baby for details.

Q. I have seen other formulas on the shelf at the grocery store. What are they used for?

These would be classified as the "gourmet formulas." Most are made for babies with particular problems. A few are made as optional products, which are not based on a medical necessity. See the following section for more on gourmet formulas.

The Gourmet Formulas

1. Lactose Free Formula

Lactose intolerance occurs in older children and adults. Babies are rarely born with this problem. Lactose intolerance can occur temporarily after an infant has a stomach virus. Some stomach viruses break down the human enzyme "lactase" which digests the lactose sugar, creating a temporary intolerance. This can go on for one to six *weeks* after the virus.

When babies are allergic to formula, it is usually the milk *protein* that is the problem, as it is the most allergenic part of the food. It is rare for a baby to have a problem with the milk sugar (lactose). Human milk has lactose in it and it is perfect nutrition.

2. Similac Expert Care for Diarrhea

This delicacy is made for babies who are experiencing a stomach virus. Not only has the lactose sugar and cow's milk protein been removed, but 6 grams of fiber are added per liter of formula. You're thinking, why give fiber to a child with the runs? Believe it or not, fiber actually bulks up watery stools. This formula can be used for the duration of a stomach bug to cut down on the water loss that occurs with intestinal infections.

3. Enfamil NEWBORN

The Enfamil company came up with a clever way to avoid having for-

mula-fed newborns take a Vitamin D supplement.

Enfamil "NEWBORN" is the same product as the Enfamil "Infant" formula except it has a higher amount of Vitamin D per serving. By using this special newborn formula, a baby under three months of age gets the appropriate daily dose of 400 IU of Vitamin D by drinking just 27 oz/day. Babies need to drink at least 32 oz/day of the standard Enfamil Infant formula (or any other brand of infant formula) to get the adequate amount of Vitamin D.

So, here are your options: either buy this special newborn formula (and the company hooks you into buying Enfamil products going forward) or give your newborn a daily Vitamin D supplement until he drinks at least 32 oz per day if he uses any standard kind of formula. The latter is much less expensive.

DIFFERENCES BETWEEN BREAST MILK & FORMULA

To understand the differences, you need a brief chemistry lesson here. Milk contains fat, protein, and sugar. Use the following table as a reference:

	Human Milk	Cow's Milk formula	Soy Formula	Protein Hydrolysate
Calories	20 cals/oz	20 cals/oz	20 cals/oz	20 cals/oz
Protein % of calories	5%	10% Nonfat milk, whey	10% soy protein	10% of calories casein hydrolysate
Fat % of calories	54%	50% Vegetable oil	50% Vegetable oil	50% of calories Vegetable oil
Carbohydrate % of calorie	41% Lactose	40% Lactose	40% Corn syrup/ Sucrose	40% of calories Corn syrup/ Sucrose
Live cells Antibodies	Yes	No	No	No
DHA, ARA	Yes	Yes	Yes	Yes

Special notes:

1. Human milk has lactose sugar.
2. Soy formulas replace cow protein with soy protein and are lactose free.
3. Protein Hydrolysate formulas are hypoallergenic because the protein is pre-digested.
4. All formulas in the table contain the recommended daily iron requirement for babies. Avoid low-iron versions of formula unless specifically directed by your doctor.
5. Note that 50% of the calorie intake comes from fat.
6. All formula companies have added very long chain polyunsaturated fatty acid derivatives of Omega-3 and Omega-6 (DHA and ARA). These are present in breast milk and some studies suggest they promote vision/brain development. (For more on this topic, see DHA nearby).

4. Enfamil AR / Similac for Spit-Up

All babies spit up a little. But babies who suffer from heartburn (a.k.a. gastoesophageal reflux or GERD), look like the Exorcist. Thickening the formula can help keep it from coming back up. So pediatricians often recommend parents add a teaspoon of rice cereal to each bottle to make the formula heavier. After trying this at home, however, I can tell you that the formula gets clumpy and it requires minor surgery on the rubber nipple to get it out of the bottle. No fun.

Enfamil AR or Similac for Spit-Up solves this problem by adding rice starch to their regular cow's milk formula. This is much easier to use, reducing your frustration. You will still need to use bottle nipples with a larger hole to get the formula to flow, however.

It is an old wives' tale that adding rice cereal will make your baby sleep through the night. But those old wives would be correct if they are speaking about babies with reflux.

5. Organic Formulas

These are the certified "antibiotic, pesticide, and growth hormone free" products on the market. Brands include: Earth's Best, Similac Advance Organic, Parent's Choice. Are these organic formulas worth the hefty price tag? It's your call. The good news: stores like Wal-Mart now sell generic organic formula at lower prices.

6. Formula with probiotics

Gerber Good Start brand is the only formula that contains active living bacteria cultures like the stuff found in yogurt. Good Start Protect has Bifidobacterium lactis, a "good germ" similar to what resides in the guts of babies who are breastfed. Good Start Soothe contains Lactobacillus reuteri (L reuteri), the probiotic shown to reduce symptoms of colic. The potential benefits include fewer illnesses, less severity/frequency of diarrhea, and yes, maybe less colic. And there do not seem to be any significant risks with this type of formula. (*Weizman*)

Are the health benefits worth the added cost? Maybe, but only time and more research will tell. A cheaper option: Buy a L reuteri probiotic supplement and toss it into whatever your baby is eating once a day. (see Appendix B, Alternative Medications, for details)

FYI: If you use a probiotic-enhanced formula, be sure to mix it with water less than 100 degrees or you will kill all those little good germs!

FORMULA FOR PREEMIES

There are higher-calorie formulas made especially for babies who are born before 34 weeks gestation or less than four pounds. These formulas have more calories, more protein, more calcium, and more phosphorous than standard formulas. Some babies will switch to standard formula, but the premature formulas can be used for a whole year if necessary for growth. *(AAP Committee on Nutrition)*

7. Formula with prebiotics

Similac Advance Early Shield and Enfamil Premium and Enfamil Newborn tout that their formulas contain "prebiotics." Found naturally in human breast milk, prebiotics feed good germs in the gut. Hence, probiotics (see above) are good bacteria, while prebiotics are food for good bacteria. Prebiotics may aid in digestion, boost immunity to disease, and reduce allergies–but most of the research on these benefits is only in its infancy.

8. Older baby and toddler formulas

According to formula companies, toddler formulas are designed for older babies who are eating solid foods. This product contains more calcium than standard infant formula. The pitch: babies over nine months have a higher calcium requirement than younger infants.

The issue: companies are trying to hook parents with "next step" products for 9-24 month olds and "toddler formulas" designed for one to three year olds. The formulas, with added vitamins, are pitched to parents as an allegedly better substitute for cow's milk.

Is any of this necessary? We say no. Follow-up (for nine to 24 month olds) and toddler formulas (for one to three year olds) are generally a waste of money. The calcium content of standard infant formulas is appropriate for birth to 12 months of age. After one year of age, a baby can drink whole or 2% milk–and milk is 85% cheaper than toddler formula! The American Academy of Pediatrics Committee on Nutrition concurs. They do not recommend using toddler follow-up formulas for healthy children who have low risk of nutritional deficiency. (*Georgieff*)

Q. Do you have a preference of powder, concentrate, or ready-to-feed?

As we mentioned above, we pointed out the cheapest option formula is powder. But is it best for baby? The answer: it's complicated. And cost isn't the only factor to consider.

The American Dental Association suggests using ready-to-feed formula to avoid excess fluoride intake (see discussion of this in the previous chapter). Or if you choose powder or liquid concentrate formula, the ADA recommends mixing it with purified, demineralized, deionized, distilled, or reverse osmosis filtered water.

Powdered formulas are heat-treated but cannot be commercially sterilized like ready-to-feed formula. Thus, powdered formulas contain low levels of microorganisms. One particular germ, Enterobacter sakazakii, can cause serious infections in babies who are low birth weight, born prematurely, or immune compromised. (*Centers for Disease Control*)

Given those concerns, we STILL recommend powder formula as the best option for baby. But we do so with the following caveats:

1. Mix powder formula with purified, demineralized, deionized, distilled, or reverse osmosis filtered water that is boiled (the water must be over 158 degrees to kill the germs). It's okay to use your own tap water if you have a reverse osmosis filter, or it contains less than 0.3 ppm of fluoride–ask your local water department for details.

2. Cool or chill the prepared formula slightly before giving it to your baby (test it on your inner wrist to check the temperature).
3. Use the prepared formula within 24 hours of preparation.
4. Toss any unused formula after a feeding.
5. Don't use a blender to prepare it—blenders can harbor bacteria.
6. Refrigerate any bottled water after opening it to prevent germs growing in the water.
7. Don't use powder formula if your baby was low birth weight, premature, or is immune compromised.

It's perfectly fine to use liquid concentrate or ready-to-feed formulas, but they are significantly more expensive.

FYI: the nutrients are the same for all types of formula!

Old Wives Tale

The ready to feed formula is easier to digest.

The Truth: The ready to feed is convenient, a little thicker, and a lot more expensive. All products are digested exactly the same way.

Q. Do I need to sterilize the bottles, boil water, or use bottled water to mix the formula?

No, maybe, and yes.

You don't need to sterilize bottles. Yes, we do suggest a run through the dishwasher when you first open the packages. Thereafter, you can clean bottles with warm, soapy water. That's clean enough.

You don't need to boil the water you use to mix liquid-concentrate formula because the American water supply is pretty clean. You DO need to boil the water you use to mix powder formula (see the previous question). Note: if you have well water, you need to get your water tested before your baby arrives to make sure it isn't contaminated.

Yes, we do recommend bottled water to mix formula—see the above discussion in the previous question for more details. We also discussed this issue (fluoride and formula) in the previous chapter, Chapter 5, Nutrition.

Helpful Hint

Look at the mixing instructions on the formula can. Powder requires one scoop per two ounces of water. Liquid concentrate is one ounce of formula per one ounce of water. Ready-to-feed is ready to go (DON'T ADD WATER). This may seem obvious to you. But if you screw up, your baby gets either half of the calories he needs or rocket fuel.

My mother-in-law (who was a very bright woman) mistakenly bought ready-to-feed formula for her third baby (my future husband) and added water because she thought she had purchased concentrate. Her astute pediatrician identified the problem at the baby's two-week well check when he wasn't gaining weight. Sure, this baby ended up nearly six feet tall as an adult, but we figure he could have topped Shaq's height if this mistake was caught earlier.

Q. Which bottles/nipples do you recommend?

Walk into any baby store and you'll see the Wall of Bottles—a mind-numbing array of baby bottles and nipples, each claiming to be the best choice for your newborn. While we review baby bottles in depth in our other book, *Baby Bargains*, here is a quick primer.

Bottles come in several different types: glass, plastic and polycarbonate. The latter came under scrutiny in recent years, as some states pushed to ban polycarbonate bottles containing a chemical called Bisphenol-A. (BPA) We will cover this controversy in Chapter 15, the Environment and Your Baby, but here's the take-away message: major chains (including Babies R Us and Wal-Mart) no longer sell BPA bottles, so it's not a concern now if you are buying new bottles for the first time.

Which nipples are best? Lactation consultants we've interviewed seem to like the Avent nipples best. They believe there is less nipple confusion when alternating between breast and bottle. Note: There are newborn nipples (low flow), older baby nipples (higher flow), and cross cut nipples (highest flow). You can switch to the older baby nipples at four months. The cross cut nipples are better for babies with reflux who drink thickened formula.

As a side note, bottle technique is sometimes as important as the type of bottle you choose. Example: lactation consultants recommend holding the bottle in a more horizontal position so babies have to work a bit harder to get the milk. Why? Bottles are usually much easier to feed from so babies get "lazy."

Reality Check

Feeder bottles (solid food dispensers) are unnecessary. Your baby needs to learn how to eat, *not drink* his solid food. (See the next chapter for more).

Q. How much and how often do I feed my baby?

For the first few days of life, a newborn might take an ounce or two every few hours. After the first few days, offer him three ounces in a bottle and see what he does with it. From day three to two weeks old, babies usually eat about 2-3 ounces every 3-4 hours. They gradually want more to eat over the next several weeks. But as you might guess by the standard bottle size, babies eventually max out at 8 ounces per feeding.

How will you know when your baby wants more to drink than what you have offered? Easy. He will finish off what you gave him and look for more! And the beauty of babies is that most of them just eat what they need to and then stop when they are full. So if you follow your baby's lead, he will probably eat just the right amount.

Using the "Big Picture" guidelines below, you will have a decent idea of how much and how often you can expect your baby to drink.

The Big Picture: Formula Feeding for the First Year

Birth to 2 weeks: (15-24 oz)

Newborns tend to eat two to three ounces every three to four hours. For the first two weeks, wake your baby if it has been more than four hours since the last feeding. Once baby has regained birth weight, he can sleep as much as he wants (good luck)!

2 weeks to 2 months: (17-32 oz)

You will see a gradual increase in volumes at feedings. By two months, babies usually take around four ounces per feeding, about every three hours.

2 to 4 months: (21-40 oz)

Your baby will eat six to eight ounces per feeding, and *max out at about 40 oz per day at about four months of age.*

When the volumes go up, the number of daily feedings go down. So, a baby who chugs eight ounces at a feeding can eat five times a day and sleep through the night. Parents often ask if they can space out the frequency of daytime feedings. NO! Use common sense here–if your baby eats every two to three hours during the day, you will all be sleeping at night. (Get used to it. This frequency of meals continues into preschool, when kids still eat three meals and two snacks a day.)

Babies who take smaller volumes at each feeding will need to eat more often. These tend to be babies who suffer from heartburn (**GERD**). We'll have more on this in Chapter 8, The Other End.

4 to 6 months: (25-40 oz)

Babies continue to take a ballpark of 40 oz per day of formula. Even if you begin offering your baby a nibble or two of solid food, *there should be no reduction in the volume of formula.* Initially, you should view complementary solid food as dessert.

6 to 9 months: (28-36 oz)

You'll be going full speed ahead on solid food. Your baby will start to wean–decreasing volumes of formula as his intake of calories from solid food increases. By seven to nine months, you will see this start to happen.

9 to 12 months: (20-30 oz)

Your baby will decrease drinking formula to a minimum of 24 oz per day. At one year of age, your baby will usually drink three 8 oz bottles. This will then be replaced by whole or 2% milk that is Vitamin D fortified. *The goal is 16 oz a day (which is two cups a day) of milk.* The equivalent in dairy products is also fine.

It's time to kick the bottle habit at a year. Don't get stuck here. You don't have a baby anymore. You have a toddler. If you want a baby in your house, go have another one. Yes, your child will be quite capable of drinking via a cup or a cup with a straw. He will not go thirsty.

Other Liquids

Q. Does my baby need any water?

Not until six months of age.

The reason: your baby is already getting water. It's naturally in breast milk and added to prepared formula. Your baby gets plenty of water. After six months of age, your baby should start to drink some water every day. How much? Even though there is no official guideline, we think four to six ounces of water a day is adequate.

No matter what other liquid babies are drinking or how it is prepared (breast milk, ready-to-feed formula, or powder/liquid concentrate formula), babies *over six months of age* should all drink some fluoride containing water (0.7ppm) on a daily basis. Again, four to six ounces a day is our best estimate on what is needed.

If your baby has no source of fluoride-containing water in his diet for whatever the reason (using fluoride-free bottled water, reverse osmosis filtered tap water, etc), then you should discuss getting a fluoride supplement with your doctor or dentist. For details on this whole fluoride issue, check out the section on Vitamin Supplements in Chapter 5, Nutrition.

DR B'S OPINION

"If you are going to offer juice, do it after six months of age. Offer no more than six ounces per day. Diluting it half and half with water is even better. I also suggest introducing juice in a cup not a bottle."

Reality Check

Bottled water is not any safer than tap. A Dutch study compared bottled water from 16 countries. 37% of the samples were contaminated with bacteria and 4% were contaminated with fungus! Hence, for older children, tap water is preferred, since it usually contains fluoride. The only reason that we recommend using *distilled* bottled water to prepare formula is to ensure your infant doesn't get too much fluoride.

Q. When can I give my baby juice?

What's the rush?

Pediatricians, as a general rule, are not very enthusiastic about juice. Sorry, juice producers of America. Here are the reasons:

1. ***Juice provides little nutrition.*** Vitamin C has to be added to many juices to give them any nutritive value. Otherwise, juice is just a form of liquid sugar.
2. ***Juice is filling,*** which decreases a child's appetite for more nutritious foods.
3. Drinking juice throughout the day (especially in a bottle) causes sugar buildup on the teeth. This, in turn, creates ***high dental bills.***
4. ***A sugar-loaded diet causes diarrhea.***

BOTTOM LINE: Children with poor weight gain, chronic diarrhea, or rotten teeth often are juice-a-holics. The American Academy of Pediatrics recommends no more than six oz of juice a day for 1–6 years of age.

Helpful Hint

A sneaky way to get those vegetables in: drink them. Although we aren't big fans of juice, combination carrot-orange juice is a tasty option most kiddos like. And it's an excellent source of Vitamin A and C. Tropicana Healthy Kids Orange Juice also contains

DR B'S OPINION: SIPPY CUPS

Yes, I know they are popular: the no-spill sippy cup. I have never been a fan of these because the sucking mechanism to get the fluid out is similar to a bottle. Dentists dislike sippy cups because the flow of liquid heads straight to the back of the top front teeth. In short, sippy cups can promote tooth decay.

I'd prefer to have your baby drinking from a straw if he hasn't quite mastered the art of drinking from a cup.

Vitamin A, C, E, and has calcium added. Another great product: Vruit (web: americansoy.com). A blend of both fruit and vegetable juices, they are 100% juice and come in kid-sized boxes.

Q. When can my baby drink from a cup?

You can try introducing a cup any time after six months of age, but there is certainly no rush.

Your long-term goal is to have your baby drinking from a cup at his first birthday. Most babies get the hang of it by 12 months.

Reality Check

Once your baby has teeth, you need to wipe them or brush them after the last feeding (before bedtime). Your baby shouldn't be falling asleep while he is eating by the time he has teeth anyway. (See Chapter 9, Sleep for details.)

Q. When and how do I switch to cow's milk?

At one year of age, cold turkey.

Your baby still needs a high fat diet because his brain development is on overdrive. The American Academy of Pediatrics recommends whole or 2% milk until *two years of age*. Previously, it was recommended that all children drink whole milk until age two. But the guidelines recently changed because many toddlers already eat a high-fat diet and obesity begins early in life. You and your child's doctor can decide whether whole or 2% is best for him, depending on your family history and your child's growth. (*American Heart Association*)

After the second birthday, your child should drink what the rest of the family is drinking. This should be *skim milk (nonfat or 1%)* for everyone. The fat will clog your baby's arteries just like it clogs ours.

Q. What do you think of alternative dairy products compared to cow's milk?

While some products have nearly the same calories as whole milk, less of those calories come from fat (and 12 to 24 month olds still need more fat than you do). The preferred dairy beverage of choice is whole or 2% cow's milk. Here is a comparison:

8 OUNCE SERVING	WHOLE MILK (3.5% FAT)	SKIM MILK (0.1% FAT)	SOY MILK	RICE MILK
Calories	150 calories	80	150	130
Total fat	8 grams	0	4	2
Sodium	115 mg	125	140	105
Carbohydrate	11 grams	12	22	26
Cholesterol	35 mg	0	0	0
Protein	8 grams	9	7	1
Vitamin A	yes	yes	yes	yes
Vitamin C	yes	yes	no	no
Vitamin D	yes	yes	yes	yes
Calcium	50%	50%	60%	<10%
Other nutrients			iron	B12

2% or "reduced fat" cow's milk contains 2% fat and about 120 calories per 8 oz serving.

Q. What do you think of organic milk?

It's expensive.

Some families prefer to buy organic, pesticide free products. Others don't. There is no public health group that recommends the use of organic milk over store brand cow's milk. Some parents have concerns about bovine growth hormone in "regular" milk causing precocious puberty. Currently, medical evidence is lacking to support this claim. It's your call.

While organic milk is fine, we don't recommend raw or unpasteruized milk. We discuss the hazards of raw milk in Chapter 13, Infections.

Q. Is it okay to use formula after a year of age?

It is not the appropriate diet for a child over age one. For babies who are failing to thrive, your doctor might recommend a dietary supplement (such as Pediasure, Carnation Instant Breakfast). Using formula for convenience when you are out and about isn't harmful, but is unnecessary. Using formula for nutrition is a waste of money.

Now that you're an expert at liquids, let's move on to a topic that truly indicates your baby is growing up: eating solid food! Up next, your guide to solid foods, food allergies and more.

Solids
Chapter 7

"Raising kids is part joy and part guerrilla warfare."
~ Ed Asner

What's in this Chapter

- How to tell if your baby is ready to eat solid food
- What is rice cereal?
- Getting started: first foods
- Making your own food
- Food allergy Special Section
- Six months and beyond
- The big picture—how much to offer and when
- Food labeling

This is the chapter you have been waiting for! After months of feeding your baby a liquid diet, you're looking forward to those photos with peas all over your baby's cute little face. And friends and relatives can get into the act of feeding baby too.

You are welcome to read this chapter at any time, but know that solid food doesn't enter the picture until your baby is four to six months old. Note: Although it's fine to try a limited amount of solid food between four and six months, breast milk or formula is the mainstay of nutrition.

When your baby is taking larger amounts of solid foods (six to nine months of age), solid food will start to replace some of the nutrients that liquid nutrition offers.

Before we get going, let's define some terms based on what you will see in the baby food aisle and in this chapter.

Note: Prepared commercial baby food is not in any way superior to making your own food for baby. But for simplicity's sake in this chapter, we will often describe serving sizes and stages of complexity of solid food the way baby food manufacturers do.

- **Stage 1 Food.** The first solid food given to babies. Pureed. Prepared "Stage 1" baby food comes in 2 oz serving sizes. Only single ingredients. Examples: squash puree, peaches, rice cereal.
- **Stage 2 Food.** Chunkier texture. Prepared "Stage 2" baby

food comes in 4 oz serving sizes. Some combinations. Examples: mixed grain cereal, berry medley.

- **Stage 3 Food.** Very chunky. Prepared "Stage 3" baby food comes in 5 or 6 oz serving sizes. Combination meals. Example: turkey rice dinner.
- **Finger foods.** Food your baby can feed to himself. Good for independence, small muscle and eye-hand coordination skills. Examples: teething/biter biscuits, small pieces of fruit/vegetables, crackers, pasta wheels, Cheerios, ground meat, canned chicken.
- **Table food.** What you eat.

Babies progress through the solid food experience based on four issues:

1. ***Food allergies.*** Start with the least allergenic foods first.
2. ***Mouth muscle (oral motor) skills.*** Does your baby know what to do with a bit of food on his tongue? You'll have to see what your baby can do. Babies cannot eat solid food until they know how to swallow it.
3. ***Texture complexity.*** Start with pureed foods, move up to chunks, then pieces. Babies cannot move up to pieces of food until they know how to gum it or chew it before swallowing. Some babies develop preferences for certain textures (or lack of texture).
4. ***Volume.*** Start with a tablespoon or two once a day. Your baby will work his way up to several ounces of solid food at a "meal," three times daily from six to twelve months old.

We'll cover all of these issues in detail later in this chapter.

Q. My mother wants to feed my two-month-old solid foods. I've heard this is a bad idea. Help!

Your mother will tell you that she fed you rice cereal at two months of age and you did fine. Here is your ammunition to keep the baby spoon out of Grandma's hands:

1 STARTING SOLID FOODS WILL NOT MAKE YOUR BABY SLEEP THROUGH THE NIGHT. Most babies start sleeping through the night by four months of age. It is not because their tummies are full of rice cereal, but because they are developmentally able to by that age.

2 INTRODUCING SOLID FOODS BEFORE FOUR MONTHS OF AGE CAN LEAD TO OBESITY. New research suggests that a parent who jumps headfirst into solid foods is more likely to misinterpret a baby's fussiness for being hungry–and overfeed her. (*Huh*)

3 INTRODUCING SOME SOLID FOODS BEFORE FOUR MONTHS OF AGE CAN LEAD TO DIABETES. Recent studies suggest that babies who first eat wheat or barley (gluten-containing grains) before four months of age or after seven months of age) can develop an inappropriate autoimmune response that leads to Type 1 Diabetes. (*Snell-Bergeon*)

4 SOLID FOOD DOES NOT PROVIDE ANY NECESSARY NUTRIENTS FOR AN INFANT UNDER FOUR MONTHS OF AGE. Breast milk and formula are the only items that should be on the menu for babies from birth to at least four months.

PREEMIES & SOLID FOOD

Because eating solid food requires a certain level of oral motor skill, many premature babies are not ready to eat solid food until their adjusted age (based on due date) is at least four to six months old. Also, preemies tend to need lots of extra calories for catch up growth. Liquid nutrition is a much better source for calories than solid food.

These products contain 50% fat and thus, are loaded with calories (20 calories per oz). So unless you are serving lard for dinner, you will never get that many calories in solid food! Breast milk and formula also contain all the essential nutrients a young infant needs (with the exception of Vitamin D– see Chp 5, Growth and Nutrition for the discussion on that issue).

5 **TELL GRANDMA THAT YOUR DOCTOR TOLD YOU NOT TO START SOLIDS UNTIL FOUR TO SIX MONTHS OF AGE.** Use your doctor as an excuse any time. We don't mind.

solid food

Q. My baby is four months old now. Is he ready to eat solid foods?

It depends. The advice on this topic can be confusing, but experts at the AAP and the National Institute of Allergy and Infectious Diseases recommend starting solid food sometime between four and six months of age when a baby shows signs of readiness. *(NIAID)*

But you may hear contradictory advice—even the AAP doesn't agree with itself on when to start solid foods. While the AAP Nutrition Committee says go for it, the AAP Breastfeeding Committee says to wait to start solids until six months if your baby is breastfed (because it promotes continued breastfeeding).

Here are the key questions: Is he exclusively breastfed? Does your doctor suggest it? Does your baby know what he is doing when you put a spoonful of solid food in his mouth?

Your baby is ready when he knows what to do with food on his tongue (**ORAL MOTOR SKILLS**). Some babies are ready at four months; some aren't ready until six months. Your baby will tell you if he is ready. Give a spoonful of baby cereal (or any pureed food on the "Stage 1" list in this chapter) a try. If he swallows it, he's ready. If he spits it back out at you, try again next week. Again, the take home message: ***there is no hurry to start solids.***

BOTTOM LINE: There is a great deal of variability amongst babies (and their doctors) about when they are ready to eat solid food. Anywhere between four to six months is fine. But remember, this isn't a race. Don't rush. And once you get the green light to start solids, remember they are "complementary foods," not the main source of your baby's nutrition. Breast milk/formula is still the priority.

Reality Check

One-third of parents do not listen to the pediatrician's advice and start feeding babies solid food *before* four months of age. The reasons are unclear. Perhaps it's a pushy grandparent or the myth that solid food will help a baby sleep through the night. Whatever the case may be, please wait until your baby is at least four months of age. Trust us.

Getting started: First Foods

What are Stage 1 foods? Stage 2? We'll give you the answers below. Before we get rolling, however, let's answer that age-old question: IN WHAT ORDER do you introduce these foods?

The answer: there is no right or wrong answer. It makes sense to start with Stage 1 foods because they are the LEAST allergenic and they are pureed. Then work your way up with textures and serving sizes. Offer single-ingredient food first (Stage 1 and 2) before offering a combination meal (Stage 3). According to the American Academy of Pediatrics, "no comprehensive research has been conducted on which specific complementary foods [solids] to provide or in which order." (*AAP Committee on Nutrition*)

Q. What is the first solid food I should offer?

Warning: controversial content ahead.

Despite what you may hear, rice cereal does NOT have to be the first solid food your baby eats. In fact, some experts suggest ***meat*** as your baby's first food. Why? Because the two key nutrients your baby needs from solid food are iron and zinc. Meat contains both nutrients in abundance . . . plus iron and zinc in meat are better absorbed by the body than in iron-fortified infant cereal. Clearly, your baby isn't ready for a steak, but you can puree meat into the texture of Spam or a nice pate.

If you prefer to go the traditional route, rice cereal is a good first food for most babies. It's easy to prepare, a decent source of iron and zinc, and almost no one is allergic to it.

The American Academy of Pediatrics Nutrition Committee recommends iron-fortified infant cereals and pureed meats as good first foods. (*AAP Committee on Nutrition*)

Reality Check

If your family maintains a vegan or vegetarian diet, you do not HAVE to offer meat to your baby at all. There are dietary alternatives to meet your baby's/growing child's nutritional needs. If you plan on feeding your baby a purely vegan diet, chat with the pediatrician about potential vitamin supplements for iron, zinc, calcium, Vitamin B 12, and Vitamin D.

Q. What is rice cereal?

Rice cereal for babies is packaged in a box as dry flakes and sold in the baby food aisle. The brand doesn't matter, as long as it is labeled iron-fortified infant cereal.

Mix it with either expressed breast milk or formula—otherwise it tastes like cardboard. (Truth be told, even when you doctor it up, it still tastes like cardboard!) Be sure you read the packaging. *Some rice cereal already has formula added*. This can be a problem for a baby with a cow's milk allergy. Make sure the cereal is pretty watery—not the thick texture you would eat. Make about two tablespoons worth. If that isn't enough, you can always make more.

Q. Does rice cereal contain arsenic?

Yes, arsenic has been found in baby rice cereal, as well as in brown and white rice and other rice-containing products like rice milk and rice cakes. For details, check out Chapter 15, Environmental Health. In a nutshell, we think rice cereal for infants is safe.

Q. How should I give my baby his first solid meal?

Offer it as a snack *after* your baby has had breast milk or formula. If you try to feed him solid food when he is hungry, you won't be able to shovel it in fast enough. By six months of age, your baby could probably win a chugging contest with the speed he guzzles down 160 calories (eight ounces of liquid).

Try one feeding a day of a "Stage 1" food for three or four days before embarking upon other foods or cereals. However, your baby should eat a high-iron containing food every day so infant iron-fortified cereals or meats are good options to try first. We encourage you to experiment with tastier cereals (oatmeal, barley, and other grains). These grain cereals also offer another advantage: FIBER. Rice cereal contains no fiber . . . therefore, if your baby eats a fair amount of it, he may become constipated.

Q. What other foods should I offer first?

Remember, there are no rules on which "order" to progress through these foods.

Iron-fortified infant cereals and Stage 1 foods are sensible first foods to introduce because they are pureed and the least allergenic. Stage 1 foods include carrots, sweet potatoes, mashed potatoes, squash, green beans, peas, bananas, peaches, pears, plums, applesauce, lamb, turkey, chicken, pork, pureed beans, and whole milk yogurt (If your baby has been diagnosed with a cow's milk protein allergy, ask your baby's doc first before offering her yogurt!)

See the nearby box on first foods. Make sure to offer each new food individually before combining them.

Q. How often do I introduce a new food?

Introduce one new food by itself every three to four days. You are introducing foods slowly because you are looking to see if your baby has any food allergies (see a discussion on this topic later in this chapter). *The AAP recommends no more than three new foods per week.*

Q. How often do I feed my baby solid foods?

Here is a ballpark figure: one solid meal daily at four through six months, two at seven months, and three solid meals daily by eight to nine months.

Start with one feeding a day and work up to three feedings a day (by nine months old).

Until about eight to nine months, always feed your baby his breast milk or formula first. Then offer solid food as a between meal snack. Remember, until your baby eats several jars of food, he's drinking his calories. When your baby is only eating one kind of solid food, a single feeding of solid food per day is fine. When he has a repertoire of foods, you can feed him three times a day.

BOOKMARK THIS PAGE! BABY FOOD BY STAGE

Fruits and Vegetables, Stage 1:
- Applesauce
- Apricots
- Asparagus
- Avocados
- Bananas
- Broccoli
- Carrots—cooked, pureed
- Green beans
- Guava
- Mashed potatoes
- Mango
- Melons
- Nectarines
- Papaya
- Peaches
- Peas
- Pears
- Plums
- Prunes
- Pumpkin
- Squash
- Sweet potatoes *(alone or sneak into pancake mix for Stage 3 food)*

Fruits and Vegetables, Stage 2:
- Bell peppers
- Blueberries
- Grapefruit
- Kale and other greens
- Kiwi
- Oranges
- Pineapple
- Rhubarb—cooked
- Spinach—cooked
- Strawberries
- Tomatoes

Dairy, Stage 1:
- Whole milk yogurt

Dairy, Stage 2:
- Cottage cheese
- Mac & cheese
- Soft cheeses (cream cheese, sour cream)

Dairy, Stage 3:
- Yogurt and fruit smoothies
- Shredded cheese

Grains, Stage 1:
- Iron-fortified infant cereal
- *Rice*
- Barley, oatmeal
- Wheat cereal
- Millet cereal
- Quinoa cereal

Grains, Stage 2:
- Cheerios/Oatios or generic
- Cornmeal: *polenta, cornbread, corn tortillas*
- Oat bran cereal/muffins
- Pasta such as wagon wheels
- Puffed kashi
- Rice cakes

Grains, Stage 3:
- Whole grain pancakes
- Whole grain waffles
- Whole wheat crackers

Meats, Beans, Legumes Stage 1:
- Beans: *red, kidney, white, black-eyed, navy, etc*
- Beef; Chicken; Lamb; Pork; Turkey
- Lentils; Split peas
- Tofu
- Garbanzo beans

Meats, Beans, Legumes Stage 2:
- Edamame; Egg; Fish
- Sunflower seed butter

Meats, Beans, Legumes Stage 3:
- Lasagna
- Hummus
- Peanuts, treenuts—but only as a spread, butter or sauce (whole nuts are a choking hazard).

DR B'S OPINION: BABY FOOD COOKBOOKS

I bought a baby food cookbook for my husband, our chef, when our first child was born. (Being in the kitchen actually makes me nervous!) The recipes amused him. The recipe for carrots was:

1. Steam carrots. 2. Puree. 3. Serve.

My advice–don't bother buying a baby food cookbook. Just use a food processor or blender and puree your home cooking. You can pour the food into ice cube trays (perfect serving size) and freeze them. It's easy to thaw out and serve.

Reality Check

To give you some perspective: rice cereal has 60 calories per 1/4 cup (5 calories per tsp) and a jar (2 1/2 oz) of "Stage 1" carrots has 25 calories. Your baby would need to eat almost 3/4 cup of cereal or six whole jars of carrots to replace one bottle or breastfeeding session. You'll be lucky if your baby eats two tablespoons of cereal or 1/2 jar (1 oz) of carrots in a feeding session in his first weeks of starting solids.

solid food

Old Wives Tale

Introducing fruits before vegetables will give your baby a sweet tooth.

The truth: Your baby will either like vegetables or not. The order of introduction has nothing to do with it. When your baby is a toddler, he won't eat *anything*.

Q. My six-month old started solids and now his skin is turning yellow—HELP!

You are what you eat!

Babies are often first introduced to a series of yellow vegetables (carrots, squash, sweet potatoes). All of these vegetables are rich in Vitamin A (carotene). This vitamin has a pigment that can collect harmlessly on the skin producing a condition called **CAROTINEMIA**. The difference between this condition and jaundice (high bilirubin level) is that jaundiced babies have a yellowing in the whites of their eyes. Sweet potato lovers don't have that. See Baby411.com (click on "Bonus Material") for a great picture.

Q. Can I make my own baby food?

Absolutely. There is nothing special about commercially prepared baby foods, other than being ready-to-eat. It's actually preferable to offer food from your table. That way, your baby will get used to your cooking! Yes, you can use seasonings, herbs, and spices. Just limit the amount of salt, and use iodized salt if you must add it. It's not that hard. Trust me, I'd never make it on "Top Chef" but even I could make baby food. And it doesn't take that much time . . . you just need a blender or food processor. If you are on the go, pick up a cheap handheld baby food grinder or mill for about $10.

Q. Is baby food in squeezable packages safer or more healthy?

Baby food is baby food—regardless of the packaging. But, squeezies are extremely popular with parents and kids on-the-go. Because babies and older kids can suck the pureed solid food directly out of the package, they don't require parental assistance. A parent can hand a squeezie to a hungry child sitting in the back seat of a car and keep on driving through rush hour traffic. And, some parents report that pureed veggies are the only kind their kids will eat. So where's the downside, right?

For babies, learning how to eat foods of different textures is important. So, while squeezies are certainly a convenient option, they should not be the only way you introduce solid foods to your fledgling eater. They also cost significantly more than jarred baby food (which already rivals a three star Michelin restaurant's prices in cost per ounce).

As for safety and health questions, makers of squeezable packages point out the containers are BPA-free (more on this controversy in Chapter 15, The Environment and Your Baby.) From a nutrition standpoint, baby food in squeezable packges is the same as that in jars.

Bottom line: squeezable baby food is fine when used in moderation.

Q. Is it ever a good idea to pre-chew food for my baby?

Um, no. Celebrity Alicia Silverstone was captured on video doing that, but remember she starred in *Clueless*.

Seriously, yes, some cultures practice "premastication," but there is no need to take the health risk in the modern age of utensils and food blenders. Mixing baby food with an adult's saliva increases the chance of spreading germs that can lead to infection, as well as germs that can lead to cavities.

Q. What do you think of organic baby food?

It's a lifestyle choice.

As we have discussed, some parents make this a priority. Others don't. What does the science show? We will save that discussion for Chapter 15,

BEHIND THE SCENES: WHAT IS "ORGANIC"?

The USDA regulates the labeling of all of these "natural" products so that people know how natural a product really is. Organic products are meats, poultry, eggs, and dairy products made from animals that did not receive antibiotics or growth hormones or fruits and vegetables grown without pesticides or petroleum based fertilizers. Organic farms are certified by a government inspector. Here are the rules:

- *100% Organic* must have a USDA seal on it.
- *Organic* is made of 95% to100% organic ingredients.
- *Made with Organic Ingredients* is made of at least 70% organic ingredients.

The Environment and Your Baby.

If you do opt for going organic, we advise you to prepare your own baby food from organic fruits and vegetables rather than to buy commercially prepared organic baby food, which is very expensive.

If you do buy prepared baby food, know that all the conventional brands (not just organic) make their Stage 1 foods preservative- and additive-free. The Stage 2 and 3 foods do add other ingredients, so you may want to check the packaging.

We'll delve into what we know about food-borne environmental exposures in Chapter 15, The Environment and Your Baby.

Special Section: Food Allergies

Q. How do I know if my baby has a food allergy?

Look for an impressive rash, profuse vomiting, horrible diarrhea, or blood/mucous in poop (the poop looks stringy, like snot from the nose).

Allergic reactions are not subtle. If your baby has a few dots of a rash or a diaper rash, it's not because of the food you just introduced.

Most allergic responses occur within minutes or at most four hours after an exposure. (Although it's quite rare, some serious reactions can occur up to three days after an exposure.) (*Sampson*) A chemical in the body called **HISTAMINE** is released in massive quantities with an allergic reaction. Histamine can cause a tingling or itchy mouth, mouth or lip swelling, shortness of breath, and dramatic diarrhea. You may also see hives (raised borders of red plaques that look like mosquito bites with circles around them). See our web site at Baby411.com (click on "Bonus Material") for a picture.

The extreme scenario is called an **ANAPHYLACTIC REACTION.** This is when loss of consciousness and airway swelling occurs—obviously, this is life threatening and you need to call 911. This is very unlikely to ever happen, particularly with a Stage 1 food—they are extremely well tolerated.

Infants who are more at risk for food allergies are those with parents who are very allergic. These babies' risk of having a food allergy may be as high as 20%. Compare that to the general population, which has about a 2% risk of food allergies. Children who have asthma have a higher risk of having a more serious allergic reaction if they have a food allergy.

DR B'S OPINION: PICKY-EATER TODDLERS

After years of watching babies grow up to be picky-eater toddlers, I can tell you those who acquire a taste for mom or dad's cooking early on, eat a broader range of healthy food in the toddler and preschool years. If you were a couple who usually ate out or ordered take-out in your pre-baby years, now is the time to make a permanent change in your food lifestyle. As I alluded to in Chapter 5, Nutrition, it really does take a family to eat healthy.

Q. What is food intolerance?

This term refers to an adverse reaction to a food or food product, not an allergic response.

Allergic reactions produce histamine. Food intolerances do not. If a baby has intolerance to a food, he might have stomach cramps or bloating. You'll probably avoid that food in the future, but he'll never have a life-threatening (anaphylactic) reaction if he is exposed to it.

(Example: An adult with lactose intolerance has gas or diarrhea when he drinks milk, but doesn't get hives).

Q. What foods are more likely to cause food allergies?

1. ***PEANUTS/Peanut Butter.*** We'll discuss this in detail next.
2. Egg whites. (the *white* part—egg protein is the problem)
3. Shellfish (crab, lobster, shrimp, scallops, oysters).
4. Fish.
5. Tree nuts (walnuts, cashews, etc).
6. Wheat.
7. Cow's milk.
8. Soy.
9. Citrus fruits, berries.
10. Cocoa.
11. Sesame seeds are rapidly emerging as a new top food allergy.

Food Allergies Stats

- 2.5% of newborns have a cow's milk allergy. 80% outgrow it by age five.
- 1.5% of children are allergic to eggs. 80% outgrow it by age ten.
- 0.8% of children are allergic to peanuts, but of those with the allergy, only 20% will outgrow it.
- Most food allergies occur in the first three years of life (8% of all children).
- Only 2% of adults have a food allergy, and of those, 50% are allergic to either peanuts or tree nuts. (*Sampson, AAP*)

Q. Can my baby have a cow's milk protein allergy if I am breastfeeding?

Yes. Food proteins are passed into mom's breast milk, and cow's milk protein is no exception.

Babies with a milk protein allergy may have blood streaked poops, diarrhea, and poor growth. If your baby is fed a cow's milk-based formula, this allergy may pop up in the first few weeks of life. In breastfed babies, it may not be a problem at all. Or, it may take a few months to become apparent because there is less exposure to the cow's milk protein.

If you are nursing and your baby is diagnosed with a cow's milk protein allergy, you will need to eliminate ALL dairy from your diet. That means no milk or dairy products—no cream in your coffee, no parmesan cheese sprinkled on your spaghetti, etc. We discussed this in Chapter 6, Liquids.

And yes, your baby may not get her doctor's blessing to eat dairy solid food products like yogurt or cheese until she outgrows the allergy.

Q. My baby was diagnosed with a cow's milk protein allergy. I am nursing and I've removed all milk and dairy products from my diet. But he is still having blood in his poop. Am I doing something wrong?

No, you are probably doing everything right. It takes at least six to eight weeks for the irritated, inflamed gut/rectum to heal. So, even if your baby is not ingesting any more milk protein, it can take time to see the results in his poop. The good news: most parents report that the baby seems happier and less uncomfortable after the dietary changes occur. Babies with persistent bleeding should see a pediatric gastroenterologist (a specialist in childhood intestinal disorders).

Food allergy testing is usually not helpful in situations where the baby is only having bloody or mucousy poop. Most babies will not have positive allergy tests. But their symptoms gradually improve when their diet changes.

Reality Check

Many babies with a cow's milk protein allergy also are allergic to soy protein. Milk from other mammals (like goat's milk) can also be problematic for these babies. Nursing moms often opt for rice milk or coconut milk in their diets.

HIDDEN SOURCES FOR DANGEROUS FOODS

If you have a food allergic child, the world can be a scary place. Are you aware of how peanuts and other potential food allergy dangers are hidden in other products? Candy and cookies, as well as fresh baked goods, are a flash point—undeclared soy, wheat, nuts, and eggs are common in baked goods. Today most processed foods are required to list allergy facts, but some products still are not covered by these laws.

And let's talk about restaurants. Unfortunately, there is no law requiring restaurants to disclose the use of allergenic foods as ingredients. As a parent, you have to take charge: inform the waiter of your preference to avoid peanuts (or a child's allergy) and ask what dishes are a problem. If you get a blank stare in return, ask to see the manager. Ditto for quick-serve restaurants.

Watch out for stealth uses of allergenic foods like peanuts—for example, some Chinese restaurants seal their egg roll wrappers with peanut butter!

Now, we're not trying to make you overly paranoid here. But as a parent, you have to be vigilant—especially when your child goes over to friends' or relatives' homes. If in doubt, speak up and don't forget to warn all your friends and relatives every time you drop off your child. In fact, it may be a good idea to get a MedicAlert bracelet for your child when he gets older. It reminds him of his allergy as well as the adults he's with for the day. For more information, check out the web. Food Allergy Network's website (FoodAllergy.org) has a brochure you can download called "Preventing or Delaying the Onset of Food Allergies in Infants." It also provides an FAQ, alerts and school resources.

Q. So when can I feed my child a peanut butter and jelly sandwich?

Okay, let's talk peanuts and peanut butter.

Here's the scary fact about peanut allergy: it can be life threatening. That's right, some kids with a peanut allergy can die from ingesting less than one peanut. Another scary fact: only 20% of kids who have peanut allergy will outgrow it!

So here is the latest advice on babies and food allergies. The American Academy of Pediatrics and the National Institute on Allergy and Infectious Diseases both recommend you offer solid food (including high-allergy ones) at four months of age and beyond. This includes children who are born to families who have a history of food allergies.

Yes, you read that correctly. Experts believe exposure to high allergy foods early in life may be protective instead of sensitizing! This reverses the advice of years past, when doctors urged parents to hold off introducing high-allergy foods until later.

For example, a study on peanut allergies in the November 2008 *Journal of Allergy and Clinical Immunology* found that Israeli children who got their first taste of peanuts between eight and 14 months of age were LESS likely to have a peanut allergy than their British peers who didn't start eating peanut products until after 14 months. In fact, the British kids were TEN times more likely to have peanut allergies! (*Du Toit*)

A quick caveat here: eating whole peanuts are a no-no until after age three because they are a choking hazard. Raw honey is off limits until one year of age due to a risk of botulism. *(AAP Committee on Nutrition, NIAID.)*

BOTTOM LINE

Although we don't suggest offering peanut butter as the first food out of the gate, you can and should offer those high allergy foods before your baby's first birthday. (Practically speaking, peanut butter is pretty tough to swallow for a young child so a nice peanut sauce is a safer bet.) If your baby has eczema, wheezes, or has a milk protein allergy, you should definitely chat with your baby's doctor before offering those high allergy foods.

Reality Check

Do people with food allergies have other allergy problems? Sometimes. The most common allergy pair is eczema and a food allergy. In fact, eczema can be aggravated by a food allergy. The most serious combination is asthma plus a food allergy. Those children are more likely to have a scary respiratory emergency (wheezing/ana-

Food allergies and eczema

Food allergies are one of the key precipitating factors for eczema. 37% of kids with severe eczema have a food allergy. The eczema improves when the food offender is eliminated from the diet. The vast majority of food offenders are the top 8 foods on the list earlier. (*Eigenmann*)

phylaxis) with an allergic reaction to a food, because that is the way their body responds to an allergen. That doesn't happen to everyone, mind you. However, kids with these combo allergies need to be particularly careful to avoid allergenic food(s).

Feedback from the Real World: Ben's Story

Want to hear something really scary? How about the story of Ben, (Denise's son), and how we discovered his life threatening peanut allergy. When Ben was one year of age, we decided we could add peanut butter into his life. Being a confessed peanut nut (I've searched the Southern U.S. for the best peanut butter pie–haven't found it yet but I'm still looking), we thought this would be a tasty addition to his diet. Besides we had no history of severe food allergies in our families.

Shazam! He immediately swelled up like a tomato. This was our first experience with an allergic reaction. Hives hit him like a ton of bricks. We practically threw him in the car and raced down the mountain (yes, we did live in the mountains at the time) to the doctor's office. There we were informed that he was allergic to peanuts. After treating the hives, the doctor mentioned that this would probably be allergic for life and the next time could be life-threatening anaphylaxis (after eating one peanut he could stop breathing and die). We next visited with an allergist who confirmed the diagnosis with a "peanut challenge" test.

So what now? Well, we see the allergist once a year. And we have to carry an epinephrine injectable pen with us everywhere we go. In fact, there is an Epi-Pen at school, at Nanna's, at our house and in my purse. We had to teach Ben to read labels on food, never share at school and never, ever take food samples without first checking with us (Sam's Club is a nightmare sometimes!). It's no wonder a recent study showed that kids with a peanut allergy suffer from more stress than kids with diabetes.

The good news: scientists are working on a form of oral immunotherapy, using the same strategy as allergy shots for seasonal pollen allergies. Food allergic patients would take increasing amounts of the food substance they are allergic to on a regular basis. This therapy, however, is still several years away from being reality.

Helpful Hints

1. If your baby does have a food allergy, get educated about hidden sources of the problem food.

2. Know how to read an ingredient label. Products containing milk include: casein, sodium caseinate, whey, or lactoglobulin.

3. Be a detective. Deli slicers are often contaminated with milk because both cheese and lunchmeat are sliced on the same machine. Many candies without peanuts are processed in the same location as those with peanuts.

Q. What is the best way to prevent food allergies?

Breastfeed for at least four months. Since human milk is made for human babies, it is the least likely to be problematic.

Is there any benefit to a breastfeeding mom avoiding high allergy foods in her diet? No. A fair amount of research has been done on nursing mothers eliminating highly allergenic foods from their diets to prevent "sensitizing" their infants. It is true that the breakdown products of foods mom eats end up in her breast milk. However, this exposure does not put a baby at any greater risk of developing a food allergy. A nursing mom only needs to limit her diet if a problem is identified.

Q. Okay, so when can I try these high allergy foods with my baby?

Again, your baby can try any solid food, even the high allergy ones (eggs, fish, peanut containing products) after four months of age. Just be sure to offer only one new food every three to four days so you can identify the food if there is a problem.

Reality Check

The recommendations for starting highly allergenic foods represent a MAJOR change from past years' advice on this topic. So have a discussion with your child's doctor if you have questions or concerns. It is particularly important to talk to your doc if your baby already has eczema, wheezing, or a milk protein allergy.

Q. What is a good reference if my baby does develop a food allergy?

Check out the Food Allergy Network at www.foodallergy.org. Or call, (800) 929-4040.

Q. How are people tested for a food allergy?

There are four basic ways to test for a food allergy, but be aware that there is no perfect science:

1 **ELIMINATION DIET.** Eliminate the food from the diet for three to six weeks; see if there is an improvement in symptoms (i.e. eczema, diarrhea, etc).

2 **SKIN TESTING.** Skin prick tests detect a true allergic response (see IgE below) to a food. If skin testing shows an allergic response, RAST testing can be done for confirmation.

3 **CAP-RAST TEST.** Blood test detects an elevation of the body's IgE antibodies (an allergic response chemical). RAST testing is useful because it can identify some food allergies. However, not all food allergies cause an elevation of IgE levels. In English: a positive test is useful. A negative test does not rule out a food allergy. The newer CAP-RAST tests have been shown to be 95% predictive in food allergies for milk, eggs, peanuts, and fish.

4 **FOOD CHALLENGE.** When a person is known to be allergic to a certain food, periodic (annual) RAST testing may show a decrease in allergy response levels. A person can try a certain food again in a controlled medical setting to see if he is still allergic to a particular food. (This does not mean at your kitchen table). (*Sampson*)

CELIAC DISEASE: ON THE RISE

Celiac Disease, a disorder caused by an abnormal immune response to a protein found in certain grains called gluten, used to be rare. Today 1% of the U.S. population has Celiac.

Here is what you need to know. People with celiac disease have an unfortunate combination of genetics (predisposition that is passed down from family) and exposure to gluten. The exposure leads to injury of the intestinal lining and then, difficulty with digestion (malabsorption). The result: chronic diarrhea, failure to thrive, vomiting, and bloating to name a few symptoms. But, some people have no or subtle symptoms while their guts are being irritated.

Wheat, barley, and rye grains all contain gluten protein. And, there are a variety of other gluten-containing foods that might surprise you–who knew Communion wafers could be a problem? See the list below for more problematic foods.

As babies start to eat cereal grains (wheat, barley, and rye), Celiac Disease can become apparent. More subtle symptoms include trouble gaining weight or anemia.

If you have a family member with this disorder, or notice a change in your baby after introducing these foods, check in with your baby's doctor. Children with Down syndrome, diabetes, and other genetic syndromes are also at risk and should be tested if they have worrisome symptoms. The first thing to do is a couple of blood tests (IgA endomysial antibody and IgA antitissue transglutamate) after a child is on a gluten-containing diet for at least two to four weeks. If the blood tests are abnormal, a biopsy of the small intestine (done via an outpatient procedure) confirms the diagnosis.

FYI: Recent research shows that feeding babies gluten-containing foods *prior* to four months of age increases the risk of developing celiac disease. It's yet one more reason to wait on starting solid foods until at least four months of age.

Gluten-containing foods:

Always contains gluten

Wheat (einkorn, durum, faro, graham, kamut, semolina, spelt), rye, barley, malt, malt flavoring, malt extract derived from barley, malt vinegar, triticale

May contain gluten

Breading, brewer's yeast, broth, bouillion, brown rice syrup, cake frosting, candy, coating mixes, Communion wafers, certain condiments, croutons, dates rolled in oat flour, drink mixes, flavored teas and coffees, flour/cereal products, gravies, imitation bacon, imitation seafood, licorice, marinades, matzah/matzah meal, some medications, some oats, panko, pasta, processed lunch meats, rice pilaf, roux, some salad dressings, some sauces and spreads, some seasonings, seasoned chips/nuts/seeds, self-basting poultry, smoke flavoring, soup stock, soy sauce (often made with soy and wheat), stuffing for poultry, some nutritional supplements. *(Hill)*

Q. Can you outgrow a food allergy?

Most kids outgrow food allergies to milk, eggs, soy, and wheat by the time they are five years old. Over 50% of kids will outgrow their food allergies by the age of one. The foods that tend to be lifelong problems are peanuts, tree nuts, fish, and shellfish. (*Wood*)

Q. Are there any other foods my baby shouldn't eat?

Yes. Here are three:

- *Honey*: Wait on honey until your child is one year old. Honey contains *clostridium botulinum* spores that can cause botulism in an infant. (Infants' digestive systems are relatively sterile compared to ours and can't kill the spores).
- *Choking Hazards:* Raw carrots, celery, popcorn, potato chips, nuts, hard candy, hard meat, fruits with seeds, raisins, hotdogs, and grapes (unless cut lengthwise). Wait on these foods until your child is really good at chewing (two to three years).
- *Artificial sweeteners:* There is no official party line on this one, but there is no reason to offer these products to babies.

Six months and beyond

Q. My baby is six months old now. What can he eat?

Start at Stage 1 foods. Then advance to Stage 2-3 Foods and start feeding him off of your plate.

If your child is doing well, expand his diet. You will work your way through the different food groups and textures, while increasing the volume of food as your baby demands it.

Now is the time to start good eating habits, and give your baby a feeling that mealtime is enjoyable. (That means, don't worry about making a mess.) Solid foods should still be a supplement and not replacement of calories. Your baby will tell you he is done by turning his head, spitting out his food, and/or throwing it on the floor.

Once you get through Stage 1 foods, move on to Stage 2 and Stage 3 foods. Beware, your baby may not like the textures. They are chunkier than the Stage 1 pureed foods.

So, if the food on your plate looks good to your baby, let him try it. This includes a variety of safe ethnic foods. You will know he is ready because he will be watching every spoonful that goes into your mouth. Don't worry about herbs and spices you use in seasoning—just limit adding salt or sugar. Your baby needs to get used to your methods of food preparation.

See our handy list earlier in this chapter for fun food ideas.

Q. My baby is nine months old. What can he eat now?

Almost anything. This includes "finger foods."

Your baby is ready to feed himself when he uses his index finger and thumb to grasp things, otherwise known as the ***pincer grasp.*** Finger foods include: Cheerios, pieces of banana, pieces of pears or peaches, small

pieces of cheese, whole wheat toast, soft meats and boneless fish, wagon wheel pasta, graham or whole grain crackers, and teething biscuits. And you thought solids were messy before...do not make a big deal out of it—just clean it up. Kids sense frustration and will have mealtime anxiety if you make it an issue. Your child can be toothless and enjoy solid and finger foods. They can gum just about anything.

As far as amounts, your baby should be taking enough solid food at a sitting to cut back on the volume of liquid nutrition. Aim for three solid meals per day (six to 14 ounces of solid food). See the "Big Picture" table at the end of this chapter.

Feedback from the Real World: Multiples

Cutting the finger foods ahead of time reduced my stress. Patience is not exactly a baby or toddler's strong suit! Less fussing and crying made mealtime a little more enjoyable for me.—*Agustina, mom of Gael and Malena, 18 month old twins*

Helpful Hint

Now is a good time to take that CPR class you have been meaning to take. It's unlikely you will ever need to utilize your skills, but it's always good to be prepared.

Q. My nine month old refuses any food that has a texture to it. Help!

This is called **TEXTURE AVERSION.**

Some babies prefer smooth, pureed foods well into their second year of life. If he is otherwise developing normally, I'd consider your baby a little eccentric, but normal.

Babies with texture aversions, adverse reactions to sensory stimulation, and developmental delays may be worth talking to your doctor about (see **PERVASIVE DEVELOPMENTAL DISORDER, SENSORY PROCESSING DISORDER**).

Q. My one year old refuses to let me feed her, but can't use utensils yet. Any ideas?

One way is to let her use a spoon while you shovel in the food with your spoon. If she clues in to this trick, try letting her dip foods. Yogurt, applesauce, guacamole, and beans will stick easily to a cracker that your baby can lick off.

Remember, getting your toddler to eat anything is a real challenge.

Q. What are the food expectations for a one-year old?

To join the family at the dinner table, and eat what the family is eating.

The goal is for your child to graduate to table foods (what you eat) at one year of age. He should eat three meals and two snacks per day. He should drink whole or 2% milk (16 oz or dairy serving equivalent), juice (less than six oz per day), and water out of a cup. Say goodbye to bottles.

Q. Is it okay for my baby to eat fish?

Yes. The few restrictions are: shark, swordfish, king mackerel, and tilefish. These fish contain high levels of mercury, so the Food and Drug Administration has recommended that these be avoided for young children. It is also recommended to contact your local health department about any warnings on fish caught in area lakes. Canned tuna is okay in small amounts (less than six ounces/week).

The Big Picture For Liquid And Solid Nutrition

AGE	LIQUID NUTRITION	SOLID NUTRITION	SOLID SERVING SIZE
4-6 months	32-40 oz **5-6 meals**	Stage 1 foods* Iron-containing foods* **0-1 feeding/day**	2-4 Tbsp (1-2 oz) 1-2 items at each meal. *Pureed foods.* **0-4 oz/day**
6-9 months	28-36oz **4-5 meals**	Stage 1, 2, 3 foods Iron-containing foods **1-3 feedings/day**	2-4 Tbsp (1-2 oz) Two or three items at each meal or a whole Stage 2 jar. *More textures.* **6-14 oz/day**
9-12 months	20-30 oz **3-4 meals**	All of the above Table foods **3 meals/day**	3-4 Tbsp (2 oz) Three items at each meal, or a Stage 3 jar. *Bite size pieces.* **10-18 oz/day**

**Solid nutrition from 4–6 months depends on your baby's readiness.*

Key Points To Remember:

- Prepared baby food jars: Stage 1= 2oz serving. Stage 2 = 4 oz serving. Stage 3 = 5-6 oz serving.
- Remember that breast milk and formula have 20 calories per ounce. A 2.5 oz jar of Stage 1 carrots has 25 calories.
- Do not reduce the amount of liquid nutrition until your baby eats enough solid food to replace the calories. This gradual taper begins somewhere between six and nine months. This is when a solid meal is at least a four to six ounce serving.
- Every baby is different!

The Other End

Chapter 8

"Gil, why are you standing there?" "I'm waiting for her head to spin around."

~ Parenthood

What's in this Chapter

- Normal newborn poop
- The top 5 worrisome poops
- Trade secrets for constipation relief
- Fun fiber foods
- Spit up, regurgitation, and vomit
- What is gastroesophageal reflux (GER)?
- Top 5 worries about vomit
- Urine and bladder infections
- Burping, hiccups, and gas

This chapter addresses a subject taboo at most dinner tables. We are going to have a candid discussion about poop (as well as gas, burps, pee and spit up, too). Why spend a whole chapter on poop? Let's be honest–you'll have LOTS of questions about this subject. And you'll be looking at lots of it too! The average baby goes through 2300 diaper changes in the first year alone.

Parents have concerns because baby poop does not look like theirs. If it does, your baby has a problem. And as you might imagine, changing at least eight diapers a day also results in a pre-occupation with diaper contents.

Before we go too far, it's a good idea to go over the terminology we'll be using in this chapter:

- **Stool.** Your digested food garbage that is eliminated through your anus. Stool also has bacteria germs in it (these germs help us digest our food). Just so we're on the same page–it's also known as poo, poop, feces, caca, Number 2, bowel movement . . . for this book, we will use the term **POOP.**

- **Urine.** The garbage that your kidneys clean out of your bloodstream that is eliminated through your urethra (the hole in the penis or the hole above the vagina). Urine is sterile (germ free). Otherwise known as pee, pee-pee, wee-wee, wet diapers, urinating...for this book, we will use the term **PEE**.

- **Gas.** The air inside the intestines that is a by-product of the food transit through it. When babies eat 24 hours a day, their intestines move 24 hours a day, *and* make a whole lot of gas. The gas slows down when the intestinal transit slows down, around six weeks.
- **Burps.** The air that gets swallowed comes back out of the esophagus. Because babies exclusively suck and swallow their nutrition for the first four months of life, burping feels good after a big meal. Some babies suck very aggressively and ingest a large air bubble. When this air bubble comes up, often so does the whole meal.
- **Hiccups.** This is caused by a muscle spasm of the diaphragm (the muscle that divides the chest and abdomen). All babies have some hiccups. This sometimes is a sign of sensory overload (i.e. over stimulation). There is nothing wrong with your baby. You may just want to soothe him.

Newborn Poop

Q. What should my newborn's poop look like?

Black tar.

In the first 24 hours of life, your baby should pass a poop called **MECONIUM**. This has the color and texture of black tar. It looks like this because the baby has swallowed some blood while inside the womb. The black tar contains some digested blood. (Good to remember if you ever see poop that looks like this again from your baby or a family member).

As your baby starts to eat breast milk or formula, the poop will change color and texture. This happens on about the fourth day of life. (Remember, they don't eat much the first few days.)

Q. My newborn is breastfed. What should his poop look like?

Grey Poupon (or crab mustard, as my Baltimore friends would say).

Breast milk poop is very watery. In fact, many parents worry that their baby is having diarrhea if they have never changed a breastfed baby's diaper before. It's watery because the breast milk is so easily digested, it goes right through the intestines and leaves very little solid garbage to be pooped out.

Parents often wonder how they will know when their baby is having diarrhea. The answer is the *frequency* of poop increases. Breastfed babies often poop with every feeding for the first six weeks of life. Some babies will poop less frequently than that, sometimes only once every few days. Do not worry unless the consistency of the poop looks like yours.

The color is often yellow. But, ***any shade of yellow, green or brown is okay.*** Florescent green is okay too.

DR B'S OPINION: GREEN POOP AND FOREMILK?

Some mothers hear that green poop is a sign that their baby is only getting the foremilk and not the richer hindmilk. (For a discussion of foremilk and hindmilk, see Chapter 6, Liquids). While this may be true, a better way to tell if a baby is getting hindmilk is to look at the feeding patterns and growth charts, not the poop color. Babies who get foremilk only tend to be snackers who eat frequently (they don't fill up as well). They also gain less weight if they miss out on the fatty hindmilk.

Q. My newborn is formula fed. What should his poop look like?

Strained peas.

Formula poops tend to be greener than breast milk poop. But, as we mentioned, any shade of yellow, green or brown is okay.

Formula poops are also thicker and pastier than breast milk poop. It takes longer to digest formula in the intestines, so more water is absorbed before the "final product" comes out.

Q. How often do formula fed babies poop?

Formula fed babies poop less often because the "transit time" through the intestines is longer. These babies may poop three or four times per day or once every couple of days. The frequency slows down even more at six weeks of life.

RED FLAGS: Worrisome Poop

If you see/note any of these, call your doctor immediately:

1. Your baby doesn't poop in the first 24 hours of life (see **MECONIUM PLUG OR ILEUS**).
2. Your baby's poops look bloody, tarry, or mixed with mucous (see **BLOOD IN STOOL**)
3. Your baby's poop looks like yours. (see **CONSTIPATION**)
4. Your baby has a stomachache and poop that looks like grape jelly (see **INTUSSUSCEPTION**)
5. Your baby's frequency of poop increases two or three fold (see **DIARRHEA/GASTROENTERITIS**)

Q. My baby grunts and his face turns red when he poops. Is this normal?

Yes.

Try lying down and pooping some time. See what your face looks like. This does NOT mean your child is constipated. There is actually a term for this phenomenon–The Grunting Baby Syndrome.

Q. My three-week-old usually poops with every feeding. Now, he hasn't gone in 24 hours. Is he constipated?

No.

Please read this carefully. Constipation is diagnosed by the FIRMNESS of the poop, NOT THE FREQUENCY (or infrequency) of pooping. *Concerned parents often think their baby is constipated when they are not.* Newborns to six week olds usually poop several times a day. Occasionally, though, they may take a day off. That's when you call the doctor in a state of panic. The answer is, "Be prepared for the Mother Load." Some babies may poop once or twice a week. That's fine, as long as it is soft when it comes out.

Your baby is constipated when the poop looks like logs, rock balls, marbles, or deer pellets. See below for tricks of the trade for relieving constipation.

Old Wives Tale

The iron in formula causes constipation.

The truth: There isn't enough iron in formula to make a baby constipated. And without the iron, your baby won't grow. If your baby is constipated, try some of the tricks below.

Trade Secrets For Relieving Constipation

1 **RECTAL THERMOMETER TRICK.** If your baby is straining and not having any success, insert a rectal thermometer in his anus for about a minute. Trust me–this is the most dispensed phone advice by any pediatrician's office. You can read the exact details on how to insert a rectal thermometer in Chapter 15, "First Aid." This usually provides the inspiration your baby needs to get moving. (And no, they don't mind having it done like you would!)

2 **PRUNE JUICE COCKTAIL.** If your baby is regularly irregular, he may need some extra fiber to move things along. Try one teaspoon of prune juice per feeding (mixed in formula or given separately to breastfed babies) until you get the desired consistency of poop. You can adjust the volume to what your baby needs (that is, anywhere from one to five teaspoons a day). Prune juice has both fiber and sorbitol (sugar) that pull water into the poop to make it softer. Hint: Buy store brand prune juice–not the stuff in the baby food section. "Baby" prune juice is mixed with apple juice and is very expensive by comparison.

3 **KARO COCKTAIL.** Some pediatricians recommend using karo syrup instead of prune juice to pull water into the stool. I don't use it because there are some anecdotal reports of botulism spores in karo syrup (similar to the concerns we discussed about honey in the feeding chapter).

4 **WASH IT OUT.** Sometimes, babies need drink a little water to soften up the poop. I wouldn't offer more than an ounce or two, though, to an infant under six months of age.

5 **GLYCERINE BULLET.** For immediate relief, use a glycerine suppository to get dramatic results. These suppositories can be purchased without a prescription at the grocery store or pharmacy. Frequently, the label will

read "infant" suppository. The suppository looks like a bullet made of soap. Insert it directly into the anus. It dissolves as you push it in. Be prepared for the fireworks.

If these tricks don't work, call your doctor. Pediatricians always have a few more tricks like this up their sleeves!

Q. My six-week old breastfed baby used to poop at every feeding. Now she only goes once a day. Should I be worried?

No. This is normal and you should be thankful.

Babies are born with intestines that work 24/7. They work that way to keep the nutritional juices flowing. By six weeks of age, things start to slow down. This is called slower intestinal transit time. Mature breast milk is also mostly digested, so there is very little garbage to eliminate.

As long as the poop is soft, your baby is fine. So be grateful you have fewer diaper changes!

New Parent 411

We said it before and let's say it again: babies poop less often after six weeks of life!

Solid Food Equals Solid Poop: Older Babies

Q. My five month old started rice cereal and now she is constipated. Help!

Rice cereal has this effect on some babies. Offer only one feeding a day of rice cereal and introduce higher fiber cereals and foods sooner rather than later. Pureed prunes are a Stage 1 food and add both fiber and taste to rice cereal. See below for more fun fiber foods.

Q. How much fiber does my child need to eat?

The equation is Age in Years + 5 = Total daily fiber requirement (in grams)

This equation doesn't apply for babies under a year of age. Breast milk contains no dietary fiber, thus there are no requirements for babies from birth to six months. From six to twelve months, fiber is introduced in the diet via solid foods. The daily needs varies from baby to baby and there are no established guidelines. But studies have shown that children who are constipated eat significantly less fiber than their "regular" peers. (*McClung*)

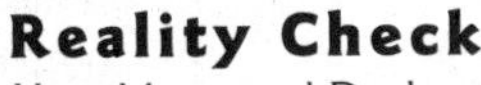

Reality Check

You, Mom and Dad, need 25 to 30 grams of fiber per day no matter how old you are. Most Americans do not eat enough fiber. The way to get your child to eat fiber is for you to have it in the house and eat it yourself. If you don't realize this yet, your baby is watching every move you make!

Q. Which foods are high in fiber and more importantly, which ones will my child eat?

THE OTHER END

This is my favorite fiber food list. Some foods will be off limits under a year of age and are designated with an asterisk (*)–these are choking hazards. Kids usually find the bread/grain category the most appealing. Take careful note of serving sizes. The sizes listed below are sometimes more than even a one year old will eat.

PRODUCT	SERVING SIZE	FIBER GRAMS/SERVING
Bread/Grains		
Whole wheat Bread	1 slice	2 grams
White Bread	1 slice	0
Pepperidge Farm		
HeartyWheat Crackers	3 crackers	1 gram
El Galindo Wheat Tortillas	1 tortilla	9 grams
Hodgson Mill		
Whole-wheat pasta	2 oz	6 grams
Brown Rice	1/4 cup	0.9 grams
Cereal		
Baby Rice	1/4 cup	0
Baby Oatmeal	1/4 cup	1 gram
Baby Mixed	1/4 cup	0
Cheerios	1/2 cup	1.5 grams
Quaker Oat Bran	1/2 cup	2.4 grams
Quaker Oatmeal Squares	1/2 cup	2.5 grams
Kellogg's Nutragrain bars	1 bar	1 gram
Wheat germ	1 Tbsp	1 gram

(I like wheat germ because you can sneak it into food and your child might not even notice)

Fruit (raw)

Note: The peel is often the part of the fruit that contains the fiber. Since most kids hate the peels, the fiber ends up in the garbage disposal and not in your child.

Apple (with peel)	1/2 medium	1.8 grams
Apricots	1/4 cup	0.8 grams
Banana	1 whole	2.7 grams
Blackberries	1/4 cup	1.8 grams
Dried Cranberries*	1/4 cup	1.5 grams
Grapefruit	1/4	1 gram
Grapes	1/2 cup	0.5 grams
Orange	1/2	1.5 grams
Pear (with peel)	1/2	2.1 grams
Prunes	1/4 cup	3.5 grams
Raisins*	1/4 cup	2 grams
Raspberries	1/4 cup	2 grams
Strawberries	1/4 cup	0.8 grams
Watermelon	1/2 slice	0.5 gram

* *Choking hazard! These foods are only for children aged three and older.*

PRODUCT	SERVING SIZE	FIBER GRAMS/SERVING
Vegetables/Legumes		
Broccoli	1/4 cup	1.4 grams
Corn	1/4 cup	1 grams
Green beans	1/4 cup	0.7 grams
Green peas	1/4 cup	2.2 grams
Lima beans	1/4 cup	3 grams
Pinto beans	1/4 cup	3.7 grams
Refried Beans	1/4 cup	3 grams
Squash (baked)	1/4 cup	2 grams

Q. Now that my nine month old eats a large amount of solid food, what should his poop look like?

Soft and solid.

The more your baby eats like you do, the more his poop will look like yours. It should always be easy for your baby to pass. It has a cow patty appearance when your baby sits on it after he poops.

By the way, some foods don't get completely digested as they pass through the intestines. It's normal to recognize last night's corn, carrots, etc. in your child's poop.

RED FLAGS: Worrisome Poops For Older Babies

1. **Streaks of blood.** If the streak is on a hard, firm poop, it's probably due to a tear in the anus as the poop was passed. It's worth checking out, though.
2. **Streaks of blood/mucous.** This is more concerning for infection, particularly if poop is loose/diarrhea. Be prepared for a homework assignment (providing your doctor with a fresh poop specimen). This can also be a sign of a food allergy, especially if the poop looks slimy and stringy like snot from the nose. Sorry to gross you out.
3. **Clay (white) colored poop.** The official name is **ACHOLIC STOOL.** This can occur in conjunction with a stomach virus. But inform your baby's doctor.
4. **Looks like meconium again.** Black, tarry poop can be a sign of bleeding in the upper part of the intestinal tract (because the blood has had time to get digested). This may indicate irritation and inflammation in the intestines. Your doctor will do a test to check for blood in the poop.
5. **Grape Jelly poop.** The doctor term for this is actually "currant jelly stool." This is a medical emergency. It is a worrisome sign of **INTUSSUSCEPTION** where the intestines have kinked.
6. **Bulky, REALLY stinky, greasy, floating poops.** This may indicate difficulty with absorption (see **MALABSORPTION**).

Helpful Hint

Pepto Bismol makes poop look black like meconium. Pepto Bismol is *not* currently recommended for infants. Just thought you'd be interested for your own sake.

Q. My baby just had a BLUE poop. Help!

Your baby is not an alien. It's either natural or artificial food coloring.

To the best of my knowledge, blue poop is never a sign of illness. Blue colored kid juices (Hi-C) and kid yogurts are often the culprits.

Beets cause a dramatic red hue in both poop and pee.

Q. I am interested in toilet training my baby. Is it too early to think about this now?

Yes, in our opinion. Your baby will be in diapers for a long time.

Being toilet trained is a developmental milestone, just like learning to talk and walk. Milestones can be encouraged, but the child has to achieve it on his own. Your child needs to be able to sense the urge to pee and poop (not just after he has gone). His only incentive to be toilet trained is the desire to be clean (regardless of how many toys you buy him). If he runs around in a poopie diaper and could care less, he is miles away from this milestone.

Girls usually train around 2 1/2 years of age. Boys train around 3 or 3 1/2 years. There is no need to purchase a potty seat any time soon. All it will do is collect dust in your bathroom. Good news: we cover this topic in depth in the sequel to this book, *Toddler 411* (see back of this book for details).

We should note there is another school of thought on this topic: Elimination Communication (EC). Proponents say babies give subtle clues that they need to poop or pee and it is up to the parent to respond to those cues. These babies go diaper-less, and parents put them on the pot every time they think their kid needs to go. If you want to learn more about this method, check out DiaperFreeBaby.org. We admit our skepticism about EC—it seems that the parent is potty-trained, not the child.

Spit Up, Regurgitation, And Vomit

Q. My newborn spits up all the time. Should I be worried?

No. Most babies spit up after meals. They are born with a loose muscle between the esophagus (swallowing tube) and the stomach. This muscle, called the *lower esophageal sphincter* (see picture at right), will tighten up by about six months of age. Until then, liquids travel down into the stomach. Then some will return into the esophagus and mouth. By definition, most babies have **GASTROESOPHAGEAL REFLUX (ACID REFLUX OR GER)**. They spit up effortlessly and with small volumes.

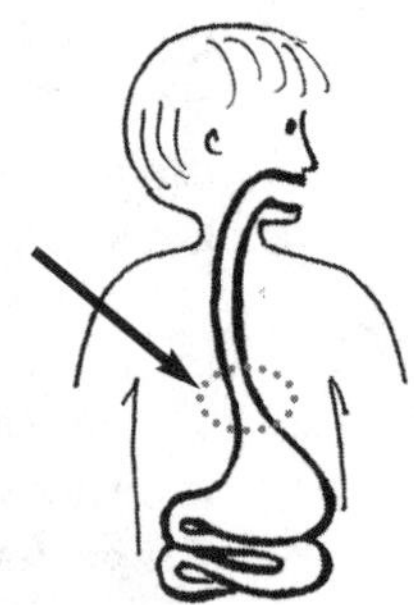

GER is not a problem (other than forcing you to spot treat all the shoulders on your shirts). According to Dr. R. Jeff Zwiener, Medical Director of Pediatric Gastroenterology at Dell Children's Medical Center of Central Texas, GER only becomes a problem called **GASTROESOPHAGEAL REFLUX DISEASE (GERD)** if it leads to these unpleasant consequences:

- irritation of the esophagus (esophagitis), making babies irritable, fussy, or refuse to eat.

- respiratory/airway problems that make babies wheeze, gag, choke, or have trouble breathing.

RED FLAGS: When to worry about acid reflux

1. If your baby spits up large volumes consistently, he won't gain weight (see **GERD TREATMENT**).
2. If your baby cries or arches after feeding, with or without spitting up. The stomach acid is irritating his esophagus (See **GERD TREATMENT**).
3. If your baby has Exorcist-style, projectile vomiting after every meal, call your doctor immediately (see **PYLORIC STENOSIS**).

Q. My baby is four-months old now and is spitting up more than he did when he was younger. Should I be worried?

No.

It takes about six months for the sphincter muscle to tighten up. As your baby takes larger volumes of breast milk/formula, larger volumes will come up. Hence, it gives the appearance that your baby's reflux is getting worse instead of better. The spit up is usually at an all-time high around four months of age.

Q. Okay, my baby is nine-months old and still spitting up. Should I be worried?

No. You're just at the end of the bell curve. Many babies graduate from spitting up by six months, but there are a few stragglers. Almost all babies stop spitting up by one year of age.

Reality Check

No, it's not just your baby who is an Olympic-caliber spitter. Consider this:

Of all babies 0-3 months of age, 50% spit up.

Of all babies 4-5 months of age, 67% spit up.

Of all babies 6-7 months of age, 21% still spit up.

By 12 months of age, less than 5% of babies are still spitting up. (*Edmunds*)

Q. How can I tell if my baby is suffering from acid/gastroesophageal reflux?

Everyone is usually miserable from this. Your doctor can help you make the diagnosis on this one.

This is usually the problem behind fussy, "colicky" infants. Most parents are convinced that their infant either has horrible gas pains, a milk allergy, or colic. They also think that they are inadequate as parents because their baby is always fussy and they haven't figured out how to make her feel better. Some adventurous parents will unsuccessfully try Mylicon drops (an over-the-counter medicine which makes big gas bubbles into little gas bubbles), switching formulas, or eliminating dairy from breastfeeding Mom's diet before scheduling an appointment with their doctor.

How do we make the diagnosis? We look at the time the fussiness occurs, and what seems to make it worse. *The first rule: babies with reflux*

don't always spit up—(spitters are really easy to diagnose). Some babies experience heartburn when the stomach acid comes up into the esophagus with the milk. If it doesn't make it all the way up to the mouth, you won't see it. Babies with heartburn often cry during and shortly after feedings. They can also cry when lying down (for example, on the changing table) because this allows the acid to come up. They may try to arch their backs or thrust their heads back to alleviate the pain. This happens around the clock, making a very unhappy baby.

Colic is ruled out by the frequency of the behaviors. Babies with colic are also unhappy. However, they are only unhappy for three hours a day (say, around 5 pm to 8 pm). Colic starts at three weeks of age and lasts until three months of age. If your baby has been fussy since two weeks of age and is always fussy, it's probably not colic and most likely acid reflux. (See Chapter 11, Discipline and Temperament for more about colic).

Milk allergy or intolerance is ruled out by exploring some details about baby's poop. A true milk allergy causes mucous and/or blood in loose

Tricks Of The Trade To Treat Acid Reflux

If your baby is uncomfortable from the heartburn associated with acid reflux, or is not gaining weight, there are many options to reduce the severity of the symptoms. Start by using the following tricks at home. If that doesn't work, consider a medication (which will require a prescription).

1. Keep your baby upright for 20 minutes after feedings. This lets the food travel out of the stomach into the small intestine before moving baby around.

2. Let your baby plan his mealtimes. Babies often figure this out themselves. They have more discomfort with large meals, so they learn to become snackers. It's not great for parents' schedules, but is more comfortable for baby.

3. Have your baby sleep in an inclined position. Keeping the head upright 30 degrees keeps food going downwards instead of upwards. How? One solution is a Tucker Sling (tuckersling.com) which allows your baby to be inclined safely and securely for sleep. While some babies under three months do well in their car seats, some reflux babies actually have more problems because they slump down, increasing the pressure on their bellies. For infants *over* three months of age, you can prop up the crib mattress with a purchased wedge or pillow UNDER the mattress. It's not terribly effective, though, because many babies roll all over their crib.

4. For formula fed or expressed breast milk babies: thicken it up. Thicker milk is heavier and stays down better. If you formula feed: add one teaspoon of rice cereal to each four oz bottle of formula (or use Enfamil AR or Similac with added rice starch—see Chapter 6, Liquids). FYI: The rice cereal trick doesn't work well with breast milk since the enzymes in breast milk break it down before the baby has a chance to drink it.

poop, really horrible eczema, or worse—hives or immediate vomiting. If you have a fussy baby with normal poop, the food is unlikely to be the problem. A therapeutic trial of changing formula or Mom's dairy elimination will not improve a reflux baby's symptoms.

Q. Can't we just do a test to look for acid reflux?

Yes, tests are available. Here's an overview:

An Upper GI or "barium swallow imaging study" (see Appendix C, Lab Work and Tests) can be done to rule out other problems that cause regurgitation. If the baby happens to reflux while the test is being done, you have an answer. But having a "normal" barium swallow can simply mean your refluxing baby didn't do it during the test.

An esophageal pH probe can be inserted through the baby's nose to his esophagus and acid levels can be monitored for 24 hours. While the test is about 70% accurate, performing the test on all babies is impractical

5. Medications. Babies use the same antacids as adults. Many products are over the counter for adults, but are by prescription-only for kids. Some products are not approved by the FDA for use in children, but are routinely used by both pediatric gastroenterologists and pediatricians. Although a 2011 review of the scientific literature questioned the effectiveness of proton pump inhibitors (or "PPI's") for infants with GERD, most docs will try these meds to see if they work. (*van der Pol*) The options are listed below. (For details, see Appendix A on medications.):

Histamine 2 Receptor Antagonists: Zantac (Ranitidine), Axid (Nizatidine)

Proton Pump Inhibitors (PPI's): Prilosec, Zegerid (Omeprazole), Prevacid (Lansoprazole)

If you reach the point that your baby needs medication, he likely has a pretty irritated esophagus lining from constant stomach acid burns. The medication prevents further insults, but it takes at least a week for the irritation to heal. So, don't expect a miraculous change in your baby's behavior after just one dose of medicine. Give the medicine for a week to see if it is working.

Helpful hints: The medication is dosed based on your baby's weight. In some cases, if your baby gains a pound or two, he may no longer be getting a therapeutic dose of his meds. Remind your doctor to recalculate his dose every month or so. And medications like Prilosec that have to be specially mixed (compounded) may separate after a couple of weeks. Get a two-week supply and refill it frequently.

Parents are often leery of giving medication on a daily basis to their babies. Understandable. However, these medications are safe to use daily, as a general rule. One rare adverse effect is the potential for an intestinal infection called C. difficile. Be sure to contact your baby's doctor if he develops bloody diarrhea while taking the medication. Once your baby outgrows the problem (about six months old), the medicine is no longer needed.

for obvious reasons—keeping this lovely tube in a baby's nose for a day is no fun, nor is the time baby isn't allowed to eat (several hours).

Then, there's always the option of doing an endoscopy. That involves anesthesia—a tube with a camera at the end of it that is inserted through the baby's mouth and throat to look at the esophagus. Biopsies (tissue samples) can also be taken at the same time to make the diagnosis. This test is 100% accurate, but very expensive.

Given the unpleasant and imperfect nature of these tests, most doctors rely on a simple examination of baby (and parent reports) to make an acid reflux diagnosis.

What's your baby's I-GERQ score?

Here's a free and painless way to assess for possible reflux disease (GERD) in your baby. It's called the I-GERQ-R score. If your baby experiences many of these symptoms, she may be suffering from at least mild heartburn.

This quiz is pretty good at screening for babies who have troublesome heartburn. But it's not 100% accurate and some normal, healthy babies who "fail" the test do not need treatment.

Take the quiz and get your baby doctor's opinion on the problems she is experiencing. Her doc may suggest following her for worsening symptoms, additional testing, or treatment. (*Orenstein*)

The test is on the following page.

DR B'S OPINION: GERD . . . AND PATIENCE

Having a baby with GERD can be miserable for everyone. Feeling helpless and sleep deprived (thanks to the symptoms worsening when reclined) makes any parent rethink the number of kids they want to have. These are normal feelings. I promise it gets better with time. Patience is key. And call on friends and family for help.

If your baby clearly has GERD and is not improving with medication, he may need a higher dosage.. FYI: Most of these meds are not FDA-approved for infants. Hence, dosage can be hit or miss. Check out the Midwest Acid Reflux Children's Institute (medicine.missouri.edu/illustrator/marcikids/) for advice on higher dose GERD medications. Then discuss this with your baby's doctor.

(I-GERQ-R; Author I-GERQ, Susan Orenstein, MD, © 2004, University of Pittsburgh) To be filled out by primary caregiver of baby. Please read each of the questions carefully, answer to the best of your ability, and do not skip questions. There are no right or wrong answers.

Infant Gastroesophageal Reflux Questionnaire

1. ***During the past week, how often did the baby usually spit-up (anything coming out of the mouth) during a 24-hour period?***
   Less than once / 1 to 3 times /4 to 6 times /More than 6 times

2. ***During the past week, how much did the baby usually spit-up (anything coming out of the mouth) during a typical episode?***
   Did not spit up
   Less than 1 tablespoonful
   1 tablespoonful to 2 ounces
   More than 2 ounces to half the feeding
   More than half the feeding

3. ***During the past week, how often did spitting up (anything coming out of the mouth) seem to be uncomfortable for the baby, for example, crying, fussing, irritability, etc.?***
   Never / Rarely/ Sometimes
   Often /Always

4. ***During the past week, how often did the baby refuse a feeding even when hungry?***
   Never / Rarely/ Sometimes
   Often /Always

5. ***During the past week, how often did the baby stop eating soon after starting even when hungry?***
   Never / Rarely/ Sometimes
   Often /Always

6. ***During the past week, did the baby cry a lot during or within 1 hour after feedings?***
   Never / Rarely/ Sometimes
   Often /Always

7. ***During the past week, did the baby cry or fuss more than usual?***
   Never / Rarely/ Sometimes
   Often /Always

8. ***During the past week, on average how long did the baby cry or fuss during a 24 hour period?***
   Less than 10 minutes
   10 minutes to 1 hour
   More than 1 hour but less than 3 hours
   3 or more hours

9. ***During the past week, how often did the baby have hiccups?***
   Never / Rarely/ Sometimes
   Often /Always

10. ***During the past week, how often did the baby have episodes of arching back?***
    Never / Rarely/ Sometimes
    Often /Always

11. ***During the past week, has the baby stopped breathing while awake or struggled to breathe?***
    No / Yes

12. ***During the past week, has the baby turned blue or purple?***
    No / Yes

13. ***Overall, how would you rate the severity of your baby's Gastroesophageal Reflux Disease (GERD) symptoms during the past week?***
    No symptoms
    Very mild
    Mild
    Moderate
    Severe
    Very severe

Again, if you have concerns, fill out the quiz and ask your baby's doctor to evaluate your child for possible heartburn or GERD.

BOTTOM LINE

Most babies outgrow their symptoms of acid reflux when the esophagus muscle tightens up (around six months of age). A few babies will continue to have problems up to their first birthdays. Babies who suffer with daily reflux symptoms from 6-12 months of age are more likely to have feeding problems in their second year of life (even if the reflux is gone). (*Nelson*)

Reality Check

Your baby does not have acid reflux because your Great Uncle Harry has acid reflux. Nor will your baby develop a hiatal hernia because of acid reflux. However, there are a few babies with GERD who grow up to be adults with GERD.

Insider Tip: Acid Reflux . . . a reason for wheezin'

Some babies with acid reflux have respiratory symptoms such as chronic cough and wheezing. This happens because the milk is coming up and irritating the baby's airway. Again, even babies with severe reflux may not be spitting up large volumes of milk. If a baby is having this much trouble with reflux, doctors are pretty aggressive about a treatment plan (for good reason!).

The flip side: if your baby wheezes and a diagnosis of asthma is being considered, get him evaluated for acid reflux (GERD)–that may be the reason he wheezes.

Q. Occasionally, my baby will throw up his whole feeding. Should I worry?

No.

When babies eat aggressively, they suck in a lot of air. When that big air bubble comes back up with burping, often the whole feeding does too. Unlike adults, babies often throw up and then want to eat again.

The only time to worry is when the whole feeding gets thrown up at *every* feeding. This is a red flag for **PYLORIC STENOSIS** (see picture at right). This is a medical emergency caused by a narrowing of the muscle between the stomach and small intestine (called the *pyloric sphincter*). It usually occurs at six to eight weeks of age because the muscle seems to narrow over time.

RED FLAGS: Vomiting

1. Vomiting bile. Bile is a fluorescent green/yellow color that can indicate a blockage in the intestines. It is especially worrisome if associated with stomachache or a bloated looking tummy, or fever. Call your doctor ASAP.

2. **Vomiting blood or "coffee grounds."** In newborns, blood in baby's spit up is often from Mommy's cracked and bleeding nipples. Beyond that time, blood in vomit warrants a call to the doctor. Blood that has been partially digested by the stomach looks like coffee grounds when it is thrown up. Both of these symptoms can be caused by bleeding in the esophagus or stomach.

3. **Vomiting repeatedly over six hours**. Excessive vomiting can be caused by stomach viruses (see **GASTROENTERITIS**), food poisoning (see **BACTERIAL ENTERITIS**), or an intestinal blockage (see **ACUTE ABDOMEN**). Most of the time, it's a stomach virus. It's time to check in with your doctor after six hours because your baby can get dehydrated.

4. **Vomiting associated with fever and irritability.** This is how meningitis presents in a baby. Babies have a unique "window" to the brain with their soft spot (fontanelle) on their heads. A full, bulging soft spot occurs with meningitis. Call your doctor immediately.

5. **Morning vomiting.** Babies don't get morning sickness. It's incredibly rare, but vomiting exclusively in the morning is a symptom of increased pressure in the skull. This can be caused by abnormal fluid collections or a mass (i.e. **HYDROCEPHALUS, BRAIN TUMOR**). Both of these abnormalities cause a full, bulging soft spot (fontanelle). This definitely needs to be checked out.

Q. What should I feed/let my baby drink while he is vomiting?

Nothing.

When your baby is actively vomiting, give him nothing to eat or drink unless you want to see it come right back out.

Wait until it has been at least an hour since the last vomit to test the waters. Start with Pedialyte or a generic brand oral rehydration solution sold at most grocery stores and pharmacies (or see the recipe to make your own in Appendix B).

This is basically Gatorade made specifically for babies. Give one teaspoon every five minutes. Don't let your baby chug as much as he wants. He will be very thirsty. If he takes a full bottle worth on an unsettled stomach, it's destined to be thrown up. He'll get about two ounces an hour for the first couple of hours. If the Pedialyte test fails (more vomiting occurs), call your doctor.

Once the Pedialyte stays down, resume formula or breast milk.

Q. What are the signs of dehydration?

Lethargy, dry skin and lips, sunken soft spot (fontanelle), and peeing less often (less than three wet diapers in 24 hours—or no wet diaper in eight hours).

Another measure is weight loss, which is checked in the doctor's office. If your child is vomiting and/or having diarrhea, *start tallying how many wet diapers your baby is having*. Your doctor will ask you that question when you call or come in for an appointment. For more info, check out Chapter 15, "First Aid."

Pee/Urine

Q. My newborn urinated only once in his first day of life. Is this normal?

Yes.

All you can expect is one wet diaper on baby's first day. We just want to know that the pipes are working. Your baby might pee twice on his second day of life. The wet diapers will start to accumulate once your baby is drinking more. By day four of life, you should get at least four wet diapers. This should reassure you that your baby is getting something to drink when you are breastfeeding.

Q. These diapers are so absorbent, how can I tell if my baby has urinated?

Put a tissue in the diaper and you can see the pee.

In the first week of life, keep track of wet diapers. This information is also useful if your baby is vomiting and has diarrhea.

Another hint: diapers with pee in them feel heavier than dry ones.

Q. My newborn looks like he has blood in his pee. What is it?

Take a closer look. Does it look like brick dust? Is it powdery and on the *surface* of the diaper?

If the answer is yes to these questions, it's not blood. These are **URIC ACID CRYSTALS**. When newborns are a little dehydrated (in the initial 10% weight loss mode), the pee is more concentrated and less watery. This causes one of the ingredients of pee, uric acid, to separate out. That's what you are seeing. Uric acid crystals are nothing to worry about if it is just one newborn diaper. Call your doctor if this is persistent or you see it in an older baby. For a picture of this, see Baby411.com/bonus (click on Visual Library).

Q. My newborn looks like she has blood in her diaper. What is it?

This is the equivalent of a menstrual period. It's not in the pee.

Baby girls' bodies respond to their mother's hormones. There is frequently some bleeding and vaginal discharge in the first few weeks of life. This is normal.

Q. I've heard that baby girls are prone to bladder infections. How can I prevent them?

Good hygiene.

A brief anatomy lesson here. Girls have a very short tube (urethra) that attaches the bladder to the outside. The urethral opening sits just above the vagina. Just below the vagina is the anus. Remember that poop has bacteria in it and urine is sterile. If the poop ends up in the nooks and crannies surrounding the urethra, the bacteria (usually E.coli) can climb into the urethra and grow in the bladder causing a bladder infection. Girls in diapers are particularly prone to infections. The best ways to prevent infection are:

- *Change a baby girl's poop diaper ASAP.*
- *Wipe "front to back."* Dads–this means start cleaning your daughter at the urethra and wipe downwards to the anus. Never go the other direction! Gently separate the labia and be sure to clean well in there.

Boys rarely get bladder infections because the urethral tube is much longer from the bladder to the opening (the urethra tube is inside the penis and the opening is at the tip). It's much harder for those bugs to travel that far.

Q. How do you diagnose a bladder infection in a baby?

Foul smelling urine, cloudy urine, and particularly, *fever in a baby with no obvious symptoms* (i.e. no runny nose, cough, or diarrhea).

This is one of the top reasons why we want to hear from you if your baby under three months of age has a fever. *Untreated* bladder infections can quickly lead to kidney infections (and even meningitis) in infants under six months of age.

If your baby is in diapers, and has a fever with no obvious symptoms, your doctor will need a urine sample to look for infection.

Q. Are some babies more prone to bladder infections than others?

Yes. Although most bladder infections occur due to poor hygiene (poopie diapers) and bad luck, about 30-45% of all children who have a bladder infection have a rare abnormality of the urinary system that causes urine to flow backwards into the kidneys. This is called **VESICOURETERAL REFLUX (VUR)**. See pictures at right.

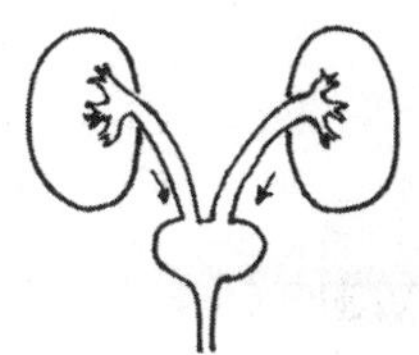

Normal urine flow.

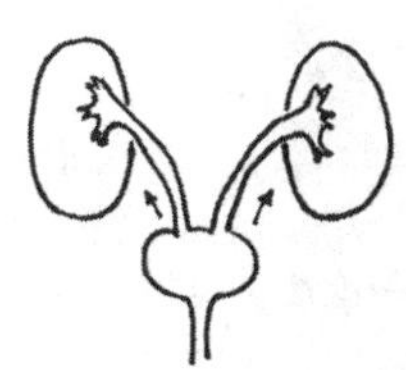

Vesicoureteral reflux.

There are five grades of VUR, with Grades 4 and 5 being the most severe. Kids with the most severe VUR are at the greatest risk of kidney infection and permanent damage. The good news: most children with VUR outgrow this disorder by age seven–even 70% of kids with Grade 3 VUR will outgrow it.

However, those with Grade 4 or 5 are the least likely to outgrow VUR and may need surgery to correct the problem.

Because of the potential for permanent kidney damage, pediatricians have always been cautious about little ones who have bladder infections.

Historically, ***any*** child with his or her first bladder infection ***before reaching puberty*** would have been tested for VUR. That testing involved an ultrasound of the kidneys (easy and relatively cheap) and either a Voiding Cystourethrogram "VCUG" or a radionuclude DMSA scan (more involved and expensive). See Appendix C, Labs and Tests for details on these studies. If the child was diagnosed with VUR, she was prescribed a low-dose antibiotic to take at bedtime to prevent future infections. This antibiotic was taken every night until she outgrew her VUR (monitored by repeating these fun imaging studies annually.)

Recently, this evaluation and preventative antibiotic treatment for kids with VUR has come under fire. Evidence shows that kids with severe VUR will likely be sicker, and have their first urinary tract infection before being potty trained. So, is it worth the time, money, and discomfort of the procedure to test every child with their first bladder infection? And should all babies who have VUR be on a nightly dose of antibiotics until they outgrow the condition? Even children who have mild to moderate (Grade 1-3) VUR may never have another infection and may not end up with kidney damage anyway.

The American Academy of Pediatrics updated their position on this issue in 2011, but not all urologists agree with their advice.

Here is what all experts can agree on: any infant under two months of age with a bladder infection needs to be tested for this abnormality. Other children at high-risk for having VUR should be tested. That includes those with: more than one bladder infection, a bladder infection with bloodstream infection, poor urine stream, a bladder infection with unusual bacteria, abnormal urinary tract on prenatal ultrasound, or continued symptoms after being on antibiotics over three days.

Here is the summary of recommendations for who should get tested for VUR:

- All children under two months of age who have a fever with a bladder infection.
- Kids ages two to 24 months old with more than one bladder infection with a fever.
- Children whose infections do not clear up quickly. *(Finnell)*

And, newborns who have abnormalities detected on a prenatal ultrasound (Grade 3-4 hydronephrosis, hydroureter, abnormal bladder) should have a VCUG screening test for reflux shortly after birth. (*AUA 2010*)

Reality Check

There is a 60% chance of a child having vesicoureteral reflux if a parent has the disorder. There is a 30% chance of having VUR if a brother or sister has the disorder. (*AUA 1996*)

Siblings (or offspring) of affected children may be screened as well. The American Urology Association says that healthcare providers may opt to screen healthy siblings of children with reflux via a kidney (renal) ultrasound. Then a VCUG test should be performed if an abnormality is detected on the kidney ultrasound. It's also an option to just observe siblings and then promptly evaluate these kids if they have a bladder infection. The same logic applies to offspring of adults who had reflux in childhood.

BOTTOM LINE

Your doctor may want to screen your child for VUR, even if she doesn't fall into the high-risk category. There is no harm in following the precautionary principle. (*AUA 2010*)

Burping

DR B'S OPINION

"Note that the burping technique involves rubbing. I watched my brother burp his twins once and considered reporting him to child protective services. Patting and hitting aren't really necessary!"

Q. Do you have any tips on burping my baby? I spend 20 minutes trying to burp him and nothing happens.

It's either going to happen or it won't. It's not your technique or patience that does the trick.

Burps are the result of swallowed air during feedings. Once your baby is an efficient eater (by four months old), he's also likely to be an efficient burper.

For the first few months of life, stop in mid-feed to burp your baby. There are basically three techniques.

1. Baby is upright on your shoulder, and you rub upwards on her back.
2. Baby is sitting in your lap, upright, and you rub upwards on her back.
3. Baby is lying face down on your lap, and you rub upwards on her back.

If it has been more than ten minutes, the burp ain't happening on your watch. Unfortunately, your baby may sleep for 20 minutes, then wake himself up when he burps. Welcome to parenthood. Just do what you can.

Hiccups

Parents ask a lot of questions about hiccups. Here is what you need to know:

1. Hiccups don't hurt.
2. Don't worry about hiccups—doctors don't.
3. Only ***excessive*** hiccupping is associated with acid reflux (GERD).

Gas

A nice way to exit this chapter.

Q. My baby has more gas than me. Should I be worried?

No.

Your baby has more gas because he sucks in a lot of air and because his intestines are on high alert 24 hours a day.

Most of the time, babies don't really care that they have gas. And don't be embarrassed, it's the only time in your child's life when people will think it's cute when he toots.

New Parent 411: Helping your baby pass gas

Here are three tips from seasoned parents:

1. Infant massage. This is a comforting way to help your baby relax. Pressing gently on baby's belly sometimes gets the gas out.

2. Warm bath. This also works by relaxing your baby.

3. Mylicon (simethicone) drops. This over the counter medication is safe for babies, including newborns. It makes big gas bubbles into little gas bubbles. Some parents swear by it, others see absolutely no difference in their baby's demeanor. Gripe water, a combo of ginger and fennel, is also a popular remedy.

Q. What can I do about my baby's gas? Are Mylicon drops okay to use?

Not much, and sure, it won't hurt.

Gas is one of the biggest obsessions of newborn parents. Some parents believe it is the root of all evil . . . the reason that the baby is unhappy . . . the reason why nobody is sleeping. The truth is–IT'S NOT THE GAS. But, if you feel compelled to do *something* (which is a common feeling of all parents), it's okay to try those Mylicon (simethicone) drops. See above for gas tips.

The good news; the gassy phase will pass by age two or three months.

Q. I'm breastfeeding. Will eliminating high fiber foods from my diet fix my baby's gas problem?

No, but it will give you, Mom, a constipation problem.

This is rarely the cause of baby's gas. You can try an elimination diet, but it's usually not the problem.

Q. My baby is colicky. Is it because of gas?

No. Gas gets a bad rap.

See Chapter 11, Discipline and Temperament, for information on colic. Eliminating gas won't solve your colic problem.

Section 3

Sleep, Development & Discipline

Sleeping Like A Baby

Chapter 9

"Whoever coined the phrase, 'sleeps like a baby' never slept with one!"
~ *Anonymous*

What's in this Chapter

- The science of sleep
- Newborn sleep issues
- Sleep safety tips
- Deciding on your family's sleep routine (family bed vs. solitary sleep)
- Setting up good habits
- Undoing bad habits
- Top 10 Mistakes parents make
- The Sleep Gurus
- Naps
- Special situations—Multiples and Preemies

Who needs sleep?
well you're never gonna
get it

Who needs sleep?
tell me what's that for

Who needs sleep?
be happy with what
you're getting
There's a guy who's been
awake since
the Second World War

—Barenaked Ladies

New (and veteran) parents struggle with their baby's sleep habits—it's a fact of life. Everyone warned you about it, but you weren't buying it. At first, the excitement of being a parent gives you the momentum to make it through the first few weeks of sleep deprivation. Then, the novelty begins to wear off. You are exhausted and desperate for a good night's sleep. You'll ask friends and relatives for tricks that worked for their babies. It's no wonder that books on infant sleep are a booming section at Amazon.

If you are reading this chapter before your baby is born, good for you. You will be prepared for what lies ahead. If you are already in the desperate category—don't worry—we can help you, too.

Before we give you all of our sage advice on this subject, it is *essential* that you understand the science of sleep.

Knowing the basics will help you appreciate the advice and avoid the common mistakes parents make.

The Science Of Sleep

Q. Do newborns have the same sleep patterns that adults do?

NO. That's why you cannot expect them to sleep like we do. Here are four important concepts you need to understand:

1 **TYPES OF SLEEP.** There are two basic types of sleep: REM and Non-REM. REM stands for **R**apid **E**ye **M**ovement. Here are the differences between the two.

	NON-REM SLEEP	REM SLEEP
Muscle movements	relaxed	active (stretches, sucks, vocalizes)
Brain activity	relaxed	active (dreams)
Occurrence	1st part of night, PM nap	2nd part of night, AM nap

Newborns spend 50-80% of their sleep in REM sleep while adults spend only 25% of their sleep in REM. The result: babies are very active when they are asleep. And that pattern continues even now. Your baby will be noisy and moving around, but he is not awake.

BOTTOM LINE: Your baby's sleep activity and noises do not mean you need to feed or help him.

2 **SLEEP CYCLES.** Humans go through a series of sleep cycles throughout an evening's rest. Adults tend to bunch all the Non-REM cycles first, and then go through REM cycles. Babies do more flip-flopping of Non-REM and REM cycles. Each sleep cycle has a beginning and an end, where a person goes from light sleep to deep to light again, before entering the next cycle. Humans recheck their environments and body comfort at that time. At the end of each sleep cycle, a partial wakening occurs. Babies may whimper or briefly cry out during this time.

BOTTOM LINE: Leave your baby alone when he has a partial wakening. He will enter into his next sleep cycle if you leave him alone. If you intervene, you will wake him up. As the saying goes, let sleeping babies lie.

3 **LENGTH OF CYCLES.** The average adult sleep cycle lasts 90 minutes. The average newborn sleep cycle lasts 60 minutes.

BOTTOM LINE: Your baby has shorter sleep cycles than you. It can take several months until he has mature sleep patterns like an older child.

4 **CIRCADIAN RHYTHM.** The human body has a biological clock that registers 24.5 to 25 hours in a day. This is called a circadian rhythm. It is affected by both light exposure and a body chemical called melatonin. Babies follow their mother's circadian rhythm in the womb probably

because of melatonin levels. Once outside the womb, they have exposure to light and must form their own circadian rhythm.

BOTTOM LINE: It takes several weeks for a baby to get their circadian rhythm sorted out. If you lived in the dark for nine months, you'd probably be a little confused too.

Newborn Sleep Issues

Q. Okay, now I understand why my newborn has erratic sleep patterns. But, how can I get my baby to sleep at night instead of during the day?

This is called Day-Night Reversal. It usually takes three or four weeks to resolve.

The best way to help your baby through this is to stimulate him during the day and keep things low key at night. Talk to your baby during daylight hours and encourage any wakeful periods he has. At night, do your feeding routine with little interaction. Only turn the lights on if you have a poopy diaper to clean. If your baby decides he wants to have a slumber party, he can party (coo, grunt, etc) on his own. You don't have to be by his side to entertain him.

These nocturnal habits usually resolve by three to four weeks of age. See "Sleep Tips" below in this chapter for more advice on the first couple weeks of life.

Q. How much should a newborn sleep?

About 14 to 18 hours total a day.

But here's the cruel part: most newborns will not sleep more than four hours at a stretch. They need to eat frequently and their little bodies know it.

Check out the table in the setting up good habits section later in this chapter to get an idea of how sleep changes through the first year of life.

BOTTOM LINE: Most newborns have six or seven stretches of sleep every 24 hours. Feedings occur in between these stretches.

Helpful Hints

Three Sleep Tips for the First Two Weeks of life

◆ ***Wake your newborn up if he has slept longer than three hours during the day.*** When your baby has day-night reversals, he may have his one long stretch of sleep in the middle of the day. Discourage this! Otherwise, you will be in for a long night of cluster feedings.

◆ ***Do not let your newborn sleep more than four hours straight during the night.*** He needs nutrition to grow. He also needs to stimulate your milk supply to come in if you are breastfeeding. Once he has regained his birth weight and your doc gives you her blessing, you can let the baby sleep at night (he won't, but it's fine if he does).

◆ ***Your job is to sleep when baby sleeps.*** Become nocturnal. Don't even think about doing laundry when your baby crashes in the afternoon. Go to bed!

Q. When can I expect to sleep through the night?

Now that you are an expert in "sleep-ology," you can appreciate the following fact: it takes (on average) *17 weeks of life* for an infant to develop mature sleep patterns. Yep, that's about four months. Think about that for a moment.

The definition of "sleeping through the night" is six hours of uninterrupted sleep. That will feel like a great night's sleep by the time you get there! (*Kleitman*)

FYI: Even parents with school-aged kids will be awakened by middle-of-the-night announcements ("I just had a nightmare, Mom"...... you get the picture). The concept of "sleeping through the night" is only a fuzzy and abstract concept that exists for childless couples.

Old Wives Tale
Giving your baby rice cereal helps him sleep through the night earlier.

The truth: Food has nothing to do with it.

DR B'S OPINION

"If your full term, healthy baby is still not sleeping six hours straight by six months of age, you need help. Read the section 'Undoing Bad Habits' later in this chapter."

Q. My friend says that their baby slept through the night at four weeks of age! That's not fair! How can this be?

Odds are, your friends are exaggerating—or will soon be proved wrong when their baby reverts back to a normal sleep pattern (that is, waking up during the night). Sure, lightning sometimes strikes and a one month old will sleep through the night . . . for one night. Or even a month. But then, as we'll discuss later, she may relapse into waking up during the nighttime.

Another explanation for these wild claims: dads. When we hear about a baby that miraculously slept through the night from birth, this claim usually comes from the proud new dad. Of course, the baby wasn't sleeping but daddy was—mom still had to get up several times a night!

By the way, some babies *will* sleep up to 12 hours a night as early as two months of age, but it's not the norm. If your baby is a terrific sleeper, don't brag about it—you'll jinx yourself for the next baby!

Q. How do I get my newborn to fall asleep? He seems to have trouble relaxing.

It would be nice to have the baby who awakens to feed and then goes right back to sleep. More likely, you have the baby who eats and then fusses until you help him return to the Land of Nod.

After you and your baby get to know each other better, you will figure out what helps him settle down.

Newborns are born with immature nervous systems. That means, they don't have the ability to pull it together, relax, and fall asleep. The most reliable way babies know how to settle down is to suck. See the next box for our Newborn Sleep Tips.

NEW PARENT 411: TOP 5 TIPS FOR GETTING A NEWBORN TO SLEEP

1. **Suck to soothe**. If you are so inclined, your breast may become the human pacifier. If this approach is not for you, use your finger or a pacifier in your baby's mouth to encourage sucking. This is fine for the first few months of life (more on pacifiers later in this chapter).
2. **Move around.** Rocking, swaying, and bouncing (you will have the veteran-parent-bop down quickly) are effective.
3. **Sing**, in or out of tune.
4. **Snug as a bug.** Swaddling, sleeping in a bassinet, or even sleeping in a car seat may do the trick.
5. **Go for a car ride.**

Q. How long should my newborn sleep in a bassinet?

Two or three months max.

You are not setting up any permanent habits the first two months of life. Babies become aware of their surroundings around three to four months of age. That's when you need to set up a permanent routine.

For now, newborns prefer to be snug. They like to sleep in bassinets, co-sleepers (small bassinet that attaches to an adult's bed) or even their infant car seat (all are fine) until they decide they want to stretch out. I recommend transitioning over to where you want your baby ultimately to sleep around three months of age. Another factor: some playpens with a bassinet insert have weight limits that are usually exceeded by two or three months of age.

FYI: Newborns never sleep for more than a few hours at a time. Hence, sleeping or napping for a short time in a car seat is fine. However, once baby starts sleeping for longer stretches (and wants to stretch out!), move him out of these contraptions and into a crib.

Old Wives Tale

Too much holding and rocking will spoil your baby.

The truth: You cannot spoil a newborn. Remember, babies don't have the ability to settle on their own. Do what it takes to get your baby to sleep. *However, you need to grow as your baby does. Your six-month-old will be quite capable of settling down on his own.*

Reality Check

Many babies will sweat while they are asleep. Don't be alarmed if your baby awakens in a pool of water (well, you might want to check the diaper, too).

Q. My baby will only sleep on me. If I put him down anywhere (bassinet, etc.) he wakes right up. What do I do?

Remember, babies are not born with self-soothing skills. They are used to being snug, warm, and next to your heartbeat. While you can simulate that environment (you can even buy a device that makes heartbeat noises), your baby may still do his best sleeping when he is skin to skin with you.

During the day, it's fairly easy to do this. Wearing your baby is very stylish. In fact, there are some beautiful fabric slings out there these days. Just continue your daily activities with your baby in tow.

During the night, it's a bit more of a challenge. You'll need to come up with a safe way for both of you to get some sleep. One solution: a co-sleeper bed that attaches to your mattress. That way, each of you will sleep in your own space, but you are still next to each other.

You are not setting up any bad habits. By two or three months, your baby will want to stretch out and won't need to be a fashion accessory anymore. You're welcome to continue using the sling as long as you'd like for transportation or nursing, but we'd suggest discontinuing its use as a sleep aid at three months.

Q. How do sleep patterns and needs change as baby grows?

Check out this information as well as the handy sleep requirements chart on the next page for details. Remember, these are general guidelines. No need to freak out if your baby doesn't follow these numbers to a tee!

◆ *Birth to two months.* Newborns sleep 14-18 hours a day. They have day-night reversals, and rarely sleep for more than a four-hour stretch at a time. Yes, you have our blessing to do whatever it takes to get your baby to fall asleep and stay asleep, as long as it is safe. Swaddling, rocking, nursing to sleep, wearing your baby as an accessory (in a sling), going for a car ride, using a pacifier, etc. You are not spoiling your baby or setting up any permanent bad habits. Remember: your baby does not have the neurologic maturity to pull it together, relax, and fall asleep on his own yet.

◆ *Two to four months.* On average, babies sleep 12-14 hours a day. They are usually taking three naps per day. Babies who prefer catnapping may take

Sleep requirements, birth to 2 years (in hours)

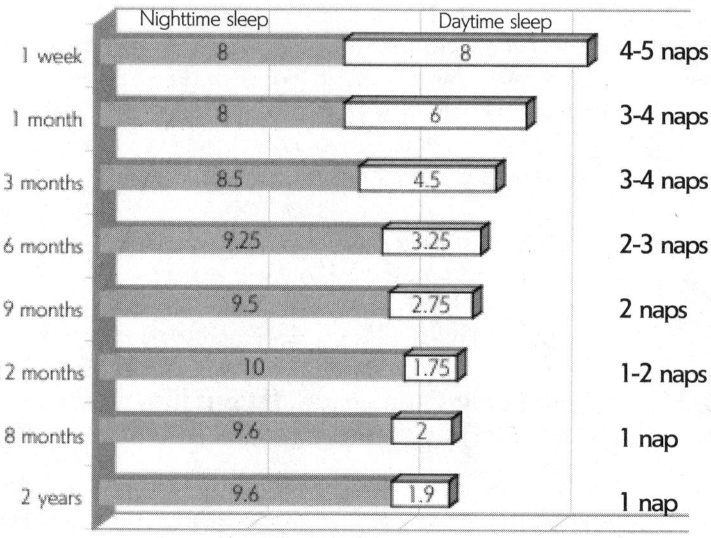

four shorter naps. If you are lucky, your baby may sleep for a six-hour stretch at night. It is still too early to train your baby to sleep. Your goal: set up *healthy sleep routines*. We'll have more on this subject later in the chapter.

◆ ***Four to six months.*** The average four to six month old sleeps a total of 11.5-13.5 hours a day, with two naps included. Your baby should be sleeping AT LEAST six hours at night. Some babies will sleep up to 12 hours at night. Yes, everyone in the house should be getting sleep by now. . .but if this is not happening, you need help. Do not be convinced that your baby NEEDS to be up at night. In fact, everyone will be happier if your child is sleeping at night. Sometimes parents aid and abet their baby's bad sleep behaviors. We'll discuss the reasons why babies this age continue to wake at night later in this chapter.

◆ ***Six to 12 months.*** On average, these babies sleep 11–13.5 hours per day, with two naps included. Many babies sleep ten to 12 hours straight at night. Yes, your prayers were answered! If your baby is still waking up for night feedings or comfort, you need help. See "Undoing Bad Habits" later in this chapter.

Feedback from the Real World: Multiples

Keeping your sanity with one newborn's erratic sleep habits is difficult enough. Imagine the juggling act when you have two (or more) newborns! You can't control or force them to sleep, but you can encourage them to eat (sometimes!) and that helps synchronize their sleep. Here's what worked for us: wake the sleeping baby for a feeding within 30 minutes of the first baby waking up. Feeding twins at the same time gives you more time to rest between feedings especially in the beginning when feedings are so close together.

–Agustina, mom of Gael and Malena, 18 months

Sleep Safety Tips

Q. I've heard about sudden infant death syndrome (SIDS). What is the official recommendation about infant sleep position?

The "Back to Sleep" Campaign is promoted by the American Academy of Pediatrics and various other health organizations. The official recommendation is that babies sleep on their backs from birth to at least six months of age to reduce the risk of SIDS (90% of SIDS cases occur in babies under six months old).

Our own parents put us on our bellies to sleep. Any grandparent will tell you that a baby sleeps better on her tummy. They are right. However, numerous studies have proven that this sleep position significantly increases the risk of sudden infant death. It seems to be caused by the infant smothering herself–a pocket of carbon dioxide forms around the baby's face when she is face down in a mattress or soft bedding. Babies don't have the neck muscles to move their heads and, sadly, that's how some SIDS deaths occur.

Before the Back to Sleep Campaign began in 1992, 5000 babies died per year in the U.S. from SIDS. Today, that number is down by over 50%. Let's take a look at a graph that shows how the SIDS rate plummeted as parents stopped putting baby to sleep on their stomach:

US SIDS rate versus the % of babies sleeping on their stomach

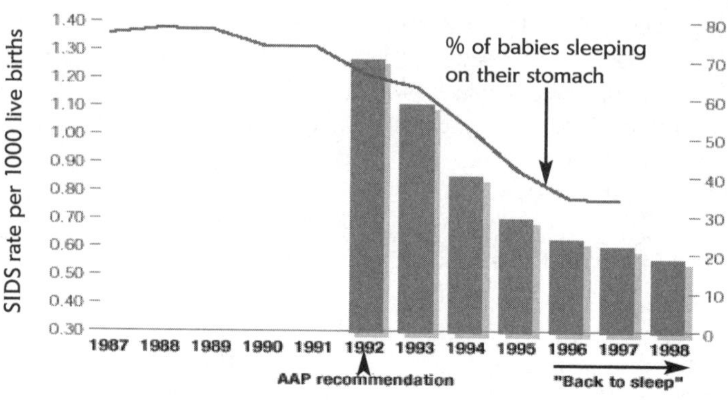

Source: Contemporary Pediatrics, Vol 17, No. 9

Q. Are there any other known risk factors for SIDS?

Yes. Here are the top six:

1 **ROOM TEMPERATURE.** Stuffy rooms with poor ventilation are a SIDS risk. The cooler the room, the better. SIDS occurs more frequently in the winter months when babies are bundled and the heat is on. Believe it or not, the recommended "safe" room temperature to reduce SIDS risk is 68 degrees. And a fan in the baby's room can also reduce the SIDS risk. (*Coleman-Phox*)

2 **SOFT BEDDING.** All those beautiful bedding sets need to stay out of the crib. Heavy quilts, pillows, bumper pads, and blankets cause the ambient temperature of the crib to go up. Babies can also smother themselves in soft bedding. All your baby's crib needs is a sheet and mattress.

3 **SMOKING.** Babies whose parents smoke have a higher risk of SIDS. So, if you can't do it for yourself, stop smoking for the most important thing in your world.

MEMO TO GRANDPARENTS: BACK TO SLEEP

Here's a scary fact: babies who are used to sleeping on their backs and are placed on their sides (and roll over) or stomachs to sleep have a significantly greater risk of SIDS than those babies who are used to sleeping on their tummies.

The message: make sure that your childcare provider or occasional grandparent-as-babysitter puts your baby on his back to sleep. They may have missed the memo on the Back-To-Sleep Campaign!

4 **ETHNICITY.** Native Americans and African Americans have a much higher risk of SIDS than other babies. New research suggests a genetic defect may be passed on in certain ethnic groups who carry the gene.

5 **FAMILY HISTORY.** There may be a higher incidence of SIDS when a previous family member has had it.

6 **BIOCHEMICAL ABNORMALITY.** Recent studies point to a deficiency in serotonin (a neurotransmitter necessary for a baby's arousal system) as a reason why some babies do not wake up during life-threatening situations (like when they're sleeping face down and not getting enough oxygen.) This is a major medical breakthrough, but there's no practical way of testing babies for this disorder right now. (*Paterson, Duncan*)

Obviously, there are risk factors on this list that you cannot control. But try to avoid the ones you can—like bedding, sleep position, and smoking.

Reality Check: Pacifiers Reduce SIDS Risk

Believe it or not, there is substantial evidence to show that pacifiers actually reduce the risk of SIDS. It is unclear why, though. It may be that the pacifier keeps a baby's airway open. Or, sucking on a pacifier prevents a baby from forgetting to breathe. FYI: 90% of SIDS cases occur between one and six months of life. (*AAP SIDS Task Force*) For a quick look at the latest recommendations to avoid SIDS, see the Top Ten Take-Home Messages on Sleep Safety later in this chapter.

Helpful Hints

◆ ***What should you do with that baby quilt you got as a gift?*** Use it as a wall hanging. Or buy a special quilt rack for your baby's nursery. You can always use it on the floor as baby gets older. Put a few toys out and encourage some supervised tummy time. Another alternative: some crib bedding makers are substituting lighter-weight blankets for thick quilts in their sets.

◆ ***Don't borrow a crib or use a hand-me-down.*** Over two million cribs have been recalled in recent years for safety hazards. As a result, the federal government rolled out tough, new crib safety standards a few years ago. The take home-message: we strongly recommend buying a new crib for your baby instead of using a hand-me-down or that garage-sale find.

Q. What bedding items are acceptable to place in the crib?

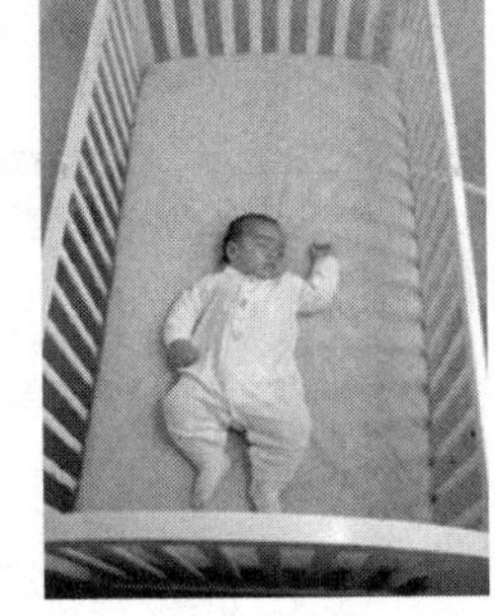

A fitted sheet over a mattress is all you need. We like to call it the Naked Crib. See nearby picture for an example.

What about blankets? While it is acceptable to swaddle a newborn to eight-week old baby in a receiving blanket, we discourage any other loose blankets for babies under a year of age.

A baby can just sleep in a sleeper or be swaddled. Or consider a "wearable blanket" (an example is the SleepSack from HALO Innovations, halosleep.com). These provide warmth but cut the

SIDS risk, as babies can't crawl under them or become entrapped. Again, the key goal here is to not over-heat your baby—putting your child in a wearable blanket and cranking up the thermostat is a no-no.

What about crib bumpers? Safety experts, including the American Academy of Pediatrics, discourage using them. The risk of SIDS with crib bumpers is greater than the protection bumpers offer from minor injury. (*Thach*) And, no, you don't need a mesh crib bumper to keep a baby's arm or leg from getting stuck between the crib rails. The risk of a trapped limb in the crib slats is minor compared to SIDS.

Save your money, skip the bumper.

Reality Check

Another item you DON'T need: a sleep positioner—a device pitched to parents as a way to keep their baby sleeping on their back. Sleep positioners have been responsible for 12 U.S. infant deaths over the past 13 years, due to suffocation or the baby rolling onto his belly. Both the American Academy of Pediatrics and the Consumer Products Safety Commission advise against their use.

Q. I've heard that standard crib mattresses are a risk for SIDS and organic mattresses are safer. Is this true?

Short answer: no. Evidence-based medicine says conventional crib mattresses are not a significant risk factor for SIDS. And buying an organic mattress is not going to prevent SIDS. We'll delve into this debate a bit more in Chapter 16, The Environment and Your Baby.

Q. Is it okay to swaddle a baby in his crib?

Yes, with a few caveats. You need to know *how* to swaddle and know *when* to stop.

Your friendly nurses from the hospital probably taught you the "burrito wrap" technique of swaddling your baby. If not, see the box on the next page. It's fine to wrap your baby's arms snugly but leave the legs loose enough for him to move them around. Experts advise this technique to possibly prevent hip dislocation from spending hours positioned like a mummy. A good tip if Baby Houdini lives with you: The Miracle Blanket ($30; miracleblanket.com). This is one blanket your baby will not be able to squirm out of.

Newborns like to be snug for the first six to eight weeks of life. Think about it. They are used to being in a confined space. Swaddling works well, until baby wants and needs to stretch out. But, after eight weeks, ditch the swaddling trick. It is important for a baby to move and turn during sleep—otherwise you will end up with a flat-headed baby.

Q. Okay, I put my baby on his back to sleep. What do I do if he rolls over?

Let him sleep!

Your baby probably won't figure out how to roll over until he is at least four months old. Once he starts, you can't stop him. The next morning, you will find him in a completely different position than the way you left him!

If it makes you feel any better, once babies are good at clearing their nose and mouth by turning their heads, the risk of SIDS is lower.

HOW TO SWADDLE A BABY—AKA BABY BURRITO WRAP

And now, the seven steps to swaddling your baby:

1. Take a square receiving blanket and turn it diamond shaped on a flat surface.
2. Take the top corner and fold it towards the center of the blanket. You now have a horizontal line at the top.
3. Place your baby on the blanket with his neck at the level on the horizontal line.
4. Bring the bottom corner up to the baby's belly button.
5. Bring one side corner over the baby and fold over the other side of the belly.
6. Bring the other side corner over the baby and fold over on the other side. *Voila*!
7. Remember to keep the legs loosely wrapped to allow the hips to develop normally.

Q. I'm concerned my baby might choke if he sleeps on his back. Should I be?

No.

Babies have a gag reflex that protects their airway when they vomit (all humans do). There is no increased choking risk.

As a side note, babies with gastroesophageal reflux do better with their heads elevated 30 degrees (about the angle of an infant car seat). They experience less heartburn that way. (That's the way I sleep, too, after overindulging on Tex-Mex food). These babies sleep better with a wedge under their mattress (an example is the Tucker Sling, tuckersling.com, discussed in Chapter 8, The Other End), or may sleep in their car seats for the first several weeks of life.

Q. Can I cheat, and let my baby sleep on his side?

We can't recommend it. Babies who sleep on their sides may accidentally roll onto their tummies. And babies who are not used to being tummy sleepers have an 18 fold increased risk of SIDS if they end up sleeping that way.

Q. Can I buy one of those breathing motion detectors and let my baby sleep on his stomach?

These products are not worth the expense—a gadget can't prevent SIDS. It leads to more parent anxiety and disrupted sleep when the alarm goes off accidentally. The motion detectors you buy at the store are not the same as "apnea monitors" that some premature infants use after they are sent home from the hospital.

Q. My baby has a flat head and a bald spot on the back of her head from this sleep position. Is this permanent?

No. This is called **POSITIONAL PLAGIOCEPHALY** and most kids do not need helmets to fix the problem. As your baby starts to roll over, the head shape will round out. All babies lose their hair around four months, and then grow new hair in.

You can help with the head shape issue by scheduling daily tummy time. This also promotes neck and back muscle strength. And, it helps them learn how to roll over. (It's easier to roll from stomach to back than the reverse). For details on tummy time and positional plagiocephaly, see the section on Flat Heads and Tummy Time in Chapter 5, Nutrition & Growth

Q. Is there any risk to having a family bed?

When it comes to infants, the answer is yes. Babies who sleep in a family bed are at greater risk of SIDS and Sudden Unexplained Infant Death (SUID) The family bed increases the risk of smothering and entrapment, both of which can be fatal. Waterbeds, comforters, pillows, and exhausted or intoxicated parents in the family bed are suffocation hazards. That is why the American Academy of Pediatrics supports *room* sharing, but NOT *bed* sharing for infants.

However, toddlers (older than one year) can safely sleep in a shared family bed if this is your preference.

For room sharing and safe infant sleeping, try these two tricks:

- Use a co-sleeper mattress that hooks up to yours so baby has his own space.
- Move the crib next to your bed and take the side rail down.

BOTTOM LINE

Here are the latest American Academy of Pediatrics recommendations to prevent SIDS:

1 **NO TO SIDE SLEEPING.** Babies who sleep on their sides are more likely to roll onto their tummies and increase their risk of SIDS. And infants who are back sleepers that sleep on their tummies increase their SIDS risk by 18 times.

2 **NO TO BED SHARING.** The risk of smothering or entrapping an infant is greater when parents and baby share a bed.

3 **YES TO ROOM SHARING.** The AAP encourages room sharing to support breastfeeding and reduce SIDS risk.

4 **YES TO PACIFIERS.** For unknown reasons, the binky is protective. Just know when to start (after breastfeeding is well established) and when to stop (when the risk of SIDS is over) using it.

Top Ten Take-Home Messages on Sleep Safety

1. Put your baby to bed on his back.
2. Keep soft bedding out of the crib.
3. Keep the room temperature cool (68 degrees).
4. Keep the room well ventilated. Consider using a fan.
5. Don't over bundle your baby with too many clothes. Swaddling in one light blanket is okay. No need for a hat or cap.
6. No smoking.

7. Use a crib made after 2000.
8. Buy a new, firm crib mattress.
9. Make sure the mattress fits into the crib snugly, without gaps.
10. Lower the mattress height to the lowest level *before* your baby starts to pull on the railings to stand up.

Deciding On The Family's Sleep Routine: a.k.a. The Family Bed vs. Solitary Sleep Debate

This debate is worthy of an introduction before we get to the details. Where your baby sleeps is completely your decision. We are not making any judgments on parenting styles (that means you, Attachment Parents.)

Here are two things you need to know.

The American Academy of Pediatrics endorses room sharing—but not bed sharing—as a way to promote safe sleep and successful breastfeeding. Attachment Parenting International states that paying attention to a baby's needs at night is the priority, not the sleep location.

We'll give you the information to make an educated decision about what is best for you, with your baby's health and wellness in mind.

Your options:

- **The Family Bed (Co-sleeping):** Parents and children sleep together in the same bed.
- **Solitary Sleep:** Each child sleeps separately in his own sleep space (crib, bassinet, co-sleeper mattress).
- **The Desperation Move:** Parents prefer that their baby sleep in his own bed, but end up having him in their bed out of sheer exhaustion and frustration with their inability to get their baby to sleep in his crib. (See undoing bad habits section later in this chapter.)

Q. What are the advantages of a family bed?

Convenience is a big advantage. And, many parents who practice attachment parenting view the family bed as a way to maintain secure parent-child bonds and work the nighttime parenting shift.

For a breastfed newborn, it's very easy to eat at night. As soon as he stirs, his mother is there for him. This is also convenient for Mom, who might fall asleep shortly after (or during!) those middle-of-the-night feeds. Recent data suggest that co-sleeping babies nurse more frequently and take larger volumes of breast milk at night than their solitary sleeping peers.

Many parents choose this option simply because it feels good to snuggle up with their baby.

Just a bit of trivia: in the U.S., 12.8% of infants regularly sleep in a family bed. And it's hard to know how accurate that figure is, as some folks may not admit to sleeping in a family bed when surveyed.

DR B'S OPINION

"Having a well-adjusted and happy child has nothing to do with where he sleeps!"

Q. What are the disadvantages of the family bed?

Potential for SIDS and SUID (Sudden

Unexplained Infant Death).

The American Academy of Pediatrics policy position warns against family bed sharing with infants due to the increased risk of death. They strongly encourage infants to have their own sleep space.

Solitary sleep advocates argue that co-sleeping families get poor sleep and prolong the time before a baby starts sleeping through the night. They also feel that co-sleeping interferes with a baby's ability to become an independent being.

BOTTOM LINE

An eighteen-year study on parent-child bed sharing

A landmark study evaluated children who slept in a family bed as infants and young children and compared them to their solitary sleeping peers. These children were studied from birth through age 18 years. *The data showed that co-sleeping had no statistically significant problems or benefits.* (Okami)

Q. What are the advantages of solitary sleep?

Safer sleep for babies. And, better quality sleep for parents and children.

Bed sharing for infants, in short, is risky business. And as stated above, breastfed babies who co-sleep are up more often at night to feed.

Q. What are the disadvantages of solitary sleep?

Consistency is required.

A baby who is used to sleeping alone in his own bed may have more sleep disruptions when families travel or sleep away from their home. It also requires taking a portable crib on trips or making arrangements to borrow one at your destination.

Babies who sleep alone need a consistent sleep ritual to wind down.

Q. With all of these night feedings, my baby ends up falling asleep on me.-Will this be a problem in the future?

For the first two months, do anything that is safe for your baby and buys you some sleep.

Babies are very malleable for the first two to three months of life. You are not setting yourself up for having long-term sleep problems. If your baby nurses and falls asleep on you, just try to peel him off of you and put him into his bassinet afterwards.

However, your goal should be to have a consistent sleep routine by four months of age.

Setting Up Good Habits (Two to Four Months)

Note: as we discuss the steps to establishing good sleep routines, these are general age ranges for healthy, thriving babies. Babies who are born prematurely or those with medical problems (such as failure to thrive or acid reflux) may go through these sleep milestones a little later.

For the first two months of life, when it comes to you and your baby's sleep, you gotta do what you gotta do—nursing, rocking, infant swing, a car ride, etc. You know the drill.

Guess what? Your baby is now nearly four months old. It's time to stop those old habits.

Why? Your baby is becoming more aware of her environment. She will respond better when things are *predictable*, anticipating what is next. She will also start to form sleep *associations*. That means your baby will rely on certain routines to fall asleep. Those routines are the good sleep habits you want to keep. And now is the time to punt the bad habits. Think about it—you really don't want to be rocking your five-year-old to sleep every night, do you?

For the nitty gritty on forming good sleep habits, check out our Ten Commandments for establishing a sleep routine in the box in this chapter.

Q. When can I start to schedule my baby's naps and bedtime?

Between two and four months of age, your baby will start to have some regular sleep and feeding patterns (finally). Keep a sleep/feeding diary for a week and you'll know your baby's preferences.

Then you can put your baby down for naps and bedtime *before* she shows you that she is tired (cranky, rubbing eyes—you've seen it all before). The key word in that previous sentence is BEFORE. Once you see those sleepy signs, she is actually overtired.

Start your wind down routine before that happens by aiming for nap/bedtime about 20 minutes earlier than what your sleep diary shows. Not only will you have some idea how to schedule your day, but you'll give your baby the best shot at falling asleep on her own.

You're in the driver's seat now and can put your baby on a schedule she already likes—yes, YOU have the power!

Q. My three month old only falls asleep while feeding. How do we change that habit?

You will be walking a fine line between two and four months of age. Your goal is to *separate* the eating experience from the sleeping experience. Your baby may not need to eat to fall asleep, but you won't know until you try! And if you fail the first time, try again the next week. Your baby is maturing at the speed of light. At this stage, a week older is a week smarter.

In the middle of the night when you hear your baby cry . . . walk, don't run, to your baby's bedside. She might just go back to sleep without your intervention.

You can also try soothing your baby without offering food if you have frequent night wakenings. Your baby may not need to eat every time and is just relying on you to help him get back to sleep. If you are breastfeeding, let Dad try to be the soother. There will be less expectation of food if he shows up. But if it has been more than four hours or so since the last feeding, you will probably have a hungry baby on your hands who needs to eat.

The Big Transition: (Four to Five months)

Q. My four month old still needs help falling asleep. What do I do?

You can gradually cut the virtual umbilical cord. Your goal is for your baby to fall asleep on her own–without feeding or rocking her to sleep.

Now that she is four months old, set up a consistent sleep ritual. If she falls asleep during the feeding, wake her up before putting her in bed so she is aware of where she is going. You are creating a healthy bedtime ritual–and one that lets your baby be in charge of falling asleep.

Give her at least ten minutes to try to fall asleep on her own. Yes, she may protest (code word for cry) and that is okay. She is learning how to self-soothe. If she cannot fall asleep, go back in and do as little as possible to relax her. Try patting, singing to her, and cuddling her for a few MINUTES (not hours). Rocking her until she is dead weight on your shoulder or nursing her to sleep is the last resort.

INSIDER SECRETS: TOP 10 COMMANDMENTS FOR

1 **TEACH YOUR BABY TO FALL ASLEEP ON HIS OWN.** Remember those sleep cycles? The cycle consists of light to heavy to light arousal before entering the next cycle. At the end of each cycle, humans re-check their environment and change body position (move a pillow or blanket, roll over). By three to four months of age, your infant will be aware of his world. If he falls asleep on a parent's shoulder and gets moved to a crib, or falls asleep when he is drinking or sucking a pacifier, that is what he will be expecting when he arouses at the end of his sleep cycle. Translation: be careful of sleep "crutches" like the pacifier. Put your child in a crib or bassinet when he is sleepy . . . but before he falls asleep. If the child always falls asleep on your shoulder, he will expect to see that shoulder at the end of every sleep cycle.

2 **BE CONSISTENT. KIDS DO BEST WITH ROUTINES.** Predictable is comfortable. You will learn that rapid transitions and unexpected activities promote anxiety and outbursts in your child (see Chapter 11 "Discipline & Temperament" for details). Have a routine for both nap and bedtime and stick with it by the age of four months.

3 **YOUR CHILD SHOULD ALWAYS SLEEP IN THE SAME PLACE FOR NAPS AND NIGHTTIME.** That's not the car seat or the infant swing anymore. Reality check: yes, every now and again your child may fall asleep in a car seat, especially after a long trip on the weekend for example. That's OK on an occasional basis. But when you are at home, keep the sleep place the same.

4 **NAP TIME AND BEDTIME SHOULD BE APPROXIMATELY THE SAME TIME EVERY DAY.** That goes for vacations, visits to relatives, etc.

The exact method of transitioning to a better sleep pattern varies for each baby. Basically, you do as little as possible and give your baby more time to work things out on her own. Thirty minutes is a reasonable amount of time by five months of age.

If your healthy, thriving baby still does not fall asleep on her own by five months, you can use the "progressive waiting" or "rapid extinction" methods so she can figure out how to self-soothe (more info later in this chapter). The same rules apply for frequent night wakenings.

Consistency is key. Do the same ritual for both nap and bedtime.

Q. I've heard babies are more likely to sleep through the night if their tummies are full. What do you think of "dream feeds"?

For newborns, feeding and sleep patterns are intimately related. Babies under two months of age need to eat frequently, usually every two to three hours day or night. That means they can't sleep very long because they get

ESTABLISHING A SLEEP ROUTINE (2 TO 4 MONTH OLDS)

5 **ALWAYS FOLLOW YOUR SLEEP RITUAL.** Bath, feeding, (teeth brushing), story-time, songs, prayers...you might do the abbreviated version of a book or song if it has been a long day, but still do it.

6 **START YOUR SLEEP RITUAL BEFORE YOUR CHILD IS TIRED.** Don't wait for the yawns and eye-rubbing to begin the routine.

7 **EARLY TO BED, LATE TO RISE.** Sounds like it wouldn't work this way, but it does. Babies actually sleep better when they go to sleep early. An "overtired" baby does not sleep longer —so, you are not buying time to sleep in by putting your baby down later in the evening. Trust me on this one.

8 **GET RID OF THE PACIFIER BY FOUR TO SIX MONTHS OF AGE.** Your baby is very aware of his world. If he falls asleep with a pacifier in his mouth, he will cry when it falls out. At 3am. And 5am.

9 **BABIES NEED REFRESHER COURSES ON SLEEP ETIQUETTE AFTER TRAVEL, ILLNESS, OR TEETHING.** When consistency is broken, it takes a few days to get back on track. If you don't remind your baby of what to do, he will remain on a disrupted sleep schedule.

10 **DON'T TREAT YOUR FOUR MONTH OLD LIKE A NEWBORN.** Your baby will take advantage of your naiveté. Many four month olds are capable of falling asleep on their own if given the opportunity to do so.

DR B'S OPINION: FOUR MONTH OLDS AND SLEEP

Your four-month old baby is aware of his surroundings. If he falls asleep in your arms and you sneak him into bed, he will awaken at the end of his sleep cycle (every 90 minutes) looking for comfort. If your child is awake when you leave the room, he will fall asleep alone and content. You'll hear him on your baby monitor discussing his day with inanimate objects. Your baby is growing up—realize and adapt to this!

hungry. Babies start to stretch out feedings at night (and give parents a small break) at two to four months.

However, as babies get older, their ability to sleep through the night has more to do with their brains than their guts. Your healthy, growing four month old is capable of sleeping at least six hours without needing to eat. Don't let her fool you. The key to Mr. Sandman's house resides in your ability to teach your baby self-soothing skills . . . not stuffing her full of milk.

For a full-term, healthy thriving baby (who doesn't have acid reflux), here are some helpful feeding parameters:

- Four month olds: Can sleep SIX hours without needing to eat.
- Five month olds: Can sleep NINE hours without needing to eat.
- Six month olds: Can sleep TWELVE hours without needing to eat.

Some parents will try to feed a sleeping baby (a.k.a. Dream Feed) before they go to bed, hoping to catch that six-hour stretch during the hours they want to actually sleep. For example, instead of your baby fasting from 8 pm–2 am, he fasts from 11 pm–5 am. While this sounds great in theory, I am not a big fan of this strategy. I think it sets up a habit of feeding a child when he isn't hungry, and it in no way guarantees you'll sleep until 5 am. Second problem: cavities. Many parents continue night feedings long after their baby has teeth (around six months of age). Unless

DR B'S OPINION: IS CRYING IT OUT CRUEL?

I encourage you to give your baby a chance to fall asleep on her own. Obviously, you have to do what you feel comfortable with . . . but it is not cruel or inappropriate (from a child development perspective) to give a healthy baby the freedom to self-soothe from four to six months of age. Otherwise, I'd never advise it!

Yes, there are parenting circles that vehemently oppose this sleep training approach. They like to cite research that it causes permanent emotional damage to the child. I'm here to say that is absolutely untrue. In fact, a recent study looked at five-year-old children who went through sleep training as babies and guess what? They were completely normal, well-adjusted kiddos. *(Price)*

you plan on brushing your child's teeth after that dream feed, you will be paying for your dentist's kids to go to college.

If your baby learns how to soothe himself, you'll have better odds of sleeping through the night.

Undoing Bad Habits (Five to 12 months and beyond): Solving the Sleep Problems

If you have a healthy baby who is still not sleeping at least six hours a night, or you are bringing your child to bed with you out of desperation (and not choice), this section is for you. Admitting you have a problem is the first step! Don't say we didn't warn you: if you set up healthy sleep routines up front, you won't have to endure the (often) highly emotional experience of sleep training.

The International Pediatric Sleep Education Task Force found that 25% of ALL parents report problems with their baby's sleep patterns . . . no matter what country they live in. You are not alone. (*Touchette*)

sleep

Behind the Scenes

Is there a correlation between parents' behavior and infant's sleep?

A recent Canadian study showed that many infant sleep disorders were based on parents' excessive intervention in comforting them to sleep. These parent behaviors with their five month olds included:

1. Putting a baby in bed *after* he was asleep.
2. Remaining in the room *until* the baby was asleep.
3. Taking the baby out of his bed to comfort him.
4. Parent feelings of inadequacy.

A significant percentage of these babies continued to have sleep problems well into their third year of life.

BOTTOM LINE: Don't just wait for your baby to outgrow his sleep issues—it may be a long time waiting. And the issues may belong to the parent and not the baby. (*Willinger*)

DR B'S OPINION: SLEEP STATS TO KNOW

These stats are based upon my 18 years of experience working with babies of all shapes and sizes:

- At least 50% of healthy four month olds can fall asleep on their own.
- At least 75% of healthy five month olds can fall asleep on their own.
- 100% of healthy six month olds can fall asleep on their own.

Q. My baby started sleeping through the night at three months old. She is five months old now and waking up in the middle of the night again. Help!

Babies who are early to start sleeping through the night (less than three months old) frequently start up again when they become aware of their surroundings.

These are babies who never needed the sleep rituals before. They just fell asleep eating and were placed into bed. Now, they are alert little beings and need to learn how to fall asleep on their own.

When your former perfect baby starts having night wakenings, it will be at the end of a sleep cycle (a multiple of 90 minutes after bedtime). That's when you know your baby's current sleep routine has backfired. Start using a sleep ritual that lets your baby fall asleep on his own.

Q. My baby uses a pacifier to fall asleep. When should we stop offering it?

We'll discuss the Great Binky Debate in the section on Soothing a New Baby in Chapter 11, Discipline and Temperament. But when it comes to healthy sleep routines, we suggest saying goodbye to the binky by six months of age.

In the first two or three months of life, babies have very few ways to soothe themselves. Parents usually figure out within the first few days of bringing their baby home that a pacifier buys everyone some sleep. This approach is fine for the first few months.

BUT, do not use a pacifier beyond six months of life. Trust me. This is the time when you need to set up the routines you plan to keep. What if someone stole your pillow while your were sleeping? If the pacifier falls out in the middle of the night, your baby will be looking for it.

You don't want to have a baby who is capable of sleeping through the night waking *because* the pacifier is out. If the pacifier isn't there to begin with, he won't be looking for it.

Helpful Hints

- Don't place dozens of pacifiers in your baby's crib so he can find one on his own.
- Don't go in every 90 minutes to put a pacifier back into your baby's mouth.
- Don't buy a glow-in-the-dark pacifier so your baby can find it at

Continued on page 230

DR B'S OPINION: BEEN THERE, DONE THAT

I am a parent of young children. I have walked in your shoes. I know that irrational thoughts seem rational at 3 am. It SEEMS EASIER to just bring your baby in bed with you or nurse them to sleep. But it is not the right answer anymore.

Once you are on the other side (sleeping through the night), you'll say, "What was I thinking?" I am happier and so are my children when we have all slept at night.

THE TOP TEN MISTAKES PARENTS MAKE WITH INFANT SLEEP ROUTINES

1. Sneaking baby into bed. Your baby falls asleep in your arms, and then you sneak him into his crib. Compare this to the following scenario, courtesy of acclaimed sleep expert Dr Ferber. You fall asleep on the couch in front of the TV. Your spouse picks you up and carries you into your bed. When you wake up in your own bed, you are disoriented and alarmed. Your baby feels the same way–and hence, wakes up and wants your arms back!

2. Falling asleep while eating. Your baby falls asleep when he is drinking (breast or bottle). When he stirs, he is in a different place and not eating anymore.

3. Falling asleep with a pacifier. Here is the comparison, again credit to Dr Ferber: You fall asleep with your head on your pillow. In the middle of the night, your spouse steals your pillow. When you wake up, you are confused and probably annoyed. (*Ferber*)

4. The Trained Night Feeder. Your baby gets used to eating a snack or a meal in the middle of the night, so he continues to be hungry at that time. Equate this to working the nightshift and having your lunch break at 3 am. Yes, your body will work up an appetite if you are used to it. Stop eating at 3 am, and your body will no longer be hungry. Parents frequently continue these feedings well beyond six months of life because they don't know any better and their babies continue to demand it.

5. Inconsistent schedules. Babies are creatures of habit. Adjust your schedule as much as possible around your baby's. Don't change your baby's bedtime because you got home late from work and missed spending time with him. Pushing back your baby's bedtime for selfish reasons is always a recipe for disaster. Tomorrow is another day.

6. Missed naps. The better your baby sleeps during the day, the better he will sleep at night. Being overtired actually creates sleep disturbances. So, don't run errands when it is your baby's naptime.

7. Late to bed equals EARLY to rise. This is really true, even though you would think the opposite. As we've said, overtired babies sleep poorly.

8. Interventions at partial wakenings. Just because your baby stirs at night, does not mean he needs your help. We all stir at the end of each sleep cycle (every 90 minutes). If you go in "to help," you will wake your baby up. If these partial wakenings are waking you up, turn off the baby monitor. If your baby really needs you, you will hear him. As Dr. B's husband would say, "Everyone sleeps better with the monitor off!"

9. Bringing baby into bed when you don't want him there. Babies get used to routines. If you consistently bring your baby into your own bed when he cries, this is what he will expect. He will continue to cry until he gets what he wants. If the expectation is not there, the behavior won't exist. Make a plan between BOTH parents and STICK WITH IT.

10. Not letting your baby learn how to self-soothe. The ability to soothe one's self is a learned skill. This skill can be mastered by six months of age, if your baby is given the opportunity. Yes, both thumb sucking and comfort objects (see below) are acceptable. Those Old Wives are correct about "spoiling" if you coddle your *older* baby.

sleep

night. I promise that your six-month-old can fall asleep without the pacifier.

- Don't get stuck treating your older baby like a newborn!

Q. My eight month old can only fall asleep nursing/taking a bottle. When will he outgrow this?

Your baby has been capable of it since four or five months of age. But he will continue to do it much longer if you let him. Feeding has become his crutch to fall asleep.

Again, for the first two months of life, anything goes. The optimal time to change this behavior for a full-term, healthy baby is around four months. But if you missed the window of opportunity, it's not too late. Babies are resilient and adaptable. If he falls asleep while feeding, wake him up just enough so he knows he is getting into bed and you are leaving the room. Be prepared for some protesting the next few nights, but he will adjust soon.

It's much easier to change these behaviors now. Your child isn't going to wake up one morning and move on from this routine—you need to actively change it. (I once consulted with a family whose five YEAR old still drank milk to fall asleep every night. Don't let this be your kid!)

Q. Are comfort objects okay to put in the crib?

Yes, at one year of age.

Comfort objects are also called transitional objects because they help a baby transition from needing their parents 24/7.

You can offer a comfort object during the day at any point, but it's safest to use—a little blanket or ***small*** stuffed animal that can go to bed with your baby, starting at one year of age. Remember, SIDS occurs in babies under age one. Just make sure the comfort item you select is small/light enough that it is not a smothering or suffocation hazard.

Q. My nine month old still has a middle of the night feeding. Is there something wrong with him?

He is a trained night feeder. There is nothing wrong with him. You've just allowed him to get part of his nutritional needs met during the night beyond when he needs them. Healthy, full term babies are all capable of fasting for up to 12 hours at night by six months of age. As long as your baby is growing well, read on.

Stop the night feeding and he will stop being hungry. That's easy to say, right? Offer water at 3 am and see what happens. It's likely to be rejected the first night. And yes, your child will protest. The second night, offer water again. The protesting will be less lengthy. By the third night, your baby won't bother to wake up.

Reality Check

It's likely that your nine-month old has at least one tooth. Therefore, offering milk at night without brushing his teeth afterwards may be a set up for cavities (milk has sugar in it). Be honest—you aren't getting out the toothbrush at 3 am after your child has crashed on your shoulder. The answer: STOP THE NIGHT FEEDING.

Q. What sets off disrupted sleep patterns?

Travel, teething, and illness. Any change in routine will disrupt a child's perfect sleep pattern.

Q. How do I get my baby back on track after a disrupted sleep schedule starts?

A quick refresher course in the preferable, normal sleep routine is helpful.

It may take just one or two nights, but be consistent with the routine you want to re-establish. Let him fall asleep on his own. Do not offer an additional night feeding. Do not bring him into your bed if he usually sleeps in his crib.

If you continue to intervene (a.k.a resorting to whatever it takes to get everyone back to sleep), your baby will demand his new "normal" routine. And trust me, these disrupted and sleepless nights are not what you or your child wants in the long run. As a doc, I am very comfortable recommending either "progressive waiting" (a.k.a. Ferberizing) or "rapid extinction" depending on how you feel about it. More on this below.

Q. My nine month old sleeps through the night, but she likes to start her day at 5 am. Can we change that?

You can adjust it somewhat, but some kids are early risers. Some tips:

First, pick a reasonable time to start the day–like 6 AM (sorry about that!). When you hear your little one making noise at 5AM, wait until 5:15 or 5:20 before going to her. The next morning, wait until 5:45. By the third morning, you can begin the day at 6 AM.

Next, try to put her down a little earlier at night. Early to bed often means late to rise-the opposite of what you might think.

Finally, try putting a few board books in her crib. She can look at them for a while until the sun comes up. Some babies will decide to play, others will go back to sleep. But let her decide what to do. Your presence signals the beginning of the day.

Helpful Hint

A baby's bedtime usually falls between 7pm and 8:30pm. Just because your baby or toddler is bouncing around the living room doesn't mean he isn't tired. Don't fall for this trick! Wired = tired.

Q. There are so many books written about infant sleep. What do you think about them?

The market has spoken: babies and their parents are desperate for a good night's sleep! If you are looking for more information, there are a few books that are worth reading.

Here are *our* opinions of the leading sleep authors and their books. You are welcome to read all of them and decide for yourself what works for you and your family. And, if you are a co-sleeping, attachment parent family, you can just skip right past this section of the chapter. First, the nearby table sums up the background and theory of each guru. Then below we offer a more detailed description of each.

I SOLVE YOUR CHILD'S SLEEP PROBLEMS, FERBER. *Theory*: "What parents view as abnormal wakenings in the night are actually normal. What they do to treat the 'abnormal' wakenings—namely going in to help their child go back to sleep—is actually causing the disturbance."

For the first four months of life, parents need to create positive sleep associations, routines, and rituals. If your baby is not sleeping through the night (six hours of uninterrupted sleep) by five or six months of age, it is time to train or un-train (break bad habits) your baby to stop the night wakenings.

Note: Babies under four months of age are not neurologically mature enough to settle and console themselves. This method is not intended for that age group.

Ferber Method, in a nutshell:

1. Do not let your baby fall asleep feeding, rocking, or being stroked by you.
2. Provide the identical sleep ritual (books, songs, cuddling) at nap and bedtime.
3. Have your baby sleep in the same place for naps and bedtime.
4. Avoid sleep crutches. (i.e. pacifiers)
5. Put your baby down relaxed, but not asleep.
6. Progressive waiting. If your baby protests, you make a brief appearance at increasing intervals (add five minutes each time) to reassure your baby that you have not abandoned him. This is NOT intended to console your baby. In fact, he will yell louder. Eventually your baby falls asleep on his own.

Pros: This method works! And it works quickly—usually in three or four nights. Dr. Ferber is truly one of the world's experts on sleep disorders in children. His book thoroughly explains the science of sleep at a level that parents can understand. He explains his method clearly with good detail and examples.

This book also addresses the gamut of all childhood sleep disorders, not just infant sleep problems. It is an excellent reference for night terrors, bed-wetting, sleep walking, etc.

Cons: Yes, your child will cry. Yes, the first night will be ugly. The second night is less ugly. The third night is manageable. The fourth night, your baby has a smile on his face and so do you. Your baby will be fine. Parents are always guilt-ridden when they hear their baby crying. More on this later.

As in every method, there are occasional setbacks. Illness, teething, and travel create sleep disturbances. Kids need an occasional refresher course (shorter than the initial training) to return to the normal routine!

Grade: A

Reality Check

There is no one-size-fits-all approach to infant sleep training. But babies thrive on consistency and routines. And, setting up good sleep habits up front prevents sleep problems down the road.

2 HEALTHY SLEEP HABITS, HAPPY CHILD, WEISSBLUTH. *Theory*: Good sleep is critical to good behavior and functioning. Overtired children have a lower frustration tolerance (short fuses), more behavior problems, and more difficulty falling asleep. Parents, with good intentions, perpetuate their child's poor sleep habits unintentionally with their actions. Common pitfalls are thoroughly explained.

Weissbluth Method, in a nutshell:

1. Set an earlier bedtime to get baby down BEFORE he is overtired. This may limit the evening playtime after a working parent comes home, but makes for a happier child.
2. Naptime should be preserved at all costs.
3. Let your baby learn the process of falling asleep by letting him do it on his own.
4. ***Rapid extinction***. If your baby is already in a vicious cycle of being overtired, end this cycle abruptly by letting him cry until he falls asleep on his own (after four months of age). This strategy is called the "Let Cry" Plan, and it takes one night to accomplish.
5. Weissbluth offers the "Maybe Cry" and the "No Cry" Plans which are more gradual approaches for parents who can't handle crying.

sleep

Table: Sleep Gurus Compared

AUTHOR/BOOK	BACKGROUND	THEORY	GRADE
Ferber Solve Your Child's Sleep Problems	M.D.-Director of Sleep Lab, Boston Children's Hospital, Harvard	Ferber method. Intervals of intervention extinguish night wakenings. Progressive waiting.	**A**
Weissbluth Healthy Sleep Habits, Happy Child	M.D.-Founder of Sleep Disorders Program Children's Memorial Hospital, Chicago	Sleep deprivation creates a vicious cycle. Break cycle cold turkey. Rapid extinction.	**A**
Mindell Sleeping Through the Night	PhD, Director of the Sleep Disorders Center at Children's Hospital, Philadelphia	Ferber with a dash more reality—finding that "golden moment" by setting limits	**A**
Sears The Baby Book	Pediatrician	Attachment parenting. Babies belong in contact with parents 24/7—asleep and awake.	**B-**
Pantley The No Cry Sleep Solution	Mother of 4	Pantley method. Comfort baby until he is almost asleep.	**C**
Ezzo/Bucknam On Becoming Babywise	A pastor and his friend, an obstetrician turned pediatrician	Parent-directed feeding. Don't let the baby dictate when it is time to eat.	**F**

Pros: This method works quickly—in one or two nights. Dr. Weissbluth provides an understandable, in-depth discussion of sleep physiology. He teaches you how to set up healthy sleep habits so you won't have to resort to breaking bad habits down the line.

The author provides true stories that will hit home with many of the parents that read this book. There is even a chapter written by a psychiatrist that is very insightful about parenting styles and how these styles impact a child's sleep routine.

Cons: Breaking the vicious cycle can be one very long night of crying (both on the part of the baby and the parent). Many parents don't have the stamina to let their child cry for more than 15 minutes, even if it is in their child's best interest. (See why parents can't let their child cry later in this chapter). In Weissbluth's defense, he expands his alternatives to letting the child cry for those parents in his latest edition.

Grade: A

3 **SLEEPING THROUGH THE NIGHT, MINDELL.** *Theory:* Ditto Ferber and Weissbluth, sprinkled with a bit more reality.

Mindell Method, in a nutshell:

"All you want is that golden moment when your child falls asleep independently. How you get there doesn't really matter."

1. Set up a sleep routine and be consistent about it.
2. Allow your child to fall asleep on his own.
3. Check on your baby as frequently or infrequently as you and your baby can tolerate.
4. Resist the temptation to resort to past sleep crutches at the beginning of the night (like rocking or nursing to sleep) once you've started to let your baby self soothe. It's okay to do whatever it takes (rocking, nursing to sleep) in the middle of the night until the sleep training process is complete.

Pros: Mindell's method gives a bit more wiggle room for parents who are squeamish about the whole crying thing. However, her take home message is essentially the same. As she says, "Setting limits for your child is part of being a good parent . . . it's a tough job, so don't feel guilty when your child doesn't like what you just told him to do." Her writing style is warm and engaging. It's the easiest to read, and thus, probably my favorite of the sleep books.

Cons: Mindell gives the green light to prolonged pacifier use (up to age four!) and dream-feeds. Since I don't really care for either of these sleep crutches, we'll have to agree to disagree on these points.

Grade: A

4 **THE BABY BOOK, SEARS.** *Theory:* Babies need positive sleep associations. To Dr. Sears, this means your baby should be skin to skin with you during sleep. Dr. Sears once said in a Child magazine interview (1998), "Why would a parent want to put her child in a box with bars in a dark room all by herself?"

PROGRESSIVE WAITING OR RAPID EXTINCTION?

Let's break this down so you understand how to implement these techniques in the real world. Both progressive waiting and rapid extinction work. It just depends on your tolerance level. Will you suffer in small doses over a period of nights (progressive waiting) . . . or suffer one long sleepless night (rapid extinction). *Note*: the parent is the one in agony. Your child is going to be just fine.

Progressive Waiting (a.k.a. Ferberizing)

1. Get your child relaxed, put him in his crib, and say goodnight.
2. Your child will start complaining.
3. On night one: Wait three minutes before returning to the nursery.
4. When you enter the nursery, make your response short and sweet (no more than 60 seconds). Tell your child you love him and say goodnight. Do NOT pick him up, rock him, or feed him. Leave the room. The purpose is for you to see that your baby is just fine and for your baby to know you have not gone to Brazil.
5. Your baby cries louder. (No surprise here.)
6. Wait *five minutes* before returning.
7. Repeat step 4.
8. Your baby sounds possessed. (They usually get louder once you leave).
9. Wait *ten minutes* before returning.
10. Repeat step 4.
11. Wait ten minutes before returning (this continues for the rest of the night).

This process requires *your baby* to do the work to fall asleep (yes, he is quite capable). The first night will be very difficult to tolerate. **Don't back down once you have committed to this plan.** When your baby wakes up the next morning, he will be happy to see you.

The second night is much easier. The night's events will last half as long as the first night.

The third night may last only ten minutes. By the fourth night, your baby will have adjusted to his new sleep schedule.

Rapid Extinction

Get your child relaxed, put him in his crib, and say goodnight.

If you are looking for steps #2 or #3, you won't find them. Yes, this is one long night. But guess what? Your baby will figure it out and move on to a new, healthier sleep routine of falling asleep and staying asleep.

Some final thoughts:

1. These techniques only work when your baby is neurologically mature enough to settle on his own—five or six months old. If you set up healthy sleep routines in the first place, you won't have to break the bad ones.
2. I always recommend doing this over a weekend. Otherwise, you will be cursing me the next day at work.
3. You can't give in or give up once you start.

Method: The family bed fosters attachment parenting. There is no reason to force your baby to sleep through the night or discontinue night feedings.

Pros: Many cultures use the family bed. If this is your plan, this is the guidebook. Attachment parenting, for those who desire it, is rewarding for both parents and baby.

Cons: As discussed earlier, there are safety concerns for babies who sleep in a family bed. Co-sleeping should also be a choice both parents vote for. Sometimes, only one parent is in favor of the family bed (the mother). Dad agrees to the family bed because his wife is exhausted from the frequency of having to get up for breastfeeding sessions. Eventually, Dad moves out to the couch or the spare bedroom to get some sleep.

Our opinion: we know that there is no one-size-fits-all approach to infant sleep training. We don't have a problem with attachment parenting advice, but the way the Sears' present their method as the *preferred* way to have happy well-adjusted child. We think parenting should be guilt-free.

Grade: B-

5 THE NO CRY SLEEP SOLUTION, PANTLEY. ***Theory:*** Babies develop associations with sleep that become a crutch (co-sleeping, feeding to fall asleep). Pantley says breaking these bad habits by letting the baby cry is insensitive and cruel. The focus is on establishing good routines and earlier bedtimes before missing the window of opportunity.

Method: Author provides 20 ideas that promote good sleep associations and routines. She tested her method on 60 families with infants.

Pros: Some families just can't listen to their baby crying. This book provides some ideas for establishing sleep rituals.

We agree with many of the author's comments on establishing sleep routines, although none of them are unique to her book. She does a nice job of addressing how to transition a co-sleeping child to his own bed.

She suggests that parents compile data on their own child and then make a personal plan for addressing their child's sleep disturbances.

Cons: Author admits that following her approach may take up to *eight weeks* to be successful. Perhaps a prescription for Prozac could be included for the parents when they buy her book. Most sleep-deprived parents are at the end of their rope at week ONE!

Ms. Pantley focuses on families who choose attachment parenting and the family bed. Her answer to reducing night feedings is to pretend to be asleep—not very realistic.

Grade: C

6 ON BECOMING BABYWISE, EZZO AND BUCKNAM. ***Theory:*** Parents mistakenly create a high need baby by having a "child-centered universe"—only the child's needs are prioritized. According to the authors, parents who feed their babies "on demand" create this flawed system. The result? Exhausted parents and breastfeeding failure.

As an alternative, the authors promote a family-centered lifestyle where

the needs of the family are the priority. The parent makes the schedule (known as "parent directed feedings" or PDF). The parent is the one who initiates *feedings, wake time*, and *naptime* for the baby—which need to occur in that exact order. The authors emphasize the importance of starting this routine in the first days of life. The first edition of this book was extremely rigid in scheduling a newborn's feedings.

The most recent edition of Babywise (5th editon, 2012) is more flexible and attempts to move away a bit from fixed hyper-scheduling. The authors tell parents to look at the newborn's hunger cues and the clock, and then assess whether or not it is time for the baby to eat. Hence, your baby doesn't need to nurse every 20 minutes, and if he does, he may not be getting enough breast milk. We agree with this. The 2012 edition offers tips on breastfeeding challenges and includes healthy baby growth charts. And, the authors discourage letting babies under four weeks of age go any longer than four to five hours between a feeding. The memo to parents: do not deprive your baby of food in an attempt to get him to sleep through the night.

The whole premise here is that good sleep patterns arise from good feeding patterns. The order should be eat-awake-sleep, not awake-eat-sleep. *Babywise* recommends putting your newborn into bed awake from day one.

Babywise Method, in a nutshell:

1. From birth to eight weeks of age, feed the baby every 2-3 hours. That is timed from the beginning of one feeding until the beginning of the next. Aim for a full feeding, not a snack.
2. Aim for a "first morning feeding" by eight weeks, which regulates the day and night's sleep schedule. If the baby awakens before the scheduled "first morning feeding," wait to see if he will fall back asleep without feeding.
3. Naptime is scheduled for the last one to one and 1/2 hours of each eat-awake-sleep cycle. Put your newborn down awake. Fussing or crying for 15-20 minutes is acceptable in the settling down process.
4. Stretch out feeding schedules after eight to twelve weeks. Sleep clusters will expand because the baby has been trained since day one.
5. There will be situations where you will have to deviate from routine.

Pros: According to the authors, 95-97% of their babies are sleeping through the night at 12 weeks of age. (Babies who were born prematurely and those with acid reflux take longer.) They offer up results of their own study of 520 babies (which does not appear to be published in a peer reviewed medical journal). One message we like: the importance of nurturing the family relationship.

Cons: The first edition of this book was so contrary to mainstream pediatric practice that the American Academy of Pediatrics issued a rare alert about this book.

However, the kinder, more flexible 5th edition is much more in line with what the AAP recommends for feedings.

The biggest red flag: the idea of leaving a *newborn* to settle on his own for 15-20 minutes is anathema to most pediatricians (and parents). Newborns are incapable of self-soothing. You can't ignore them and let them cry it out eight times a day. For that reason alone, I can't recommend this book.

Grade: F

DR B'S OPINION: WHICH SLEEP METHOD IS BEST?

By far, my patients' families have had the most success with progressive waiting or rapid extinction (the methods found in Ferber, Weissbluth, and Mindell's books). Which works better for the individual child depends on the parents' ability to cope. Some parents prefer to go into the nursery to check on their baby. Others prefer to avoid seeing the drama unfold. Either way, the baby learns to self-soothe. If you have a video baby monitor, you may be more willing to wait it out outside the nursery.

Yes, your baby will probably (okay, almost definitely) cry. If you avoid our "top ten mistakes" and follow through with your plan, the crying is a one night to one week (at most) experience. Your baby is resilient and has the wings to fly. Give her the chance to use them!

For parents who "just can't let their baby cry," I offer these words from Dr. Weissbluth: "Have the courage to do what is best for the child."

As Dr. Mindell points out in her sleep book, sleep training will NOT a) cause your child harm, b) affect your child's attachment to you or c) make your child emotionally scarred for life. In fact, studies have shown that kids who sleep well are well adjusted and have fewer behavior problems than kids who are up several times a night. Studies have also found that "young children are ***more securely*** attached to their parents following sleep training." (*Mindell*)

Anti-CIO (Cry It Out) activists claim that infant crying causes elevated stress hormone (cortisol) levels and permanent damage. However, the studies that critics refer to were NOT done on the impact of sleep training techniques. Those studies looked at babies who cry all the time (not just at bedtime) beyond three months of life to detect early signs of neurological or developmental delays. (*Rao, Stifter*)

According to Dr. Mindell, "The positive results of weeks and months of a good night's sleep clearly outweigh a few nights of sleep training. Not only are babies happier and more alert during the day after a good night's sleep, but moms and dads are also better parents when they get the sleep they need."

I'd argue that a few nights of crying is insignificant compared to MONTHS (or, gulp, years!!) of disrupted sleep. That, I believe, takes a huge toll on growth, development, and parent-child relationships.

Q. I tried letting my child "cry it out" and it didn't work. Help!

There are a couple of reasons why attempts at sleep training fail:

1. A determined child.
2. A tired parent.

Let's tackle the child issue first. Yes, some babies protest more than others. It is completely normal for a child to push back when he is asked to change and try something new.

Most babies will cry for 45 minutes and then fall asleep. A few, really vocal ones, may go on for an hour or two. Most babies will adapt to self-soothing after a few nights. A few, really determined ones, may protest for a week or more.

We understand that if you are living with the vocal, determined baby that you will only have so much will power to follow through with this self-soothing, baby-in-charge-of-falling-asleep game plan. If this is your situation, it's okay to go in for a brief intervention. Do some snuggling or singing but don't completely rock your baby to sleep...because then you just taught your baby that a long tirade achieves the objective: a parent's shoulder to fall asleep on.

Note: although most babies adapt very quickly, there are a handful of kids who may not be ready for this approach quite yet. For those babies, take a complete break from sleep training and try again in a few weeks.

Now, let's talk about you. Most parents are unsuccessful because they are either too exhausted or don't feel right about letting their baby cry. We know it can be nerve-wracking.

Here is my pep talk to give you the incentive to persevere.

1. What you are doing currently is not working.
2. Nothing is medically wrong with your child.
3. Nothing will happen to your child if he cries.
4. Your child will not hate you or feel you have abandoned him. Your baby will be HAPPY to see you the next morning and you'll be happier to see him.

Feedback from the Real World: Multiples

One parent wrote of her nine-month-old twins:

"You'll be interested to know that they slept through after the second night. I guess they were as ready as I was."

Here's another reader comment from a mom of twins:

"'Crying it Out' is a frightening term to most parents. But truth be told, fear is often times worse than the actual event itself. It was such an intimi-

Five Reasons parents can't listen to their baby cry

1. You feel like you are helpless and not "doing anything" for your baby (not true).
2. You are a working parent and feel guilty (don't).
3. You think you will cause your baby to have long-term emotional scars (you won't).
4. You think you are an inadequate parent if you can't get your baby to settle down (you aren't).
5. You think something must be wrong with your baby (probably not).

dating undertaking for us, but once we started, it only took two nights before they learned how to self-soothe. And contrary to what you might think, the crying twin rarely awakens the other twin. They have been sleeping through the night since six months for 12+ hours a night!"
–Agustina, mom to Gael and Malena, 18 months old

Q. I know I am being a wimp, but I don't think I can listen to my baby cry.

Be strong. You can do it.

As a baby sleep consultation expert, here is my perspective. Yes, your baby is mad that he is not getting his way. You will see a lot of this behavior in the years to come (a preview of the toddler and teenage years)! Remember when you were 16 and your parents didn't let you borrow the car? Did you still love them? Your child will still love you, even when you set limits on his behaviors (including sleep).

I know, easy for us to say. But as moms, we've been there and know what you are going through. Follow the advice in this chapter and you can do it.

Feedback from the Real World

From Helen G. in Austin, TX: "If you are really bothered by letting your baby cry without seeing what is going on, buy a video baby monitor. That way you will know if there is a serious problem (his leg is stuck between the crib slats) . . . or if he is just testing you."

So now that we've picked apart all of the sleep gurus, it's our turn to summarize our approach to sleep. Yes, it's the BABY 411 SLEEP PLAN. Drum roll please . . . we've cleverly used the acronym S.L.E.E.P. (Heck, you all are so exhausted, it would be hard to remember otherwise!)

S Set up a sleep routine. Babies and kids thrive on consistency. Follow the SAME routine at naps and bedtime. Make it short and sweet. Example: one book, one song, one minute of rocking, bed.

L Less is more. The less you intervene, the more everyone sleeps. Babies who learn to self-soothe won't need you to help them fall asleep or go back to sleep after every sleep cycle.

E Empower the child. Babies (by four to six months) are capable of going to sleep, and falling back asleep on their own . . . if you let them!

E Earlier bedtime. Babies who are overtired have more trouble falling asleep. The earlier they go to bed, the better and longer they sleep.

P Plan together and stick to it. Make a plan *with* your spouse that you BOTH agree to follow. And then don't cave at 3am. If you need to do a sleep "intervention," start it over a weekend so no one has any excuses.

Feedback from the Real World

"Consistency is key. Keep your bedtime wind-down routine simple, and one that works for both you and your partner. Don't lock yourself into an elaborate ritual that you will later regret!"
–Agustina, mom to Gael and Malena, 18 months old

Nap Schedules

Q. How much should my baby be napping?

Here's the timeline:

- *Birth to two months:* three to four naps per day (mostly waking up to eat and going back to sleep)
- *Two to four months:* Three or four naps per day
- *Four to six months:* Two or three naps per day
- *Six to 12 months:* Two naps per day

Babies usually cut back to one afternoon nap a day shortly after their one-year birthdays. Some will keep that nap until kindergarten. Most (like my own kids) give it up by three years old.

Q. When will my baby be on a nap schedule?

By four months, maybe earlier. Follow your baby's lead.

At two months of age, you will have more predictability in your lives. Your goal, at this point is to start having a schedule by four months of age. You follow your baby's plan and work around it. In general, babies are awake for a couple of hours and then it's time for a nap.

Naptime can begin within 30-45 minutes of your daily goal. But try as much as you can to be consistent. Overtired babies are not exactly the life of the party. Things happen and delays sometimes are unavoidable. Just be prepared. . . you will pay for it!

Remember, from birth to two months, anything goes. If your baby falls asleep in the car, that's fine. This is a popular parent trick. But by four months, avoid it.

Put your baby down awake and follow your same sleep routine as at bedtime. View naptime as your baby's downtime. If he chooses to talk for 30 minutes instead of sleep, so be it.

By six months, you should have the nap thing down. If you don't, it's time for an intervention. The only difference with naps versus night sleep is that if your intervention goes on for more than an hour, that is the end of naptime. As a result, you may have a baby who is not actually sleeping during naptime for a few days.

Q. How long are naps supposed to be?

Thirty minutes to three hours.

It depends on the child. By four months of age, your baby should have two to four naps per day. The more naps, the shorter they all are in duration. Once she is down to a couple of naps a day, one is likely to be a morning catnap and the afternoon nap may be a three-hour marathon.

By a year of age (12-21 months), the morning nap is lost, and your baby will probably take a 90-minute to three-hour afternoon siesta.

Q. My baby never naps at daycare and comes home cranky. Help!

Some babies just don't do well with group naptime. They prefer solitude.

See if your daycare center is willing to put your baby in a private area to take his naps. If this is not a possibility, you may need to rethink your childcare options or aim for a very early bedtime.

Q. My nine month old talks and plays during his second nap of the day and rarely falls asleep. Is it time to cut that nap out?

It's reasonable for naptime to last one hour. What your baby chooses to do with it is up to her. She is having downtime (and likely, so are you). She may look at books, talk to her dolls, or complain. But she still needs that opportunity to rest or sleep. The second nap is usually dropped around 12-21 months.

Q. I have an older child that is in school. My baby's naptime falls right at the time I pick him up from school. He either misses his nap or falls asleep in the car, only to be awakened when we get home.

Naps are an important part of your baby's schedule. Enough that it is worth looking into carpool options. Perhaps you could drive in the morning and a friend could pick your child up from school. Don't sacrifice that nap if you can help it.

Q. My baby takes a late afternoon nap and then wants to stay up all night. I don't. What should I do?

It's wise to *end* that afternoon nap by 4 pm or 5 pm at the latest. Otherwise, your baby won't be tired enough to go to sleep at a reasonable hour. Try putting your baby down for the last nap of the day by 1pm or 2 pm. If your baby plays in his crib for an hour and then finally falls asleep, you will probably need to wake him up to stick to the game plan.

Beyond The First Year

Q. How long will my baby sleep in his crib before graduating to a big bed?

As long as he still likes it.

That can be as old as three years of age. We don't recommend toddler beds or convertible beds because they are a waste of money. When your child starts trying to climb out of his crib, take the mattress out and put it on the floor. Put up a safety gate in front of his doorway. That way, he'll have free reign of his room, but not the whole house.

Q. We have a one year old and are expecting again. Should I take the older baby out of the crib when the new one arrives?

No.

A bassinet will buy you a couple of months with the newborn. Then, see if the older child still likes his crib. If the answer is yes, borrow or buy a crib for the younger baby until the older one graduates (see information above about purchasing a new mattress).

Otherwise, you are asking to have a toddler roaming free around your house at night.

Q. Can we use a small travel pillow in the crib?

After a year of age, it's okay.

Special Situations

sleep

Q. I have twins. Is it okay to let them share a crib?

Yes. Until they start waking each other up.

For the first two months, both babies will sleep snugly and not get in each other's way. After two months, it's probably wise to give them the space they need to move around–that means two cribs. It's fine to have them share a room.

Q. Do you have any recommendations for how to get both babies to sleep through the night?

The answer is the same as for single babies. Set up the right routines and rituals.

The only difference is with feeding times. See Chapter 6, Liquids for how to coordinate night feedings with multiples.

Q. I have a baby who was born prematurely. Will it take longer for him to sleep through the night?

Yes. It may be as long as 17 weeks beyond your baby's *due date*, not his birth date.

Premature babies are neurologically immature. They also need more calories for "catch up growth." Night feedings will be necessary for a longer period of time than full term babies need.

Q. My baby has acid reflux (GERD). Will this make any difference in his ability to sleep through the night?

Yep. Babies with reflux take longer to sleep through the night for a few reasons. For starters, their heartburn symptoms are worse at night when they are lying down. You can't really blame them for having trouble falling asleep. If your baby is taking medication to control the symptoms, be sure he hasn't outgrown his dose of medication (get the dose re-calculated by your doctor every month). You don't want your child lying there in misery.

And crying can make the acid reflux worse. So it's probably not the best idea to let your baby cry it out for an hour. It's okay for five or ten minutes, but not for the duration an otherwise healthy baby would cry. The good news: most kids outgrow reflux by six months of age. Get the green light from your doc or gastroenterologist, and then proceed with your sleep plan.

BOTTOM LINE

Some final thoughts: the National Sleep Foundation found that infants and young children are not getting enough sleep (and neither are their parents—but you already knew that). Tired kids are not only cranky, but they are less interested in learning new information. Make sure both you and your baby get enough sleep!

Development

Chapter 10

"I have found the best way to give advice to your children is to find out what they want and then advise them to do it."

~ Harry S Truman

What's in this Chapter

- What does development mean?
- How do I know my baby is developing normally?
- What is the Denver Developmental Checklist?
- Failing milestones and Early Childhood Intervention
- Autism
- Intellectual (cognitive) development
- Social & emotional development
- Fostering development
- Keeping kids safe while they explore
- Developmentally appropriate toys and books

"There should be a warning label in bold at the beginning of this chapter: 'Caution: all overachievers and/or first-time parents. Your baby may not develop at the same rate as we have listed in this chapter as normal. You should neither jump off a bridge nor sign your child up for Sylvan Learning Center. These are just averages.'"

—Adventures in the Life of NGL, blogger and fan of *Baby 411*

Okay, you've heard the conversations on the playground: "Janey was walking at only ten months." "Well, my little Henry was saying his first words at four months." You know—competition starts early. Now if you're pregnant as you read this you're probably wondering when they should start walking and talking. If you have a child already, you may be one of those quiet moms who doesn't join in the above boasting conversation. But, you may still be wondering if your baby is behind. That's what this chapter is here to tell you.

When can your child roll over, when should he, and when is he developmentally delayed? And what is important to worry about and bring up to your doctor during well check visits? This chapter provides the key to understanding how your child's brain works. Knowing what to expect will help you know how to respond to your child's needs as he is growing. This is required reading before you get to the next chapter, "Discipline and Temperament." We'll refer back to

this stuff, so don't jump ahead.

Your first lesson: DO NOT COMPARE YOUR BABY TO OTHER CHILDREN. We know, you just can't help it. You watch other kids in playgroups, at the park, and in your own family and then look at your baby. Don't do it. Every child reaches her developmental milestones at her own pace. Yes, there is a certain timeline to reach these milestones, but there is a broad range of "normal."

Q. What does development mean?

The way a child evolves in muscle skills (large and small muscles), language skills, social and personality skills, and intelligence. This is different from the term "growth" which refers to physical body changes. We'll define some key terms on this topic next.

1. Gross Motor Development. This refers to using large muscle groups to function (i.e. arms, legs, torso). *Milestones*: rolling, sitting, crawling, climbing, walking, running, throwing, and kicking a ball. *FYI: Gross motor development is mastered in a "Head, shoulders, knees, and toes" direction. Remember these milestones by the numbers 3-6-9-12:*

- Three-month-olds have achieved *head* control. (no more head bobs)
- Six-month-olds have *shoulder* and *trunk* support. (rolling over, sitting up)
- Nine-month-olds have *knee* control and can stand up holding on, and walk with support.
- 12-month-olds have control of their feet and toes, standing alone and taking steps.

2. Fine Motor Development. This skill involves using small muscle groups to function (i.e. fingers). *Milestones*: batting with hands, grabbing, picking up objects, feeding oneself, holding food utensils, holding writing utensils, coloring, and writing.

3. Oral Motor Development. The ability to use mouth and tongue muscles. *Milestones*: swallowing, chewing, and talking. Newborns only have the ability to suck, swallow, and cry.

4. Language Development. This refers to the ability to communicate with others. The prerequisites for language development are oral motor development and the ability to hear and process language (see receptive language skills below). *Milestones*: cooing, babbling, stringing sounds together, imitating noises, and using words purposefully. There are two different areas of language development:

- *Receptive* language skills. The "input" that babies get in the form of words is understood long before they start talking. Babies can follow directions (if they are in the mood) before they say any words.
- *Expressive* language skills. This is language "output." When people refer to a child having language delays, it is usually an expressive language delay (i.e. they aren't talking yet). If there is a concern for an expressive language delay, your doctor should always

check to be sure there is not a receptive language delay, too (a hearing problem, or an **AUDITORY PROCESSING DISORDER**).

5. Social-Emotional Development. This is how a child adapts to his world. *Milestones*: smiles responsively, knows parents, asks to be held, laughs, imitates, plays peek-a-boo, anxiety towards strangers, anxiety from being separated from loved ones, seeks independence.

Social skills are a learned process. And, parents are the most important role models for a child. Children interact in social situations quite differently at different ages.

6. Cognitive (Intellectual Development). This refers to how a child figures out his world. Babies are like big sponges. They absorb vast quantities of information on a daily basis and learn how to decipher it all. And you thought your learning curve was steep with this new parent experience. Imagine what your baby's brain is going through!

Milestones: follows people and objects in field of vision, expresses needs, explores toys, prefers routines, knows how to get people's attention, understands cause-and-effect (that is, banging this toy makes noise), object permanence (things still exist even if not in view), remembers frequent visitors, limited problem solving skills.

Q. How do I know that my baby is developing normally?

You visit your pediatrician or family doctor for well baby checks. Or schedule a special appointment to address any developmental concerns you might have.

Many parents think that well baby checks are "just for shots." They're not. At every well baby check, your doctor will ask a series of questions to be sure your baby is developing all five types of skills at an appropriate pace. Docs don't usually ask developmental questions at sick visits because those are "problem-focused" appointments.

If a delay in any of the developmental areas is detected, it may be followed for a period of time to see if your baby "catches up" or a referral may be made to a specialist in that particular field.

This is an extremely important part of both the parent and doctor's job description. If you have concerns about your child's development, don't be shy about it. There is never a downside to getting your concerns checked out.

Early intervention makes the greatest impact in lifelong outcomes. For more on this, see the section "Learn the Signs. Act Early."

Q. I've heard the term "developmental milestones." What does it mean?

These are individual skills that your baby progressively masters as he matures.

The series of questions your pediatrician asks are based on expected milestones at specific ages. Some babies will show off and demonstrate their new tricks in the office. In most cases, however, doctors rely on your descriptions for the rest. Remember, there is a range of time for when milestones are achieved.

Q. Can I have a milestone checklist so I can follow along?

Yes. The Denver Developmental Checklist is considered the gold standard to assess milestones. We have included the test items in a box below.

Remember, no obsessing over this list. Do not tape it to your baby's crib and check off his accomplishments. This is by no means a perfect test, but

BOOKMARK THIS PAGE! THE BABY 411 ALL-IN-ONE

Developmental checklists are designed to identify developmental delays in infants and young children. In general, the areas are divided into the following categories:

- Gross motor skills (large muscle groups)
- Fine motor skills (small muscle groups)
- Language including all forms of communication (indicating wants, facial expressions, understanding language, and vocalization)
- Personality/intellectual development

Because children accomplish these milestones at a range of ages, mastery of a particular milestone will vary over a period of time (i.e. walking may be mastered between 9-15 months of age). The cutoff for 'normal' is at the level where over 90% of children have achieved a milestone at a particular age.

For babies born prematurely (if your child was born before 36 weeks gestation and your child is under 2 years old): Subtract the number of months missed in pregnancy from the baby's current age and check at the adjusted age.

Gross Motor:	**Age achieved:**
Lifts head	0 to 2 months
Holds head steady	1.5 to 4 months
Pushes chest up while lying on stomach	2 to 4 months
Rolls over	2 to 4.5 months*
No head lag when pulled to sitting position	3.5 to 6 months
Bears weight on legs when held in standing position	3 to 7.5 months
Sits alone	5 to 8 months
Stands holding on to something	5 to 10 months
Pulls self up to standing position	6 to 10 months
Gets to sitting position independently	6 to 11 months
Walks holding on to furniture ("cruises")	7.5 to 12.5 months
Stands alone briefly	9 to 13 months
Stands alone	9.5 to 14 months
Walks alone	11 to 14.5 months

**Note: Rolling over is a less reliable milestone now that babies spend most of their time on their backs with the anti-SIDs campaign.*

**Note: Crawling is not listed on the developmental checklist because many children skip crawling and are developmentally normal.*

it is a helpful guide for doctors to screen for developmental delays.

There is a very low criterion to "pass" a test so that children with normal skills are not falsely considered delayed. In light of this, if a child does "fail" a test on the Denver Checklist, it is quite likely he has a developmental delay in a certain area. In such a case, the doctor will investigate this further either in her office or via referral to a developmental specialist.

DEVELOPMENT CHECKLIST

Fine Motor:	Age achieved:
Brings hands together	1.5 to 3.5 months
Grasps objects	2.5 to 4.5 months
Reaches for objects	3 to 5 months
Transfers objects hand to hand	4.5 to 7.5 months
Grabs objects with whole hand ("rakes")	5 to 8 months
Able to feed self a cracker	4.5 to 8 months
Grabs object between thumb and finger ("crude pincer grasp")	7 to 10.5 months
Bangs objects together	7 to 12 months
Mastery of pincer grasp ("fine pincer")	9 to 14 months
Drinks from a cup	10 to 16.5 months

Language/Communication:	Age achieved:
Eyes focus on objects in front of them	0 to 1.5 months*
Eyes follow objects to the sides	0 to 2.5 months*
Baby regards person's face	0 to 1 month*
Baby smiles in response to person smiling at them ("social smile")	0 to 2 months*
Responds to loud noise	0 to 1.5 months
Makes happy noises	0 to 2 months
Laughs	1.5 to 3.5 months
Makes squealing noises	1.5 to 4.5 months
Baby smiles without prompting	1.5 to 5 months
Turns to someone's voice	3.5 to 8.5 months
Says "dada" or "mama" but doesn't mean it	6 to 10 months
Imitates speech noises (baby talk/jabber)	6 to 11.5 months
Says Dada or Mama and means it	9.5 to 13.5 months
Indicates wants non-verbally ("point & grunt")	10.5 to 14.5 months
Says 3 or more words besides Mama/Dada	11.5 to 20.5 months

**Note: A newborn's vision is 20/200. They can only see about 8 to 12 inches in front of their faces. So, to test these items, you need to be very close to your baby's face.*

Personality/Intellectual development	Age achieved:
Plays peek a boo	6 to 9.5 months
Looks for hidden object	5 to 8 months
Initial shyness with strangers ("stranger anxiety")	5.5 to 10 months
Plays pat a cake	7 to 13 months
Plays ball with someone	9.5 to 16 months

Putting it all together

Here are the questions your baby's doctor will ask you at each well check during the first year. Complete these checklists ahead of time if you want to make sure your baby is tracking where he should be (or if you want to look really smart!).

Two weeks

Large muscle:

Does your newborn move his arms and legs?	Yes	No

Language/communication:

Does your newborn look at your face?	Yes	No
Does your newborn startle to loud noises?	Yes	No

Two months

Large Muscle

Can your baby lift/hold her head up?	Yes	No

Language/communication

Does your baby smile back at you when you smile at her?	Yes	No
Does your baby follow you with her eyes?	Yes	No
Does your baby make happy noises ("coos")?	Yes	No

Four months

Large Muscle

Does your baby hold his head up steady?	Yes	No
Can your baby lift his chest up while lying on his stomach?	Yes	No
Can your baby roll over?	Yes	No
Can your baby bear weight on his legs when he is held in a standing position?	Yes	No

Small Muscle

Does your baby notice his own hands?	Yes	No
Does your baby reach/bat at objects?	Yes	No
Can your baby grasp or hold a rattle or toy?	Yes	No

Language/communication

Does your baby laugh or squeal?	Yes	No
Does your baby look for you across the room?	Yes	No

Six months

Large Muscle

Does your baby hold his head up when pulled to sit up?	Yes	No
Can your baby sit up by himself?	Yes	No
Can your baby roll over?	Yes	No
Can your baby bear weight on his legs when he is held in a standing position?	Yes	No

Small Muscle

Does your baby reach for objects?	Yes	No
Can your baby grasp or hold a rattle or toy?	Yes	No
Does your baby transfer objects from hand to hand?	Yes	No

Language/communication

Does your baby laugh or squeal?	Yes	No
Does your baby turn to your voice?	Yes	No
Can your baby imitate speech noises (baby talk/jabber)?	Yes	No
Can your baby make single syllable noises ("ba" or "ga")	Yes	No

Nine months

Large Muscle

Can your baby sit up by herself?	Yes	No
Can your baby stand up, holding onto something?	Yes	No
Does your baby pull herself up to standing position?	Yes	No
Does your baby crawl, scoot, or walk holding onto furniture (cruise)?	Yes	No

Small Muscle

Does your baby transfer objects from hand to hand?	Yes	No
Does your baby pick small items up with her whole hand (raking)?	Yes	No
Can your baby feed herself a cracker?	Yes	No
Can your baby pick up small items between her thumb and index finger (pincer grasp)?	Yes	No

Language/communication

Does your baby turn to your voice?	Yes	No
Can your baby imitate speech noises (baby talk/jabber)?	Yes	No
Can your baby make single syllable noises ("ba" or "ga")?	Yes	No
Can your baby say "mama" or "dada" without meaning it?	Yes	No
Does your baby try to get your attention?	Yes	No

Social/intellectual

Does your baby play peek-a-boo with you?	Yes	No
Can your baby wave "bye-bye"?	Yes	No
Does your baby look for objects that are hidden or that have dropped?	Yes	No
Is your baby afraid of strangers?	Yes	No
Is your baby bothered when you leave her?	Yes	No
Does your baby look to get your approval in new situations?	Yes	No

One Year Old

Large Muscle

Can your child stand while holding on to something?	Yes	No
Does your child crawl, scoot, or walk holding onto furniture (cruise)?	Yes	No
Can your child stand alone?	Yes	No
Can your child take steps or walk alone?	Yes	No

Small Muscle

Does your child feed himself?	Yes	No
Does your child hold his own cup?	Yes	No
Does your child pick up small items between his thumb and index finger (pincer grasp)?	Yes	No
Does your child bang objects together?	Yes	No
Can your child put objects into a container?	Yes	No

Language/communication

Comprehension:

Does your child respond when you call his name?	Yes	No
Does your child understand what you are saying to him?	Yes	No
Does your child look where you point when you say, "Look at the _______."	Yes	No

Expression:

Does your child say "mama" or "dada" and mean it?	Yes	No
Does your child say one word besides mama or dada?	Yes	No
Does your child babble like he is speaking a foreign language that you cannot understand?	Yes	No
Does your child take turns "talking" to you, as if you are having a conversation?	Yes	No
Does your child try to get your attention?	Yes	No
Does your child communicate his needs without words?	Yes	No
Can your child shake his head to say "no"?	Yes	No

Social/intellectual

Does your child play (pat-a-cake, high-five) with you?	Yes	No
Does your child imitate you (e.g. pretend to talk on the phone, clean up, or use the remote control)?	Yes	No
Does your child wave bye-bye?	Yes	No

Autism Screening Questions:

Does your child have constant repetitive behaviors, like flapping of the hands?	Yes	No
Does your child have an unusual preference for a hard object, like preferring to carry a phone around instead of a doll or blanket?	Yes	No
Does your child avoid eye contact?	Yes	No
Does your child act like he is in his own world?	Yes	No
Is your child bothered by cuddling?	Yes	No

If you answer YES to more than one of these autism screening questions, please be sure to inform your doctor.

Q. What is the significance if my child fails in his milestones?

Maybe something, maybe nothing.

This is a non-committal answer, but it is the truth. Some children will have an isolated delay in one particular developmental area (that is, just motor

skills, just expressive language skills, etc.). With a little help and encouragement, these kids catch up to their peers and you might never notice a problem later on. For others, it may always be an issue. For instance, a child with gross motor delays may grow up to be a non-athletic kid. A child with expressive language delays may turn out to have a learning disability. Both of these children might also be a varsity football player or the valedictorian. It just might take a little more work for that kid to succeed in those areas.

The children we are most concerned about are those with delays across the board, termed "global developmental delays." These children are more at risk to never catch up to their peers. When children continue to have global delays by the age of three years old, they are ultimately diagnosed as intellectually disabled. There is a range from mild to severely affected children. Doctors evaluate these children for genetic and metabolic (the way the body breaks down certain chemicals) defects when they are diagnosed.

Autism

Q. I've heard a lot about autism in the news. What is it, and when do I worry?

AUTISM SPECTRUM DISORDERS (ASD) are a collection of several disorders that cause children to have two abnormal areas in common: social and communication skills, and repetitive/restrictive behaviors. Previously, specialists used the terms **PERVASIVE DEVELOPMENTAL DISORDERS (PDD), PERVASIVE DEVELOPMENTAL DISORDER, NOT OTHERWISE SPECIFIED (PDD-NOS),** and **ASPERGER'S SYNDROME** separately to describe people who fell onto the autism spectrum. Without question, there is a very broad range of severity within ASD. A child may have normal intelligence and language, but be socially awkward and have panic attacks if his sandwich is cut in triangles instead of squares. Or a child may appear out of touch with reality and spend his entire day rocking and flapping his hands. Both children have autism. And that is why the newest psychiatric diagnostic bible (DSM-5) eliminates these other diagnostic terms and gives everyone on the spectrum the same diagnosis–autism.

As you might suspect, children with severe problems are diagnosed much earlier than kids who can communicate but have trouble with social skills.

Children are usually diagnosed by 18-24 months of age when language delays are obvious. Many mildly affected children may not be diagnosed until preschool (or sometimes even later!)

LEARN THE SIGNS, ACT EARLY.

The Centers for Disease Control recently launched a campaign called "Learn the Signs. Act Early." It empowers parents with information on what is normal child development and what isn't. The key point: early diagnosis and intensive therapy leads to the best developmental outcome for the child. Kids who get help before age three (and earlier is even better) have the best chance of overcoming developmental challenges. You can access their info at www.cdc.gov/actearly or at 1-800-CDC-INFO.

However, clues to the diagnosis appear long before that time. Some early clues include: not smiling back at people, poor eye contact, not imitating, not gesturing (waving bye-bye), not responding to being called by name, and not trying to communicate/connect/engage with other people by one year of age.

There are also some unusual behaviors. Cuddling may not be soothing. In fact, a child with autism may get very upset by being touched. Bright lights and noises often bother them. Because they are bugged by the outside world, they may turn inwards and find comfort in repetitive behaviors (rocking, head banging, spinning). Children with autism may have little interest in playing with toys. Or they may play in an odd way–such as using a phone as a comfort object.

BOTTOM LINE: Children with autism have autism long before their first birthdays, even though their "official" diagnosis usually occurs in their second year of life. Remember this fact when we discuss the now debunked measles (MMR) vaccine controversy. (see Chapter 12, "Vaccines" for details).

Q. My baby bangs his head frequently. Does he have autism?

No. Many babies have behaviors that they perform repeatedly. The repetition is soothing for them. It becomes a red flag (see below) when the behavior goes on all day long and replaces meaningful play. And with autism, there are other also other atypical behaviors (lack of social skills, poor language, etc.). By the way, babies have the same self-preservation instincts that we do, so they really won't hurt themselves by head banging.

RED FLAGS for Autism

Although autism is usually diagnosed by age two or so, clues are apparent much earlier. Here are some things to be watching for by a child's first birthday.

- Lack of eye contact. Babies should make eye contact (and smile back at you) by two months of age.
- Failure to respond to name by first birthday.
- Constant repetitive behaviors (hand flapping, etc).
- Preference for unusual comfort objects (that is, not a doll or blanket).
- Lack of symbolic play or imitation–pretending to talk on the phone or use the TV remote.
- No babbling by first birthday.
- No gesturing by first birthday.
- Lack of social skills. Babies should try to engage and get someone's attention.

WHERE TO GET HELP

- *Head Start and Early Head Start programs:* ehsnrc.org
- *Parent training:* patnc.org
- *Early Intervention for children birth to three years:* nectas.unc.edu

Insider Tip: Testing

All children who are being evaluated for autism should have chromosome testing done (karyotyping). A small percentage of kids with ASD have a chromosomal abnormality called Fragile X Syndrome. Other, less common chromosome abnormalities have also been linked to autism. Knowing that your child has Fragile X or another genetic defect may be useful someday when targeted gene therapy is a reality. That's a hot area of research right now.

Q. Is there a test for autism?

There's currently no blood test or imaging study that detects autism. An autism diagnosis is based on the symptoms that a child displays (and lack of findings/results that would suggest a different diagnosis). However, testing for chromosome defects or metabolic disorders may be useful if there are other family members who have autism or the child's physical examination is concerning. Doing a blood lead test is helpful if a child has had a significant environmental exposure. (Kids with lead poisoning don't really have autism, but their bizarre behavior may be misdiagnosed as autism.)

What is NOT useful? Tests that look for heavy metal exposure in the hair/urine/poop, food allergy tests that look at "IgG" levels, or any "alternative lab" where you get your child's test results back on a pretty, four-color grid.

Your pediatrician can do an assessment in her office. If autism is suspected, your child's doctor can make a referral to a developmental pediatrician or multidisciplinary assessment program.

The American Academy of Pediatrics has an extensive Autism Toolkit to help educate families. You can ask your doctor for these materials or go online to aap.org for more information.

Q. I have a friend whose child has autism. She said he was "perfectly normal" until he was about 18 months old. Does this happen?

There are a small minority of children with autism who have completely normal milestones and then regress, which is known as "late onset autism." These children most likely have a distinct genetic abnormality that turns on or off without any trigger.

However, for most kids with autism, parents and doctors just miss (or dismiss) the early signs in the first year of life and the child's atypical development only becomes apparent at 18 months.

Doctors rely heavily on parents to point out concerns. And parents (especially first timers) don't know what is normal and what isn't.

One of my patient's mothers told me that she only realized how unusual her son's development was after she watched her second child, without autism, breeze through her milestones. Even the most vocal autism activist mom of all, Jenny McCarthy agrees. Her son was five months old when he first smiled at her (that's abnormal), when all of her friend's babies smiled at two months of age (that's normal).

Some parents report that their child with autism spoke a few words and then "lost" the ability to say them. If you delve a bit deeper, the child may have randomly said a few things, but was not consistently using words like "juice" or "no" to communicate his needs.

There is growing research in language development that looks at brain anatomy. Primitive brain parts control early language development from birth to 18 months. At 18 to 24 months, the mature brain parts turn on and language takes off. With children who have autism, mature language does not take off. But from a parent's perspective, it may look like a loss of skills.

And again, children with subtle atypical behaviors may be harder to diagnose early on. Reviewing home movies of a child once the diagnosis is made often shows that early signs are overlooked. (*Maestro*)

OLD WIVES TALE

The MMR Vaccine causes autism.

False. See Chapter 12, Vaccines, for an expanded discussion!

Q. Okay, so what causes autism?

The million-dollar question.

In the 1980's, one in 10,000 kids were diagnosed with autism. Today, one in 88 American eight-year-olds have some form of autism. Boys outnumber girls four to one. The U.S. is not the only country seeing this trend. It is increasingly diagnosed worldwide.

For starters, is it really an epidemic? Or, are more people being diagnosed? Many children who were diagnosed with mental retardation thirty years ago are children who are diagnosed with classic autism today. And mildly disabled kids with autism today are children who never would have had a diagnosis thirty years ago. Those verbal, but socially awkward, children account for the majority of new autism cases.

So what are the hotbeds of research into the causes of autism?

1 **GENETICS.** There no question that genetics play a role. Autism runs in families. I have a family in my practice and all four children have a diagnosis on the autism spectrum.

Studying twins is an obvious way to detect genetic disorders. If one identical twin has autism, up to 90% of the time, so will the other twin. To date, studies suggest there is more than just one "autism gene"—there appear to be several.

Children with autism have several different abnormalities with their DNA. However the X chromosome is one of interest because of the high prevalence of boys with autism. (*Jamain*)

Fragile X Syndrome, which is a known genetic cause of autism, also points to a defective X chromosome in autism spectrum disorders. And Rett Syndrome, which is a disorder causing developmental regression and autistic behaviors in girls, is caused by a defective MECP2 gene located on the X chromosome. (*Chahrour*)

We also know that kids with autism and defects on Chromosome 11 have dysfunctional "neurexin 1 protein." Researchers are looking into how this defective protein affects fetal and infant brain growth.

Finding these specific genetic defects may help in genetic counseling as well as therapies in the future. Animal studies are already underway for targeted genetic therapy in both Fragile X and Rett Syndrome.

2 **ABNORMAL BRAIN GROWTH.** Children with autism spectrum disorders have problems with brain growth. Babies are born with immature

brains that grow rapidly and make nerve connections called synapses . . . like an information superhighway. In the normally growing brain, some branches of this superhighway get "pruned." In the autistic brain, this pruning process seems to be defective. This may explain why babies who are autistic have abnormally rapid head growth under one year of age. No one has yet figured out what causes that defective nerve growth. Of note, boys with autism have higher levels of hormones (insulin-like growth factor) which may contribute to their larger head size, weight, and body mass index. (*Mills*)

3 **ENVIRONMENTAL TRIGGERS.** Is there some environmental exposure that sets off abnormal brain development in a genetically predisposed baby? Maybe. And that exposure may happen at or shortly after conception, before a mother even knows she is pregnant. The embryo has a critical period of brain development at 20-24 days after conception. That is when the developing brain is most sensitive to injury. Studies done by the Environmental Working Group have detected over 280 environmental toxins in umbilical cord blood, so clearly pregnant moms are exposed to a variety of toxins–could one of these be the autism trigger? We don't know.

Viral infections during pregnancy may also be a key environmental trigger that causes abnormal genes in the fetus. Those infections include rubella, CMV, and influenza (yes, "the flu"). (*Fatemi*) Having prolonged fevers during pregnancy also seems to be a risk factor. *(Atladottir)*

Researchers are also exploring whether or not air pollution exposure during fetal development and the first year of life is a possible autism trigger. *(Volk)*

What about vaccines as an environmental trigger? Researchers and scientists have taken a long, hard look at vaccines–and there is conclusive evidence that vaccine exposure is NOT the turn-on switch for autism. (*AAP*) Flip over to Chapter 12, Vaccines for an extended discussion.

The bottom line: there's evidence that newborns who are later diagnosed with autism already have abnormal levels of certain proteins in their brains. So, whatever the trigger is (if there is one), it has been fired before the baby even enters the world.

4 **PREMATURITY.** A developing brain is quite vulnerable. Premature, very low birth-weight babies (under three pounds) have a 25% chance of developing an autism spectrum disorder. (*Limperopoulos*)

5 **OLDER PARENTS.** Another possible reason for the increase of autism: the trend of parents having babies at a later age. Moms who conceive after the age of 40 have a 30% increased risk of having a child with autism. Dads who conceive after the age of 40 have a 50% increased risk of having an autistic child. (*Croen*) Scientists speculate that an older dad's sperm may have defective genetic material, possibly altered by environmental toxins. Dads who are 20 years old at conception pass on 25 different gene mutations. Dads who are 40 at conception pass on 65 genetic mutations.

6 **CLOSELY SPACED PREGNANCIES.** A 2011 study compared to children who were conceived at least three years after their sibling was born, to closer spaced pregnancies and found that babies conceived less than 12 months after the birth of the first-born child were THREE times more likely to be diagnosed with autism spectrum disorder. Babies conceived from 12

to 23 months after the birth of the first-born child had almost two times the risk of autism. And, even babies conceived 23-35 months after the first-born child had a slightly greater risk of autism.

Unfortunately, researchers have no idea why the odds are greater when the spacing between pregnancies is shorter. Perhaps it's because a woman's nutritional stores have not had enough time to be replenished. Or maybe women who have put off parenthood until later in life have more closely spaced babies–and parental age itself is a risk factor for having a child with an autism spectrum disorder.

Thus study alone should not necessarily influence your decision on how long to wait between pregnancies. However, the current recommendation from the Centers for Disease Control is to wait at least 18-23 months between pregnancies for a mother and baby's optimal health. *(Cheslack-Postava)*

7 **OBESITY.** Researchers at UC Davis and Vanderbilt medical school published a 2012 study that found women who were obese (Body Mass Index of 30 or greater) at the beginning of their pregnancies were more likely to have a child diagnosed with autism. Perhaps the altered metabolism affects the intrauterine environment, and thus affects the intricate process of fetal brain development. More research is definitely needed in this area. *(Krakowiak)*

8 **FOLIC ACID DEFICIENCY.** A 2013 Norwegian study showed that women who took folic acid (or prenatal vitamins) at least four to eight weeks before becoming pregnant lowered the risk of having a child with an autism spectrum disorder by 40%. We've known for a long time that folic acid is clearly necessary for proper brain and nervous system development (deficiencies in pregnancy cause spina bifida). So, it isn't a crazy stretch to think this nutritional deficiency in pregnancy could also lead to autism. *(Suren)*

Follow our website at Baby411.com for new information on this topic.

Q. My child has autism. What therapy do you recommend?

The first place to start with is your child's medical provider. He/she can help with both diagnosis and referrals locally in your community. National resources to help you get started include:

The Centers for Disease Control: cdc.gov/ActEarly
American Academy of Pediatrics: aap.org

Early, intensive therapy with developmental specialists is key. Please beware of unproven (and possibly dangerous) therapies that promise a cure for autism. We realize that parents will do anything to help their kids. But we also know that leaves them prey for unscrupulous folks selling snake oil.

Other developmental differences

Q. My baby has Down syndrome. What steps do I take to get help for him?

Down syndrome is the most common of all the known chromosome abnormalities that cause intellectual disability. So it's important to get your baby hooked up with developmental specialists from the start. The AAP recommends that kids with Down syndrome receive early intervention services from 0–3 years of age. That's good news because it means most insurance companies will foot the bill for it!

Down syndrome also causes other potential health problems that need to be assessed. Most large pediatric hospitals and academic centers offer a Down syndrome clinic where an affected child can see all his specialists on the same day (convenient, one-stop shopping!)

Here is a checklist for the health issues associated with Down syndrome:

- *Growth*: Assess at regular well child visit intervals.
- *Sleep*: Evaluate for sleep apnea (snoring, restless sleep) beginning at 1 year of age.
- *Thyroid screening*: Assess as part of newborn metabolic screening, recheck at 6 months of age, 1 year of age, and then annually.
- *Hearing screen:* Formally assess in newborn period, recheck at five years of age, 13 years of age, and then annually. Referral to specialist between 1–2 years of age. Assess for frequent ear infections.
- *Vision screen:* Referral to specialist by six months of age. Formally assess as needed until 13 years of age, and then annually.
- *Heart defect screening:* Heart ultrasound (echocardiogram) performed at prenatal visit. Referral to specialist for periodic assessment in teenage years and adulthood.
- *Blood count:* Newborns need a complete blood count, recheck annually between 13–21 years of age.
- *Celiac disease screening:* Perform at two years of age. Repeat assessment if symptoms of gluten intolerance develop.
- *Periodontal disease screening:* Referral to dentist for regular dental visits every six months.
- *Neck/spine stability screen:* Assessment by neurologic exam, and possibly a screening x-ray. (*AAP*)

For more information and parent resources on Down syndrome, check out the Association for Children with Down syndrome at acds.org.

Q. If my child has a developmental delay, where can I get help?

Want to use a service that makes house calls?

Most states offer an early childhood intervention (ECI) program—Google your state name and "early child intervention" to find a local agency. Your child's development will be screened over the phone. If he qualifies as having a delay, a specially trained physical therapist (large muscles), occupational therapist (small muscles), or speech therapist (language, mouth skills) will show up at your doorstep and do a formal assessment. If help is needed, regular therapy will be scheduled.

Like most government programs, needs often exceed resources of early intervention agencies. Our advice: be a strong advocate for your child. ECI is a great program in theory, but your child may need more intensive services than what the program can offer. If your child qualifies for speech therapy once a month but really needs it once a week, speak up or seek alternative programs.

Besides ECI, another option is to get a referral from your pediatrician to a private specialist in your area. Easter Seals also has a national program that provides services based on ability to pay. Contact them at easter-seals.org or at (800)-221-6827.

Denise's opinion: We've all been at the park and noticed a child who seems to be "hyper" or "slow" or "aggressive" or non-communicative. But no matter how tempting it is, keep your opinions to yourself. Besides, behavior problems on the playground probably have more to do with kids who are tired or hungry than with some kind of serious brain dysfunction.

As the parent of a learning disabled child, I can tell you that no outsider would have known he was anything but normal until he got closer to school age. And kids who *seem* to have delays and problems often sort them out and have no issues by the time they reach kindergarten.

But if you notice your child doesn't seem to be keeping up with other kids his age physically or socially, be sure to bring it up to your doctor at the next well visit. If you don't say anything, your doctor may not notice subtle signs in a ten or 15-minute visit.

Feedback from the Real World

Special babies, Extraordinary Parents: Meredith's Story

"When we first learned of Meredith's diagnosis (developmental delays) our first worry was that there would be nobody to take care of her in the future when we were gone. We now realize that dwelling on that is giving up any hope for the present. When Meredith was finally able to throw a ball, we celebrated all the years in therapy that got her to that moment. When she was able to catch the ball, we marveled that it happened the very next day."—Sarah Barnes and Jim Hemphill, parents of Meredith Hemphill, age 6 (diagnosis: agenesis of the corpus callosum).

Q. My baby was born prematurely. Does the same developmental checklist apply to him?

Yes, but not at first.

Your baby's chronological age will be adjusted by subtracting the number of weeks born prematurely. So, the expectations will be lower initially. Your baby's "age" won't need to be corrected once he is 2 1/2 or 3 years old.

FYI: Because very low birth weight babies (under three pounds) are at greatest risk of developmental delays, they should have a formal developmental screening (in a developmental assessment program or Early Childhood Intervention) at nine to 15 months corrected age, and again at 21-30 months corrected age.

Babies who are born between 32 to under 37 weeks are at higher risk for having learning issues (particularly reading skills) than babies born full term. So, even if your kiddo was a "late preterm infant," he should still be followed closely for developmental delays. (*Chyi*)

Now that we've talked about general developmental milestones and delays, we want to explain a bit about intellectual development and social/emotional development. We'll explore theories from two prominent doctors with their thoughts on the stages your child will go through throughout his life.

How Your Baby Learns

Ever wonder how your baby learns all the amazing things she does? How does she go from being a little lump at birth to a smiling, talking, walking dreamboat by her first birthday? Dr. Jean Piaget, the father of the major accepted theory for cognitive (intellectual) development, believes that a child's brain processes and understands information in different ways at different ages. As a parent, it's helpful to know what "stage" of brain development your child is at, *because your child's reasoning will be different than yours*. And if you are educated about those differences, hopefully, you'll be less perplexed and frustrated by them.

So here is the big picture, stage by stage:

Sensorimotor: Age birth to two years

Babies learn by hearing, feeling, tasting, smelling, moving, and manipulating (that is, using their Five Senses). Babies are **EGOCENTRIC**. In their minds, the world revolves around them. They continue to think this way until about age six or seven years old (although you might think that some adults haven't outgrown this stage yet!).

◆ ***Birth to one month:*** A newborn comes equipped with immature reflexes (sucking, rooting, grasping). He will learn how to use and coordinate them. Newborns have no concept of "self."

◆ ***One to four months:*** Babies realize that they have body parts, and can control them. If you see your baby staring at his hand, it's because he has discovered it.

◆ ***Four to eight months:*** Babies are more interested in the world. They realize their actions can make other people do things. They start to manipulate objects and explore with their mouths. But, people and things don't exist unless they are within a baby's visual field. They do well with routines and predictable events with their limited memory banks.

◆ ***Eight to 12 months:*** Babies grasp the concept of *object permanence*. A baby realizes that a person still exists even when he leaves a room. The same goes for toys, food, etc. A baby this age has a limited repertoire of techniques to explore a new situation. He uses his *memory* of what worked in the past to approach something unfamiliar.

◆ ***12 to 18 months:*** Toddlers have more sophisticated approaches to problem solving (although it won't feel that way to their parents). They experiment systematically. Toddlers go through a trial and error method of attack. Things are explored more with hands than with mouths. They CAN follow directions. (It's a matter of whether or not they CHOOSE to).

◆ ***18 to 24 months:*** As these kids approach two years of age, they can do "trial and error" in their minds, and figure out the solution to a problem (i.e. simple puzzles). They will figure out language, and start to pretend.

Pre-Operational: Age two to seven years

Kids have the concept of symbols representing things (i.e. language, pretend play). Their level of reasoning is based on *their* viewpoint. They are not capable of taking someone else's perspective. They have primitive logical thinking. For example, a full juice cup will look like it has more in it than a half-full water glass.

Concrete Operational: Age seven to eleven years

Kids this age can think logically, order and classify items, compare, and sequence information. But, everything is black and white—there is no *gray* zone.

Formal Operational: Age 12 to Adulthood

This is the age of abstract reasoning— when a child can "think outside of the box." A teenager can take a hypothetical situation and reason it out. (*Brainerd*)

Your Baby's Social and Emotional Growth

As one of the most influential psychologists of the 20th century, Erik Erikson continues to influence our view of social and emotional development today. His theory suggests that personality development rests on how a person deals with a series of stages in his life. A person's sense of identity depends on the outcome of eight crises or conflicts. If a person does not successfully resolve a particular conflict, the unresolved issue persists in later life.

People can also regress to prior stages during times of stress (that is, a four-year-old returns to the Terrible Two's when a baby sister is born).

Again, the big picture....

Trust vs. Mistrust: Birth to 18 months

Infants learn to trust their parents. They learn that their needs are met. Babies who do not get appropriate care have a sense of distrust and apprehension around others.

Autonomy vs. Doubt: 18 months to three years

Children are seeking independence and are trying to gain confidence in their abilities. This happens while parents are trying to set limits on inappropriate behaviors. (This meeting of the minds is also known as the Terrible Two's). Children need some autonomy to rely on their own skill, or else they will begin to doubt themselves.

Initiative vs. Guilt: Three to six years

Children thrive on decision-making and accomplishments. If parents do not support these experiences, the child feels guilty for trying to be independent.

Industry vs. Inferiority: Six to 12 years

Children gain confidence in their skills and want to learn. With failure or lack of support, children feel inferior to others.

Identity vs. Role Confusion: 12 to 18 years

Simply put, teens either figure out who they are and what they want (sense of self) or they are confused and reliant on their peers. (*Harder*)

Now you know the theories behind how babies develop. So you're probably wondering how to put them to work. This is the section for you. Here we're going to discuss how to foster appropriate development for each age and stage. Keep in mind the idea is not to "train" your child to be the next Beethoven, Mary Cassat or Bill Gates.

Birth to Two Months of Age

Q. So what is a general idea of how my baby will develop in the first two months?

Here is a thumbnail sketch.

You may think that your newborn spends his whole life eating and sleeping, but he is actually learning a great deal. Babies are born with an immature nervous system (brain, spinal cord, nerves). So, most of what you see develop is not dramatic in the first two months of life. Instead, development is happening with a baby's neurological system. *Milestones*:

- ***Newborn reflexes.*** Babies suck and turn their head instinctively when you rub their cheeks. They will also grasp anything placed in the hands. If you gently drop their heads back, they will flail their arms out and open their eyes. These reflexes should go away by six months of age.
- ***Motor skills.*** Babies are born with poor head and neck stability. Over the first two months of life, they gain better head control. They should move both arms and legs equally well. A dominant side or hand preference is NOT normal.
- ***Vision.*** Newborns have 20/200 vision. They are not blind. But, they can only see clearly about eight to ten inches in front of them. Putting your face right up to theirs is very entertaining for them. Babies like contrasts (hence, all of the black and white toys at trendy baby stores). By the time your baby is two months old, he will be able to see one to two feet in front of him. He should also be able to fix his eyes on an object and follow it side to side.
- ***Hearing.*** Newborns are born with normal hearing. They startle to loud noises. Babies recognize their parents' voices. They have heard you inside the womb.
- ***Social.*** Newborns are interested in your face. By two months of age, if you smile at your baby, he will smile back (called a social smile). Under six weeks of age, any smiling is a mere coincidence, or gas.
- ***Language.*** Initially, babies cry to express all of their needs. As they approach two months, babies will start to "coo" (ooo and ah noises). They may even start to laugh and squeal.

Q. What kind of developmental stimulation should I provide my birth to two month old?

Give them lots of time with you. Here is a breakdown:

1. Sensorimotor:

- Give your baby interesting things to follow with her eyes (your face, colorful toy).
- Listen to music; play with rattles, music boxes.
- Let your baby touch different objects (your face, your hair, the dog).
- Give your baby short bursts (five minutes) of time on her tummy (a.k.a. Tummy Time) to work on shoulder and stomach muscles. Not only does it strengthen neck and shoulder muscles, it also prevents the flat head issues we discussed earlier in the book (**POSITIONAL PLAGIOCEPHALY**). Many babies hate tummy time at first because it's a lot of work for them! The earlier and more often you do it, the more comfortable they get with tummy time. Get down on the floor with her and give her some encouragement (and entertainment).

2. Language:

- Start a *reading ritual*. Set aside reading time EVERY day until your child packs up and goes to college. There is a great deal of research that proves infants who are read to at early ages have stronger language and cognitive skills than their peers.
- Infants respond best to rhymes and good illustrations. See the end of this chapter for a list of good books for kids age birth to one-year-old.

3. Social:

- Spend time talking and smiling at your baby.

Q. My newborn does not have good head control yet. Is it okay to use an infant baby carrier (Snugli/Baby Bjorn)?

Yes. Holding your baby in your arms 24/7 gets old quickly. These carriers provide enough head support and allow you to use two hands to get something done.

Q. My two month old's eyes cross frequently. Should I worry?

No. A baby's eye muscles are weak initially and frequently are not in sync with each other.

Doctors start testing for lazy eye muscles (see **AMBLYOPIA**) from six to nine months of age. If you notice that one eye turns in, turns out, or only one eye has a "red eye" effect in photographs, let your doctor know. Note: a two month old can follow your face as you move it in front of him. A three month old can follow it for a full 180 degrees.

Old Wives Tale

Letting an infant bear weight on his legs will make him bowlegged.

The truth: Babies like to bear weight on their feet with your support. It's fun–and it won't make them bowlegged.

Two to Four Months of Age

Q. What milestones should I expect my two to four month old to achieve?

- *Gross Motor.* Your baby should have good head control by three months of age. If you lift his body from a lying position, his head should come up at the same time and not lag behind. He may or may not roll over. By four months old, he should bear weight on his legs if you stand him up. Most babies can lift their heads up when lying on their stomachs.
- *Fine Motor.* Your baby will start to realize that his hands are useful. At first he will bat at objects, then start to grab successfully around four months. (This is when moms usually stop wearing hoop earrings and pull their hair back). Your baby should also be able to bring his hands together.
- *Language*. Babies are really experimenting with their voices at this age. They will move on from cooing to laughing and squealing. They may start to "blow raspberries" (spray saliva). This is particularly fun at mealtime. They also experiment with the volume of their voice.
- *Vision*. Your baby's vision improves to about 20/40 by four months of age. So he will be able to see you across the room.
- *Social/Personality.* Your baby will try to imitate social contact with you. Smiling, tickling, and laughing are very entertaining for your baby.

Q. What developmental stimulation can I provide for my two to four month old?

- *Motor*. Give your baby more tummy time (five to ten minutes) several times a day. He will let you know when it's time to turn over. Activity gyms are fun because they can start to bat and grab at the objects.
- *Language/Social.* Keep that reading ritual going. When you are out and about, talk to your baby. He is your companion, so treat him like one. Tell him where you are going and what you are doing. You may feel silly telling him what you are putting in your grocery cart, but all those vocabulary words will be recorded in his growing brain.

Reality Check

A recent study looked at three-month-old babies' brain activity in response to hearing simple phrases. Guess what? Their little brains lit up when they heard phrases they had heard before! While you may not hear your baby talk back to you for a while, there is a

lot going on in there. This study validates the importance of talking to your baby early in life. (*Dehaene-Lambertz*)

Four to Six Months of Age

Q. What developmental milestones will I see with my four to six month old?

- *Gross Motor.* Your baby will sit up with your assistance, then "tri-pod sit" with his hands supporting him between his legs. Eventually, he will sit up without support.

- *Fine Motor.* Your baby has mastered grabbing. He will start to use his fingers more than just his hands. He will "rake" objects to get them into the palm of his hand by six months. He will also start to transfer objects from one hand to the other by six months old.

- *Oral Motor.* Your baby will figure out how to maneuver his tongue to swallow solid food by six months of age (see Chapter 7, "Solids"). This is one of several reasons why it is not recommended to offer solid food before this age.

- *Language*. Your baby will start making the first recognizable sounds of language. Consonant sounds usually progress from B's to D's to M's. This means, you'll first hear "ba-ba" then "da-da" then "ma-ma". The "Ba-Ba" occurs around six months of age. Your baby should also turn to you when you are talking to him by six months.

- *Social/Cognitive.* Your baby is very aware of his surroundings. He knows his family and friends. He knows his room and his crib. Four month olds already thrive on the routine and the expected. But even at six months of age, your baby will not have the concept of "object permanence." So, if you leave the room or a toy leaves his sight, it no longer exists.

Q. My six-month-old is sitting up but he never rolled

NEW PARENT 411: READING PROGRAMS

Reach Out and Read (reachoutandread.org) is a national program that encourages 15-20 minutes a day of reading to young children. In participating doctors' offices, books are given free of charge at well child visits from infancy to five years of age. This allows parents to build a developmentally-appropriate reading library in their homes.

You can also seek out local libraries and national bookstore chains that offer free story times for both infants and toddlers.

The benefits of reading to children at an early age are clear. Set aside special time everyday for reading with your little one!

over. Should I be worried?

No. Welcome to the anti-SIDS generation.

It is easier to roll from tummy to back, than from back to tummy. Babies of our generation spend significantly less time on their tummies because of the "Back to Sleep" campaign to prevent Sudden Infant Death Syndrome. As a result, babies these days often master rolling over about the same time as sitting up (or skip rolling over entirely). Rolling over used to be a four-month milestone. Sitting up is a six-month milestone.

Q. What can I do to foster my four to six month old's development?

- *Gross Motor.* Because babies of this age group aren't quite sitting alone yet, the stationary Exersaucer toys are great. They give babies a sense of independence, and free up their hands to play. However, we don't recommend using them for more than ten or 15 minutes at a time. Some studies have shown that babies who can't see their feet and legs because of the trays on these toys can have delays in walking. Also, be sure to give babies lots of floor time to work on rolling and balancing.

- *Fine Motor.* Give your baby large plastic or plush toys to grab, manipulate, and mouth. Yes, mouth is used as a verb here. Everything your baby examines will go into his mouth to test out. Toys that make noise are fun. The plush caterpillars that have different sounding objects in each segment are popular.

- *Language.* You know the drill by now. Read to your child on a daily basis. Use board books and those designed for tub time (that is, they're waterproof)—these give your child a tactile experience as well. But, for safety reasons, no chewing on vinyl books.

RED FLAG: AVOID WALKERS

The American Academy of Pediatrics strongly discourages the use of walkers. Canada went so far as to ban walkers in 2004. Why? Babies drive these things without taking a driver's ed course. Walkers allow babies to get places that their knees or feet would never take them. This sometimes means falling down a flight of stairs.

New walkers now have some safety devices built in meant to keep them from falling down stairs. Because of the newer safety requirements, there has been a marked decline in the number of injuries caused by walkers.

Even with the new safety standards, Pediatricians see numerous head injuries every year as a result of walkers. Even if a child doesn't fall down the stairs, she can still run into low tables and chairs and knock items off tables (like hot drinks and glass vases, for example). And older, used walkers without the new safety devices are definitely death traps.

- *Social/Personality.* Babies are keenly aware of facial expressions. Get a cheap plastic mirror for hours of fun—your baby will sit there and stare at himself.

Six to Nine Months of Age

Q. What are your expectations for a six to nine month old?

- *Gross Motor.* The main milestone over these three months is locomotion. Your baby will figure out how to get where he wants to go. That may be achieved by rolling, crawling, or "cruising" (walking while holding onto furniture). Some babies skip crawling. Because of this, if you look at the Denver Developmental Checklist, you'll notice that crawling isn't listed. Meanwhile, your baby should also be able to get from lying down to sitting, and from sitting to standing up (holding on to something).
- *Fine Motor.* Your baby will refine his reaching and grabbing skills. The crude "raking" will change to a "pincer grasp" (picking things up between index finger and thumb). Things like lint and dirt on the floor will suddenly become very interesting. This correlates with the ability to self-feed (see finger foods in Chapter 7, "Solids").
- *Oral Motor.* Your baby should be able to maneuver his tongue and chew food with teeth (or gums).
- *Language*. Your baby should be progressing into the D's and M's. We expect a nine month old to say "Dada" and "Mama", but don't expect them to know the meaning of those words until about 14 months. Everything you are saying is recorded in your little one's big brain. His receptive language is quite good (that is, he understands what you are saying). *Your nine month old understands the word, "No." Whether he chooses to respond to it is another story.*
- *Cognitive/Social*. Ah, the light has turned on. Somewhere between six and nine months, your baby will have achieved "object permanence." This is a MAJOR concept. He realizes that people and things still exist, even if he can't see them anymore. So, if you leave the room, he will look for you. This, understandably, creates some anxiety (see "separation anxiety" in the next chapter).
- *More social issues.* Another concept that arises is *stranger anxiety*. Not only will your baby want to know your every move, but he won't want to hang out with anyone but you. Don't get too frustrated. When your baby is so independent that he wants nothing to do with you, you will look back fondly at these days. Your baby also is picking up social cues. He will smile to engage others. He might wave bye-bye by nine months of age. He also is starting to figure out how to express his needs non-verbally. Finally, your baby will start testing the limits of his world. At nine months old, your real parenting job begins. You need to set limits on your baby's behaviors STARTING NOW (see Chapter 11, Discipline).
- *Vision*. Your baby's vision is 20/20 by six months of age.

Old Wives Tale

A baby who skips crawling and walks first won't be able to do higher math.

The truth: Where did this one come from? I crawled before I walked and still couldn't figure out calculus—so there. It has no bearing on intelligence.

Q. What developmental stimulation can I provide for my six to nine month old?

- *Gross Motor*. Provide a SAFE environment for your baby to move around in (see safety section below). Your house is now his playground.

- *Fine Motor.* Provide SAFE toys for your baby to feel, touch, maneuver, and taste. Babies explore with their hands first, then their mouths. If you are buying toys, pick ones that make sounds or lights when manipulated. Before you rush to Toys R Us, look around your kitchen. Old measuring cups, Tupperware, seasoning bottles (sealed shut), pots, pans, and wooden spatulas are often a hit with this age group. If you actually venture to a restaurant, those individually wrapped crackers are a real crowd pleaser until your meal arrives.

- *Language*. Do you have a Barnes & Noble Member Card or Amazon Prime? Now would be a good time to take the plunge—reading books to your baby is key to language development. Use your local library as your baby gets older, but for now buy some cardboard books (called board books) of your own. Your baby's library will double as his teething toys.

- *Even More Language*. When you speak to your baby, use single words and short phrases. Otherwise, you will sound like the teacher in the Peanuts cartoon to him. Your baby will start to show you

development

DR B'S OPINION: BABY SIGN LANGUAGE

We know that children are capable of understanding language and communicating non-verbally long before they are able to speak. So, teaching an older baby or toddler hand gestures to communicate makes sense. And there is scientific proof that signing is beneficial. One study found that infants and toddlers that were "sign talkers" spoke earlier and performed slightly higher on IQ tests at age eight that their non-signing friends. (*Brenner*)

While your baby may only learn a few signs, sitting down with your child to learn any new skill has its merits. You don't need to buy a book to learn sign language. You can create the hand gestures on your own (check out *Meet the Fockers* on Netflix sometime). If you choose not to teach your child sign language, do not fear...your child will master the universal "point and grunt" skill to tell you what he wants.

what he wants. Instead of saying, "Oh, do you want the rubber ducky?" say, "Duck?" That will teach him the vocabulary word he is looking for. The same language rules apply for discipline. Instead of saying, "Oh, no, Honey, don't bite Mommy's shoulder!" say, "No biting." (Yes, there is more coming on this in the next chapter).

- *Social/Personality.* Your baby is a social being and is very responsive to family members. Your baby will imitate the way you respond to situations. He follows your lead. Be a good role model. Since your baby now has object permanence, playing peek-a-boo is fun. It's also fun to hide toys under a blanket and let your baby look for them. How easy it is to amuse a child this age!

Nine to Twelve Months of Age

Q. What are the developmental milestones for a nine to 12 month old?

- *Gross Motor.* Your baby should definitely have his sea legs. He should be able to stand holding on to someone's hand or a piece of furniture. He probably will be able to pull up to stand and get back down to a sitting position. One day, you'll go into the nursery and be shocked to find your baby standing up in his crib grinning at you. Your baby may or may not be taking his first steps at his birthday party. It's still within developmental limits to be walking by 15 months old.

- *Fine Motor.* Your baby should be good at picking up small items. He will also start banging objects together. Babies this age get really good at pointing.

- *Oral Motor.* Your baby should learn how to drink liquids from a cup. Ideally, she will be able to drink from a real cup, but most parents seem to prefer the no-spill sippy variety. Drinking from a straw is also something that works well for a child this age. By one year of age, your baby should graduate from a bottle to a cup (see Chapter 6, "Liquids" for details).

- *Social/Personality.* As your baby approaches his birthday, he will be very good at expressing his needs non-verbally. There is a universal "point and grunt" that babies around the world know how to do. As his expressive language improves, there will be less frustration due to communication barriers.

- *Anxiety.* Separation anxiety peaks at nine to 12 months, then again at 15 to 18 months. Remember that anxiety stems from the fear that you are leaving permanently. Ease these fears by kissing your baby goodbye and telling him when you will be back. Keep it short and sweet, and make your exit.

- ***Language.*** From nine to 12 months, your baby may start to say "Mama" and "Dada" and mean it. He may also say a word or two (but it's more likely to happen if you have a girl). Regardless of sex, your baby will speak with great confidence in some foreign language. If you listen to him (via monitor) in his crib at night, you should hear a whole monologue going on. This singsong intonation of speech is called "jabbering." Even though there aren't any vocabulary words, you know your baby has been listening to you.

Babies start to imitate their parents' activities. You may catch him pretending to dust and sweep. You may have a cleaning buddy!

Your baby will make it clear that she wants to be in charge and independent (in simple terms, it's her way or the highway). It is important to begin discipline and setting limits.

Your child will have conflicting moods. He may happily leave you behind, but then call for your help. Your availability as a consultant teaches your child to turn to adults for problem solving. Your child's sense of self (ego) is developing. Praising your child for small accomplishments gives him confidence.

Q. My one year old son isn't talking yet. All of the girls in his playgroup are yakking up a storm. Should I be worried?

Girls are talkers. Boys are walkers.

There is no question that girls learn language skills more quickly than boys. And once we start talking, you can't shut us up! Boys tend to reach motor milestones more quickly than girls—hence the roughhousing and athletic skills that you see later on. It's very interesting to watch. Clearly, parents have some hand in the way children develop along gender lines, but a lot of it is pre-determined.

However, if your one year old son or daughter has no signs of non-verbal communication skills (babbling, pointing/grunting), it's time to get it checked out.

Q. We speak two languages in our house. Will our child learn both?

Yes. She will have excellent receptive language skills in both languages (that is, she'll understand both) long before she speaks either language.

NEW PARENT 411: CAR SEATS & HEAD CONTROL

Children should be at least two years of age to sit forward-facing in a car seat. Why? A child under two lacks neck support to avoid injury in a car accident when forward-facing. Hence, rear-facing is safer. That's the official advice from the American Academy of Pediatrics—a child should ride rear-facing until age two. The good news: most car seats (both infant and convertible) work rear-facing to 30 or 40 lbs.

Q. What can I do to foster my baby's development from nine to 12 months?

- *Gross Motor.* Offer a wide-open space for your child to roam. Start playing with a ball. Toys that can be pushed are fun for babies who are walking (lawn mower, grocery cart, baby buggy).
- *Fine Motor.* Play pat-a-cake. Offer toys that your baby can bang together. It's also fun to get "cause and effect" toys (your baby pushes a button that causes a toy to move or make a noise; Jack-in-the-Box). Now is the time to buy "the classics." These toys are called stacking cups (plastic cups of various sizes) and shape sorters (cylinder with plastic shapes and matching holes in the top). Toys that can be filled and dumped are also entertaining.
- *Social*. Let your child participate in activities of daily living. While you are cooking dinner, let your baby "cook" his own meal on the floor with old pots and pans. While you are cleaning up, give him a towel, too. Start reviewing body parts with your child as a part of his vocabulary. You can also begin giving jobs to your baby. He should be able to follow one-step directions (such as "Bring me the ball.")
- *Language*. Books, books, and more books. Picture books with a single picture and word on each page encourage vocabulary words. Remember to converse with your child as your companion. Continue to identify items in single words and short phrases. Singing songs helps with language skills, and helps pass the time in traffic. Your baby doesn't mind if you can't carry a tune.

If you're looking for a great resource on the best toys to buy for your child, check out the *Oppenheimer Toy Portfolio* (web: toyportfolio.com). The book and accompanying web site rate and review toys, books, videos, software and music for kids. You can find age appropriate toys that are geared toward stimulating your child's development.

Don't forget friends' toys. When you take your child to another kid's house for a play date, they get exposed to a whole other set of toys. Some parents even get together and toy swap so their kids get different toys but don't have to spend oodles of money on them.

Feedback from the Real World: Multiples

"Don't buy two of everything!Twins learn to share early on. Instead, have a few different options and swap them around to keep them entertained."*–Agustina, mom of Gael and Malena.*

Q. When should I buy shoes for my baby?

When he is a good walker.

There is no medical reason to wear shoes. Most babies use their toes to grasp the floor when they are trying to walk. For this reason, we encourage your baby to travel the house in bare feet. If you are out in public, by all means, put shoes on your child. You don't need to buy expensive shoes. But, it is a good idea to get your child's foot measured when you buy that

first pair of shoes to ensure proper fit.

The hottest trend: Robeez. These are soft leather moccasins meant for protection and flexibility. Did we mention, pricey? Does your baby NEED these shoes? No. They are not a medical miracle. But they are a nice alternative to socks if your child will be exiting his stroller on your travels.

Helpful Hints

- *Take a CPR course* and have any caregivers who are taking care of your child take one, also. The biggest potential problem for a child after nine months is choking. Kids this age do not get the famous Heimlich maneuver– they get back blows to force out the foreign object. You'll want to find out how to perform this if you don't know already.

- ***Have Poison Control's phone number by your kitchen phone.*** The national number is: 1-800-222-1222. You can find your local Poison Control number from the American Association of Poison Control Centers' web site at aapcc.org. Always call poison control first if your child has ingested something. FYI: It is no longer recommended to have syrup of Ipecac in your medicine cabinet. Not all toxic chemicals should be removed by vomiting because they can burn the esophagus and mouth when coming back up.

Q. Where can I get information about toy safety? I have heard about baby product recalls.

Check out the U.S Consumer Product Safety Commission Hotline on the web at cpsc.gov or toll free at 1-800-638-2772.

Q. When can my baby start watching TV?

I'm so glad you asked! As one of the authors of the 2011 American Academy of Pediatrics policy statement on media use in kids under age two, I can answer this question and explain the rationale behind it.

The short answer: the AAP discourages *passive* media programs viewed on all screens (TV, DVD's, smartphones, tablets, etc.) for kids under two years of age. *(AAP)* Note: the AAP's advice is specific to passive screen time, where a child is simply viewing a show. There is currently no official AAP position on apps or computer games, where a child is engaging in activity (interactive media).

Once children turn two, the AAP recommends limiting total recreational screen time to two hours a day. *(AAP)* Despite that recommendation, 90% of kids under age two watch TV every day and 26% even have a TV in their bedrooms. (*Kaiser Family Foundation*)

Why are the experts so negative on TV? What's the harm, you say? Sure, we know that a 30-minute kiddie show might buy you time to take a much-needed shower. And don't "educational" shows help kids learn?

Here's why TV and other forms of passive media is bad for babies under age two:

1 **WATCHING A SHOW ON A SCREEN IS A LOW ENERGY ACTIVITY**. If a screen is turned on, your child is sitting down (unless you are doing an aerobics video). The average school age child watches an astounding three

hours a day. Yep, that's three hours sitting on their butts. Do you want to start this couch-potato habit in infancy?

2 **IT'S ONLY EDUCATIONAL WHEN YOU CAN UNDERSTAND IT.** Studies have shown that educational programming is beneficial for kids… BUT only for children who understand the content. The magic age to understand TV is two years old. While there are some very bright 18 month olds who "get it," the majority of kids don't, and thus do not gain any knowledge by watching. It gets lost in translation. The reality: those baby videos that *claim* developmental stimulation have no data to back up those claims (heck, why spend money doing a study when the product sells like hotcakes). Bottom line: even Sesame Street, which is an educational show, is not appropriate for your baby to watch. (*Anderson*)

3 **SCREEN TIME DISPLACES OTHER ACTIVITIES.** The time kids are watching screens is time they are not spending with their family, engaging in conversation, playing with someone, or playing independently. These are important activities for kids of all ages. (*Vandewater*) *That* is the harm of TV for babies. We know you can't sit down and play with your child 24/7. But realize that independent or solo play is a valuable use of your child's time. That is how kids fine-tune skills that they need in this world (like problem-solving or using their imagination.)

4 **SCREEN TIME INTERFERES WITH TALK TIME.** If a parent and child are in the same room (even if both are working on individual tasks) and screens are off, a parent is more likely to chat with a child. That "Talk Time" is a necessary part of learning language and social skills. When screens are on, parents talk time goes down by 85%.

5 **MANY PROGRAMS ARE INAPPROPRIATE FOR CHILDREN.** For instance, the evening news can be very graphic and disturbing (and don't think your baby/child isn't watching because it's "your" show). Even children's programs can be problematic. Have you watched a cartoon lately? The average cartoon has 20 violent scenes per hour. The violence that occurs does have an impact. Studies have shown a direct influence on children's behaviors after watching cartoons. (*AAP*)

So, here are some suggestions:

- ***After your child turns two or older, limit your child's screen time (a daily limit is good).*** Have house rules and stick to them.
- ***Know what your child is watching.*** Any PBS show is usually a good bet. Cartoon Network shows require a parent preview. Yes, that means sitting down and watching without your child to see if that show is appropriate. You can also cheat and go to commonsensemedia.org to get expert and parent reviews of programs.
- ***Participate WITH your child.*** Talk about what you are seeing. Stress to your child the "make believe" part. As your child gets older, explain the advertisements.
- ***Keep screens out of your child's bedroom.*** Let's get real here—your kids will learn how to master just about any screen you put in front of them…probably better than you. So, any screen that lives in a child's room gives your little one free access without

supervision. Bad idea.

- ***No screens at meal times***—no exception for kids' shows OR the news or checking your Facebook page. This not only interferes with important time together as a family, but it also encourages people to continue eating after they are full.

BOTTOM LINE

Many baby videos and websites have clever marketing pitches—watch THIS video and your child will be smarter! Stronger! Wealthier!

The truth: your baby will be smarter if *you sit down for 15 minutes and play with him*—no screen time required. Children learn much better when they are actively participating in a learning activity. No kiddie program will make your child an Einstein or a Mozart.

Reality Check

Have a media management plan for everyone in your family—that includes YOU. Screen time is distracting for parents. That all-important "talk time" gets reduced when a parent is watching her own adult show or even has the TV on in the background while preparing dinner. And even if the show on the screen is intended for grown-ups, a child playing in the same room will look up at the screen about every 20 seconds and be less attentive to his play. Just turn it off and watch your shows later.

And don't get us started on parents who check email, latest stock quotes, or Facebook posts on smartphones while their little ones play on the playground, or worse, in the pool. Turn it off!

development

Q. But I just need 15 minutes to take a shower or prepare dinner. Is a little screen time okay to entertain my child?

We hear you—as parents of four children ourselves, we know there are times you just want to take a shower. Or cook dinner. Yes, this means taking your attention away from your child.

But what is your child to do during this brief period of time? We know the simple answer is to turn on a kid TV show or DVD as a babysitter. While there are no studies that suggest this will leave a permanent scar on your child, here is an alternative:

It's called *independent play.* Crazy, eh?

Yes, you have our blessing to let your child find something to do with his time! And yes, it stimulates your child's creativity and problem solving skills. He can be sitting in the bathroom while you take a shower. Or on the floor in the kitchen with some age-appropriate toys (plastic bowls and wooden spoons do nicely).

We'd argue this is time well spent. Our kids have become the Entertained Generation—if they aren't plugged in, they're bored. The take home message: you do NOT have to entertain or find entertainment for your child 24/7. Let them play on their own.

Q. What about iPads and educational Apps? Are these ok?

Great question. The AAP has no official recommendation on interactive media and young children—yet. AAP policies are based on scientific evidence and in this case, science lags far behind the pace of technology.

Our advice: the answer depends on how much you trust your baby with an expensive piece of equipment (does AppleCare cover drool damage?) and how you decide to manage your family's media time. Trust us, once the cat is out of the bag, your child will be as addicted to it as you are.

There are some great interactive apps that let kids test cause and effect, learn vocabulary words, and practice problem-solving skills. Just know that an app can never replace some toys. There is real value in figuring out how to take two blocks in your hands and stack them up on top of each other so they don't fall over. You can't do that on an iPad. Remember that young children are tactile learners and need to experience real people and real things–not just virtual ones.

Q. What do you think of "Mommy and Me" and other community programs for babies?

For babies, these are a mixed bag. For the most part, Mommy gets more out of these programs than babies less than one year of age. Look for programs that focus on singing, story time, and finger plays. The more motor oriented programs (Gymboree, Little Gym) are more appropriate for toddlers (over one year in age). One tip: watch a class or two before you sign up so you aren't wasting your time.

Q. Should my baby take an infant swim class?

Sure. It can be a fun way to bond with your baby and get out of the house. And it may actually help prevent a drowning.

Recent research suggests that swim classes may be an important part of drowning prevention–which is why the American Academy of Pediatrics now recommends beginning swim lessons when a child shows signs of interest and developmental readiness. Children ages 1-4 who have had some formal swimming instruction are less likely to drown.

The other keys to prevention include pool fencing, adult supervision (and we really mean supervision–without distraction), and a CPR-trained parent or caregiver sitting poolside. (*Brenner*) For more water safety information, check out colinshope.org, an advocacy group founded by a family who lost their son, Colin, in a drowning accident at a community pool. Not only is it chock full of useful information, it's near and dear to my heart because Colin was my patient.

Many community pools offer "parent and me" classes. Check with a local office of the Red Cross or your city's parks and rec department for more info.

NEW PARENT 411: FINDING THE BEST TOYS

The best place to find great toys are to look in your own home. Old bowls, wooden spoons, measuring cups, and Tupperware can entertain a child more than you think.

But, if you are in the market for toys, it is worth doing a little research. The Oppenheimer Toy Portfolio is a great resource. Visit their website at toyportfolio.com.

Reality Check

By swimming instruction, we are NOT endorsing the Infant Swimming Resource (ISR) programs where babies are repeatedly immersed in water until they learn to roll to their backs and float. Look for Red Cross approved lessons.

Q. What books do you recommend if I want to learn more about child development?

Touchpoints by Dr. T. Berry Brazelton. He has a beautiful style to approaching development, developmental stimulation, and the challenges within these topics. Brazelton has a "cup is half full" way of viewing your child's struggles with growth and independence.

BOTTOM LINE

The most critical developmental stimulation for your baby is *the time you spend with him*. You don't need to buy expensive toys

NEW PARENT 411: TOP 14 SAFETY TIPS

Now is the time to make your home safe. Put this one on the Honey-Do List.

Children start to explore their world as a natural part of their development. Make their world safer so they can accomplish their goals. Here are the Top Safety Tips:

1. ***Safety gates need to be at the top and bottom of the stairs.*** The best and safest option is to permanently install gates (instead of using pressure gates).
2. ***Electrical outlets need to have plastic safety covers.***
3. ***Get down on the floor*** and look at the world through your child's eyes. Electrical cords and telephone cords need to be moved behind furniture.
4. ***Toxic cleaning products in lower cabinets need to be moved.***
5. ***Cabinet locks on cabinets*** with knives, glass containers, and china.
6. ***Coffee tables and fireplace hearths with corners need safety bumpers.***
7. ***Anchor bookshelves to the wall.***
8. ***Get toilet lid locks so your baby cannot fall in.***
9. ***Set your hot water heater to 120 degrees or less.***
10. ***Get cord shorteners*** or wall brackets to avoid dangling drapery cords.
11. ***Remove any toys hanging over the crib*** by the time your baby is five months old.
12. ***Keep medicine out of reach.*** Be especially watchful of grandparents who come to visit. They are more likely to a) be taking a medication and b) be leaving it out on a bathroom counter.
13. ***If you drop something, pick it up.*** Otherwise, your baby will do it for you and stick it into his mouth.
14. ***If you are a gun owner*** (remember I live in Texas, y'all), ***lock 'em up.*** Guns should *never* be accessible to children. Store ammunition elsewhere and lock it up, too.

or park him in front of "developmentally appropriate" DVD's. Nor do you need to enroll your baby in a special preschool program. We'll discuss preschool at length in our *Toddler 411* book (see the back of this book for details). For now, just concentrate on spending time with your baby.

Q. Can you give me some ideas for age appropriate toys for babies?

Here are some guidelines:

Infants birth to six months:

Look for: bright primary color, clear lines, features, human faces
Fine Motor (manipulatives): soft blocks, rattles, squeeze toys, keys on a ring, activity gyms.
Other sensory activities: Tape recordings of you singing or reading a story, music boxes, mobiles, mirrors, hand held puppets

Infants six to 12 months:

Look for: things safe to go in the mouth, things to stack, pour, dump, things to push, turn, or press, things to open and shut
Gross Motor Play (large muscles): Push toys, Low climbing platform
Fine Motor: soft blocks, easy puzzles, squeeze-squeaky toys, pop-up boxes containers to empty and fill, nesting cups, water toys
Other sensory: music boxes songs, tapes, tapes of you

This list is derived from The Consumer Products Safety Commission guide called *Which Toys for Which Child: A Consumer's Guide for Selecting Suitable Toys, Ages Birth Through Five*. Check out their website at cpsc.gov for your own copy.

Recommended books for birth to age one

We suggest buying the board book versions if you can find them. Not only will your baby enjoy listening to the stories, but he'll want to help turn the pages. He's also likely to use them as a teething toy at some point (as we discussed earlier). If you want the books to have a decent lifespan, go cardboard.

Here are some favorite titles:

Margaret Wise Brown: *Good Night Moon, Runaway Bunny, The Big Red Barn*
Eric Carle: *The Grouchy Ladybug, The Very Busy Spider, The Very Hungry Caterpillar*
Eric Hill: *Where's Spot?*
Bill Martin, Jr.: *Brown Bear, Brown Bear, What Do You See?*
Golden Books: *Pat The Bunny, The Pokey Little Puppy*
Nancy White Carlstrom: *Jesse Bears' Yum Yum Crumble*
Dr. Seuss: *Mr. Brown Can Moo! Can You?*
Sandra Boynton: *Barnyard Dance!*
Tedd Arnold: *Five Ugly Monsters*
Jan Pienkowski: *Little Monsters, Oh My a fly!*
Paul Strickland: *Dinosaur Roar!*
Stephen Losordo: *Cow Moo Me*

Discipline & Temperament

Chapter 11

"Any child can tell you that the sole purpose of a middle name is so he can tell when he's in trouble."
~ Dennis Fakes

What's in this Chapter

- Figuring out your baby's temperament
- The high maintenance baby
- Tips for soothing the savage beast
- Pacifiers
- Colic
- Infant massage
- Tips on planting the seeds of discipline
- Separation anxiety
- Masturbation
- Thumbsucking
- Biting and being bitten

Every parent will go through it. You can see it coming. Your son snuck out last night to hang with his buddies after you explicitly told him he couldn't. So he's grounded. You took the car keys. He has to bum a ride to school or, worse, take the bus. Maybe you remember when you did exactly that or something like it.

Okay, so you don't have to worry about this scenario yet, but you do need to set up the foundation for what seems like a lifetime of discipline. And now that you know all about child development, you can take all that knowledge and apply it to guiding your child's behaviors today and into the future.

But before we get to discipline, we'll need to discuss temperament. Call it the "getting to know the real you" section of the book. Once you figure out your little angel's temperament, you can tailor your discipline issues to fit him like a glove. Or at least that's the theory.

Believe it or not, your baby's doctor may be a good resource to help you sort through these issues. If she doesn't have all of the answers, she can point you in the right direction to get the answers.

Temperament and discipline issues are the toughest part of your job description. Here is a general list of what you will be facing this first year:

AGE	FUN CHALLENGE
0-3 months	Learning your baby's temperament
	Colic
3-4 months	Night feeding/sleep issues
9 months	Separation anxiety
	Stranger anxiety
	Night wakenings
	Limit setting
12 months	Aggressive behaviors (biting, hitting)

(*Harriett Lane Handbook*)

Temperament: Getting to know YOUR baby

Every baby is different. We know that's not news to you. No matter how much advice you get, or how many books you read, no one can tell you what YOUR child's emotional needs will be. You will realize when you have a crying baby on your hands that you'd better figure out your child ASAP . . .or check into the nearest mental health facility.

Q. What are the typical temperaments of babies?

Landmark research done in the 1970's described the three main types of temperaments. Every child doesn't fit into only one category all the time, but here are the groups:

1 **EASY CHILD.** Surprisingly, 40% of kids fit in this category. These babies have regular eating, sleeping, and elimination habits. They are usually happy and easy going. They are interested in exploring new things and don't mind change.

2 **DIFFICULT CHILD.** Only 10% of kids fit in this category. These babies have more irregular eating, sleeping, and elimination schedules. They have trouble with change, transitions, and new experiences. These babies are intense.

3 **SLOW TO WARM UP CHILD.** About 15% of kids fit here. These kids are also difficult because it takes them a while to adjust to change in environment or care provider. They hide in their shells when they encounter a new situation.

4 **THE REST.** Thirty-five percent of kids don't fit into any of the above categories and have "mixed" temperaments. (*Thomas*)

BOTTOM LINE

Figuring out what type of baby you have will help you to *anticipate* how your child will react to certain situations. Plus, you'll have a better idea on how to make his world (and yours) a better place. For example, a difficult baby needs extra time getting into his car seat without a fight. Plan extra time in your schedule for coaxing if you have some place you need to be.

Real world parent story: It always amazes us to watch our child-less friends decide to go somewhere (like a restaurant). They just pick up their keys, lock the door and poof! They're gone. For parents of children, it is a 20 (or 30 or 40) minute odyssey that first involves finding shoes/socks, coats, toys, books, etc. Then someone has to have a diaper change. It then takes more time to buckle in the car seat, only to discover a child has forgotten their toy and then the process repeats. As a parent, outings require the pre-planning that usually goes into staging a small-scale military invasion—remembering to bring that diaper bag (honey, do we have any wipes?), wallet, purse, keys . . . as well as your sanity. Then add in a "difficult" baby and you may as well just stay home.

DR B'S OPINION

"View your baby's temperament . . . as a cake mold. While you can't break the mold, you can control how the cake is baked. How you interact with your baby can positively impact his future!"

Q. When will I be able to figure out my child's temperament?

By the time a baby turns one, most parents have his number—you know what kind of child you have on your hands.

Of course, some temperaments are more difficult to live with than others. But all have their strengths. When you are feeling frustrated with your baby, think about how successful he will be in the future with those traits!

Here are seven questions to help you understand your child's temperament:

1. ***Adaptability***: How does your baby respond to change or new situations?
2. ***Regularity***: Does your baby follow a schedule with sleep and mealtimes?
3. ***Mood***: Is your baby's attitude positive or negative about life?
4. ***Persistence***: Does your baby persist at activities or give up easily?
5. ***Sensitivity***: Is your baby sensitive or oblivious to environmental changes (like noises, smells, tastes, lights)?
6. ***Intensity***: Is your baby laid back or intense?
7. ***Energy***: Is your baby energetic or quiet? (*Kurcinka*)

Q. As a doc, what is your view of infant temperament?

There are high-maintenance babies and low-maintenance babies. If you are blessed with a high maintenance baby, recruit family and friends to help out.

High-maintenance babies require more physical and emotional strength from their parents. These babies get walked around, rocked, and soothed more than their low maintenance friends. Parents of these babies are exhausted and frequently at wits end. They have irrational thoughts about giving their baby up for adoption. Don't worry—you are not alone.

Low-maintenance babies need little intervention, and therefore need little discussion here.

Q. Can you predict a child's future personality based on their temperament as an infant?

Yes.

Elements of a child's temperament will persist through a lifetime. However, all humans adapt to succeed in the face of life's challenges. The way you respond to your child has a *tremendous* impact on your child's personality. It's that heredity vs. environment thing—both have an influence on behavior.

Q. I have an extremely active baby. Can you tell if he has Attention Deficit Disorder (ADD)?

No.

Attention Deficit Disorder is a diagnosis based on the shortened attention span of a child compared to peers his age. All babies under one year of age have fleeting abilities to pay attention to anything for very long. It's virtually impossible to make a diagnosis of ADD in a child less than three years of age.

Will your very active baby ultimately have ADD? Only time will tell. As we discussed in the previous chapter, armchair quarterbacks (namely, other parents at your local park) may be quick to offer a diagnosis for your child on this subject. Don't listen to them!

Q. Why is my baby crying?

Because he can't talk. The average baby cries one to four hours a day.

If you had no other way of communicating you'd be crying, too. Babies are trying to tell you something when they cry. It's your job to play detective and figure out what it is. Yes, there are certain types of cries (I'm hungry, tired, in pain), and that will give you some clues. The truth is, when you spend 24 hours a day with your crying baby, you will get each other figured out—we have no doubt about it. Welcome to Hell Week—you are about to be initiated as a parent.

Read the next box for a reasonable cry management approach.

Reality Check

A recent study done at a clinic for babies with colic showed that two-thirds of the babies referred actually had gastroesophageal reflux (that is, heartburn). (*High*)

BOTTOM LINE

The mistake most parents make is that they give their newborn more credit than they deserve. Newborns have simple needs. Your baby is not nearly as sophisticated as the baby in E*TRADE commercials. They don't cry because you are a bad parent, because they are lonely, or because you have gone back to work and they are mad at you.

Most of the time, your baby just can't pull it together to fall asleep and needs some soothing. Depending on your baby's temperament, that may mean a little—or a lot—of soothing.

NEW PARENT 411: THE 3 RULES OF CRY MANAGEMENT

Rule #1: DON'T PANIC—the most important advice!

Rule #2: Go through your baby's To Do List. Is your baby crying because she:

- Needs to eat?
- Needs a diaper change?
- Is overtired and having trouble falling asleep?
- Is a high-maintenance baby and doesn't know what she wants?

Rule #3: Rule out medical causes if crying persists over two hours straight. A good rule of thumb is that medical reasons for crying are generally not fixed by holding and rocking your baby. For example, your baby may be saying:

- I'm having heartburn. (This is probably the most common medical reason—see **GASTROESOPHAGEAL REFLUX DISEASE**).
- I have colic. I do this every night. (See later in the chapter for more discussion on colic.)
- I have a fever. (If your baby is under *three* months old, call your doctor ASAP.)
- I have gas, constipation, or milk intolerance (Memo to new parents: usually this is NOT the cause, but every parent is convinced that this is the problem).
- I have a really serious medical problem (also rare, but that's why you should call your doctor).

discipline

Old Wives Tale

Picking your newborn up every time he cries will spoil him.

The truth: Your newborn does not have a neurological maturity to relax and settle down on his own. You need to do the work to comfort him—*given his age*. From birth to two months, you do whatever it takes. There is no such thing as spoiling a newborn. As babies reach four to six months of age, they are quite capable of self-soothing. Wait to see if your baby can settle on her own before intervening.

Top Ten Tricks for Soothing a New Baby (under three months of age)

1 **LET YOUR BABY SUCK ON YOUR FINGER.** Sucking is incredibly soothing for newborns. Pacifiers are okay, too. (More on this below).

2 **DO THE BABY BURRITO WRAP.** Swaddle your baby in a receiving blanket. They are used to being snug in the womb, without limbs flailing around. See the How to Swaddle a Baby box in Chapter 9, "Sleep" for a how-to lesson.

3 **ROCKING.** Either sitting in that expensive rocking chair you bought, or walking around and gently swaying baby back and forth in your

arms. (Much as YOU would like to be sitting in that chair, babies often prefer you to walk around.) Singing or humming is also helpful.

4 **GO FOR A WALK IN THE STROLLER.** A change of scenery often helps baby and parent.

5 **GO FOR A CAR RIDE.** When parents call me about prolonged (over two hours straight) crying, I tell them to go for a car ride. If a few trips around the block don't make the crying stop, I'll tell them to keep on driving to the nearest emergency room.

6 **USE A VIBRATING INFANT SEAT OR INFANT SWING.**

7 **TAKE A TRIP TO THE LAUNDRY ROOM.** Put your baby in his car seat and place on top of the dryer. Turn on the dryer. Vibration is particularly helpful for colicky babies. Don't leave your child unattended, however.

8 **GIVE YOUR BABY A BATH.**

9 **TRY SOME INFANT MASSAGE** (see later in this chapter for more info).

10 **PUT YOUR BABY IN BED AND LEAVE HIM ALONE.** If you have tried everything and now you are crying, too, it's time to let your baby cry it out. They are truly exhausted at this point and will fall asleep on their own.

Feedback from the Real World: Multiples

"My twin stroller turned out to be my best friend, both indoors and outdoors. I used it whenever my two hands weren't enough. If necessary, I could simultaneously bottlefeed them in the stroller. During bath time it was the best way I found to focus all my attention on the one in the water and know that the other one was safe and secure in the stroller next to me. It was also my crutch anytime they were crying in unison. I would strap them in and do laps around my kitchen and living room which calmed them every time!"–*Agustina, mom to Gael and Malena, 18 months old*

The Great Binky Debate

Q. Is it okay to use a pacifier?

Sucking is soothing. And it is one of the few skills a newborn possesses. That's why pacifiers and thumb sucking are such popular pastimes for the diaper-clad set.

Yes, by four to six months of age, babies have other ways to calm themselves. And by the time babies reach their first birthdays, they are more than developmentally ready to lose the binky and move on. But do they *need* to? And, is there any harm in clinging to the pacifier after a birthday

or two (or more)?

We've all seen binky-addicted preschoolers. Case in point: years ago, then five-year old Suri Cruise graced the tabloids with a binky in her mouth (which sadly clashed with her Dolce&Gabbana handbag).

So let's tackle the Great Binky Debate! Where do the experts weigh in? Pediatricians, lactation consultants, speech pathologists, and orthodontists all have their own opinions.

The American Academy of Pediatrics states that pacifiers offer some protection against Sudden Infant Death Syndrome, which occurs exclusively in babies under one year of age (90% of cases occur in babies less than six months of age). That's all the AAP says on the matter.

However, pacifiers are a known risk factor for ear infections. They are also a sleep crutch, requiring a parent to repeatedly return to the crib-side for re-insertion when the child pops it out of his mouth. For those reasons, many pediatricians advise kicking the pacifier habit sooner rather than later.

The International Lactation Consultant Association (ILCA) has no official position. Although many lactation experts feel that pacifiers sabotage breastfeeding success, research shows that pacifiers don't have an impact—that is, when a family is motivated to breastfeed. (*Jaafar*)

Do pacifiers cause speech impediments? The research is inconclusive, according to Shelley Solka, MS, CCC-SLP, an Austin-based speech language pathologist. "Pacifier-using children plug themselves up and don't have a chance to use their words," she said. "Instead they point and grunt to communicate. Speech starts developing earlier than parents think and if a child is using the pacifier, they may not experiment with sounds and putting sounds together to make words." Her perspective: with respect to speech development, it's best to get rid of the binky in infancy.

Perhaps the greatest concern about pacifiers is their potential impact on a child's teeth and mouth structure. You'd think the major orthodontic organization in the country would have something to say on the matter, but they don't. So, we asked Randy Kunik, DDS, an orthodontist in Austin, TX, for his advice on binkies as well as thumb sucking. Here are his answers:

Q. Is there any harm in letting my child use a pacifier beyond a year of age?

Dr. K: As long as parents use a "Nuk" style pacifier after a year of age and the baby is not turning it upside down, there is no significant dental issue in using them until 24 months of age. It's rare to see any long term consequences if discontinued before then.

Q. How old is "too old" for a binky?

Dr. K: From a purely dental standpoint, any child over 24 months is too old for a pacifier. Kids who use pacifiers between two and three years of age risk having additional nasty habits such as tongue thrusting or lip sucking. These habits can adversely alter the growth of the mouth and teeth, which makes future ortho-

DR B'S OPINION

"I cringe when I see a three-year-old walking around the mall with a pacifier in his mouth. In fact, my husband gets great joy in pointing these kids out to me to see my reaction."

dontic treatment more complex. It may take longer to correct the problems and may be difficult to maintain permanent results.

Q. Are there any other dental risks?

Dr. K: Yes. Pacifiers are germ-laden. The bacteria S mutans can be present on a pacifier and increase the risk of caries (dental decay)...especially if a parent licks the binky after it drops on the floor. (Yuck, right? It's gross but many parents use this "cleaning" tactic.)

Q. What do you say to parents who say, "My child might need braces even if he doesn't use a pacifier"?

Dr. K: Well, it's true that your child may need braces anyway. But long-term binky users or thumb suckers (and the associated habits of tongue thrusting and lick sucking) can create some really challenging orthodontic problems, particularly in people who have longer, less round facial structures. Those cases require oral surgery for optimal results. Bottom line: prolonged binky use or thumb sucking may be the tipping point that results in oral surgery and not just braces if a child is already genetically predisposed to having tooth misalignment.

Q. Which is worse? Pacifiers or thumb sucking?

Dr. K: Pacifiers (beyond three years of age) cause more orthodontic damage, but truthfully, it is much easier to break a pacifier habit than a thumb sucking habit. Thumb sucking pushes the erupting permanent teeth outwards, increasing the risk of injury. And, if the finger or thumb isn't clean, thumb or finger sucking increases the risk of bacterial and fungal infections.

Q. How old is "too old" for thumb sucking?"

Dr. K: From an orthodontist's perspective, a child needs to stop by kindergarten. By age six, there is a much greater risk of significant and complex orthodontic problems.

BOTTOM LINE: The longer the pacifier remains in your baby's world, the harder it will be to kick the habit. Babies adjust very quickly to life without a pacifier and forget about it within a day or two.

Linda's tip

If you are breastfeeding, it's probably wise to wait until things are going well (at least four to seven days) to introduce a pacifier. That way your baby

DR B'S OPINION: PACIFIERS

Pacifiers are okay to use for babies *under six months of age*, at most, a year. After one year of age, there are absolutely no medical or developmental benefits—only risks. While it's not a dental issue before age two, binkies can lead to ear infections and interfere with a good night's sleep for everyone in the house.

learns good sucking etiquette at your breast first.

Another concern: WHICH pacifier to use. A newborn who uses an "orthodontic" pacifier (such as "Nuk" brand) may suckle (or bite!) at mom's breast the same way, leaving her mom with some very sore and cracked nipples. I recommend "Soothie" brand pacifiers (soothie-pacifier.com) for newborns since they're shaped like the human nipple—lowering the odds of gnarly nipples! Orthodontic pacifiers are fine for a seasoned breastfeeding team.

Colic

Q. What is colic, anyway?

It's the "C word" in new parent circles. But what is it, exactly? Colic is known as the Rule of Three's. It starts around three weeks of age. The baby cries for about three hours straight from about 5–8 PM every night (otherwise known as the "UN-happy hour"). And it lasts until the baby is three months old. About 15% of all babies are afflicted with this malady.

Q. What causes colic?

Although scientists have been studying colic for years, no one knows exactly what causes it. Many experts think the problem is due to immaturity of the gastrointestinal or digestive system. So over the years, doctors have tried treating it with medications to reduce gas, relax the intestinal muscles, or cause sedation. None of these medications really help. The best treatment for colic is time....all babies eventually outgrow colic.

Some babies who seem "colicky" actually have a medical diagnosis. So it is important to check in with your baby's doctor if you've got a chronically fussy baby on your hands. Some babies have heartburn (gastroesophageal reflux disease or GERD). Those babies are usually miserable all day and night or around feedings—not just for a three-hour period everyday. Other babies may have a cow's milk protein allergy and don't start to show signs of discomfort until several weeks of being exposed to the milk protein going through mom's breast milk or in standard cow's milk-based formula.

Insider Tip

The difference between a baby with colic and one with heartburn (gastroesophageal reflux, GERD) is that colicky babies act this way for specific periods during the day. Babies with heartburn do it all day long.

Q. My baby has colic. Help!

We know you want to do something. As parents, we are compelled to help our babies feel better even when the doc tells us there is no treatment but time. After browsing the net, you'll no doubt find many colic treatments that make miraculous (and unregulated) claims.

My advice before starting any treatment is to ask yourself this question: Am I treating my child to make myself feel better (because I feel I am doing something), or does the therapy really work?

Q. Do any alternative therapies for colic really work?

Maybe, but more research is needed to prove it.

A 2011 study examined the scientific evidence supporting the most popular complementary and alternative therapies for colic and here's what they found: Of 1764 studies done between 1991-2008, fifteen were reasonable enough to review. Of those, just eight were considered "well designed". And, only two treatments had more than one single study showing beneficial results. *(Perry)*

Therapies included spinal manipulation, massage therapy, reflexology, herbal remedies (chamomile, fennel, licorice, vervain, mint tea or fennel seed extract), sugar solutions, and probiotics. Of those, the most effective therapies were fennel-containing remedies, sugar solutions, and probiotics.

Fennel may relax the gut and increase the gut's motility. Sugar solutions may have a pain-relieving effect. And probiotics may kick-start a colicky baby's (presumably) immature gut.

All of these remedies deserve more study.

Q. Is it worth it to try probiotics for my colicky baby?

Yes! Sold in capsules or powder, probiotics are the good germs in your body that help improve intestinal function. Babies are born germ-free and then acquire good germs in the gut to help digest food (you have millions in your adult gut as you read this).

One of the first studies published on colic and probiotics compared 90 exclusively breastfed babies with colic. Half received over-the-counter gas drops (simethicone) and the other half got one capsule a day of a probiotic containing the germ Lactobacillus reuteri (commonly known as L. reuteri). (*Savino*)

The results? Pretty darn impressive . . . the gas drops group saw a 7% reduction in crying. *The probiotics group had a 95% reduction in crying.* No, that isn't a typo. *Babies who cried two to three hours a day were crying less than an hour after one month of treatment.*

Several studies have shown similar results. While we won't promise that it will cure your baby's colic, probiotics are certainly less expensive than hiring a babysitter every night for two months! A two-month supply of L. reuteri is about $12.

The product I recommend for my patients is a powder form of L. reuteri from Nature's Way. The dose is a half-teaspoon a day, immersed in a few drops of water (or mixed in expressed breast milk or formula).

Q. Do you have any other tips to help us survive the next

DR B'S OPINION: GRIPE WATER & COLIC

Based on limited evidence of safety and effectiveness, I recommend trying "gripe water" (a combination of ginger and fennel) or a daily dose of L. reuteri probiotics to combat colic. Both products are available in pharmacies and online. I don't make any promises, though.

10 weeks of colic?

We know it is a nerve-wracking experience. So, here are a few tips to help you keep your sanity:

1. Recruit loving friends and family to come over from 5 to 8 pm a night or two a week. You leave.
2. If #1 isn't an option, put your baby in his crib and step outside for a few moments.
3. Put your baby in a sling or carrier and run the vacuum cleaner. You probably haven't had a chance to clean the house in a while anyway. We're not being cruel, just realistic here.
4. Seek professional help for yourself if you can't take it anymore—this is not a sign of weakness or poor parenting skills.
5. For those parents who are really desperate, and will spend any amount of money to stop the crying, there is a product called "Sleep Tight" which attaches to the baby's crib to simulate the vibration and noise of a car going 55mph. For a mere $140, it can be yours. Check out www.colic.com or call 1-800-NO COLIC. Another idea: those vibrating bouncer seats ($30 to $40) have been the saviors of more than one parent of a colicky baby.

Tips and tricks for dealing with colic could fill an entire book–and, in fact, one doctor has already written an excellent book on this. Dr. Harvey Karp, a retired pediatrician in Santa Monica, CA, has developed a terrific method for soothing colicky babies. His *Happiest Baby on the Block* book (Bantam, $13.95) focuses on five steps to mimic the baby's experience in the uterus: swaddling, side/stomach position, shhh sounds, swinging and sucking. We highly recommend Karp's book.

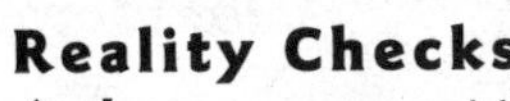

Reality Checks

◆ ***A common parent thought is, "I can't listen to my baby cry."*** That is exactly the way nature intended it to be. All animals have a certain noise that is disturbing to their elders and that prompts them to take action. As a doctor, I listen to children cry all day long in my office and completely tune it out. When I get home and my own children cry, it drives me nuts. Parents (including me!) need to learn to take their own emotions out of the picture. View crying as a form of self-expression and it won't raise your blood pressure. Remember this rule: Most of the time, YOUR CHILD IS FINE.

◆ ***Parents at the end of their rope need to walk away from their baby. NEVER SHAKE a baby.*** Babies who are colicky or high maintenance have a significantly higher risk of being abused. A baby's brain is very fragile. If he is shaken, the motion can lead to blindness, brain damage, or death.

Q. When should I encourage my baby to have a favorite toy?

The official term is *transitional object*. You can introduce it starting at six months of age, but it is safest to keep it out of the crib until a year of age.

Remember that *object permanence* concept from Chapter 10, Development? Babies start to realize that parents still exist when they leave their viewing field between six and 12 months of age. The transitional object or toy is the friend that travels with your child when you aren't there. They are making an emotional "transition" to seeking an alternative source of comfort. The object may be a doll, blanket, or even a piece of parent's clothing.

Your child will likely have his comfort object for a while. He will give it up before going to his first slumber party (age seven to eight years is normal).

Helpful Hint

Try to pick a transitional object you don't mind carrying around everywhere. One of my patients clung to his mother's satin nightie. Another important point: buy EXTRA objects. Once your child has a favorite "lovie" (such as a stuffed animal or blanket), be sure to buy extra identical ones. Odds are, the lovie will get lost or destroyed—and that isn't a pretty scene. Having back-ups is important for everyone's sanity. Also: be careful when you attempt to wash a lovie—a much-loved stuffed animal can easily fall apart in a washing machine. Hand washing or using the delicate cycle (and not drying) is important.

Q. What do you think about infant massage?

Everyone benefits from a massage.

The power of touch has known therapeutic value. Not only are babies soothed, but parents are too. Learning infant massage teaches parents how to feel more comfortable holding and handling their babies.

Infant massage classes are very popular. Check with your local hospital or parenting magazine for information in your area.

DR B'S OPINION

"Spouse massages are also very important. Often our energies get focused on the baby and our spouses get treated like chopped liver."

If you've ever seen those kids who seem to have their parents wrapped around their little finger (think Veruca Salt from *Charlie and the Chocolate Factory*), you know you want to avoid that fate. But how can you prevent that future behavior in your cute little baby? Even though you now know how your baby's brain works, you still may not have all the right answers in every discipline situation. Why? Because your child is really smart and has figured YOU out. So let's move on to setting up a good discipline foundation that can hopefully take you through the tougher times to come.

Planting The Seeds Of Discipline

Q. At what age should I start to discipline my baby?

By nine months of age.

Planting the seeds of discipline is CRITICAL. From birth to eight months, your parenting job is easy. It is physically exhausting but doesn't require too many mental strategies to succeed. At about nine months old, you will start playing chess with your child and will continue to play for a lifetime. Here are the rules of the game:

Discipline is the process of teaching your child to be an independent being. Your job is to give your child a **SUPER-EGO**. This is a Freudian term that refers to self-control and self-regulation—a person's internal control that limits inappropriate behavior from occurring. In other words, your discipline implants a device in your child's hard drive that he will carry with him wherever he goes. That way, your child will do the right thing even when you aren't around.

Let's review your child's development. A nine to 12 month old is exploring, not purposefully destroying, his environment (your house). He uses his memory of what has worked before to approach the unfamiliar, so everything ultimately ends up in his mouth (and hence, a safety hazard). He has figured out how to get other people to repeat behaviors (if you scream when he bites you, he will bite you again). He is egocentric—the world revolves around him (how could a phone call be more important than him?) He wants independence, but doesn't quite have the motor skills to accomplish his goals (refusing to let you feed him). He has developed a sense of trust with his parents and caretakers. He doesn't want anyone to leave him, even to go to the bathroom (separation anxiety). Are we having fun yet?

When the baby I just described is *your* baby, it's time to get to work.

BOTTOM LINE

Consistency is the key to making a discipline plan work. If there is an adult who ignores a behavior that other adults reprimand, the behavior will continue to occur.

discipline

Q. What should be included in our House Rules?

Anything dangerous or potentially painful to the child or others.

These are behaviors that are *never* acceptable. These include pulling on cords, touching the stove, putting fingers in electrical outlets, turning on bathtub water, biting, hitting the dog and so on. Look around your house and add to your list.

Q. What is a discipline management plan?

How adult caretakers will respond to inappropriate behaviors.

NEW PARENT 411: PLANTING THE SEEDS OF DISCIPLINE

1. Make your house kid safe, so you don't have to say "No" to everything your child touches.
2. Make up a set of "House Rules" that all caretakers enforce.
3. Make up a discipline management plan with consequences—again, that all caretakers enforce.
4. Know that your nine-month old understands the word "no", but wants to be sure you really mean it. Yep, this is "testing limits."

Remember, you are planting the seeds of discipline. Don't expect a tree to grow overnight. You won't see your child's behavior change immediately. It takes months (and sometimes years!) to see the fruits of your labor. Be calm and consistent.

Everyone has his or her own style. Most parents will think back to their own parents' approach and remember what worked. You and your partner need to come up with a uniform strategy that both of you feel comfortable enforcing.

Q. Do you think it's okay to spank my child?

No.

We never recommend using physical force to punish a child. Your child learns from you. If you are violent when you are angry, your child will be that way, too. We know that your first reaction when your child hits you is to hit back—DON'T. You're older than your child remember?

BOTTOM LINE: The goal of discipline is to *teach*. If you want a well-behaved child, you need to be well behaved as their role model.

Q. At what age does the Terrible Two's start? My one year old is already acting terrible.

The Terrible Two's is a misnomer. It actually starts when your child declares independence from you. This behavior starts around 12 to 18 months and lasts until age three or four.

My advice is to have a glass of wine at dinner for the next two years. Just kidding—sort of. My other advice is to give your child the opportunity to feel like he is in control of his world. You are really in charge, but he doesn't need to be reminded of that 24 hours a day. When there is an opportunity for *him* to choose something, let him (picking out a snack, a toy to play with, etc.). Also, don't bother to discipline for minor infractions. It's not worth it and limits the amount of conflicts that arise.

Q. What is a temper tantrum and how should I respond to it?

A physical release of anger. You need to let it happen.

Tantrums are frequently seen in toddlers, but some kids like to start early. When your child is at the end of his rope, he may have an emotional breakdown. This involves kicking, screaming, crying, and flailing around on the floor.

Your job is to give him a safe place to have it out. Do not respond to your child while he is in the midst of this performance. When he is done, you can scoop him up and discuss things.

Just for fun, as parents, we also like to rank our children's temper tantrums much in the way scientists score hurricanes. There are Category 1 and 2 fits, which like minor hurricanes involve a minimal amount of damage. Then there are the serious tantrums—up to and including the big ones we like to call Category 5.

Once we took our two year old to a train show, something he absolutely loved. Until it was time to go. They were closing it down and turning out the lights (we had been there for an hour or more). Suddenly, our son launched into the most amazing Category 5 tantrum—a one-hour scream-fest. You just had to marvel at the intensity of it all. Of course, at the time, we wanted to give back our parent license and go into the Federal Parent Witness Protection Program.

11 Tips For Developing A Discipline Style

1 **Avoid as many conflicts as possible**. Make your house kid safe. Don't push your child past his threshold. For example: running too many errands, missing naptime, waiting forever at a restaurant. For eating out, we have a ten-minute rule–if the wait is over ten minutes, it's time to go elsewhere. Obviously, eating early is a good way to avoid lengthy waits for a table.

2 **Anticipate conflicts**. If you see your child heading towards the stereo, move him elsewhere or offer him a toy. Obviously, parents develop a sixth sense for this–soon, you'll be able to scan a room and predict the future (that is, zeroing in on your baby's next conflict).

3 **Anticipate attention-seeking behavior**. Be prepared for trouble when your attention is turned elsewhere. If your child gets into trouble when you are cooking dinner, let him "cook" on the kitchen floor.

4 **Pick your battles**. Saying "No" twenty times a day loses its effectiveness. Believe it or not, I had a parent tell me her child thought his name was "No." Categorize behaviors into major errors, minor ones, and those too insignificant to bother with. Minor infractions are negotiable with an older child.

5 **Act Immediately**. Discipline when the behavior occurs, not after the fact. Otherwise, your child won't remember what he is getting in trouble for. Never say: "Just wait till your father/mother gets home!"

6 **Make your comments short and sweet**. Speak in short sentences such as "No hitting." This is much more effective than, "Johnny, you know it's not nice to hit the dog." Believe us, you lost Johnny right after "you know."

7 **Focus on the behavior, not the child**. Be sure to state that a particular behavior is bad. NEVER tell your child that HE is bad.

8 **Remind your child that you love her or him**. Always end your intervention with a positive comment. It reinforces the reason that you are teaching her how to behave.

9 **Use age-appropriate and temperament-appropriate discipline techniques**. You need to adapt to your baby and find a discipline style that works well with your individual child. What works at nine months might not work when your child is two. He's had time to figure out your strategy!

10 **Don't yell**. It's not the volume of your voice, but the tone that gets your point across. Remember *The Godfather*? He never needed to yell. Some of the most effective discipline we've ever seen has been whispered.

11 **Catch your child "being good."** Praise for good behavior is so important and helps encourage more of it. Think of it as fertilizer for her conscience.

Reality Check

A word of caution: If you give in to a situation when your child has a tantrum, you have just taught him that a tantrum is an effective way to get what he wants. Be strong!

Q. What sets off a temper tantrum?

Anything and nothing.

Look at your child's world through your child's eyes. He has poor language skills and can't tell his parents everything he needs and wants. He hasn't mastered all his motor skills to accomplish certain tasks. He isn't sure where his activity boundaries are and is told "no" numerous times a day. Add in an egocentric perspective that Mom and Dad can read his mind (if he thinks it, everyone must know what he is thinking). Finish with the unattainable goal of complete independence.

Being tired, bored, and hungry are also contributors to ugly behavior.

So, when you pick out the wrong pajamas at bedtime and your child explodes, don't think it's just the P.J.'s.

Special Situations: Tips & Tricks

Q. How do I deal with separation anxiety? Can I just sneak out of sight?

Before, you could leave the room and your baby might not have cared. Now, if you leave the room, he wants to know where you're going. This is about the time you will keep your bathroom door open so your baby does not panic every time you answer nature's call. (That bathroom door often remains open for the next several years. I have to remind myself when we have company to close mine. But I digress). It is CRITICAL that you tell your baby where you are going. You will think it is better to "sneak out" of the house when you leave, so your baby doesn't cry. But, you are NOT helping your baby with his anxiety—you only make it worse. He doesn't know if you are leaving for a minute or for a lifetime. If your baby is prepared for your departure, he will protest for a few minutes and then move on.

Q. My child freaks out with strangers. How do I make him more comfortable?

Be patient. All babies, but especially the slow-to-warm-up ones, are afraid of strangers. They need some time to check out these people and make sure they are okay. And "strangers" to a baby might include a grandparent who lives out of town.

To help the situation, let your baby watch this person before handing him over. Then, stay in your child's view for a while after the hand off.

It's probably a good idea to have consistent caregivers while your child is in his stranger anxiety mode (nine to 15 months).

Q. My baby is playing with his genitals. How do I make him stop?

He is normal and you don't need to stop him.

The official term is **MASTURBATION**. It is amazing how quickly babies find these body parts, and yes, it does feel good to touch them. P.S. Erections are also normal.

For now, there is little you can do to limit this behavior. As your child gets older (18 months) you can start explaining to him that it's okay to touch down there, but only when he is at home/in his room. This is a good segue into a discussion that no one else touches or looks down there except for Mom, Dad, and Doctor.

Masturbation is in the same category of self-soothing behaviors as thumb sucking. You won't be able to eliminate these behaviors, but you can limit where and when they are occurring.

Reality Check

Boys aren't the only ones exploring their pleasure zones. I had a female patient who would ride the high chairs at restaurants. Needless to say, her parents didn't take her out to eat much.

Q. My nine-month old enjoys having food fights in our kitchen. Help!

A budding John Belushi. Children start to play with their food when they are no longer eating it. When the food starts to fly, mealtime is over. Your child will quickly learn that he is excused from the dinner table when more food ends up on the floor than in his mouth.

Q. My one year old sucks his thumb. How can I stop it?

You can't. The thumb goes everywhere your child does. This is another self-soothing activity. As your child gets to be around 18 months, you can reason with him about where it is appropriate to thumb suck (in his bedroom) and where it is not (out in public). This will limit the behavior to certain times when your child needs to have some down time. Check out our other book, Toddler 411, for ways to end a preschooler's thumb sucking habit.

Q. My child holds his breath when he gets angry. What do I do?

Nothing. At worst, he will faint. It is human nature not to inflict harm on oneself. If your child holds his breath long enough, he will lose consciousness and start breathing spontaneously. This sounds really cruel, but a *breath-holding spell* is potent ammunition for a little kid to get his way. If you want to win the battle, you can't give in.

Note: If your child has numerous breath-holding spells, check in with your doctor. Occasionally, this can be related to iron deficiency anemia.

Q. My child is biting me. What do I do?

Don't bite back. And whatever you do, don't scream.

When babies are teething, they often start to gnaw on whatever is available. This may be a parent's shoulder or Mom's nipple (OUCH!). It's not malicious. But, if you respond dramatically, it will encourage your baby to bite again.

Your response: Take your baby off your body and place him on the floor. Calmly and sternly say, "No biting." Do not pay any attention to your baby for one minute. Your baby yearns for your attention so this is a good punishment. Lick your wounds later, out of sight from your baby.

It may take 20-30 times before your baby gets the message, but he will.

Q. My child is biting/being bitten at daycare. What do I do?

Talk to the daycare director and do an observation in the classroom.

There is a biter or hitter in every room. A good childcare program will be constantly watching the children and be able to prevent Hannibal Lecter, Jr. from successfully drawing blood from another child.

Reality Check

My son's kindergarten teacher had a wonderful motto. "If I'm doing my job, I don't have to discipline these kids." The point is, children who have the opportunity to bite or hit are those that aren't being watched closely enough by an adult caregiver. If your child is biting, do an observation in the classroom.

Q. We are traveling with our baby. Do you have any tips?

For starters, lower your expectations. Then you can be pleasantly surprised when things go smoothly. How your baby does with a travel adventure depends on his temperament.

Regardless of the mode of travel, bring a "goodie" bag packed with old favorites and new toys/books to explore. Remember the New Toy Rule: whipping out a special new toy your child has never seen before can provide a valuable distraction. It still works on our babies and one of them is in middle school now. If your baby likes music, take an iPod with some fun songs.

And try to travel at off-peak times—traffic delays and delayed flights make the experience that much more challenging. Here are our tips:

- ***Get a seat for your baby, if possible.*** The National Transportation Safety Board recommends that kids under age two be restrained in their own seats while in the air, but the FAA does not require it. Check to see if your airline will discount that seat—it's rare but worth a try.
- ***Feed baby on takeoff and landing.*** Babies don't know that yawning will equalize pressure in their ears as cabin pressure changes. Drinking works the same way as yawning.
- ***What about drugs?*** Parents often ask about giving Benadryl (diphenhydramine) to make their babies sleep through the flight. If your baby is under six months old or your flight is less than six hours long, I don't suggest it. If you are taking an international flight, it is a consideration but check with your doctor first.
- ***Can my baby fly with a cold or ear infection?*** Yes. For either issue, using decongestant nose spray (see Appendix A, "Medications") before takeoff reduces nasal secretions and makes cabin pressure changes less unpleasant (see Chapter 13, "Infections" for more info).

Finally, here's when you know you're getting through to your kids: My four-year-old was watching a football game on TV with my husband. One of the teams called time out. My daughter astutely asked, "Daddy, why is the team in Time Out?"

Section 4

Sickness & How to Avoid it!

Vaccinations

Chapter 12

"No man is an island, entire of itself; every man is a piece of the continent, a part of the main..."

~ John Donne (1572-1631)

What's in this Chapter

- The Top 15 Vaccine Questions
- The vaccination schedule
- Vaccine preventable diseases
- Optional vaccines
- Controversies and Misconceptions
  - -MMR and Autism
  - -Rotavirus
  - -Thimerosal
  - -Vaccine shortages
  - -Aluminum
- Where to get more information

It's time to jump right into a hot topic you'll find in parent circles—vaccines. Nothing seems to stir the blood these days more than a good ol' fashion debate on vaccinating your child.

A head's up: since there is so much misinformation out there on vaccines, you need to be armed with detailed, accurate information. And like the rest of this book, that is what you will get in this chapter. The information we provide is based on scientific evidence and solid peer-reviewed research. Remember our mantra: show us the science! Your child is too precious to make such important decisions on anything less. This chapter is ***not*** based on personal anecdotes, conspiracy theories, "research" done in people's basements (we are not kidding), or the crusades of B-list celebrities.

However, before we get to our take on this debate, let's go back in time a bit. Well, more than a bit. How did the human race survive when other early humans didn't? Yes, making tools and finding food most efficiently played a big role.

But here's another key element: we built civilizations. And we developed a sense of responsibility . . . to ourselves and to our society.

Every time we respond to a tragedy in our nation—whether it be 911, Hurricane Katrina or Sandy, or the Boston Marathon bombing—we are reminded of how we are not just individuals living in our own little worlds. It's part of our civic duty to lend a hand and take care of our neighbors.

So, what's this pontificating have to do with vaccines? Again, it is responsibility to work together as a community. . . .this time, the subject isn't terrorism or storms, but something that can be just as terrifying: infectious diseases.

Consider a bit of history: in the 1890's, people would have seven or eight children in their families and only half of them would survive childhood. Just go to an old graveyard some time and look at the ages listed on the headstones. Many of the diseases that killed those children are now prevented by vaccination. It's a fact: vaccinations have increased the life expectancy of our nation's children. That's why our grandparents and parents embraced vaccines.

Here's a crucial point: the key to a vaccine's success is that *everyone* in the community gets vaccinated. Vaccines won't work if a large number of folks just choose to opt out of the system and their responsibility. Germs are rather simple creatures . . . they just look for a new person to infect. They don't play politics.

Please keep this in mind as you read about vaccinations. Your decision (and every other parent's decision) affects your child. And society as a whole.

Reality Check

The concept of "public health" has been around since antiquity. Obviously, rulers had a vested interest in keeping their subjects healthy so they had a society to rule. Through the years, governments have been responsible for managing numerous programs. The most important advances in public health have been vaccination programs, water purification, and waste disposal/sanitation systems. The only way for public health to work, though, is for all members of the community to follow the same rules.

Q. Who came up with the idea of vaccinations in the first place?

It took centuries of observation as well as trial and error. (And sometimes,

OUTBREAK: IT COULD HAPPEN TODAY

Let's get even more serious here. European settlers who came to the New World had a very effective (yet unintentional) way of clearing locals off the land they intended to settle. They brought their germs from the Old World and infected Native Americans. In some cases, entire groups of native peoples were wiped out by disease. Why? They had no immunity.

Fast forward to the present day. One obvious real-world example: swine flu (H1N1). Here's a new virus that in a matter of weeks spread around the world and killed thousands. Thanks to today's modern air travel system, a bug can go from a regional problem to a worldwide epidemic in a blink of an eye. Swine flu, like many of the diseases we vaccinate for, is a VIRUS. Besides a vaccine, there is little we can do to stop the spread of infection—despite our scientifically advanced world. (*Fenn*)

error meant death.) The first real step was describing the disease, in this case, smallpox. Smallpox was a deadly disease that, historically, wiped out entire civilizations. The earliest descriptions can be found as far back as the ninth and tenth centuries among Turks. In fact, "inoculation" or the infecting of a person with the disease in hopes of introducing a mild form and then creating immunity was practiced first in Asia. In the 1700's an English aristocrat, Lady Mary Wortly Montagu, was living in Constantinople and learned of the practice of inoculation (known then as variolation). She had her son inoculated and subsequently, brought the practice back to England.

At about the same time, an English country doctor, Edward Jenner, made an interesting connection: milkmaids who had been exposed to cowpox (a common disease in cattle at the time) never seemed to get smallpox infections during epidemics. He began to study the idea that vaccinating humans with cowpox virus would make them immune to smallpox. In 1798 he published a paper on his idea and called it "Vaccination." Not to say, by the way, that Dr. Jenner's idea was accepted with completely open arms. In the nineteenth century there did emerge a group opposed to vaccination led by Mary C. Hume. See, even the anti-vaccination lobby has been around a long time! Of course, in those days, you could be prosecuted for refusing to vaccinate. (*UCLA*)

People were inoculated with a small amount of cowpox virus on their arm. It caused a localized infection at that site (hence, the scar that we forty-somethings and above bear). And true to Dr. Jenner's hypothesis, it provided protection against smallpox disease. In 1972, the United States stopped vaccinating against smallpox because it was no longer a threat to the population. In 1977, the last case of smallpox occurred in Somalia. In 1980, the World Health Organization declared the world free of smallpox, thanks to a global effort to immunize all children.

The success of the smallpox vaccine and other scientific discoveries led to the evolution of many vaccines. These new, safer vaccines are extremely

DR B'S OPINION: TODAY'S PARADOX—ARE VACCINES TOO SUCCESSFUL?

Vaccinations are one of the greatest achievements in medical history. They have significantly decreased infant and childhood mortality. Yet, amazingly, doctors have to convince some of today's parents that immunizing their child is extremely important, not "optional."

Most parents have not spent a night in a pediatric intensive care unit with a child who has HIB meningitis, watched a child gasping for breath with whooping cough, or seen a child die with a Strep infection as a complication of chickenpox. I have. Sadly, every pediatrician has had one of these experiences and has known that the child's illness or death could have been prevented by vaccination. I don't want *your* child to be that child. And I refuse to let a child become a statistic because of online myths or fear mongering.

That's the bitter irony of today's vaccine "debate." As a vaccinated society, we've made diseases like measles so rare that parents have no idea today how devastating it was and still can be.

effective in preventing diseases and epidemics that our grandparents and parents can still remember.

Q. Why do you care whether I vaccinate my child or not?

For starters, I want your baby to be protected.

But I also want you to realize that the decision to vaccinate your child impacts the health of other children in the community. Choosing NOT to vaccinate your child is choosing to put your child AND your community's children at risk. As a parent, you want to make the right choices for your child to protect them. I want you to ask questions. I want you to be informed. And I want you to get your child vaccinated. YOUR decision impacts ALL children. Why?

There are two critical points for vaccination to work:

1. *You need to be vaccinated.*
2. *Your neighbor needs to be vaccinated.*

This concept is called herd immunity. And yes, you are a member of a herd. When 90-95% of "the herd" is protected, it is nearly impossible for a germ to cause an epidemic. Think of germs as rain. Vaccination is a raincoat. Even with a raincoat on, you can still get wet. You need an umbrella, too. The umbrella is "herd immunity." Those who don't vaccinate expect someone to share their umbrella when it rains. But society can only buy umbrellas TOGETHER. And raincoats aren't made for newborns—they need umbrellas!

Some parenting decisions have little or no impact on the community at large. Deciding whether or not your child eats organic baby food, goes to preschool, or sleeps in a family bed is entirely up to you—your decision only affects your child.

However, your decision whether or not to vaccinate your child affects *all* our kids. If you are a parent who is considering delaying or skipping vaccinations altogether, please realize the impact of your decision.

If more than 10% of American parents choose to "opt out" of vaccines, there's no question that our entire country will see these horrible diseases

FIVE BIGGEST MISCONCEPTIONS ABOUT VACCINES

Pop online to any of the anti-vaccine web sites out there today and you'll find a plethora of misconceptions, untruths and worse about vaccines. Here are the top five we hear most often:

1. Diseases disappeared before vaccines were introduced. *No!*
2. Vaccines cause illness and death. *Reactions are very rare.*
3. Vaccine preventable diseases are rare. *No!*
4. Too many vaccines, given too soon overload the immune system. *No!*
5. There is a government conspiracy to inject autism-causing agents into our children. (The Jenny McCarthy movement.) *Dr. Strangelove, check your messages!*

SOURCE: CDC AND DR. BROWN'S PATIENTS.

of bygone days return. Fortunately, very few parents decide to do this (see the stats below).

What is most concerning today is that there are pockets of under-vaccinated children. Birds of a feather flock together. Like-minded parents who don't vaccinate their kids tend to live in the same community and send their kids to the same schools. With lower immunization rates, there is no herd immunity. We have these "Ground Zero" areas to thank for recent measles and whooping cough outbreaks. (*Omer*)

Reality Check: The good news

While parents are asking more questions, they are still choosing to vaccinate their kids. The most recent CDC survey (2011) showed 99.2% of U.S. children aged 19 to 35 months are being vaccinated. Yes, 99.2%. Despite all the media stories on vaccine "controversy," only a tiny fraction of parents—less than 1%— are choosing to forgo vaccinations.

The Top 15 Vaccine Questions

1 **WHAT ARE VACCINES?** Vaccines are materials that are given to a person to protect them from disease (that is, provide immunity). The word vaccine is derived from "vaccinia" (cowpox virus), which was used to create the first vaccine in history (smallpox).

Modern medicine has created many vaccines. Vaccines PREVENT viral and bacteria infections that used to cause serious illness and death.

vaccinations

2 **HOW DO VACCINES WORK?** Here is your microbiology lesson for today. Your immune system is your body's defense against foreign invaders (viruses, bacteria, parasites). Vaccines prepare your body to recognize foreigners without getting infected. A vaccine revs up your immune system to make antibodies (smart bombs with memory) for the signature of a particular germ. So, if your body sees the real germ, voila! You already know how to fight it off.

There are three types of vaccinations: inactivated, live attenuated, and inactivated bacterial toxins.

SEVEN TRUTHS ABOUT VACCINES

Let's contrast those misconceptions about vaccines with these truths:

1. Vaccines save lives. They have single-handedly reduced infant mortality rates.
2. Lower immunization rates mean higher disease & mortality rates.
3. Misinformation is everywhere—online, media, and playgroups.
4. The decision NOT to vaccinate is a decision to accept the consequences of the disease.
5. The decision NOT to vaccinate is a decision to put your community at risk for epidemics.
6. Like any medication, vaccines are not 100% risk-free.
7. Your parents/grandparents respect vaccines because they have seen these diseases.

- ***Inactivated vaccines*** do not contain any living germs. An immune response forms against either a dead germ, part of the germ (recombinant DNA), or a protein or sugar marker that sits on the outer layer of the germ (its signature). Very cool. These vaccines are safe to give to immune-compromised people. The only down side is that several doses of the vaccine are needed to provide full, lifelong protection against disease. Some of these types of vaccines include: ***Flu, Hepatitis A & B, HIB, Pertussis (whooping cough), Inactivated Polio, Prevnar.***

DR B'S OPINION

"I vaccinated my own kids to protect them. I wouldn't do anything differently for your kids. I consider my patients to be my own children. I would not sleep at night if I knew they were not protected against preventable disease."

- ***Live attenuated vaccines*** are weak forms of the germs that cause infection. An immune response occurs just as if your body had the infection. So one or two doses of vaccine gives you lifelong protection. These vaccines are not given to immune compromised people because they can make them sick. Examples include: ***MMR, Oral Polio, Smallpox, Tuberculosis, Varicella (chickenpox), Rotavirus.***

- ***Toxoids*** (inactivated bacterial toxins) are vaccines that create a defense against the toxin (poison) that a bacteria germ makes. Examples of toxoid vaccines include: ***Diphtheria, Tetanus.***

3 WHAT ARE THE DISEASES WE ARE PROTECTED AGAINST WITH VACCINATION?

Good question. You are probably unfamiliar with most of these diseases since we don't see them much anymore in the U.S. After you read about these diseases later in this chapter, thank your parents for immunizing you.

As you read through the vaccination schedule, note that some diseases are viruses. Antibiotics kill bacteria only. Doctors have no medications to cure the viral infections. See section on "vaccine specifics" for details on all of these diseases and the vaccines.

Doubt the effectiveness of vaccines? Let's look at the facts. Here is a chart that compares the annual infections by vaccine-preventable diseases in the 1900's compared to 2010 in the United States. (*CDC*)

	CASES OF DISEASE PER YEAR		
DISEASE	1900'S	2010	TYPE OF GERM
Smallpox	29,005	0	virus
Diphtheria	21,053	0	bacteria
Tetanus	580	8	bacteria
Pertussis	200,752	21,291	bacteria
Polio	16,316	0	virus
Measles	530,217	61	virus
Mumps	162,344	2528	virus
Rubella	47,745	6	virus
Congenital rubella	152	0	virus
HIB	~20,000	270	bacteria

DISEASE	PRE-VACCINE	2008	TYPE OF GERM
Hepatitis A	~117,333	11,049	virus
Hepatitis B	~66,232	11,269	virus
Strep pneumoniae*	~16,069	4,167	bacteria
Rotavirus**	~62,500	7500	virus
Varicella	~4,085,120	449,363	virus

**cases under age 5*
***number of hospitalizations under age 5*

Rather amazing, no? Diseases that used to kill *thousands* (if not hundreds of thousands) now only harm a handful of people—thanks to vaccines.

4 HOW ARE VACCINES TESTED TO MAKE SURE THEY'RE SAFE? Vaccines are researched extensively for an average of 15 years before being approved for use.

A pharmaceutical company conducts medical research trials in a series of stages. Once safety is proven, the vaccine is tested in several thousand volunteers to make sure the vaccine actually works. These volunteers are followed for at least one year to be sure that no serious side effects occur.

Nothing in this world is 100% foolproof, including vaccine science. But the research trials that occur before licensing are very rigid. If you think there are a lot of vaccines on the market, imagine how many didn't make it through the research phase of development.

The Food and Drug Administration (FDA) governs this whole process. The FDA is the watchdog for any medication that is sold over-the-counter or by prescription. There are extremely high standards that must be met before any product is allowed for human use.

After a vaccine is approved for use, long-term follow-up studies are done to assess for side effects, adverse reactions, and potency over a lifetime.

Reality Check

Given the FDA's mixed track record, you may be skeptical about trusting the government when it comes to vaccine safety. But in truth, the system is in place to protect consumers. Although conspiracy theorists might disagree, the FDA really is on our side.

To improve drug and vaccine safety, the Institute of Medicine has called for an overhaul of how the FDA works—in the future, the FDA will do more ongoing safety reviews of medicines and make all clinical study results public. This should help boost public confidence in the FDA and vaccine safety.

5 WHY IS MY CHILD GETTING MORE SHOTS THAN I DID? Simple answer: we've been successful inventing vaccines to fight more diseases. It's one of the important advances in modern medicine—vaccines prevent disease, injury and death. More vaccines are a good thing!

An important point: many of the vaccine preventable diseases are viruses. These viral infections cannot be treated with medicine once an infection occurs (for example, Hepatitis B).

Vaccines that protect against bacterial diseases are often serious ones, and resistant to many antibiotics (for example, Prevnar).

And even though the number of shots has gone up, the total load on the immune system has gone down. Today's vaccines are smarter and better engineered than the shots from a few decades ago.

In fact, the total number of immunologic agents in ***the entire*** childhood vaccination series today is less than what was in just two vaccines in 1980!

Our children are getting smarter, safer vaccines today and better protection than we ever got as kids.

6 **ARE WE GIVING TOO MANY SHOTS, TOO SOON?** This is a false mantra of the anti-vaccine crowd: they say babies are receiving too many shots (compared to say, 1980) and too soon (infants can't handle all these shots, they say).

So, let's look at this scientifically. On any given day, your baby is exposed to literally thousands of germs (it doesn't matter how spotless your house is). Exposing your child to five to eight different germs in the form of vaccines is a spit in the bucket.

Young children have better immune responses to vaccines than adults and older children. So they will form adequate immune responses to various vaccines *simultaneously*. (This is studied extensively before a vaccine is licensed). Even if your baby got 11 shots at the same time, he would only need to use about 0.1% of his immune system to respond to them. (*Offit*)

Giving several vaccines at once does not damage, weaken, or overload the immune system. Vaccines boost the immune system.

Also, the diseases that the vaccines protect against are the most severe in infants and young children. Your doctor wants to get those vaccinations in as safely and effectively as possible. That's why the timing is so important (and why a staggered or delayed vaccination schedule is a bad idea—more

REASONS NOT TO VACCINATE

There are very specific medical reasons to discontinue or hold off on certain vaccinations:

1. ***An immune-compromised patient or family member.***
2. ***Had disease (for example, if you've had chicken pox, you don't need the vaccine).***
3. ***Encephalitis or degenerative brain disorder.***
4. ***Allergy to vaccine or an additive in vaccine.***

If your baby has a food allergy to eggs or gelatin, or an allergy to antibiotics (such as Neomycin, Streptomycin, Polymyxin B), notify your doctor before any vaccinations are given. Several vaccines are grown in chick embryo cells and therefore contain a small amount of egg protein: flu vaccine (Flushield, Fluzone, Fluvirin), MMR, rabies (RabAvert), and yellow fever vaccine (YF-VAX). The MMR vaccine also includes gelatin.

Rabies, MMR, Chickenpox and Polio vaccines include several different kinds of antibiotics to prevent contamination of the vaccine itself. Check with your doctor if your child is allergic to any antibiotics. (*Schuval*)

While there is a scant amount of egg protein in the MMR vaccine, it is still safe to give to a person with an egg allergy in your pediatrician's office. (*Pickering*) And, although the flu vaccine contains trace amounts of egg protein, it is also still possible for some egg-allergic people to get it. Patients should consult their allergist for testing and administration.

on that in the controversies section of this chapter.)

Q. Can't you just give one big shot that has all the vaccines in it?

Medical science is working on it!

There have been a few combination vaccines licensed for use. The largest combination vaccines are Pediarix (DTaP, IPV, Hepatitis B) and Pentacel (DtaP, IPV, HIB). The reason there isn't just one big shot is that some vaccines are ineffective when they are sitting together in a solution. Your baby may still need more than one shot, but if your doctor uses a combo vaccine at least it will be fewer shots than if they are all administered separately.

More combination vaccines are on the horizon.

Helpful Hints

Top Five Tips to Make Shots Less Painful

1. Distraction. Blow in your child's face, or pull out a new toy.

2. A spoonful of sugar. Put a little sugar water on a nipple or pacifier. It is a known pain reliever (analgesic).

3. Acetaminophen (Tylenol). It's a great pain medicine. Be sure to check with your doctor for the correct dose for your baby's weight. And, for your baby's immune system to respond optimally to his shots, wait a few hours after the shots to give a dose.

4. Numb it. There is a prescription anesthetic cream called EMLA that can be applied one hour before shots are administered. The downsides: a) Pain is not just from the needle going through the skin but also from the fluid injected into muscle. b) You may not know where to place the cream.

5. Freeze it. There is a cold "vapocoolant" spray that can be placed on the skin just before the injections. A few doctors use it. It works slightly better than the distraction technique. (*Reis*)

7 **WHAT GROUP MAKES DECISIONS ABOUT VACCINATIONS FOR CHILDREN?** There are four governing panels of experts in infectious diseases that make recommendations for vaccinations. These smart folks include: American Academy of Pediatrics (AAP), American Academy of Family Physicians (AAFP), Advisory Committee on Immunization Practices (ACIP), and the Centers for Disease Control (CDC). Because there are several groups involved in this effort, there is some variability in vaccination schedule recommendations.

8 **MY BABY HAS A COLD. SHOULD I HOLD OFF ON VACCINATIONS?** No! This is a common misconception of parents. Even if your baby has a minor illness, he can still get his shots. We cannot stress how important it is to get your child vaccinated in a timely manner. So don't let a sniffle or two make you reschedule an office visit for shots. Your child can also get his shots even if he is on antibiotics.

9 **CAN I CHOOSE NOT TO VACCINATE MY CHILD?** Yes, but we wouldn't advise it. Choosing not to vaccinate is not a risk-free choice. It's choosing to expose your child to potentially serious infection. It's also choosing to expose other children in your community to serious, preventable diseases.

And if you think your child will be safe because everyone else vaccinates his or her kids, you'd be wrong (and very selfish, we might add). You can also choose not to stop at a stop sign, but we wouldn't advise it!

Reality Check

Vaccine requirements for school entry vary by state. There is no one consistent policy. All 50 states allow vaccine exemptions for medical reasons, 48 states allow exemptions for religious reasons and about 21 states allow exemptions for philosophical reasons. (*Johns Hopkins Hospital*)

10 **I'VE HEARD THAT GETTING A DISEASE PROVIDES IMMUNITY FOREVER AND VACCINATIONS MIGHT NOT PROVIDE LIFELONG PROTECTION. WOULDN'T IT BE BETTER TO GET THE DISEASE? ISN'T THAT A MORE "NATURAL" WAY OF CREATING IMMUNITY?**

No.

The diseases we prevent by vaccination are not minor illnesses (this includes chickenpox). For instance, would you rather have your child get meningitis and die or get the vaccine? Getting chickenpox or any other disease the "natural way" is a much greater health risk without any significant benefit. And just think of the discomfort, pain and perhaps serious injury that come with getting any of these diseases.

It is true that some vaccinations require a booster dose to keep antibody levels high. That is why we need a tetanus, diphtheria and pertussis booster every ten years.

11 **WHAT WOULD HAPPEN IF WE STOPPED USING VACCINATIONS?** That's an easy one. The diseases would come back.

Vaccinations keep us from getting sick from these infections. But, all of the infections we protect against are alive and well in our world. As of today, the only disease we have completely eliminated is smallpox. And when it was eliminated, we stopped vaccinating for it.

Anyway, it's a simple fact: when immunization rates drop, epidemics occur. Just look at states with lower immunization rates—their rates of pertussis (whooping cough) are twice the number seen in states with higher percentages of immunization rates. And, children whose parents opt out of vaccines face a 23x greater risk of getting whooping cough. (*O'Brien*)

Reality Check

In 1990, low immunization rates led to a measles epidemic of 55,000 cases and over 100 preventable deaths in the U.S. The U.S. saw a measles epidemic again in 2008—over 90% of these cases were unvaccinated children, two-thirds of which were by parental choice. But a few of the cases were infants who were too young to be vaccinated (and exposed to an infected child in the doctor's waiting room). This serves as a reminder that vaccine-preventable diseases have not disappeared.

12 **WHAT ARE THE TYPICAL SIDE EFFECTS OF VACCINATION?** Fever, fussiness, redness or lump at the site of the injection.

Inactivated vaccines cause an immediate immune response. The body mounts a response to the foreign invader as if it were being infected. The

result, typically, is a fever within 24 hours of vaccination. Babies sometimes feel like they are coming down with a cold or flu (body aches, pains). Some babies prefer to sleep through the experience; some choose to tell you how they feel (fussiness, crying). All of these symptoms resolve within 24 to 48 hours of vaccination.

Live attenuated vaccines (MMR, Varicella) cause a delayed immune response. This occurs one to four *weeks* after the vaccination is given. Long after the doctor's visit, your child may wake up one morning and have a fever. This may be accompanied by a rash that looks like measles (pimples) or chickenpox (clear, fluid filled pimples). The rash can sometimes be dramatic. Both the fever and the rash tell you that your baby is forming an immune response to the vaccination. Babies are not contagious and aren't too bothered by the rash. You don't need to call your doctor. This reaction is expected.

Redness at the injection site is common. In particular, the fifth booster dose of the DTaP (at age five years) can cause a pretty dramatic area of redness. No worries. We do get quite a few phone calls about it, though!

A firm lump may develop at the injection site if some of the fat in the arm/leg gets nicked as the needle goes into the muscle. This is called **FAT NECROSIS**. It usually goes away within six to eight weeks. It doesn't hurt.

RED FLAG

If your baby has a fever *more* than 24 to 48 hours after being vaccinated, it's not from the vaccination. You need to call your doctor. The only exceptions are the MMR and chickenpox vaccines given at one year of age.

It's okay to give your baby acetaminophen (Tylenol) to help reduce the fever and discomfort of vaccinations. The dose is not listed on the package. It says to "consult a doctor." That's because doctors don't want you giving this medicine to a baby *three months or younger* with a fever without checking in first. Other than with shots, you need to call your doctor about fevers in this age group—see the section on fevers in Chapter 15, "First Aid" chapter.

13 **WHAT ARE THE WORST REACTIONS TO VACCINATION?** These are called adverse reactions. This is the equivalent of an allergic reaction to a medication—and fortunately, they are all quite rare. With each generation of newer vaccinations, the risk of serious reactions is almost eliminated. Adverse reactions include:

1. Death.
2. Anaphylactic reaction.
3. Encephalitis.
4. Fever related seizure (convulsions).

Both the CDC and FDA keep close tabs on adverse reactions to vaccines via a Vaccine Adverse Event Reporting System (VAERS). Both doctors and patient families may submit a VAERS form if any adverse reaction occurs.

Keep in mind that medical illness reports do not prove an association of a particular illness with a specific vaccination. The job of both the CDC and FDA is to review each report that occurs and see if there is a pattern of subsequent illness after vaccination. VAERS data is publicly available at vaers.hhs.gov. To report a possible reaction, you can download a form at the same site. There is also a Clinical Immunization Safety Assessment Network comprised of six U.S. academic medical centers that evaluates adverse reactions to vaccines (vaccinesafety.net).

While we would be remiss if we didn't tell you that vaccinations have some risks associated with them, we want you to remember that the risk of adverse reaction is *significantly* lower than leaving your baby unprotected.

In 1988, recognizing that there are rare, serious reactions that occur as a result of vaccinating children, the U.S. Department of Health and Human Services created the Vaccine Injury Compensation Program. This program attempts to determine whether adverse reactions from vaccines are responsible for injuries or death and then to provide the victim with compensation. Since 1988 there have been about 15,000 claimants. Considering there are four million babies born each year and most have been vaccinated, the odds of an injury are staggeringly tiny.

Another statistic to mull over: 1.9 billion doses of vaccine were given in the U.S. from 1991 to 2001. Only 2,281 cases of allergic reactions were reported. (*Zeiger*) (Compare that statistic to one in 50 adults who have a food allergy!)

We agree that an adverse reaction only has to happen to one child for it to be heartbreaking. But if we look at the big picture, we can point to the millions of children who might have experienced illness, chronic disability, and death if diseases like smallpox or polio were not controlled by vaccinations.

RED FLAGS

Call the doctor if your baby does the following after a vaccination:

1. Inconsolable crying over three hours.
2. Fever over 105 degrees.
3. Seizure activity.
4. Extreme lethargy.

Q. How do I know that the CDC and FDA are on "our" side?

Ah, the government conspiracy theory—the belief by some that the government is part of a vast conspiracy to hurt children with bad vaccines . . . and enrich pharmaceutical makers who make vaccines.

Yes, years ago, some members of vaccine advisory committees had ties with vaccine producers. These people were invited to the table because they brought a wealth of knowledge with them (example: vaccine research scientists).

Today, no one working for the vaccine watchdogs (CDC, FDA, AAP, ACIP, or AAFP) receives any grant or research money from pharmaceutical companies. So there is no real or perceived financial incentive to allow a bad vaccine to stay on the market. If there is concern about a vaccine, it will be pulled from the market immediately (see the example of the rotavirus vaccine later in this chapter).

To further ensure unbiased recommendations, the National Immunization Program (NIP) and the Vaccine Injury Compensation Program (VICP) parted ways in 2005 so there would be no perceived "conflict of interest."

Here is another consideration: why would these groups want our nation's children to suffer chronic illness, pain, or even death? Think about it. It is in *nobody's* interest to increase infant morbidity and mortality rates.

14 **WHO KEEPS A RECORD OF MY CHILD'S VACCINATIONS?** You and your doctor. Your doctor keeps a record of vaccinations in your child's records. And some states have an immunization registry that also keeps records of vaccinations.

But ultimately, YOU need to have a copy of these in your personal medical record file. You will need proof of vaccinations for many things. Any childcare or school program requires this information. Summer camps and athletic programs want the records too. If your child becomes a healthcare professional, joins the military, or is a food handler, he will also need this information.

Helpful Hint

It's a good idea to have a medical passport for your child. This should include an immunization record, growth chart, list of medical problems, list of surgeries, drug allergies, and name and dosage of any medications that are used regularly (such as asthma medicine). Some medical practices now offer a patient portal that allows you to keep track of your own records. If so, we encourage you to take advantage of it!

Q. How do I know when my child needs booster shots?

Your doctor will remind you at each well child visit.

We wish pediatricians were more like dentists or veterinarians, who long ago figured out how to send out reminders of needed visits. Sadly, only a minority of pediatric practices have electronic reminder or recall systems. Most do not usually send out reminder cards to let you know your child is due for shots. What most practices do is provide the schedule in an information packet at your child's *first* visit. Your doctor will tell you at each well check when to return. This system works pretty well unless you start missing well-child visits. Then your child gets behind on his vaccination series. You can try to catch your child up on shots when he is in for a sick visit if this happens.

Reality Check

Wanted: a national immunization registry.

There is no uniform system of tracking immunization status and sending reminder cards to patients' families. One solution: a national immunization registry. Advocates of this plan feel it will improve our country's immunization rates. Those opposed to the plan think it invades personal privacy and creates a government health care tracking system. So, like most governmental decisions, it may take years to resolve.

15 **WHAT VACCINES ARE REQUIRED AND WHICH ONES ARE OPTIONAL?** The answer varies state to state. It also varies depending on the frequency of disease in particular counties within a state. We have provided a table of the most recent requirements in the U.S. on our web site Baby411.com (click on "Bonus Material").

Q. Can I take my baby out before she gets her first set of shots?

Yes, just be smart about it.

Pediatricians usually recommend limiting human contact with babies under four weeks of life. Why? Because if your newborn gets any fever (of 100.4 or greater), that is an automatic ticket to the hospital for two days (see Chapter 15, First Aid for details). Even if your baby has the cold that the rest of the household has, we still need to rule out a serious infection. That said, you aren't quarantined, but use discretion when planning your outings. In cold and flu season, avoid crowded places for the first three months of life.

With respect to an unvaccinated baby, the biggest threat these days is whooping cough. Whooping cough is spread by cough and sneeze droplets of an infected person. Babies get a series of four shots over the first two years of life to protect them from whooping cough. To keep everyone inside that long is crazy! But being cautious until she gets her first shot at two months isn't a bad idea.

Vaccination Schedule

The schedule for vaccinations is below. For details on these specific vaccines, see the next section. Note: If you want to know what shots your baby is due for, use the CDC's free Immunization Scheduler. Go to: www2a.cdc.gov/nip/kidstuff/newscheduler_le/and just type in your baby's birth date!

Disease And Vaccine Specifics

Let's talk specifics—here is a breakdown of the vaccines and the diseases they are designed to stop. View our website at Baby411.com for a visual library of these diseases (click on "Bonus Material").

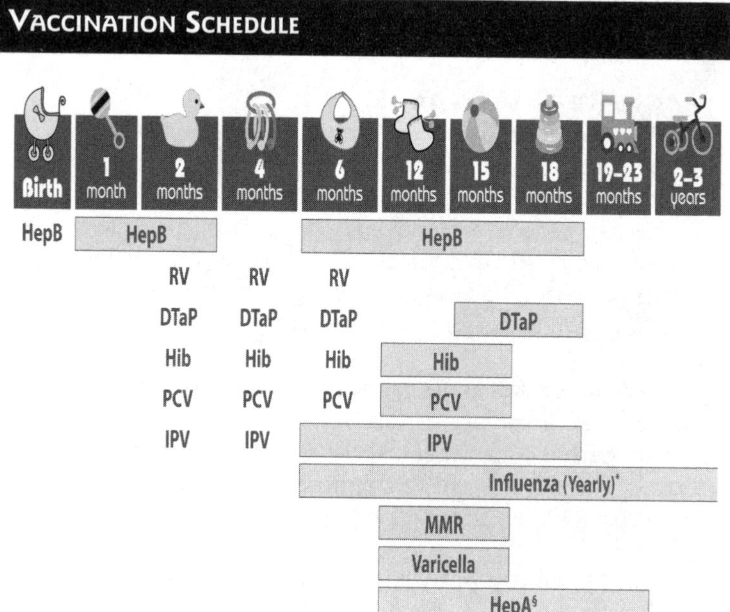

Diphtheria, Tetanus, Pertussis

◆ ***Diphtheria***: This is a *bacteria* that causes a serious throat infection. It invades the tonsils, kills the tissue, and creates a thick pus lining that can block off the airway. It also produces a toxin that enters the blood and injures the heart, kidneys, and nerves. It is spread by respiratory droplets (coughs and sneezes). There is a 10% mortality rate from infection, even today. *Before the vaccine, up to 20,000 Americans died per year.*

◆ ***Tetanus***: This is a *bacteria* that causes wound infections. It is not contagious person to person. Tetanus bacteria produce spores that are found in the soil and dust around the world. These are resilient little germs, so we will never eliminate them. Tetanus spores can enter open wounds (especially puncture wounds, animal bites, and umbilical cord stumps) and make a toxin that attacks nerves. The affected nerves cause muscles to spasm (called "tetany"). These spasms prevent breathing and swallowing (lockjaw). There is a 30% mortality rate from infection.

◆ ***Pertussis (Whooping Cough):*** This *bacteria* causes irritation and inflammation of the throat. This swelling prevents mucous from being coughed up and creates a blocked airway, particularly for those with the smallest airways (infants). Pertussis infection initially looks like the common cold. Over time, infected people have coughing fits or spasms. As a person tries to get a breath in, he makes a characteristic "whoop." Infants, who have smaller airways, are unable to breathe at all. So instead of whooping, they stop breathing and their faces turn red or purple. Children often throw up during a coughing fit. In Asia, this illness is known as the "100 Day Cough." The infection is spread by respiratory droplets. *Prior to vaccine development, there were 200,000 cases a year in the U.S. There were 10,000 deaths annually, mostly in infants.* In 2010, there were over 21,000 cases reported in the U.S. and 26 deaths. Over 75% of the hospitalizations were in infants under six months of age and most of the deaths were in babies.

vaccinations

DTaP: The vaccine

This is the vaccine that protects against **D**iphtheria, **T**etanus, and **P**ertussis (whooping cough).

The combination vaccine has been around since the 1940's. The original vaccine (DTP) was called a "whole cell" vaccine because the vaccine was derived from a whole dead whooping cough germ. This vaccine was effective, but caused a significant number of high fevers and convulsions. A newer, safer formulation (called the "acellular" vaccine or DTaP vaccine) came out in 1991. The immune response is formed to a piece of the bacteria (its signature).

The primary vaccination series is five total doses. The primary doses are given at two, four, and six months of life. The fourth and fifth booster doses (given to toddlers and before kindergarten) are more likely to cause a fever or redness at the injection site because our bodies recognize it and have an immune response ready to go. After the fifth dose of DTaP, a single Tdap booster is given to preteens and anyone else who has never received it. And as of 2012, pregnant women should get Tdap with each pregnancy to protect herself and her baby. The tetanus and diphtheria booster (Td) is then given every ten years.

Here is the tricky thing about pertussis protection–it is short lived, whether you endure the actual disease or get the vaccine. Immunity wears off after about five years. That leaves susceptible teens and adults as reservoirs of infection to expose infants who aren't fully protected yet. So it's important for moms, dads, and other adult caretakers (under age 65) to get their Tdap vaccine!

Q. Is it true that whooping cough epidemics still occur?

Yes. In fact, whooping cough is alive and well. 2010 was a particularly bad year, especially in California, where they saw almost 10,000 cases. Then in 2012, there were almost 42,000 cases–11% of which were in Washington state (a hub of anti-vaccine sentiment). Most troubling of all, babies still die from this disease.

Here are some things you should know:

1. Whooping cough epidemics occur about every three to four years.
2. Immunity to whooping cough wanes in teens and adults despite vaccination during childhood. The good news: since 2005, a whooping cough vaccine for teens and adults is available. The bad news: only 8% of American adults have gotten their booster shot!
3. Many cases of whooping cough are undiagnosed and untreated in older people. Have you ever had a cough that just "hung on" for several weeks? You may have had whooping cough and not known it.
4. Dropping immunization rates allow the disease to spread quickly through a community.
5. Infants are given their first whooping cough (pertussis) vaccination at two months of age. But, they don't have effective protection against the disease until they have received three doses of the vaccine (at six months of life). Yes, it is the youngest children who are the most susceptible and unfortunately, they also have the highest risk of serious illness and death.

BOTTOM LINE: If you or anyone in the family has a chronic cough, get it checked out. It's important for you and your baby. And please get your baby vaccinated.

Polio

This *virus* attacks the spinal cord and brain. It has particular affinity for the nerves that control leg muscles and the diaphragm muscle (that helps you breathe). Polio infections leave people paralyzed, or needing a machine to breathe for them. Prior to our modern day ventilators, people survived the illness by living in iron lung machines. The virus spreads through the stool of infected people. This was a common summertime epidemic, and whole households would get the infection. Before the vaccine, there were 20,000 cases of paralysis per year in the U.S. Since 1979, there have been no cases of naturally occurring polio infection in the U.S. We still give the polio vaccine because the infection is an airplane flight away.

The top three countries where polio is still endemic are: Nigeria, Pakistan, and Afghanistan. There has been an extraordinary effort to eradicate the disease, like smallpox. Seeing what countries are involved, you can understand why this is such a challenge! While this may happen in our lifetime, polio is still a threat.

Polio: the Vaccine

In the U.S., we give the inactivated form of the vaccine (a shot). The vaccine that was given from 1963-1996 was a live vaccine (a drink) that carried a small risk of acquiring vaccine-associated polio disease.

There were a few cases annually of vaccine associated polio disease when the live (oral) vaccine was used. In 1997, doctors switched to an all-inactivated vaccination series (IPV; that is, not live). IPV does not cause polio disease.

Polio vaccine is a four-dose series. The first doses are given at two and four months of age. The third dose is given at 6-18 months. The final dose is given before entering kindergarten.

Haemophilus Influenza B (Hib)

vaccinations

This is a *bacteria* that causes a potentially fatal throat swelling (epiglottitis) and **MENINGITIS** (infection of the brain lining). Despite the name, there is no relationship to influenza, the flu virus—yes, we realize that is confusing. HIB is spread by respiratory droplets (sneezing, coughing). Prior to vaccine development, there were 20,000 cases of HIB infection annually in the U.S. and 500 deaths. Most infections occurred in children less than five years old. Survivors of meningitis may be permanently deaf, blind, or intellectually disabled. About 5% of children with HIB infections die, and 20% suffer permanent disability. The development of the HIB vaccine is a true success story of modern-day medicine. The vaccine was licensed in 1985. By 1992, HIB infections were virtually eliminated (less than 200 cases per year).

In 2008, Minnesota reported an outbreak of five cases of HIB—one child, whose parents chose not to vaccinate, died. Of the five cases, three of the children were not immunized due to parental concern about vaccines and the desire to delay or space out vaccinations. One child had an immune deficiency, so his body did not mount an adequate response to vaccination and therefore he was unprotected. Another child who died received two doses of the vaccine, yet was too young to get the third dose of the primary vaccination series. Pennsylvania also had seven children with HIB infection, three of whom died. Of the seven children, six had received no HIB vaccinations and one three-year old child, who died, had received just one dose (more than one dose is needed to provide adequate protection).

Minnesota hasn't seen this many annual cases of HIB since 1992. Health officials attribute the outbreak to two causes: 1) unvaccinated children by parental choice and 2) a HIB vaccine supply shortage at the time. Toddlers are supposed to receive a booster dose of HIB vaccine. Because of the shortage, HIB vaccine was given preferentially to infants.

HIB: The vaccine

The HIB vaccine can be given either individually (in three or four doses)

or in a combination product. The combination vaccine, Comvax (which combines Hepatitis B and HIB), is a **three** dose series of shots for complete protection. ALL other HIB vaccines require **four** doses to complete the series. Children form a good immunity with either of these products.

According to the CDC immunization schedule, babies complete a primary series of vaccinations for HIB at two, four, and six months of age. A HIB booster dose is given to toddlers at 12-15 months.

Measles, Mumps, Rubella

◆ *Measles:* This is a *virus* that infects the entire body. Infected people start out with cold symptoms and pink eye. It causes a dramatic head-to-toe rash, then the infection spreads to other organ systems. These include the intestines (diarrhea), lungs (pneumonia), and brain (encephalitis). The highest rate of these complications is in children under age five.

The virus is highly contagious and is spread through respiratory droplets (coughs and sneezes). The virus is so hearty, it can remain alive and infectious in the air and on surfaces for up to two hours.

Measles was as common as chickenpox used to be. *Before the measles vaccine, there were an amazing four million cases per year and 500 deaths per year in the U.S.* Today, measles is more common in other countries (particularly England, Germany, Austria, Italy, Australia, Switzerland, Israel, China), and international travel easily brings it to America. Twelve children recently adopted from China had measles infections when they landed on U.S. soil.

2008 saw one of the largest U.S. measles outbreaks in the past ten years—135 cases. *91% percent of the children who contracted measles were unvaccinated-by-parent choice.*

It all started when one of those children (a seven year old boy from San Diego), returned from a trip to Switzerland with measles. He went on to infect his unvaccinated siblings and classmates. He also infected infants (who were too young to be vaccinated), whose only mistake was to be in a doctor's waiting room on the wrong day. Some children were hospitalized, fortunately none died.

Great Britain (which does not have a mandatory-for-school vaccination program) had a more substantial outbreak in 2008—1348 cases and one death, compared to 56 cases in 1998. Why such a rise? Immunization rates at the time, were only about 80% for the MMR shot on that side of the pond. Not coincidently, Britain was the epicenter for the MMR vaccine controversy, which first erupted in 1998—more on that later in this chapter (see controversies).

Even today, there is no treatment for measles. If you'd rather let your child get the measles than give them the shot to prevent it, you've never seen measles!

◆ *Mumps*: This is a *virus* that attacks the salivary glands. Mumps infect the glands located along the jaw line and causes a marked swelling. It also infects other body parts that swell up, including the testicles, ovaries, and brain. Mumps attacks the brain (meningitis) about 15% of the time. It can cause deafness and intellectual disability in survivors. Like measles, mumps is spread through respiratory droplets. *Before the mumps vaccine was developed, there were up to 200,000 cases per year. We usually see fewer than 600 cases a year in the U.S.*

◆ *Rubella* (**GERMAN MEASLES**): This is a highly contagious *virus* that causes mild infection in children, but fatal or disabling infection in unborn fetuses. Rubella spreads through respiratory droplets and causes a runny nose, swollen glands, and a rash in children. If a pregnant woman gets rubella, the fetus can die in the womb (miscarriage) or be born with severe intellectual disability, deafness, or blindness (called congenital rubella syndrome). *An epidemic in 1964 (prior to the rubella vaccine) affected 20,000 babies.* The good news: the CDC took rubella off the U.S. disease "threat list" in 2005 because only nine cases were reported in 2004. Three cases were reported in the U.S. in 2012. We need to continue vaccinating since this disease is not eliminated worldwide.

MMR: the vaccine

The vaccines for measles, mumps and rubella are given together as the MMR vaccine. In the past, these vaccines were also manufactured separately. Since 2009, the only vaccine product on the market is the combination MMR vaccine.

Because the MMR vaccine is a live-attenuated vaccine, your child may develop a rash that looks like measles (red pimples) and/or a fever, one to four weeks after being vaccinated. There are two shots in the MMR vaccination series. The first dose is given at 12-15 months of age. A booster dose is given before entering kindergarten.

Hepatitis A

This *virus* attacks the liver. And there is a vaccine to prevent it. It's spread through infected poop, contaminated water and food. It spreads rapidly in childcare centers due to all the kids in diapers. Fortunately, children infected with Hepatitis A have a relatively minor illness. Some children don't even have symptoms. Adults, however, get very sick. Prior to the Hepatitis A vaccine, there were over 100,000 cases per year in the U.S.

Hepatitis A: the vaccine

The Hepatitis A vaccine was approved in 1995 and became part of the routine childhood immunization series in 2005. Vaccinating toddlers against Hepatitis A not only protects them but also prevents the spread of the disease to others in childcare centers. The vaccine is very effective: Israel has seen a 98.5% reduction in disease since they began Hepatitis A universal vaccination.

Kids get the vaccine starting at age one. It is a series of two doses given at least six months apart.

Hepatitis B

This is another *virus* that attacks the liver. There are various types of Hepatitis. The most noteworthy are A, B, and C. Each type of virus is spread

differently. Hepatitis B is spread through blood and body fluid (saliva, vaginal discharge, and semen) contact. It is extremely contagious. Yes, it is spread primarily by sexual contact and by exposure in the healthcare field. However, children are most at risk of exposure to Hepatitis B during birth if their mother has the disease.

The infection causes skin to turn yellow because the liver is unable to metabolize bilirubin as it should (see earlier in this book for a discussion of bilirubin). It causes stomach upset and lack of appetite. Some people with Hepatitis B recover quickly, while others die. Others have a chronic infection that goes on for 20 years until they die. And some people become carriers of the disease once they survive the infection.

Don't think of this disease as one that only happens to IV drug users or people with several sex partners. 16% of people who get Hepatitis B have neither of these risk factors.

Reality Check

There are over ***1 million*** Hepatitis B carriers walking around the U.S.

If this isn't enough to convince you to protect your child, Hepatitis B also is a known cause of liver cancer. Yes, the Hepatitis B vaccine is the first cancer vaccine. Before the vaccine became part of the childhood immunization series in 1991, 30,000 children were infected with Hepatitis B annually in the U.S.

Hepatitis B: The vaccine

Giving the vaccine as a part of the childhood immunization program ensures that your child gets immunized and has lifelong protection. Babies born to mothers who have Hepatitis B need to get the vaccination and immuneglobulin shot within 12 hours of birth to prevent infection. If they don't get these shots, newborns who get infected by their moms have a 90% chance of getting Hepatitis B.

The Hepatitis B vaccine is a three-dose series. The first dose is routinely given before hospital discharge. The second dose is given one or two months later. The third dose is given six to 18 months after the first dose.

Varicella (Chickenpox)

This is a *virus* familiar to most of us. Before routine use of chickenpox vaccine in 1995, about four million people got chickenpox every year in the U.S. Some of you reading this book probably remember having this illness. *What most of you don't know is that chickenpox also led to 10,000 hospitalizations and 100 deaths annually.*

The varicella virus spreads by respiratory droplets and by the fluid found in the skin lesions. It is incredibly contagious. The virus attacks the whole body via the bloodstream. Infected people feel tired and run a fever, then break out in classic clear fluid-filled blisters that arrive in clusters. The average number of skin lesions is 350. Does it make you feel itchy just thinking about it? People are contagious for seven days, on average.

The virus itself can cause pneumonia and encephalitis. Even more prob-

DR B'S OPINION: CHICKENPOX CAN BE DEADLY

During my residency, I cared for a seven-year-old patient with chickenpox who came to our emergency room with a secondary Strep infection–she died two hours later. That experience has left an impact on me. When parents perceive that chickenpox is just a minor illness, I tell them that story. Attending a "chickenpox party" to knowingly give your child this illness is not a sign of being an empowered parent. It's a sign of ignorance.

lematic is that Strep bacteria have a field day with the open wounds when the blisters pop. These secondary infections can be deadly.

The vaccine has prevented 95% of severe chickenpox infections. And in kids under nine years of age, death from chickenpox is down by a whopping 90%. And vaccinated people who get chickenpox despite the vaccine have a very mild illness (less than 50 pox; occasional fever; lasts for just a few days).

Varicella (Chickenpox): The vaccine

The varicella vaccine is a live-attenuated vaccine. Hence, it contains a weakened form of the germ that causes chickenpox. As a result, some children will get a rash that looks like chickenpox one to four weeks after being vaccinated.

Some parents wonder if a recently vaccinated child can spread chickenpox to someone else (particularly someone who has an immune deficiency). Since the chickenpox vaccine came out in 1995, several million people have been vaccinated. There have been *three* documented cases of vaccine-associated chickenpox. Yup, three. The risk is so low that even if your child develops a rash after his shot, he can still attend daycare. (*Pickering*)

There is a small risk of getting shingles (reactivated chickenpox) later in life. At the time of this writing, evidence suggests that you are more likely to get shingles if you get the actual disease than if you have been vaccinated.

Parents also wonder if the vaccine will provide lifelong protection. While we don't have an entire generation's worth of data, we do have data on people who participated in the original studies of this vaccine dating back to 1975–and yes, those people have shown good immunity.

The American Academy of Pediatrics and Centers for Disease Control recommend two doses of vaccine for the most complete protection. The first dose is given at 12-15 months and the booster dose is given at 4-6 years, in preparation for kindergarten.

Can older children get the chickenpox vaccine? Yes, the varicella vaccine should be given to anyone over a year of age who has never had chickenpox.

Strep Pneumoniae

This is a *bacteria* that is in the Strep family. It is not the Strep that causes Strep throat. It's a distant cousin. This bacteria causes meningitis, pneumonia, blood infections (sepsis), sinus infections, and ear infections. The

Prevnar vaccine protects against the top 13 strains of Strep pneumoniae (there are 90 total) that cause serious infection.

Respiratory droplets spread the bacteria. Once the bugs get in, they head for the respiratory system (ears, sinuses, lungs) or the brain. They travel via the blood en route to these places. Infected people run a high fever when the bacteria are in the bloodstream. Fortunately, many infections are treated before meningitis occurs. *Prior to the Prevnar vaccine, there were over 16,000 cases of serious Strep pneumoniae infections a year in American children under age five. In babies, Strep pneumoniae is the #1 cause of bacterial meningitis.* The highest risk groups for serious infection are infants and the elderly.

There are antibiotics to treat Strep pneumoniae, however, doctors are seeing more drug-resistant strains. It's survival of the fittest for germs–and these germs are some of the smartest around. Twenty percent of the Strep pneumoniae strains in the vaccine are resistant to Penicillin. Ten percent are resistant to three OR MORE types of antibiotics. Daycare children are at higher risk for Strep pneumoniae infection, particularly the drug-resistant strains.

Strep pneumoniae (Prevnar or PCV 13): The vaccine

Prevnar is recommended as part of the routine immunization schedule by the American Academy of Pediatrics. There has been an 87% reduction in serious Strep pneumoniae disease (meningitis, blood and pneumonia infections) since the immunization program began in 2000. Interestingly, we have also seen a 50% reduction in pneumonia in the elderly since there is less Strep out there.

Prevnar is a four dose series. The first three doses are given at two, four, and six months of age. A booster dose is given at 12-15 months.

Rotavirus

Rotavirus is a *virus* that comes to visit every winter.

Doctors always know rotavirus has arrived in a community. The littlest patients come into the office with so much watery diarrhea that parents cannot keep up with diaper changes. The vomiting part is pretty miserable, too. Because there is so much water lost in the poop, infants are at high risk of becoming dehydrated.

Before widespread vaccine use in 2006, Rotavirus infection caused about 50,000 hospitalizations of young American children every winter. There were also about 30 deaths per year in the U.S. from rotavirus. Worldwide, rotavirus kills 440,000 kids every year.

You can see why docs have long wanted a vaccine for this disease! Looking at data on diarrhea season (that's a fun job, eh), it's clear that rotavirus vaccine has made a significant impact in reducing the number and severity of cases. (*CDC*)

Rotavirus: The vaccine

The FDA approved the rotavirus vaccine (called Rotateq) in February 2006. It's a live, attenuated vaccine given in the form of oral drops at two, four, and six months of age. While it is an optional vaccine in all states, we STRONGLY recommend your child get the vaccine (especially if he attends daycare, where rotavirus infections spread like wildfire). Rotarix, another

FDA approved rotavirus vaccine, is a two-dose oral drops series.

The most common side effect of the rotavirus vaccine is mild diarrhea within a week. Past rotavirus vaccines had a very rare, nasty side effect: bowel obstruction (intussusception); see the controversies section later in this chapter. However, since the vaccine came out, tens of millions of doses been given worldwide and results are promising–the risk of bowel obstruction is no greater in vaccinated babies than in the general population. Nonetheless, parents should be looking out for severe abdominal pain/irritability or blood in the poop/grape jelly poop after vaccination.

One word of caution: rotavirus vaccine is a live vaccine. Babies cannot receive the vaccine if they have a rare immune disorder called Severe Combined Immune Deficiency (SCID). And if any caretaker is immune-compromised (for example, on chemotherapy) there is a theoretical risk of an adult getting the disease from exposure to the vaccinated baby's stool. About 9% of babies will shed the weakened virus in their poop four to six days after the first dose of the vaccine. Less than 0.3% shed it after the second or third doses. Let your doc know and you can discuss your individual situation.

Influenza (Flu)

This is another *virus* we see every winter. It is an infection that attacks the respiratory tract. Worse than the common cold, flu causes higher fevers, body aches, headaches, and a crummy feeling in general. The runny nose and cough arrive later and last longer than a typical cold. Secondary bacterial infections (ear infections, sinus infections, pneumonia) occur more often with the flu than with your garden-variety cold virus.

Besides being generally unpleasant to endure, the flu can be deadly. The highest risk groups for serious health complications from the flu are children under two years of age and adults over age 65.

Influenza: The vaccine

The only state that requires flu vaccine for school is New Jersey. Yep, you can't go to school in New Jersey without proof of being vaccinated against the flu. While that sounds draconian, keep in mind that school-aged kids are often ground zero for a flu epidemic–while they are at low risk of suffering severe health complications, school-aged kids are most likely to spread the flu to others in the community who ARE at risk.

The Centers for Disease Control's latest recommendations for "Who should get flu vaccine?" are: EVERYONE who is six months old and up. But, here are the people who are most at risk:

1. 50-years or older.
2. Immune-compromised (weak immune systems)
3. Suffering from chronic illness (asthma, heart disease, diabetes), age six months old or older.
4. Health care workers.
5. Pregnant women during flu season (November-March).
6. Children ages six months old to 18 years old.
7. Household contacts and caretakers of any child aged birth to five years.

The flu vaccine currently used for kids under two years of age is an inactivated vaccine, in the form of a shot. They won't get the flu from it. It provides immunity two weeks after getting the vaccine. The vaccine is effective for one year. The particular influenza virus strains that show up every year is different, so we have to get vaccinated for the new bugs in town each autumn.

Kids under nine years of age who get the flu vaccine for the first time need two doses given one month apart. One cautionary note: children with egg allergies should first consult their doctor about the flu vaccine.

Currently, there is only one flu vaccine that is "preservative free" and allowed for use in infants as young as six months old. It's called Fluzone (Aventis Pasteur). The other flu vaccines contain a trace amount of thimerosal (0.025 milligrams per dose). However, the acceptable limit of exposure is over 12 times this dose (0.2-0.4mg). See the section "Controversies" later in this chapter for more information on thimerosal.

Insider Tip

There is a live inactivated flu vaccine nasal spray called Flumist, currently FDA approved for healthy children ages two years and up…to age 49 (in case you are squeamish about shots and wanted to know your options). The nasal spray vaccine provides comparable protection to the injectable one–and it doesn't hurt. Flumist is produced in single-use nasal syringes. No preservatives are necessary (hence, Flumist is thimerosal-free).

Reality check

Every spring, the World Health Organization determines the three or four strains of influenza virus that are most likely to show up in the Northern hemisphere in the upcoming winter flu season (based on those circulating in the Southern hemisphere). So each year, the seasonal flu vaccine protects against three or four different types of flu. That's why the flu vaccine is slightly different every year.

Q. I'm pregnant. Is it safe for me to get the flu vaccine?

YES! And, it will protect both you and your unborn baby.

The flu shot (not the nasal spray) is FDA approved for pregnant women during ANY trimester of pregnancy.

A pregnant woman is at greater risk of complications from the flu because her body is in a functionally immune-compromised state (which allows her body to let a fetus with foreign DNA grow inside of her). So protection via vaccination is pretty important.

Moms-to-be who get their flu vaccine also protect their babies, once they are born. In fact, newborns and infants whose moms got flu vaccine during pregnancy have a 40% lower chance of being hospitalized for flu. (*Eick*)

Smallpox

Q. Will my baby get the smallpox vaccine?

No. The World Health Organization declared the world "smallpox-free"

in 1980 (a major accomplishment). We no longer vaccinate for this disease.

Currently, there is no plan to resume smallpox vaccination. If bioterrorism becomes an increasing concern, we may hear about this vaccine again. Check our website at Baby411.com for more info and updates.

Controversies

Let's face it, controversy drives TV ratings and web traffic. No one is interested in hearing about things that work as they should—and vaccines are a good example. Vaccines have been a hot topic for the last decade or so. Unfortunately, rare adverse events and theoretical concerns tend to make more headlines than the remarkable success story of vaccinations. These problems are then seized on by vaccine opponents and spread online through the web like a, well, virus.

So, let's address this head on. Here are the controversies you might hear about with vaccines:

Does MMR Cause Autism?

Q. I've heard that the MMR vaccine might cause autism. Is this true?

No.

Parents also hear that vaccinations cause multiple sclerosis, diabetes, asthma, and SIDS. None of these are caused by vaccination. The government operates a safety monitoring system (VAERS, FDA, CDC)—watching for any possible adverse effects from vaccines. *No one wants to increase autism rates.*

One small case report of only eight patients in 1998 led a research group to feel that the combination MMR vaccine might cause autism. (*Wakefield*) But, don't try to find the article online because the journal that published the article later retracted it when a former member of the research lab revealed

DR B'S OPINION: MMR & AUTISM

I follow the developmental milestones of all my patients carefully. I have concerns for autism long before a patient turns a year of age. But I keep these concerns to myself because many of these worrisome children ultimately catch up developmentally. It is only when I am sure of the diagnosis do I sit down with my families to discuss these lifelong developmental disorders.

I have never had a developmentally normal patient come in for his one year well check, get his MMR vaccine, and come back at his 15-month checkup as an autistic child. The 15-month-old who is autistic is a child I was worried about long before the one-year well check.

In another study, doctors noticed the same results. Developmental specialists viewed footage of children's first birthday parties (who had not received the MMR vaccine yet). The specialists accurately identified the children who were later diagnosed with autism.

that the data reported in the study was fabricated! (*Newsweek.com*) Twelve years later, the lead author lost his license to practice medicine in England and was accused of fraud. The whole thing was a hoax.

Before this came to light, several reputable scientists tried to replicate the findings of this now discredited researcher. No one ever could—and know we know why!

Unfortunately, frightened parents chose to skip the MMR vaccine and measles epidemics occurred both in England and the U.S. as a result of these unfounded claims.

Bottom line: Don't base health decisions for your child on one research study or what the media reports! Talk to your child's doctor about any vaccine safety concerns.

DR B'S OPINION: IS IT TIME TO MOVE ON?

Vaccines have received intense scrutiny over the past fifteen years in the search for a cause of autism. The best scientific minds, worldwide, have looked for a link and none has been found. Many autism researchers have moved on to look for more promising leads. Some families, however, have not moved on and want more research dollars earmarked for this debunked theory. So, yes, you will continue to here about this controversy and we want you to realize that a) science has devoted much brainpower, time and money to this concern and has concluded there is no link and b) many families with a child who has autism do not feel that vaccines have anything to do with their child's disorder. Here are some noteworthy comments:

"The question has been asked and answered and it's time to move on ... we need to be able to say, 'Yes, we are now satisfied that the earth is round.' ... we need to listen to experts and not actresses. The media culture, feeling compelled to give both sides of an argument has lent a legitimacy to the anti-vaccine movement that is very overweighted. They're a small number of people with very loud voices. The vast majority of parents of children with autism are very supportive of the importance of vaccines. . . . the media need to show both sides to make it look like both sides are equal. One side is backed by evidence, one side is not."

Alison Singer, Founder and President of the Autism Science Foundation and mother of a child with autism spectrum disorder

"It would be nice if autism advocacy organizations actually advocated for children with autism...Instead, they are anti-vaccine organizations, and the fact of the matter is vaccines have nothing to do with autism... it's high time that these organizations stopped deluding people into thinking that vaccines do have something to do with autism and started focusing on the real causes of autism."

Paul Offit, M.D. Director of the Vaccine Education Center, Children's Hospital of Philadelphia

Q. If the MMR vaccine doesn't cause autism, why is the diagnosis made around the same time as the vaccination?

One of the criteria used to make a diagnosis of autism is a language delay. Because children do not have significant expressive language under a year of age, doctors have to wait until 15 to 18 months to confirm a language delay and make the diagnosis. That's about the same time as the MMR vaccination, which leads some parents to wonder about autism and vaccination.

Rotavirus

Q. I've heard about a vaccine that was taken off the market. What was the problem with it? It makes me nervous about other new vaccines.

The original rotavirus vaccine was approved in August 1998 after a study was done on 10,000 individuals. It looked like a safe vaccine. That vaccine was then given to 1.5 million children over a period of nine months. During this time, there were 15 reports of bowel obstruction (intussusception) that occurred within a week of being vaccinated. There were no deaths. The CDC immediately pulled the vaccine off the market and initiated an investigation.

Although this was certainly a setback for new vaccinations, it proves that the adverse events reporting system (VAERS) works. Modifications have been made to the license process as a result of the rotavirus vaccine. This was the first vaccine recall in over 20 years.

As we mentioned earlier in the chapter, a newer rotavirus vaccine debuted in 2006–it was studied in 70,000 infants in Latin America and Europe before getting the nod by the FDA. After several years of use, this vaccine has clearly proven to be very safe. But given the history of the previous rotavirus vaccine, the FDA still closely monitors for any cases of bowel obstruction.

The Thimerosal (Mercury) Controversy

Q. I've heard there is mercury preservative in the vaccines. Is this true?

Not anymore. It was removed from all required childhood vaccines by 2001. This deserves repeating: ***YOUR baby will not be getting required vaccines that contain mercury (thimerosal) as a preservative.***

Despite the fact that vaccines have been mercury preservative-free for over a decade now, speculation persists about vaccines ***previously*** containing mercury and links to autism. This speculation continues even after the Institute of Medicine published a conclusive report in 2004 negating any association between vaccines and autism. (The IOM spent four years studying both the mercury question and the MMR combo vaccine question and published a series of eight reports on the subject).

Because of ongoing concerns, we present to you: more than you ever wanted to know about thimerosal!

BOTTOM LINE: Thimerosal will remain on blogs and anti-vaccine websites forever, but the preservative does not remain in any of the required childhood vaccines that YOUR baby will get.

Q. I heard that I should still ask my doctor if the vaccines for my baby are thimerosal-free. What do you suggest?

We think you should ask as many questions as you need to feel comfortable. Remember that since 2001, the entire childhood vaccine series went thimerosal (mercury) preservative-free. If your doctor has a 2001 vintage vaccine vial sitting on the shelf (which would be long expired by now), I'd have bigger concerns about your doc than his vaccine supply.

Here are the specific rules regarding thimerosal use in vaccines: the FDA requires manufacturers of *routine* childhood immunizations to no longer use thimerosal as a *preservative*. This rule does NOT apply to flu vaccine because (technically) this vaccination is optional (except in New Jersey) and not "routine."

Why does flu vaccine need thimerosal or any other preservative? First, understand the flu vaccine is reformulated every year to reflect the anticipated flu strains. Since millions of doses of flu vaccine are needed every year, the most efficient way to produce the shot is in multi-dose vials, which require a preservative.

Hence, *some* flu shots (not the flu nasal spray) contain the preservative thimerosal. However, there are single-dose preparations of flu vaccine that are mercury preservative-free. These can be given to young children and pregnant women. Ask your doctor for a thimerosal-free flu vaccine if you are concerned.

Even though thimerosal is safe, it would be ideal for all flu vaccines to be thimerosal preservative-free—this would put any concerns to rest. However, the technology just isn't there yet.

What about other vaccines? Do they contain thimerosal? There are four vaccines that use thimerosal in the production process—but it is extracted before the final product is bottled. As such, these vaccines must list that TRACE amounts of thimerosal (less than 0.003mg) may exist in the vaccine. There is probably little or no thimerosal in the finished product, but the manufacturer must declare it.

We have no concerns about these vaccines, but if you are completely freaked out about the thimerosal thing (despite the proof that they are safe), there are other alternatives to these specific vaccines made without any thimerosal:

- Tripedia (one brand of DTaP),
- Pediarix (one brand combo of DTaP/HepB/IPV),
- Trihibit (DTaP/HIB),
- Engerix-B (one brand of Hep B).

The FDA has a chart online that tracks any thimerosal content in vaccines: vaccinesafety.edu/thi-table.htm We have a link to the chart on our web site Baby411.com (click on Links).

FYI: many vaccines such as the combination measles, mumps, and rubella vaccine (MMR,) never used thimerosal in the production process or as a preservative.

Reality Check

Worried about the mercury preservative (thimerosal) in your child's flu vaccine? Consider this: *there is five times more mercury in a tuna fish sandwich, than in a thimerosal preservative*

THIMEROSAL 411

Preservatives and stabilizers are used in vaccines so that the vaccinations remain potent and uncontaminated. A popular preservative *used* to be a chemical called thimerosal, which contained trace amounts of *ethylmercury*. Thimerosal use began in the 1940's.

A quick chemistry lesson: Certain compounds have completely different properties even though they may be related. For instance, take the alcohol family. *Methanol* is anti-freeze; *ethanol* is a Bud Light. Keep this in mind when we discuss mercury. We are all exposed to small amounts of mercury. The type of mercury that has raised health concerns is called *methylmercury*. High concentrations of methylmercury can be found in tuna, swordfish and shark from contaminated waters. The information known about mercury poisoning comes from unfortunate communities that have experienced it. Example: there is a large amount of data from the Faroe Islands, near Iceland. The people there would eat whale blubber contaminated with toxic levels of methylmercury and polychlorinated biphenyls (PCBs). Children, especially those exposed as fetuses during their mother's pregnancy, seemed to have lower scores on memory, attention, and language tests than their unexposed peers. (They were *not* diagnosed with autism or Attention Deficit Disorder, however.) (*AAP Technical Report*)

Chronic exposure to liquid methylmercury causes Mad Hatter's Disease, named for hat makers who used liquid mercury in the hat-making process. The disease consists of psychiatric problems, insomnia, poor memory, sweating, tremors, and red palms. Chronic mercury poisoning also impairs kidney function.

Methylmercury is a small molecule that can get into the brain—it takes almost two months to break down in the body. Ethylmercury (the type of mercury that was previously used as a vaccine preservative) is a large molecule that cannot enter the brain and is rapidly eliminated from the body within a week.

Because of the increased number of vaccinations that children get, the potential *cumulative* exposure to mercury became a concern in 1999.

There are three federal groups that set standards for acceptable daily mercury exposure (Environmental Protection Agency, Food and Drug Administration, Agency for Toxic Substances and Disease Registry). When the exposure was calculated, the cumulative dose was higher than acceptable levels set by the EPA only (the other groups' standards were higher). The Food and Drug Administration mandated the removal of thimerosal (ethylmercury) at that time for concerns extrapolated from data on methylmercury.

Vaccines still contain other preservatives (more on this in the additives section later in this chapter).

flu vaccine. (*EPA*) And the type of mercury (methylmercury) found in tuna is the one that has health concerns. Also: a baby who is exclusively breastfed for six months of life consumes about 0.36 mg of methylmercury from breast milk. That's 15 times the quantity of mercury in one flu vaccine!

vaccinations

Bottom line: as a doc, I am much more concerned about your baby's mercury exposure from the environment than what's in a flu shot. Here's a look at the numbers:

	AMOUNT OF MERCURY	TYPE OF MERCURY
Tuna, 5.6oz can	0.115 mg	METHYL
Breast milk, 1 liter	0.015 mg	METHYL
Flu vaccine with Thimerosal	0.025 mg	Ethyl

Q. Does thimerosal cause autism?

No. The Institute of Medicine reached this conclusion in 2004. What proof do we have?

Thimerosal has been removed from vaccines since 2001, but the rates of autism are still skyrocketing. A 2008 survey of autism rates in California confirms that mercury is essentially out and autism rates are still going up. If thimerosal was the cause and it was removed from vaccines seven years ago, autism rates would be going down by now. Why? Because autism spectrum disorders are usually diagnosed by three years of age. By now, any reduction in autism should have been obvious if thimerosal caused the disorder. *(Schechte)*

1. Mercury preservatives were removed from vaccines in Denmark in 1992. Canada and the European Union followed suit shortly thereafter. However, their autism rates are going up too.
3. Mad Hatter's Disease (mercury poisoning) and autism are very different disorders. See chart below.
4. A study of 100,000 kids in England compared those receiving thimerosal containing vaccines to those who did not. The ones who had the t-free shots had HIGHER rates of autism. (*Communicable Disease Surveillance Center*)
5. A 2007 study showed that children between seven and ten years of age who got those mercury containing vaccines (before 2001) have no significant differences in tests of attention and processing information. Although the study did not look specifically at autism, it showed that mercury preservatives did not make much of an impact on brain functions in general. A follow up study that specifically addresses autism is now underway. (*Thompson*)

Did thimerosal cause autism? Notice the differences between autism and mercury poisoning (*Nelson*):

	AUTISM	MERCURY POISONING
Motor	Repetitive movements	Wobbly, shaky gait
Vision	Normal	Impaired
Speech	Delay, repetitive sounds	Articulation problem
Sensory	Hyper-responsive	Loss of sensation
Psychiatric	Aloof, likes sameness	Psychosis, depression
Head size	Large	Small

Q. Are there other additives in the vaccines?

Yes. And you should know about them.

As we have already discussed, vaccines contain the active ingredients that provide immunity. But there are inactive ingredients that improve potency and prevent contamination. Below is a list of additives and why they are there. These products are present in trace amounts and none have been proven harmful in animals or humans. (*Offit*)

- Preservatives: Prevent vaccine contamination with germs (bacteria, fungus). Example: 2-phenoxyethanol, phenol, (thimerosal, prior to 2001).
- Adjuvants: Improve potency/immune response. Example: aluminum salts.
- Additives: Prevent vaccine deterioration and sticking to the side of the vial. Examples: Gelatin, Albumin, Sucrose, Lactose, MSG, glycine.
- Residuals: Remains of vaccine production process. Examples: Formaldehyde, Antibiotics (Neomycin), Egg Protein, Yeast Protein.

See our web site (Baby411.com, click on "Bonus Material") for a list of ingredients for the routine childhood vaccination series.

Reality Check

If vaccines contain ingredients like aluminum or formaldehyde, wouldn't it be better if vaccine makers got rid of these additives? Shouldn't vaccines be "greener"?

This is a red herring argument against vaccines—current vaccines are safe, even with tiny/trace amounts of preservatives or additives like aluminum. And your baby is exposed to many of these ingredients every day . . . simply by eating or breathing.

Q. Why is formaldehyde in vaccines?

Small amounts of formaldehyde are used to sterilize the vaccine fluid so your child doesn't get something like flesh-eating Strep bacteria when he gets his shots.

We know when you think of formaldehyde, you think of that ever-present smell wafting from the anatomy lab in high school. But what you probably don't know is that formaldehyde is also a naturally occurring substance in your body. And if you use baby shampoo, paper towels or mascara, or have carpeting in your home, you've been exposed to formaldehyde. The small amount used in vaccines is not a health concern. (*Dept of Health and Human Services*)

DR B'S OPINION

"We have spent a lot of money studying vaccines. Now let's spend our research dollars on finding a cause for autism.

A colleague of mine, Dr. Jill Nichols, said it best: 'This is not the case of two sides to every story. It is a case of fact vs. opinion.'"

Q. Is it true that anti-freeze is used in vaccines?

No.

There is a chemical used in some vaccines (called polyethylene glycol) that is also found in antifreeze, as well as toothpaste, lubricant eyedrops and various skin care creams. Polyethylene glycol is used in the production process to purify vaccines (it is used in one flu vaccine, among others).

Q. Is it safer to delay vaccines or use an alternative vaccination schedule?

Easy answer: no.

The CDC publishes a recommended vaccine schedule for American children. Many, many doctors, scientists, and researchers work together with the CDC to decide what is the best timing to give shots. The goal: protect babies as soon as it is safe and effective to do so. This schedule was not created out of thin air.

Between anti-vaccine activists shouting "too many shots, too soon" and Dr. Bob Sears hawking his book, new parents wonder if it would somehow be safer to wait on shots altogether or stagger them out on "Dr Bob's schedule."

Here's a nasty little truth about alternative vaccination schedules: they are all fantasy. There is absolutely no research that says delaying certain shots is safer. Dr Bob is making up "Dr Bob's Schedule" all by himself. He even admits that. In an interview with iVillage, he commented, *"My schedule doesn't have any research behind it. No one has ever studied a big group of kids using my schedule to determine if it's safe or if it has any benefits."*

A 2010 study actually did study children whose vaccinations were delayed and found there was absolutely no difference in their development to children who'd received their shots on time. (*Smith*) A 2013 study showed further evidence that giving numerous shots at the same time and giving the recommended vaccination schedule has no impact on a child's risk of autism. *(DeStefano)*

I'd much rather follow a schedule that has been extensively researched for both safety and effectiveness by experts in the field of infectious diseases.

What we do know about alternative vaccination schedules is that delaying shots is playing Russian Roulette with your child. The simple truth is that you are leaving your child unprotected, at a time when she is the most vulnerable.

DR B'S OPINION: ASK YOUR DOC ABOUT HER KIDS

As parents, our job is to protect our kids as best we can. I get it. I am a parent, too. And I certainly understand, after browsing the internet and hearing parent chatter, that you may have more questions and concerns about vaccinations.

At the end of the day, you've got to put your trust in someone to help guide you in some of those decisions. I hope you and your baby's pediatrician have a good relationship and this person can answer questions that concern you on any topic. Our job is to advocate for and protect your child. If I ever had any doubt about vaccines, or anything else that might harm your child, I guarantee that I would be the first to stop doing it. I treat my patients like my own children. So I suggest asking your doctor the most important question you can ask regarding vaccines: Did you (or would you) vaccinate your own children?

I vaccinated both my children, and would do it again without hesitation.

We realize that parents who choose to delay or opt out on vaccines are not bad parents. They are scared parents. What we are trying to help you realize is that the fear you *should* have is for the diseases that vaccines prevent. If you are on the fence about vaccinations, please take the time to research the diseases—see earlier in this chapter for details.

Q. If I want to do a staggered vaccination schedule, how should I do it?

I suggest setting up a consultation with your own pediatrician to discuss what both of you feel comfortable with doing. Remember, the ultimate goal is to have your child vaccinated in a timely manner.

Q. Didn't the government concede that vaccines caused a child's autism?

During the equivalent of a class action lawsuit against the government (called the "Omnibus Autism Proceedings"), one child, Hannah Poling, received a monetary settlement. The court did not hear her case. Hannah's case was being reviewed to serve as one of the test cases for a suit to represent 5000 families who believe vaccines caused their child's autism. During the review process, it was determined that Poling *did not* represent a test case because she had a rare, underlying genetic mitochondrial disorder that caused her deterioration and autism. For rare kids like her, *any* stress could have caused her to deteriorate. This is the equivalent of being born with an aneurysm, a ticking time bomb that could go off at any moment. Although she was not diagnosed prior to being vaccinated, experts recommend that even children with known mitochondrial disorders still be vaccinated.

Bottom line: the government did NOT concede that vaccines cause autism in the Poling case.

Vaccine Shortage

Q. I've heard there is a vaccine shortage. Is this true, and why did this happen?

Yes, our country has experienced shortages in many of the childhood vaccinations. Most vaccines are available now, though.

One reason for vaccine shortages: there are fewer vaccine makers than in years past. Now that you have read about all the controversies with vaccines, would you want to be a vaccine manufacturer? There used to be 15 pharmaceutical companies that made vaccinations. Now there are only four. When the others left the market, the remaining companies were forced to increase production for the needs of our entire country.

Helpful Hints

Where to get more information

Our advice: don't type in "vaccinations" in a Google search. You will end up with inaccurate information from concerned groups who do a great job of creating parental anxiety. The following sites will provide *accurate* information:

- ***CDC's National Immunization Program***
  cdc.gov/nip, (800) 232-2522
- ***American Academy of Pediatrics:*** aap.org, (800) 433-9016
- ***Immunization Action Coalition***immunize.org
- ***Vaccine Education Center, Children's Hospital of Philadelphia***
  vaccine.chop.edu

Here is an excellent reference book written for parents:

Vaccines and Your Child. Separating Fact from Fiction. Offit, P. and Moser C. New York: Columbia University Press. 2011.

ALUMINUM 411

Now that the mercury (thimerosal) saga is coming to an end, anti-vaccine crusaders have come up with a new bad guy: aluminum. Yes, trace amounts of aluminum salts are used in some childhood vaccines. Here's all you need to know (and more) about aluminum. Bottom line: we are not worried about it. Here's the 411:

Aluminum is everywhere. It's one of the most common metals in our earth's crust. So it is naturally present in our water, soil, and even in the air. Fruits, vegetables, nuts, flour, cereal, dairy products, and yes, even baby formula and breast milk... all contain some aluminum. Do you wear antiperspirant? It's in there, too. To avoid aluminum exposure, you'd have to quit wearing antiperspirant . . . and basically leave the planet.

Why is aluminum used in vaccines? Aluminum enhances the immune system's response to the vaccine. It's been used safely for several decades. By using aluminum salts, some inactivated vaccines require fewer booster shots for the body to mount an adequate immune response.

Are there any health concerns with aluminum in vaccines? No. There is significantly less aluminum in vaccines than what babies are exposed to in the environment. Both the National Vaccine Program Office and the World Health Organization have determined that the aluminum content in the childhood vaccination series is safe. Humans rapidly eliminate aluminum salts from the body. The small amount of aluminum that accumulates in human brains (about 50-100 mcg in an adult brain) comes from food sources. *(Mitkus)*

Does aluminum poisoning cause autism? No. People with aluminum poisoning have bone problems (osteomalacia) and anemia, as well as neurologic issues. These include memory loss, fatigue, depression, behavioral changes, and learning impairment. Aluminum has also been proposed as the cause of Alzheimer's Disease. To date, however, there is little evidence that aluminum causes that disorder. *(Dept of Health and Human Services)*

Feedback from the Real World

Vaccination Revealed, by Ginny Butler, Pregnancy and Newborn magazine March 2009:

"We live in an Information Age. We mothers can become experts in digital photography, gourmet cooking and up-to-the-minute runway fashion, merely by spending some time online. However, when we're making decisions that may be critical to our children's health and our communities' stability, obtaining correct information is vital."

Ryan's Story

Frankie Milley, a founder of Meningitis Angels (web: meningitis-angels.org), offered up this heartbreaking story about vaccines:

How much aluminum is in vaccines? Very little. If your baby follows the standard immunization schedule, he is exposed to about **four to six mg** of aluminum at six months of life. By comparison, he's also exposed to **10 mg** of aluminum if he is breastfed, **40 mg** if he is fed cow's milk-based formula, or **120 mg** if he is fed soy formula. None of these are very large amounts, by the way. To put things in perspective, there's about 200mg of aluminum in a standard antacid tablet. In fact, the average adult ingests seven to nine mg of aluminum everyday. Here's a look at how much aluminum is in breast milk/formula, compared to vaccines:

Amount of aluminum exposure (milligrams per liter) (*Vaccine Education Center*)

	AMOUNT OF ALUMINUM
Breast milk	0.01–0.05 mg/L
Cow's milk based infant formula	0.06–0.15 mg/L
Soy based infant formula	0.46–0.93mg/L
Prevnar vaccine	0.125 mg/dose
DTaP vaccine	0.17–0.625 mg/dose
HIB vaccine	0.225 mg/dose
Hep A vaccine	0.225–0.25 mg/dose
Hep B vaccine	0.25–0.5 mg/dose
DTaP/IPV/HIB vaccine	1.5 mg/dose

Is it a good idea to space out vaccinations that contain aluminum salts? No. Since aluminum-containing vaccines do not cause any health risk, separating or spacing out these vaccines has no benefit. In fact, there is a risk to spacing out the vaccines—your baby will go unprotected against real vaccine-preventable disease.

vaccinations

On June 22, 1998, a vaccine preventable disease called Meningococcal meningitis took the life of my only child, my son, Ryan. Thousands of children will develop meningitis each year and many will die. But death isn't the only outcome: children who survive are often left with limb amputations, organ damage, and the list goes on.

The two types of meningitis that are most common are meningococcal and pneumococcal (Strep pneumoniae). There are vaccines for both.

This vaccine preventable disease took away my identity, my right to ever be the parent at a wedding, to hold a grandchild, and to have the comfort of a child in my old age. We must work together in the United States to protect our children from epidemics which other parts of the world see everyday. Because epidemics are a plane ride away. And vaccinations save lives.

Yes, vaccines prevent sickness—but you can't be vaccinated against every infection. Up next, the infection hit parade, including a special focus on ear infections, when your child can go back to day care and more!

Common Infections

Chapter 13

"A family is a unit composed not only of children but of men, women, an occasional animal, and the common cold."
~ Ogden Nash (1902-1971)

What's in this Chapter

- What are Viruses?
- What are Bacteria?
- Antibiotic Resistance
- What you always wanted to know about the Common Cold
- When your child can return to childcare or playgroup
- Germ Hit Parade
- Special feature—Ear infections

This chapter answers that age-old parent question: "So, when can my child go back to child care/playgroup?" Yes, it's time to take a look at the germs that like to invade us. Infectious diseases are a large part of pediatrics. Adults have their share of infections, but the numbers pale in comparison to kids (a.k.a. human culture dishes). FYI: diseases that are not caused by infections are covered in the next chapter, "Common Diseases."

Common infections are usually caused by one of two issues–viruses and bacteria. We'll cover both in this chapter.

Most infections that your child will get are viruses. These are infections that go away on their own, without medication. One of the advantages of being a pediatrician is that in the case of viruses we do nothing, and our patients usually get better! Many parents don't understand what viruses are and feel compelled to DO SOMETHING. It often takes more time to explain to a parent that their child will get better without a prescription, than it takes to diagnose the ailment.

You will be an honorary microbiologist after reading this chapter. It will prepare you for the numerous infections coming your way. We'll go over viruses and bacteria since those are the biggies. Fungi, mites, lice, and parasites are discussed in "Things that make you itch just thinking about them" in this chapter. Fun, no?

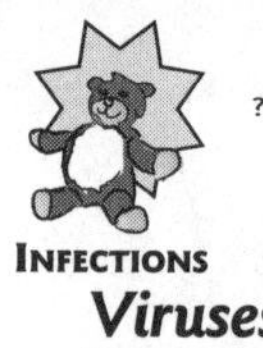

Viruses

Q. What is a virus?

These are tiny germs that need our body cells (called the "host") to survive and prosper. Viruses are like little copy machines. Their genetic coding allows the virus to reproduce quickly in the host.

Most viruses enter our bodies, reproduce for a few days, then leave to infect someone else. Examples include the cold virus and hand/foot/mouth diseases (see the table at the end of this section for a complete run-down of viruses with their common and scientific names). A few viruses like to stick around, lie dormant, and then reactivate to torture us again, such as herpes and chickenpox. Rarely, a virus kills their host—one example is HIV.

Here's some cocktail party trivia for you: according to the International Committee on Taxonomy of Viruses (7th Report, 2000), there are more than 1550 virus species, divided into 56 families. Within each family, there are sometimes thousands of relatives for each virus. These identified viruses are just a small portion of what is actually out in the world.

Q. Where do viruses live when they aren't infecting someone?

Viruses can be airborne or live on surfaces for a period of hours to days. Germs live on surfaces called **FOMITES.** Fomites include door handles, grocery carts, gas pumps, changing tables, shared toys, etc.

BOTTOM LINE: Your mother was right—WASH YOUR HANDS!

Q. Is antibacterial soap a good defense against infections?

Yes, but let's talk about the ingredients and then you can decide if you want to use them. Antibacterial soaps contain an effective antiseptic chemical called triclosan. (Hospitals used triclosan-containing hand cleansers for decades before they popped up in household products and hand gels.) Experts are increasingly concerned that widespread use of triclosan may lead to antibiotic-resistant super germs. There are also possible health risks regarding exposure and the body's hormone regulation. According to the Centers for Disease Control, triclosan is present in the urine of 75% of Americans over the age of five. Scary, no?

NEW PARENT 411: WHY EVERYONE IN THE HOUSE GETS SICK WHEN A CHILD HAS A VIRAL ILLNESS

Everyone gets sick because of what families do in their own homes. We hug, kiss, share drinks, touch door handles, touch hand towels, etc. We also wash our hands less in our homes than when we are out in public.

BOTTOM LINE: Think twice before you decide to finish what is left over on your child's plate. Is that half-eaten chicken nugget really worth it?

Then, there are alcohol-based hand sanitizers, which are also effective in keeping germs at bay. Hand sanitizers that use *at least* 60% alcohol as the active ingredient are a convenient alternative to soap and water if hands are not full of dirt. The only controversy related to these popular hand gels is that some products contain far less than 60% alcohol—which means they won't work.

As you might guess, we have mixed feelings about antibacterial soap. Are they "too much of a good thing?" We certainly do not want to help create new breeds of bacteria that are harder to kill.

Ultimately, the decision is up to you. We suggest using 60% alcohol-based hand sanitizer for when you are out and about or at the diaper changing table. But in most other circumstances regular soap will do just fine.

Denise's opinion: On a personal note, we have found that in the Fields' household, antibacterial soap aggravates our chronic dry skin (we live in a very arid climate) and eczema. We stick to regular Dove soap and wash frequently. Also those alcohol based hand sanitizers like Purell are very painful if you have cracks from eczema. We avoid them as well.

Q. Do we pass viral infections back and forth in our house?

No. Once everyone is infected, everyone is immune to that particular germ.

Q. Why is my child always getting sick?

Because he is being exposed to infectious germs he has no immunity to.

There are literally millions of germs out there. Every time your child gets an infection, he creates antibodies to a specific bug. But until your child has a large immune memory in his body's "hard drive," he will get almost every illness that comes down the pike. Most infections are spread through respiratory droplets (snot and cough secretions), saliva, and poop. Babies don't have good manners. They cough and sneeze on each other. They also explore toys in their mouths, leaving the germs behind for someone else.

Reality Check

Babies begin to get sick when they start venturing out in the world. Here are some astounding statistics:

- The average number of viral infections per year for kids under age five is EIGHT. Yes, you read that right.
- Each illness lasts seven to ten days.
- Most infections occur between October and April.
- That's 80 days of illness packed into six months of the year.

BOTTOM LINE: That's right, expect an infection every other week in the winter. And that's just the AVERAGE. If you win the sick kid lotto, you could be in for more. Astounding, eh?

Q. Why is my second child sicker than my first?

Because your older child is bringing home infections to share.

Firstborns often live in a bubble for their first year of life (unless they are in childcare). Second babies don't have that luxury. They get carted around to big brother or sister's activities. And big bro/sis share whatever infections they have acquired with the little ones. So, it is natural for a second child to get more illnesses earlier in life than the first.

Q. Why do we only see the flu virus in the wintertime?

Viruses prefer certain times of year to attack.

When a virus arrives in a community, it spreads in an epidemic fashion for a period of weeks, then disappears. Doctors know what virus has arrived because every patient has the same illness for a few weeks. Yep, it's a fact of life–viruses are always coming to town, it's just a matter of when they arrive every year. Here are the seasonal patterns of viral epidemics:

Summer: Coxsackievirus (hand/foot/mouth), Enteroviruses (stomach, skin, respiratory, eye)
Fall: Parainfluenza (croup), Rhinovirus (common cold)
Winter: Influenza (the flu), Rotavirus (stomach virus), RSV (bronchiolitis)
Spring: Parainfluenza again, Varicella (chickenpox)

What causes these seasonal patterns? There are various factors that influence the annual epidemics of these viruses. Scientists have been studying this for years. It seems to be a combination of atmospheric conditions and host (that's us) behaviors that lead to the perfect conditions for a virus to attack. Interestingly, viruses can be found infecting people in their "off-season," but not at epidemic levels. *(Dowell)*

Q. How do viruses cause infection?

Remember, viruses need us to survive. They jump at the chance to enter any body orifice (eyes, nose, mouth, anus, vagina, urethra). Most often, they are spread via the nose or through cough droplets, saliva, poop, or sexual relations.

Garden-variety viruses enter our body, replicate, and leave. This makes it hard to detect a virus or use a medicine to stop a viral infection–by the time you realize you have been attacked by a virus, the virus itself may have moved on.

The symptoms we experience are due to our immune response to the infection. For example, the common cold virus (rhinovirus) attacks the nose. Our immune system sends white blood cells there to fight the infection. The result of the bug/white blood cell battle is mucous production.

Once we have symptoms, the virus has already replicated numerous times in our body. It's usually too late to do anything. Fortunately, most viral infections are not serious and our bodies recover from the invasion.

BOTTOM LINE: Think of a virus as a speedboat. It zips in and out of our body.

Q. How do doctors know that a child has a viral infection?

Your baby's doctor will make a diagnosis based on symptoms (the problems/complaints you describe) and the signs of infection (the abnormal findings on physical examination). *Most experienced physicians are able to accurately make the diagnosis of a typical viral infection on this information alone.*

Q. Are there any tests that can detect a viral infection?

There are a few special tests for certain viral infections, but most tests look for signs of a *bacterial* infection.

The problem with viruses is that they are extremely small. We can't see them with a regular microscope. And often, the virus is already out of the body so it can't be caught. The few tests we have available for specific viral infections usually look for an immune response to a particular virus (antibody levels). There are a few rapid lab tests for influenza virus ("the flu"), Epstein-Barr virus ("mono"), viral respiratory infections like RSV, and viral diarrheal infections like rotavirus. And occasionally, some viruses like herpes, can be caught growing in a culture specimen.

But most of the time, your doctor can't just do a blood test to see if your baby has a virus. If a complete blood count is done on a child with a viral infection, the results are usually normal. The white blood cell count does not rise in response to a virus. In fact, some viruses cause a decrease in the number of cells that fight infection (termed *viral bone marrow suppression*). Influenza is classic for causing a low white blood cell count. White blood cells can be further differentiated by their shape under a microscope. The types of white blood cells that mount an immune attack to viruses are predominantly *lymphocytes*. Seeing a high number of lymphocytes is one of the only useful bits of information in a blood count to diagnose a viral infection.

BOTTOM LINE

Lab work and x-rays are rarely necessary to diagnose a run-of-the-mill virus in your baby. If a child does not improve as expected, though, doctors need you to call or follow up to explore things further.

Q. Are there any anti-viral medications?

Yes. There are a few available. But all of these medicines must be given within the first 24 to 48 hours of symptoms because they act by inhibiting the replication of the virus. It is useless to take an anti-viral medicine more than three days into a viral illness.

For most viruses, there is no anti-viral medication available to clear the infection. The ones that ARE available include:

1. Tamiflu (Oseltamivir) for Influenza A and B
2. Symmetrel (Amantadine) for Influenza A
3. Flumadine (Rimantadine) for Influenza A
3. Zovirax (Acyclovir) for chickenpox, shingles, or Herpes virus
4. AZT, Abacavir for HIV infections
5. Formvirisen for CMV eye infections

Q. How long do most viral infections last?

You can expect a typical virus to cause symptoms for seven to 14 days.

Usually a fever is present for the first two to four days of illness. While there is a fever, your child is contagious. The virus is actively growing/replicating. The fever stops when the virus stops replicating. But our bodies will feel the impact of the infection for about a week.

Q. Is there any way to prevent a viral infection?

Yes—with vaccination.

We are fortunate to have vaccinations to prevent some of the most serious viral infections known to civilization: smallpox, polio, Hepatitis A, Hepatitis B, measles, mumps, rubella, Rotavirus, chickenpox and Human Papilloma Virus (HPV).

The Common Cold

Q. What is the common cold?

Answer: a viral infection usually caused by our friend, rhinovirus ("rhino" is the Latin word for nose.)

Here is what you need to know:

1. The virus enters the host body through the nose and goes to work.
2. Fever and body aches occur when the virus starts reproducing.
3. Snot (mucous production), cough, with or without sore throat follows.
4. Symptoms last for up to 14 days, with day three or four being the worst.
5. The snot can change from clear to green and still be just the same old virus (not a sinus infection, which we'll discuss later in this chapter).

So, how long with cold and flu symptoms last?

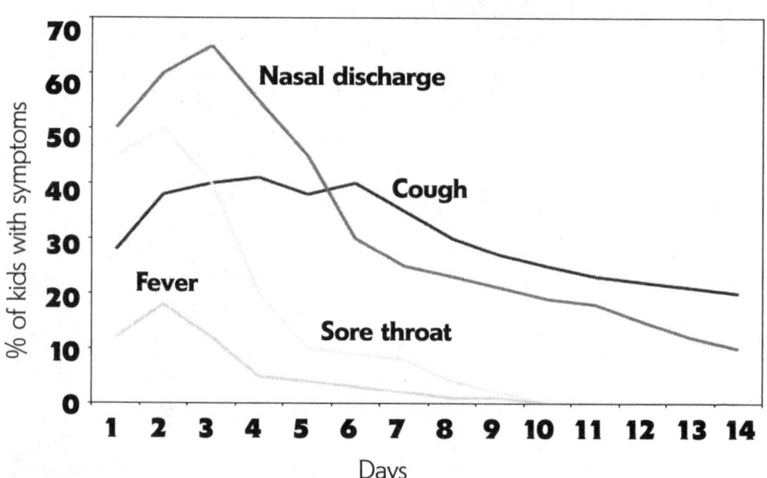

Source: Dr. S. Michael Marcy & Kaiser Permanente from data presented in JAMA

DR B'S OPINION: COLD MEDS AND INFANTS

The Food and Drug Administration prohibits the sale of over-the-counter cough and cold meds for kids under age two. I never recommended them anyway. Infants under six months of age can have a paradoxical reaction to antihistamines (instead of sedating a baby, these medicines can leave your child wired). The decongestants used in most of these medicines can act similarly to caffeine. I personally would rather deal with a snotty sleeping baby than a snotty awake baby.

Q. How is the common cold diagnosed and treated?

A cold virus or upper respiratory infection is diagnosed based on the symptoms that the patient has. There is currently no test for it.

For babies, the best treatment is to use saline nose drops as much as needed. Saline is salt water. (See home remedies in Medications, Appendix A.) A mist or two in each nostril before feedings and bed helps loosen the mucous and often makes babies sneeze. The beauty of saline is that it is safe and nearly impossible to overdose on it!

Remember, antibiotics will not cure a cold.

Top Remedies to Treat a Cold

- Saline nose drops.
- Running a humidifier in baby's room to help loosen the mucous.
- Having baby sleep in car seat or with head of mattress elevated (place a pillow or wedge *under* the mattress).

Reality Check

There are over 100 rhinoviruses. Once your child has a rhinovirus infection, he is immune to that one. But there are 99 more that he isn't immune to. Get the picture?

Q. I can feel a rattling in my baby's chest. Are you sure the infection isn't in his lungs?

Yes. It's air moving through snot that you hear and feel. See transmitted upper airway noise info in the section on breathing problems in Chapter 15, "First Aid."

Q. How long is a baby contagious with a cold virus?

In general, the first three days of illness.

With viruses in general, people are contagious while they have a fever. The infection is spread via hand-to-hand contact with snot (mucous). It is also spread from cough and sneeze droplets.

Q. When my baby has a cold, he has a runny nose for almost two weeks. I'm afraid to take him back to playgroup because the other moms seem upset. When is he no longer contagious?

With the common cold virus or upper respiratory infection, the virus is

DR B'S OPINION: VAPO-RUBS

Some parents love to use this stuff. But here's what you need to know: it is not approved for use in children under two years of age. Camphor, one of the active ingredients, gets absorbed through the skin and can potentially cause seizures in babies. See Appendix B "Alternative Medicine" for information on menthols/peppermint oil.

HUMIDIFIERS & VAPORIZERS: COLD VS WARM MIST DEBATE

A humidifier and vaporizer both do the same thing–they add humidity to dry air. Vaporizers have a place to add medicine to the mist but this feature is rarely used today. Kids who have asthma and need breathing treatments have a high-tech machine called a nebulizer.

Warm mist humidifiers are unnecessary and they make the nursery feel like the Bahamas. There is also a risk of an older baby burning his hand on a warm mist machine.

BOTTOM LINE: Buy a cheap, cool-mist humidifier. It loosens up mucous so babies can sleep when they have a cold. Just be sure to clean it every few days.

For a discussion of which humidifier models are best, ratings and buying advice, see the web site for our other book *Baby Bargains* (BabyBargains.com).

spread in the first three or four days of illness (usually when kids have a fever). After that, it's just snot. You can return to playgroup.

Q. My baby has swollen glands. What is that?

Lymph nodes. Our bodies have chains of lymph nodes that look like a string of pearls. These chains are located throughout the body, but mostly in the neck, armpits, and groin. Each area works to protect a particular body area. For instance, the neck nodes are dedicated to the head, ears, nose, and throat. These tiny glands are jam packed with the cells that fight off infection. When there is an active infection in the body, these glands rise to the occasion, swelling to several times their normal size. They can be tender and can remain enlarged for up to six weeks after the infection is gone.

Swollen lymph nodes point us in the direction of where an infection is located.

Q. What is the significance of green snot? I always thought that it meant a bacterial infection.

Bacterial sinus infections cause green nasal secretions, but green snot alone does not diagnose sinusitis. The nasal secretions are a result of our

The difference between a cold and a sinus infection

The common cold causes a short lived fever with several days of snot. A sinus infection causes prolonged fever and prolonged snot.

immune system (white blood cells) fighting with either a virus or bacteria. The discoloration tells us that the battle has been going on for a while.

The change from clear secretions to yellow/green secretions WHEN ACCOMPANIED by fever, headache, fussiness, or prolonged symptoms (over two weeks of illness) is suspicious for a bacterial sinus infection.

Bacteria

Q. What are bacteria?

These are much larger germs than viruses. These bugs can live on their own without a host. Most bacteria do not cause illness, and live in harmony with us. Some bacteria cause infection only in susceptible humans (those that are "immune compromised"), or when they end up in places they don't belong (e.g. intestinal bacteria in the urinary tract causes a bladder infection). And there are only a few bacteria that live to hurt us.

Q. I have heard about "good bacteria." What are they?

The bacteria that live in and on our bodies are called *normal flora.*

These bacteria live on our skin, and in our mouths, nostrils, vagina, and intestines. Babies are born relatively sterile (bacteria free). But it only takes a day or two in the real world to become colonized with bacteria. Here are the typical bacteria that are in you and your baby's body:

- ***Skin bacteria:*** Staph and Strep
- ***Nostril bacteria:*** Staph and Strep
- ***Gut bacteria:*** Lactobacillus and E coli, among many others
- ***Vagina and gut bacteria:*** Group B Strep
- ***Mouth bacteria:*** too numerous to mention here

Q. How do bacteria cause infection?

They enter through any body opening under favorable conditions. These conditions include open wounds, mucous in the nose from viral infection, fluid in Eustachian tubes with a common cold virus, poop and bacteria pushed into the urethra/bladder opening. Other bacteria get in via respiratory secretions, saliva, or sexual activity.

Then they grow and fester in our bodies. Unlike viruses, they like to stick around.

Bacteria either invade our body tissues or produce a toxin (poison) that injures our bodies. Each bug has a particular body part they prefer to hang out in (throat, intestine, bladder, eye, etc)

Q. I have heard the term "secondary bacterial infection." What does it mean?

Bacteria often capitalize on a person who already has an active viral infection.

The viral infection is the *primary* infection. The bacteria that come in later are termed *secondary* infections. This is an important concept to understand why a) you are at risk for bacterial infections when you have a cold

infections

or flu, b) you don't often get bacterial infections when you are well, and c) why many bacterial infections are not contagious to others.

BOTTOM LINE: Think of bacteria as tugboats. They are slower moving than viruses. Their lack of speed and tendency to stick around make them susceptible to antibiotics.

Old Wives Tales

◆ **Going out in the rain causes pneumonia. False!**
The truth: Having a viral infection (cold or flu virus) predisposes a person to getting a secondary bacterial infection (pneumonia is a bacterial infection in the lungs). The weather has nothing to do with it.

◆ **The wind or ceiling fans cause ear infections. False!**
The truth: If your baby has a cold (or any viral infection), she is more susceptible to getting an ear infection (or another bacterial infection). Like the old wives tale about the rain and pneumonia, the wind has nothing to do with ear infections.

Q. Are bacterial infections contagious?

It depends on the bug and the host.

Not all bacteria jump from person to person. Some just set up shop in one body and grow until they are killed off.

And some bacteria will only cause infection in people who are susceptible

HOW A DOC CAN TELL A BACTERIAL INFECTION FROM A VIRUS

1. **Your child is sicker.** Bacterial infections, in general, make people sicker than viruses.
2. **Your child's fever lasts longer than four days.** Viral illnesses usually cause fever for three to four days maximum (except influenza which last up to a week).
3. **Your child's fever is really high (over 105).** Viruses cause high fevers, too. But there is a greater chance it's a bacterial infection when you could fry an egg on your child's back.
4. **Your child has a localized area of infection.** Bacteria pick a body part to live in. The most common bacterial infections in childhood include: ear, sinus, throat, eye, lung, bladder/kidney, lymph node, intestine, blood, or the brain.
5. **Your child has abnormal lab work.** If there is not an obvious source of infection on examination, and he looks really sick with or without prolonged or high fever, some tests will be done. A complete blood count shows an elevation of the cells that fight infection (total white blood cell count over 15,000, and a high percentage of **neutrophils**–see lab section in Appendix C for details). Or, white blood cells in urine, spinal fluid, etc. indicate that infection is there (white blood cells are never found in normal urine or spinal fluid).

(either because they already have a viral infection or their immune systems are compromised—such as premature infants, the elderly, people on chemotherapy, AIDS patients).

As a general rule, assume your child is contagious if he has a fever. The fever tells you that the body's immune system is actively fighting the bug.

But your doctor can tell you if the particular bacterial infection is contagious to others (or read the final section of this chapter) For example, Strep throat (Group A Strep) infection IS contagious. An ear infection caused by Strep pneumoniae is NOT contagious.

DR B'S OPINION

"If you can get a child over three months old to smile at you, he isn't that sick. There is a scientific study that has proven this. In practice, I can tell you it's true."

Q. Can you find out which bacterium is causing an infection?

Yes.

Because bacteria don't leave the body, doctors can potentially catch the bacteria and identify them under a microscope or grow them on a culture plate. Blood, urine, stool, spinal fluid, eye discharge, ear discharge, throat pus, sputum (mucous coughed up), and vaginal discharge to name a few, can be examined. Bacteria living in our bodies can grow on a culture plate in about 48 hours.

The only problem is that we can't always get a specimen from the location of the infection (like an ear infection). Fortunately, a limited number of bacteria cause certain infections. Once the source of the infection is identified (eye, ear, sinus, lung, etc.), doctors have a pretty good idea which bacterium is wreaking havoc.

Q. How do doctors know which antibiotic will kill a bacterial infection?

Doctors select an antibiotic that kills the bacteria most likely causing the infection. Antibiotics are not all the same. They are each potent against specific families of bacteria. (See Appendix A, "Medications.")

If bacteria grow on a culture plate (from an available specimen), doctors get exact information for antibiotic selection. The growing bacteria are placed on several "sensitivity" plates. These plates contain a growth medium and an antibiotic. If the bacteria can't grow on a particular antibiotic plate, the right medication to keep the infection from growing in the body is found.

Antibiotic Resistance

Q. I've heard a lot about drug resistant bacteria/antibiotic resistance. What is it?

Darwin's Survival of the Fittest.

Bacteria adapt to survive. There is a constant challenge to create more anti-microbials (antibiotics) to kill off the smart drug-resistant bugs.

Many people don't understand the concept of antibiotic resistance. They think that a *person* who is taking antibiotics will develop a drug resistance. *Drug resistance refers to the bugs.* When so many antibiotics are being used in the community, the bugs know our ammunition. Those that survive are drug resistant. The idea is that we can't overuse our weapons—otherwise we will be left with no defense. We need to use our antibiotic weapons judiciously.

Reality Check

Penicillin resistant strains of bacteria, particularly one called Strep pneumoniae (see Prevnar in the last chapter on vaccines) began emerging in 1991. Now 20% of Strep pneumoniae strains are resistant to Penicillin and 10% are resistant to at least three types of antibiotics. Strep pneumoniae cause five to seven million ear infections annually.

Q. What can be done to stop drug-resistant bacteria?

- Give the Prevnar vaccine to children at high risk of getting Strep pneumoniae infection (children under age five).
- Use a higher dose of the first-line antibiotic (amoxicillin).
- Save the big gun, broader spectrum antibiotics for persistent infections.
- Only use antibiotics when it is really necessary.

Q. When should antibiotics NOT be prescribed?

1. The common cold or "upper respiratory infection."
2. A sore throat caused by a virus (as opposed to Strep throat which is caused by a bacteria).
3. Green snot (see the common cold section earlier in this chapter).
4. Because someone else in the house is on antibiotics.

The abuse of antibiotics

Here are a couple of startling stats: In 1980, U.S. healthcare providers wrote four million prescriptions for amoxicillin (a popular antibiotic) for children. By 2010, that number jumped to 18 million.

In fact, amoxicillin was the most prescribed medication to kids under age two. And except for albuterol (a medication for wheezing), three other antibiotics—azithromycin, amoxicillin-clavulanate, and cefdinir—rounded out the top five list of medications prescribed to young children. *(Chai)*

It is clear that doctors over-prescribe antibiotics. Want to know the

DR B'S OPINION: CAN WE TALK?

Parents and doctors need to communicate better. If a bacterial infection is diagnosed, an antibiotic is in order. Viruses are not cured by antibiotics.

Doctors need to do a better job of explaining viruses. Parents need to do a better job of accepting the fact that their child will get better on his own. And this may mean missing work to take care of a sick child. A miracle "pill" isn't always available to restore your child to perfect health in mere hours!

number one reason doctors site for over-prescribing? Parent expectation that an antibiotic will be prescribed!

Truth be told, it's not just the parents' fault. One study showed that doctors often misperceive what a parent expects at an office visit (and try to satisfy them). (*Mangione-Smith*)

Old Wives Tale

I am on an antibiotic for an upper respiratory infection. My child is sick, too. He needs antibiotics.

The truth: Not everyone with a cold develops a sinus infection. That is probably why you are taking an antibiotic. Your child should be checked for a secondary bacterial infection if he has a fever, crankiness, or prolonged symptoms (beyond ten to 14 days). It was common 15 to 20 years ago that if one person in a house had a Strep infection, then doctors prescribed antibiotics for the ENTIRE family. Now, we realize that is NOT the answer. Giving antibiotics to healthy folks only strengthens the bugs' resistance to drugs.

When can Johnny go back to childcare/playgroup?

DISEASE	TREATMENT	RETURN TO CHILDCARE?
Common cold	None	When fever is gone.
Influenza	+/- Anti-viral Rx	When fever is gone.
Croup	+/- Steroid Rx	When fever is gone.
Hand-foot-mouth	None	When fever is gone.
Herpes stomatitis	None	When lesions are healed.
Conjunctivitis/Pink eye	None if viral infection	When eyes are clear.
Bacterial conjunctivitis	Antibiotic eye drops Rx	After 24 hrs. of treatment.
Stomach virus	None	When poop is formed.
Viral rashes	None	Depends on the infection.
Chickenpox	+/- Antiviral Rx	When all lesions crusted (1 wk).
Fifth disease	None	Not contagious once rash appears.
Impetigo	Antibiotic Rx	After 24 hours of treatment.
Food poisoning	Depends on the bug	When poop is formed.
Giardia	Anti-parasitic Rx	When poop is formed.
Ringworm	Anti-fungal Rx	After 24 hours of treatment.
Scabies	Body wash Rx	After 1 treatment.
Head lice	OTC shampoo	After 1 treatment.
Pinworms	Anti-parasitic Rx	After 1 treatment.

KEY–Rx: prescription medicine; OTC: over-the-counter medicine. (*Donowitz*)

Putting it all together...

Now you know the usual suspects. Here is how doctors put it all together. When a child has a fever, your doctor looks for infection. (There are other causes for fever, but infection tops the list). The symptoms IN ADDITION TO the fever are what lead to the diagnosis. (Vomiting, diarrhea, cough, runny nose, decreased appetite, rash...) The constellation of symptoms and findings on physical examination are often enough information to make the call. Lab work and x-rays are sometimes needed to help figure out the source of infection.

New Parent 411: Antibiotics

Just because YOU are on an antibiotic, does not mean your child needs to be on one. Whole families can get infected with a virus. But not everyone gets a secondary bacterial infection from the virus. Remember that secondary infections are not contagious. So, even if you now have a sinus infection, your baby most likely will still have just a cold.

Viral infections for the most part do not require any medication and are fought off by our body's immune systems. Bacteria, fungi, mites, and parasites respond to medication, which helps eliminate the infection. The medication selection is often based on the usual suspects for a particular illness. If an infection doesn't clear up or the patient is pretty sick, cultures can help identify the particular bug and the right medication.

Bacterial infections are frequently secondary infections that capitalize on a weakened immune system that is fighting a virus (ear infections, sinus infections/adenoiditis, pneumonia). Doctors worry about secondary infections when a child with a viral infection suddenly gets worse (i.e. new fever, new green snot, new irritability, new respiratory distress).

Viral Infections

And now, for your listening pleasure, the viral hit parade! In just a bit, we'll have a special section on ear infections. But first, here's an overview of the viral infections that most impact babies:

I. Respiratory Viruses

The Flu (Influenza)

Disease: Respiratory illness caused by either Influenza A or B. A different strain causes epidemics every year. Influenza causes more severe respiratory illness than the common cold. There is a higher risk of secondary bacterial infections in infants, people with chronic lung disease, or other chronic diseases.

Symptoms: High fever, body aches, and chills. Then runny nose, cough and sore throat.

Diagnosis: Based on symptoms. White blood cell count is low (less than 4,000) with mostly lymphocytes. Rapid flu assay is available, but it is only about 50% accurate in identifying the flu.

Treatment: An anti-viral medication can be given to children over one year old if diagnosis is made within 48 hours of becoming ill.

Contagious: From 24 hours before symptoms start, and while person has symptoms. Spread via respiratory droplets, fomites.

Incubation period: 1-3 days after exposure

Season: Winter

Prevention: Annual flu vaccine offered each fall season. Recommended for everyone, starting at six months of age. (*Pickering*)

Bronchiolitis (RSV)

Disease: RSV stands for Respiratory Syncytial Virus. (Or, as one of my patient's dads says, "Really Sucky Virus".) It can infect anyone, but causes more severe illness in infants, especially babies born prematurely. As opposed to the common cold or upper respiratory infection, RSV attacks the tiny branches of the lower lung airways (bronchioles). Swollen bronchioles make the air flow turbulent through them, creating a wheeze with inspiration, similar to the mechanism of asthma. RSV infection can be serious enough to require hospitalization.

Symptoms: Fever, runny nose, breathing faster than normal and wheeze, but no "distress." Infants and premature babies may have more "respiratory distress" (see glossary). About 30% of children who wheeze with an RSV infection will have asthma. The cause is debatable. Does the RSV infection causes long term damage to the airways, predisposing to asthma; or are the kids who wheeze with RSV really asthmatics with sensitive airways? Regardless, damage to the bronchioles from RSV takes a long time to heal. Symptoms can go on for weeks.

Diagnosis: Based on symptoms. A rapid assay test is available, usually only in hospitals.

Treatment: Some kids respond to asthma medication (Albuterol) via a nebulizer machine to aerosolize the medication. Some kids need oxygen, which requires hospitalization.

Contagious: 3 to 8 days, but sometimes up to 3 weeks. Spread by fomites, respiratory droplets.

Incubation period: 2 to 8 days.

Season: Winter, early spring

Prevention: For children under age 2 who were born prematurely (less than 32 weeks gestation), those from 32-34 6/7 weeks old with a higher risk of RSV exposure, or who have chronic lung disease, RSV-Antibody (Synagis) provides immunity for one month. The medication is a shot given monthly through RSV season. (It's about $1000 a shot, and the series is usually six injections). (See Appendix A "Medications" for details on Synagis.) (*Pickering*)

infections

Croup

Disease: A viral infection that attacks the voice box area. The smaller the child, the smaller the airway tube, the more problematic when the airway is swollen.

Symptoms: Fever. Cough is a classic "bark", like a seal. Always worse at night when lying down. This is a three night illness. With babies, significant swelling can occur. A squeal is heard. Persistent squealing (stridor) more than five to ten minutes is a medical emergency. Adults with croup have laryngitis instead of a bark because adults' airway tubes are larger.

Diagnosis: The bark is usually enough to prove it. A neck x-ray is occasionally done to identify the swollen area.

Treatment: Turn on the shower in a closed bathroom. The steam works well. Humidifier in room. For more severe cases, steroids (taken by mouth or a shot) help reduce the airway swelling. A breathing treatment (racemic epinephrine) also relaxes the airway for kids with stridor.

Contagious: 4 to 7 days. Spread via direct contact, fomites, respiratory droplets.

Incubation period: 2 to 6 days.

Season: Fall. (*Pickering*)

2. Mouth And Tonsil Viruses

Hand-Foot-and-Mouth (Coxsackievirus)

Disease: A virus that causes ulcers in the back of the mouth, and sometimes a rash on the palms, soles, and around the anus.

Symptoms: Fever, lack of interest in eating. Rash can be flat red dots or raised like pimples. Ulcers in the *back of mouth.*

Diagnosis: The ulcers in the back of the mouth are classic. No diagnostic testing is done. See Rash-o-Rama on Baby411.com for a picture.

Treatment: Avoid citrus and salt. Acetaminophen (Tylenol) or Ibuprofen (Advil) for discomfort. Make up a concoction of liquid Benadryl and Maalox (1 tsp of each), then give about 0.8 ml of the mixture before feedings. This coats the ulcers.

Contagious: Up to 7 days. Spread through saliva, poop, and fomites.

Incubation period: 3 to 6 days.

Season: Summer, fall. (*Pickering*)

Oral Herpes Stomatitis

Disease: Viral infection caused by HSV Type 1. (Type 2 is genital herpes–a completely different infection). Once a person is infected, the HSV-1 lies dormant for life and can re-activate as a cold sore. Cold sores appear on the outer lip and last for a week. Cold sores spread HSV-1 to others. The worst case scenario is a newborn who contracts HSV infection (75% of these are from genital herpes type 2, but 25% are HSV-1). These babies are at high risk of getting an infection of the brain (**ENCEPHALITIS**) from HSV.

Symptoms: Fever over 102 for a week. VERY poor fluid and food intake (at risk of dehydration). Numerous ulcers in mouth, gums, tongue called **GINGIVOSTOMATITIS.** The pain is so severe, some children avoid swallowing their saliva. These kids feel awful.

Diagnosis: Can be made just by looking at the mouth lesions (very impressive looking). Can also be grown (takes 3 days) in a culture by taking a specimen from the ulcer base. It's not always cultured because by the time the culture grows out, it's too late to treat the infection.

Treatment: FLUIDS. Acyclovir, an antiviral, is used if the diagnosis is made within 48 hours. Gingivostomatitis is usually diagnosed too late (after two days of illness) to use an antiviral medication. Cold sores can be treated with anti-virals.

Contagious: VERY! For 7 days. Spread via saliva and direct contact with the lesions.

Incubation period: 2 to 14 days.

Season: Year round.

Prevention: Avoid contact with child if someone has an active cold sore. (*Pickering*)

Reality Check

If Great Aunt Suzy has a cold sore, kindly ask her not to hold your newborn. If you have a cold sore, don't touch your lips and don't kiss your family members.

3. *Viral Sore Throat*

Disease: A viral infection that causes the tonsils to be swollen. Caused by many different viruses. Adenovirus often causes pink eye (viral conjunctivitis), runny nose, and ear infections in addition to a sore throat.

Symptoms: Fever, decreased appetite, redness or pus (white patches) on tonsils.

Diagnosis: Based on age group and associated symptoms. No lab test. Strep test rarely done because it is rare for babies under age two. It is extremely rare for babies under age two to get Strep (bacterial) throat.

Treatment: To treat the symptoms only. Acetaminophen (Tylenol) or Ibuprofen (Advil), lots to drink.

Contagious: While child has a fever. Spread by direct contact, respiratory droplets, fomites.

Incubation period: 2 to 14 days.

Season: Winter, spring, summer. (*Pickering*)

4. *Gastrointestinal Viruses*

There are many types of viruses that are known collectively as the "stomach virus." They are all treated the same way—lots of fluids to prevent dehydration. The most notorious one of all is Rotavirus. It comes every winter.

Viral gastroenteritis (Rotavirus)

Disease: Rotavirus enters the stomach and intestines. Prior to 2006, almost all kids got this infection by three years old. (And people can get it more than once). The kids at greatest risk are infants. They lose so much water in the diarrhea that it's hard to keep the fluid intake greater than the losses. That's why some babies get admitted to the hospital for IV fluids.

Symptoms: Fever, vomiting, and extremely watery diarrhea (often more than 20 times a day). This lasts for about a week.

Diagnosis: Usually obvious by the volume of diarrhea! Assay test is available.

Treatment: Lots of fluids. See Diarrhea section in Chapter 15, "First Aid."

Contagious: VERY. FOR THE WHOLE TIME YOUR CHILD HAS DIARRHEA. Spread via contact with infected poop, fomites. Spreads like wildfire through childcare centers and households.

Incubation period: 1 to 3 days.

Season: Winter (starts southwest and moves northeast every year—the opposite of birds)

Prevention: Rotavirus vaccine, given at two months of age, with one or two doses to complete the series.

Viral gastroenteritis (Norovirus)

Disease: Another common stomach virus that prefers group settings like cruise ships, nursing homes, and child care centers. The cause of about 15% of all gastroenteritis in the U.S.

Symptoms: Nausea, vomiting, abdominal cramps, non-bloody diarrhea, occasionally fever.

Diagnosis: Health department does testing when there are a large number of people affected in an outbreak.

Treatment: Lots of fluids. See Diarrhea section in Chapter 15, "First Aid."

Contagious: VERY. FOR THE WHOLE TIME YOUR CHILD HAS DIARRHEA. May return to childcare when symptom free for 48 hours. Spread via contact with infected food, water, poop, fomites (contaminated surfaces), and person-to-person contact.

Incubation period: 12 to 48 hours.

Prevention: Good hand washing with soap and water for at least 20 seconds. Alcohol based hand sanitizers are not an acceptable substitute for this resilient little virus. (*MMWR*)

5. Viral Exanthems (viruses that cause rashes)

See rashes section in Chapter 15, "First Aid" for more info on treatment.

Roseola (Herpes virus 6)

Disease: A virus that the entire world population over one year of age has had. Because it is a Herpes virus (this is NOT genital herpes HSV 2), it stays in our bodies forever. We all shed this virus in saliva and respiratory droplets daily. Mom's antibodies (immunity) are passed to baby and provide protection against illness for 9 to 12 months. When immunity wanes, babies get this infection. The only time you see a roseola "epidemic" is if you hang out with a bunch of one year olds.

Symptoms: Fever over 102 for about four days with no other signs of infection. Kids are usually in good spirits. *When the fever breaks, the rash comes out.* The rash can be subtle or dramatic. It is mostly flat, with some raised areas. Red, blotchy. On chest, back, arms. Not itchy, goes away within hours to a few days.

Diagnosis: Obvious after the rash comes out. The fever often prompts lab work (CBC, urinalysis) to prove that there is not a bacteria causing the fever.

Treatment: None. Acetaminophen (Tylenol) or Ibuprofen (Advil) for the fever.

Contagious: We are all contagious because we shed the virus for a lifetime once we are infected.

Incubation period: Ten days.

Season: When is your baby's first birthday?

Chickenpox (Varicella)

Disease: Caused by Varicella-Zoster virus, another type of Herpes virus. Like all Herpes viruses, it lies dormant forever in previously infected people. Because chickenpox can cause serious infection and death, vaccination became the standard of care in 1995. The vaccine is given to all children at one year of age and anyone (including adults) who has never had chickenpox. The vaccine is not 100% effective in preventing infection. But people who get infection despite vaccination have a very mild form of the disease. Babies under three months of age are usually protected via Mom's immunity (as long as she had chickenpox). Both immunized and infected kids can get Zoster (shingles) infection later in life (reactivation of Varicella). Shingles infects only one group of nerves (called a dermatome). A group of lesions come up in one patch. These blisters are more painful than itchy. They contain the virus and are contagious.

Symptoms: A full blown case causes fever, body aches, and a rash of tiny fluid filled blisters (called **VESICLES**) that appear in crops. New crops come up over a period of 3 to 4 days. The average number of pox is 350. Very itchy. Secondary Strep skin infections can occur. Watch for red areas surrounding pox, or a new fever after the initial fever breaks.

Diagnosis: Classic rash. Virus (found in vesicle fluid) will grow in culture in 2 to 3 days.

Treatment: Acyclovir, an anti-viral, can be given within 48 hours of illness. It will shorten the course of illness by a couple of days and reduces the total number of lesions (not dramatically though)

Contagious: VERY. FOR ONE WEEK. Child is contagious for 24 hours before the rash comes out and until all lesions (which contain the virus) are crusted over. Spread via respiratory droplets and direct contact.

Incubation period: 10 to 21 days. If you know when your child has been exposed, look for infection 10 days later and for the next 11 days. If you make it out of that window, you are safe.

Season: Winter, early spring

Prevention: Vaccination.

Slapped Cheek (Parvovirus)

Disease: Also known as **FIFTH DISEASE** or **ERYTHEMA INFECTIOSUM**. Occurs more in school age children. Questions arise more with exposure in pregnancy than anything else. The biggest problem with this infection is that it can cause miscarriage. If a pregnant woman (usually in the first 20 weeks) is not immune to Parvovirus and gets the infection, her fetus is at risk. Unfortunately, by the time we know a child has had Parvovirus (i.e. the rash appears), he has already exposed everyone. Note: If you are pregnant and have been exposed to any child with parvovirus, notify your obstetrician.

Symptoms: Mild or even undetectable when a child is contagious. Low fever, body aches, or headache. Ten days after the infection is gone, a classic rash erupts. The red cheeks look as if someone slapped them plus a lacy, mostly flat, red rash on chest, arms, and legs. The rash can last several weeks. When older kids and adults get infected, they may get joint pains that last for weeks.

Diagnosis: Easy once the rash has erupted. Antibody levels can be checked for evidence of recent infection.

Treatment: None.

Contagious: Hard to know when contagious because often there are no symptoms. Spread via respiratory droplets, blood products.

Incubation period: 4 to 21 days.

Season: Winter, spring.

Reality Check

Beware of mosquitoes. There were over 1100 cases of West Nile Virus (WNV) in 2012, and over 40 deaths. Before you pack your bags to Antarctica (the only place in the world that is mosquito-free), know that very few mosquitoes carry WNV and less than 1% of people who are bitten by WNV-carrying bugs will get seriously ill. Just remember the 3 D's of prevention:

- Drain any standing water near your home.
- Dawn and dusk are peak mosquito feeding hours. Stand indoors.
- Defend and protect your family with DEET or Picaridin-based insect repellants.

Bacterial Infections

1. Sinus Infections

Disease: Caused by the same bacteria that cause ear infections. Sinus infections are a secondary bacterial infection after a person has a common cold or flu. The virus sets up fluid in the sinus cavities behind the cheeks and above the eyes. More common in older children.

Symptoms: Prolonged runny nose over 14 days. New onset of discolored nasal secretions (snot) after 10 to 14 days of illness. New fever. Nighttime cough.

Diagnosis: Mostly by examination. Occasionally sinus x-ray is helpful.

Treatment: Same antibiotic choices as for ear infections, but often needs longer course.

Contagious: No.

2. Lung Infections (pneumonia)

Disease: Lung tissue inflammation that can be caused by bacteria or a virus. Bacterial pneumonia is a secondary infection after a viral illness (cold or flu).

Symptoms: High fever, wet cough, respiratory distress, vomiting. Child is getting worse instead of better with an illness, or new fever after initial fever resolved from an upper respiratory infection.

Diagnosis: Abnormal lung exam, chest x-ray, elevated white blood cell count

Treatment: Antibiotics. Rarely hospital admission—for labored breathing, need for oxygen.

Contagious: Depends on the bug.

3. Skin Infection (Impetigo and cellulitis)

Disease: Skin infection caused by bacteria that normally live on the skin that get under the skin. Bacteria capitalize on open wounds (bug bites, raw nostrils, burns).

Symptoms: Wound gets red with a golden, crusty, weeping discharge over it with impetigo. The skin is red, warm, and tender with cellulitis.

Diagnosis: Based on symptoms. Bugs can also grow in a culture if drainage from wound is obtained.

Treatment: Impetigo can be treated with prescription antibiotic cream. Extensive impetigo and cellulitis are treated with antibiotics given by mouth.

Contagious: Impetigo—yes. Spread by direct contact with wound. Not contagious after 24 hours of antibiotic therapy. Cellulitis is not contagious.

Incubation period: 7 to 10 days.

Season: Year round.

Special alert: Drug-resistant Staph infection. "MRSA" (Methicillin Resistant Staph Aureus) is a bacterial skin infection that is a real problem to treat.

Disease: Skin infection caused by Staph (bacteria) that is resistant to several antibiotics and can spread through the whole household.

Symptoms: Infections look like spider bites, boils, or red, tender areas.

Diagnosis: Suspicious looking lesions can be lanced to drain as well as obtain culture to check for the germ and its susceptibility to antibiotics.

Treatment: Topical or oral antibiotics, IV antibiotics for serious infections. People who are carriers (not infected) may harbor MRSA in their noses.

They can be treated with topical antibiotics to the nose.

Contagious: Yes. Spread via carriers of MRSA, or those infected with it spread to another person's skin.

Prevention: Wash hands thoroughly with soap and water or alcohol based hand sanitizer. Keep cuts/scrapes clean and covered with a bandage until healed. Avoid contact with other people's wounds or bandages. Do not share personal items like towels, washcloths. (*CDC*)

Season: Year round.

4. Eye Infections "Pink Eye" (Bacterial conjunctivitis)

Disease: Infection of the eye lining. Can be caused by either viruses or bacteria. Bacterial infections usually cause yellow or green eye discharge. Viral infections usually cause watery eye discharge. One bacteria, Haemophilus influenza, causes pink eye, sinus infections, and ear infections at the same time. About 30% of babies under age two with bacterial pink eye will also have an ear infection to go with it.

Symptoms: Red, itchy eyes with discolored thick fluid draining or matting the eyes shut.

Diagnosis: Based on exam. Occasionally, a culture is done of the fluid.

Treatment: Antibiotic eye drops if infection is bacterial. No treatment for viral pink eye.

Contagious: VERY. Spread by direct contact with eye discharge. Use separate hand towels.

Incubation period: Varies. For viral pink eye, 2 to 14 days.

Season: Year round.

5. Food Poisoning (E. coli, Salmonella, Shigella, and others)

Disease: Bacterial infection spread through contaminated food (and infected people's mouths and poop). Salmonella bacteria is the most common cause of food poisoning (80% of the time). E. coli Type 0157: H7, although less common, can be particularly serious. This bug releases a toxin/poison that causes **HEMOLYTIC UREMIC SYNDROME** (HUS). HUS causes severe anemia, low platelet count, and kidney failure. It is a reversible condition, but can be fatal. These kids are *really* sick with abdominal distention, pain, bloody diarrhea, and **PETECHIAE.** E. coli 0157 comes from cow and deer poop. Ground meat can have bacterial contamination throughout. Because of that, the meat needs to be cooked thoroughly to kill any of these bugs. Whole muscle cuts are only contaminated on the surface of the meat, which are always cooked well. (The poop gets spread to the meat during hide removal or evisceration). (*Pickering*)

Symptoms: Vomiting, diarrhea mixed with blood or mucous. Fever. Body aches. Abdominal pain.

Diagnosis: Stool culture, blood and white blood cells in poop, some blood test abnormalities.

Treatment: FLUIDS to avoid dehydration. Some bacterial infections need antibiotics to clear. Some bacterial infections should NOT be treated with antibiotics as it causes the person to remain a "carrier" of the infection.

Contagious: Spread through contaminated food/water (poultry, undercooked eggs, alfalfa sprouts, unpasteurized milk, undercooked hamburgers), breast milk, fomites (e.g. raw meat on countertop), direct contact with infected poop, saliva. Salmonella is also spread via pet iguanas and turtles, who are carriers. People, especially infants, who get Salmonella will often remain carriers for months after the infection.

Incubation Period: Varies on the bug, usually 6 to 72 hours.

Season: Year round.

Prevention: Never eat a hamburger that can moo back at you (it needs to be well done). Avoid fresh fruit/vegetables and water when traveling to developing countries. Drink only pasteurized milk and apple cider. Be careful in the kitchen. Food preparation should be separated from baby products (bottles, nipples, etc.). Avoid pet iguanas or turtles.

BOTTOM LINE

Yes, we know it is trendy in some circles to drink unpasteurized milk. People who prefer this product believe that the pasteurization process takes out some of the "natural" ingredients ... like bacteria that can cause serious illness or death. Louis Pasteur is rolling over in his grave right now. Please purchase pasteurized milk and dairy products!

Reality Check

There was an E. coli outbreak a few years ago blamed on petting zoo exposure. Kids touched animals that had rolled around in cow manure. The kids later touched their mouths with their contaminated hands. Note: wash your child's hands thoroughly after going to a petting zoo.

6. Bladder Infections or Urinary Tract Infections (E. coli and others)

Disease: A bacterial infection caused by intestinal bacteria that get into the bladder. Bacteria (e.g. E. coli) routinely come out in our poop. They only cause infection when they creep into our bladders. Babies who are in diapers are susceptible to bladder infections (especially girls) because the poop collects where the opening to the bladder sits (urethra). Some babies are prone to bladder infections because of an abnormality called **VESICOURETERAL REFLUX.**

Symptoms: Fever, fussy mood, lack of other symptoms to explain fever

Diagnosis: Abnormal urinalysis, urine culture grows bacteria. Certain children with bladder infections have an evaluation done of their urinary tract system to rule out abnormality.

Treatment: Depends on the age and severity of infection. Babies under three months of age are hospitalized because of a higher risk of kidney infection and meningitis from infection.

Contagious: No.

Prevention: Clean poopie diapers as soon as possible. Wipe girls front to back.

7. Meningitis

Disease: Inflammation of the tissues that line the brain. This can be caused by viruses or bacteria. Bacterial meningitis is a life threatening illness. There are different bacteria that cause meningitis in various age groups. Meningitis can be caused by more than one type of bacteria. The top two that you need to know about are discussed below:

Group B Strep

Disease: With a newborn, the bacteria you will hear the most about is ***Group B Strep.*** This bacteria is normal flora in the intestines, bladder, and the vagina of mothers. It uniquely causes infection in newborns as they pass through the birth canal. Pregnant women are routinely screened at 35 to 37 weeks to check for the presence of Group B Strep (GBS). If Mom is a carrier, she is given IV antibiotics during labor to suppress the growth of this bacteria. If Mom goes into labor before 37 weeks, has broken her water more than 18 hours, or has a fever greater than 100.4, she also gets IV antibiotics because of the risk of Group B Strep infection. (Women who have planned C-sections don't have to worry about this stuff.) Doctors watch all newborns closely, but those with GBS-positive Moms get watched even more closely. A standard protocol is to get a complete blood count and blood culture on a newborn if Mom is GBS-positive and didn't get pretreated with antibiotics (i.e. a quick labor), baby is born less than 35 weeks gestation, or if a baby starts misbehaving (temperature instability, respiratory distress). There is also potential for a late onset GBS infection up to three months after delivery.

Diagnosis: Bacteria can be seen in blood or spinal fluid under a microscope (see Gram stain in lab section). Blood or spinal fluid cultures give the definitive answer in 2 to 3 days.

Treatment: IV antibiotics. Penicillin works well.

Contagious: Spread via birth canal.

Incubation period: 0-3 months.

Season: N/A.

Prevention: Prophylactic antibiotics to Mom while in labor.

infections

Strep pneumoniae

Disease: This type of Strep is also known as *pneumococcus* (very confusing). This bacteria has been the top cause of bacterial meningitis in infants. (It also causes ear infections, blood infections, sinus infections and pneumonia). Strep pneumoniae has developed resistance to many antibiotics. This is why the Prevnar vaccine (for Strep pneumoniae) was a welcome arrival back in 2000. Since then, we have seen an 87% disease reduction in bloodstream (bacteremia) infections and meningitis.

Symptoms: High fevers (usually more than 103), *without obvious symptoms*, irritability. If the infection is caught early while it is in the blood, treatment prevents travel to the brain (meningitis).

Diagnosis: Blood infections (bacteremia) by an elevated white blood cell count over 15,000 (often over 20,000) and a blood culture which may grow the bug. Meningitis is diagnosed by an abnormal spinal fluid (white blood cells in it) and a culture that grows bacteria.

Treatment: Blood infections get treated with an antibiotic shot initially, then oral antibiotics. Meningitis requires IV antibiotics and hospitalization.

Contagious: Spread by respiratory droplets. Strep pneumoniae lives everywhere. Some people are carriers. Children get infected when they already have a viral upper respiratory infection.

Incubation period: 1 to 3 days.

Season: Winter mostly.

Prevention: Prevnar (PCV-13 strains) vaccine for infants and children under five who are high risk. There is also a Pneumococcus vaccine (23 strains) for high risk children and elderly people. High risk: sickle cell disease, children with no spleen, kidney disease, immune compromised, HIV. (*Pickering*)

Things That Make You Itch Just Thinking About Them

Note: We will also discuss some of these lovely germs in Chapter 15, First Aid in the section on rashes. Go to our online Rash-o-Rama at Baby411.com (click bonus material) to see pictures.

Fungal Infections

Disease: Fungi are plant relatives (yeast, mold) that don't need light to live. Fungi prefer places where there is little competition (i.e. low bacteria levels). And, some fungi thrive on people whose defenses are down (i.e. immune compromised). We get infected in the following ways:

1. ***Fungus infestation.*** These are the accidental tourists. These fungi thrive on our skin, but don't go any deeper than that (**RINGWORM, ATHLETE'S FOOT, JOCK ITCH**). They are passed from person to person, or via a pet. These fungi just happen to be at the right place at the right time.

2. ***Opportunistic infection.*** These fungi grow when other factors alter our body defenses to fungi. Infants are susceptible to fungal infections (**THRUSH, YEAST DIAPER RASH**) because their bodies are relatively free of bacteria flora. Kids are also at risk for yeast diaper rash after having a course of antibiotics because the antibiotic not only kills the bad bacteria, but also the good normal flora. Other fungal opportunities include people on chronic steroids or with diabetes.

3. ***Invasive infection.*** This virtually never happens to normal, healthy people. A fungus invades the blood or lungs after its spores are inhaled.

Diagnosis:

Ringworm. Classic circular area with raised red border, and central scale. Fungus visible under microscope. Culture will grow in 2 to 3 weeks.

Ringworm of scalp. Patch of hair loss with overlying scale, or dots of hair loss with stubs of broken hair, or big ugly pus pockets (kerion) in the scalp. More in African American kids (fungus likes the hair texture). Culture grows in 2 to 3 weeks.

Thrush. Classic white plaques on a red base in the cheeks, gums, tongue. Looks like milk you can't wipe off. Diagnosis based on examination.

Yeast diaper rash. Raw meat red area with satellite pimply dots. Won't improve with Desitin. Found often when thrush is present in the mouth.

Treatment:

Ringworm. Anti-fungal cream for 2 to 4 weeks.

Ringworm of scalp. Anti-fungal medicine by mouth for 1-2 months (cream won't kill it). The fungus imbeds in the hair follicle and is very hardy. We see some drug resistant strains.

Thrush. Anti-fungal mouthwash for 1 to 2 weeks. Sterilize all nipples, pacifiers.

Yeast diaper rash. Anti-fungal cream for 1 to 2 weeks.

Contagious: Until treated for 24 hours with anti-fungal medicine.

Ringworm. Direct contact with infected person or animal (itchy dogs). Fomites too.

Ringworm of scalp. Direct contact with combs, hairbrushes, bed sheets.

Thrush. Direct contact with infant's mouth (spreads to Mom's nipples).

Yeast diaper rash. Opportunistic infection. Not particularly contagious. (*Pickering*)

Scabies (Mite Infection)

Disease: An infestation caused by mites, tiny bugs that are somewhere between parasites and ticks. The female scabies mite burrows into our skin and lays her eggs. She lays 200 eggs in eight weeks. When the eggs hatch, the babies burrow into our skin and start eating. This is the ITCHIEST rash ever. Even after treatment, people are itchy for weeks afterwards.

Symptoms: The mites usually burrow between our fingers, elbow creases, armpits, belly button area, and genitals. In infected kids under two years old, they prefer the neck, palms, and soles. What you will see is a streak made out of tiny bumps—they start out gray, but are usually red by the time a person seeks medical attention.

Diagnosis: If the rash is classic, diagnosis is made on examination alone. For unclear cases, a scraping of a burrow can be done. It may reveal the mite, mite egg, or mite poop under the microscope.

Treatment: A scabicidal body wash (Elimite-5% Permethrin) is available by prescription. ALL FAMILY MEMBERS GET TREATED. Clothing and bedding used for four days before treatment need to be washed and dried on the hot cycle. Disinfecting the house is a waste of time.

Contagious: Until treated with Elimite. Spread by direct contact, especially by holding hands. Co-sleeping is also an easy way for the whole family to get infected with scabies. Mites cannot survive off of humans for more than 24 hours.

Incubation period: 4 to 6 weeks.

More mite facts:

Chiggers are mites who like pores and hair follicles of people. These are self-limited infestations, but are also very itchy.

Dust mites do not cause infection. They feed off of the dead skin that we slough off on a daily basis. Some people are allergic to dust mite poop and have chronic nasal congestion as a result of it (see environmental allergies). (*Pickering*)

Lice

Disease: Infestation by a human louse. Head lice enjoy feeding on us via human hair. They don't have wings. They migrate from one head to the next by crawling over. They can't survive away from hair for more than 24 hours. The adult females lay eggs in the hair shafts (less than 1/4 inch from the scalp). Adults live about one month. The eggs become thriving nymphs in about one week. Head lice prefer the straighter hair of Caucasian people. Outbreaks happen more in school age children, but younger kids can acquire lice at childcare centers.

Symptoms: Itchy scalp, white flakes that are firmly adherent to the hair shaft.

infections

Diagnosis: Adult lice are brown and visible with the naked eye—but they move quickly. The diagnosis is made most often by finding white nits (empty eggshells). Nits stick firmly to the hair shaft close to the scalp. Dandruff is rubbed off easily, nits are not.

Treatment: An over-the-counter shampoo called Nix (1% permethrin) kills adult lice and the eggs. Two treatments, one week apart (to kill any baby lice that survived the first round). Since the nits are empty eggshells, removing them is more of a cosmetic issue than a therapeutic one. The phrase "nit-picking" comes from the tedious task of removing the sticky nits that are close to the scalp. Many little lice are resistant to current over-the-counter treatment.

Contagious: Until treated. "No-nit" policies in childcare facilities are not necessary.

Incubation period: 6 to 10 days.

Creative treatment for resistant head lice: If living *adult* lice are found (not nits), then re-treatment is in order. The list of alternatives include prescription 5% Permethrin (Elimite), Malathion (a pesticide), Bactrim (an antibiotic), Ulesfia (benzyl alcohol), Sklice (ivermectin), and products that smother the lice (Vaseline, olive oil, mayonnaise). A combination of tea tree oil, eucalyptus oil, and olive oil (1 teaspoon of each mixed together) applied to the scalp may also prove effective for kids over age three.

For more information on lice: www.headlice.org

Pinworms

Disease: Pinworms live in our intestines and lay eggs on the outside of the anus. Infection is spread when worm-ridden Johnny scratches his bottom and plays in the sandbox. Suzie plays in the sandbox later and picks up the eggs on her fingers. Her fingers go in her mouth, and voila! Suzie has pinworms too!

Symptoms: The female pinworm comes out to the anus at night and lays her eggs. This causes a symptom called pruritus ani (Latin for "itchy tushie"). Itchy vagina also happens from pinworms.

Diagnosis: Often based on symptoms alone. Parents can go on a worm hunt. The female comes out of the anus about two hours after a child is sleeping. Put clear Scotch tape on a toothpick and obtain a specimen.

Treatment: Two doses of Vermox (Latin for "worm-out") prescription, given two weeks apart. Doctors often treat the whole family. Bathing in morning helps remove the eggs.

Contagious: Until treated. Infected people often re-infect themselves by scratching their anus and ingesting more eggs.

Incubation period: 1 to 2 months (egg is ingested, then matures into an adult egg-laying female in 1 to 2 months). (*CDC*)

Parasites

Another stomach infection is called Giardia. This is a parasite spread via water. Yes, this includes swimming pools, hot tubs, and area lakes. Someone with the infection who is swimming in the water can share it. It frequently haunts childcare centers. Prolonged or foul-smelling diarrhea deserves to be tested for parasites.

Special Feature: Ear Infections

Is your child earning frequent flier miles at the doctor's office? Are you exhausted by the constant ear infections your poor baby has had to endure? Then this section is for you.

Q. Why is my baby prone to getting ear infections?

Thanks to your baby's facial structure, her Eustachian tubes are not working right. The Eustachian tubes equalize pressure changes in the ear and clear the fluid created from infection or allergies. Babies are born with round heads to get through the birth canal. As a result, the Eustachian tubes (connection between the ears and the back of the nose) *lie horizontally* in kids until three years old. This keeps the tubes from draining effectively. As a child grows, his head and face elongate. The Eustachian tubes ultimately slant downwards (and work better).

When a child gets a cold or upper respiratory infection, the virus causes the lining of the Eustachian tubes to swell, making the tubes even more inefficient. Bacteria like to grow if the fluid sits there long enough. The body's immune response to the bacteria creates pus, and that is the definition of a middle ear infection (**ACUTE OTITIS MEDIA**). Older children and adults rarely get ear infections because their Eustachian tubes drain more effectively.

Your Baby's Ear, in a nutshell

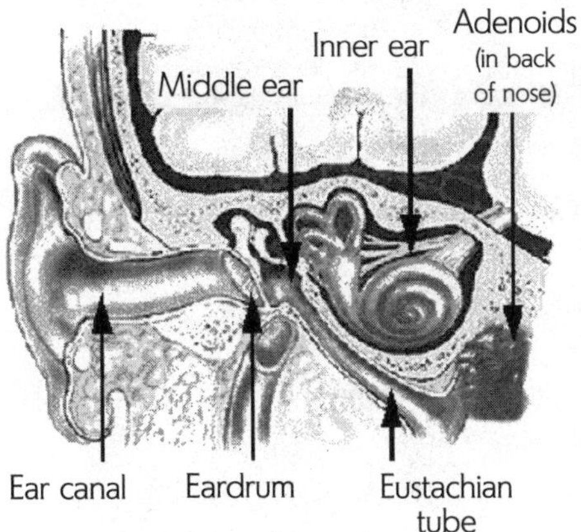

Notes:
1. The ear is divided into three parts—the inner, middle, and outer areas.
2. The Eustachian tubes attach to the middle part of the ear.
3. The eardrum (tympanic membrane) is a piece of tissue that separates the middle and outer ear.
4. The eardrum protects the delicate middle ear bones and nerves.

Ear Infection Facts

- By the age of three, 75% of all children have had at least one ear infection.
- 40% of all antibiotics prescribed for children are for ear infections.
- The peak age of ear infections is six to 18 months of age.
- 90% of ear infections are caused by bacteria; 10% by viruses.

Q. What is the difference between an ear infection and swimmer's ear?

An "ear infection" generally refers to a *middle* ear infection (**ACUTE OTI-**

infections

TIS MEDIA). The pus/infection sits behind the eardrum (see diagram on the previous page). A "swimmer's ear" (**OTITIS EXTERNA**) refers to an infection of the skin lining the *outer* ear (the canal where Q-tips don't belong!).

Middle Ear Infection (Acute Otitis Media)

A normal looking eardrum is grayish and translucent. The bones that control hearing (the ones you learned about in junior high science class) are visible behind it. An infected eardrum has pus behind it and is swollen and red. The pus and swelling obscure the view of the middle ear. *Think of the infection as being a zit.* It has to drain before it gets better. It can either rupture the eardrum and drain (undesirable) or drain down the Eustachian tube (desirable). The use of antibiotics taken by mouth clears the pus and decreases the chance of the zit bursting (**PERFORATED EARDRUM,** see more on the next page).

TOP 7 RISK FACTORS FOR EAR INFECTIONS

Parents often ask if there is anything that can be done to prevent an ear infection from happening. Here are the risk factors:

1. **The common cold/upper respiratory infection.** By definition, fluid must be present in the Eustachian tubes to allow bacteria to grow. Having a cold is the perfect set up for fluid accumulation in the sinuses and Eustachian tubes.
2. **Daycare.** Children get more cold viruses when they are around other kids. Naturally, kids in daycare will get more colds, thus more ear infections. And the bacteria that live there are more likely to be drug resistant bacteria.
3. **Second hand smoke.** Smoke is irritating to the whole respiratory tract, from the nose down to the lungs. Irritation of the Eustachian tubes causes swelling of the tissues and inefficiency in clearing fluid.
4. **Pacifier use.** Constant sucking seems to create a backup of fluid in the back of the throat and Eustachian tubes.
5. **Bottle propping.** Babies who lie down and hold their own bottles allow fluid from the back of the throat to end up in the Eustachian tubes. The fluid is a set up for infection.
6. **Native American.** The facial structure of this ethnic group predisposes them to Eustachian tube dysfunction.
7. **Cleft lip/palate.** This facial structure predisposes them to Eustachian tube dysfunction.

If you're looking for more information on common ear, nose and throat problems in childhood, check out the web site of the American Academy of Otolaryngology Head and Neck Surgery at EntNet.org/kidsent.

Swimmer's Ear (External Otitis)

This is a skin infection caused by either pooled water that collects in the ear canal of kids who swim under water or skin irritation from being scratched (from a Q-tip). Both situations allow bacteria to penetrate the skin and cause infection. *Swimmer's ear causes extreme pain with touch or movement of the outer ear* (the part you can see). There is swelling, redness, and sometimes debris in the canal. The eardrum is normal. These infections usually clear up with antibiotic eardrops.

Q. My baby's eardrum popped! Will he have permanent hearing damage?

No. Perforated eardrums heal like a piece of skin that has been cut.

Remember the zit analogy? The eardrum is under pressure with all that pus behind it. When the pimple pops, it lets the pus drain out. The perforation hole is usually small and not completely ruptured. The ear feels better if this happens. The infection still needs to be treated, though. The doctor may prescribe antibiotic drops and oral antibiotics if this occurs. It should heal up without any long-term consequences as long as the infection is treated.

Q. Will my child get an ear infection from lying in bath water?

No.

Bath water is fairly clean and very little collects in the outer ear canal. But it's a good idea to wipe the water out of the ears. It's not a major player in

New Parent 411: Ear Treatment Guidelines

The American Academy of Pediatrics revised their treatment guidelines for ear infections in 2013. Here's a look at the rules:

Infants under six months of age with acute middle ear infections will still get treated with antibiotics. They are more likely to suffer complications from ear infections. But, providers should adhere to strict guidelines for what constitutes an acute ear infection.

Kids ages six months to two years with *clear cut infections* are also treated, but when the diagnosis is in question, a wait and see approach is in order. Your doctor may ask you to return for a follow-up visit or have you fill a prescription in a couple of days if your child's symptoms don't improve.

The guidelines attempt to limit antibiotic use in kids with mild to moderate symptoms and avoid use when the diagnosis itself is in question (not all ear infections are so black and white).

Ask your doctor for his or her opinion about this issue. Record his thoughts here:.

causing swimmer's ear. And it has absolutely nothing to do with middle ear infections (which happen on the other side of the eardrum).

Q. My child was just in the doctor's office two days ago. Now he has an ear infection. Didn't the doctor see it then?

Back to the zit thing. Ears can go from normal to bulging with pus in a matter of hours.

Q. Can I buy one of those ear scopes (otoscope) and examine my own child's ears?

Sure. But you might not know what you are looking at.

An acute middle ear infection may present itself in one of several ways. The obvious bulging red ear is one you'd be able to diagnose. But not all of them look like that. They are more subtle. It doesn't just take the light of an otoscope to make the diagnosis. It takes the experience of looking at thousands of ears for comparison.

Don't be disappointed if you buy an otoscope, feel sure that you have diagnosed an ear infection, and find that your pediatrician has a different opinion.

Q. I've heard that not all ear infections require antibiotics to go away. Do we have to treat every ear infection with antibiotics?

Not all middle ear infections require antibiotics.

A small percentage (10%) of ear infections are caused by viruses. And up to 60% of bacterial ear infections will clear on their own without any consequences. However, bacterial ear infections clear more quickly with antibiotics.

A 2011 study in the *New England Journal of Medicine* looked at the standard recommendations for treating ear infections in children ages six to 23 months of age. Their conclusion: little kids feel better faster when they are treated with antibiotics. (*Hoberman*)

That said, the American Academy of Pediatrics came out with its own guidelines in 2013 regarding treatment of ear infections. Their message to healthcare providers: be judicious about diagnosing ear infections based on stricter criteria and only treat true infections. Their message to parents: be patient. Every illness does not improve with antibiotics.

And for kids over age two, a provider might diagnose an ear infection and send a child home without a prescription. She might tell the parent to give the child a pain medication and come back the next day for a recheck. If the ear looks worse or unchanged, she prescribes antibiotics. If the ear is improved, no therapy is required.

DR B'S OPINION

"I always pick the least potent antibiotic that will work in a given situation. The only way to have the 'big gun' when you need it is to avoid using it when you don't need it."

Q. What happened in the days before antibiotics when children had ear infections?

Some children did just fine. Others did not.

Untreated bacterial infections can lead to *hearing loss* (from chronic fluid accumulation, chronic infection, and chronic ear drum perforations), *mastoiditis* (infection invades the skull bone), and *brain abscesses/meningitis* (infection extends to brain and spinal fluid). In the old days before antibiotics, 80% of ear infections would go away on their own. But the last 20% of ear infections that were untreated led to these significant complications. (*Rosenfeld*)

Q. What antibiotics are typically used to treat ear infections?

The right drug for the bug.

The most common bacteria that cause middle ear infections are:

- Strep pneumoniae (now less common thanks to Prevnar vaccine).
- Moraxella
- H. Influenza *non-typable* (a cause of pink eye with an ear infection)
- Group A Strep

There are basically four antibiotic classes that kill all of these bugs. As a general rule, doctors prescribe amoxicillin (in the Penicillin class) as their first choice. It is a broad-spectrum antibiotic that is well tolerated by most kids, has been around for a long time, and is relatively inexpensive (about $10 for generic). It works about 85% of the time, depending on the amount of drug resistant bacteria living in your neighborhood. That's a pretty good track record.

If it has been *less* than 30 days since a previous ear infection, doctors may select a different class of antibiotics because the bacteria may be resistant to the amoxicillin (that is, the same bug may have grown back after being off medication).

If there is pink eye associated with an ear infection, there is a good chance that H. influenza is the bug. This bug is resistant to amoxicillin about 50% of the time (again, depending on your neighborhood). So, a doctor may choose a different antibiotic in this situation.

Q. My child was on amoxicillin before and it never works.

Your child is not resistant to amoxicillin–the bacterium he is being infected with is resistant. Children in daycare settings tend to have more ear and sinus infections with drug-resistant bacteria. That does not mean that amoxicillin will *never* work. For instance, Group A Strep (which causes Strep throat) is almost always cured with amoxicillin.

Q. My child is pulling on his ears. Should I be worried about an ear infection?

No. It's not a reliable indicator.

Parents frequently rely on ear pulling as a sign of an ear infection. There was an excellent study done on this suspicious behavior that showed ear pulling predicted ear infections only 5% of the time. 95% of the time, babies pull on their ears because they can! (*Baker*)

Q. Why do I have to bring my child back for an "ear check" after he has been treated?

Because infants can't tell you that their ears are better.

The antibiotic prescribed should kill the bacteria. But there are smart, resistant bugs that will survive. That's one reason why the doctor wants to see your child back two to three weeks after the diagnosis.

The other reason is that residual sterile fluid (**SEROUS OTITIS MEDIA**) can remain for a long time after the bacteria is gone. This is basically pus that is dissolved, but not dried up. The fluid is not infected, but can create two problems:

- It puts a child at risk for getting another middle ear infection down the road.
- It inhibits sound waves from getting through the middle ear (**CONDUCTIVE HEARING LOSS**). It's like walking around with earplugs in all day long. Chronic fluid (more than three months duration) is a problem for a child who is trying to learn his native language (**EXPRESSIVE LANGUAGE DELAYS**).

Q. My child feels better after just a couple of days taking amoxicillin for his ear infection. Why do we have to continue the medicine for ten days?

Antibiotics start to clear an infection within 48-72 hours. However, it can take five to ten days to kill off all of the bacteria. Stopping an antibiotic early allows a germ to re-grow and cause infection (and pain) to return. Doctors are trying to shorten the course of antibiotics because of the growing number of antibiotic resistant bacteria. If you doctor prescribes a shorter course (five days) of medicine, be sure to follow up with an appointment to make sure the infection has cleared.

Q. We are flying with our baby tomorrow and he was just diagnosed with an ear infection. Should we cancel our trip?

No. Go have fun.

RESIDUAL EAR FLUID

The pus from the ear infection gradually dissolves and gets reabsorbed by the body. The name for this sterile (bug-free) fluid is called **SEROUS FLUID** or serous otitis. 70% of children will still have serous fluid two weeks after an ear infection. Up to 40% of kids will still have serous fluid one month later, and 10% have fluid three months after infection. (*Peter*)

The serous fluid does NOT need to be treated with antibiotics to clear up. However, kids with residual fluid need to be re-evaluated to make sure the fluid goes away. As mentioned earlier, chronic fluid in the ears interferes with language development (in the short term).

If a child has chronic fluid in the ears, over three months duration, an Ear/Nose/Throat specialist may want to drain the fluid by popping the eardrum with a needle. Frequently, if the drum is popped, a PE tube is inserted to prevent further accumulations of fluid.

As anyone who's traveled on a plane knows, the pressurized air in the cabin requires you to "clear" your ears (by chewing gum, yawning, etc). Babies have the same needs–their middle ear must accommodate to the pressure change. When a child has an acute ear infection, pus fills in the middle ear space and the eardrum cannot move. The ear won't hurt. In fact, the pressure change might make the drum pop to release the pressure (and that's okay–see perforated eardrum earlier in this chapter).

It is more problematic when an ear infection is starting to clear up. Then there is both air (normal) and fluid (not normal) in the middle ear. The eardrum will try to accommodate to the pressure change and will be only partially successful. This HURTS. Don't cancel your trip; just be prepared for some discomfort on take off and landing. Nursing, feeding your child a bottle or sucking on a pacifier can help relieve the pressure.

Q. How many ear infections are too many?

Great question. For this answer, we've recruited Dr. Brown's husband, Mr. Dr. Brown (an Ear, Nose, and Throat specialist) for some advice:

"Most kids outgrow the problem of ear infections by about three years of age. (See earlier for information on why this is). So theoretically, we can all wait until your child turns three. But there are some important considerations that compel doctors to take a more active approach." Here are some key questions:

1. **How many courses of antibiotics are too many?** Antibiotics can have unpleasant side effects like diarrhea and yeast infections. Being on antibiotics frequently leaves a child susceptible to bacteria that are smarter (the drug-resistant strains) and allows bacteria in the community to see our weapons. From an economic standpoint, every ear infection costs parents a visit to the pediatrician, missed work, and another round of antibiotics.
2. **How old is the child?** If a child is in the midst of language acquisition (nine months to age two), it's critical for him to hear what people are saying to him. Otherwise, the infections can contribute

DR B'S OPINION: WHEN TO CALL IN AN ENT

Here is how I would approach making a referral to an Ear/Nose/Throat (ENT) Specialist for a child with recurrent ear infections (other than the "too many" criteria above).

Scenario 1: If a child already has had three ear infections by Thanksgiving, that doesn't bode well for the rest of the season (cold and flu season will continue through March). Refer now to an ENT.

Scenario 2: If a child gets ear infections sporadically through the winter and gets his fourth infection in April, wait and see if the ear infections stop as the season ends.

Scenario 3: If a child gets two ear infections during the summer months and a third in September, the child gets one more chance before referring. But I prepare the family for the possibility.

to short-term expressive language delays. In the long run, these kids do catch up and have normal language skills.

3. **How miserable is the child?** Ear infections hurt. That leads to disrupted sleep for the whole family. This important point tends to get overlooked by both parents and doctors.

Reality Check

It's important to look at what is in the best interest of the child. There is some variability amongst doctors, but a reasonable answer to what is "too many" is the following:

- Four infections in the peak (winter) season
- Three infections in the off peak (summer) season
- Three months of persistent residual fluid (serous otitis media)
- Three back-to-back courses of antibiotics for the same ear infection.

Too many ear infections buy your child a trip to see the Ear, Nose, and Throat specialist. These doctors assist in decision making for children with recurrent ear infections. If necessary, they can place pressure equalization tubes in the eardrum to reduce the number of ear infections (we'll discuss this more in detail later in this chapter).

Ear infections occur mostly in cold and flu season. (Remember, bacteria are secondary infections for a child with fluid in his ears already). So, it's expected that more infections will happen then. Kids who get middle ear infections in the off-season are time bombs for the winter.

Q. How can I prevent ear infections from happening?

There are a few things you can do:

1. **Feed your baby in an upright position.** Milk can get into the Eustachian tubes if a baby is lying horizontally while eating.
2. **Avoid pacifiers after six months of age.** There is some good data to suggest this is a risk factor for ear infections. (*Post*)
3. **Don't smoke.** Smoking is a respiratory irritant—both to the smoker and his family. It causes swelling of the Eustachian tubes, which can lead to infection.
4. **Infection control during the cold and flu season.** Good hand-washing and flu shots for the family are helpful. The Prevnar vaccine for your child helps limit some (not all) infections.
5. **Reconsider your childcare options.** There is no question that children in daycare settings get more infections (and with drug-resistant bugs). When families have reached the end of their ropes, doctors may discuss this subject.

Q. Can we just start an antibiotic when my child has a cold? What about preventative antibiotics through the winter months?

Doctors used both of these methods in the past. And to a certain degree, they worked. However, the price paid is too great. This approach created drug-resistant bacteria.

The Infection Hit Parade: Viruses and Bacteria

So, let's sum up this chapter. Here is a list of the top infections, as caused by viruses and bacteria:

Viruses That Cause Infection

Here is a list of the most common VIRUSES that cause infection in babies ages birth to age one.

Viral Respiratory Infections
1. The Common Cold or upper respiratory infection (Rhinovirus)
2. The Flu (Influenza)
3. Bronchiolitis (RSV)
4. Croup (numerous viruses)

Viral Mouth And Tonsil Infections
1. Hand-Foot-and-Mouth (Coxsackievirus)
2. Herpes Stomatitis (Herpes Type-1)
3. Sore throat virus (Adenovirus)

Gastrointestinal Viruses
1. Stomach virus, or "stomach flu" (Rotavirus, Norovirus)

Viral Exanthems (Viruses That Cause Skin Rashes)
1. Roseola (Herpesvirus-6)
2. Chickenpox (Varicella)
3. Slapped Cheek or Fifth Disease (Parvovirus)

Bacteria That Cause Infection

Here are some of the bacterial infections in babies birth to age one. For details, please see earlier in the chapter.

1. **Ear Infections** (Strep pneumoniae, H. Influenza, and others)
2. **Sinus Infections** (Strep pneumoniae H. Influenza, and others)
3. **Eye Infections** (H. Influenza, Strep pneumoniae, and others)
4. **Throat Infections** (Group A Strep)
5. **Lung Infections** (Strep pneumoniae, Staph, and others)
6. **Food Poisoning** (E. Coli, Salmonella)
7. **Bladder Infections** (E. Coli, and others)
8. **Meningitis** (Group B Strep, Strep pneumoniae)
9. **Skin infections** (Staph, MRSA, Strep)

Things That Make You Itch Just Thinking About Them

1. **Fungus:** Ringworm, Thrush, Yeast diaper rash
2. **Mites:** Scabies, Lice
3. **Parasites:** Giardia
4. **Worms:** Pinworms

Q. Can I prevent an ear infection from happening by using a decongestant or antihistamine to dry up all that snot?

No.

You would think that if you got rid of the fluid, the ear infection could be prevented. This idea was studied about 30 years ago and it didn't prevent ear infections. There is a reason it doesn't work. When there is infection, the Eustachian tubes are full of fluid *and* get swollen. This prevents them from draining effectively.

Q. What are "tubes"?

The official term is Pressure Equalization (PE) Tube.

The alternative to antibiotics for recurrent ear infections is to insert PE tubes into the eardrums. These tubes are the length of a pencil point and the diameter of angel hair pasta (i.e. really small). The procedure is relatively simple. An ENT Specialist makes a tiny hole in the eardrum, cleans out any fluid/pus, and inserts the tube. The tube falls out on its own after a lifespan of 6-18 months. The eardrum heals beautifully 99% of the time.

Children have this procedure done in a day-surgery facility. They do require anesthesia, but don't require an IV, breathing tube, or ventilator. Why anesthesia? It's helpful not to have a squirming child when someone is poking a hole into the eardrum. The procedure takes about five minutes. Kids are usually back to themselves again later that day.

Many parents are incredibly fearful of having PE tubes placed. They are afraid of the procedure, the anesthesia, or the risk of having an opening in the eardrum (you have to keep water out of the ear). Most of these concerns should be clearly addressed by your ENT doctor.

Helpful Hints: Understanding PE Tubes

Think of PE tube placement as a *procedure* and not surgery. I think the word surgery really freaks people out.

- This is a simple, quick procedure. For adults, it could be performed in an office setting.
- The risk of anesthesia is no greater than the risk of all the antibiotics your child has been taking.
- You'll no longer need to see the pediatrician every week. My frequent fliers stop visiting my office after they have PE tubes placed. I always enjoy seeing my patients, but I see some kids too often.

BOTTOM LINE

As a general rule, PE tubes are a life changing experience for the whole family. Even the most anxious parents report how "easy" the experience is, how much better their child feels, and wonder why they waited so long to do it. I've never had a family tell me they regretted the decision to get tubes!

Whew! That was a load of viruses and bacteria. Now, it's on to other medical problems that are NOT caused by infectious bugs. The next chapter explores the most common diseases that affect babies.

Common Diseases

Chapter 14

"Sooner or later we all quote our mothers."
~ Bern Williams

What's in this Chapter

- Eyes: Lazy eye
- Lungs: Asthma, Bronchiolitis
- Heart: Murmurs
- Blood: Anemia, Sickle cell disease, Iron deficiency, Lead exposure
- Skin: Eczema
- Muscles/Bones: Intoeing, Bowed Legs, Flat feet, Torticollis, Hip Dysplasia
- Endocrine: Diabetes
- Allergies: Seasonal, Environmental
- Genitals: Penile, labial adhesions
- What's that smell? Unusual odors

This chapter is devoted to the most common medical problems in infants ages birth to one. Some topics have been discussed in other chapters. (See the index if you can't find the disease you are looking for in this chapter). The common thread of these medical problems is that they are not caused by an infectious bug.

We've organized this discussion by body system—first up, it's the eyes.

Eyes

Q. I'm worried my baby has a lazy eye. How do you check for that?

By examining the eyes every time you visit your doctor.

Under three months of age, babies can looked cross-eyed occasionally. The muscles of both eyes aren't working together yet.

After three months, both eyes should move together. There are two medical reasons for why they don't:

1. **Strabismus.** The muscles that move the eye are weak.
2. **Amblyopia.** The eye itself is weak or injured.

Often a parent will notice this at home. Doctors check by covering up one eye and checking that the other eye can focus on an object. A child looks away or tries to remove the examiner's hand when the unaffected eye is covered. Cool new trend: high-tech vision screening devices. These gadgets can detect vision problems—even in squirming toddlers. While the American Academy of Pediatrics supports early vision screening, major insurance plans have not embraced this technology yet. In other words, you may need to pay out of pocket for it. Our advice: it's worth it.

Children who fail a screening test should see an eye specialist (ophthalmologist). If a lazy eye goes untreated, permanent problems can occur. Eye doctors prefer to assess these problems before three years of age.

Helpful Hint

There is a benign condition called **PSEUDOSTRABISMUS** where kids just have narrowly set eyes. This is not a medical problem.

RED FLAG

If your child has a dramatic new problem with an eye turning in, go see your doctor ASAP. This can be a sign of a brain tumor. Don't panic yet, just get it checked out.

Lungs

Q. What is asthma?

In short, it's like hay fever in the lungs.

Asthma is a process of swelling, muscle tightening, obstruction, destruction, and mucous production in the big and little airways of the lungs. This chain of events occurs due to a revved up immunologic/allergic response to *infections, allergies, weather, and emotions*.

The narrowed airways interfere with the air exchange (getting clean air in and dirty air out) that occurs with each breath. As a result, children are "air hungry." Their bodies try to get more air in by breathing fast and pulling the rib muscles in when breathing. The characteristic wheeze comes from air traveling through a narrowed passageway.

Asthma attacks (termed exacerbations) occur intermittently depending on what a child is hypersensitive to. Often, kids with asthma have flare ups with upper respiratory infections. This makes for a very long, bad winter.

Q. How do you diagnose asthma?

Asthma is a diagnosis made by physical examination.

If a child is caught wheezing three or more times in his life, he carries a diagnosis of asthma. The first and second time a child wheezes, it might be bad luck. The third time, it's a trend.

There are reasons other than asthma that make children wheeze. Babies can get RSV bronchiolitis (see more below) or another infection that results in wheezing. Older babies can get a raisin (or other small object) stuck in their airway and wheeze, too.

Your doctor can get a chest x-ray to rule out an infection or a foreign body in the airway. Blood tests aren't particularly helpful. Probably the best information to confirm a diagnosis is a child's response to asthma medication. If their lungs clear up with asthma medication, they likely have the diagnosis.

Q. My doctor said my child has "Reactive Airway Disease." Is that asthma?

Basically, yes. It's just a nicer term to use for a younger child who has not been diagnosed asthmatic.

Doctors tend to hedge on the diagnosis of asthma in a child before the first birthday. Some infants get hit really hard with an RSV infection and wheeze for what seems like months. By definition, they have airways that are "reacting" to infection—by getting swollen and full of mucous.

Still other babies with severe acid reflux (**GERD**) will wheeze when the airway gets irritated. This type of wheezing resolves when they outgrow their reflux.

Doctors use this term for little ones who haven't proven themselves to be true asthmatics yet.

Q. My husband had asthma as a child. What are the chances that my baby will have it?

There is definitely a genetic predisposition to asthma and other allergic disorders. There is probably a 25% chance your child will have asthma. That means there is a 75% chance he won't. Given the odds, it doesn't pay to worry.

Q. My baby had RSV bronchiolitis this winter. What are the chances that he will have asthma?

Thirty to forty percent.

It is true that kids who wheeze with RSV tend to wheeze again (asthma) in their lifetimes. This is a chicken or the egg dilemma. We just don't know which came first.

Interestingly, not all kids who get RSV wheeze. And of the kids who do wheeze with RSV, not all of them respond to asthma medication. So, there may be just a subset of kids who would have wheezed anyway who have trouble with RSV infection. See the RSV section in Chapter 13, "Infections," for more details.

Q. Are there any other factors that cause asthma?

Besides genetics, there's nothing else that is solidly proven to predispose a child to asthma. However, a few interesting studies have recently been published on this subject. Research suggests babies who are born four months before peak cold and flu season seem to be at higher risk of developing asthma later in life. One study points to RSV, while others point to the common cold (rhinoviruses) as the culprits. (*Stein*)

Other studies have found correlations with using the European equivalent of acetaminophen (Tylenol) in babies or exposure in the womb and development of allergies and asthma later in life. None of these studies prove that acetaminophen causes asthma. It's an age-old rule of science: correlation does not prove causation. (*Beasley, Allmers, Persky, Bakkeheim*)

But, considering that several studies have found similar results, it makes sense for babies and pregnant women to only take acetaminophen when they absolutely need it.

Q. How do you treat asthma?

◆ *For immediate rescue:* A **BRONCHODILATOR** (albuterol) very quickly relaxes the airways. This is usually inhaled via an inhaler device or a nebulizer machine (a souped-up vaporizer). For infants, the nebulizer provides the most immediate, effective relief. This medication can be given for prolonged periods in an office or emergency room setting. It can be administered every four to six hours at home.

◆ *For prevention of attacks:* Kids who wheeze more than twice a week or one night a month need a medication to keep their asthma in check. Persistent symptoms mean chronic destruction to the lungs, which we now know, can be permanent. An **INHALED STEROID** (Budesonide/Pulmicort) is administered via nebulizer daily for these high-risk kids. (*Expert Panel Report II*) Children with severe, persistent wheezing may need a round of steroids given by mouth. Other oral medications, called Singulair and Cromolyn, are also used to prevent flare-ups (See common medications Appendix A for more info.)

Asthma is categorized by the severity of symptoms into ***Intermittent, Mild Persistent, Moderate Persistent,*** and ***Severe Persistent***. The National Asthma Education and Prevention Program revised their guidelines in 2007 to standardize asthma treatment. The treatment plans are divided by the severity of the symptom categories. See below:

SEVERITY	SYMPTOMS DAY/NIGHT	RX TO MAINTAIN CONTROL
Intermittent	2 or less days/week Uses rescue meds < 2 days/week	No daily medications Use rescue meds as needed
Mild Persistent	>2 days/week but not daily 1-2 nights/month Uses rescue meds >2 days/week	Low-dose inhaled steroid 2nd choice: Singulair or Cromolyn
Moderate Persistent	Daily symptoms 3-4 nights/month Uses rescue meds daily	Medium-dose inhaled steroid
Severe Persistent	Continual symptoms >1 night/week Uses rescue meds several times a day	Four Steps (see below)

Steps with severe persistent asthma:

1. *Medium-dose inhaled steroid or*
2. *Step 1 plus long-acting rescue or Singulair*
3. *High dose inhaled steroid plus long-acting rescue or Singulair*
4. *Step 3 plus oral steroids (National Institutes of Health)*

Reality Check

Most insurance plans cover the cost of a nebulizer machine for a patient who needs one. They know it's less expensive to buy a $100 machine than to pay for an ER visit or hospitalization.

Q. What are the chances my child will outgrow asthma?

50/50.

Those odds aren't bad for a chronic illness. Unfortunately, no one can predict if and when your child will outgrow it. As a general rule, kids who have asthma before the age of five tend to outgrow it. Children who are diagnosed with asthma when they are older are more likely to have it in adulthood. (*Behrman*)

Q. What are the long-term consequences of asthma?

Asthma can cause permanent airway damage. This is a recent discovery in the medical world.

Kids who have *occasional* asthma flare-ups do fine in the long term. If a child has *chronic* wheezing, normal parts of the lung can be damaged—and don't recover. So, doctors are more aggressive about treatment for a child with persistent symptoms. Chronic obstructed airways also decrease the amount of oxygen getting to the body on a daily basis.

Q. My child has eczema. My doctor told me he has a higher risk of developing asthma. Why?

Because allergic diseases can occur as a group. This particular problem is called **ATOPY.**

Atopy or atopic disease refers to a classic triad of asthma, eczema, and seasonal allergies. Of the kids who have eczema, 30% get either asthma or seasonal allergies (but 70% won't get either). (*Behrman*)

diseases

Q. My child wheezes. Could he have Cystic Fibrosis?

Yes, but it is very unlikely. Cystic Fibrosis is a genetically inherited disorder that affects one in 1600 children. It causes an abnormality in body cells that impair absorption of chloride. The result of this is that the lungs pull in too much sodium. Normal airway secretions get thick and don't move. Chronic lung infections develop. Other body systems are affected by this cell abnormality, particularly the intestines, pancreas, and reproductive system.

If your baby wheezes chronically, and especially if he is having trouble gaining weight, a screening test for cystic fibrosis may be in order. A simple assessment of a baby's sweat will give the answer. (*Behrman*)

Heart

Q. What is a heart murmur?

A murmur is an extra noise that is heard when your doctor listens to the heartbeat with a stethoscope. The normal heartbeat is actually a series of sounds best described as "lub-dub." A murmur is an extra noise that may sound like rushing water ("p-ssh") or a squeak ("eek"). The quality, duration, and location of that noise help your doctor determine what is producing it.

If the cause isn't obvious by simply listening, your doctor may recommend that a heart specialist (pediatric cardiologist) see the baby. Tests, such as an electrocardiogram (EKG) or echocardiogram ("echo" or ultrasound examination of the heart), may be recommended to gain additional information about your baby's heart.

Q. My doctor heard an "innocent" heart murmur in my baby. Should I be worried?

No.

We recruited one of our favorite pediatric cardiologists, Karen L. Wright, M.D., to field this one. She says, "An innocent murmur is the sound of normal blood flow passing through the heart chambers and blood vessels. These sounds are commonly heard in infants, and are no cause for alarm. If your baby is doing well and an innocent murmur is detected, your baby's doc will let you know and make a note to check on this during future visits. If there is any concern, or reassurance is needed, your baby's doctor can arrange for you to see a pediatric cardiologist."

Q. My baby has a heart murmur and is going to see a specialist. Should I be worried?

Normal heart

Be appropriately concerned, but not alarmed. Most heart murmurs are innocent (see above) and are not a problem.

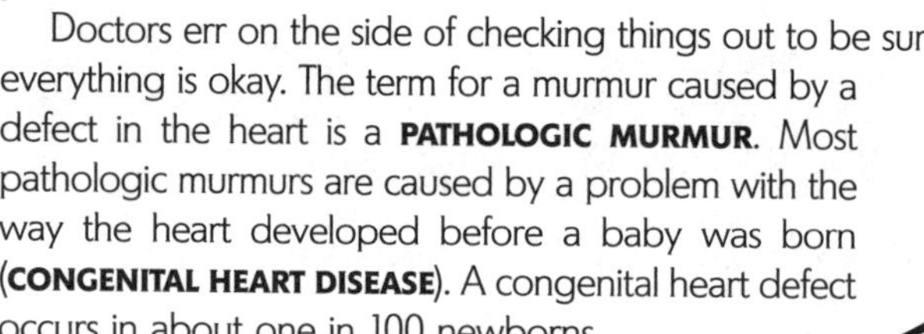

Doctors err on the side of checking things out to be sure everything is okay. The term for a murmur caused by a defect in the heart is a **PATHOLOGIC MURMUR**. Most pathologic murmurs are caused by a problem with the way the heart developed before a baby was born (**CONGENITAL HEART DISEASE**). A congenital heart defect occurs in about one in 100 newborns.

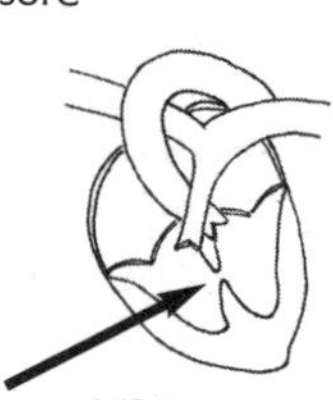
VSD

According to Dr. Wright, "The vast majority of those defects are pretty mild, and do not significantly interfere with a child's life. In fact, some of these defects truly go away on their own. A common type of congenital heart defect is a hole between the pumping chambers of the heart, called a **VENTRICULAR SEPTAL DEFECT (VSD)**. Most of these holes are small, and will often close as the baby's heart grows."

Other, less common defects may require either a procedure or surgery to correct. These defects are beyond the scope of this book. But if you are looking for more information, check out cincinnatichildrens.org/heartcenter/encyclopedia

Q. Are there other types of heart problems seen in babies?

SUPRAVENTRICULAR TACHYCARDIA (SVT) is an abnormally fast heart rhythm and it can make babies pretty ill. Fortunately, it's rare.

A baby's normal heart rate is already fast (up to 180 beats/minute), so it can be difficult to tell what is *too* fast. But if a baby is unusually fussy, feeding poorly, or breathing rapidly, SVT is one thing to think about. Get it checked out by your doc.

Blood

Q. What is anemia?

Let's discuss what red blood cells are first.

Red blood cells (which come from bone marrow) carry oxygen to our body tissues and remove carbon dioxide. Hemoglobin is the name of the protein that performs this function in each red blood cell. The key ingredient of hemoglobin is iron.

"Anemia" means there are not enough red blood cells circulating in the bloodstream. The causes of anemia are either *excessive destruction* or *inadequate production of red blood cells*.

Examples of *excessive destruction* of red blood cells include:

- More blood is being lost than made (such as menstruating women).
- Abnormal red blood cells are made and destroyed (such as sickle cell disease).

Examples of *inadequate production* of red blood cells include:

- Bone marrow production slows (such as bone marrow suppression by virus).
- Iron deficiency limits production due to lack of a key ingredient (that is, iron-deficiency anemia).
- Lead poisoning (technically, this is competition for iron's place in the red blood cell).
- Poor nutritional intake of key vitamins like B12/Folate.

The number one cause of anemia in childhood is iron deficiency. Kids who are severely anemic are pale and fatigue easily. Anemia sometimes presents with odd symptoms, like breath-holding.

Q. My baby had an abnormal newborn screen. We found out he has "sickle cell trait." What does that mean?

Let's be geneticists for a moment. Babies get one set of genes/DNA from Mom, and one set from Dad. Some diseases require one defective gene to affect someone (**AUTOSOMAL DOMINANT**). Some diseases require *both* genes to be abnormal to manifest themselves (**AUTOSOMAL RECESSIVE**).

Sickle cell disease is an autosomal recessive disease. People with one defective gene and one normal gene are called carriers. They carry the trait (gene) for the disease but are not affected by it. About 8% of the African-American population are sickle cell carriers.

Both sickle cell trait and disease can be detected by that first newborn blood test sent to the state laboratory (see Newborn Screening Tests in Chapter 1). It's detected by the type of protein chain that makes up red blood cells.

This is only a problem when your child gets married. If he marries a woman who also has sickle cell trait, his children are at a high risk for having sickle cell disease. (*Behrman*)

Q. My baby has sickle cell disease. Can you explain what that means and what I should worry about?

Sickle cell disease is caused by abnormal protein (hemoglobin) in red

blood cells. This protein causes the red blood cell shape to be deformed. Instead of an oval shaped cell, these cells look like half moons (like the "sickle" on the old Soviet Union flag).

Sickle cells die more quickly, have trouble carrying oxygen, and clog up blood vessels. This blood vessel clogging kills the tissues that the blood vessel supplies (muscle, bones, spleen, lung, kidney, intestine).

The consequences in infancy and early childhood are the following:

1. **Chronic Anemia:** This shows up by age three months. Folate supplements are given to promote red blood cell formation.
2. **Dactylitis:** Infants get hand and foot swelling from clogged blood vessels.
3. **Non-functional spleen:** The spleen filters red blood cells as well as white blood cells (infection fighters). Because of the spleen's job, it takes the greatest hit as far as clogged vessels. We can't rely on the spleen being a functional organ in a child with sickle cell disease. This leaves children prone to infection, particularly with Strep pneumoniae and H. influenza bacteria. These kids need Prevnar vaccine, flu vaccine, and the Pneumonia (pneumococcal) vaccine that elderly people get.
4. **Failure to thrive:** Because of a chronic lack of oxygen to the tissues, these children are shorter and smaller than their peers.

There are a variety of medical problems associated with sickle cell disease as a child gets older. For more information, see sicklecelldisease.org.

Q. My nine month old had a routine blood test performed. He has iron-deficiency anemia. What did I do wrong?

You probably haven't done anything wrong.

However, there are some parent mistakes that can cause this problem:

1. **Exclusively breastfeeding** without introducing cereal after six months of age.
2. **Replacing breast milk or iron-containing formula with regular cow's milk before the first birthday.**

Q. How is iron deficiency anemia treated?

With a high iron diet and an iron supplement (we discuss this in detail in Chapter 7, "Solids").

If your child is diagnosed with iron-deficiency anemia, your doctor will prescribe an iron supplement. Don't try to treat anemia by yourself without professional help. Why? Because iron, in high doses, can be toxic.

As a result, although vitamins containing iron are available without a prescription, the infant drops are located at the pharmacist's counter. The pharmacist dispenses these medications so he can counsel you on the correct dosage.

Also: there is a difference between the recommend daily allowance for iron (*maintenance iron dosage)* and the dose required for *replacement therapy* for those with low iron stores (iron-deficiency anemia). Doctors usually treat a child with iron-replacement therapy and then recheck their blood counts in three months.

Helpful Hints

Getting your child to take his iron supplement.

- Iron supplements universally taste bad. The brand name products taste a little better. Icar and Feostat brands taste best.
- It's okay to mix the medicine in juice. Just make sure your child drinks *all* the juice. Vitamin C actually helps the iron get absorbed into the bloodstream.
- DO NOT MIX WITH MILK. The calcium in milk competes with iron and can block absorption.
- Iron can cause a temporary gray/brown stain on the teeth. You can use baking soda on a toothbrush to remove it.
- Iron can make poop look black. It's not blood. Don't worry.

Q. We live in an old house. I'm worried about lead exposure. When should I get my child tested?

The appropriate time to get tested depends on when your child becomes mobile.

Most children who have lead poisoning live in homes built before 1978. These older homes have lead paint and lead pipes. Chipping paint is a very popular item for kids to pick up and eat. There is also lead in the soil surrounding these homes.

Screening for lead exposure is usually performed at nine to 12 months of age. In high-risk areas (urban, older homes), all children have a blood test done routinely. In low risk areas, doctors will screen with a risk-factor question list. If there is a possible exposure, a blood test is performed.

For more information, check out the Environmental Protection Agency's website at epa.gov/lead/index.html or call the National Lead Information Center (NLIC) at 800-424-5323.

While the Environmental Protection Agency recommends consumers turn to professionals to have their homes tested for lead, there are also a number of home tests available on the market. For under $10, you can purchase a lead test kit that includes swabs with a chemical that changes colors when it comes in contact with lead. Unfortunately, the accuracy of these tests has not been proven independently. And each $10 test kit only tests one area in your home (hence, you will end up buying several test kits.) If you're looking for a reputable professional testing lab in your state, check out the EPA's website at epa.gov/lead. Once you contact a certification officer in your state, he will be able to provide a list of certified labs.

Feedback from the Real World

I cared for a family who carefully de-leaded their home built in 1910 before moving in with their young children. Unfortunately, a central air conditioning unit was installed AFTER the move and it spewed old dust from the attic into all of the children's rooms. The children required medication to remove the lead from their bloodstreams. They are all doing fine now.

Skin

Q. What is eczema?

This falls into the allergic disease category. Eczema is a broad term to describe dry, scaly, itchy skin that appears in patches. It is often referred to as "the itch that rashes." In other words, kids have particularly sensitive, itchy skin. The itching is what produces the rash that you see.

The sensitive skin flares up with *dryness*, *exposure to perfumes/dyes*, or *allergies to metals/plants*.

The rash appears in different places depending on the age of the child. Younger kids tend to get it on their elbows, knees, and face. Older kids get it in their elbow and knee creases. We have more on managing eczema in Chapter 4, "Hygiene" and below.

LIVING WITH ECZEMA: 7 TIPS & TRICKS

As a parent of a child with severe eczema, we've been there, done that. Here are our tips:

1. Moisturizing soap: The cheapest in this category is good old Dove soap. Other options are Cetaphil, Aveeno, and Neutrogena. Avoid alcohol-based hand gels—they sting cracked skin.

2. Avoid perfumes and dyes: If it smells good, don't use it on your child. That goes for laundry detergent too. Use All Free and Clear or an equivalent product.

3. The thicker and greasier the moisturizing cream, the better: My personal favorite is Creamy Vaseline. Eucerin cream, Aveeno, CeraVe, and Cetaphil are also popular choices among dermatologists. You need to lube your child up several times a day. As soon as you get your child out of the bathtub, apply the moisturizer (I'm serious—have the tube ready).

4. Apply 1% hydrocortisone cream to really red areas twice daily: 1% hydrocortisone cream is a low-potency steroid cream available without a prescription. It is very safe to use on a daily basis when flare-ups occur.

5. Give a sedating antihistamine like diphenhydramine (Benadryl) at bedtime, for babies over six months: it will help reduce the amount of scratching that goes on when you aren't watching your child.

6. No bubble bath—most contain dyes and perfumes that can aggravate eczema. Instead, consider oatmeal bath treatments (Aveeno makes one). If you bathe your child every night, do it in lukewarm water. Consider bathing every other night in winter. The combination of frequent baths and dry heated air can cause flare-ups.

7. If you have tried all of this and your child is still miserable, it's time to check in with your pediatrician. They can recommend prescription products that are safe and effective. Don't hesitate to see a dermatologist if you and your pediatrician can't keep your baby's eczema under control.

Q. How do you get rid of eczema?

It's a long battle. In fact, it's a more realistic goal to keep it under control than to get rid of it.

The key to managing eczema is to keep the skin moist. Eczema always flares up in the wintertime because of cold, dry air.

Q. My baby has severe eczema. Should I be worried about using steroids all the time to treat eczema?

No, these are not the dangerous steroids that some professional athletes use. Topical steroids are extremely good anti-inflammatory medicines. They act by reducing the irritation of the skin, thereby reducing the itching. Long-term use (for months or years), especially with high potency products, can cause unwanted side effects.

It's always a good idea to use the lowest potency steroid creams and ointments for the least amount of time. Doctors move up on the strength level until they find one that works, and taper back down when the eczema improves. Ointments work best, followed by creams and lotions. High potency steroids should *not* be used on the face. And always use the product as prescribed. More is not better.

There is another alternative to topical steroids (approved for use in kids over age two) called immunoregulators. They are sold under the brand names Elidel and Protopic. They are an alternative for short-term or intermittent use to treat eczema. Because any medication has potential adverse effects, ask your doctor his/her opinion.

There is also a class of medications that are called emollients. They act by repairing the skin's top layer and reducing inflammation and itching. For details, see Appendix A.

Finally, you may want to consider food allergy testing. You may improve the skin by eliminating an allergenic food.

Q. Is there a link between eczema and asthma?

Yes, for some people.

Eczema is an allergic disorder. About 70% of kids who have eczema have a parent, brother or sister who has some type of allergy (hay fever/seasonal allergies, eczema, asthma).

About 30% of kids with eczema will have the classic triad of **ATOPY** (eczema, seasonal allergies, and asthma). But 70% of kids have eczema without any other type of allergic disease. (*Behrman*)

It's just something to pay particular attention to.

Q. Will my baby outgrow eczema?

Chances are, yes.

About 70% of kids will outgrow eczema. But no one can predict if and when your child will outgrow it. Chances are better if your child gets eczema as a baby. Kids who get eczema later in life have a greater chance of having it into adulthood.

Muscles/Bones

Q. My baby's feet turn in. Will he need to wear special shoes or a brace?

No.

The official term for this is called **INTOEING**. This is very common and usually corrects itself as your child becomes a good walker.

Old Wives Tale

Pigeon toed children need to wear corrective shoes.

The truth: It was trendy 30 to 40 years ago to have kids wear corrective shoes or braces (for example Forrest Gump) if they turned their feet in while walking. Since then, doctors discovered feet get better whether a child wears this apparatus or not–so why put a child through the trauma of special shoes or braces.

Q. My one year old is bow-legged. Will he always walk like this?

No.

Kids have some trouble finding their center of gravity. When they first start walking, they bend their knees to support their body weight. As they get older, they often go the opposite direction and look knock-kneed. It's nothing to worry about unless one leg is misshapen or both legs look severely deformed.

Q. My baby seems to have flat feet. My husband has flat feet, too. Do we need to see a podiatrist?

Your child can thank your husband for his feet. And no, you don't need to see a podiatrist yet.

The term "flat feet" refers to a lack of a natural arch in the bones of the feet. Some flat feet are flexible (the arch is seen when standing on tip-toe) and some are rigid (always flat). The feet that are always flat can cause some discomfort when kids become teenagers and adults. But placing a shoe insert (**ORTHOTIC**) into a toddler's shoes is not going to change the results down the line. The American Academy of Pediatrics feels orthotics are not necessary for kids with flat feet.

Q. My doctor says my baby has TORTICOLLIS. What is it and what do I do about it?

Here we go with the Latin again. This term literally means "twisted neck." It is caused by a tightening of a neck muscle (**STERNOCLEIDOMASTOID MUSCLE**) on one side of the neck. This neck muscle tightening occurs while the baby is still in the womb. The fetus may get stuck in one position for several weeks, forcing the baby's head to tilt towards the shoulder.

The muscle tightening gets worse after birth if babies sleep in the same position all the time. You may notice that your baby prefers to turn or tilt his head to one side. Babies who are at greater risk for this are boys, large birth weight babies, twins/multiples, breech, moms with uterus abnormalities, and first pregnancies. (*Stellwagen*)

If your child has torticollis, his head and neck movements will be limited. And if you don't actively do something about it, his head and facial shape may be affected. See the next box for home exercises to work on. Do the exercises at each diaper change, if you can.

Here are a few other practical tips (warning: your baby will not like any of them) (*Barrow Neurological Institute*):

- Place your baby to sleep on alternating ends of her crib.
- Place your baby's head on alternate ends of the changing table.
- Put toys on the side of the stroller/swing/crib where your baby's neck rotation is most limited. This forces him to work to see those toys.
- When carrying your baby, alternate which hip or arm used.
- Try to interact with your baby on the side where his neck movement is limited.
- Tummy time. Tummy time. And more tummy time.

If you do not see improvement in six to eight weeks, it's time to call in a physical therapist to help you.

Physical therapy is very effective in treating more severe cases of torticollis.

EXERCISES FOR TORTICOLLIS

Here are two exercises you can do at home to fix this problem.

It's easiest to remember if you do the exercises after each daytime diaper change. Your baby will respond best if he has a full tummy and is relaxed. You can do the exercises on the changing table or on your lap.

1. ***Tilt the head, ear to shoulder, stabilizing the chest with one hand.*** Hold for 10 seconds and repeat on the other side. Repeat three times on each side.

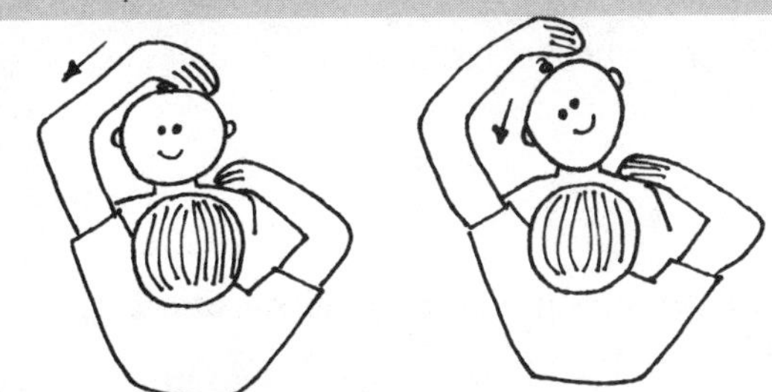

2. ***Turn the baby's head, chin to shoulder, while stabilizing the chest with one hand.*** Hold for 10 seconds. Then repeat in the other direction and hold for 10 seconds. Repeat three times on each side. (*Stellwagen*)

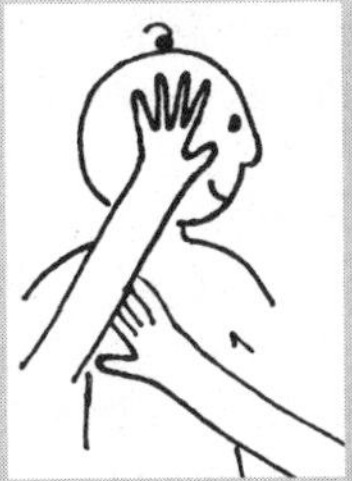

For the few kids who fail that intervention, BOTOX injections and minimally invasive endoscopic surgery have both been used to release the affected muscle.

Q. My baby girl was born breech and the doctor wants to do a special test on her hips. Should I worry?

No, but you should do the test. The concern: developmental dysplasia (dislocation) of the hips or DDH. In some babies, the hip joint forms abnormally and so the top of the thighbone does not stay in the joint. The result is that the bone is either loose or entirely out of the joint. The dislocation may be apparent at birth, or be identified as the joint loosens with time and activity.

There are certain babies who are at increased risk of this deformity: girls who are born in a breech presentation have the highest risk. First-born children and those with a family history of hip dysplasia are also at risk.

If DDH is diagnosed in infancy (the earlier the better), it is fairly easy to treat and correct. If DDH is not diagnosed or not treated, it can cause joint pain and arthritis. That's why pediatricians carefully examine a baby's hips and order a simple ultrasound test on babies who are born breech, who have a family history of DDH, or who have a concerning hip examination. Radiologists suggest doing a hip ultrasound at six weeks of life for these babies. A follow up x-ray of the hips may be in order at six months of life for some at-risk babies.

Reality Check

Notify your baby's doctor if your baby:

- Has uneven leg creases on the thighs.
- Has legs that are a different length.
- Seems to use one leg less than the other.
- Limps or waddles when walking.

FYI: Experts are increasingly concerned that tightly wrapping a baby's legs while swaddling (aka the baby burrito wrap) may increase the risk of DDH. So it's a good idea to leave some wiggle room for the legs. Allow the legs to bend up and out at the hips.

Endocrine

Q. Diabetes runs in my family. How can I get my baby tested for it?

Let's discuss diabetes first.

Diabetes mellitus is a chronic disease due to impaired sugar metabolism. There are two types (Type 1 and Type 2). They are divided by the cause of the disorder and the treatment. Although both can be inherited diseases, Type 2 tends to "run in families" more often.

Here is a brief explanation of the malfunction:

Since a person with diabetes doesn't breakdown sugar properly, the sugar ends up in vast quantities in the bloodstream. The body tries to eliminate the sugar by filtering it through the kidneys and into the urine. The sugar pulls excessive amounts of water with it into the urine. The result?

- Elevated blood sugar level.
- Excessive urination (with sugar found in the urine).
- Excessive thirst to keep up with fluid loss in the urine.
- Weight loss (from poor metabolism and fluid losses).

Type 1 Diabetes is also known as *Juvenile Diabetes*, or *Insulin Dependent Diabetes*. This is an autoimmune disease—that means the cells in the pancreas that make insulin get killed off by a person's own body. Insulin is the chemical in our body that metabolizes sugars.

There are some genes that have been identified in people with Type 1 diabetes and genetic defects can be passed on to offspring. Treatment is life-long with insulin injections and dietary modifications. Onset of Type 1 Diabetes is usually around school age (six to seven years old). It is extraordinarily rare to be diagnosed with diabetes while a child is still in diapers.

Type 2 Diabetes is also known as *Adult Onset Diabetes*. This type of diabetes is caused by the body's impaired response to insulin—this impairment is related to obesity.

As you can tell by the name, this USED to be an adult disease. Unfortunately, there is a virtual "epidemic" today of Type 2 Diabetes in preteens and teens. Children at risk are obese (defined as a Body Mass Index greater than 85%—see Chapter 5, "Nutrition and Growth" for details on the BMI) as well as other family members with Type 2 diabetes. Treatment includes dietary modifications and medications taken by mouth. FYI: There is a higher risk of developing this disorder among African-Americans, Hispanics, and Native Americans. (*Behrman*)

Interestingly, there seems to be an increased risk of developing diabetes if babies are exposed to wheat and barley *before* four months or *after* six months of age. The theory is that introducing these foods too early or too late can trigger an autoimmune response that damages the body's insulin-making islet cells. *(Snell-Bergeon)*

BOTTOM LINE

Diabetes is not a disorder of infancy. But, offering wheat and barley between four and six months of age may prevent diabetes later on.

If you have a family history of diabetes it's a good idea to watch your child's growth. Eating a healthy diet and avoiding obesity is even more important in your family.

As your child gets older, a screening test for diabetes can be done by obtaining a urine and blood sample.

For more information, check out this web site: diabetes.org.

Allergies

Q. My husband and I both have seasonal allergies. What are the chances that our baby will have allergies?

50%.

For each parent who has allergies, a child has a 25% risk of developing them himself. This refers to seasonal allergies, asthma and eczema. Some doctors might also put food allergies on this list, too. The earliest manifestations of an allergic child are eczema and food allergies. Asthma is usually diagnosed after a year of age. Seasonal allergies come even later.

Reality Check

The hereditary patterns of allergies do *not* apply to *drug* allergies. Just because you have an allergy to Penicillin doesn't mean your child will have one too.

Q. My baby seems to have a runny nose all of the time. Does he have seasonal allergies?

No.

Allergies ("hay fever") that cause a runny nose can be divided into perennial (all year long) or seasonal categories.

- ***Perennial allergies.*** These are year round allergies caused by something a child is exposed to on a daily basis. This is something inside your house, not outside your house. The most common causes are dust mites or cat dander. Molds are found both inside and outside the house year round.
- ***Seasonal allergies.*** These are allergies caused by something that's in the air outside of your house. These pollens include weeds, trees, and grasses that come in seasonal patterns. Most children under one year of age do not get *seasonal* allergies. Allergies, by definition, are a body's hyper-response to an allergen they have seen before. In the first year of life, a child has never seen these pollens before so there is no response.

BOTTOM LINE

Newborns do not have seasonal allergies when they are congested for the first six weeks of life. Nor does a nine month old have a ragweed allergy.

Most of the time, a chronic runny nose is caused by one viral upper respiratory infection after another. Although there are conflicting viewpoints,

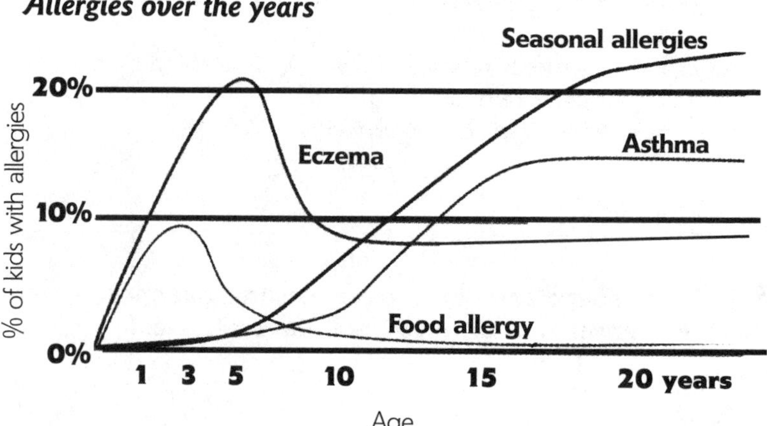

Source: *Contemporary Pediatrics, August 2007*

FELINES ARE OUR FRIENDS

Although most people have heard that having a cat causes allergies, recent research shows that early exposure (first year of life) to cats and dogs may actually prevent allergies. Kids who grow up on farms have significantly less problems with allergies, presumably due to their constant exposure to animals and the germs they carry.

some doctors feel that perennial allergies or food allergies may cause a chronic runny nose year round in kids under age two.

Helpful hint

For perennial allergies (for example, dust mites), allergists often recommend plastic bedding covers, air filters, etc. These products are available through medical supply companies. Check out the following resources for a product catalog: National Allergy Supply, Inc. (800-522-1448, web: natlallergy.com) or Allergy Asthma Technology Ltd. (800-621-5545, web: allergyasthmatech.com).

Genitals

Q. My son is circumcised, but he doesn't look circumcised anymore. What do I do?

See Chapter 4, "Hygiene" for a frank discussion on **PENILE ADHESIONS.** Some parents will comment that they see a white blister (called a bleb) on the skin, or a red swollen area, or that the penis just doesn't look right. These are usually all the same problem. The white blister is dead skin that has collected and is allowing the skin to stick together. The red swollen area may be the penis trying to unstick on its own. The penis doesn't look right because you can no longer see the helmet part.

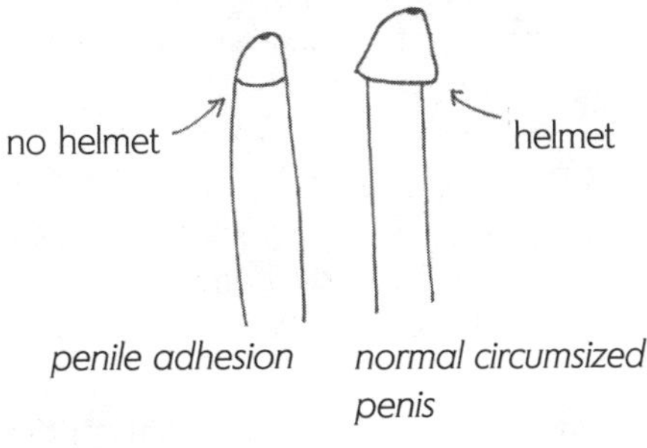

Q. The skin of my daughter's genitals is sticking together. My doctor said not to worry about it . . . but I am worried.

Don't worry. This is a common problem called **LABIAL ADHESIONS**. The labia and vaginal areas stay lubricated and open when estrogen is being produced. Young women produce estrogen when they start menstruating. So pre-pubertal girls are prone to labial adhesions until they go through puberty.

The only time this is a problem is when the labia are so fused together that the urethral opening is blocked too (that's where the urine comes out). See the graphic on the below to understand what we're talking about.

Labial adhesions are treated by using a prescription estrogen cream twice daily on the area for a couple of weeks. After that, apply petroleum jelly (Vaseline) on a daily basis to keep the area moist and open. Very rarely, a surgical procedure is necessary to open the area.

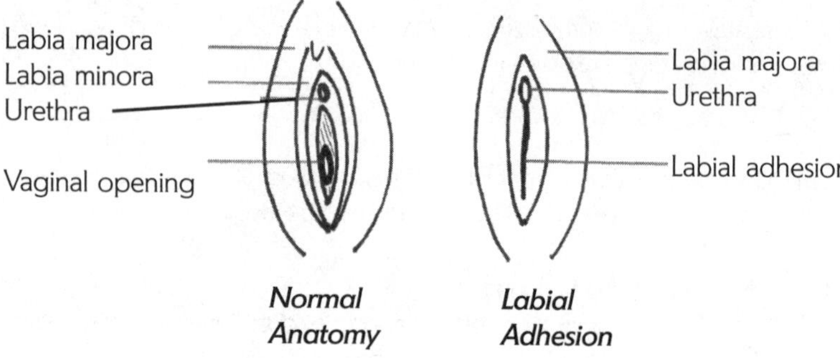

What's that smell?

Have you ever gone to a wine tasting and tried to describe the "nose" of a wine? When babies smell unusual, parents go to great lengths to come up with adjectives to explain the odor to their doctor.

We hesitate to explain this category of disorders in a chapter entitled "Common" diseases. But there are some very rare metabolic disorders that are associated with unusual body odors. It is important that you are aware of them, and seek medical care if you notice any of the following smells:

- ***Body odo**rs*: Barn-like, mousy, musty, horsey, wolf-like, sweaty socks, cheesy.
- ***Breath odors:*** fruity/sweet, fishy, ammonia-like, clover, musty fish, raw liver, foul.
- ***Urine (pee) odors:*** mousy, musty, horsey, wolf-like, barn-like, maple syrup, caramel, boiled Chinese Herbal medicine, yeast, celery, malt, brewery, sweaty feet/socks, ripe cheese, tomcat urine, dead fish, cabbage.
- ***Stool (poop) odors:*** foul, vile. (*Fleisher*)

Note that other problems may cause you to turn your nose: poisonings and infections.

BOTTOM LINE: Bad odors are worth checking out.

Now that you've been briefed on the most common diseases that affect children, let's talk the environment. The next chapter covers top environmental health concerns, including food, water, air quality and more.

The Environment and Your Baby

Chapter 15

What's in this Chapter

- Top health concerns
- Food: Formula, high fructose corn syrup and more
- Fish
- Water
- Home: BPA, Phthalates, lead
- Formaldehyde
- Radon
- Crib mattresses
- Air quality: indoors and out
- 28 tips to reducing eco-hazards

Before having a baby, you might have given only a passing thought or two about how the environment affects your health. Like many things in your life, however, a baby changes everything . . . including your perspective on this topic.

Whether you are a card-carrying member of the Sierra Club or just an occasional Whole Foods shopper, going green is now mainstream. Heck, when even Wal-Mart has an organic produce aisle, you know things have changed.

Just because folks are paying more attention to the environment doesn't change the rather stark facts about eco hazards: babies born today are exposed to more environmental pollutants than any previous generation in history. And babies are more susceptible than adults to adverse health effects from these pollutants.

Eighty thousand chemicals have been used in commerce since the 1960's. Three thousand are used in high volume production of consumer products and foodstuffs. Most of these chemicals were invented in the past 30 to 40 years. MANY of them have never been tested for their effect on your health.

Even more scary: we don't know basic toxic info on more than HALF of these chemicals . . . and even less is known about how these chemicals affect the development of young children. (*Goldman*) The American Academy of Pediatrics issued an ultimatum in 2011: revamp the Toxic Substance Control Act

of 1976 to protect pregnant women and children who are particularly vulnerable to the affects of toxic chemical exposure. (*AAP Council on Environmental Health*) We are still waiting for our government to respond . . . until then, figuring out what may have real health concerns and how to reduce or limit our exposure is mission critical for researchers.

Warning: This chapter may be hazardous to your *mental* health. Environmental health is an emerging science. Many factors contribute to certain diseases . . . so we cannot necessarily say exposure to pollutant X causes disease Y. There are also more questions than answers, and more shades of grey than pure black and white. As you know, we are fairly non-alarmist folks who make recommendations based on solid scientific evidence. However, when solid science is lacking, it's more challenging to offer advice.

Bottom line: we'll try not to freak you out.

What's important is that you weigh the evidence (or lack thereof) so you can make a more educated decision if you are concerned about reducing your child's exposure to environmental hazards.

Our key goal: this chapter should help you consider the HEALTH risks of various eco decisions (Organic versus regular milk? Should I get my home radon tested?). Of course, many of these decisions have other environmental factors (sustainability, etc)–we'll leave that discussion to the numerous other books and web sites out there dedicated to living a green life.

So, let's get rolling. We have divided this chapter into four sections: food, water, home and air (indoors and out). First, let's talk about why babies are vulnerable to eco toxins.

Q. Why are children vulnerable to environmental toxins?

Babies and children are not little adults–their growing bodies work differently. And while they may live in the same macro-environment as their parents, they live in a completely different micro-environment (that is, the carpeted floor of a home in Hometown, USA). This can make a significant impact on what environmental hazards babies are exposed to on a daily basis.

Here are the top nine reasons why the environment can be hazardous to your baby's health:

1. ***Breathing:*** Babies breathe at faster rates than adults, so they take in more air. They also breathe lower to the ground where chemical matter settles.
2. ***Fluid intake:*** For their body weight, babies drink the adult equivalent of 1.75 gallons of fluid a day.
3. ***Food intake:*** For their body weight, babies eat three times more food than adults.
4. ***Oral exploration:*** Babies stick stuff in their mouths–and it's not always food. So they are at risk of ingesting pollutants, like lead in the soil.
5. ***Gut absorption:*** To add insult to injury, a baby's gut absorbs more toxins than an adult's. Case in point: lead. A baby's gut absorbs 50% of lead that's been ingested, whereas the adult gut only absorbs about 10%.
6. ***Surface area:*** Compared to adults, babies have twice the surface area per pound to absorb chemicals.
7. ***Location:*** Babies spend many more hours on the floor, grass,

carpeting, and wood decking. These offer more opportunities for exposure where chemical matter settles.

8. ***Developing bodies:*** Embryos, fetuses, babies, and young children are uniquely sensitive to environmental exposures that can permanently interfere with how organs and body systems develop.
9. ***Lifetime burden:*** Babies born today have a longer lifespan, giving them a longer opportunity for adverse health effects from exposures to arise. (*AAP*)

Q. Where are these pollutants?

Well, they are lurking everywhere. That's encouraging, huh? Sometimes we think ignorance may be bliss. But seriously, it's important to know where the greatest potential health hazards lie, so you can limit your baby's exposure where possible in a practical way.

- *Food:* Additives, antibiotics, hormones, arsenic, methylmercury, PCB's.
- *Water:* Lead, methylmercury, industrial chemicals.
- *Home:* phthalates, bisphenol-A (BPA), lead, arsenic, flame retardant.
- *Air*: Radon, carbon monoxide, second hand smoke, radio frequency/electromagnetic fields, industrial chemicals.

Q. What damage can they do?

Some exposures have very defined health risks. Others are a bit murkier, or have only been proven to have adverse effects in animal studies—not humans. Environmental health is a very young scientific field. Compared to other fields, scientists have only just started to look at the effects of natural and man-made environmental exposures. And while some health risks are obvious (for example, smoking increases your risk of lung cancer) there are very few long-term studies that have been able to tease out one individual exposure as a direct cause of one particular disease.

Here is how the major categories of health risks are divided:

- ***Carcinogens:*** These agents are known to cause cancer. (Examples: arsenic, tobacco, solvents like benzene).
- ***Mutagens:*** These agents increase the rate of change ("mutation") in genetic material. This can lead to defective cells and cancer. (Example: ionizing radiation).
- ***Teratogens:*** These agents alter a fetus during development in the womb. Abnormalities are present at birth. (Example: alcohol).
- ***Neurotoxins:*** These agents damage or interfere with nerve/brain function. (Example: lead, methylmercury, Polychlorinated Biphenyls or PCB's, organophosphate pesticides). The scary part: there is a spectrum of neurotoxicity. Severely affected people will have obvious symptoms. Those with lower amounts of exposure may have more subtle symptoms such as a shorter attention span or slightly lower IQ.
- ***Endocrine disruptors:*** These agents mimic the body's natural chemical messengers (hormones) and can potentially interfere with body responses in the reproductive system and thyroid gland. (Example: phytoestrogen).

- ***Irritants and allergens:*** These agents cause allergic responses in the airway and/or the skin. (example: Volatile Organic Compounds or VOC's).

Q. What are the top health concerns?

Certain disease rates are on the rise. While we can't blame the environment for everything, these diseases are currently hotbeds of research for the possibility of environmental triggers. These include:

- ***Asthma.***
- ***Leukemia.***
- ***Male reproductive system problems*** such as testicular cancer in Caucasian men (up 60% in the past 30 years), hypospadias (abnormal penis development has doubled in the past 30 years), and falling sperm counts.

THE TOP TOXINS

Industrial chemicals

Toxins: polychlorinated biphenyls (PCB's), dioxin, solvents.
Source: industrial waste.
Exposure: prenatal, breast milk, seafood, air.
Health Risk: lower IQ, lower developmental scores, endocrine disruptor.

Pesticides

Toxins: organophosphate, organochlorine, pyrethroids, carbamates, boric acid, copper chromium arsenate (CCA), N,N-idethyl-m-toluamide (DEET).
Source: pesticides, insecticides.
Exposure: food, household exposure, water, air.
Health Risk: nausea, vomiting, muscle weakness, allergic reaction, neurotoxin, carcinogen, endocrine disruptor.

Metals

Toxins: arsenic, cadmium, lead, manganese, methylmercury.
Source: contaminated water from industrial waste, old homes with lead paint.
Exposure: food, water, blinds, treated wood, imported pottery, toys/jewelry, lead pipes.
Health Risk: anemia, learning problems, kidney problems, lower IQ, carcinogen.

Volatile Organic Compounds (VOC's)

Toxins: benzene, xylene, styrene, formaldehyde, aliphatic and aromatic hydrocarbons.
Source: household products, air pollution.
Exposure: rug/oven cleaners, paints, lacquers, paint strippers, dry cleaning.
Health Risk: nasal congestion, eye irritation, headache, nausea, vomiting, possible carcinogen. (*AAP*)

- *Neurodevelopmental disabilities* such as dyslexia, ADHD, and Autism Spectrum Disorders.
- *Obesity*.

Q. If I can't avoid these pollutants, how much exposure is acceptable and how much is "too much"?

Unfortunately, the threshold of "acceptable limits" of exposure changes as more research is done. For instance, 40 years ago experts used to think that some lead exposure (levels under 40 mcg/dl) was perfectly safe. We now know that *any* level of lead exposure can have subtle, but permanent effects on the brain. (*Canfield*) And for some pollutants, it also depends on *when* the exposure occurs.

Food: Additives, Contaminants, Facts and Fables

Formula

Q. Does soy formula cause man boobs or ADD?

Soy formula has been through some controversies. Some researchers think soy formula may interfere with reproductive or immune functions when given in high doses to infants. Why? Soy formula contains phytoestrogens, which is a plant version of estrogen. While this chemical has been shown to lower the risk of certain cancers in adults, it is unclear what effect it is has on infants. However, there is NO proof that soy formula is harmful to babies. In 2006, the Center for Evaluation of Risks to Human Reproduction reviewed all the concerns regarding soy formula. One committee member said it best, "After 40 years of soy exposure we haven't seen a blip on the radar screen. Right now, we don't have a problem." (*Wall Street Journal*)

As for soy formula and Attention Deficit Disorder, this fear stems from a study that purported to show a link between one ingredient in soy formula (manganese) and neurological disorders like ADD. But let's take a closer look at that study. Researchers fed baby rats extremely high doses of manganese—some 38 times greater than the level found in formulas. Surprise! These toxic doses caused developmental problems in the rats. The bottom line: Soy formula has been around for over 40 years and is considered acceptable by both the AAP and the Food and Drug Administration. If you give toxic doses of anything to rats (or people), bad things happen to them! (*Tran*)

Breast milk contaminants

Q. I've heard there is rocket fuel in breast milk. Is it true? Is it dangerous?

Perchlorate is an industrial pollutant, a byproduct of weapons, rocket and fireworks production. Twenty states around the country (especially those with military production facilities that made Cold-War era missiles and rockets) have significant perchlorate pollution in local groundwater and wells.

The health concern for babies: perchlorate exposure can interfere with proper function of the thyroid gland. That in turn can lead to growth and brain development problems.

Perchlorate has been found in more than just water—it's also been detected in cow's milk-based formula and, yes, even breast milk. That's because the chemical has creeped into the food supply chain.

So, what can you do to avoid perchlorate exposure? The answer: not much.

There is currently no federal legislation that requires states to test their water and ensure tolerable levels of perchlorate. That's because the EPA found that most water supplies do not have high levels of perchlorate. However, individual states do have some regulations for perchlorate—check with your local state or water district for details.

The hard truth: human breast milk also contains many other environmental contaminants. No, it is not practical to test your milk for these chemicals. And yes, it is still the healthiest form of food for your baby! The benefits far outweigh the risks. And remember that the alternative, infant formula, has a small amount of perchlorate too.

Organic Food

Q. Which fruits and vegetables contain the most pesticides?

The Environmental Working Group (ewg.org or foodnews.org) has compiled the "dirty dozen" list of produce that contains the highest pesticide load. If you have an organic food budget (let's face it, going organic is very expensive), these would be the top organic foods worth the splurge.

Here is the list, in order of the most to least contaminated:

#1 Peach	#7 Cherries
#2 Apple	#8 Kale
#3 Sweet bell pepper	#9 Lettuce
#4 Celery	#10 Imported grapes
#5 Nectarine	#11 Carrot
#6 Strawberries	#12 Pear

Want to see the entire list of 47 produce items? Go to foodnews.org. You can sign up for a free iPhone app or PDF of the Shopper's Guide to Pesticides and take it shopping with you.

Reality Check

It is widely accepted knowledge that children are more sensitive than adults to many pollutants. When it comes to pesticides, children are about ten times more sensitive. (*AAP*) The question that remains is if the pesticide exposure in foods has significant adverse health effects. At the moment, there is no major evidence of that. *(Forman)*

Q. Is it worth it to buy organic formula, milk and dairy products?

Six Ways To Reduce Pesticide Exposure From Foods

Don't want to spend your entire paycheck on organic groceries? Here are some tips to reducing pesticide exposure:

1. Scrub produce with a brush under running water to get rid of any obvious residue.
2. Peel whatever produce you can. (FYI: this often removes the fiber benefit, though).
3. Don't eat the outer leaves of leafy vegetables (e.g. lettuce, kale).
4. Grow your own garden and don't use pesticides.
5. If you are buying imported produce, only purchase produce that can be peeled.
6. Buy produce that's in season. (*AAP*)

Organic milk and dairy products claim to be free of pesticides, antibiotics, and hormones. But organic milk can cost almost twice the price. Is it worth the cost? As we've already discussed, children today are exposed to more environmental pollutants than past generations. Is it worth it to limit these exposures when it comes to milk?

First, let's discuss the three questionable ingredients consumers are concerned about in their milk and dairy products:

- ***Pesticides***: Pesticides are in both water and soil. So there will be some in just about anything our children eat or drink (including breast milk and yes, organic products). Organic milk promises to be chemical free, but because chemicals remain in the soil for so long, even organic milk may contain pesticides. Organic farmers may also use organic pesticides. *Bottom line: compared to say, apples, the pesticide residue in all milk products is rather low.*

- ***Antibiotics***: All milk products are screened for antibiotic residues. If residue is detected (which happens in about 1 in 1000 tankers of milk), the milk is rejected for sale. Hence, conventional milk should also be antibiotic-free. Our concern here: even though the finished product is antibiotic-free, antibiotic use in livestock is contributing to antibiotic resistance. Doctors have tried to limit antibiotic overuse in humans; it is time to reduce use in animals too. Your grocery store purchases drive the marketplace. *Bottom line: while there is probably no antibiotic residue in milk, buying organic milk encourages milk manufacturers to avoid using antibiotics.*

- ***Hormones***: Even in "juiced" cows, all milk has about the same composition (see below for more discussion on bovine growth hormone.).

So, is organic worth almost twice the price? If you look strictly at health risks, organic milk doesn't have much advantage over conventional milk (with the possible exception of the antibiotic issue discussed above).

To us, the main argument for choosing organic when it comes to formula, milk, and dairy products is this: when it comes to young children, dairy is their biggest food group. If you are going to spend your organic dollars somewhere, this would be the most cost-efficient for the volume your child consumes.

Q. Is it worth it to buy organic baby food?

There are three choices here: buy organic jarred baby food, conventional jarred baby food or make your own.

The argument for making your own is simple: it is easy to do and costs less than the jarred stuff. Plus your applesauce will just be applesauce (no additives, sugar, etc).

But is using conventional jarred baby food hazardous to your baby's health? No. Processed food (including jarred baby food) is actually subject to *stricter* federal regulation than fresh produce. So, jarred baby food should have *less* pesticide residue than what you might find in the regular (conventional) produce aisle. And some baby food manufacturers make their products pesticide-free even if they are not labeled as "organic." (*AAP*)

Bottom line: there isn't much difference between regular and organic baby food. If you decide to go organic, we advise you make your own baby food, using organic fruits and vegetables (see the discussion earlier for the fruit that's most likely to have pesticide residue).

Q. Should I buy organic meat?

There are plenty of reasons to choose organic meat, but the key health issue is antibiotics.

Antibiotics are given to healthy animals to prevent disease and improve growth. In fact, at least 40% of the antibiotics used in the United States are used in animals that are destined to become our next meal. Antibiotics used in the food industry are indirectly a problem for humans because they allow antibiotic resistant bacteria to evolve.

So while there is no direct health hazard from eating conventional meat, there is an indirect health risk. If you want to buy antibiotic-free meat simply on principle, look for meat labeled USDA Organic.

Q. I've heard rice cereal contains arsenic and it's dangerous. True?

Yes, arsenic has been found in baby rice cereal, as well as in brown and white rice and other rice-containing products like rice milk and rice cakes.

Inorganic arsenic is a potentially harmful chemical that is all over our universe, thanks to natural causes (like being part of the earth's crust) as well as human causes (like burning coal). Because of its ubiquitous nature, it is in our air, water, and soil...and thus in our food supply. The arsenic levels in a particular food can vary widely, depending on its origin.

Inorganic arsenic is known to cause cancer. It's also possible that fetuses and young children who are exposed to arsenic may have lower IQ scores. *(Centers for Disease Control)*

However, the Food and Drug Administration has not advised people to change their diets at this point. The FDA is looking into this further and then will provide recommendations. You can keep tabs on them here:

fda.gov/ forconsumers/consumerupdates/ucm319827.htm

Bottom line: Like all environmental health issues, it's wise to limit exposures whenever possible. It's fine to give your baby products made out of rice. But, providing a varied diet consisting of other grains will reduce his arsenic intake.

RBGH

Q. Will my baby go through puberty early if she has milk or yogurt with bovine growth hormone?

No.

Some dairy farmers give bovine growth hormone to lactating cows to increase their milk production. There are no direct associations to early puberty or cancer. All cows, in fact, make this hormone naturally. Even though these cows are "juiced," the composition of conventional milk vs. organic milk is almost the same. Pasteurization destroys 90% of the bovine growth hormone. Additionally, bovine growth hormone is species-specific. So even if there is some bovine growth hormone in commercial milk, it does not affect humans. *(Forman)*

Despite the lack of scientific evidence, consumer demand drives retail decisions. Wal-Mart, Kroger, and Safeway brands are now all synthetic bovine growth hormone-free. And Starbuck's only uses hormone-free dairy products at their stores.

Reality Check

Northern American girls have had earlier menstrual cycles since 1840 when nutrition improved. Some experts think early puberty these days is due to the obesity epidemic—which turns on hormones earlier than it should. So, if milk is to blame at all, it's because kids over age two are drinking whole or 2% when they should be drinking skim! Also: puberty standards have also changed over the years in the US to compensate for African American girls who do tend to go through puberty earlier than Caucasians.

Nitrates

Q. I've heard it's not safe to make your own baby food out of carrots, beets, and spinach. Is this true?

No, that is false.

It is safe to make your own baby food out of root and leafy vegetables. Just don't offer those food items to babies *under three* months of age because their guts are too immature to appropriately breakdown a chemical called nitrates. (This should be a non-issue, because we don't recommend starting solid food until at least four to six months of age).

Nitrates are the product of nitrogen fertilizer and animal waste breakdown that ends up in our water supply and soil. Nitrates aren't toxic, but the bacteria in a baby's gut converts them to *nitrites*, which can be a health hazard. Nitrites interfere with the oxygen carrying capacity of red blood cells, and can cause Blue Baby Syndrome (**METHEMOGLOBINEMIA**).

Bottom line: You can make your own baby food out of beets, broccoli, cabbage, carrots, and spinach as long as your baby is at least four months old.

FYI: If you have well water and a septic system, be sure to get it tested for nitrates. You don't want to give this to a baby under three months of age for the same reasons outlined above!

High fructose corn syrup

Q. Is high fructose corn syrup safe?

Yes, it's safe.

High fructose corn syrup (HFCS) is found in many processed foods, from soda to pancake syrup. Over the years, HFCS has replaced many other types of sugar in foods for one simple reason: it's cheap.

At the same time, however, concerns have been raised about HFCS: is it contributing to our nation's obesity epidemic?

Here's the latest science: high fructose corn syrup does not cause obesity or any other malady.

However, like natural sugar, you should limit how much HFCS you offer to your baby. And since HFCS is found mostly in processed foods, it is more nutritious to stick with fresh foods for overall health reasons.

Reality Check

A recent study found that countries with HFCS-containing food supplies have 20% higher rates of Type 2 Diabetes. In short, processed-food-loving Americans have the highest rates of Type 2 Diabetes. It's not necessarily the HCFS that is the problem, but the types of diets that are rich in HCFS.

Q. Does high fructose corn syrup (HFCS) cause autism?

No.

This novel theory sprung from the blogosphere in 2009. Some autism advocates claim HFCS is contaminated during the manufacturing process with mercury. While it is true that some food makers use strong chemicals to clean equipment, that doesn't mean HFCS is contaminated with mercury or any other chemical. And, no, mercury poisoning does not cause autism either!

Artificial sweeteners

Q. Do artificial sweeteners cause cancer?

No. The National Cancer Institute says that consumption of Splenda, Nutrasweet, and Equal have no increased risk of cancer. Saccharin, however, has been linked to bladder cancer in animal studies.

Food coloring

Q. Does food coloring cause Attention Deficit Disorder?

Several years ago, scientists looked at a possible link between food coloring and attention problems. The "Feingold Hypothesis" failed to pan out and the theory basically died. In 2007, researchers resuscitated this theory in a study published in the journal Lancet. Children who drank beverages with red or yellow dye, or sodium benzoate (a common preservative) had more hyperactive behavior than their peers. Kids who drank sugary drinks had no change in their behavior, by the way.

We don't recommend changing your life on the basis of one study, but it's not a bad idea to limit processed foods (which usually contain food coloring and preservatives).

At the time of this writing, the FDA has agreed to evaluate the current scientific evidence on food coloring and potential health problems. We will keep you posted of their findings on our blog at Baby411.com (as well as our Baby 411 app, Twitter, and Facebook accounts).

Grilling

Q. Is it okay for my baby to eat grilled foods? Does BBQ cause cancer?

Cooking foods quickly at high temperatures–by grilling, frying, or broiling–produce heterocyclic amines (HCA). HCA's are on the National Institutes of Health's list of chemicals "reasonably anticipated to be carcinogens."

However, we believe it is okay to enjoy BBQ *in moderation*. Here are a couple of tips:

- Certain foods produce more HCA's than others. Chicken produces the most, hamburgers the least.
- Fat drippings on the grill create (warning: big chemical word ahead) polycyclic aromatic hydrocarbons (PAH). These are also carcinogens. Charred meat has more PAH's . . . so, it's wise to limit fat drippings and scrape off any charring.

Sodium nitrate

Q. I've heard that lunchmeats and hot dogs processed with nitrites/nitrates are dangerous. Is it worth it to buy preservative-free meats?

Sodium nitrite keeps you from getting botulism from a frankfurter or other processed meats like lunch meat, bacon, ham, and smoked fish. It also makes the meat look more appetizing (otherwise your hotdog would look sickly grey).

The health concern: nitrites can convert to nitrosamines, which are known animal carcinogens (but only *potentially* carcinogenic in humans). U.S. food manufacturers now add ascorbic acid or erythorbic acid to nitrite-containing meat products, which prevents that chemical conversion to nitrosamines. So the health concern is much lower now than twenty years ago.

However, processed meats like hot dogs and lunchmeats contain more salt (and often more fat) than unprocessed, preservative-free products. For that reason alone, we recommend limiting them in your baby's diet. (*CSPI*)

Fish

Q. I've heard there is mercury in certain types of seafood. How can I reduce my baby's exposure?

Yes, fish can absorb methylmercury from coal-fired power plant waste that ends up in nearby rivers, lakes, and oceans. And excessive methylmercury intake during brain development of a fetus or young child can lead to language, attention, and memory problems. In addition to methylmercury, seafood can also be contaminated with polychlorinated biphenyls (PCB's).

However, fish is also a very healthy food choice and contains Omega 3 Fatty acids that promote brain development.

So, how do you avoid toxins in fish? Stick with the safest fish and avoid risky varieties:

Safest fish:

- Butterfish, catfish, domestic crab, crawfish, shrimp, fresh or canned salmon, pollock, tilapia, whitefish.
- Freshwater trout.

Risky fish:

- Freshwater fish (with the exception of trout) are more likely exposed to industrial waste products.
- Predators (shark, swordfish, tuna, king mackerel, tilefish) who live a long time build up methylmercury.
- Fatty fish (mackerel, carp, catfish, lake trout) are more likely to contain PCB's.

If you are really interested, you can see how much methylmercury is in fish at this website: cfsan.fda.gov (click on seafood). And if you want a handy wallet card to take to the grocery store with you, check this out: nrdc.org/health/effects/mercury/walletcard.PDF

Here are some specific recommendations on fish for both your baby and you if you are breastfeeding:

- Completely avoid eating shark, swordfish, mackerel, and tilefish.
- Eat less than 12 ounces a week of shellfish, canned fish, small ocean fish, or farm-raised fish.
- Eat six ounces or less a week of white albacore tuna. Canned light tuna, and specifically Carvalho Fisheries and King of the Sea are lower in methylmercury.
- Eat six ounces or less of local fish if you are unsure of local water contamination. (*FDA*)

Home

Water

Q. Is it worth it to get a water filtration system?

It depends on the type of system. Those little filters that attach to faucets aren't going to do very much. Tap filters may remove lead and other toxins, but not excessive fluoride. And if you don't take care of them properly and replace the carbon filters regularly, bacteria will end up growing in the filters.

Our advice: It's cheaper to merely run your tap water for two minutes in the morning before you use it—that flushes any lead out.

Reverse osmosis filters do remove both toxins and fluoride—but these are much more expensive and need to be installed house-wide.

Here's our recommendation: get your community's water quality report (most are posted online on water company home pages). If your community has a serious problem with contamination, then a whole-house reverse osmosis filter would be a useful investment. The same is true if you are relying on well water: get it tested and treat it if necessary.

Bisphenol-A (BPA)

Q. Are plastic baby bottles safe?-Do I still need to worry about BPA?

Prior to 2009, all the best-selling clear, hard plastic baby bottles were made of polycarbonate, which contained a chemical called Bisphenol A (BPA). It is the BPA that makes the hard, clear plastic bottles . . . well, hard and clear. BPA is also used in the linings of cans for liquid foods (more on that later).

BPA's chemical bond with polycarbonate breaks down over time, especially with repeated washing or heating of the bottle. As a result, BPA leaches out of the plastic and ends up in the liquid—that is, the breast milk or formula.

BPA is an endocrine disruptor. It can mimic the natural female sex hormone, estradiol. While most data about BPA comes from animal research, these studies show even low level exposure of BPA *may* be linked to everything from early puberty and breast cancer, to attention and developmental problems.

We don't know all the answers about BPA—the research is evolving. But, the FDA banned BPA in baby bottles and sippy cups in 2012 over potential health concerns. When you go bottle shopping today, the plastic bottles you see in major chain stores are all BPA-free. As long as you don't use hand-me-down baby bottles, you should be in the clear.

Q. Are there any other sources of BPA I need to be aware of?

A minor source of BPA: the linings of food cans, specifically baby formula. BPA is used in the epoxy lining of metal cans—when it comes to formula, this means *liquid* infant formulas (ready to feed and liquid concentrate).

So how dangerous is BPA in the lining of metal formula cans? Well, there's about ten times more BPA in those old baby bottles compared to liquid formula cans. So the risk is much less.

And remember the *powder* formula cans are made out of cardboard. Their lining does not have any plastic, nor any BPA.

Why do formula makers use BPA in the can lining? Well, there is no other alternative that can withstand the heat generated from the required sterilization process. A FDA subcommittee is currently reviewing this issue and may come up with alternatives in the future.

For now, know that regulatory agencies in the U.S., Canada, Europe, and Japan all believe that the current levels of BPA in food packaging is not a health risk to anyone, including babies.

So how do you lower exposure to BPA? The National Toxicology Program has these recommendations to reduce BPA exposure:

- Avoid plastic containers with #7 on the bottom (some–but not all–that have a #7 recycling number may have BPA).
- If you own polycarbonate plastic containers, do not wash them in the dishwasher with harsh detergents.
- Do not microwave polycarbonate plastic food containers. BPA may break down from repeated use at high temperatures.
- Eat less canned food. Opt for fresh or frozen foods.
- Use glass, porcelain, or stainless steel containers, particularly for hot food or liquids.

Phthalates

Q. There's buzz about other harmful plastics. What should I know to protect my baby?

The other big plastic issue you should be aware of: phthalates.

Phthalates are plasticizers that make plastic soft and durable. The health concern? Phthalates are considered endocrine disruptors (weak estrogens and androgen-blockers) and animal carcinogens. While there is much controversy about phthalates, there is still no scientific consensus that they are dangerous to humans.

Phthalates are used just about everywhere. For example, you'll find them in plastic cooking wrap, plastic food packaging, baby shampoos, diaper rash creams, and toys. Phthalates can be both ingested and absorbed through the skin. Babies have been found to eliminate the breakdown products of phthalates in their urine.

The good news: both the U.S. and Canada require toys and products that are intended for use in the mouth (pacifiers, teething toys, bottles) to be phthalate-free. And newer U.S federal legislation has tighter restrictions on phthalate use.

The Consumer Product Safety Commission is in charge of enforcing this ban, and for the record, do not find a significant health risk to young children. According to the CPSC, a child would have to suck/mouth a phthalate-containing toy for at least 75 minutes a day to have any significant health consequences.

Our advice: If you want to reduce phthalate exposure, use a napkin or paper towel when you heat food in the microwave and do not use second-hand soft plastic toys.

Lead

Q. Is it safe to decorate with holiday/Christmas lights?

Yes.

Readers have asked about this after seeing holiday lights sold in the state of California plastered with a warning label about lead. So is the lead in holiday lights dangerous? And why is it there in the first place?

Lead is used in the manufacturing process of holiday lights to stabilize the plastic bulbs (so the plastic doesn't burn and set your tree on fire). The lead acts as a flame retardant—which is a good idea.

Bottom line: unless your baby is eating or chewing on holiday lights, she is NOT in any danger of lead poisoning.

Q. Because of the lead toy scare, I am hesitant to buy toys for my baby. How can I be sure they are lead-free?

In response to the Toxic Toy Fiasco of 2007, Congress passed a Consumer Product Safety Improvement Act. This law requires toys and products intended for use by children under 12 years of age to contain less than 0.009% lead. The law also requires testing for lead and other heavy metals.

New children's products (including toys) made after February 2009 are required to be certified to meet this new standard—this includes both American made and imported items.

The best course: buy NEW toys, certified to meet the current standards. All toys sold in major chain stores would qualify. Avoid hand-me-downs from friends, relatives or older siblings.

Q. Are there any other sources of lead exposure I should know about?

Yes.

Here's a surprise: your garden hose most likely contains lead. Lead is used to stabilize the hose material (which is made of polyvinyl chloride).

If water has been standing for a while in the hose, the lead concentration in the water is higher. If you are filling up a baby pool in your backyard with that garden hose, you should let the water run for a minute before you start filling. Yes, your baby will probably play *and* drink that water. If you are in the market to buy a new garden hose, buy one that is labeled "safe for drinking".

We discuss lead exposure in old homes in Chapter 14, Diseases.

Formaldehyde

Q. I saw a news story about formaldehyde in baby shampoo and other hygiene products. Are these safe for my baby?

Yes.

In very small amounts, formaldehyde is not considered a health hazard. For example, it is used in mascara, paper towels, and carpeting. There is also a trace amount in some vaccines.

Concerns about formaldehyde in baby care products arose after a 2009 study by the Campaign for Safe Cosmetics, an environmental advocacy group. The study found that half of the baby products tested (shampoo, soaps, lotions, diaper wipes) contained some formaldehyde.

We should note that none of these products intentionally add formaldehyde. The chemical is a byproduct of the production process. Among the more ironic findings: the product that had the most formaldehyde was Huggies ***Naturally*** Refreshing Cucumber & Green Tea Baby Wash!

Bottom line: this is not a serious health risk.

Cleaning products

Q. Are cleaning products safe to use?

Home cleaning products have been scrutinized in recent years, as an entire industry has grown around eco alternatives to conventional cleaning chemicals.

So is there a health risk here? Well, if your baby accidentally inhales, drinks, or bathes in a cleaning product, that's a real problem. Yes, they are toxic and, in some poisoning situations, fatal.

As for other potential health hazards from everyday, appropriate use . . . that's a bit more difficult to say. At this point, there's no scientific evidence linking everyday use with health problems.

If you'd prefer to go the green route, check out web sites like EarthEasy.com for extensive lists of eco alternatives and homemade recipes for cleaning products.

Want to know what's in your common household cleaning products? Check out the National Library of Medicine's website at hpd.nlm.nih.gov for details.

Carpeting

Q. Is it safe to install new carpeting in our home?

New carpeting, as well as the padding and adhesive that goes with it, can release Volatile Organic Compounds (VOC's). VOC's can irritate eyes, nose and/or throats as well as cause coughing or trouble breathing.

Also: carpeting is a nice place for pesticide residue, molds, and dust mites to settle. This is the same place your baby will be crawling and rolling for several hours a day. Our advice: considering putting down a playmat or washable area rug over the carpeting in rooms where baby plays.

Q. Is it safe to get my carpets cleaned?

You may have heard the claim that carpet cleaners causes Kawasaki Disease (KD; an immune disorder that causes blood vessel swelling).

However, scientific evidence suggests that an infectious agent causes KD, not carpet cleaning.

Although carpet cleaners do not cause KD, it's still a good idea to wait until your carpets are completely dry before your baby plays there. You may also want to use a no or low solvent cleaner.

Pesticides

Q. Is it safe to use pesticides in our home?

Here is what we know for certain, according to the Centers for Disease Control: "Home pesticide use overall has been linked to childhood cancers such as soft tissue sarcomas, leukemias, and cancer of the brain." Some studies have specifically linked organophosphate pesticides to lymphoma and leukemia, but the study results are controversial and inconclusive. (*CDC*)

We've got some tips to reduce your child's exposure: If you have to use pesticides, set traps or treat the *outside* of the house first. This should be done BEFORE use of any an indoor insecticide spray or "bombs." The pesticide residue will collect on upholstery, rugs, carpeting, and even stuffed animals. And only treat for pests when there is a problem. Skip scheduled or routine pesticide applications.

It's also a good idea to avoid doing routine pesticide treatments on your lawn—only treat your lawn when there is a problem.

Q. Is it safe to use insect repellent on our baby?

Yes, we cover this answer in detail in Chapter 4, Hygiene.

Radon

Q. Should I have my home tested for radon?

Yes.

Radon is an odorless, colorless, tasteless radioactive gas formed from the decay of naturally occurring uranium in the earth's rocks, soil, and water. Radon gets into homes from cracked foundations, granite walls, and porous cinderblocks. Exposure is usually more of a problem in homes with basements.

Because radon exposure is a known carcinogen, you should get your home tested. For more info, check out the Environmental Protection Agency's website at epa.gov/radon or call 800-767-7236. (*AAP*)

Crib mattresses

Q. Are organic crib mattresses safer than traditional mattresses?

In short, no.

Yes, conventional crib mattresses do utilize synthetic ingredients such as polyurethane foam, polyvinyl chloride (aka vinyl), phthalates, and flame retardants.

Rumors have circulated the Internet for years that sleeping on a conventional crib mattress was related to Sudden Infant Death Syndrome (SIDS). The theory: inhaling all the fumes from a traditional mattress caused SIDS. Scientific research has debunked this theory: SIDS is NOT caused by foam or coil crib mattresses.

However, we understand why parents would want to limit exposure to these chemicals–and let's face it, your baby will spend a good amount of time on his mattress.

An entire alternative crib mattress industry has sprung up in recent years to fill this demand–companies are now selling "organic" mattresses filled with soy-based foam, latex, coir (coconut husks) and more. Most of these mattresses are covered with organic cotton covers or food-grade polyethylene plastic. And, of course, these mattresses are much more expensive than traditional crib mattresses: $300 to $600, compared to conventional mattresses that start at $100.

One major negative to some organic mattresses: they have covers that are NOT waterproof. As you probably can guess, diapers leak, babies spit up (and more) in their crib. A waterproof cover is critical to keep bacteria from growing inside the mattress. Hence some folks buy an all-organic mattress but then use a waterproof protector that contains many of the same "bad" chemicals they were trying to avoid in the first place.

So where's the science that says organic is better for mattresses? There isn't much. Most of the "proof" circulating around the web comes from a company in New Zealand, which is selling its own special mattress cover which it claims protects against SIDS.

Our opinion: we don't think an organic mattress is going to reduce the risk of SIDS. If you buy an organic mattress and don't have a waterproof cover, the occasional pee that escapes the diaper will enter your organic mattress and leave a nice nesting ground for bacteria. (*Sherburn*)

Bottom line—-here's what we'd recommend:

- Get a mattress with a vinyl cover that is triple-laminated (basically thicker). The cover should be listed as waterproof, not just water resistant.
- Use a waterproof pad over the mattress. Some "sheet savers" (Ultimate Crib Sheet) have waterproof backing that would provide extra protection to keep liquid out of the mattress.
- Don't use a hand-me-down mattress, since it might have not been water-protected.
- Consider changing out the mattress with each child (new baby, new mattress). No matter how hard you try, some leakage might happen.
- If you want to limit chemical exposure, look for mattresses that are GREENGUARD certified. These mattresses are tested to meet strict standards for low chemical emissions.

Q. Is it safe to have a sandbox for my baby?

Here's the health concern for sandboxes: synthetically-made play sand can contain asbestos-like fibers. Asbestos is a known carcinogen (exposure

can cause cancer later in life). Real sand from the beach is fine.

Except for the state of California, manufacturers do not have to list whether or not the sand is real or synthetic, and whether or not it is asbestos-free. Our advice: buy only natural river, beach, or silica-based products for your baby's sandbox. If you know where the sand is coming from, go for it. (*AAP*)

Q. Are chlorine-free diapers any safer for my baby?

There are no adverse health effects from conventional disposable diapers that contain chlorine. Deciding whether or not to buy chlorine-free diapers is more of an eco decision than a health one.

Air: indoors and out

Carbon monoxide

Q. Should I install a carbon monoxide detector?

Yes.

Carbon monoxide poisoning can be quite serious. It's health effects can range from headaches and dizziness to coma and even death. People are exposed to carbon monoxide from woodstoves, fireplaces, charcoal grills, poorly ventilated combustion appliances, motor vehicle exhaust, and tobacco smoke. (*AAP*)

Bottom line: it's not a bad idea to have a detector in your home, since carbon monoxide is odorless and invisible. Be sure to get one that is UL certified. Good brands include American Sensors and Kiddie; check ConsumerReports.org for the latest ratings.

Tobacco smoke

Q. If I smoke outside the house, my baby will not be exposed to secondhand smoke, right?

Wrong. Sorry to ruin the fantasy here but . . . your baby is very likely to be a secondhand smoker unless you wear a towel over your head and clothing while you are smoking outside. The smoke is pervasive and will settle on your hair and clothing. Once you re-enter your house and pick your baby up onto your chest or shoulder, your baby will be breathing in the particulate matter from the smoke.

Besides the obvious long-term health hazards to a child, the immediate health consequence is often wheezing. Babies and young children exposed to tobacco smoke are more likely to have symptoms of asthma.

Factoid: Poor air quality has a direct link to asthma. Air pollution can cause new cases of asthma–and can trigger symptoms in people with existing asthma. Clearly, there is a genetic susceptibility (that is, you have a greater chance of having asthma if other family members have asthma/allergic disorders). But environmental pollutants don't help.

Electric and magnetic fields

Q. I worry about exposing my baby to electric and magnetic fields. Should I worry?

Electro magnetic fields (EMF's) are invisible lines of force created by electric charges. Power lines, electric appliances, cell phones (and towers), the earth's magnetic field, and even humans, emit these EMF's.

Low frequency fields don't have enough energy to cause damage to you or your baby's DNA or body organs. (*NIH*) Hence, your hair dryer, coffee maker, and microwave are probably safe. But researchers continue to look at possible connections between EMF's (including cell phone use) and brain tumors and certain types of leukemia. The greatest concern is the distance of the body organ (example, the brain) from the EMF source (say, the cell phone).

One suggestion to avoid EMF exposure and cell phones: use a Bluetooth headset to talk to grandma instead of the cell phone. It's not a bad idea for you to do this as well.

28 tips for reducing eco hazards

We know that going green can sometimes be impractical and costly. Here are some easy, common sense things you can do to reduce your family's exposures to environmental pollutants.

1 **HAVE FORCED AIR FURNACES, FUEL-BURNING APPLIANCES** (gas water heaters, stoves, clothes dryers) **PERIODICALLY CHECKED** by a professional as the manufacturer recommends.

2 **PILOT LIGHTS PRODUCE CARBON MONOXIDE SO MAKE SURE THEY ARE WORKING PROPERLY.**

3 **DON'T USE GAS STOVE TOPS OR OVENS AS A HEAT SOURCE.**

4 **VENTILATE SPACE HEATERS PROPERLY.**

5 **DON'T USE HIBACHIS OR BBQ GRILLS INDOORS.**

6 **DON'T LEAVE A CAR RUNNING IN THE GARAGE**, even when the door is open.

7 **LIMIT THE AMOUNT THAT YOUR BABY TALKS/LISTENS DIRECTLY ON YOUR CELL PHONE.**

8 **LIMIT THE TIME/INCREASE THE DISTANCE BETWEEN YOUR BABY AND SMALL APPLIANCES.**

9 **If you have to use pesticides,** set traps or treat the outside of the house instead of using an indoor insecticide spray or "bomb" indoors. The pesticide residue will collect on upholstery, rugs, carpeting, and even stuffed animals.

10 **Treat for pests only when there is a problem.** Skip scheduled or routine pesticide applications in your home and on your lawn.

11 **Scrub produce with a brush** under running water to get rid of any obvious residue.

12 **Peel whatever produce you can.** (FYI: this often removes the fiber benefit, though).

13 **Don't eat the outer leaves of leafy vegetables** (for example, lettuce, kale).

14 **Grow your own little garden, and don't use pesticides.**

15 **If you are buying imported produce, only purchase produce that can be peeled.**

16 **Buy produce that's in season.**

17 **Completely avoid eating shark, swordfish, mackerel, and tilefish.**

18 **Eat less than 12 ounces a week** of shellfish, canned fish, small ocean fish, or farm-raised fish.

19 **Eat six ounces or less a week of white albacore tuna.** Canned light tuna, and specifically Carvalho Fisheries and King of the Sea are lower in methylmercury.

20 **Eat six ounces or less of local fish** if your community's fishing advisories are unknown.

21 **Avoid plastic containers with #7 on the bottom** (some—but not all—that have a #7 recycling number may have BPA)

22 **If you own polycarbonate plastic containers, do not wash them in the dishwasher with harsh detergents.**

23 **Do not microwave polycarbonate plastic food containers.** BPA may break down from repeated use at high temperatures.

24 **Eat less canned food.** Opt for fresh or frozen foods.

25 USE GLASS, PORCELAIN, OR STAINLESS STEEL CONTAINERS, particularly for hot food or liquids.

26 CONSIDER USING MORE ECO-FRIENDLY CLEANERS.

27 RUN YOUR TAP WATER FOR A COUPLE OF MINUTES IN THE MORNING BEFORE USING IT.

28 DON'T SMOKE.

Here are some useful websites if you are looking for additional info:

Environmental Health and Toxicology of the National Library of Medicine www.sis.nlm.nih.gov/enviro.html

Household Products Database householdproducts.nlm.nih.gov

We dedicate this chapter to Michael Shannon, M.D., FAAP. Thank you for your sage advice and guidance. You are missed.

Section 5

First Aid

Top 12 Problems & Solutions

FIRST AID

PROBLEMS & SOLUTIONS

Chapter 16

"It's no longer a question of staying healthy. It's a question of finding a sickness you like."
~ Jackie Mason

WHAT'S IN THIS CHAPTER

1. YOUR FIRST AID KIT
2. TAKING VITAL SIGNS
3. THE TOP 12 PROBLEMS & SOLUTIONS

- ABDOMINAL PAIN
- ALLERGIC REACTION
- BLEEDING AND BRUISING
- BREATHING PROBLEMS (RESPIRATORY DISTRESS)
- BURNS
- DIARRHEA AND VOMITING
- FEVER
- POISONING
- RASHES
- SEIZURES
- DOES IT NEED STITCHES?
- TRAUMA (ACCIDENTAL INJURY)

Are you afraid your pediatrician will fire you for calling too much? Although doctors entertain this thought occasionally, we never act on it (well, almost never). Phone calls are a part of the job. Most phone calls come from new parents. You are not alone.

The purpose of this chapter is to help you troubleshoot the most common problems you will encounter on the front line of your baby's medical care. It should help you determine when to call the doctor. It also prepares you for what the doctor will ask when you call.

This chapter does not replace the need to check in with your doctor. Pick up the phone if you are worried. But being educated helps you worry less and trust your instincts more.

Helpful Hints
On Call Etiquette

How can you make the most of a call to your baby's doctor? As a doctor who has spent one third of her life on call, here are some important points to consider:

1 **THE ON-CALL DOCTOR IS NOT IN THE OFFICE.** Doctors leave the office at the end of the workday and carry a cell phone for after hours calls. Doctors also go to sleep. (It's often disrupted sleep—but we try). If you call about your child's diaper rash at 2 am, the doctor won't be as perky as when you call during office hours. (FYI:

Some offices utilize nurse call centers to handle minor middle-of-the-night questions and save the more pressing emergencies for the physicians.)

2 **TELL THE ON-CALL DOCTOR ABOUT PAST MEDICAL PROBLEMS.** Most pediatric and family doctor practices have SEVERAL doctors on staff. After hours, there is usually one doctor (who picks the short straw) that is on-call. This may or may NOT be your regular doctor. As a result, the on-call doctor may not know your child. If the practice has an electronic health record and the on-call doc can access it from home, then he might be able to see your child's chart. But, as a general rule, assume that he doesn't. (Nurse call centers don't have access to your child's chart either.) Explain any previous medical problems, surgeries, or hospitalizations. It might have a bearing on the particular problem at hand.

3 **TELL THE ON-CALL DOCTOR ABOUT ALLERGIES TO MEDICATIONS.** If your child has an allergic reaction to a medication, put it in YOUR family medical records. Don't rely on an on-call doctor or your pharmacy to know this information.

"The pink medicine" or "some antibiotic" is not adequate. Most doctors inquire about drug allergies before any medicine is prescribed—but we appreciate it if you tell us.

4 **HAVE A PHARMACY PHONE NUMBER READY.** Yes, many docs have smartphones and can Google a pharmacy phone number—but it is helpful if you have your preferred pharmacy phone number available for us. Often, there is more than one Walgreen's on a major street, so being as specific as possible is helpful. That way, I can call in your prescription after I talk with you.

5 **DON'T CALL FOR REFILLS, REFERRALS, OR APPOINTMENTS AFTER HOURS.** Universal doctor rule—we don't do these things without patient charts or schedules available. Medical emergencies are the only exception to this rule.

6 **DON'T LEAVE YOUR HOUSE OR GET ON THE PHONE AFTER PAGING US.** Believe it or not, this happens. If it's truly an emergency, keep your phone line clear or your cell phone within reach. During cold and flu season, it may take a while for the doctor to return your call (the on-call doctor may get several calls per hour). But we appreciate it if we can get through to you when we call you back.

7 **DON'T USE CALLER ID TO CALL THE ON-CALL DOCTOR BACK WITH ANOTHER QUESTION.** Okay, for the doctor, this is just creepy. If you call back through the appropriate answering service or voicemail system, you will always get your call returned. There is a protocol for a reason, folks—there is often a queue of patients who may need callbacks. If your caller ID shows the doctor's home or cell phone number, don't use it.

8 **DON'T EXPECT OR DEMAND THAT ANTIBIOTICS BE PRESCRIBED OVER THE PHONE.** There is a good reason why antibiotics aren't available over the counter. A child needs to be seen to make a diagnosis of a bacterial infection. Remember the drug-resistant bacteria problem. (This is men-

tioned in Chapter 13, Infections). Doctors usually prescribe "supportive relief" (such as acetaminophen (Tylenol)) until your child can be evaluated.

9 **IF YOU HAVE A QUESTION ABOUT A MEDICATION, HAVE THE BOTTLE IN HAND WHEN YOU CALL.** Just common sense here. We will probably ask you to read the information on the bottle to us.

Q. What should I have in our first aid kit at home?

Here is your grocery list:

- Band-Aids (lots of them—they become badges of courage)
- sterile, non-stick dressing and tape
- "butterfly" bandages or thin adhesive strips
- Ace wrap
- a roll of gauze dressing
- rectal thermometer
- petroleum jelly
- acetaminophen (Tylenol)
- ibuprofen (Motrin, Advil)
- antibiotic ointment
- diphenhydramine liquid (Benadryl)
- saline nose drops (home made or store bought)
- decongestant nose spray (Afrin)
- 1% hydrocortisone cream
- A list of emergency phone numbers, including the National Poison Control Center (800-222-1222) or your local poison control number.
- baking soda
- tweezers
- measuring spoon, cup or dropper; you'll want one with cc/ml measurements for those tiny infant doses. (See Chapter 5, Nutrition & Growth for a list of common measurements)

first aid

Q. Should I take a CPR course?

Yes!

Learn how to handle emergencies before they happen. Even if you can't remember exactly what to do, you will be more prepared to take action if something bad happens.

It's also helpful to learn how to take your child's vital signs. This information is very useful for when you call your doctor for advice.

Q. How do I take my child's vital signs?

Vital signs include the heart rate (pulse), respiratory rate (breaths per minute), temperature, and blood pressure. The only thing you cannot do at home is the blood pressure.

1. **Temperature:** Know how to take a rectal temperature. (See fever section later in this chapter for details.)
2. **Pulse:** Feel your baby's pulse in the inner part of the elbow or in the groin. Count the number of pulsations for 15 seconds and multiply by four. This gives you the beats per minute. Below is a

list of average heart rates for your baby's age:

Average heart rates for babies, birth to three years of age:

Birth to one week: 95–160
One week to six months: 110–180
Six to 12 months: 110–170
One to three years: 90–150
(Compare these to an adult's heart rate of 60–100 beats per minute.)

3. **Respiratory Rate:** Watch your baby's chest as it moves in and out. Count one breath for each time he breathes in for 30 seconds and multiply by two. This gives you the number of breaths per minute. Babies have very erratic breathing, so you won't get an accurate count if you only look for ten or 15 seconds. Below are the details.

Average respiratory rates by age:

Newborns: 25–50
One week to one year: 24–38
One to three years: 22–30
(Compare to an adult's respiratory rates of 12–16 breaths per minute.) *(Gunn)*

Helpful Hint

When a child runs a fever, all the other vital signs are elevated, too. Parents worry about the heart racing when children run a fever. That is to be expected and normal.

How Can Docs Make a Diagnosis Over the Phone Without Examining a Child?

Your doctor will rely on you to provide the signs and symptoms (the clues).

Doctors are very systematic in the way they make a diagnosis. A professor once told me that 90% of the time, a diagnosis can be made purely on the history of the problem. Only 10% of the time will the physical examination of the patient be necessary to make the diagnosis. It's true. I usually know what I will find when I examine the patient just by listening to the story. But this requires some detective work. I always ask the same questions for each complaint to get a history of signs and symptoms (that is, location/type of pain, length of fever, appetite or lack of, sleep disruption, runny nose, cough, vomiting, etc.) When you call, expect to be interrogated.

Nervous parents often focus on one particular aspect of a disease process while doctors are trying to figure out the big picture. (See fever section later in this chapter). Doctors need to know about various symptoms to put the puzzle together. Let the doctor help point you in the right direction!

The Most Frequent Phone Calls

First, here's some doctor lingo: ever heard the guys on Grey's Anatomy say a patient was "in triage?" Triage just means to sort out by severity of the condition. The point: phone calls are triaged by the doctor into the following categories:

- **Priority 1:** Needs immediate evaluation and treatment–NOW.
- **Priority 2:** Needs appointment the next day.
- **Priority 3:** Watch and wait. Needs appointment if there is no improvement or worsening of symptoms.
- **Red flags:** Denote symptoms that are medical emergencies.

We've adopted this system in this chapter to give you a general idea of how problems are managed. But every problem is unique. If you have concerns, call your doctor.

Abdominal Pain

Q. My baby has a stomachache. When do I need to worry?

It's hard to tell when an infant has a stomachache, unless he is vomiting or has diarrhea. Some reliable signs include irritability during/after feedings, pulling up of the legs, or a tense, full belly. There are also medical problems that have nothing to do with the stomach that cause abdominal pain (such as bladder infections).

Abdominal pain is divided into acute (a new event as of yesterday or today) or chronic pain (the problem has been going on for over a week). Acute issues *only* are discussed below.

Priority 1: Needs immediate evaluation and treatment—NOW:

The most serious problems are called surgical emergencies or an "acute abdomen." A piece of bowel may be kinked, blocked, or infected. Babies with these problems look sick and are often inconsolable. Concerning symptoms include: swollen and/or tender belly, lack of interest in eating, persistent vomiting, unusual looking diarrhea, and difficulty settling down. These problems need to be addressed quickly. See the Red Flags on the next page. Diagnoses include: **INTESTINAL OBSTRUCTION, INTUSSUSCEPTION, INCARCERATED HERNIA, APPENDICITIS, PYLORIC STENOSIS.**

Priority 2: Needs appointment the next day.

Most problems fall into the non-urgent category. These symptoms are less severe and babies are consolable. Symptoms include: gas, trouble settling after a feeding, crying/straining while attempting to poop, and one or two episodes of vomiting. Observation and medical evaluation is in order if things are not improving. NOTE: In babies under a year of age, it's better to be cautious and contact your doctor if you are worried.

Diagnoses include: **GAS, CONSTIPATION, EARLY VIRAL GASTROENTERITIS**

Helpful Hints

What the doctor will ask you about ABDOMINAL PAIN:

1. Does your baby have a fever?
2. Is your baby vomiting? What does the vomit look like?
3. Does your baby have diarrhea? Is it watery, bloody, mucousy, look like grape jelly?
4. Does your baby's tummy look like he is pregnant? Does it hurt to touch?
5. How long has the pain/vomiting/diarrhea been going on?
6. Does your baby have at least three wet diapers (urine) a day?
7. Is your son's scrotum swollen?

RED FLAGS

Call your doctor immediately if you see the following symptoms with abdominal pain:

- Fever and pain without diarrhea.
- Projectile vomiting or bright green/yellow vomit.
- Diarrhea that is bloody/mucousy/grape-jelly like.
- Tense, distended belly.
- Pain more than two hours in duration.
- Prolonged vomiting (see vomiting section later in this chapter).
- Prolonged diarrhea (see diarrhea section later in this chapter).
- Less than three wet diapers a day.
- Swollen scrotum.
- Crying with urination.

Feedback from the Real World

My four-year-old daughter slept for 12 hours once and awakened with the tensest belly I had ever seen. She was very uncomfortable and was having difficulty walking. She screamed when I tried to touch her belly. She had no interest in eating. Being quite convinced that she had an acute abdomen, I called one of my pediatric surgeon friends to evaluate her in the ER. As we drove to the hospital, she proclaimed that she needed to pee NOW. I pulled off the highway onto the shoulder. She urinated in my portable car trashcan. She had had a full bladder. She felt much better and asked if we could go out to lunch after visiting the doctor. We sheepishly walked into the ER together. She skipped to the exam room. I apologized for calling my friend to look at my perfectly normal child. His comment was, "Well, she does have a *cute* abdomen!"

Lessons learned here:

1. Sometimes benign processes (like a full bladder, constipation, etc.) can look like an acute abdomen. Doctors prefer to check out suspicious patients rather than wait.
2. It's hard to be objective when dealing with your own child.

Allergic Reaction

Q. I think my child is having an allergic reaction. Do I need to go to the ER?

Clarify the reaction. Do you see a rash or is he having difficulty breathing?

Priority 1: Needs immediate evaluation and treatment—NOW:

RED FLAGS

Anaphylactic Reaction

Call 911 for a child who is drooling, anxious, having obvious labored breathing (stridor), lip swelling, sweating. Another serious allergic reaction is called Stevens Johnson Syndrome. This is an extensive rash accompanied by mouth ulcers. This requires immediate medical attention.

If your child is having an anaphylactic reaction, do not attempt to drive to the hospital. Call 911 and get immediate help. Most ambulances are equipped with medicine to handle these reactions immediately.

Diagnoses: **ANAPHYLACTIC REACTION, STEVENS-JOHNSON SYNDROME**

Priority 2: Needs appointment the next day.

Most rashes are less of an emergency. (See details of other rashes in the rash section later in this chapter). Allergic reaction rashes can have various configurations. They are all itchy. Rashes (except Stevens-Johnson Syndrome, see above) can be evaluated by a doctor when the office is open. These include:

- ***Hives:*** raised mosquito bites with flat red circles around them or large flat red areas with raised edges (for example, a drug allergy).
- ***Erythema multiforme:*** extensive, small, flat, red patches with raised edges (for example, a drug allergy).
- ***Eczema:*** red plaques with a scaly rough appearance overlying it (for example, a food allergy).
- ***Contact dermatitis:*** red pimples or blisters in a patch or streak (for example, poison ivy).

See our web site at Baby411.com for a visual library of common rashes.

Reality Check

Have your child in front of you when you speak to the doctor on the phone. You will be asked to describe what you see over the phone.

What the doctor will ask you about ALLERGIC REACTIONS:

1. Is your baby having any trouble breathing?
2. What does the rash look like? Where is it on the body?
3. When did you first see the rash?
4. Is the rash itchy?
5. Is your baby currently taking any medication?
6. Has your baby been exposed to any new foods, laundry detergents, clothing, or soaps?

Helpful Hints

- Unless your child is having an anaphylactic reaction (see above), give diphenhydramine (Benadryl) and schedule an appointment.
- Stop any other medication until a doctor sees your child.

- Don't give diphenhydramine (Benadryl) in the morning before your appointment—otherwise the rash will be gone.
- Try to think of any new medication or food your child may have had recently.

Reality Check

FYI: An allergic reaction is caused by a release of a chemical called histamine. Diphenhydramine (Benadryl), an ANTI-histamine, effectively clears the results of histamine (the rash) until the medicine wears off (about six hours). Histamine levels stay elevated for several DAYS. So, don't be surprised to see the rash "come back" after the medicine wears off. You will need to use the antihistamine medicine for a few days.

Causes of allergic reactions: Food allergy, medication allergy, bug bites, poison ivy (rhus dermatitis).

Bleeding And Bruising

Q. My child bruises easily. Should I be worried?

No, not usually.

Bruising in high trauma areas is not worrisome (shins, knees, elbows, forehead). We worry much more about bruising on the torso—most falls do not cause bruising to this area.

Easy bruisability can be a sign of low platelet count (platelets help your blood clot). Bruising is much more worrisome when it is seen with **PETECHIAE.** (pe-teek-ee-eye). See box on the next page. Bruising accompanied by excessive bleeding can indicate a blood clotting disorder.

See our web site at Baby411.com (click on Bonus Material) for a picture.

Common Diagnoses include: Trauma/injury, temporary bone marrow suppression from a viral infection.

Uncommon Diagnoses include: Hemophilia, von Willebrand's disease Leukemia, Idiopathic Thrombocytopenic Purpura, Henoch-Schonlein Purpura, Meningitis.

Priority 1: Needs immediate evaluation and treatment—NOW:

1. A fever with petechiae rash
2. Petechiae AND bruising, with or without a fever
3. Bruising and lethargy
4. Excessive bruising (beyond the knees/elbows)
5. Uncontrollable bleeding

Priority 2: Needs appointment the next day.

1. Bruising with no other symptoms
2. Recurrent nosebleeds

What the doctor will ask you about BRUISING OR BLEEDING:

1. Where are the bruises?
2. Are there any other rashes on his body?
3. Does he bleed excessively? Does anyone in the family have bleeding problems?

NEW PARENT 411: ALL YOU EVER WANTED TO KNOW ABOUT PETECHIAE BUT WERE AFRAID TO ASK

Petechiae are flat, purplish, pinpoint dots that almost look like freckles. When you push down on them, they remain colored (that is, they do not blanch). Petechiae are caused by broken blood vessels. They arise for the following reasons:

1. ***Pressure***: Straining while pooping, giving birth, coughing, or vomiting forcefully.
2. ***Infection***: Strep, meningitis, Rocky Mountain Spotted Fever.
3. ***Low platelet count:*** Leukemia, Idiopathic Thrombocytopenic Purpura, temporary bone marrow suppression from a viral infection.

If there is a good reason to have petechiae (such as repeated coughing), and they are located above the level of the chest only, you can relax a bit, but still call your doctor.

If there is not a good reason, your baby needs to be seen quickly to rule out the serious medical problems on this list.

4. Has he been unusually tired or been running a fever with no explanation?

Q. My child is having a nosebleed. What do I do about it?

Lean your child's head *forward*, not backwards. Apply pressure to the base (soft part) of the nose for ten minutes. If this doesn't work, you can spray some medicated decongestant nose drops into the nostrils (Little Noses or Children's Afrin are two brand names). This causes the blood vessels to shrink and stop bleeding.

Most nosebleeds stop in about ten minutes. If it goes beyond that, call your doctor.

Q. My child just vomited blood. Where is it coming from and should I be worried?

If it looks like fresh red blood, it can't be coming too far from the mouth. Blood that comes from the stomach is partially digested and will look like coffee grounds. Be prepared to describe the vomit. Lack of an obvious explanation for the blood needs an evaluation.

What the doctor will ask you about VOMITING BLOOD:

1. How old is your baby?
2. Are you breastfeeding? Are your nipples cracked and raw?
3. Have you been suctioning your baby's nose with a bulb syringe?
4. Has your baby been vomiting forcefully?
5. What does the vomit look like? Are there streaks of blood? Coffee grounds? Mucous?

The most common cause of *Upper GI Bleeding* (official term for vomiting blood) in a newborn is Mom's cracked nipples. The blood in the spit up is really Mom's. There is a test to prove it, but one look at Mom's nipples is a dead give-away.

The next likely culprit is that dreaded bulb syringe we told you to throw away in Chapter 4. It causes an irritation in the lining of the nose, making it raw to the point of bleeding. Nasal secretions are swallowed and then spit up.

As your baby gets older, he will explore his body. His finger will find his nostrils and cause trauma. The number one cause of bloody vomit in an older child is a nosepicker's nosebleed.

Now, for more serious causes. Forceful vomiting can cause a small tear in the lining of the esophagus. A child with persistent blood in vomit needs to be examined.

Vomit that looks like coffee grounds also needs to be evaluated. In older babies, doctors worry about a toxic ingestion/poison that irritates the esophagus or stomach, ulcers, gastritis, or esophagitis. If the vomit looks like Folger's coffee, call your doctor.

Diagnoses of an upper GI bleed include: Mom's cracked nipples, esophagitis, toxic ingestion/poisoning, gastritis, ulcers

Priority 1: Needs immediate evaluation and treatment—NOW:

1. No obvious source for bleeding.
2. Vomit that looks like Folger's coffee.
3. Persistent bleeding.

Q. My baby has blood in his poop. Should I worry?

No, but Lower GI bleeding *always needs to be evaluated by a doctor*. If you see blood in the diaper, save the diaper. It's helpful to bring a fresh specimen to the office visit. If your baby doesn't cooperate, doctors have other ways to get what they need (via a rectal exam).

You will describe every detail of that poop to the On-Call Doctor. If the blood looks red and fresh, the source is close to the anus. If the blood looks darker or the poop looks like meconium, it comes from further up the pipes (small or large intestine). The age of the child partially determines the cause of the problem.

◆ ***Newborns:*** Bad *diaper rash* is often the explanation. Blood is usually found on the diaper wipe more than in the poop with an obvious raw bottom. Babies under four months of age with streaks of blood often have a *milk protein allergy*. Even exclusively breastfed babies can encounter this because the cow's milk protein can enter the breast milk. It often takes six weeks for the blood to clear once babies eliminate the cow's milk from their diets. Even if this is what the working diagnosis is, bacterial stool cultures are in order to rule out infection.

Diagnoses include: diaper rash, milk protein allergy, food poisoning (Bacterial gastroenteritis).

◆ ***Older babies:*** Babies who have started solids often get constipated. If your baby looks like he is giving birth when he pushes out a solid poop ball, he might bleed with it. An *anal tear or fissure* can be seen if you look for it. This is not serious. Put some petroleum jelly (Vaseline) on the area and check out fiber facts in Chapter 8, The Other End.

Now for more serious causes. Babies can get *food poisoning*—even

those who aren't eating off the Chinese buffet line yet. Where do babies get it? Human carriers, pets, and food exposure. Babies in daycare are at higher risk of parasite infections. Your doctor can test for all of these bugs with cultures (see bacterial infections and parasites in Chapter 13, Infections). Symptoms include diarrhea with streaks of blood and mucous.

Finally, poop that looks like grape jelly (currant jelly stool) is a medical emergency. The diagnosis is *intussusception*, where the bowel telescopes on itself and creates an obstruction. Symptoms include abdominal pain (pulling up of the legs), irritability, and grape jelly stool.

Diagnoses: Anal fissure/tear (caused by constipation), food allergy, food poisoning (bacterial gastroenteritis), parasite infection, antibiotic induced colitis (C difficile infection), intussusception

What the doctor will ask you about BLOOD IN POOP:

1. How old is your baby? Was your baby premature?
2. What did you see in the diaper? Streaks of blood mixed in poop? Solid poop with blood on the diaper wipe? Explosive bloody diarrhea? Mucous also? Grape jelly?
3. Is there a diaper rash?
4. What is your baby eating?
5. Has anyone in the house had diarrhea?
6. Does your baby look sick or well? Fever?
7. Is your baby's belly full and distended?
8. Is your baby interested in eating? Is he vomiting?
9. Has your baby been on antibiotics recently?

Priority 1: Needs immediate evaluation and treatment—NOW:

- Bloody diarrhea
- Grape jelly poop
- No obvious diaper rash or anal tear
- Former premature baby

first aid

Priority 2: Needs appointment the next day.

- Streak of blood with normal looking stool and well appearing child

Priority 3: Watch and wait. Needs appointment if there is no improvement or worsening of symptoms:

- Obvious constipation
- Obvious diaper rash

Feedback from the Real World

Dr. Brown's TRUE STORIES about food poisoning:

1. One mother was a short order cook who discovered she was a carrier of Salmonella when her newborn had it. She truly was "Typhoid Mary" (named for a woman who was a cook and a carrier of typhoid fever–a cousin of Salmonella). Sometimes parents are carriers who have had a previous infection and don't know it.
2. Unusual pets can be carriers of Salmonella. One of my patient's uncles had a pet iguana that roamed freely on the family's kitchen counter.
3. Raw eggs and chicken are also known to have Salmonella. I had a

HOW TO AVOID FOOD POISONING

Steer clear of the following foods and remember to clean cutting boards, knives, and countertops when dealing with these products. Keep a spray bottle of bleach handy in the kitchen to clean these tools. Here is what to avoid:

- ◆ unpasteurized dairy products
- ◆ unpasteurized juices (fresh squeezed OJ, apple cider)
- ◆ alfalfa sprouts
- ◆ raw shellfish
- ◆ oysters
- ◆ undercooked and raw meat or seafood
- ◆ unwashed fruit and vegetables
- ◆ undercooked eggs (sunny side up, raw cookie dough, fresh Caesar salad dressing, homemade ice cream, homemade mayonnaise)

Natural food warning: While it doesn't seem likely that you and your baby would come across the above items, think for a moment about unpasteurized juices. These are common in health food stores and some vegetarian/vegan restaurants. It can be easy to pick up a bottle of such juice without thinking about it. The same goes for unpasteurized dairy products—gourmet cheeses at health food stores sometimes fall into this category. While adults might be able to eat these products without a problem, they are much more dangerous to infants and children. Check the labels: raw milk cheese, for example, should be clearly labeled as such.

patient who acquired Salmonella when Grandma was preparing chicken gizzards next to Mom preparing a bottle for the baby.

Feedback from the Real World

There was an outbreak of the deadly E. coli 0157 bacteria (Hemolytic Uremic Syndrome) on the East Coast several years back. It was traced to an apple cider producer in New Hampshire. It had been a bad apple season, so the producer used apples that had already fallen off the trees to press for cider. Unfortunately, the cows that lived on the farm pooped on those apples and contaminated them with the E.coli. There are new regulations for cider production now. Moral of the story: Never drink unpasteurized apple cider.

A similar outbreak happened with Odwalla apple juice—a small batch of unpasteurized juice contained E.coli bacteria, sickening more than a dozen children. This juice was blended with other products as well. Be sure to look for these products—make sure ALL the ingredients in a blended juice product are pasteurized.

Burns: Water, Sun, Hot Drinks, Appliances, BBQ

Q. My child got a burn from _____. What do I do? Does he need an appointment?

Don't get out the butter . . . and yes, you may need a doctor visit.

First rule: If it blisters, it should be looked at.
Second rule: Apply cool water, not butter.
Third rule: Don't pop a blister.

Any type of burn damages the top layer of skin. This causes redness (first degree). Burns that go deeper than that create blisters (second degree) or damage to the full thickness of the skin. Your skin is your body's protection from foreign invaders such as infection. Without the skin, the body is defenseless. To help combat infection, it's always a good idea to use an antibiotic ointment (such as Neosporin) on a burn and cover it with a non-stick dressing.

For second-degree burns, a prescription product called Silvadene may be needed. Second degree burns (or worse) need to be seen by your doctor to assess the damage, look for infection, and clean away any dead skin (this debris inhibits healing and promotes infection). Any burns on the hands, genitals, and on large areas should also be seen.

Priority 1: Needs immediate evaluation and treatment—NOW:

- Extensive areas burned.
- Area looks infected (red, weeping pus, fever)

Priority 2: Needs appointment the next day.

- Second degree burns (blisters).
- Burns on the hands or genitals.

Priority 3: Watch and wait. Needs appointment if there is no improvement or worsening of symptoms:

- First degree burns.

Breathing Problems (Respiratory Distress)

Q. My baby is having trouble breathing. What do I do?

Knowing what true respiratory distress looks and sounds like is very important. Read the section below first. Then understand how calls like this are triaged. The short answer is–if your child is having labored breathing, call your doctor immediately.

Understanding the Respiratory System

Think of the respiratory system as one big tube. The opening of the tube starts at the nose. The bottom end branches into tiny tubes in the lungs. Air goes in and out of this tube with each breath.

What is an UPPER respiratory infection?

The common cold or flu viruses live in the top of the tube (nose and sinuses). The body forms mucous or snot as a result of it. A person coughs because the mucous drips down the tube towards the lungs. Coughing protects our lungs. The cough brings the mucous up so it can be swallowed (into the stomach) instead of collecting in the lungs. Upper respira-

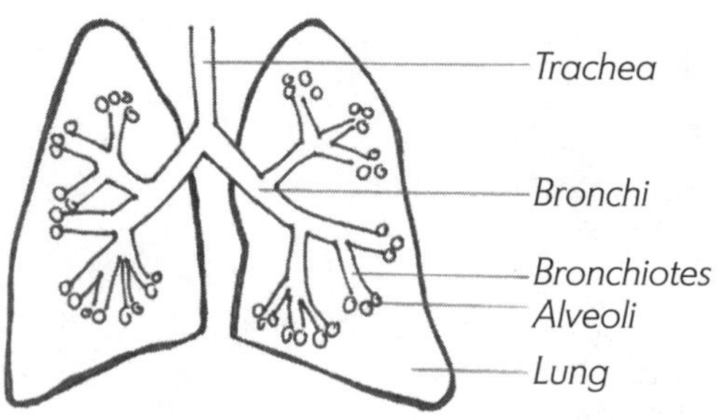

The Lungs

tory infections rarely cause labored breathing. They do cause noisy breathing, though, as air travels through the snot in the nasal passages.

Diagnoses include: Common cold, the flu (influenza)

What is a LOWER respiratory infection?

Bronchiolitis (RSV), bronchitis, or pneumonia are infections (viral or bacterial) that live in the lungs or tubes in the lungs. Because there is swelling or mucous in the tiny tubes and lung tissue, it is hard to exchange air effectively (remember that oxygen/carbon dioxide thing you learned about in science class). A person with a LOWER respiratory infection may become *air hungry*. We'll discuss this more in detail later in this section.

Rattling in the chest or ***hearing wheezing*** are NOT usually signs of a lower respiratory infection.

Diagnoses include: RSV Bronchiolitis, bronchitis, pneumonia

Any others?

There are also infections that attack the middle of the tube (larynx and trachea) where the voice box (vocal cords) is located. The tube swells in this area. Because children's tubes are smaller than adults, they are more compromised by these infections. The younger the child, the more problematic.

Diagnoses include: croup, whooping cough (pertussis)

Now that you understand the tube analogy, here the scoop.

Think about the tube. You know how your pipes are all attached in your home? When you flush your toilet upstairs, you can hear it in the kitchen. Here is the analogy: nose is to toilet as lung is to kitchen. The water is in the nose, not the lung—but it can be heard and felt down there. This is called ***transmitted upper airway noise.*** The wheezing noise is ***air pass-***

WHAT AN AIR HUNGRY CHILD LOOKS LIKE: A MUST READ

The diagnosis of an air hungry child can be made without a stethoscope. It's not what is heard—it's what is seen. A baby or child who is air hungry breathes rapidly and shallowly *(elevated respiratory rate)*, sucks in his rib cage (retractions), and flares his nostrils (flaring). A child may also make a grunting noise at the end of each breath. These are the body's way of using every muscle to pull in more air with each breath. The number of breaths taken per minute (respiratory rate) is much higher than normal. (See guide to vital signs earlier in this chapter). If a child is air hungry, call your doctor immediately.

ing through snot–it whistles.

A child who is really wheezing enough to be audible to the naked ear is in such severe distress that you will *see it* in his chest (**AIR HUNGRY**).

Helpful Hints

- Sometimes your doctor can tell what the problem is just by listening to the baby breathing on the phone. If the breathing noises are dramatic, have the baby handy when you call.
- When a person lies down, the snot from the nose drips down the back of the throat. Our body's job is to cough and keep it out of the lungs. The cough is likely coming from nasal secretions when the "cough is worse at night."

Red Flags

- Air hungry.
- Croup under age two. (See below).
- Repeated coughing spasms, followed by reddening of face, possibly a "whoop," or vomiting.
- Episodes of not being able to catch one's breath.

What the doctor will ask you about RESPIRATORY DISTRESS:

1. How long has he been having trouble breathing?
2. Could he have swallowed something?
3. Does he have a fever?
4. Is he barking like a seal? Any high-pitched squeals?
5. Look at his chest. Is he sucking in his ribcage with each breath (retractions)? Is he panting or breathing fast? Are his nostrils flaring? Is he grunting at the end of each breath?
6. Has he wheezed before? Ever stayed in the hospital overnight for it?
7. Are there coughing spasms? Any gasping for breath? Vomiting or turning red with cough?

Priority 1: Needs immediate evaluation and treatment—NOW:

- Signs of air hunger.
- Any stridor noise (see croup box nearby).
- Trouble catching breath.
- Child who has asthma.
- Child who is a former premature infant.
- Choking (see choking emergencies on the next page).

Everything You Ever Wanted to Know about Croup

A virus causes croup. It appears in epidemics every winter. A croup cough has a characteristic bark that sounds like a seal. Although impressive, this can be managed by quality time spent in your bathroom with a steamy shower running for twenty minutes. When the airway tube is markedly swollen, the bark changes to a high-pitched squeal, called stridor. Stridor requires an emergency breathing treatment and steroids to reduce the swelling or the airway. FYI: Croup is always worse at night.

Priority 2: Needs appointment the next day.

- Barking like a seal, but no squeal.

Priority 3: Watch and wait. Needs appointment if there is no improvement or worsening of symptoms:

- Chest rattling.
- Intermittent wheezing noises WITHOUT labored breathing.

Red Flag

When your child stops breathing. Call 911 immediately if your baby has any episode of true apnea (lack of breathing over 15 seconds).

Reality Check

There is a difference between apnea (not breathing) and **PERIODIC BREATHING**. Newborns frequently pause for several seconds between breaths. It is your child's job in life to give you grey hairs. Adults breathe 12 times a minute at a nice regular rate. Newborns breathe 30-60 times per minute at an irregular rate. *Newborns can pause for up to ten seconds and be feeling just fine.* To monitor the respiratory rate of a newborn, count the breaths for a whole minute.

What the doctor will ask about APNEA:

1. Is your child breathing okay now or is he having labored breathing?
2. Does he have a fever?
3. Has he had a problem with acid reflux?
4. Was he born prematurely?
5. Any recent trauma or injuries?

Babies with apnea get admitted to the hospital to be evaluated.

Diagnoses include:

1. Near Sudden Infant Death Syndrome (SIDS) event or acute life threatening event (ALTE).
2. Gastroesophageal reflux.
3. Infection (whooping cough, RSV bronchiolitis).
4. Metabolism problem.
5. Head trauma.

Choking Emergencies: 4 Tips

1 **DO NOTHING IF YOUR CHILD IS ALERT AND MAKING NOISES (CRYING, GAGGING, COUGHING).** He is effectively attempting to clear his airway.

2 **IF YOUR CHILD IS IN DISTRESS AND NOT MAKING ANY NOISE,** try to dislodge the object by putting his belly on your forearm, face down (hold him like a football). Push forcefully between the shoulder blades with the lower part of your palm five times (called back blows). *Do not perform the Heimlich maneuver on infants under one year of age.* If back blows are unsuccessful, try performing five chest thrusts. Repeat the back blows and chest thrusts until the object comes out or the baby becomes unconscious. Call 911.

3 **DO NOT BLINDLY SWEEP YOUR FINGER IN THE MOUTH AS IT MAY PUSH THE OBJECT FURTHER INTO THE AIRWAY.** Call 911 if the foreign body

does not come out.

4 If your child becomes unconscious, call 911, and begin CPR.

FYI: Need a quick visual on how to perform a back blow on a choking baby? Search "Infant CPR" on YouTube and you will be a pro in no time. We suggest viewing this video before a choking incident happens (not during it!)

Feedback from the Real World

Another True Story from Dr. Brown

I was on-call and answering a page. While I was on the phone, my nine month old son crawled over to our dog's food bowl and did a taste test. In my panic, the first thing I did was to blindly put my finger in his mouth to pull the food out. I ended up pushing it down and he swallowed it whole. After that scary (and painful) experience, he never touched the dog's food again! And I never made the mistake again of ignoring my own advice.

Cough And Congestion

Q. My baby's nose is so congested that he can't eat or sleep. What do I do?

This is the second most popular phone call. (Fever is number one). Nasal congestion happens for many reasons:

- Newborns all have nasal congestion for the first four to six weeks of life. They ALL sneeze and snort and snore. They do not have allergies (and rarely have a cold).
- Babies with acid reflux can have congestion from the milk that heads upwards behind the nose.
- Mucous pouring out the nose suggests an upper respiratory infection.

Diagnoses include: Common cold, the flu (Influenza), RSV bronchiolitis

Tricks of the trade: How To Make (And Use) Saline Nose Drops

The most safe and effective way to clear the mucous is to flush the nostrils with saline nose drops. Saline is just a salt-water solution. You can't overdose on it. You can make your own concoction (1/2 tsp salt to eight oz water). Or you can buy it for about a dollar at the grocery store. Shoot several drops in each nostril before feedings. *You don't need to suck it out with a bulb syringe.* The saline will either make your baby sneeze or loosen the mucous enough to swallow it. Babies are usually not big fans of this maneuver, but it is effective.

There are other methods of reducing the amount of mucous, but doctors always suggest saline first. Over the counter cough and cold medicines are *not recommended* under two years of age.

What the doctor will ask you about NASAL CONGESTION

1. Has he ever breathed through his nose?
2. Does he have a fever?
3. Is anyone else in the house sick? Is he in childcare?
4. Is he fussy or having disrupted sleep?
5. Does he have goopy eyes and/or green snot?

Helpful Hint

If a baby under age two has an upper respiratory infection, the flu, or especially RSV, he is at risk of getting an ear infection. Nasal discharge with fever, goopy eyes, and/or fussiness deserves a visit to the doctor to check for an ear infection.

Priority 1: Needs immediate evaluation and treatment—NOW:

- Has labored breathing or appears air hungry.
- Under four weeks of age and has a fever of 100.4 or greater (see fever section later in this chapter).
- Irritable and inconsolable.

Priority 2: Needs appointment the next day.

- Never breathes through the nose.
- Under four weeks of age, WITHOUT fever.
- Four weeks old to six months old, nasal congestion with or without fever.
- Fussy mood or disrupted sleep.
- Goopy eyes or red eyes.
- New appearance of green nasal discharge after clear discharge for at least one week.

Priority 3: Watch and wait. Needs appointment if there is no improvement or worsening of symptoms:

- Over six months of age with nasal congestion, runny nose, and cough for less than one week's duration (see fever section for other reasons to call).

Q. My child is keeping up the whole house with his cough! Make it go away.

Doctors are not miracle workers.

Nighttime coughs cause sleep deprivation for the child *and the parent*. Take a moment to review the respiratory system lecture. Coughing is a protective mechanism to keep the nasal discharge from collecting in the lungs. So for an upper respiratory infection (cold), let the cough happen during the day. The cough is worse at night because your baby is lying down. Always try saline nose drops first. Stopping the drip may stop the cough.

If the cough is keeping baby awake, your doctor may prescribe an infant cough suppressant–*prescription* cough and cold medications for children are still manufactured. However, for the same reasons that the FDA banned over-the-counter cold meds, most pediatricians don't really care for these prescription products. Letting your baby sleep in an upright position (such as in a car seat) is also helpful.

If the cough is keeping YOU awake, turn off the baby monitor!

What the doctor will ask you about COUGHING:

1. How long has he had the cough? (Over three weeks deserves an appointment).
2. Is it worse at night or in the daytime?
3. Is he having any breathing difficulties? (See that section).
4. Is he barking like a seal? Squealing?
5. Is he panting or breathing shallowly?
6. Any apnea (no breathing for 15 seconds or more)?
7. Any concern for having swallowed a foreign body?
8. Any new fever?

Priority 1: Needs immediate evaluation and treatment—NOW:

- ◆ Breathing appears labored–grunting, flaring, retractions, stridor, or elevated respiratory rate.
- ◆ Trouble catching breath with coughing episodes.
- ◆ Foreign object known to be swallowed.
- ◆ Known asthma and not responding to medication.

Priority 2: Needs appointment the next day.

- ◆ Persistent cough.
- ◆ Cough sounds productive (wet or juicy).
- ◆ Vomiting or turning red with coughing episodes, but no apnea.
- ◆ Barking like a seal, but no squeal.
- ◆ New fever with a cough and NO labored breathing.

Priority 3: Watch and wait. Needs appointment if there is no improvement or worsening of symptoms:

- ◆ Cough under three weeks duration.
- ◆ Exposure to someone with a chronic cough.

first aid

Chronic Coughs

Not all coughs are caused by infection. Prolonged coughing (over three weeks) should be evaluated. Occasionally, we discover something interesting that has ended up in a branch of the lung airway. Mr. Dr. Brown (the Ear/Nose/Throat specialist) removes toy jacks, beads, peanuts, teeth, and popcorn kernels in the airways of small children on a regular basis.

The major causes of chronic cough include: foreign object in airway asthma, sinusitis, whooping cough, tuberculosis (rare).

Red Flags

- ◆ Cough with breathing difficulties.
- ◆ Chronic cough over three weeks.
- ◆ New fever with worsening cough.
- ◆ Possible foreign body (swallowed object).

Diarrhea

Q. My baby has diarrhea. What do I do ? When do I worry?

Most of the time, diarrhea is a sign of a *stomach virus* (**VIRAL GASTROENTERITIS**). Some people call it the stomach flu. It's not THE flu. (The flu that we can get vaccinated for is influenza–a respiratory virus.) At best, your baby vomits once and the diarrhea continues for three to five days. At worst, your child vomits for 12-18 hours and has diarrhea 25 times a day for ten days (see rotavirus infection in Chapter 13, Infections). Those "24 hour bugs" don't really exist.

Food poisoning (**BACTERIAL GASTROENTERITIS**) is a concern when there is mucous or streaks of blood in the diarrhea. (See abdominal pain section earlier for details). Bacteria will cause only 10% of intestinal infections. Of those 10%, the most common culprit is **SALMONELLA**. *Other diagnoses include:* Shigella infection (bacteria), Yersinia infection (bacteria), Campylobacter infection (bacteria), C. difficile (bacteria, after an antibiotic) Giardia (parasite), Cryptosporidium (parasite), food allergy.

FYI: Chronic diarrhea (over two weeks duration) is a different problem More on this next.

Diarrhea for more than two weeks

If the diarrhea has been going on this long, your baby needs to see his doctor. Most commonly, chronic diarrhea is the result of an acute stomach virus.

Stomach viruses tear up the intestine's normal "flora" of good bacteria that help digest food. Stomach viruses can also break up a digestive enzyme called lactase, which helps the body digest milk sugar (lactose). Occasionally, infants and children can get a temporary lactose intolerance for up to six weeks after a stomach virus. Diarrhea results from repeated dairy intake and inability to digest it.

Another culprit is high juice intake. This is more of a problem with toddlers who become juice-a-holics. The high sugar content pulls water into the poop, causing increased frequency and watery stools.

Causes of chronic diarrhea include: Lactose intolerance (post-stomach virus), high juice intake, food intolerance, celiac disease, parasite infection, Inflammatory Bowel Disease.

What the doctor will ask you about DIARRHEA:

1. How old is your baby?
2. How long has the diarrhea been going on?
3. Has there been vomiting or fever?
4. What does the diarrhea look like? Watery, bloody, mucous or blood streaked?
5. Is your baby still urinating?
6. Has your baby eaten any new foods?

Priority 1: Needs immediate evaluation and treatment—NOW:

- Under three months of age.
- Blood or mucous in diarrhea.
- Grape jelly diarrhea.
- Not urinating at least three times in 24 hours.
- Unsure about frequency of urination.
- Lethargy.

Priority 2: Needs appointment the next day.

- Diarrhea more than one week.
- Age over three months and fever more than three days.

Priority 3: Watch and wait. Needs appointment if there is no improvement or worsening of symptoms:

- ◆ Watery diarrhea for less than one week, with frequent wet diapers, and over three months of age.

Q. I'm worried about my baby getting dehydrated. Should I be?

Yes.

Babies under a year old are at higher risk of getting dehydrated. *Contrary to popular belief, dehydration is caused more by diarrhea than vomiting*. The vomiting part of an illness usually stops within about 12 hours. There is only a limited amount of fluid lost from vomiting (once the stomach is empty, there's not much left to throw up). As long as the vomiting is short lived, dehydration is not a problem. Diarrhea is another story. Frequent, explosive, watery diarrhea for a week causes a tremendous amount of water loss. Your baby needs to keep up with these losses with fluid intake.

BOTTOM LINE: Although vomiting is scary, persistent diarrhea is more

HOW TO TELL IF YOUR BABY IS DEHYDRATED—A MUST READ

1 **Urine output:** When our body needs fluid, less water is released as urine. If your baby pees (urinates) at least three times in 24 hours, he is doing okay. It's sometimes hard to tell if there is pee in the diaper, though, when there is explosive poop in it. (See helpful hint on the next page).

2 **WEIGHT LOSS:** If your baby has lost 10% of his body weight, he is severely dehydrated. This is an emergency.

3 **SUNKEN FONTANELLE:** Babies under a year still have a soft spot in their skull. That is their oil gauge equivalent. If the tank is low, the soft spot is sunken. That's the first place a doctor will touch when he examines your baby.

4 **SKIN TURGOR:** You know what your skin looks like when you have been in the bathtub too long? That prune like appearance is a clue to dehydration. Nice doughy skin has plenty of water in it.

5 **DRY LIPS AND MOUTH:** When you're dry, you stop making saliva.

6 **CAPILLARY REFILL:** Press down gently on your fingernail. You will see the pink color turn white. When you release the pressure, the pink color returns in less than two seconds. In severe dehydration, that refill will take more than two seconds because the blood supply is sluggish.

7 **LETHARGY:** This is a difficult one to assess. If your baby looks like a wet noodle, it's time to visit the doctor.

likely to cause dehydration.

Helpful Hint

How to tell if there is urine in the diaper:

Put a tissue in the front part of the diaper. The urine looks yellow on the tissue because it is concentrated. You can also just opt for those disposable diapers with built-in wetness sensors.

Q. What can I give my baby to eat and drink to prevent dehydration?

Start with liquids, then slowly add solids.

Presuming that vomiting has come first in this scenario, make sure that fluids stay down before going back to solid food (if baby is over four months old). *Liquids are much more important than solids.* It's the fluid that replaces the losses. Babies make up for lost time and will eat when they are feeling better.

Your doctor may recommend a rehydration electrolyte drink (Pedialyte) to treat dehydration–see the vomiting section later for details. Once your baby has kept the rehydration drink down, return to regular formula or breast milk.

Here are some other suggestions:

1. Try Isomil DF formula for severe or prolonged diarrhea. (see formula section in liquid nutrition, Chapter 6) The DF stands for Diarrhea Formula. But it also stands for Dietary Fiber. The formula is lactose free and has a high fiber content that helps bulk up the poop.

2. Try a high fat, high fiber diet for babies over four months old. Resume solids when a baby is interested in food again. Depending on the age and what foods your baby has tried, look for high fiber foods (prunes, oatmeal, beans) and high fat foods (whole milk yogurt, avocados) to feed your baby.

3. Try yogurt or probiotics. Stomach viruses kill off the "good germs" that live in the intestines and help digest food. Replenishing the gut with good germs improves digestion. If your baby is over six months, offer four oz. yogurt daily during the illness. Another option: probiotic chewable tablets and powder packets are available over the counter. Use half of a packet or crush up a tablet daily and mix into food.

4. Try a lactose (dairy) free diet for diarrhea lasting over one or two weeks. If the diarrhea is prolonged, a secondary lactose intolerance may be the culprit (see chronic diarrhea section earlier).

BOTTOM LINE: Liquids are the priority in re-hydration. Your baby will eat solid food again when he is well.

Old Wives Tales

1. Avoid milk when your baby has diarrhea.

The truth: Your baby will have diarrhea no matter what he is eating or drinking. Give him what he is willing to drink. If the diarrhea has been going on for *over a week*, however, dairy restriction may be in order to avoid a lactose intolerance (see earlier section on chronic diarrhea).

2. Use the BRAT diet for a baby with diarrhea (Bananas, Rice, Applesauce, Toast).

The Truth: Fat and fiber are more effective in bulking up the poop than these foods. The *old* school of thought was called the BRAT diet. It was thought that a bland, carbohydrate diet was best for infants with diarrhea. The latest research suggests that fat and fiber are actually more effective in reducing water loss in diarrhea.

Q. Can I give my baby any anti-diarrhea medications?

No.

There are a couple of concerns here.

Concern #1: Infant deaths have been reported from products containing loperamide (Imodium). The medication can bring intestinal movement to a screeching halt. While it is nice to stop the diarrhea, stopping the intestines from moving entirely can be life threatening.

Concern #2: Using products containing bismuth subsalicylate as an active ingredient (Pepto-Bismol, Kaopectate) when a child has a viral illness has a theoretical risk of causing liver failure (Reye's Syndrome). That is why both of those products are only approved for children ages 12 and up. Some doctors even feel uncomfortable using Pepto-Bismol and similar medications on children under 18 years of age. Check with your doctor for her opinion.

In short, the American Academy of Pediatrics advises against using anti-diarrhea medications in infants. (*AAP*)

Reality Check

To make life even more confusing for consumers, Pepto-Bismol makes a chewable tablet for children ages two and up. The active ingredient in the product is calcium carbonate (similar to Tums). While it is safe to use that product for a toddler who has some heartburn, it is no help for diarrhea!

first aid

Vomiting

There is spit up, and then there is vomit. All babies spit up (see acid reflux in Chapter 8, The Other End). Vomiting is the forceful elimination of food and fluid that is in the stomach.

There is only a fixed amount of stomach contents. So, if a child is vomiting repeatedly, eventually he will have "dry heaves" (vomiting with nothing coming out). If a child is vomiting *bile* (fluorescent green/yellow fluid), that is coming from the small intestine and may be a concern for an intestinal blockage.

In the strictest sense, repeated vomiting causes dehydration. If your child is vomiting more than 18 hours straight, he is unable to maintain adequate fluid intake. *This rarely happens*. With most garden-variety stomach viruses, the vomiting stops within 12 hours and kids are drinking again. The greater risk of dehydration is the water lost in the diarrhea that accompanies the vomiting. Dehydration usually occurs later in the course of the illness.

All vomiting is not due to stomach upset. Babies and young children have active gag reflexes. *Forceful coughing* can result in vomiting (see **POST-TUSSIVE EMESIS**). So a baby with a common cold might vomit after

coughing. Headaches can also be accompanied by vomiting. This category includes ear infections, head injury, brain tumors, or meningitis. That's why unexplained vomiting needs to be checked out.

BOTTOM LINE: Persistent vomiting with no obvious cause should be evaluated.

Causes of vomiting include:

Gastroesophageal reflux	Early viral gastroenteritis
Pyloric stenosis	Intestinal obstruction (rare)
After coughing (post-tussive emesis)	Ear infection
Head injury	Brain tumor (rare)
Meningitis	Metabolic disorders (rare)
Bladder/ kidney infections	Food poisoning (bacterial gastroenteritis)

What the doctor will ask you about VOMITING

1. How old is your baby?
2. How long has he been vomiting?
3. Is it projectile (Exorcist-like) or just coming up effortlessly?
4. What does the vomit look like? Any fluorescent green or yellow color? Any blood or coffee grounds?
5. Does he have a fever?
6. Does he have diarrhea?
7. Is he around other children/anyone sick in the house?
8. Does he look like his stomach hurts?
9. Is he still urinating?
10. Any recent head injuries?

WHAT TO DO WHEN YOUR BABY VOMITS

1. **While your baby is actively vomiting,** DO NOT GIVE HIM ANY FOOD OR DRINK. Parents are often so afraid that their baby will get dehydrated, they offer fluids immediately. And it comes right back at them. Don't give fluids on an unsettled stomach.

2. **If it has been at least one hour since your child has vomited, offer a few sips of Pedialyte (see below).** The goal is one teaspoon every five minutes for an hour. Do not offer a whole bottle to your child. He is thirsty and will drink the whole thing—only to vomit again because his stomach isn't ready for that much. If this plan fails (that is, your baby vomits again), call your doctor.

3. **If the Pedialyte stays down, you can add to the volume one to two ounces every time your baby wants to drink.** If this plan fails, call your doctor.

4. **If your child has four hours vomit free, return to breastfeeding or formula.**

5. **After eight hours of success,** babies who are already eating solid foods can return to eating again.

Priority 1: Needs immediate evaluation and treatment—NOW:

- Vomiting with a head injury.
- Vomiting bile (bright green or yellow).
- Vomiting over 12 hours straight.
- Projectile vomiting more than three times in a row.
- Vomiting only in the mornings.
- Vomiting blood or coffee grounds.
- Appears dehydrated (see section earlier on this topic).

Priority 2: Needs appointment the next day.

- Large volume spit ups frequently.
- Recurrent vomiting.

Priority 3: Watch and wait. Needs appointment if there is no improvement or worsening of symptoms:

- Isolated episode of vomiting in well appearing child.

Q. What is Pedialyte?

Pedialyte, conceptually, is kind of like Gatorade for babies*. It's a rehydration electrolyte drink made especially for babies ages birth to one year. Parents often ask if it's okay to use for babies that young—this is exactly who it is made for! It has a high salt and moderate sugar content and tastes like salt water. Usually babies under a year don't mind the flavor. (Kids over a year are pretty smart and will refuse it.) If you want to make your own Pedialyte, check out Appendix B for a recipe you can make at home.

Do NOT give plain water to babies when they have vomiting or diarrhea. Their body salts are already depleted and giving plain water messes up the delicate electrolyte balance even more.

For older kids, try Pedialyte popsicles, flat ginger ale, or clear chicken broth.

*Note: The "oral rehydration" solutions (brand names Pedialyte or Ricelyte) have the perfect concentration of salts to replenish body electrolytes. Gatorade and other sports drinks actually have a higher salt concentration and can lead to increased diarrhea—so don't use them interchangeably.

Reality Check

Regular Pedialyte is a clear fluid. But it also comes in "flavored" varieties—which contain food coloring. Stick with the clear version. Why would you give a child who is vomiting a purple drink?

Eye Problems

Q. My newborn has goop draining from his eyes. Does he have pink eye?

No. It's a blocked tear duct.

Babies are born with narrow canals that let the tears flow out of them. Until the canals widen, the tears can get clogged. This can happen intermittently

HOW TO AVOID HAVING THE WHOLE FAMILY GET PINK EYE

Pink eye is spread by the sick person touching the infected eye and leaving the germs for someone else to touch (doorknobs, hand towels, toys). The best approach if you have pink eye in your house is to wash hands frequently and make a concerted effort not to touch your face.

through the first year of life. (See glossary for **NASOLACRIMAL DUCT OBSTRUCTION**). Just wipe away the goop with warm water.

Call your doctor if the white of the eye is red, or if the eyelids are swollen.

Q. My nine month old has goop draining from his eyes and has a cold. Does he have pink eye?

Probably.

When the eye goop is accompanied by other symptoms (runny nose, cough, fever), it's more likely to be an infection called conjunctivitis or pink eye.

Conjunctivitis can be caused by either a virus or bacteria. Bacterial infections cause goopy eye discharge (eye boogers) and viral infections cause watery eye discharge. Both are extremely contagious. Bacterial infections can be treated with antibiotic eye drops or oral antibiotics. Viruses cannot be treated and can last up to a week.

Children under age two years with bacterial conjunctivitis (goop) should see a doctor. About 30% have an ear infection or sinus infection to go along with it. The bug is usually Haemophilus influenza non-typable (a cousin of the HIB we vaccinate against). This is a smart bug often resistant to first line antibiotics.

BOTTOM LINE: A child under age two with goopy eyes needs to be seen by a doctor. There is an association of pink eye with ear infections and sinus infections.

Q. My baby's eye is red. Does he have allergies?

Unlikely.

As a general rule, babies under one year do not have seasonal allergies. A red eye is either caused by *trauma, irritation,* or *infection.* If just one eye is red, consider trauma (corneal abrasion—see below, foreign body) or irritation (soap, sun block). If it is bothersome to your baby, try flushing the eye with some lukewarm water.

If your baby looks uncomfortable, he needs to be evaluated.

Causes of red eyes: trauma, irritation, infection—viral or bacterial.

Q. My baby's eye is swollen shut. Should I worry?

Yes—if she has a fever.

Usually the cause of impressive swelling is a local allergic reaction. If a bug bite or poison ivy occurs on an eyelid, the reaction can be impressive. Proof of a bite or rash is helpful.

The concern is a serious infection called **ORBITAL CELLULITIS**. This is a sinus infection that extends into the area where the eye rests in the skull (orbit). It happens in stages, and the prognosis is obviously better if caught early. The first sign is redness and swelling of the eyelid. It then progresses to a bulging eye, with limited motion of the eye itself.

If you see this, call your doctor NOW. This is a medical emergency. See our web site at Baby411.com for a visual library picture (the picture titled "eyelid swelling" is the example you're looking for).

Q. My baby's eye is tearing constantly today. What is wrong?

Probably a corneal abrasion.

Babies can scratch their eyes accidentally. This is a superficial scratch that takes a day or two to heal. Foreign bodies (dust, etc.) can also cause similar symptoms. Doctors check for abrasions using a purple light and fluorescent dye. If a scratch is found, antibiotic eye drops are prescribed. If a foreign body is found, it can be flushed out.

What the doctor will ask you about RED EYES

1. How old is your baby?
2. Is there eye discharge? Is it watery or goopy?
3. Is there fever, runny nose, or fussiness?
4. If the eyelid is swollen, is there any bug bite or rash visible? Any fever?

Priority 1: Needs immediate evaluation and treatment—NOW:

- Eyelid swollen shut with fever.
- Question of foreign body in the eye.
- Very uncomfortable child with a red eye.

Priority 2: Needs appointment the next day.

- Goopy eyes with a cold, with or without fever

Priority 3: Watch and wait. Needs appointment if there is no improvement or worsening of symptoms:

- Newborn with eye that waters frequently, without redness.

Fever: Special Section

Fever is the number one reason pediatricians get called at night. At some point in your baby's life, he will have his first fever. And like every new parent that has come before you, you will have some anxiety. So, let's go over our advice. Note: please read this section in its entirety! If you only read a portion, you may miss key details. (Note: all temperatures are in degrees Fahrenheit).

Q. What is the definition of a fever?

Fever is an elevation of the body's regular temperature.

Contrary to what you learned in junior high science class, our body temperature is not 98.6 for 24 hours a day. It varies on a daily rhythm based on hormone levels. Our body is the coolest at 7 am (as low as 97.6) and the hottest at 7 pm (as high as 100). *The true definition of fever is a body temperature of 100.4 or higher taken rectally.*

DR B'S OPINION: FEVER-PHOBIC PARENTS

Here is a typical phone encounter on fevers:

Parent: "Doctor, my baby has a fever."
Doctor: "Yes, but what else is going on?"
Parent: "But, doctor, he has a fever."
Doctor: "I understand, but can you tell me if he has any other symptoms?"

You get the picture. I heard you. I know your baby has a fever. I need to figure out WHY he has the fever. Help me. Don't fixate on the fever. *The fever is not the problem—it's a clue for the real problem.* Be a good detective and help me look for clues. It will make for a much more productive conversation!

When an infection (most common reason for fever) enters the body, the body mounts a defense via the immune system. The immune system revs up all other body systems into attack mode. This raises all vital signs (temperature, heart rate/pulse, respiratory rate, blood pressure). A warmer body temperature actually helps fight infection. FEVER IS NOT BAD.

Because the normal body temperature is lowest in the morning and highest at night, our fever will be lower in the morning and higher at night. With a typical viral infection, we may have a temperature of 99 in the morning and be 102 at night. This is why pediatricians get phone calls about fever at night. *The fever doesn't go away and come back. It's always there. It's just lower in the morning. Fevers often last for three to four days for a viral infection.*

Fever, in and of itself, does not do any harm to the body. But it is an indicator that something (usually infection) is going on in the body. *Parents tend to focus and worry about the fever. Pediatricians worry about what the diagnosis/infection is.* Body temperatures over 108 cause brain damage. Infections do not cause body temperatures over the 106 range. (Hyperthermia, the term for body temperatures over 107, are usually caused accidentally—for example, someone locked in a car in the middle of August).

Fever is often the first sign of illness. It can take several hours to see the other symptoms blossom from the infection. So, unless a baby is under three months of age (see protocol below), you may need to watch and see how things evolve.

Fever Phobia

A study looked at parent misconceptions of fever: (*Crocetti*)

- 91% believed fever could cause harmful effects (death, brain damage).
- 44% believed that a fever over 102 was a "high" fever.
- 7% believed that a fever could rise to 110 if left untreated.
- 25% gave fever reducing medicine for temperatures less than 100.
- 85% said they awaken their child to give fever-reducing medicine.
- 44% dosed the fever reducing medicine incorrectly.
- 52% said they checked their child's temperature at least every hour when they had a fever.

BOTTOM LINE

The body is coolest at 7 am (as low as 97.6) and hottest at 7 pm (as high as 100). So, the true definition of fever is a body temperature of 100.4 or higher taken rectally.

Fever is the body's immune response to infection. The immune system revs up all other body systems and raises all vital signs. A warmer body temperature actually helps fight infection. Therefore, fever is *not* bad.

Remember, fever is not the problem, rather it is a clue to finding the problem. And fever is often the first sign of illness.

Don't be fooled that your child is fever-free in the morning if he had a fever the night before. It's just naturally lower in the morning. If you send him to childcare, you will get called to take him home when his fever spikes in the afternoon. Prepare to stay at home next day if your child has a fever at night.

Reality Check

Most of the time, newborns have a virus they picked up from a family member. But your doctor doesn't want to take any chances. Now you know why the standard advice is to limit visitors during the first four weeks after birth.

Helpful Hint

Newborns can also have problems if they have LOW body temperatures. If your newborn has a persistently low body temperature (under 97.6 taken rectally), it's best to check in with your doctor.

Q. At what temperature should I be worried?

Below is the protocol for fever in infants. The management plan is based on a child's age. The protocol is fairly universal for all babies under three months.

first aid

Priority 1: Needs Immediate Evaluation And Treatment—NOW:

◆ *Age zero to four weeks: any fever in this age group is an emergency!*

1. A rectal temperature of 100.4 or greater requires hospitalization ASAP.
2. Newborns have a unique risk of serious bacterial infections due to delivery and congenital urinary tract defects (Group B strep meningitis, pneumonia, sepsis, urinary tract infections/kidney infections). They are tested for all of these potential infections and treated with antibiotics until bacterial cultures are clear of growth. (see sepsis workup in Appendix C, Lab Tests).
3. ***Never give acetaminophen (Tylenol) to your feverish newborn. Call your doctor.***

◆ *Age four weeks to three months: any fever in this age group is an emergency!*

1. A rectal temperature 100.4 or greater requires examination and lab evaluation.
2. These infants need to be seen either in the doctor's office or in an emergency room depending on the hour. They still run the risk of having those bacterial infections that newborns get.
3. If there is an obvious source of infection (e.g. a cold), and the baby's lab work looks reassuring, hospitalization is unnecessary.

4. ***Never give acetaminophen (Tylenol) without calling the doctor.*** Exception: If your two-month-old baby received his vaccinations, and then starts running a fever within 24–48 hours, it's not a problem unless there are other symptoms going on. We expect your baby to run a fever after getting his shots. Review Chapter 12, Vaccinations, for more information.

◆ *Age three months to six months: a fever AND these problems in this age group is an emergency.*

1. A fever over 102.
2. A fever lasting more than three days.
3. A new fever, after a recent illness.
4. No obvious symptoms of viral infection (cough, runny nose, diarrhea).
5. Fussy mood/inconsolable.
6. Petechiae rash (See bleeding section earlier).

◆ *Age six months to one year:*

1. A fever of 104 or above deserves a phone call. (We know—that's way beyond your comfort level.)
2. A fever lasting more than three days.
3. A new fever, after a recent illness.
4. No obvious symptoms of viral infection (cough, runny nose, diarrhea).
5. Fussy mood/inconsolable.
6. Petechiae rash (see bleeding section earlier in this chapter.)

Priority 2: Needs appointment the next day.

◆ *Age three months to six months:*

1. If everyone in the house has the flu and your baby has the same symptoms, make an appointment if the fever persists longer than three days (or something else is concerning–i.e. dehydration, labored breathing).
2. ***You can give acetaminophen (Tylenol) for the fever. Just make sure you have figured out why your baby has the fever first.***

Priority 3: Watch and wait. Needs appointment if there is no improvement or worsening of symptoms

◆ *Age six months to one year:*

1. Obvious symptoms of a virus (cough, runny nose, vomiting, diarrhea), you can probably manage the infection without a doctor's visit.
2. ***You can give acetaminophen (Tylenol) or ibuprofen (Motrin) when your baby has a fever. Just make sure you know why your baby has the fever.***

Reality Check

After six months of age, it's not the degree of the fever that is concerning, it's what the baby looks like. Everyone looks sick when they are running a fever. If a baby still looks sick after taking a fever reducing medicine, it's time to call the doctor.

Insider Tip: Roseola

Children usually get the common childhood infection, **ROSEOLA**, between nine to 12 months of age. It causes a high fever

(103 to 104) for about three days with no other symptoms. These kids look perfectly happy and go about their daily routines. On day four, when they are fever free, the classic roseola rash (flat red patches on the chest and arms) comes out. They are not contagious with the rash. High fevers (104 or above) deserve to be evaluated, but roseola is often the culprit.

See our web site at Baby411.com (Bonus) for a visual library of rashes.

Q. My baby is running a "low grade" fever. Should I be worried?

Who started this urban legend? What is a low-grade fever? It's not in the doctor dictionary.

Parents worry about body temperatures of 99 to 100. This is not, by definition, a fever. It has no association with an infection unless your baby is 100 at 7am. In that case, it does not bode well for what the night will bring.

Q. My baby has had a fever "on and off" for several days. I thought he broke the fever. Why does it keep coming back?

Let's review. A typical viral infection will cause a fever for three or four days.

Remember, it may look like your baby doesn't have a fever in the morning, but it always comes back at night. If there is a fever at any point in a 24-hour day, your child still has fever on a daily basis. This is helpful when you are reporting symptoms to the doctor. Doctors want a record of how many days in a row your child has had a fever. It helps make diagnostic decisions.

Fever reducing medicine, acetaminophen (Tylenol) and ibuprofen (Motrin), will help bring the body temperature down for four to six hours. But once the medicine wears off, the fever will return. The medicine does not make the infection go away. (See later questions on fever-reducing medications).

BOTTOM LINE: A truly NEW fever after being fever free for a period of at least 24 hours is concerning for a bacterial infection that has capitalized on a sick person (such as ear infection, sinus infection, pneumonia). Make an appointment to see your doctor.

Helpful Hint
On Fever Curves

Another important trend doctors watch is the fever curve over a period of days. At the beginning of an infection, the fever is the highest. As the body effectively fights off the infection, the maximum fever spikes should be lower. If a fever curve trends up instead of down (fevers are getting higher on a day to day basis), this is more concerning and may prompt an evaluation.

Q. How do you recommend taking a baby's temperature?

For the target age of this book (birth to age one), you need to take the temperature with a rectal thermometer.

Most parents cringe just thinking about this task. Are you cringing? Don't. Babies really don't mind. It does not hurt or make them feel like you've invaded their space. In fact, it's a good trick to make them poop. But I digress.

Rectal temperatures are the most accurate way to check a human's

DR B'S OPINION: THERMOMETERS

Ear thermometers are not my friend. Their reliability is based upon the ability of the user to line the tip up with the eardrum. If you compare your own two ears and get two different readings, you will understand what I mean. Ear thermometers can also overestimate the degree of fever and create parent panic. I've received frantic calls regarding kids with fevers of 107 taken with an ear thermometer that turned out to be 102 or 103 when taken rectally.

Except for the ear thermometers (which OVER estimate fever), alternative methods to check temperature UNDER estimate the degree of fever. Parents often ask, "Do you add or subtract a degree from the non-rectal measurement?" My response is, "If you ever get an actual reading that is 100 or over, you know your child has a fever. That is all the information I need."

body temperature. And for infants under three months of age, one tenth of a degree will make the difference between whether you stay at home in your nice warm bed or head out for an evening of fun at your local emergency room.

If you call the doctor at 2 am and tell her that your six week old has a fever, the first thing she will ask is, "How did you take the temperature?" If you took it any way other than rectally, we make you get a rectal thermometer and call us back. Invest in one now—digital rectal thermometers cost about $5.

After one year of age, there is more flexibility about how to take your child's temperature. Trendy products on the market for toddler temperatures include a pacifier thermometer, ear thermometer, temporal artery scanners, and plastic skin stickers. Using an oral thermometer in the armpit is also okay. None of these are as accurate as a rectal temperature. But after a year of age, the actual degree of fever is much less important to making a management plan for your child. That is, a child with 101 or 103 is managed based on the *other symptoms* they have in addition to the fever.

Mom Knows Best

There was a great study that tested Mom's method of temperature taking (placing the hand on the forehead). Guess what? Mom is usually right—at least 80% of the time—with this method. Some thoughts on this:

1. After six months of age, if you say your child "feels hot," that's often enough proof of fever.
2. Trust yourself! Parents think they need to take their baby's temperature periodically to make sure he is okay. You hold your baby 24 hours a day. You will know when he feels hot. Then you can get out the thermometer.

New Parent 411: How to take a baby's rectal temperature.

Don't be embarrassed. You've never done this before. Get out your digital rectal thermometer. Place some petroleum jelly

TREATING A FEVER: DR. B'S 10 COMMANDMENTS

1 **IF YOU HAVE YOUR DOCTOR'S BLESSING, IT'S OKAY TO GIVE A FEVER REDUCING MEDICATION.** (See age discussion earlier.)

2 **BABIES FROM THREE TO SIX MONTHS CAN USE ACETAMINOPHEN** (Tylenol). It's fine for two month olds to take acetaminophen after getting vaccinations. However, many docs suggest waiting until several hours later to give acetaminophen. Giving a dose too soon may blunt the appropriate response to the vaccination. Ask your doc for dosing instructions.

3 **BABIES OVER SIX MONTHS OF AGE CAN USE IBUPROFEN** (Motrin/Advil) **OR ACETAMINOPHEN** (Tylenol).

4 **I PREFER IBUPROFEN FOR OLDER BABIES BECAUSE THE MEDICATION LASTS FOR SIX HOURS INSTEAD OF FOUR.** Since the fever will climb at night, this will buy everyone two extra hours of sleep.

5 **ACETAMINOPHEN IS PREFERRED IF A CHILD IS DEHYDRATED** or has a stomach virus (ibuprofen can upset an empty stomach).

6 **BE FOREWARNED: THESE MEDICATIONS ARE CALLED FEVER REDUCERS NOT FEVER ELIMINATORS.** At best, these medications will bring the body temperature down by two degrees. If your baby is cooking at 104, he will be feeling more comfortable at 102. That's as good as it gets.

7 **I DON'T ROUTINELY INSTRUCT PARENTS TO ALTERNATE ACETAMINOPHEN AND IBUPROFEN.** If a baby is old enough for the ibuprofen, stick with that. I only alternate medicines in babies prone to febrile seizures (see glossary for details). There is no proven benefit of alternating medicines.

8 **DON'T BOTHER PUTTING BABY IN A TEPID BATH.** If you had the chills, would you want to sit in cold water? This cooling technique is only necessary in an emergency situation (such as extreme hyperthermia, a 107 temperature). Bringing your child's temperature down with this technique is not only unpleasant, but a waste of time and effort.

9 **NEVER GIVE YOUR CHILD ASPIRIN**. It can cause liver failure when given with particular viral infections.

10 **ALWAYS USE THE MEDICINE DROPPER THAT COMES WITH THE PACKAGE.** The term "one dropperful" refers to the dropper that comes with the medicine.

first aid

(Vaseline) on the tip. With one hand lift up your baby's feet, holding them together. With your other hand, insert the tip of the thermometer into his anus about one inch. Leave the thermometer in there for one minute (or until it beeps at you). See, you and baby did just fine.

FYI: The American Academy of Pediatrics recommends using digital (rectal/oral) thermometers as opposed to glass mercury thermometers. The latter are dangerous if broken.

Q. What is the correct dose of medication? It says on the box to consult a physician.

Ever wonder why it says this on the box? It's to make sure that you call the doctor when your newborn has a fever. Now that you know when you need to call, we will tell you how to dose these medicines. Both acetaminophen (Tylenol) and ibuprofen (Advil) are dosed at five milligrams per pound per dose. See the dosing chart on the following page.

How to avoid overdosing your baby

"I have too many stories about Tylenol overdoses to share in this book. It's just not as easy to figure these medicines out as it should be."

1. Acetaminophen is the generic name for Tylenol, Feverall, and Tempra.
2. Ibuprofen is the generic name for Motrin and Advil.
3. Both acetaminophen and ibuprofen are effective fever reducers and pain medications.
4. Acetaminophen is dosed every four hours. Ibuprofen is dosed every six hours.
5. As we've said earlier, always use the medicine dropper that comes in the package. The dropper size varies between products. To reduce dosing confusion, acetaminophen liquid now comes in only one standard concentration. However, ibuprofen comes in two different strengths—infant concentrated drops and a children's syrup.
6. There is a difference in the concentration of medicine in the infant drops and the children's syrup. The infant drops are much more concentrated so you won't have to force a large volume of medicine into your baby.
7. Acetaminophen suppositories (medicine bullets inserted in the anus) are available for babies who resist taking medicine or are actively vomiting.
8. When your doctor tells you to use "one dropperful," it routinely means the dropper that comes with the package, with the medicine drawn up to the line marked on the dropper. A mother requested that we share this with you because she mistakenly thought it meant to fill the whole dropper up with medicine (look at a medicine dropper and you'll understand).
9. When you graduate to the syrup medicine, use a medicine cup to dispense. Silverware teaspoons are not an exact teaspoon measurement. They can be larger or smaller depending on your set. Medicine syringes are also helpful—they make it easier to measure and dispense medicine.

Dosing Chart

Acetaminophen:

BABY'S WEIGHT IN LBS.	6-11LBS	12-17LBS	18-23LBS	24-35LBS
Dose in mg *(80mg per 0.8 ml)*	40mg	80mg	120mg	160mg
Children's syrup *(160 mg per tsp)*	1/4 tsp	1/2 tsp	3/4 tsp	1 tsp
Suppositories (80mg)	—	1 suppository	1 1/2	2
Suppositories (120mg)	—	—	1	1 1/3

Ibuprofen:

BABY'S WEIGHT IN LBS.	6-11LBS	12-17LBS	18-23LBS	24-35LBS
Dose in mg	*	50mg	75mg	100mg
Infant drops *(50mg per 1.25 ml)*	*	1.25ml	1.25+0.625	1.25+1.25
1.875ml is a dropperful	*			
Children's syrup (100mg per tsp)		1/2 tsp	3/4 tsp	1 tsp

* *Note: Ibuprofen is NOT for babies under six months of age*

Q. Is it safe to give a fever reducing medicine longer than five days? It says on the box to consult a physician.

The medicine itself is safe to give. This warning is a way to make sure you have checked in with your doctor if your baby has a prolonged fever. A child with a fever more than four days straight should be seen by her doctor.

Q. I have given my baby acetaminophen (Tylenol) and he still has a fever.

This one is on the Top 10 List of most asked questions for any pediatrician.

The most common reason this happens is that your child has outgrown the dose of medicine you have given him. Fever reducing medicines (as well as most other types) are dosed based on the weight of a child. A few pounds can make a difference for the correct dosing.

Look at the chart above. When your doctor tells you the dose of acetaminophen (Tylenol) at your child's two-month well check, don't think that the dose will never change.

BOTTOM LINE: Acetaminophen and Ibuprofen are fever reducers (not eliminators). If your child has a high fever, it won't be completely eliminated by the medicine. The fact that the fever does not go down with medication has no implication on the severity of the illness.

Q. I've heard that fevers can cause seizures in babies. Is this true?

Yes, babies can have febrile seizures or convulsions.

A few children—less than 5% (ages six months to five years) are prone to having a seizure/convulsion as a fever is shooting up. "Febrile seizures" do not cause brain damage or lead to a seizure disorder such as epilepsy.

The seizure happens when the body temperature rises quickly. If your child's temperature is already at 104, he's most likely missed the window of having a seizure. So, you can relax now.

Yes, it is terrifying to watch a child have a full-blown seizure in your living room. Fortunately, febrile seizures last less than five minutes. And children are fine afterwards.

About 30% of children who are prone to febrile seizures have more than one episode in their lives. But after the first time, parents are much more comfortable about managing it. Parents will give fever medicine around the clock so that the temperature elevation can never rise rapidly during the course of an illness.

The first time a child has a febrile seizure, he needs to be evaluated thoroughly. Once this diagnosis is determined, treatment focuses on the cause of the fever.

Old Wives Tales

Don't give your baby a bath while he has a fever.
Don't let your baby drink milk while he has a fever.
Fevers cause brain damage.
Teething causes fever.

The Truth: None of these statements are remotely true. Keep feeding your baby breast milk or formula, go ahead and give him a bath, and unless his fever reaches the extreme temperatures mentioned earlier, relax a bit. Oh, and teething has *nothing* to do with fever.

What the doctor will ask you about FEVER:

1. How old is your baby?
2. How did you take the temperature?
3. What other new symptoms are you seeing?
4. Is anyone else in the household sick?
5. Is your child exposed to other children?
6. How many days has the fever been going on?
7. Any recent illnesses prior to the fever?
8. Any rashes?
9. Have you given any fever reducing medicines?
10. What dose of medicine did you give?
11. What does your baby look like after giving the medicine?

Red Flags

- Fever under three months of age.
- Fever over 102 in three to six-month-old.
- Fever of 104 or above in six months and older.
- Fever lasting over three days.
- Fever without obvious source of infection.
- Fever with petechiae rash.
- Fever with irritability or lethargy.
- Febrile seizure.
- Fever with a limp or limb pain.

Poisonings/Ingestions

If your child accidentally swallows a household product, call poison control immediately.

Have the phone number at each of your telephones. Do NOT try to make your child vomit. Other treatments are more effective (and vomiting can, in some cases, causes MORE harm than good).

Poison Control is an amazing resource of information on any product a curious child might ingest. They will tell you whether the product can do potential harm to the body or not. And they know the antidotes.

Occasionally, a parent is not even aware of the ingestion happening. They only know that their child is acting unusual. *Some clues to ingestion include: mouth burns, drooling, rapid or shallow breathing, vomiting without fever, seizures, extreme lethargy, or body/breath odor.*

THE MOST DANGEROUS HOUSEHOLD PRODUCTS

Here is a list of childhood favorites to keep out of reach. (Place items in high cabinets out of reach or in places with cabinet locks).

Chemicals

- cleaning products
- paint thinner
- dishwashing detergent
- gasoline

Medications

- especially Mom's prenatal vitamins (iron)
- especially visiting grandparents (heart or blood pressure medications)

Plants (some of these are common houseplants).

- Christmas favorites: poinsettias, mistletoe, holly
- wild mushrooms
- hyacinth, narcissus, daffodil, elephant ear, rosary pea, larkspur, Lily-of-the-Valley, iris, foxglove, bleeding heart, daphne, wisteria, golden chain, laurels, azaleas, jasmine, lantana

Hygiene products

- mouthwash
- nail polish remover
- rubbing alcohol
- hair dye

Food and wine

- liquor
- pottery from foreign countries (lead)

Helpful hint

If Poison Control directs you to an emergency room, take the poison/medication with you if you have it. It helps determine the ingredients and the amount that was swallowed.

Feedback from the Real World

Dr. B True Story

I cared for a patient once who ate part of a necklace a mother had brought back from traveling abroad. The beads were made of ricin, the active ingredient of poison darts (think Bond, James Bond). ***Bottom Line:*** Be careful. Babies are programmed to taste everything.

What the doctor will ask you about POISONING:

1. Is the product toxic vs. non-toxic?
2. Do you have the bottle/container?
3. Is your child having trouble breathing?

When to call:

All poisonings and ingestions are Priority 1: Needs immediate evaluation and treatment–NOW!

Rashes

Trying to diagnose a rash over the phone is always a challenge. Someday we'll just take a picture of our rashy kid and text our pediatrician. (Most docs do not currently offer telemedicine service.) But for now, you need to be the eyes for your doctor. Without actually seeing the rash, the best we can do is figure out whether the rash fits into the worrisome or the non-worrisome categories. Worrisome rashes need prompt attention. Non-worrisome ones can wait until the office opens the next day. Causes of rashes include:

- **Infection:** viruses, bacteria, fungi, mites
- **Allergy:** eczema, contact allergy (poison ivy, sensitivity to a skin care product), food/medication allergy
- **Newborn rashes:** due to hormonal changes
- **Blood cell abnormalities**

See our website at Baby411.com (Bonus Material) for a visual library of rashes.

What the doctor will ask you about RASHES:

1. How long has the rash been there?
2. Where on the body did the rash start? Is it spreading? Where?
3. Is there a fever?
4. Is it itchy? Really really itchy?
5. Anyone else in the house with a rash?
6. Is the rash flat or raised? (Can you feel it with your eyes closed?)
7. Is it scaly on top?
8. What color is the rash?

9. How big are the spots?
10. When you press on the rash, does the color turn white? Or, does it remain discolored?
11. Is your child taking any medications?
12. Has your child eaten any new foods?
13. Have you used any new skin products? (sun block, lotion, soap, detergents)
14. How old is your child?

Q. Which rashes are worrisome?

Petechiae with or without bruising. (See bleeding section earlier for details on petechiae). Petechiae are small flat freckle or pinpoint dots, purplish in color, that stay purple when you push on them.

This is really the only rash that needs immediate attention. Petechiae can be caused by forceful coughing or vomiting. But this rash can also indicate meningitis, Rocky Mountain Spotted Fever, idiopathic thrombocytopenia purpura (ITP), or leukemia. Petechiae are ***Priority 1: Needs immediate evaluation and treatment—NOW.***

Q. What are hives and what causes them?

A rash that appears due to release of a chemical called histamine. 20% of the population will get hives once in their lives. But 75% of the time, the cause is never found. (*Fleisher*)

Hives look like mosquito bites with red circles around them. Or, they look like a flat red area with a raised border. Hives vary in size and shape. They are itchy and occur anywhere on the body. The individual lesions come and go. See Chapter 14, Common Diseases for causes of hives.

What to do if your child breaks out in hives

- *Relax.* If your child is not having any trouble breathing, this can be managed at home.
- *Try to figure out what caused the hives* (foods, medications, illness).
- *Stop any medications until you see the doctor.*
- *Give an antihistamine.* Liquid diphenhydramine (Benadryl) comes in 12.5mg per teaspoon syrup. A 20 lb. baby can have 3/4 tsp. If your baby is smaller than 20 lbs., call your doctor before giving it. Babies six months up to two years of age can have 1/2 tsp of liquid cetirizine (Zyrtec) or loratidine (Claritin), which are also available over the counter.

Q. What does a drug allergy rash look like?

True drug allergies will cause hives or **ERYTHEMA MULTIFORME.** Any other rash does not require avoidance of a particular medication.

Erythema multiforme basically means "redness in multiple forms." What you see is a full body rash of red flat patches and raised borders. Many of the patches run into each other.

If you see a concerning rash while your child is on medication, hold the dose of medicine and bring the child in to be seen. A particular medication class should not be avoided unless there is a documented allergy.

first aid

RASH-O-RAMA: COMMON RASHES SEEN WITH

Viral exanthems: (rashes caused by viruses)

	Rash looks like	Where?
Chickenpox	fluid filled blisters come up in crops	all over avg. 350 lesions
Shingles	fluid filled blisters	1 patch
Measles	red, raised pimply	face to body
German measles	red, raised	face to body
Roseola	FLAT red ovals/ lace	chest, arms, neck, +/- face
Parvovirus (Fifth disease)	"slapped cheeks" Flat, red, lacy on body	chest, arms
Coxsackievirus (hand, foot, and mouth)	red dots or blisters	palms, soles, +/- buttocks
Unilateral Latero-thoracic Exanthem	raised red bumps, scaly on top	one armpit
Pityriasis rosea	raised red streaks a little scaly	back, angled like a fir tree
Special viral rashes:		
Herpetic Whitlow	blister, red around	thumb, finger
Molluscum Contagiosum	pinpoint blisters	anywhere
Bacterial infections:		
Impetigo*	red, raised with weeping golden crust	anywhere
Scarlet fever* (usually over 2 yrs old)	red, sandpaper feel, rough raised dots	armpit, groin, neck, body
Meningitis*	petechiae (purple freckles)	spreads head to toe
Fungal infections:		
Ringworm*	circle, red raised edge +/- overlying scale	anywhere
Yeast diaper rash*	raw meat red with surrounding pimples	diaper area
Tick borne illness:		
Lyme Disease*	bullseye with bite in the center	bite site
Rocky Mountain Spotted Fever*	starts out flat, red then petechiae (purple freckles)	wrist, ankles palms, soles
Mites:		
Scabies*	lines of red raised bumps (burrows) blisters in babies	head, neck, palms, soles, armpits, finger webs
Other:		
Kawasaki Disease*	red cracked lips peeling skin on fingers flat/mildly raised red spots	lips, palms, soles of feet

Denotes an infection that needs treatment

INFECTIONS, HOW LONG THEY LAST AND MORE!

Duration	Other symptoms
1 week	fever, itchy
1 week	painful
1 week	fever, pink eye
3 days	swollen glands
1 day	high fever that breaks then rash appears
2-40 days	mildly itchy, joint pains
1 week	fever, sore throat with ulcers
4-6 weeks	mildly itchy
6 weeks	mildly itchy
1 week	very painful
1-2 years	
gets worse until treated	very itchy
3-4 days	sore throat, fever
hours	fever, irritability, light sensitivity
gets worse until treated	very itchy
gets worse until treated	itchy
enlarging diameter	fever, fatigue
1-6 days	fever, vomiting irritability light sensitivity
worse until treated	**ITCHIEST RASH EVER!**
Over five days	fever for more than 5 days pink eye swollen lymph nodes in neck

Q. What does a food allergy rash look like?

Food allergies can cause hives and lip swelling if the reaction is severe. But it can also cause a flare up of a rash called eczema. Eczema is an allergic skin disorder–the equivalent of hay fever. Eczema looks like a scaly plaque lying on top of a red base. With a food allergy, the eczema can cover huge body surface areas.

Food allergies do NOT cause mild diaper rash, a few patches on the face, or heat rashes.

Q. My child has a scaly rash on his elbows and knees. What is it?

Eczema. It is sensitive skin. In infants, it likes the elbows and knees because these areas get chewed up from crawling. It also ends up in the skin folds of the elbows and knees from rubbing. See Chapter 14, Common Diseases for more details on this.

Q. Which rashes are likely to be contagious due to infection?

Most of them. Kids have wonderful immune systems (much better than ours). And rashes are created from an immune response to a particular infection.

The diseases listed on the previous pages are The Classics. There are also a variety of non-descript rashes that fit in the category of "viral and non-worrisome."

Q. I know that all newborns get rashes. Are there any I need to be worried about?

Yes. Herpes.

Moms with genital herpes have a chance of spreading it to their newborn during a vaginal delivery. (If Mom has an obvious outbreak a Caesarian section is performed.) A herpes rash in a newborn shows up within two weeks of life. The lesions look like little blisters either alone or in crops. This is ***Priority 1: Needs immediate evaluation and treatment–NOW!***

Q. My four week old has a pimply rash all over his face and chest. What do I do?

It's acne, but don't break out the Oxy 10. This rash is caused by a hormonal change in the baby. Leave it alone and it goes away by eight weeks of age.

Feedback from the Real World

Dr. Brown True Story

My son woke up one morning with three distinct red circles on his chest. I thought he had ringworm until I realized the circles matched the snaps on his sleeper pajamas. He had an allergy to the metal snaps.

Necklaces, earrings, and snaps on jeans can cause a similar reaction in people with sensitive skin.

Q. My one year old looks like he has the measles! Does he?

No. Did he come in for his one year well check recently? That rash is the response to the MMR vaccination. (Kids also get a chickenpox-like rash with the chickenpox vaccine). Be happy. This means he has formed a good response.

These rashes usually appear one to four weeks after being vaccinated.

Q. My baby has a diaper rash. What do I do about it?

See Chapter 4, Hygiene for details on how to treat diaper rash.

Priority 1: Needs immediate evaluation and treatment—NOW:

- Hives that occur while taking medication or trying a new food.
- Hives with difficulty breathing ***(Call 911).***
- Petechiae rash.
- Newborn with a blistery rash.
- Any rash with a fever.

Priority 2: Needs appointment the next day.

- Rashes that are scaly, without fever.
- Rashes that are not going away after being treated by a doctor.

Priority 3: Watch and wait. Needs appointment if there is no improvement or worsening of symptoms:

- Newborn (birth to eight weeks) with a non-blistery rash, acting well.
- Diaper rashes.
- One year old with rash after being in for his one year well check.

Seizures

Seizures are scary to watch. If your child has a seizure, ***dial 911.*** Once the episode is over, you can review this information.

Q. What is a seizure?

Involuntary muscle (motor) activity is the definition of a seizure. This is caused by an electrical brainwave that has fired incorrectly. In kids under age one, the most common type of seizure is associated with a fever that is rising quickly (See febrile seizure in the fever section of this chapter).

Causes of new onset seizures include: Febrile seizure (convulsion), head trauma/ injury, meningitis, poisoning/ingestion, metabolic disorder, seizure disorder

What To Do If Your Baby Has A Seizure

- *Call 911.*
- Put him in a safe place (a carpeted floor).
- Make sure he can breathe.
- Do not put anything in his mouth to hold his tongue (contrary to what you see on TV).

◆ Start CPR–do mouth-to-mouth resuscitation if baby looks blue.

What the doctor will ask you about SEIZURES:

1. Has your baby ever had a seizure before?
2. How old is your baby?
3. Does the baby have a fever?
4. Anyone in the family prone to febrile seizures as a child?
5. Any history of head trauma?
6. Any history of poisoning or ingestion?

Priority 1: Needs immediate evaluation and treatment—NOW:

- Known history of febrile seizures, with another episode
- Has a known seizure disorder.

Stitches (Sutures)

The key point to remember: *Stitches (sutures) need to be placed within 12 hours of the injury. So they are always considered Priority 1.* Any later than that, the wound has a much higher chance of getting infected. If your child has a wound that might need stitches, call your doctor now.

What the doctor will ask you about NEEDING STITCHES:

1. **What happened?** For example, animal bites usually are not stitched because of infection risk.
2. **How long ago did the injury happen?** If over 12 hours, wound can't be sutured.
3. **Where on the body is the cut (laceration)?** Location of the wound makes a difference because of cosmetic issues (face) and potential nerve damage (hands).

How to Clean and Care for Minor Wounds

It's not what you use, it's how you use it. Plain old soap and water is fine. You don't have to get high tech here. The key is to flush the wound and repeat this several times. Wash the wound every day until it heals. Here's how to care for minor wounds:

1. Apply pressure to the wound with a gauze pad or towel for ten minutes.
2. Thoroughly clean wound with soap and water. The most important part of the cleaning process is flushing with water repeatedly–especially with puncture wounds (bites, sharp objects). Your doctor will use a mechanism much like a Waterpik to clean "road rash" scrapes.
3. Apply antibiotic ointment for two or three days. This prevents infection and improves cosmetic results.
4. Look for signs of infection. (Redness, pus, fever).
5. For cuts in the mouth or tongue, try popsicles or ice cream (if age appropriate) to help control bleeding.

4. **If on the face, is it crossing the lip/skin line or the eyebrow line?** It may need stitches for better cosmetic result.
5. **How deep is it?** If you can see fat, it needs stitches–anything deeper than 1/4 inch.
6. **Is the bleeding under control?** If not, it needs stitches.
7. **For older wounds: Is there any pus, redness around the wound, streaks of red from the wound, or fever?** Needs to be seen for possible wound infection.
8. **Are your child's immunizations current?** Needs tetanus shot if not up to date.
9. **Does your child have any bleeding disorders?** There is a risk of large volume of blood loss.

Q. Are there any body parts that always need stitches?

Yes. Eyebrows and lip lines. The lip line means the area where the lip meets the skin. If a wound crosses this line, the lip will not line up correctly without stitches. The same is true for the eyebrow line. Cosmetically, this is a big deal.

Q. Are there any body parts that never need stitches?

It is RARE to need stitches on the lip itself, tongue, or gums. The blood flow to these areas is tremendous (which is why they bleed so much). This blood flow allows very rapid healing.

Feedback from the real world: Tongue injuries

One of our readers suggested we add some tips on tongue injuries (after her $74 adventure to the doctor's office). Her two-year-old daughter had bitten her tongue and there was a visible gap. So, Michele C., this one's for you!

As long as the tongue is not cut (lacerated) through, it usually does not require stitches and will heal up beautifully in one or two days. You don't need to visit your doctor or the ER.

Our reader recommends offering scrambled eggs, mashed potatoes, and ice cream to little ones with tongue injuries.

first aid

Q. How can I tell if the wound is infected?

Pus (white/yellow/green discharge) will start to ooze out of the wound. There will be red and tender skin around the wound site, and maybe even a streak of redness starting from the wound. There may also be a fever.

Q. Is my child's tetanus shot up to date?

If your child is receiving his immunizations regularly at well baby checks, he is well protected. He gets a tetanus shot at two, four, six, fifteen months and again at five years old. Your child is probably better protected than you.

Q. Can I get water near the stitches?

YES!

This is a common misconception. Clean the wound, even if it has stitches in it. The not-cleaned ones have crust around them, making it a challenge for the doctor to remove the stitches.

Q. When should the stitches be removed?

It depends on the location. Skin heals at different rates on the body. The doctor who puts the stitches in will tell you when they need to come out. Try to do it when suggested– a delay in suture removal can not only impair the cosmetic result, but can also be very painful if the stitches are imbedded in the skin.

To give you an idea of the variability of suture removal, stitches on the face come out in four days. Stitches on the palm of the hand come out in 14 days.

Q. What is that glue used to close wounds? Can we use that instead of stitches?

The brand names are Dermabond or SurgiSeal, and they are fairly popular alternatives to stitches. It's like superglue. It dissolves on its own and does not need any removal. Sounds great, right?

Well, it is only useful for a limited number of wounds. If the skin is under any tension (gets pulled frequently), the glue won't be able to hold the wound together. The glue is also not intended for use near the eyes.

Dermabond and SurgiSeal are products sold only to medical providers. There are some over-the-counter topical skin adhesives, but we cannot attest to their effectiveness.

Q. I've also heard about using staples instead of stitches. Is this better than stitches?

It's easier than stitches for placement, but they are painful to remove. For non-cosmetic areas such as the head, it is a reasonable option.

Helpful Hint

Cuts on the scalp and face bleed a lot. The blood flow to these body parts is much greater than any other areas. Don't be alarmed. It is only a problem if you can't get the bleeding under control.

Priority 1: Needs immediate evaluation and treatment—NOW:

- Any skin wound that you think might need stitches.
- Unable to control the bleeding after ten minutes of pressure to the wound.
- Wound in a cosmetically undesirable location.
- Looks like it is getting infected (redness, pus, fever).
- If immunizations are not current.

Priority 3: Watch and wait. Needs appointment if there is no improvement or worsening of symptoms:

- Make an appointment for suture removal.

Trauma (Accidental Injury)

No matter how good of a parent you are and how safety proofed your house is, your child will find a way to hurt himself. Welcome to parenthood–this is only one of the many reasons that your child will give you grey hairs.

This section is body part specific. The section on skin trauma/injury is covered in the Stitches section.

What the doctor will ask you about TRAUMA / ACCIDENTAL INJURIES

1. What happened?
2. Any loss of consciousness or did he cry immediately?
3. With head injury: Any vomiting or confusion?
4. With head injury: How far did the child fall and what surface did he fall onto?
5. Any bleeding or fluid draining from the nose or ears?
6. Are there any obvious broken bones, sticking out of the skin?
7. Any pain with touching or movement of a body part?
8. Any bruising or swelling?
9. Can you check the eye pupils. Are they equal?

Helpful Hint

The mechanism of injury (that is, what happened) is the most reliable factor in determining the severity of a body injury.

1. Head injury

Once babies are mobile, they run into things like the coffee table and fireplace hearth. The result is a big bruise (a.k.a. "goose egg") on the forehead. It is an impressive bump because of that vast blood supply to the head and face. Despite the appearance, goose eggs are not too worrisome.

The mechanism of injury is much more concerning. Here are the red flags for head injuries:

first aid

NEW PARENT 411: HANDLING MINOR HEAD INJURIES

◆ Put a bag of frozen vegetables on the goose egg, if your child lets you. It will be less swollen in the morning, but will change into a rainbow of colors for a week or two.
◆ Watch for signs of concussion for the next two days (vomiting, irritability from headache, confusion, lethargy)
◆ Let your child go to bed. Invariably, it's nap or bedtime when these events happen (probably because your child is tired and clumsy then). You can monitor him every few hours by watching his breathing and gently touching him to see if he stirs. Vomiting or seizure activity happens whether he is awake or asleep.

Priority 1: Needs immediate evaluation and treatment—NOW!

For injuries for a concussion or bleeding in the head.

- Child falls a distance greater than his own height.
- Child falls onto hardwood floors, tile, or concrete.
- Child loses consciousness (blacks out) after the injury.
- Child vomits more than once after the injury.
- Baby's soft spot is bulging.
- Seizure after head injury.
- Acting abnormal or confused.
- Bruising behind the ear or bleeding from the ear.
- Clear fluid draining from the nose.

Priority 2: Needs appointment the next day.

- Child falls a distance less than his height, onto a padded surface, no loss of consciousness.

Priority 3: Watch and wait. Needs appointment if there is no improvement or worsening of symptoms:

- Child has a minor accident resulting in a large bruise on the head (goose egg), no loss of consciousness, no vomiting, and is acting normally.

BOTTOM LINE

Every child who has rolled off a bed onto a carpeted floor does not need to be rushed to an emergency room. (And yes, this will happen to you!)

Which head injuries require a CAT scan?

When there is a concern for a severe head injury (bleeding inside the skull), a CT scan (Computer Tomography) is helpful to check it out. Here are the criteria:

- all kids under two years of age
- loss of consciousness for over one minute
- trauma (knife, bullet)
- abnormal neurologic examination (dizziness, weakness, abnormal reflexes..)
- vomiting
- seizures
- bulging soft spot (fontanelle)
- bruising behind the ear or bleeding from the ear
- clear fluid draining from the nose
- depressed skull fracture (i.e. a break in the skull detected on a plain x-ray)

Reality Check

Walkers cause over 6000 head injuries in the U.S. annually. Yes, the newer models have more "safety features" that keep them from rolling down stairs. But we say save your money or buy some other really cool toy.

2. Neck and back injuries

CALL 911 and do not try to move your child. He will be immobilized on a straight board until x-rays can prove that no spine damage has occurred.

3. Eye injuries

All eye injuries should be evaluated by a doctor immediately. Here are the most common problems:

- **Corneal abrasion:** surface of the eye is scratched. It heals in a day or two. Frequent tearing is a clue to this diagnosis.
- **Hyphema:** bleeding that occurs beneath the surface of the eye (a doctor sees it with special equipment). If the blood is not removed, vision can be lost. This is fairly uncommon, but it is the reason that all eye injuries need a medical evaluation.
- **Subconjunctival hemorrhage:** bleeding occurs on the surface of the eye. It can be seen on the white part of the eye. Although it looks dramatic, it's not serious.

4. Ear injuries

Outer ear: (the part you can see) can be bruised and cause permanent cartilage damage. If you see bruising, this is a ***Priority 1: Needs immediate evaluation and treatment*** call–the blood might need to be drained.

Inner ear: (the inside) can be injured when curious kids put things in their ears. Usually they don't get anywhere near the eardrum. If you see bleeding, it's likely from scratching the lining of the canal. Doctors need to see these kids, but it can wait until the office opens (***a priority 2 call***). The only emergency is if your child had a head injury and you notice blood draining out of the ear or a bruise behind the outer ear. This is a sign of a skull fracture.

first aid

5. Nose injuries

Priority 1: Needs immediate evaluation and treatment—NOW:

- A nosebleed after a nose injury increases the chances of it being broken.
- A clear drainage or bloody nose after a head injury increases the chances of a skull fracture.
- Inability to breathe through the nose after an injury may mean a severe bruise in the nose (septal hematoma)
- Nose is obviously crooked (displaced nose fracture).

Priority 2: Needs appointment the next day.

- Nose injury without bleeding or obvious fracture.

6. Mouth injuries

See stitches section for details. The bottom line: Very few injuries to the mouth require stitches. They bleed a lot but heal quickly and beautifully. Injuries that go through the inside of the mouth to the outside of the skin, or full thickness through the tongue need to be seen ***(Priority 1: Needs immediate evaluation and treatment–NOW).***

7. Tooth injuries

Injuries to baby teeth rarely need intervention. Worry only if the tooth was "knocked out" and you can't find it anywhere. That is a sign of a tooth intrusion. The tooth can get pushed back into the gums ***(Priority 1: Needs immediate evaluation and treatment–NOW; call the dentist).***

FYI: You may know about the trick of placing a knocked out tooth in milk and rushing to the dentist to re-implant it. They only do this for permanent teeth, not baby teeth.

8. Bone injuries

Q. Is it BROKEN?

The best way to tell over the phone is to know the mechanism of injury and what your child is doing with the limb. The list of red flags is below.

If there is a break (fracture), your child needs a cast. Some specialists prefer to see kids with broken bones 48 hours after the injury so the swelling will be down before casting. As long as the bone is immobilized, it is fine. A temporary (splint) cast can be applied to keep the bone fixed and comfortable.

RED FLAGS

Does it need an x-ray?

All of these are ***Priority 1: Needs immediate evaluation and treatment–NOW:***

1. Unable to move a limb without crying.
2. Limping or refusing to bear weight.
3. Impressive bruising or swelling.

BOTTOM LINE

Broken bones hurt. If you can distract your child and move or touch the area without pain, it may just be bruised.

Helpful hint

Kids have areas in their bones called growth plates. This area is located at the end of each bone that gives it growing room. These plates fuse when children go through puberty (hormone levels cause them to close). A normal x-ray of a child's bone shows a gap where the growth plate is. Occasionally, if there is a fracture along the line of the growth plate, it may not be seen when the x-ray is read. So, even if an x-ray is read as "no fracture," call the doctor if there is no improvement in your child's symptoms in five to seven days.

HOW TO IMMOBILIZE AN INJURED LIMB

- Use a scarf or large towel and wrap it around the shoulder to keep an arm in place. Pinning a long arm sleeve to the shoulder also works.
- Use a piece of cardboard and an Ace wrap to form a makeshift splint for an arm or leg.

Q. My child was walking and put his hand out to break his fall. Is the wrist broken?

Probably. Your wrist joint is not intended to sustain your body weight. Your baby needs an x-ray.

Q. I was walking with my child and holding his hand. He pulled away from me and now he won't use his arm. Is it broken?

No–it's probably dislocated.

This is called a nursemaid's elbow. The elbow joint has gotten pulled out of its socket. Some children are repeat offenders. It can be easily fixed by your doctor in a matter of seconds. For frequent fliers, parents can learn how to do it at home. It's a good idea not to pull your kids up by their arms, or jerk their arms when they resist motion. And obviously, kids with frequent dislocations shouldn't play on the monkey bars!

9. Fingers and toes

The classic injury here is the finger that gets slammed in a car door. If there is bruising or swelling, it needs an x-ray (***Priority 1: Needs immediate evaluation and treatment–NOW***). If there is a blood blister/collection of blood under the fingernail (subungual hematoma), it may need to be lanced by a doctor to relieve the pressure (***Priority 1 or 2***).

The fingers and toes are an exception for casting of broken bones. Some of these breaks only require stabilization (buddy taping) to the finger or toe next to it.

So, how do you immobilize a finger or toe? Tape fingers or toes together (buddy tape) for an injured digit. The neighbor of the injured digit gets taped to it for support.

first aid

RED FLAGS

A recap:

- any true head injury in a child under two years of age
- head injury with loss of consciousness
- head injury with vomiting
- head injury with confusion
- significant height of fall or to a hard surface
- any eye injury
- head injury with nosebleed or ear drainage
- ear injury with bruising
- limb injury with swelling/bruising and discomfort
- fall onto an outstretched arm
- jerked elbow
- neck or spine injury–call 911
- bone injury with exposed bone

BOTTOM LINE

If you are ever in doubt, call your doctor.

Notes

Section 6

The Reference Library

Medications

Appendix A

Here's a look at the most common medications used by children. Obviously, with the huge universe of possible medications, this chapter is by no means comprehensive. Instead, we focus on the most popular and widely used meds in children. We will cover both over the counter products and prescription medications. (*Murphy*) FYI: We have also designated products that are safe for moms who are breastfeeding. Let's begin with some general questions regarding administering medicine to your child.

Q. If my child throws up right after I give him medicine, do I re-dose the medicine or wait until the next dose is due?

If your child throws up less than 20 minutes after administering medicine, give the dose again. It didn't have time to get through the stomach and be absorbed into the blood stream.

Q. Is a generic medication as good as a brand name?

For the most part, yes.

When a pharmaceutical company develops a medication, the company obtains a patent for it, which lasts for 17 years. Because it takes several years of research before a medication is approved for use, a medication may be on the market for an average of eight years before the patent runs out. Once the patent runs out, any pharmaceutical company can make their own product, which is the exact duplicate of the original brand.

The potency is the same, but sometimes the taste is not. And the cost is definitely not the same. Generic medications are often much cheaper than the brand name.

Q. If my doctor prescribes an expensive antibiotic, can I ask for a generic brand at the pharmacy?

Good news. Virtually all the antibiotics used for children are now available in generic form. The only exception is cefixime (Suprax). That antibiotic, which is used primarily for bladder infections, is still only available as a brand name.

Helpful Hint

If you are paying out-of-pocket for prescription medications, speak up! Don't be shy about inquiring about the cost of the medication. Your doctor may have free samples available in the office. Or she will be able to prescribe a less-expensive generic drug if available.

Q. How do I get my baby to take her medicine?

Here are a few tricks to getting all the medicine down:

1. Give small amounts over several minutes, instead of the whole dose at once.
2. It is okay to mix certain medications in with formula or juice—but check with your pharmacist for the particulars. The only problem with this plan is that your child has to drink the whole thing. Be sure to mix the medicine in a small volume of fluid (less than an ounce).
3. For a small fee, some pharmacies will add flavorings to your child's prescription to make it more palatable.
4. Taking a prescription medicine is not optional. It may take two parents to administer medicine to one strong-willed child.

Reality Check

Just a spoonful of sugar makes the medicine go down. Here are some tips from Edward Bell, Pharm.D., BCPS:

1. White grape juice or chocolate syrup masks a medicine's after taste.
2. Graham crackers get rid of the leftover drug particles in the mouth.
3. Strawberry jam mixed with a crushed chewable tablet disguises the flavor.

Q. Is it okay to use a medicine if it is past the expiration date?

No.

For the most part, medications start to lose their potency after the listed expiration date. So the medication may be less effective (for example, Albuterol for an asthma attack).

Q. The prescription medicine was supposed to be given for ten days. We ran out of it after eight days. What happened?

Most of the time, this happens when a "teaspoon" dose is administered with an actual teaspoon from your kitchen. Your silverware spoon may hold anywhere from 4-8 ml of fluid. Buy a medicine syringe that lists both cc/mls and teaspoons on it.

Q. I have some leftover antibiotic from a prescription. Can I save it and use it for another time?

No.

First of all, you should never have leftover antibiotics. Your doctor wanted

your child to have a specific length of therapy for that medication. If your child stops taking an antibiotic "because he feels better," you run the risk of the bacteria growing back. This is particularly true of Group A Strep (of Strep throat fame). Yes, people often forget to give all of the doses of antibiotic–we're human. But try to finish a prescription as it was intended to be used.

Second of all, antibiotics that are in liquid form will only stay potent for about two weeks. They come as a powder from the manufacturer and the pharmacist mixes it with water when he fills the prescription order. If you have any medicine leftover–toss it.

Q. Are all medications administered to children of all ages?

No.

Many medications are not approved for infants under six months of age. Doctors' choices are more limited for these patients. There are also some medications that are purely for adult usage (for example, Tetracycline).

Q. How do I know if there is a problem taking more than one medicine at a time?

The official term is "drug interactions."

Your doctor or pharmacist can answer this question. Don't assume that your doctor knows all the medications your child is taking. If your child received a prescription from another doctor/specialist, it might not be recorded in your child's chart.

Reality Check

Tell your doctor if your child is taking any herbal remedies. There can be overlap in effects of herbal and over-the-counter products. For instance, Sudafed (a traditional decongestant) and ephedra (an herbal decongestant) can cause heart rhythm disturbances when taken together. It pays to ask.

Q. Can you use acetaminophen (Tylenol) and an antibiotic at the same time?

Yes. It is okay to use a fever reducing medication like Tylenol/Motrin and an antibiotic simultaneously.

Q. What does the term "off-label" mean?

It means that a pharmaceutical company has not received FDA (Food and Drug Administration) approval for a medication to be used for a particular problem or age group.

Medications are approved for use based on research studies for particular medical problems. Once a drug is available for use, doctors may find it useful to treat other ailments. In this case, a doctor might prescribe a medicine to a patient and explain that it is being used "off label."

What frequently happens in pediatric medicine is that clinical research studies are done on adults, so a medication is approved for use only in adults. When it appears to be a safe product, the medication is used in pediatric patients as well. Pediatricians feel relatively comfortable using these medications for children, but your doctor should always explain to you if he prescribes a medicine that does not have FDA approval for use in a particular age group. Good news: There is now a law requiring pharmaceutical companies to test medications in kids as part of their research.

Q. How can I find out if a generic equivalent is available for the medicine my doctor has prescribed?

Ask your doctor or pharmacist. For the medication tables below, generic availability is noted with an (*) asterisk. Note: while all medications have a generic name, not all of them are available to be purchased in generic form.

Q. How do I read a doctor's prescription? I've always wondered what they really mean.

It's written in medical abbreviations, so here's how to read it. You'll need this for the medication tables later in this appendix.

How often to take a medicine

QD or QDay: once daily
BID: twice daily
TID: three times daily (preferably every eight hours)
QID: four times daily (preferably every six hours)
QHS: once daily, at bedtime
QOD: every other day
PRN: as needed

How medicine is given

po: taken by mouth
pr: insert in rectum
ou: put into each eye
au: put into each ear

How medicine is dosed

1 cc (cubic centimeter): 1ml (milliliter)
tsp: teaspoon (1 tsp is 5 cc or 5ml)
T: tablespoon (1 T. is 3 tsp or 15cc or 15 ml)
tab: tablet
gtt: drop

Q. How do I know which medications require a prescription?

We've included some handy tables later in this chapter with information on common medicines used for treating babies. In the tables, you'll note the following symbols.

- **Rx**: Denotes that a product is available with a doctor's prescription only. If nothing is designated, assume the product in question is prescription-only.
- **OTC**: Denotes that a product is available Over The Counter (that is, without a prescription).

Q. How do I know if a medication is safe for me to take while I am pregnant or breastfeeding?

Some information is listed in the medication tables later in this appendix. Your obstetrician, pediatrician, pharmacist, and lactation consultant all have reference books in their offices with this information–if you have doubts, call them.

Breastfeeding Categories

Category 1: Okay to use while nursing.
Category 2: Okay, but use with caution.
Category 3: Unknown whether there is a risk.
NO: Definitely harmful to baby.

Pregnancy Categories

Category A: Studies have been done with first-trimester pregnancies and show no risk to fetus.
Category B: Animal studies prove medicine to be safe, but not enough data in humans yet.
Category C: Animal studies prove medicine to be harmful, but no data in humans.
Category D: Known risk to fetus, but benefit of medicine to mother may outweigh the risk.
NO: Known risk to fetus outweighs any benefit to the mother.

Drugs Of Abuse: Not To Be Used While Breastfeeding (And not recommended otherwise)

Amphetamines, Cocaine, Heroin, Marijuana, Nicotine, Phenylcyclidine

Category 3 Medications (Unknown Risk)

Medications in the following classes of drugs have potentially concerning effects on babies who are breastfed.

Antianxiety drugs
Antidepressant drugs
Antipsychotic drugs

Category 2 Medications (Okay, But Use With Caution)

Acyclovir (Zovirax)
Cetirizine (Zyrtec)
Diphenhydramine (Benadryl)
Fluconazole (Diflucan)
Ketorolac (Toradol, Acular)
Omeprazole (Prilosec)
Ondansetron (Zofran)

Category 1 Medications (Okay To Use While Breastfeeding)

Acetaminophen (Tempra, Tylenol)
Albuterol (Proventil, Xopenex)
Alcohol**
Allergy injections
Amoxicillin (Amoxil)
Amoxicillin + Clavulanate (Augmentin)
Cefadroxil (Duricef, Ultracef)
Cefazolin (Ancef, Kefzol)

Cefotaxime (Claforan)
Cefoxitin (Mefoxin)
Cefprozil (Cefzil)
Ceftazidime (Fortaz, Tazidime)
Ceftriaxone (Rocephin)
Cimetidine (Tagamet)
Codeine (Tylenol #3, Empirin #3)**
Contraceptive pills
Dextromethorphan ("DM" products- Delsym, Robitussin DM)
Digoxin (Lanoxin)
Enalapril (Vasotec)
Erythromycin* (E-mycin, Ery-tab)
Hydralazine (Apresoline)
Ibuprofen (Advil, Ibuprofen, Motrin, Nuprin)
Loratadine (Claritin)
Magnesium sulfate
Prednisone (Deltasone, Meticorten, Orasone)
Propranolol (Inderal)
Valproic Acid (Depakote, Depakene)
Verapamil (Calan, Covera-HS)
Warfarin (Coumadin)

**Medication concentrates in breast milk, but is still acceptable to use while nursing.*
***Acceptable in moderation.*

Note: Pseudoephedrine (brand names: Sudafed, Actifed), a popular decongestant, may reduce milk supply by up to 25%. Use this product with caution, especially if milk supply is already low. (Hale T, AAP Committee on Nutrition)
FYI: Because of some safety concerns, teeth whitening products are not recommended while breastfeeding.

Herbal Remedies and breastfeeding

Fenugreek and Blessed Thistle are both considered generally safe to use to improve milk production.

Herbal products that are *unsafe* while nursing include: Comfrey, Blue Cohosh, Sage, and Valerian Root.

Medication Index

1. Allergies
2. Dental/Mouth
   - fluoride
   - teething products
3. Ear Problems
4. Eye Problems
5. Fever and pain
6. Gastrointestinal
   - antacids/gastroesophageal reflux
   - constipation
   - diarrhea
   - gas/colic

- ◆ vomiting
- ◆ rehydration solutions

7. Infections
    - ◆ antibiotics (for bacterial infections)
    - ◆ antifungals (for fungal infections)
    - ◆ antihelminthics (for pinworms)
    - ◆ amebicides (for Giardia infection)
    - ◆ antivirals (for viral infections)
8. Nutrition
    - ◆ iron supplements
    - ◆ vitamins
9. Respiratory
    - ◆ asthma
    - ◆ cough and cold preparations
10. Skin
    - ◆ antibiotic creams
    - ◆ antifungal creams
    - ◆ scabies/ head lice medications
    - ◆ steroids
    - ◆ anti-inflammatory
    - ◆ diaper rash creams

Medications

1. Allergy Medicines

These medications are used for allergic reactions, itching, and nasal congestion. For skin allergy products, see skin section (10).

Antihistamines have been around for decades. They are classified by their "generation." The first generation products are very effective but also have more side effects (drowsiness, dry mouth). Second and third generation products do not cause nearly as much sedation and can be dosed once every 24 hours.

Under six months of age, doctors use all medications with caution. Antihistamines, which are usually sedating, can result in excitability in infants. Consult your doctor before using any of these products.

GENERIC	BRAND	DOSE	RX?	AGE LIMIT	BREAST
Cetirizine	Zyrtec*	QDay	OTC	over 6 months	2
Desloratadine	Clarinex	QDay	Rx	over 6 months	1
Diphenhydramine	Benadryl*	QID	OTC	over 2 years	2
Fexofenadine	Allegra*	BID	OTC	over 2 years	1
Hydroxyzine	Atarax*	QID	Rx	Infants ok	1
Loratadine	Claritin, Alavert*	QDay	OTC	over 2 years	1

KEY: Rx? Rx medications are available by prescription only; OTC is over-the-counter. * A generic is available for this brand-name medicine.

Side effects: Drowsiness, dry mouth, headache, paradoxical excitability
Serious Adverse effects: tremors, convulsions

Feedback from the Real World

You may be tempted to use diphenhydramine (Benadryl) as a sleep aid for your child. A study, appropriately called the TIRED study—Trial of Infant Response to Diphenyhydramine, showed there was no significant improvement in a baby's sleep when used in kids six to 15 months of age. Go back to Chapter 9, Sleep, if you need tips that will actually work!

2. Dental/Mouth

Fluoride Supplements

Fluoride is a mineral well known to prevent cavities. But as we discussed back in Chapter 5, Nutrition and Growth, the recommendations are confusing and a bit of a moving target when it comes to babies and young children.

Infants *under* six months of age should have little to no fluoride intake. Thus, the American Dental Association currently recommends that you prepare powdered or liquid concentrate formula with filtered tap water (reverse osmosis) or bottled water.

Infants *over* six months of age until age 16 years need a source of fluoride to significantly reduce cavities in both primary (baby) and secondary (adult) teeth. Fluoride is added to tap water in many cities and counties in the United States. Find out if your city has added fluoride to its water supply. Ideally, your water supply should have 0.7 ppm of fluoride. Once your baby is six months old, he should start drinking some water on a daily basis (about four to six ounces).

Who needs a fluoride supplement? There are just four specific situations where a fluoride supplement is recommended if baby is over six months of age AND:

1. In a household that has well water, and has no other source of fluoride-containing water.
2. Exclusively breast fed, and does not drink fluoride-containing water.
3. Formula is prepared with bottled water or uses ready-to-feed formula, and does not drink fluoride-containing water.
4. The local water supply does not contain added fluoride, and natural fluoride levels are less than 0.6ppm.

If you fall into one of those categories above, the American Academy of Pediatrics and American Dental Association recommends the following dosages of fluoride (these are based on age and the amount of fluoride in your drinking water):

How much extra fluoride does your baby need?

Age	Amt. of fluoride in community's water supply (in parts per million- ppm) LESS THAN 0.3 PPM	0.3-0.6 PPM	GREATER THAN 0.6 PPM
0-6 months	None	None	None
6 months-3 yrs	0.25 mg	None	None
3-6 years	0.5 mg	0.25mg	None
6-16 years	1 mg	0.5 mg	None

Fluoride supplements include: Luride*, Fluoritab, Pediaflor*, Poly-Vi-Flor*, Tri-Vi-Flor*. These are all available by prescription only and dosed once daily.

Possible side effects: Overuse of fluoride can cause white spots on the teeth (fluorosis). This occurs in daily doses of greater than 2 mg of fluoride /day.

Reality Check

Fluoride containing toothpaste has about 1 mg of fluoride per ribbon. Kids tend to eat toothpaste instead of spitting it out. For this reason, it is suggested NOT to use toothpaste until your child can spit (around age three). It's also a good idea to limit the volume to a pea-sized ration.

Q. Is fluoride safe? I've heard it can cause bone cancer in lab rats.

Yes it is safe. If you give toxic mega-doses of any product to rats, you will create medical problems. So just how much fluoridated water would you have to drink each day to equal the volume that the rats drank? Answer: 42 gallons a day!

Helpful Hint

Give fluoride drops on an empty stomach. Milk prevents the absorption of the medication.

3. *Teething*

The only medication we recommend for teething is acetaminophen (Tylenol), or ibuprofen (Advil) for babies who are at least six months of age or older. They are both safe and effective pain relievers.

The FDA advises *against* using topical numbing products that are rubbed on the gums to provide temporary relief. The active ingredient in all of these products is benzocaine, which can potentially cause a life-threatening blood disorder called methemoglobinemia. The brand names we are talking about are: Baby Anbesol, Baby Numz-it, Baby Oragel, and Zilactin Baby.

The FDA recalled homeopathic "Hyland's Teething Tablets" a few years ago. These tablets contain a small amount of belladonna, which is a known toxin to the nervous system. Because the tablets are homeopathic, they were not required to have FDA approval for safety or therapeutic benefit. (This is a convenient loophole in the lucrative alternative medicine industry. More on that in Appendix B, Alternative Medications).

The FDA stepped in because they received reports of children having adverse reactions (adverse reactions include seizures, difficulty breathing, lethargy, excessive sleepiness, muscle weakness, skin flushing, constipation, difficulty urinating, or agitation). Additionally, the FDA laboratory found the product to have inconsistent amounts of belladonna in it. Safety regulators felt that the amount of belladonna should be more tightly regulated—considering the health dangers it can pose.

Although the product is back on the market, we still don't recommend them.

Reality Check

Teething gets blamed on fussy moods, disrupted sleep, runny noses, and diarrhea. RARELY is teething the cause of any of these maladies! If you want a natural teething remedy, try freezing a mini bagel or banana, and let your little one gnaw on that!

4. Ear Medication

Antibiotic Ear Drops

For swimmer's ear (otitis externa) or for children who have ear infections with PE tubes, antibiotic eardrops are used. Because the medicine is not absorbed into the bloodstream, there are more antibiotic family choices. Below are the most popular antibiotic eardrops. Note: most products also contain a steroid. The steroid reduces the inflammation and swelling of the ear canal so the antibiotic can work more effectively.

GENERIC	BRAND	DOSE	RX
Acetic Acid*		QID	yes
Acetic Acid + Hydrocortisone	Vosol-HC*	QID	yes
Chloroxylenol +Pramoxine + Hydrocortisone	Oto-End*	QID	yes
Ciprofloxacin + Dexamethasone	Ciprodex	BID	yes
Ciprofloxacin + Hydrocortisone	Cipro HC	BID	yes
Ofloxin	Floxin Otic*	BID	yes
Polymyxin B + Neomycin + + steroid	Cortisporin* Pediotic	TID	yes

KEY: Rx? Rx medications are available by prescription only; OTC is over-the-counter.
* A generic is available for this brand-name medicine.

Side Effects: Irritation of the ear canal such as itching and stinging.

Swimmer's Ear Prevention Drops

These drops dry up any left over water in the ear canal after swimming. Drops are placed in the ears immediately after swimming. These are used primarily for older kids, not infants.

You can make your own concoction: 2 drops of rubbing alcohol and 2 drops of vinegar per ear.

Brand names: Auro-Dri, Swim Ear. Both products are OTC. Active ingredient: Rubbing Alcohol.

Ear Pain Drops

These are topical numbing medications. They have a modest effect in providing temporary relief of pain in the ear canal. (Remember that middle ear infections occur behind the eardrum.)

Numbing drops are absolutely not intended for use if a child has PE tubes (see Chapter 11, Infections, for more details) or has ruptured the eardrum with infection.

Brand names are: Avrodex. Active ingredient: Antipyrine, Benzocaine *Dosing: 2-3 drops to affected ear, QID Rx only.*

DR B'S OPINION

"Yes, some doctors will prescribe numbing drops for ear pain. Know that these drops do not reach the real location of the pain (which is why many ear, nose, and throat specialists don't find these drops very helpful). I think acetaminophen (Tylenol) or ibuprofen (Motrin) and a heating pad (low setting) placed on the ear are more effective pain relief."

Reality Check

Although we don't find them helpful, some doctors will prescribe numbing drops for pain relief. But do NOT use the drops prior to your doctor's appointment. It makes it hard for the doctor to see the eardrum!

Ear Wax Drops

These drops help loosen or dissolve earwax. Earwax rarely is a problem unless it is hard and stuck in the canal (impacted). If the earwax is impacted, earwax drops loosen up and break down the earwax.

Brand names are: Auro, Debrox, and Murine eardrops. OTC Active ingredient: carbamide peroxide *Dosing: 3 drops per ear, TID, for 3 days*

Colace, a stool softener, also works nicely to soften up earwax. It's available OTC.

BOTTOM LINE

We don't recommend routine cleaning with Q-tips. Q-tips can irritate the ear canal and push the earwax backwards, creating wax that is hard and stuck (impacted).

Helpful Hints

◆ Rub the eardrop bottle in your hands for a minute or two before administering the drops. Warm drops in the ear are less bothersome than cold ones.

◆ If a child has a perforated eardrum or PE tubes, many types of eardrops should NOT be used (exception: approved antibiotic drops). Check with your doctor.

Reality Check

ENT specialists frequently use antibiotic eye drops for the ears. If you get a prescription filled for your child's ear infection and it turns out to be eye drops, don't think we have lost our minds. One caveat here: It's okay to use *eye drops* for the ears, but you cannot use eardrops for the eyes!

medications

5. Eye Problems

Antibiotic Eye Drops/Ointment

These are used primarily for conjunctivitis (pink eye) and corneal abrasions.

GENERIC	FAMILY	BRAND	DOSE	RX ONLY?
Azithromycin	Erythromycin	Azasite	Qday	yes
Besifloxacin	Quinolone	Besivance	TID	yes
Ciprofloxacin	Quinolone	Ciloxan*	BID/QID	yes
Erythromycin	Erythromycin	(many)*	BID/QID	yes
Gatifloxacin	Quinolone	Zymaxid	QID	yes
Gentamicin	Aminoglycoside	(many)*	QID	yes
Levofloxacin	Quinolone	Quixin	QID	yes
Moxifloxacin	Quinolone	Moxeza, Vigamox	BID	yes
Ofloxin	Quinolone	Ocuflox*	BID/QID	yes
Tobramycin	Aminoglycoside	Tobrex* Tobradex*	QID	yes

KEY: Rx? Rx medications are available by prescription only; OTC is over-the-counter. * A generic is available for this brand-name medicine.
Note: Although the quinolone based products are not FDA approved for under one year of age, your doctor may feel comfortable prescribing them.

Side effects: Burning, itching, local irritation

6. Fever And Pain Medications

Please keep in mind the following points about fever medication:

1. If your baby is less than four weeks old and has a fever, do NOT give a fever reducing medicine–call your doctor immediately.
2. Never give aspirin to a child unless directed by a doctor. Aspirin use is associated with Reye's syndrome (liver failure) when taken during an influenza or chickenpox infection.
3. Ibuprofen is not recommended for babies under six months of age.
4. Tylenol is the brand name. The generic name is acetaminophen (other brand names include Tempra, Feverall)

DR B'S OPINION: ALTERNATING FEVER MEDS

Unless your child is prone to febrile seizures, I do not recommend alternating fever medications during the day to keep the body temperature down. I also prefer to use acetaminophen (Tylenol) for children who are dehydrated or not eating. Ibuprofen is more likely to cause stomach upset when taken on an empty stomach.

5. Ibuprofen: brand names are Motrin, Advil
6. Do not use more than one fever reducing medicine at a time, unless your doctor specifically recommends it.
7. REMEMBER TO USE THE DROPPER THAT COMES WITH THE PACKAGE OF MEDICINE. See Chapter 15, First Aid, for details on fever and when to administer medication (as well as a dosing chart).

7. Gastrointestinal Problems

Antacids/Gastroesophageal Reflux

GENERIC	BRAND	DOSE	RX?	AGE LIMIT	BREAST
Aluminum Hydroxide	Gaviscon	QID	OTC	usually not recommended	
Calcium Carbonate Supreme	Mylanta	TID/QID	OTC	ask Dr.	
Esomeprazole	Nexium	QDay	Rx	over 1 yr of age	2
Famotidine	Pepcid*	BID	Rx	over 1 yr of age	1
	(The tablet version is OTC)				
Lansoprazole	Prevacid*	QDay	Rx	over 1 yr	3
	(The capsule version is OTC)				
Metoclopramide	Reglan*	QID	Rx	severe cases only	2
Nizatidine	Axid*	BID	Rx	over 12 yr 2	
Omeprazole	Prilosec*	QD/BID	Rx	over 2 yr	2
Omeprazole+ Sodium bicarbonate	Zegerid	QD	Rx	over 18 yr	
Ranitidine	Zantac*	BID/QID	Rx	over 1 mo.	1

KEY: Rx? Rx medications are available by prescription only; OTC is over-the-counter.
* A generic is available for this brand-name medicine.

Note: Of all the reflux medications, only Zantac is FDA approved for infants. Before 2004, pharmaceutical companies had no requirements to test products on infants. Despite the lack of FDA approval, gastroenterologists and pediatricians prescribe these medicines routinely.

Side effects:

◆ Aluminum hydroxide is generally *not* recommended for use in babies due to possible side effects.

◆ Most common side effects are headache, constipation, or diarrhea.

◆ Metoclopramide (Reglan) can cause rare but significant neurological problems, sedation, headaches, and diarrhea. Because of these adverse effects, Reglan is only used in very sick babies.

Helpful Hints

◆ It is more effective to give these medications 30 minutes before a meal if you can.

◆ Zantac is the cheapest choice, readily available at most pharmacies, with the longest track record. However, it tastes like mouthwash. If

your baby spits out the Zantac because it tastes bad, it won't work.

- Prilosec liquid has to be specially compounded at a pharmacy. It will become inactive within about two weeks. You will need to refill it frequently.
- Prevacid solutabs are a popular option because they can be cut into halves or quarters for smaller kids and suspended in a few drops of water. Once a day dosing is also convenient.
- Zegerid is a popular choice among pediatric gastroenterologists because the combination product seems to improve symptoms when nothing else has worked.
- Medications in the "proton pump inhibitor" family such as Prilosec, Prevacid, and Zegerid carry an FDA warning. There is an uncommon, but potential risk of developing a diarrheal illness caused by C. difficile infection.
- As with other medications, dosing is based on a child's weight. Your baby may outgrow his therapeutic dose every few weeks/months. Ask your doctor to recalculate his dose based on his current weight.

Often times, medication isn't working because babies metabolize it at different rates at different ages. If your baby is not responding to medication and clearly has the diagnosis of acid reflux, ask your doctor to decide if your baby's medication should be adjusted.

Constipation

GENERIC	BRAND NAME	DOSE	RX?	AGE LIMIT	BREAST
Docusate	Colace	QD/QID	OTC	over 1 year	2
Glycerin	(suppository)	1 dose	OTC	None	
Guar gum	Benefiber	QD	OTC	over 6 mos	
Lactulose	Duphalac, Chronulac*	QD	Rx	Ask Dr.	
Malt soup	Maltsupex	BID	OTC	over 1 month	
Mineral oil	Kondremul	QD/ TID	OTC	over 5 years	
Polyethylene glycol	Miralax*	QD	OTC	Ask Dr.	3
Senna	Senokot	QD	OTC	over 1 mo	1

Side effects: diarrhea, bloating, gas, body salt (electrolyte) disturbances with excessive or prolonged use.

Diarrhea

GENERIC	BRAND NAME	DOSE	RX?	AGE LIMIT	BREAST
Lactobacillus	Lactinex,* Culturelle*	QD	OTC	Ask Dr.	

KEY: Rx? Rx medications are available by prescription only; OTC is over-the-counter. *A generic is available for this brand-name medicine.

Helpful Hint

Fat and fiber intake both help bulk up the stools.

BOTTOM LINE

If diarrhea has been going on more than a week, check in with your doctor. Doctors also want to know about blood or mucous in the stools. (See Chapter 15, First Aid for more).

Gas/Colic

GENERIC	BRAND NAME	DOSE	RX?	AGE LIMIT
Ginger-Fennel	Gripe Water	QID	OTC	None
Lactobacillus	L. reuteri, Culturelle	QD	OTC	None
Simethicone	Mylicon, Phazyme* Little Tummys	up to 12x day	OTC	None

Reality Check

Remember, there is no miracle cure for either gas or colic. These products are okay to try, but they may not work.

Vomiting

GENERIC	BRAND	DOSE	RX?	AGE LIMIT	BREAST
Dimenhydrinate	Dramamine*	QID	OTC	over 2 yrs	2
Diphenhydramine	Benadryl*	QID	OTC	over 2 yrs	2
Ondansetron	Zofran*	TID	Rx	over 1 mo	2
Phosphorated-Carbohydrate	Emetrol*	QID	OTC	Ask Dr.	
Promethazine	Phenergan*	QID	Rx	over 2 yrs	2

KEY: Rx? Rx medications are available by prescription, OTC is over-the-counter.
* A generic is available for this brand-name medicine.

Helpful Hints

◆ Home remedy: The equivalent of Emetrol is to give 1-2 teaspoons of heavy fruit syrup (fruit cocktail juice) every 20-30 minutes. This occasionally works to relieve nausea.

◆ Phenergan has a black box warning from the FDA discouraging its use in kids under age two.

◆ Zofran is very popular for babies and kids under age two.

Rehydration Solutions

These products are the Gatorade equivalent for babies. They are designed to replace water, body salts, and sugar lost when a child has vomiting and diarrhea. They are most helpful in the early phase of a stomach virus when a child is just starting to take fluids after actively vomiting. Doctors prefer rehydration solutions instead of plain water, juice, milk, Gatorade/sports drinks, or soda for infants. Once a child is keeping down this clear fluid, we usually suggest that your child resume breastfeeding or formula. All products are available over the counter. See Chapter 15, First Aid, for more information on using this product. See Appendix B, Alternative Medicine, for a recipe you can make at home.

Brand Names: Enfalyte, Gerber Pediatric Electrolyte, Kao-electrolyte, Pedialyte.

8. Infections

Antibiotics (Bacterial infections)

This list contains the most popular choices of antibiotics (taken by mouth). There are basically four classes of medications approved for pediatric use. There are more classes available to adults. Take special note of the class or family each medicine belongs to. If a person develops an allergic reaction to a medication, ANY antibiotic that belongs to that class is to be avoided.

In this chart, we note what these medications are typically used for (usage): Ear and sinus infections (1), Pneumonia (2), Skin infections (3), Bladder infections-UTI (4), Strep throat (5).

Note: all products are available by prescription only.

GENERIC NAME	BRAND NAME	FORM	DOSE	USAGE	PREG/BREAST
PENICILLIN FAMILY					
Amoxicillin	Amoxil, Polymox, Trimox, Wymox*	Liq/Chew	BID	1,2,4,5	B, 1
Amoxicillin+ Clavulanate	Augmentin* Augmentin ES-600*	Liq/Chew	BID	1,2,3,4,5	B, 1
(Clavulanate kills resistant bacteria strains)					
Penicillin V-K	Pen VeeK, V-cillinK*	Liquid	BID-QID	5	B, 1
CEPHALOSPORINS					
Cefaclor	Ceclor*	Liquid	BID	1,2,5	B, 2
Cefadroxil	Duricef*	Liquid	BID	3, 5	B, 1
Cefdinir	Omnicef*	Liquid	QD/BID	1,2,3,5	B, 1
Cefixime	Suprax	Liquid	Qday	1,3,4	B, 2
Cefpodoxime	Vantin*	Liquid	QD/BID	1,2	B, 1
Cefprozil	Cefzil*	Liquid	BID	1,2,3,4,5	B, 1
Ceftibuten	Cedax	Liquid	QDay	1,2,5	B, 1
Ceftriaxone	Rocephin*	injection	QDay	1,2,3,4,5	B, 1
Cefuroxime	Ceftin*	Liquid	BID	1,2,3,5	B, 1
Cephalexin	Keflex*	Liquid	TID/QID	3,5	B, 1
MACROLIDES					
Azithromycin	Zithromax*	Liquid	QD	1,2,3,5	B, 2
Clarithromycin	Biaxin*	Liquid	BID	1,2,3,5	C, 2
Erythromycin	E.E.S., Eryped*	Liq/chew	BID/QID	2,3,5	B, 1
Erythromycin + Sulfisoxazole	Pediazole*	Liquid	TID	1,2	C, 1
SULFONAMIDES (SULFA)					
Sulfisoxazole	Gantrisin	Liquid	QD	1,4	B/D, 2
		Used as preventative therapy only			
Sulfamethoxazole + Trimethoprim	Bactrim, Septra* Sulfatrim, TMP-SMX	Liquid	BID	1,2,4	C, 3

KEY: Rx? Rx medications are available by prescription only; OTC is over-the-counter.
* A generic is available for this brand-name medicine.

Side Effects:
The most common side effects include:

1. *Diarrhea.* The antibiotic kills the bacteria causing infection, but also some normal bacterial "flora" that helps us digest food in our intestines. Lack of bacterial flora can cause malabsorption (i.e. upset stomach). ANY antibiotic can cause this problem.
2. *Yeast Infections.* Again, the antibiotic kills both bad bacteria and certain bacterial flora that live in our mouths and on our skin. Lack of normal bacteria predisposes a person to yeast infections in the mouth (thrush) and in the genital area (yeast diaper rash).

Allergic Reactions:
A true allergic reaction to these medications includes hives, lip swelling, or difficulty breathing. About 25% of patients who are allergic to the Penicillin family will also be allergic to the Cephalosporin family.

Rare Adverse Reactions:
1. Stevens-Johnson syndrome (severe allergic reaction)
2. C. difficile colitis (bacterial super-infection in intestines)

Antifungals:

GENERIC	BRAND	DOSE	USAGE	AGE LIMIT	RX	BREAST
Fluconazole	Diflucan*	QD x 2 wks	Thrush	None	RX	1
Griseofulvin*	Fulvicin Grifulvin Grisactin	QD x 1month	Scalp Ringworm	None	RX	2

Side effects: nausea, headache, rash, stomach upset
Griseofulvin can cause skin sensitivity to sunlight. Used with caution in patients with Penicillin allergy.

Helpful Hint
Griseofulvin is absorbed better when taken with something rich in fat (milk, ice cream...)

Antihelminthics (For Pinworm Infections):

GENERIC	BRAND	DOSE	AGE LIMIT	RX	BREAST
Albendazole	Albenza	2 doses, 2 weeks apart	over 1 mo	RX	
Mebendazole	Vermox*	2 doses, 2 weeks apart	over 2 years	RX	1
Pyrantel	Pin-X	2 doses, 2 weeks apart	over 2 years	OTC	3

Side effects: stomach upset, headache
KEY: Rx? Rx medications are available by prescription only; OTC is over-the-counter.
* A generic is available for this brand-name medicine.

Reality Check

Often the whole family gets treated when one child has pin-worms.

Amebicides (For Giardia Infection):

GENERIC	BRAND	AGE LIMIT	RX	BREAST
Albendazole	Albenza	1 mo	RX	
Metronidazole	Flagyl*	None	RX	3
Nitazoxanide	Alinia	Over 1 yr	RX	

Side effects: nausea, diarrhea, hives, metallic taste, dizziness

Antivirals:

GENERIC	BRAND	DOSE	USED FOR	AGE LIMIT	RX	BREAST
Acyclovir	Zovirax*	4-5x daily	Varicella Oral herpes, Zoster	None	RX	1
Amantadine*		BID	Influenza A	over 1year	RX	1
Oseltamivir	Tamiflu	BID	Influenza	over 1 year	RX	3
Rimantadine*		BID	Influenza A	over 1 year	RX	3

Side effects: stomach upset, insomnia, headache. Case reports of children acting strangely while taking Tamiflu currently are being investigated. *Adverse reactions:* kidney failure with acyclovir—patient needs to be well hydrated

KEY: Rx? Rx medications are available by prescription only; OTC is over-the-counter.
* A generic is available for this brand-name medicine.

BOTTOM LINE

Because antiviral medications work by preventing replication of the virus, the medication must be started within 48 hours of when the illness began. Otherwise, it will have no effect on the course of the illness.

9. Nutrition

Vitamin supplements for children aged birth to one are used for specific situations. These include Vitamin D for newborns who drink less than 32 oz a day of formula and exclusively breastfed infants, and iron for children with iron-deficiency anemia. A multivitamin for general well being of infants is not routinely prescribed.

Vitamins

Vitamin D supplements:

BRAND NAME	INGREDIENTS	DOSE	RX?
Tri-Vi-Sol	Vitamins A, D, C	1 ml/day	OTC
Vi-Daylin	Vitamins A, D, C	1 ml/day	OTC
D-Vi-Sol	Vitamin D	1 ml/day	OTC

**Other products containing Vitamin D are multivitamins and you should consult your doctor before purchasing.*

Iron Supplements:

Iron is a necessary ingredient to carry oxygen on red blood cells. Babies are born with a stockpile of iron from their mothers. However, by six months of age, they need to consume iron in their diets to meet their daily needs (11mg/day for ages six to 12 months). Some babies need an iron supplement in addition to their food intake (see Chapter 5, Nutrition & Growth, for details of iron containing foods).

Multivitamins often contain iron (see chart above). The dose of iron in multivitamins made for infants is 9-10 mg of iron per daily dose. This meets the daily nutritional needs of a six to 12 month old. If a child has iron deficiency anemia, he needs daily nutritional iron requirements PLUS an additional amount to fill back up his depleted iron stores. The only way to get the higher dose of iron is to use the specific products listed below.

Iron Replacement Therapy

Brand Names: Fer-In-Sol*, Feosol*, Icar, Niferex
Dose: Comes in drops 15mg iron per 1 ml. Dose is based on weight. Your doctor will calculate it for you. There are also syrups for older kids, which can be confusing!
Rx: These drugs are OTC, but are behind your pharmacist's counter so they can help you select the appropriate product.
Side effects: constipation, black looking poop, nausea, stomachache, temporary teeth staining

Helpful Hints

◆ You can avoid staining the teeth by shooting the medicine in the back of the throat. If the teeth do become stained, use baking soda on a toothbrush to remove the stains.

◆ Vitamin C improves the absorption of iron. Calcium interferes with the absorption of iron. So if you are offering a drink with the iron medicine, offer juice—not milk.

◆ If you give the iron AFTER a meal, there is less stomach upset.

10. Respiratory Problems

Asthma

Asthma medications are divided into rescue medications and preventative/long term control medications. The rescue medicines are used as needed (with a certain interval between doses). A child is placed on preventative medicine if he:

1. needs rescue medicine more than twice a week
2. has his activity affected by asthma flare-ups
3. has problems at night more than twice a month

The idea is to get the asthma under control, then cut back on the amount of medications needed to minimize flare ups.

For information on asthma and home nebulizers, see the common diseases chapter.

Rescue medicines

GENERIC	BRAND	DOSE	RX	BREAST
Albuterol	Proventil, Ventolin	Syrup TID	Rx	1
	Accuneb* Nebulizer	Q4 hrs		
	Inhaler	Q4 hrs		
Levalbuterol	Xopenex	Nebulizer solution TID	Rx	2

This class of medication is called a Beta agonist. There can be effects on the body similar to caffeine. More side effects are seen with the dose given orally (syrup) than with the doses that are inhaled (nebulizer machine, inhaler). Levalbuterol is a newer product that seems to have fewer side effects than the older albuterol product.

Side effects: Increased heart rate, palpitations, nervousness, insomnia, nausea, headache.

Preventative/Long term control medicines

GENERIC	BRAND	DOSE	RX	AGE LIMIT	BREAST
Mast cell stabilizer					
Cromolyn	Intal*	Nebulizer TID	Rx	None	1
Inhaled corticosteroid					
Budesonide	Pulmicort*	Nebulizer BID	Rx	over 1yr/ask Dr.	2
Leukotriene antagonist					
Montelukast	Singulair*	Chew tab QHS Granule packets	Rx	over 1 yr	3

KEY: Rx–Rx medications are available by prescription only; OTC is over-the-counter.
* A generic is available for this brand-name medicine.

Side effects:

1. Mast cell stabilizer: bad taste, cough, nasal congestion, wheezing.
2. Inhaled corticosteroid: sore throat, nosebleeds, cough, thrush (see below for more information).
3. Leukotriene antagonist: stomach upset, headache, dizziness.

Helpful Hint

◆ Pulmicort respules (a grainy substance dissolved in liquid) can be administered in a nebulizer machine. Pulmicort is very effective for younger children and has significantly fewer side effects than its oral counterpart. Many doctors feel comfortable using this product in infants even though the product is approved for ages one year and up.

◆ Always rinse your child's mouth after he has taken an inhaled steroid. It reduces the incidence of thrush.

◆ Steroid medications are always used cautiously. Steroids given by mouth (liquid/pill) are more likely to cause systemic side effects if given for a long time (more than one to two weeks). Inhaled steroids (nebulizer or inhaler) have significantly fewer side effects because only a small amount is absorbed into the bloodstream. As with any medication, the risks of taking these medications are weighed against the potential benefit of therapy for the disease.

Risks of long-term steroid use:

1. Mood change
2. Stomach upset
3. Intestinal bleeding
4. Impaired body's stress responses (HPA axis suppression: hypothalamic-pituitary-adrenal)
5. Bone demineralization (Osteopenia)
6. Weight gain, hair growth (Cushingoid features)
7. Cataracts
8. Growth suppression. Numerous studies show that children who have to take inhaled steroids on a daily basis are about 1cm shorter than their peers. However, children with chronic problems with asthma also have poor growth. Studies have not concluded whether or not these children have "catch up growth" when steroids are discontinued. (*Shared*)

MAKE THE CALL: ASTHMA CONCERNS

If your child needs his rescue medicine more frequently than it has been prescribed, CALL YOUR DOCTOR. Here are some important points to consider:

1. Your child is air hungry and needs to be evaluated by a doctor See Chapter 15, First Aid.
2. Administering asthma medicine more frequently than recommended can be dangerous. A doctor's office or hospital can administer asthma medicine more often than prescribed because a medical provider can be monitoring a patient for side effects of the medicine.
3. If a child is having that much trouble breathing, it is likely that he needs to receive oxygen in addition to medication, which is only available in a medical facility.

Preventing RSV infection in premature babies

If you have a baby who has graduated from a Neonatal Intensive Care Unit, you may already know that RSV (bronchiolitis) can be a serious lung infection for a premature infant.

A product to prevent RSV infection is called Synagis (generic name is palivizumab). This is a synthetic antibody given by a monthly injection during the peak of RSV season (November to April). The antibody provides immunity for a period of 30 days.

Children who are at risk for more severe cases of RSV are:

1. Babies born prematurely, prior to 32 weeks gestation.
2. Babies born 32 to under 35 weeks who are under three months old during RSV season.
3. Children with chronic lung disease under age two years.
4. Children with congenital heart disease.
5. Children with certain immune deficiencies.
6. Weight under ten pounds.
7. Children of lower socioeconomic status.
8. Males.

Children who are more likely to get RSV infection include:

1. Babies under age six months when RSV season begins.
2. Babies in daycare.
3. Multiple births.
4. Babies with school age siblings.
5. Babies exposed to smoking.

The American Academy of Pediatrics recommends monthly Synagis injections during RSV season for the following babies:

1. Children under age two years with chronic lung disease (requiring treatment within six months of RSV season)
2. Babies born at or less than 28 weeks gestation and at or less than one year of age at the start of RSV season.
3. Babies born at 29-32 weeks gestation and at or less than six months of age at the start of RSV season.
4. Babies born 32 to under 35 weeks gestation, less than three months of age at the start of RSVseason, AND attends daycare or has a sibling under five years old.
5. Babies under two years of age with severe types of congenital heart disease.

Cough And Cold Medicines

The Food and Drug Administration has banned the sale of all over-the-counter cough and cold remedies for children under four years of age. Yes, there are still "children's" cough and cold products on the market, but they all now warn "do not use in children under four years of age."

Bottom line: please do NOT buy these products and then guess-timate what dose to give to your baby. There is a reason these products are not made for young children anymore. They were never very effective in doing what they claimed to do, and the risk of adverse side effects is greater than for older kids and adults.

The following discussion of these products is mostly for nursing moms . . . and for the outside chance that your baby's doctor gives you a prescription product with one of these ingredients.

Decongestant

These medications reduce or relieve congestion in the nose. They can be taken by mouth (absorbed into bloodstream) or sprayed into the nose. Oral decongestants: Pseudoephedrine, phenylephrine, ephedrine.
Side effects: Insomnia, restlessness, dizziness, high blood pressure, heart rhythm disturbances.

Nasal spray: Oxymetazoline (Afrin), Phenylephrine (Neosynephrine)
Side effects: stinging, burning, nosebleed, rebound nasal congestion with prolonged use (more than 4 days)

Nasal spray: Saline. This is a safe and effective product for all ages, starting at birth.
Side effects: None! Saline is salt water. It is effective in loosening mucus and can be used as often as needed.

Pseudoephedrine, another popular decongestant, has been replaced by phenylephrine in many over the counter and prescription products. The reason? Methamphetamine (Meth) labs use pseudoephedrine to produce illegal drugs. Federal legislation in 2006 requires products containing pseudoephedrine to be purchased from behind the pharmacy counter (not "over-the-counter"), thus limiting supplies. Pharmaceutical companies responded by just changing their formulations, to improve access to their products and their bottom line.

Antihistamine

These medications combat the effect of histamine in the body. Histamine is released as an allergy response and causes nasal congestion. Antihistamines are frequently found in cough and cold medicines because they are sedating, improve the cough suppressant effect, and dry up a runny nose.

Common ingredients: brompheniramine, chlorpheniramine, diphenhydramine, (promethazine– Rx only), carbinoxamine

Side effects: sedation, dry mouth, blurred vision, stomach upset, paradoxical excitement in infants

Expectorant

These medications make thick mucous looser. By doing this, the mucous in the bronchial tubes (lungs) can be coughed up more easily. These medications do not suppress the cough.

Common ingredients: guaifenesin
Side effects: sedation, stomach upset, headache

Cough Suppressant

These medications reduce the brain's "cough center" activity. These products are not recommended when someone has pneumonia.

Common ingredients: Dextromethorphan, codeine (Rx only), carbetapentane

Side effects: drug interactions with psychiatric medications.

Helpful Hints

A study published in the journal, Pediatrics, looked at 100 children who took over-the-counter cough medicines and whether they slept better or not. The verdict: nobody slept better (child or parent). Since kids do about the same with or without cough medicine, don't feel like you are missing out because infant cough and cold remedies are off the market.

The decision to take infant cough and cold remedies off the market came after three deaths of infants under six months of age who had about 14 times the recommended dose of pseudoephedrine decongestant in their bloodstream. We'll say it again: over-the-counter cough and cold meds should NOT be given to kids under age four, unless instructed by your doctor.

Cold Medicines For Breastfeeding Moms

Cold medicines and breastfeeding: Decongestant nose sprays (like Afrin) are usually okay for a day or two as are antihistamines. Some cough medicines are NOT okay. Pseudoephedrine, a popular decongestant, may reduce milk supply by 25%.

11. Skin (Dermatologic) Products

1. Antibiotic creams are used for wound care and minor bacterial infections (impetigo, mild cellulitis).
2. Antifungal creams are used for fungus infections (ringworm, yeast infection, jock itch, athlete's foot) on the skin.
3. Scabicides and pediculocides are used for scabies and head lice.
4. Steroids are used for contact irritations (bug bites, poison ivy, local allergic reactions), seborrhea, cradle cap, and eczema. Steroids are divided into classes by their potency. Doctors always try to use the lowest potency if possible. The higher the potency, the more the risk of side effects (the high potency products can get absorbed into the bloodstream).
5. Anti-inflammatories are FDA approved for kids over age 2 with eczema.
6. Diaper rash creams form a barrier between the irritated skin and recurrent insults caused by pee and poop.

Antibiotic Cream

GENERIC	BRAND	RX
Bacitracin, Polymyxin B	Polysporin*	OTC
Used for minor cuts, scrapes, irritations		
Mupirocin	Bactroban*, Centany	Rx
Used for impetigo and cellulitis		
Neomycin,Polymixin, Bacitracin	Neosporin*	OTC
Used for minor cuts, scrapes, irritations, and superficial burns		
Retapamulin	Altabax	Rx
Used for impetigo and cellulitis.		
Silver Sulfadiazine	Silvadene*	Rx
Antibiotic salve used for second-degree burns		

Side effects: Burning, stinging, itching.

Antifungal Cream

Uses:
1. Yeast diaper rash (monilial dermatitis)
2. Ringworm of skin (tinea corporis)
3. Athlete's foot (tinea pedis)
4. Jock itch (tinea cruris)

GENERIC	BRAND	USED FOR	AGE LIMIT	RX
Clotrimazole 1%	Lotrimin AF*	1, 2, 3, 4	None	OTC
Ketoconazole 2%	Nizoral*	1,2,3,4	Over 2 yrs	Rx
Miconazole	Vusion*	1	Over 4 wks old	Rx
	Micatin*	1,2,3,4	None	OTC
	Triple Paste AF	1,2,3,4	None	OTC
Nystatin	Mycostatin, Nilstat*	1	None	Rx
Econazole	Spectazole*	1,2,3,4	None	Rx

KEY: Rx–Rx medications are available by prescription only; OTC is over-the-counter. * A generic is available for this brand-name medicine.

Reality Check

Ringworm of the scalp (called tinea capitis) requires an antifungal medication by mouth for four to eight weeks. The fungus gets imbedded in the hair follicles and will not respond to an antifungal cream.

Scabicides And Pediculocides

GENERIC	BRAND	USED FOR	AGE LIMIT	RX
Acetic acid	Klout	Head lice	None	OTC
Benzyl Alcohol	Ulesfia	Head lice	Over 6 mos	RX
Crotamiton	Eurax	Scabies	None	RX
Ivermectin	Sklice	Head lice	Over 6 mos	RX
Lindane1%**	Lindane	Head lice, scabies	Over 1 yr	RX
Malathion	Ovide	Head lice	Over 6 yrs	RX
Permethrin 1%	NIX*	Head lice	None	OTC
Permethrin 5%	Elimite*, Acticin	Head lice scabies	None	RX
Pyrethrum***	A-200* Pyrinyl* RID, Pronto*	Head Lice	None	OTC
Spinosad	Natroba	Head lice	Over 6 mos	RX

* A generic is available for this brand-name medicine.
**Medication has significant side effects/potential for seizures. Other medications are better alternatives.
***Medication is derived from the chrysanthemum flower. Avoid use with a ragweed allergy.

Side effects: burning, itching, redness, rash

Helpful Hints for Head Lice

1. Use OTC products as directed. I know you are grossed out, but don't overdose the medicine.
2. Don't use more than one medicine at a time.
3. Use the nit combs every three days.
4. Wash clothing and bed linens in hot water and dry on the hot cycle.
5. Soak combs and hairbrushes in rubbing alcohol for one hour.
6. See Appendix B, Alternative Medications, for other possible remedies.

Reality Check

◆ When head lice enters your home, treat any family member who has an itchy scalp.

◆ When scabies enters your home, treat *all* family members, regardless of whether they have symptoms or not.

Steroids

◆ Low potency: can be used for longer periods (months) of time without side effects, okay to use on the face

◆ Mid potency: okay to use for short periods (weeks) of time without side effects, use with doctor's recommendation on the face

◆ High potency: okay to use for limited period (days) of time without side effects, do not use on the face

Note: None of these steroid creams are FDA approved for use under age two years. But they are used routinely by medical providers who feel that they are safe and efficacious.

GENERIC	BRAND	POTENCY	DOSE	RX/OTC
Hydrocortisone 0.5%	Cortaid, etc*	Low	BID	OTC
Hydrocortisone 1%	Cortaid, etc*	Low	BID	OTC
Hydrocortisone 2.5%	Hytone*	Low	BID	Rx
Triamcinolone 0.025%	Aristocort, Kenalog*	Low	BID	Rx
Desonide 0.05%	Desowen*	Mid	BID	Rx
Hydrocortisone valerate	Westcort*	Mid	BID	Rx
Hydrocortisone butyrate	Locoid*	Mid	BID	Rx
Mometosone furoate	Elocon*	Mid	QD	Rx
Triamcinolone 0.1%	Aristocort, Kenalog*	Mid	BID	Rx
Betamethasone	Diprolene*	High	BID	Rx
Diflorasone diacetate	Psorcon*	High	BID	Rx
Fluocinonide	Lidex*	High	BID	Rx
Triamcinolone 0.5%	Aristocort, Kenalog*	High	BID	Rx

KEY: Rx? Rx medications are available by prescription only; OTC is over-the-counter. * A generic is available for this brand-name medicine.

Side effects: skin irritation, decreased pigmentation, thinning of skin
Rare adverse reactions:
HPA axis (adrenal gland suppression)–only with high potency steroids

Emollients

GENERIC	BRAND	DOSE	RX/OTC
Pimecrolimus	Elidel	BID	Rx
Tacrolimus -.03%, 0.1 %	Protopic	BID	Rx

Side effects: burning, redness, itching
Rare adverse reactions: worsens warts, herpes, and chicken pox infections
Note: FDA approved for use in kids over the age of two years.

Another class of eczema medications repairs the skin's top layer and reduces inflammation and itching. Brand names include Mimyx, Atopiclair, Epiceram, Promiseb, Prumyx, and Pruclair. They are Rx only (and pretty pricey).

Side effects: burning, redness, itching
Rare adverse reactions: Atopiclair, Promiseb, and Pruclair are derived from the shea nut, so allergic reactions are possible.

Diaper rash creams

The idea behind all of the products listed below is to provide a barrier between the skin and moisture (pee and poop). When applying these creams and ointments, it is key to apply liberally and frequently.

Dr. B's opinion: I prefer creams to powders. When powder is applied, there is a risk that the baby will inhale the powder.

Diaper rash creams

A+D ointment	OTC
Boudreaux's Butt Paste	OTC
Dr. Smith's Diaper Ointment	OTC
Silvadene Used for rash that looks like a burn.	Available by Rx only.
Triple Paste	OTC
Vaseline	OTC
Zinc Oxide (brands: Desitin, Balmex)	OTC

BOTTOM LINE

Many pediatricians have a secret recipe of salves and barrier creams that pharmacies will make especially for them. If none of these over the counter products are working, it's time to visit your pediatrician for some help.

Want to know more information about medications and get updated safety alerts? Head to the FDA's website at fda.gov/cder/drugsafety.htm. In an effort for the FDA to provide more transparency, consumers can check on post-marketing drug studies, adverse events reporting, and learn how to report problems with medications.

Alternative Medicines

Appendix B

While it seems there is a drug for just about every malady, sometimes there's not. That may leave you frustrated as a parent. And some families fear that medications will have harmful side effects. This leads some to search out a "natural" or "alternative" remedy for their children.

Alternative and complementary therapies are big business (over $7 billion annually in the U.S.). Some of these treatment options have real merit and the science to back them up. Those are the therapies we will present to you. While there are many more choices in your local organic grocer's aisle, we are sticking to our comfort zone and our mantra: show us the science.

As a consumer, you also need to know a few things about natural or herbal remedies:

1. **Are they effective?** There are very few scientific studies that prove with statistical significance that herbal remedies work. The National Center for Complementary and Alternative Medicine, part of the National Institutes of Health, is starting to investigate many of these products.
2. **Are they safe?** There are no required clinical research trials that test herbal products on humans to prove that they are safe before they are sold to the public. Herbal remedies fall into the category of "foods" by the FDA (Food and Drug Administration). This is a convenient loophole for herbal product manufacturers. This means that they do not need to do any of the scientific research that a pharmaceutical company does to market their medications. This is based on federal legislation from 1994. Attempts to revise this act

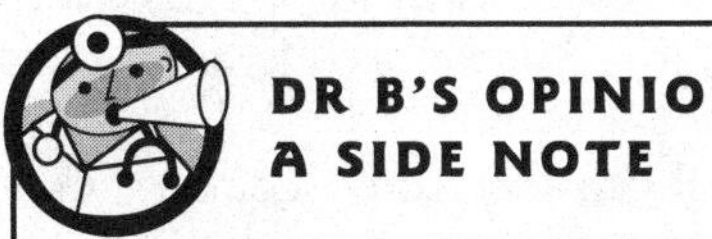

DR B'S OPINION: A SIDE NOTE

Disclaimer: I admit that my medical training did not include acupuncture, spinal manipulations, homeopathy, or herbal supplements. So I have a certain degree of skepticism in complementary therapies—particularly when used in children. But I am always open to trying new remedies if they are proven beneficial and safe.

have failed in the past due to political pressure (and money) from the dietary supplements lobbying group. (*National Public Radio*)

3. **Are production standards uniform?** Production is not standardized. The potency and purity of the product may vary tremendously. This is especially true for products that contain expensive herbs (e.g. ginseng). In fact, herbs produced in China are often laced with unlabeled products such as steroids and antibiotics to make them more potent. Also know that developing countries may sell products that are contaminated with mercury, arsenic, and lead. (*Kemper*) And, in the United States, researchers found that only 7% of the studied Echinacea supplements complied with FDA labeling standards and some of the supplements contained no measurable amounts of Echinacea! (*Gilroy*)
4. **Can I trust the label?** The claims on the label for marketing purposes do not require scientific evidence that the information is accurate. Bottom line: consumers don't have any protection against misleading information.

Compare herbs to traditional medicine. Many traditional medications are based on naturally occurring products. Penicillin is derived from a mold. Digoxin, a popular heart drug, is based on the digitalis plant. It is true that certain naturally occurring products have medical value. The difference between herbs and medications is *how they are tested and regulated*. Some herbs have absolutely no therapeutic value. And some herbs are so potent, they can be harmful. Just because it's natural, doesn't mean it is safe.

Consider alcohol and tobacco. Both have known effects on the body. Both are legal for use. But long term, chronic use of these products also can cause problems. Alcohol and tobacco are as natural as the herbs you are trying. No one knows what long-term problems *some* herbs can create.

We suggest you look at reliable resources to examine the evidence before you try these alternative meds. Here are a couple of free online sources:

- National Center for Complementary and Alternative Medicine (nccam.nih.gov)
- Cochrane Reviews (cochrane.org/reviews)

Herbs: A review of uses and precautions

Aloe Vera

Uses: Used externally for minor burns, eczema. Used internally for constipation.

Scientific Data: Good evidence that it reduces itching and promotes wound healing. Not enough data to prove it works as a laxative, treats asthma, cancer, ulcers, or diabetes.

Precautions: Risk of irreversible intestinal damage, kidney damage, electrolyte imbalance when taken internally. Not safe for use as a laxative in children under 12 yrs of age. (*Rodriguez-Bigas, NIH, Fetrow*)

Calendula

(calendula officinalis)

Uses: Used externally for skin irritation, wounds/burns, numbing drops for earaches.

DR B'S OPINION: TELL YOUR DOCTOR

A recent article in a parenting magazine stated that 12% of all children have been given alternative therapies. Patients are using these products–most of the time without their doctor's knowledge. Parents don't tell the doctor they are trying herbals because:

a) they fear that their decision will not be respected or
b) think the doctor won't know anything about the product.

The truth is, I respect parents' decisions even though I may not agree with them. As far as my knowledge about herbal remedies, I am learning as I go along. *But it is very important to tell your doctor if you are giving your child an herbal remedy. Some herbal products have significant drug interactions with other medications your doctor might be prescribing.*

Scientific Data: Some evidence that it promotes wound healing and reduces inflammation in rats. Virtually no studies in humans.
Precautions: Allergic reactions can occur, and can cause eye irritation. Not recommended for use in the eye. (*Kemper, NIH*) Not *recommended for women who are breastfeeding as effects are unknown.*

Chamomile
(anthemis nobilis)
Uses: acne, allergies, colds, colic, diaper rash, ear infections, eczema, sleep problems, sore throats, vomiting.
Scientific Data: One study shows 3-4 oz per day of a combination (chamomile, fennel, vervain, licorice, balm mint) herbal tea improves symptoms of colic. Chamomile is an antispasmodic and may help relax the gut muscles, but it's also possible that the fennel was the effective ingredient. (*Perry*) Some evidence of improved wound healing.
Precautions: Infant botulism has been reported from contaminated homegrown chamomile tea. *Allergic reactions can be severe including shortness of breath, throat swelling, and anaphylaxis.* (*Weizman, NIH*) The National Library of Medicine/National Institutes of Health discourages its use during pregnancy, breastfeeding and for children.

Echinacea
Uses: allergies, prevention of colds, sore throats
Scientific data: Study results are conflicting whether or not Echinacea prevents cold symptoms in adults. However, research shows no significant benefit in reducing length and severity of cold symptoms in children under 11 years of age.
Precautions: It can cause allergic reactions. (*Barrett, Kemper, NIH*) When taken at recommended doses, there are few side effects. These include: stomachache, nausea, sore throat, rash, liver inflammation. Many tinctures also contain high concentrations of alcohol.

Evening Primrose Oil
(Oenothera biennis)

Uses: allergies, eczema, attention deficit disorder
Scientific Data: Approved in several countries outside of U.S for eczema and atopic dermatitis. Several studies show benefit.
Precautions: Stomachache, headaches reported. (*Horrobin, Hederos, NIH*)

Fennel
(foeniculum vulgare)
Uses: colic, gas, diarrhea, colds, conjunctivitis
Scientific Data: Studies show some benefit for colic. Fennel relaxes the gut (antispasmodic) and increases intestine motility. (*Perry*)
Precautions: None (*Weizman*)

Ginger
(Zingiber officinale)
Uses: colds, diarrhea, headaches, nausea, vomiting, colic
Scientific Data: Some evidence shows it has anti-nausea, anti-vomiting effects and reduces inflammation. Ginger may help relax the gut muscles. One study shows some benefit for colic.
Precautions: heartburn. Not for use if prone to gallstones. (*Schmid, Mowrey*)

Licorice
(glycyrrhiza glabra)
Uses: allergies, asthma, cough, eczema, sore throats, canker sores
Scientific Data: Minimal data on canker sores done on 20 patients, one study on eczema.
Precautions: Long-term use has similar effects to steroids (high blood pressure, altered body salts). Heart rhythm disturbances possible. Not for use during pregnancy, or if patient has diabetes, liver, kidney disease. (*Das, Teelucksingh*)

Reality Check
Most of the licorice candy sold in the U.S. is flavored with anise oil, not real licorice!

Peppermint
(Mentha piperita)
Uses: Used externally as a decongestant (VapoRub). Used internally for cough suppressant, irritable bowel syndrome, indigestion, headaches, itching.
Scientific Data: Research shows positive effects on irritable bowel syndrome and indigestion. Peppermint is an antispasmodic and may help relax gut muscles. Peppermint actually INCREASES nasal congestion but people subjectively report that they can breathe better.
Precautions: Heartburn. Peppermint oil should not be placed in nasal passages of babies as it increases risk of apnea (they stop breathing) (*Fox, Eeles, Gardiner, NIH*) *National Institutes of Health does not recommend use of peppermint leaf or oil in young children because of side effect risks.*

Tea Tree oil
(Melaleuca alternifolia)
Uses: Used externally to treat dandruff, head lice, fungal infections.
Scientific Data: Some research shows benefit for mild to moderate dandruff, lice, and fungal infections (athlete's foot, toenail fungus).
Precautions: Toxic if taken by mouth. May mimic effects of estrogen and cause pre-pubertal boys to have breast enlargement. (*NIH*)

Zinc
Uses: common cold, diarrhea, malnutrition, gastric ulcers, acne
Scientific Data: Positive effect seen in malnourished kids with diarrhea, gastric ulcers. May reduce duration and severity of common cold if taken within 24 hours of symptoms. May prevent the common cold if it is taken daily for several months. No specific dosing information available on children or adults. (*Singh*)
Precautions: Unpleasant or "distorted" taste. Occasional nausea, vomiting, diarrhea. (*NIH*)

BOTTOM LINE

Just because it's natural doesn't mean it's safe. Get educated about these products before using them.

Q. Is it safe to use VapoRub on my baby when she has a cold?

No. Besides, it's not clear that it even helps.

The most popular brand on the market, Vicks VapoRub, is a combination of camphor, menthol, and eucalyptus oil. It is approved for use in children ages two and up (because camphor has the potential for causing seizures in young children when it is absorbed through the skin).

Once your child is at least two, you are welcome to try it and see if it works. People often report that they can breathe better when they use VapoRub because of the cool sensation in their nostrils. However, the medication does not stop snot production. Parents subjectively noted in one recent study that their snot-nosed-VapoRub-treated children coughed less and slept better than those who got treated with a placebo (a.k.a. Vaseline). And the VapoRub treated group of parents slept better. But note: over 85% of parents in the study correctly guessed if their child was using VapoRub or Vaseline. So, take the study results with a grain of salt. (*Paul*)

alternatives

PRObiotics and PREbiotics

Probiotics and prebiotics are popping up at natural and conventional grocery stores alike, thanks to the potential health benefits. But what are they?

What are PRObiotics?

These are "good germs" (bacteria or yeast) that help the body digest food. They are found naturally in yogurt, kefir, kombucha, tea, and sauerkraut. They also come in capsules or powder form. One capsule or powder packet has about 1000 times more "germs" than what is in a serving of

DR B'S OPINION: NEW STUDIES MAY SHED LIGHT ON ALT MEDS

The NIH (National Institutes of Health) has numerous scientific trials ongoing to study the effects and safety of herbal medicines. Hopefully, this will provide the data that physicians need to feel comfortable prescribing these products to their patients.

yogurt. Note: the good germs are only present when you ingest them. So once a person stops taking them, the benefits go away.

What are PREbiotics?

These are complex starches or polysaccharides in food that help the gut grow the good bacteria mentioned above. This is what sustains the healthy gut environment. Prebiotics are found naturally in whole grains, honey (a no-no under age one), bananas, garlic, onions, leeks, and artichokes. Other food and beverage products are fortified with them. Note: prebiotics basically provide the nesting ground for good germs. So, even if someone doesn't take prebiotics everyday, the benefits have longer lasting effects.

Does your baby need these products?

There's been quite a bit of hype about the health benefits of both pro- and prebiotics. Formula companies have joined the bandwagon: one major brand has added probiotics while another is touting prebiotics.

These "good germs" seem to reduce antibiotic-associated diarrhea and diarrhea from stomach viruses in infants as young as one month of age. Probiotics may also be useful for eczema, colic, and intestinal problems in premature babies.

However, it's debatable whether a daily dose is useful or not. More research is definitely needed to know when, what type, how much, and how often these products should be used for proven health benefits.

Which product should I buy?

Probiotic products are mostly bacteria from the Lactobacillus acidophilus, Lactobacillus GG or Bifidobacterium families that are similar to the germs that naturally live in our guts. A few probiotics are actually yeast-based, like Saccaromyces sp. Specific products include: Lactinex (Lactobacillus acidophilus and Lactobacillus bulgaricus), Culturelle (Lactobacillus GG), Lactobacillus reuteri, and Florastor (Saccaromyces).

Do all probiotics have the same effectiveness?

Frankly, we don't really know. Probiotics research is really in its infancy. Lactobacillus reuteri is the probiotic that was specifically used in the study done on reduction of colic in infants (see Chapter 11 for details). Lactobacillus rhamnosus and Lactobacillus GG have proven results in reducing diarrhea from rotavirus infection. Saccaromyces boulardii is also effective for diarrhea.

So, will your local warehouse club version of probiotics prevent your child's diarrhea or colic? We don't have the answers yet–the research is still evolving. Watch our blog or sign up for our eNewsletter for the latest updates at Baby411.com.

Do probiotics need to be refrigerated, or need any other special care?

Many need to be refrigerated for the germs to stay alive. Check the packaging on the item you purchase.

Give probiotics and antibiotics at different times. Otherwise, the good germs will be killed off.

If you are adding probiotics to infant formula, do not warm the bottle over 100°F, or you will kill off the good germs.

Are these products safe for my baby to use?

Despite the general belief that these products are safe, there are some serious safety concerns, particularly with young children and those with immune deficiencies. There have been a few cases of bloodstream infections among people with chronic illness. There is also some evidence that newborns and young children who take L rhamnosus have a greater risk of wheezing later in life. (*Kopp*) You also need to know that some probiotics contain cow's milk proteins, which could lead to an allergic reaction for a baby with a milk protein allergy. (*Moneret-Vautrin*)

FYI: The only probiotic that is FDA approved for use in formula is B. lactis. Other probiotics are not regulated for children.

How much and how often should I give probiotics to my baby?

Well, we're kinda shooting from the hip here since there are no official recommendations.

For colic: half teaspoon of L. reuteri powder per day to help with colic symptoms.

For diarrhea: use 1/4 or 1/2 the powder contained in one capsule of L. rhamnosus, B. lactis, or L. acidophilus per day for 5-7 days. (*Land*)

What about PREbiotics?

Prebiotics are certainly safe and they are the building blocks for good germs. So, serve up another helping of bananas or whole grains to your baby who has started solid foods. Is it worth it to buy prebiotic-supplemented formula? It's certainly not a bad idea, but we have to see more data before we recommend it over other products on the market.

Homeopathic Remedies

These are products containing diluted ingredients that are listed in the *Homeopathic Pharmacopeia of the United States* (HPUS). But according to the National Center for Complementary and Alternative Medicine, "A product's compliance with requirements of the HPUS, ...does not establish that it has been shown by appropriate means to be safe, effective, and not mis-branded for its intended use."

For more information on herbal and homeopathic remedies, check out *The Holistic Pediatrician*, by Kathi J. Kemper, M.D. (see Appendix F). She is a well-respected pediatrician who has done a great deal of research on alternative therapies.

The National Center for Complementary and Alternative Medicine, a branch of the National Institutes of Health, also has a useful website at nccam.nih.gov/health/herbsataglance.htm.

Home Remedies

Not every ailment requires a trip to the pharmacy. Here is a list of household items and remedies that often provide symptomatic relief for various problems.

Abdominal pain/gas/colic

Give your child a bath. The warm water is soothing. Playing in the bathtub is also a nice distraction technique.

Bruises

Pull out a bag of frozen vegetables and place on the site.

Common Cold (URI)

Make your own saline (salt water) nose drops. Take 1/2 teaspoon of salt and add to 8 oz. of water. Use as much as needed.

Chicken soup. Every culture has their own recipe, and for good reason. The high salt and water content is good for hydrating a child with a fever.

Pull out the humidifier. This moistens the air your child breathes, and loosens the mucous in his nose.

Cradle cap

Massage olive oil into the scalp. Then lift off the plaques.

Croup

Take your child into the bathroom. Close the door. Turn on the shower for ten to 15 minutes. The warm mist will help relax the airway.

If this technique doesn't work, walk outside with your child. The cold night air will often shrink up the swollen airway. It also changes the scenery for your child, which has a therapeutic effect too.

Croup usually occurs in the wintertime. If you live in a warm climate, this might not work for you.

Diaper rash

Good old petroleum jelly (Vaseline) works well. It provides a barrier between the skin and moisture.

Leave your baby open to air (diaper-less) in a safe place inside or outside your house.

Use a blow dryer on the lowest setting to dry baby's bottom.

Some doctors recommend applying liquid antacids (milk of magnesia, kaopectate) to the diaper rash. It might be worth a try.

Vomiting and Diarrhea

Make your own Pedialyte solution. Here is the recipe:

4 cups of water
1/2 tsp of salt
2 Tbsp. of sugar
1/2 tsp of instant Jell-O powder for flavor

Ear infections

Use a heating pad on low setting up to the ear.

Want to prevent your child's ear infections? Stop smoking.

To prevent swimmer's ear, you can make your own "Swim-ear" drops. The alcohol will dry up the water left in the ear canal. The vinegar changes the pH of the ear canal so bugs won't want to grow there. Here's the recipe:

2 drops rubbing alcohol
2 drops of vinegar

Eczema

Keeping the skin moist is the key. The best moisturizer (although not very practical) is good old petroleum jelly (Vaseline). Lube your child up head to toe.

Eye stye

Place a warm tea bag over the eyelid. It is soothing and reduces the swelling.

Sore throat

Make a milkshake or smoothie (depending on the age of your child). Cold drinks feel good and are a nice way to get the fluid intake in. This idea makes me very popular with my patients.

Warts

Try duct tape. A study showed that smothering the warts suppresses the growth of the virus that causes them. Apply a new piece of duct tape to the wart nightly and leave on for the day. It takes about six weeks.

Reality Check: Clean your humidifier

Clean your humidifier properly every few days or else you will be spewing dust particles and germs into the nursery. Be sure to check the instructions that came with your humidifier for details.

DR B'S OPINION: ALTERNATIVE MEDICINE

In today's world, I tell the parent what their child's diagnosis is, explain the diagnosis, and explain the therapy that I would advise. Then the parent often quotes recent information about alternative therapies that they found on the Internet (sometimes accurate and sometimes not) and asks what I think of it. I don't mind these interactions–I find them stimulating. They keep me on my toes. As you can tell by now, I like educating parents. But not every physician is enthusiastic about this style of practicing medicine.

As we discussed in the introduction to this book, our mantra on complementary and alternative medicine for your baby is SHOW US THE SCIENCE. If an alternative therapy is shown to be effective in a reputable scientific study, then we are happy to recommend it. But if it is just snake oil or an Internet myth, we won't hesitate to say so. See Appendix B, "Complementary and Alternative Medicine" for more details.

Notes

When The Parent Wants Tests Done

Parents frequently ask their doctor to order lab work on their child. Doctors are less interested in getting lab work done if they are comfortable in making a diagnosis. But doctors also know that a parent may bring their child in for the common cold and are actually concerned that the child has leukemia or some other devastating diagnosis. In medical terms, this is called "The Hidden Agenda." It's perfectly fine to have that agenda–you are a parent. But don't keep it a secret. Your doctor won't laugh at you. What we will do is make sure that your child does not have the problem that is keeping you up at night worrying.

What you need to know is that there is no one "test" that will uncover every disease that you have concerns about (like a total body CT scan or a comprehensive blood test panel). In the past, doctors would perform annual blood metabolic panels on adults to go on a fishing expedition for abnormalities. This is out of vogue for adults and has never been standard practice for children.

What we might do is order a particular test that would help to diagnose or rule out the concern you have.

When The Doctor Wants Tests Done

Pediatricians can frequently make a correct diagnosis of illness in a child without any tests. I wish I could say it's because we are so much smarter than our other doctor colleagues. The truth is, childhood illnesses are often infections that follow classic patterns. And rashes, which occur more in kids than adults, are helpful in determining the cause of illness.

When do doctors order a test?

1. When there is something about the child's illness history or examination that may indicate a bacterial infection.
2. When there is a concern infection is bacterial and cultures are needed to know what bug it is (so it can be treated appropriately).
3. When a child has a fever with no obvious source.
4. When a baby under three months has a fever.
5. When your doctor thinks your child has a broken bone.
6. When your doctor feels a hip "click" in a newborn. Testing (hip

ultrasound) will verify he doesn't have a congenitally dislocated hip.

7. When a child is vomiting bile or has intractable vomiting.
8. When a child has blood in his poop.
9. When a child has pain when he urinates.
10. When a child's head size is enlarging across percentiles (in other words, the head is growing much faster than expected).
11. When a child's head size is *not* enlarging.
12. When a child is failing to thrive (not gaining weight).
13. When a child wheezes for the first time and it doesn't sound like RSV bronchiolitis.
14. If an abnormality is found during a regular exam (such as distended abdomen, swollen testes).
15. When a child is drinking or urinating excessively.
16. When a child has excessive bruising.
17. When a child has petechiae.
18. When a child has a persistent fever (five days or more).
19. When a newborn is jaundiced to the level below the belly button.
20. When a child is disoriented.
21. When a child has a seizure for the first time.
22. When a child appears dehydrated and the doctor needs to decide how dehydrated he is (that is, does he need to be admitted to the hospital and get IV fluids).
23. When a child bleeds excessively–with cuts or nosebleeds.
24. When a mother has Blood Type O. Your doctor needs to know the baby's blood type so the doctor can be prepared for potential newborn jaundice problems.
25. When your doctor thinks a child has pneumonia and want to confirm it.
26. When a parent is worried.
27. When a child is limping.
28. When a child has recurrent bacterial infections (not just ear infections) such as pneumonia, sinus infections, skin infections.
29. When a child has chronic or severe problems with wheezing.
30. Anytime a child is jaundiced out of the newborn period.
31. When a child has a heart murmur that does not sound like an innocent heart murmur.
32. When a child has an irregular heartbeat.
33. When a child has a bladder or kidney infection.
34. When a child has swallowed a non-food object.

With that said, here are the most common tests we order and what they mean.

Imaging Studies

Ultrasound

The beauty of ultrasonography is that no radiation is used. The technology involves use of sonar waves and computer imaging. Doppler flow studies in addition to ultrasound pictures are helpful in looking at blood flow. Ultrasound pictures can be limited, however. Gas and fat obstructs the view.

Abdominal. Looks at the anatomy of the liver, gallbladder, spleen. Not as good at looking at intestines. Detects pyloric stenosis, intussusception, gallstones, masses.

Head. Looks for bleeding inside the skull. Wand is placed on top of the anterior fontanelle (soft spot) to see inside. Not used once fontanelle has closed. Detects intraventricular hemorrhage (IVH), a problem that can occur in babies born prematurely.

Hip. Looks at the hip joint. Detects hip dislocations (Developmental Dysplasia of Hips or DDH) in infants under four months of age.

Heart (echocardiogram with Doppler). Looks at the anatomy of the heart and the great blood vessels coming off of the heart. Detects heart defects.

Kidney (renal). Looks at the anatomy of the kidneys. Detects evidence of enlargement, fluid collection (hydronephrosis), and infection.

Pelvic. Looks at anatomy of the ovaries, uterus, bladder. Detects ovarian cysts, masses. Also detects location of a testes if it has not descended into the scrotum.

Spine. Looks for spina bifida, an abnormal formation of the spine

Testicular, with Doppler flow. Looks at the anatomy of the testes. Detects a twisted testes and can assess blood flow to the testes. Also detects some hernias.

Plain x-rays

X-rays use diffraction of low doses of high-speed electrons (radiation) to project an image. Solid or fluid filled objects appear white and air appears clear. As a general rule, plain x-rays are better at detecting bone problems, and less helpful at assessing problems with "soft tissues."

Abdomen. Looks at the anatomy of the intestines, liver, spleen. Detects intestinal obstructions, malrotations, constipation. Can detect some foreign bodies (swallowed objects that are metal).

Chest. Looks at the anatomy of the heart, lungs, ribs. Detects fluid (blood, pus) in lungs, masses in lungs, enlargement of the heart, rib fractures, foreign inhaled objects.

Extremities. Looks at the bones of the arms and legs. Detects fractures (broken bones), fluid or swelling occasionally. Less helpful in detecting problems with muscles, tendons, and joints.

Neck. Looks at the anatomy of the throat (epiglottis, tonsils, adenoid, trachea). Detects swelling of these areas, location of some swallowed objects.

Skull. Looks at the anatomy of the skull bones. Detects craniosynostosis, fractures.

Sinus. Looks at the anatomy of the sinus cavities of the face. Detects *acute* sinus infections by identifying an air/fluid level. Not helpful in detecting chronic sinus infections.

Spine. Looks at the anatomy of the vertebrae from the neck to the buttocks. Detects fractures, slipped discs, scoliosis.

CT/MRI with or without contrast

Computerized Tomography (CT) uses x-ray technology (radiation) to look at cross sectional slices of the body in a two-dimensional picture. Magnetic Resonance Imaging (MRI) uses a magnetic field to detect the body's electromagnetic transmissions. MRI's produce narrow slices of the body without radiation.

As a general rule, these studies are better at detecting abnormalities with soft body tissues and less helpful with bone problems. The decision to perform a CT versus an MRI is based on the particular problem that is being assessed.

Abdomen. Looks at the anatomy of the liver, spleen, pancreas, gallbladder, intestines, kidneys. Detects masses, tumors, abscesses–including appendicitis, fluid collections, trauma.

Chest. Looks at the anatomy of the lungs and heart. Detects masses, tumors, fluid collections, congenital abnormalities, trauma.

Extremity. Looks at the anatomy of the arm or leg. Detects fractures, torn ligaments, masses, tumors, osteomyelitis (infection).

Head. Looks at the anatomy of the brain. Detects masses, tumors, obstruction of spinal fluid flow (hydrocephalus), evidence of stroke (cerebrovascular accident), evidence of trauma, bleeding.

Lymph node. Looks at the anatomy of a concerning (swollen) lymph node. Detects pus (infection), masses, congenital cysts.

Pelvic. Looks at the anatomy of the ovary, uterus, bladder. Detects masses, tumors, fluid collections.

Sinus. Looks at the anatomy of the sinus cavities. More helpful imaging study than plain x-rays. Detects obstruction to flow in the sinuses, chronic sinus infections, masses/polyps.

Special studies

Barium swallow/Upper GI. Looks at the anatomy of the upper gastrointestinal tract (esophagus, stomach, upper small intestine). Detects anatomic abnormalities, hiatal hernias, pyloric stenosis, ulcerations, narrowings. Although gastroesophageal reflux may be seen (barium goes backwards), it doesn't tell you the severity of the reflux. It also does not rule out reflux as a diagnosis.

Bone scan. Nuclear medicine study (uses a radio-isotope to be visualized on x-ray). Looks at the all of the bones of the body in one study. Hot and cold "spots" detect areas of inflammation. Detects: infection, tumors, avascular necrosis, child abuse.

DMSA Scan. Special nuclear medicine study that uses a radio-isotope dye visualized on x-ray. Looks for scarring of the kidneys. Detects: chronic kidney scarring and damage due to kidney infections.

Voiding Cystourethrogram. Looks at the flow of urine from kidney to ureters to bladder to urethra. Detects vesicoureteral reflux in children prone to bladder infections. (*Gunn*)

Laboratory Tests

Blood tests

Amylase. This test looks at the level of an enzyme that the pancreas makes. Detects: pancreatitis

Basic Metabolic Panel. This is a battery of tests that includes *sodium, potassium, chloride, bicarbonate, blood urea nitrogen, creatinine, glucose*. This combination of tests assesses body fluid and salt (electrolyte) balance as well as kidney and adrenal function.
Detects: Dehydration, kidney dysfunction, diabetes, hypoglycemia, adrenal dysfunction

Bilirubin. This test assesses the level of this substance circulating in the bloodstream. Newborns uniquely have higher levels than any other time in life because:

1. Newborn metabolism is not functioning at 100%.
2. Newborns are not eliminating bilirubin in their stool yet.
3. Newborns have bilirubin load due to prematurity, birth trauma, or blood type incompatibility.

A total level is assessed as well as *direct* and *indirect* levels. These indicate the cause of the total elevation. Beyond the newborn period, any evidence of jaundice prompts a lab evaluation.
Detects: Hyperbilirubinemia, Hepatitis, Biliary Atresia, gallstones, hemolytic anemia

lab tests

Blood culture. see below

Blood sugar (glucose). This test assesses the body's metabolism of sugar. A random level above 110 is concerning for diabetes. In newborns, a level less than 40 is concerning for hypoglycemia. Levels less than 60 in children is concerning for hypoglycemia.
Detects: Hypoglycemia in large birth weights, babies whose mothers have gestational diabetes or diabetes, body temperature irregularities, lethargy
Detects in children: Diabetes, hypoglycemia

Blood type. This test determines what proteins sit on the surface of a patient's red blood cells. There are A and B proteins. The AB blood type means both A and B protein are present. The O blood type means there are no proteins present. Rh typing refers to the presence (+) or absence (-) of another type of protein that sits on the red blood cell surface. These tests are necessary when a blood transfusion is needed. In an emergency situation, however, everyone gets O (-) negative blood. Most hospitals no longer test a newborn's blood type on a routine basis.

C-Reactive Protein (CRP). This is a substance that circulates in the bloodstream when there is an inflammatory process going on. It is one of several "acute phase reactants" whose numbers change by at least 25% when there is active inflammation. It is not specific for any one disease, but it is accurate. It detects inflammation, infection, trauma, or tumors.

Cholesterol level. See lipid panel

Complete Blood Count (CBC). This refers to a test that looks at the number of white blood cells, red blood cells, and platelets that are circulating in the bloodstream..

1. *White blood cell count (WBC).* These cells fight infection, but also rise with inflammation. An elevated count is concerning for a bacterial infection. A depressed count is due to decreased bone marrow production (where white blood cells are made)—usually caused by viral infections (e.g. influenza, mononucleosis).

2. *White blood cell count differential.* Not only is the number of white blood cells counted, but the types of white blood cells are identified in a CBC. The types of cells also give your doctor clues as to the disease process going on.

- *Neutrophils (PMN's)*- Cells that fight bacteria. If more than 50% of the WBC's are this type, the likelihood of a bacterial infection is greater.

- *Lymphocytes*: Cells that fight viruses. If more than 50% of the WBC's are this type, the likelihood of viral infection is greater.

- *Eosinophils*: Cells that fight parasites. Also revved up by allergies. If more than 10-15% of these cells are present, it prompts an investigation.

3. *Hematocrit/Hemoglobin.* These measurements assess the amount of red blood cells in the circulation. Low levels detect anemia.

4. *Platelet count.* These cells help clot the blood. A low level detects a cause for bleeding problems. A low level can also suggest bone marrow suppression (where platelets are made) or an autoimmune disorder. Platelet counts can be elevated with infection or inflammation.

FYI: When all thee cell lines (white, red, platelet) are depressed, there is a concern for leukemia.
Uses: infection, inflammation, leukemia, anemia, bleeding disorder

Comprehensive Metabolic Panel. This is a large battery of tests that assesses adrenal, kidney, liver, gallbladder, fluid and electrolyte balance, and a measure of general nutrition. Many physicians pick a select number of these tests and not the whole panel. These tests include:

Albumin
Alanine Aminotransferase (ALT)
Bicarbonate
Blood Urea Nitrogen (BUN)
Chloride
Glucose
Potassium
Total Protein
Alkaline phospatase
Aspartate Aminotransferase (AST)
Bilirubin
Calcium
Creatinine
Phosphorous
Sodium

Detects: Liver dysfunction, hepatitis, gallbladder dysfunction, kidney dysfunction, dehydration, diabetes, adrenal dysfunction, malnutrition.

Chromosome analysis. This test assesses a patient's chromosomes, the part of each cell that contains genes. Blood, tissue, or an amniotic fluid sample can be tested.
Detects: Chromosomal abnormalities related to developmental delays/congenital defects; determines the sex of a baby born with ambiguous genitalia.

Coagulation studies. These tests detect an abnormality in the clotting "cascade" or chain of events that allow blood to clot. These tests include: Bleeding Time, Factor levels, Prothrombin time (PT), Partial thromboplastin time (PTT)
Detects: Bleeding disorders–such as Hemophilia, von Willebrand's disease

Coombs test. This test looks for antibodies (reaction) to a person's blood type. In newborns whose mothers have O Blood type, many hospitals perform a Coombs test on the baby routinely. There is some mixing of mother's and fetus's blood in the placenta, which can cause a Type O mother's blood to create antibodies to a type A or B baby. These antibodies can potentially kill some of the baby's red blood cells creating an extra bilirubin load in the newborn.
Detects: Blood type incompatibility in newborns

Electrolytes. See Basic Metabolic Panel

Erythrocyte Sedimentation Rate (ESR). This test looks at how fast it takes for red blood cells to settle at the bottom of a test tube. It is a very nonspecific test, but an elevated level suggests further testing. It is a non-specific sign of inflammation.
Detects: inflammation, infection, pregnancy, malignancy, anemia

Liver function tests. This is a battery of tests that evaluates how the liver is working. It looks at products the liver is in charge of metabolizing and producing. Some tests look at the breakdown product of liver cells (but these products are also seen in muscle breakdown) so they are not specific in detecting liver disorders.
Alanine Aminotransferase (ALT)
Aspartate Aminotransferase (AST)
Total protein
Albumin
Bilirubin
Detects: Hepatitis, liver failure, drug toxicity, heart attack.

Monospot/EBV titers. For monospot, see rapid assays below.

Epstein-Barr Virus (EBV) titers detect a person's immune response (antibodies) to an EBV infection (mononucleosis). Because different types of antibodies are formed through the course of infection, this test differentiates a recent infection and a prior one.
Detects: Acute mononucleosis, prior mononucleosis.

Lipid panel/cholesterol. This battery of tests looks at how the body metabolizes fat. Poor fat metabolism is associated with coronary artery disease (heart disease) in later life. In children, often a random (non-fasting) cholesterol level is an acceptable screening test. If that level is elevated, a full panel is done with the child fasting prior to the test. Tests:

Cholesterol	HDL
LDL	Triglyceride level

Detects: Hypercholesterolemia, hepatitis, metabolic disorders, bile duct obstruction, nephrotic syndrome, pancreatitis, hypothyroidism

Reticulocyte count. Reticulocytes are baby red blood cells. They circulate in the bloodstream while they mature. This test looks at the number of these present in the blood. A high level suggests good bone marrow production in response to anemia.
Detects: Body's response to anemia

Thyroid function tests. This is a battery of tests that assesses the function of the thyroid gland. An indirect way of testing thyroid gland function is to look at a Thyroid Stimulating Hormone (TSH) level, a hormone produced by the pituitary gland. If the thyroid gland is not functioning well (hypothyroidism), the TSH level is elevated to stimulate the gland to work harder. This is a test included in all state metabolic screens to detect congenital hypothyroidism.

T3 (triiodothyronine) level	Thyroxine Binding Globulin
T4 (thyroxine) level	Free T3, Free T4 levels
TSH	

Detects: Hypothyroidism, Hyperthyroidism

Viral titers. There are a few viruses for which a patient's antibody response can be detected. These tests are useful to make a diagnosis or confirm immunity to a particular virus.

CMV	Hepatitis A, B, C
HIV	Parvovirus
Rubella	Syphilis
Toxoplasmosis	Varicella

Urine tests

Urinalysis. This is a test that looks at the components of urine and detects any abnormal components. Urine is normally a sterile fluid, thus should not contain any bacteria or white blood cells (which fight infection). Urine does not breakdown sugar or protein, so it should not contain any of those substances. Urine is produced in the kidneys, so some abnormalities will point to a kidney dysfunction.

In children, obtaining a urine specimen can be a challenge. A urine specimen needs to be clean to be able to make any decisions based on its findings. The preferred method of obtaining this specimen is to insert a small catheter in the urethra of a non-toilet trained child. If the reason for testing urine is not to look for infection, a collection bag may be placed over the urethra. Tests:

Specific gravity	pH
Color, odor	White Blood Cells
Red Blood Cells	Glucose
Protein	Nitrite

Microscopic analysis for bacteria

Detects: Bladder infection, dehydration, kidney disease, diabetes, adrenal dysfunction, metabolic disorder, kidney stones

Skin tests

PPD. This is the preferred test for exposure to tuberculosis. PPD stands for purified protein derivative, which refers to a synthetic protein "signature" that belongs to the tuberculosis bacteria. If a person has had an exposure to tuberculosis, their antibodies will also respond to this skin test. A positive test requires further evaluation and testing.

Stool tests

Occult blood. This test detects blood in the stool. A small amount of stool (poop) is placed on a special developing card. When a processing fluid is added to the specimen, it turns blue in the presence of blood.

Detects: Gastrointestinal bleeding (e.g. food allergy, infection, ulcer, inflammatory bowel disease, polyp)

Spinal fluid (CSF) tests

Cerebrospinal fluid (CSF) is a liquid that bathes the brain and spinal cord. It transports important chemicals through the central nervous system. A specimen of this fluid helps diagnose viral infection, bacterial infection, tuberculosis meningitis (infection of the tissues protecting the brain), brain infection, and obstruction of the spinal fluid collecting system.

CSF is obtained by performing a lumbar puncture or "spinal tap." This sounds scary, but it is a similar concept to having an epidural placed in childbirth. A small needle is inserted between two vertebrae in the back. A small amount of fluid is collected, and then the needle is removed.

We look at the pressure of the fluid, the appearance of the fluid (should be clear/watery), the sugar/protein levels, and if there are any cells in the fluid (white, red, bacteria).

A culture of the fluid is also done (see below).

Sweat test

A specimen of sweat is obtained by warming the skin on the arm or thigh and obtaining a small amount of sweat.

Detects: Cystic Fibrosis

Cultures

This group of tests takes a particular body fluid and incubates it (creates ideal growing conditions for bugs). If there is a germ in a specimen, there is a chance to identify it. Germs that grow are very accurate for infection growing in the patient (except for contaminated/dirty specimens). But, lack of growth in culture does not necessarily rule out an infection.

Most germs will grow out in a culture within three days. Fungus infections, however, may take up to one month to grow.

Blood. Detects BACTERIAL infections
Urine. Detects bacterial infections
Spinal fluid. Detects primarily BACTERIAL infections, some VIRAL infections
Stool. Detects BACTERIAL, PARASITE, AMOEBA infections
Throat. Detects BACTERIAL infection
Sputum. Detects BACTERIAL infection
Abscess. Detects BACTERIAL infection
Viral. Detects limited number of VIRAL infections (such as Herpes, Varicella, Chlamydia)
Fungal. Detects FUNGUS infections

Rapid Antigen Assays

As a group, these tests identify responses that infections have to certain chemicals. You might think of them in a similar way to a home pregnancy test. A positive test accurately confirms infection. But a negative test does not rule *out* infection. These "assay kits" also look like a home pregnancy test. The earlier these tests are done in the course of an illness, the less accurate they are.

Strep. Throat swab specimen
Monospot. Blood specimen
Influenza. Nasal secretion specimen (not covered on some insurance plans)
RSV. Nasal secretion specimen.
Rotavirus. Stool specimen (*Loeb*)

Glossary

Really Big Latin Words

Appendix D

Abdominal tumors. There are some solid tumors that occur more frequently in children than adults. These include Wilm's tumor and neuroblastoma. Patients with these tumors may (not always) have enlarged, firm bellies with a mass that can be felt. Other symptoms include weight loss, lack of appetite, or unexplained fevers.

ABO incompatibility. See Coombs test in Lab section.

Accessory Nipple. See supernumerary nipple.

Acholic stool. Official term for a clay colored poop. In isolation, it may have no significance. But, it can indicate a problem with the biliary system (liver, gallbladder, pancreas) if it is associated with other symptoms—particularly jaundice (yellowing) of the skin. Diagnoses can include hepatitis infection and biliary atresia. If you see this, check in with your doctor.

Acne (neonatal). Skin inflammation due to hormonal changes in the newborn period. Onset is usually by four weeks of age and lasts until about eight weeks of age.

Acute abdomen. Term that refers to an emergency requiring surgical intervention to alleviate an intestinal problem. Examples of these problems include: appendicitis, intussusception, intestinal obstruction.

Acute life threatening event (ALTE). Term that describes an episode of lack of breathing (apnea) that requires intervention to resume spontaneous breathing. If an event like this happens, a thorough evaluation is done to determine the cause of the event.

Acute otitis media. Infection in the middle ear space. This is primarily caused by bacteria. When the infection comes up quickly, it is called "acute." Symptoms include fever, cranky mood, and vomiting. Occasionally, children may also seem dizzy. Ear infections that smolder for a long period of time are called "chronic" and do not have the same symptoms.

Acrocyanosis. The blue discoloration frequently seen on the hands and feet of newborns. This is due to the body circulation transitioning from fetal to newborn. It doe not indicate any problem with the heart or circulatory system. Blue discoloration only on the feet or legs (not hands) can be a sign of a circulation problem (Coarctation of the Aorta) and needs to be evaluated.

Air hungry. The inability of a person to get enough oxygen in with each breath. The person then tries to get more air in with each breath by using chest wall muscles and increasing the number of breaths taken per minute. This is also known as **respiratory distress.**

Ambiguous Genitalia. It's hard to tell whether the baby has boy parts or girl parts. We'll test chromosomes, hormone levels, and get an ultrasound to look for internal genitalia (ovaries/uterus or undescended testes).

Amblyopia. (Known as lazy eye). A reduction of vision in an eye that is not correctable with glasses. This problem can be caused by a weakness of an eye muscle (strabismus). It is important to detect this eye problem early (under age two or three years) so it can be treated.

Anal fissure. A crack in the anus opening usually due to passage of a hard poop. The crack causes discomfort and occasionally blood in the diaper or on a diaper wipe.

Anaphylactic reaction. An allergic response to exposure to a particular item (that is, medication, food). The response is extremely serious and life-threatening. These body responses include: difficulty breathing, heart failure, loss of blood pressure.

Anemia. A reduced amount of hemoglobin that carries oxygen on red blood cells. Because the body is less capable of getting oxygen, symptoms include tiredness, pale appearance, and quick fatigue.

Ankyloglossia (tongue tie). The tongue is attached to the base of the mouth too close to the tip. Not all babies with tongue tie need intervention. If it is so tight that it interferes with feeding or talking, the tissue band can be clipped. This is more likely to be a problem if the tip of the tongue is forked.

Anomaly. Fancy word for abnormality, usually malformed prior to birth (congenital anomaly).

Anterior Fontanelle. See Fontanelle.

Antibiotic induced colitis. Inflammation of the lower part of the intestine which, rarely, can be caused by antibiotics. Symptoms of colitis include blood and mucous in the poop, diarrhea, and cramping. If someone has been on an antibiotic just prior to the onset of these symptoms, a specimen of poop can be checked for this problem.

Apnea. Pause, or temporary absence in breathing. Frequently babies born prematurely have these events when they just plain forget to breathe. This is called **apnea of prematurity**. Preemies eventually outgrow this problem. Until they do, they are placed on an apnea monitor which alarms when breathing stops. Some babies also need caffeine (in medication form) to stimulate them to breathe.

Appendicitis. Inflammation of a small piece of the intestine called the appendix. The appendix is usually located in the lower RIGHT side of the belly, but this varies occasionally. When the appendix gets swollen, symptoms include: vomiting, diarrhea, fever, and abdominal pain that worsens over time. Appendicitis is extremely rare in the birth to age one group.

Asperger's Syndrome. A term that is no longer used to describe a developmental disorder that is part of the Autism Spectrum Disorders. Historically, children with Asperger's have better communication and language skills than those more severely affected.

Asthma. The swelling of the big and little airways in the lungs. The swelling can occur due to allergic response. The episodes happen intermittently. Symptoms include: coughing and labored breathing (respiratory distress).

Atopy. A classic triad of allergic disorders: eczema, asthma, and seasonal allergies (termed "allergic rhinitis"). Not everyone is unlucky enough to have all three problems, but some people are.

Atresia. Means that something is completely absent or is significantly narrowed

Anal atresia. Anus (opening of the intestines to the outside).
Biliary atresia. Bile ducts.
Choanal atresia. Nasal/throat.
Duodenal atresia. Small intestine.
Esophageal atresia. Esophagus.
Ileal atresia. Small intestine.
Tricuspid atresia. Heart valve.

Autism. A developmental disorder that is characterized by poor or no language development, lack of normal social skills and repetitive self-soothing behaviors. The disorder has a genetic basis in at least 10-15% of the cases. The newer term, Autism Spectrum Disorders (ASD) more appropriately describes the umbrella diagnosis that encompasses the broad range from mild to severely affected individuals.

Autosomal dominant. A genetically inherited trait that requires only one parent to have an abnormal gene to pass it on to a child. If one parent carries an autosomal dominant gene, the chances are 50% that a child inherits the gene.

Autosomal recessive. A genetically inherited trait that requires both parents to have the gene to pass it on to a child. If both parents are carriers of the autosomal recessive gene, the chances are 25% that they will have an affected child. If both parents have the disease, chances are nearly 100% that they will have an affected child.

Bacterial gastroenteritis. (See gastroenteritis)

BAER. Brainstem Audio Evoked Response. An objective hearing test that measures the electrical activity of the inner ear in response to sound. This is a universal screening test done on newborns. It is recommended by the American Academy of Pediatrics and currently mandated in most states.

Balanitis. An inflammation of the tip of the penis, which becomes inflamed an irritated. Balanitis can be caused by an infection.

Bladder infection (see UTI)

Blocked tear duct. See nasolacrimal duct obstruction.

Blood in stool. A symptom that may be caused by a variety of reasons. Blood can be found in poop due to skin irritation (diaper rash), a crack or tear in the anus (see anal fissure), inflammation in the intestine (milk protein allergy), intestinal infection (see gastroenteritis), or intestinal obstruction (intussusception). As you can see, the problem may be a minor or serious one. It always should be checked out by your doctor.

Brain tumor. Abnormal mass of cells that grow in the brain tissue. Although not all tumors are malignant (fast growing, aggressive), even benign tumors can be life threatening depending on the location that it arises. Symptoms in infants and young children include morning headaches accompanied by vomiting, increasing head size, behavior changes, imbalance, seizures, and new onset eye abnormalities.

Branchial cleft cyst. An abnormality in fetal development of the throat that results in a cyst that occurs on the neck

Breath-holding spell. An episode where a child holds his breath when upset or angry. Usually occurs after one year of age. The episode ultimately results in a child losing consciousness and regaining normal breathing. Rarely, these episodes are due to anemia–but worth checking out if the episodes occur frequently.

Breech position. Occasionally, a baby will decide to exit the womb with his butt, foot, or feet first–instead of the usual head first (vertex) position. Because this can increase the risk of complications at delivery, it is preferable to deliver these babies by C-section. Babies who are breech in the womb, particularly girls, have a *slightly* increased risk of having **hip dysplasia** (also known as developmental dysplasia of the hips or DDH). There is an association between abnormal formation of the hips as a fetus leading to the unusual butt/foot first position for delivery. See **hip dysplasia.**

Bronchiolitis. Swelling in the tiny airways in the lungs (bronchioles). In children, this is caused primarily by a virus called RSV (Respiratory Syncytial Virus). When the little airways are swollen, it can be difficult to exchange oxygen poor air with oxygen rich air. In severe cases, particularly infants under a year of age or those born prematurely, some children need medication to reduce the swelling (see bronchodilators in medication appendix) and supplemental oxygen.

Bronchitis. Swelling in the larger airways of the lungs (bronchi). In children, this swelling is usually caused by a virus or bacterial infection.

Broncopulmonary dysplasia (BPD). Term used to describe chronic lung disease that occurs primarily in babies who are born prematurely who require prolonged breathing assistance with a mechanical ventilator. The longer the baby is dependent on mechanical ventilation, the poorer the prognosis. Babies with BPD may have poor lung function, wheezing, and higher risk of severe complications with Respiratory Syncytial Virus (RSV) infection. Lung function, however, usually improves over the first several years of life.

Cafe au lait spots. As the name implies, these are light brown (coffee with milk) colored birthmarks. They occur in babies of all races. Most of the time, there is no significance to these marks. When a child has more than five of these birthmarks, there may be an association with a disorder called **neurofibromatosis.**

Carotinemia. A benign yellow discoloration of the skin due to a large dietary intake of carotene containing foods (carrots, sweet potatoes). The whites of the eyes remain white, as opposed to what is seen with jaundice–**see jaundice**.

Cataracts. A clouding of the eye's lens. This can occur at birth (congenital cataracts). If a newborn has cataracts, it can be detected by the lack of a 'red reflex' on an eye examination. A referral to a pediatric ophthalmologist is made.

Celiac disease. A disorder of the intestines which causes poor digestion and absorption of foods. The underlying problem is due to an abnormal response to 'gluten' containing foods (e.g. wheat, oat, rye grains). The classic symptoms of this disorder include foul smelling, chronic diarrhea and failure to thrive (lack of weight gain). Treatment is a lifelong gluten-free diet.

Cephalhematoma. Literally, a head bruise. This often occurs in newborns as a result of birth trauma. Some of these bruises are quite large and take one to two months to completely go away. In the process of healing, these areas can become very hard and firm. Since the bruise is a collection of blood, it sometimes creates an additional bilirubin load and can lead to jaundice in some newborns.

Cerebral palsy. An abnormality of the brain center that controls muscle tone and movement. Cerebral palsy does not cause any abnormalities in IQ. However, there are children who have *both* intellectual disability AND cerebral palsy.

Choanal atresia. Lack of communication between the back of the nasal passages and the throat. This can occur in one or both sides of the nose. If both sides are blocked, a newborn will have severe breathing problems. Newborns only know how to breathe through their noses for the first four months of life.

Clavicle (collar bone) fracture. When Mom is small and baby is big, it can be difficult to get the baby out of the birth canal. The baby's shoulder pulls out and can break the clavicle (collar bone) in the process. It heals nicely without a cast. The area can feel crunchy under the skin, then it feels like a hard lump. The lump is healing bone and goes away after several weeks.

Cleft lip and palate. The roof of the mouth and/or the upper lip does not completely form in a fetus. These defects can occur together or separately in 1 in 1000 births. There is some hereditary predisposition. Rarely, this defect is associated with other congenital defects. Frequently, a team of providers manage babies with these defects (Ear, Nose, and Throat doctors, Plastic Surgeons, Dentist, and Occupational Therapists). See Appendix F for web sites on this issue.

Club foot. An abnormality in the formation of the foot of the fetus. The result is a stiff foot that turns markedly inwards. Pediatric orthopedic surgeons are consulted and a cast is made to correct the position of the foot.

Coarctation of the Aorta. A narrowing or kink in the great artery (aorta) that leaves the heart and supplies the body with oxygen rich blood. This is a defect that occurs during fetal development (prior to birth). If the abnormality is severe, it is diagnosed in newborns who have weakened/no pulse in the legs. If the abnormality is small, it may go undetected until later in life. It is repaired by surgery.

Colostrum. A first "milk" that a mother produces. This product is rich in antibodies and cells. It has fewer calories than mature milk which arrives on about the fourth day after birth.

Conductive hearing loss. Difficulty hearing due to a problem with the transmission of sound waves to the part of the ear that controls hearing. Sound waves can be blocked due to fluid sitting behind the eardrum (see serous obits media) or a significant amount of earwax sitting in the ear canal. The good news about conductive hearing loss is that the problem can usually be fixed and normal hearing is restored.

Congenital. This refers to an abnormality in the *formation* of a certain organ/body part that occurs in the development of an unborn fetus. These abnormalities may be due to either hereditary problems or environmental exposures during pregnancy. The lay term for these disorders is **birth defect.**

Congenital Adrenal Hyperplasia. An abnormality in the gland that produces steroids in the body (adrenal gland). This can cause severe metabolism problems of body salts. This abnormality is routinely tested in the newborn metabolic screen.

Congenital heart disease. A defect in the structural development of the heart or the great vessels that attach to the heart. Because heart development occurs in the first trimester of pregnancy, many congenital defects can be identified on a prenatal ultrasound. Some abnormalities will resolve on their own. Some require surgical repair. The disease incidence is 1:1000. The most common defects are the least serious ones. Remember, there is a difference between an innocent heart murmur (no defect) and a pathologic murmur (caused by congenital heart disease).

Congenital nevus. (Known as moles, birthmarks) A mark on the skin which is present at birth, or appears within the first year of life. The most concerning moles are ones larger than 10 to 20 cm (really big) that are present at birth. These have more potential risk of skin cancer and removal is usually advised.

Congestive heart failure. When the heart is unable to perform adequately, the blood flow accumulates in the lungs and liver. So, symptoms of heart failure include shortness of breath and enlarged liver size. In children, symptoms include failure to thrive, sweating with feedings, shortness of breath, and excessive fatigue.

Conjunctivitis. An inflammation of the lining of the eyelid. Otherwise known as "pink eye." The inflammation can be caused by a virus, bacteria, allergies, or irritation. All types of conjunctivitis cause redness and some discomfort. Here are the major types of conjunctivitis:

Allergic. An allergic response usually due to a sensitivity to something in the air (e.g. pollens). Usually causes watery, somewhat itchy eyes. Antihistamines treat the symptoms.

Bacterial. A bacterial infection in the eye (often accompanied by ear and sinus infection). Causes thick yellowish eye discharge and may even cause the eyes to be caked over or "matted." Antibiotic eye drops treat the infection.

Viral. A viral infection in the eye (that may be accompanied by a sore throat). Causes watery and very itchy eyes.

Irritation. Eyes become inflamed because of a chemical irritant (e.g. shampoo).

Constipation. The texture of poop is significantly hard, and is passed either in small pieces or in a very large mass of small pieces stuck together. Contrary to popular belief, constipation is NOT defined by the infrequency of poop (although this can contribute to the problem). There is no defined length of interval for which a person needs to poop—it can vary considerably. If the poop is soft when it comes out, your baby is unlikely to be constipated.

Craniosynostosis. A baby's skull bones have gaps that allow for the brain's growth in the first one to two years of life. This abnormality is a premature closure of the gaps (sutures) that occurs in about 1 in 1800 children. The reason why this occurs is unknown, but is not due to any birth trauma or complication. Early closure can cause deformities in the skull and facial shape, inhibition of brain growth, and increased pressure within the skull.

Cystic Fibrosis (CF). This is a genetic disease that causes body glands to produce abnormal secretions. Lung, sinus, pancreas, intestine, and reproductive organ problems occur because of it. One in 20 Caucasians are carriers of this genetic abnormality. The disease incidence is 1:1600 for Caucasian babies (it is much less common in other races). Many women now receive genetic testing during pregnancy for CF, although it is not a routine screening test.

Developmental Dysplasia of the Hip (DDH). See hip dysplasia.

Diarrhea. Frequent passage of watery or very soft poop. In a breastfed baby, diarrhea is defined more by the dramatic increase in frequency of poop than by the texture.

Duodenal atresia. Congenital abnormality of the first part of the small intestine to form. It's often associated with other abnormalities. Babies are diagnosed with this disorder before birth by an abnormal ultrasound (extra amniotic fluid found) or shortly after birth when they start vomiting bile. This requires surgical repair.

Eczema. A skin disorder that causes redness and scaling. The underlying problem seems to be allergic in nature, and children with eczema have flare-ups with exposure to perfumed products and certain chemicals. Eczema can be associated with other allergic disorders such as asthma, seasonal allergies, and food allergies but it can also occur without any other problems.

Egocentric. The inability to see things from someone else's point of view. This is a child's view of the world from age two to about seven years.

Emesis. The technical term for vomit.

Enamel hypoplasia. A thinning of the enamel of the teeth found in babies who are born prematurely. And, there appears to be less "catch up' growth of that enamel in babies born prematurely compared to their full term peers. This may result in increased risk of cavities.

Encephalitis. Brain inflammation usually caused by a virus or a bacterial infection.

Engorgement. The Milkman Cometh. Period of excessive breast milk production around three to five days after childbirth. Women's breasts feel full and often uncomfortable until milk demand and milk supply equilibrate.

Epispadias. Congenital abnormality of the formation of a boy's urethra (tube connecting the bladder to the outside). The hole is located on the top side of the penis, instead of in the center. This requires surgical repair.

Epstein's pearls. Tiny cysts (white bumps) found on the roof of the mouth in newborns. These are common, non-problematic, and go away on their own.

Erb's palsy. An injury to the nerves that supply the arm. This occurs as a result of a difficult delivery requiring the baby's head to be pulled forcefully. On examination, the arm will hang limp. The nerve injury usually heals in a year, but may require surgery or physical therapy.

Eruption Hematoma. This is just a bruise under the gum line that can occur as the tooth is breaking through the gums. It can look pretty darn impressive–swollen and blue or purple. No worries. It means a tooth will be arriving soon.

Erythema toxicum. A normal newborn rash that looks like flea bites (white pimple with red around it). These tiny bumps come and go.

Esophagitis. The inflammation of the upper part of the gastrointestinal system (esophagus).

Expressive language delays. A child whose ability to speak words is behind his peers. A child with this delay may have completely normal ability to understand and process language that he hears (see receptive language).

Failure to thrive. When a baby or child falls below the 3rd percentile on the weight curve. When the problem is a chronic one, height and head size also drop on the growth curves. Failure to thrive prompts a thorough medical evaluation.

Fat necrosis. An occasional complication from vaccination injection. As a needle goes through the fat under the skin, it can injure it and create a firm lump. This lump may be present for several weeks after the injection is given. It is painless and not harmful.

Flaring (nostrils). When an infant or young child is having trouble breathing (respiratory distress), he will use any additional methods his body can to get in more air. Nostrils will flare with each breath to try to capture more air. Thus, this is a red flag for respiratory distress.

Flat angiomata. Official term for an "angel kiss" birthmark on the forehead or eyelids. These are flat, reddish colored marks that eventually fade. The color becomes more dramatic with crying or anger.

Fomites. Objects handled by a person with an infection that subsequently allows passage of the germs to someone else.

Fontanelle. A space between the bones of the skull that allows room for the baby's head to pass through the birth canal and room for the baby's brain to grow after birth. The main fontanelle is on top of the head (anterior) and is sometimes called the baby's "soft spot." There is a smaller fontanelle in the back of the head (posterior). The anterior fontanelle closes between nine to 18 months of age.

Food poisoning (see gastroenteritis)

Foreign body/object. Term used to describe an object which has no place being where it is in someone's body. Kids have a way of putting objects like small toys in their noses, ears, etc. as well as swallowing them.

Foremilk. A breastfeeding term used to describe the milk that is released in the first several minutes of nursing. It is less fatty than what comes out later (see **hindmilk**). If your breastfed baby is a snacker, he may not be getting the richer milk. For these babies, its better to nurse on one breast per feeding.

Frenulum. The tissue that connects the tongue to the base of the mouth. (see **ankyloglossia**).

Frenulectomy. The process of clipping the tissue at the tongue base to correct a 'tongue tie' or ankyloglossia. This procedure can be performed in an office setting if the baby is less than a few weeks old.

Galactosemia. A rare metabolic disorder that makes a baby unable to digest galactose, a milk sugar. Newborns are routinely tested for this disorder in the state metabolic screen. If present, a baby needs a special formula diet. Breastmilk contains galactose, so it is not possible to breastfeed. Babies who have galactosemia and continue a normal diet can have intellectual disabilities.

Gastroenteritis. An inflammation of the stomach and intestines caused by either a virus or bacteria. The inflammation can cause both vomiting and diarrhea. Viral gastroenteritis is commonly known as the "stomach flu" and tends to cause watery diarrhea. Bacterial gastroenteritis is commonly known as "food poisoning" and tends to cause diarrhea mixed with blood or mucous.

Gastroesophageal reflux (GER, acid reflux). The backflow of food and liquids from the stomach into the esophagus (and often all the way to the mouth). This is a common problem for newborns up to age one year. The muscle that separates the esophagus and the stomach (lower esophageal sphincter) is relatively loose in infants, allowing food to travel down to the stomach (good) and back up to the esophagus (not good). Once food contents make it to the stomach, they are mixed with stomach acid. So, when this partially digested food goes backwards, the stomach acid can irritate the esophagus, cause discomfort, and sometimes wheezing or coughing (GERD–Gastroesophageal Reflux Disease). Most babies outgrow this problem by age one.

Gingivostomatitis. Inflammation and irritation of the gums and lining of the mouth caused by the Oral Herpes virus. The amount of inflammation is usually extensive and may lead to refusal to eat or drink anything.

Glaucoma. Increased pressure behind the eye. Babies with hemangiomas near the eye need to be evaluated by an ophthalmologist because they are at risk for glaucoma.

Heart murmur. A noise heard in addition to the normal heart sounds audible with a stethoscope. The murmur can be due to normal heart function (termed innocent, benign, or transitional). Or, it can be due to a structural defect of the heart or great blood vessels coming off of the heart (termed pathologic). The type of noise, location of the noise, and other abnormalities found on physical examination help determine the cause of the murmur. All murmurs do not require an echocardiogram and a cardiologist evaluation to determine the cause.

Hemangioma. See Strawberry Hemangioma.

Hemolytic Uremic Syndrome. (Also known as HUS). A group of medical problems caused by some food poisoning (E coli, Shigella) infections. The problems include severe anemia, low platelet count, and kidney failure. HUS typically occurs in children ages four months to four years of age.

Hemophilia. A genetically inherited blood clotting disorder. People with this disorder lack a chemical clotting "factor" that impairs the body's chain reaction to clot blood when bleeding occurs. In general, this is a disease of males and women are only carriers (i.e. not affected) because the gene for the disorder is on the "X" chromosome.

Henoch-Schonlein Purpura. (Also known as HSP) Inflammation of the blood vessels (vasculitis) after a viral illness. Symptoms include a dramatic rash of raised bruised areas on the legs. Joint pain, abdominal pain, and blood in the urine also occur. Although the disease sounds and looks serious, 90% of children recover completely without any treatment. Occurs mostly in children aged four to 10 years.

Hernia. The term used to describe a bulging out of tissue or organ where it is not supposed to be. It occurs due to a weakness of a muscle wall. The most common types include:

Diaphragmatic hernia—abdominal organs protrude into chest
Femoral hernia—intestines protrude into thigh
Inguinal hernia—intestines protrude into groin
Umbilical hernia—intestines protrude into belly button

The risk of all hernias is that the organ that is bulging out will get stuck in that position and cut off the blood supply to it. Umbilical hernias rarely get stuck (incarcerate), thus rarely require any treatment.

Hemorrhagic disease of the newborn. A relatively common (one in 200) problem of newborns who have a Vitamin K deficiency. Infants with this disorder can have severe bleeding. Because of this risk, all newborns receive a shot of Vitamin K shortly after they are born.

Hindmilk. Another breastfeeding term. This refers to the fattier milk that comes out after several minutes of nursing. This milk can actually look yellow (like fat). Don't be alarmed–it's good stuff.

Hip dysplasia. Also known as congenital hip dyplasia, or developmental dysplasia of the hip. This is a congenital abnormality where the leg bone is out of its socket at the hip. It is easily treated with a brace if detected in the first few months of life. Babies who are **breech** have a slightly higher risk of having this disorder.

Hirschprung's disease. A congenital abnormality where the nerves of the rectum (intestinal exit) don't form. As a result, newborns cannot poop (stool) without assistance. Infants with severe constipation may have a partial defect and are also tested for this disorder. Treatment is surgical.

Histamine. A chemical compound the body produces in an allergic response. Histamine causes the characteristic "allergy symptoms" that people experience such as hives, itchy eyes, and congestion.

Human Papilloma Virus (HPV). A virus that is transmitted through sexual contact. HPV can live in the undersurface of the foreskin of an uncircumcised man. HPV is also a known factor in the development of cervical cancer in women.

Hydrocele. A fluid collection in a boy's scrotum. Rarely, it is associated with a **hernia**. Most of the time, the fluid is present at birth and goes away on its own by six months of life. It makes the boy's scrotum look unusually large.

Hydrocephalus. An abnormally large collection of cerebrospinal fluid (CSF), the fluid that bathes the brain and spinal cord. This can be caused by excessive production, blockage of the collection pathway, or decreased absorption in the body. Symptoms include: bulging fontanelle (soft spot), headache, vomiting, enlarged head size, loss of developmental milestones, and abnormal neurologic exam.

Hypospadias. A congenital abnormality where the urethra (tube that connects the bladder to the outside) opening is on the underside of the penis instead of in the middle. This requires surgical repair, usually after six months of age. Because the foreskin is used to perform the repair, these babies are not circumcised.

Hypothyroidism. A poorly functioning thyroid gland produces a suboptimal level of thyroid hormone. Thyroid hormone is an essential chemical needed for body metabolism. Babies with congenital hypothyroidism can become mentally retarded (cretins) if they are not treated. This is one of the screening tests performed in the state metabolic screen. The incidence of congenital hypothyroidism is one in 4000 newborns.

Idiopathic Thrombocytopenic Purpura (ITP). The destruction of platelets due to an autoimmune response in the body. Can occur after a viral ill-

ness. Because platelets are needed to clot blood, a low count causes bruising and **petechiae**. Some children need medication to help the body increase platelet production in the body, others bounce back on their own. The good news is that almost 90% of kids do beautifully and have no further problems after the one episode.

Imperforate Anus. A congenital abnormality where the anus (opening of the intestines to the outside) does not form completely. This abnormality is often associated with a combination of abnormalities called VATER syndrome. It is repaired surgically.

Inflammatory Bowel Disease (IBD). Chronic swelling of the intestinal lining that results in bloody diarrhea. Crohn's Disease and Ulcerative Colitis are types of IBD. It is rare for a child under age two years to be diagnosed with this disorder.

Inguinal hernia. (see **hernia)**

Inhaled steroid. Medication used to control chronic asthma symptoms. The medication is administered via a machine that aerosolizes it (nebulizer) or via a hand-held "inhaler." The inhaled method is preferable because most of the medication goes to the location it is intended to help (i.e. the lungs). Very little of the medicine gets absorbed into the bloodstream—this means there is less of the unwanted side effects and more therapeutic benefit.

Intestinal obstruction. This is a general term to describe the blockage of the intestine. The gastrointestinal tract is like a big pipe, and in these terms, obstruction is a clogged pipe. This can occur due to intussusception, volvulus, malrotation (congenital defect), and hernias. Because the area is blocked, blood flow to the intestines decreases and may cause death of that tissue. This is a surgical emergency or an "acute abdomen." Symptoms include distended belly, vomiting bile.

Intraventricular hemorrhage (IVH). Bleeding within the brain area called the ventricles due to a weak, fragile matrix of blood vessels and blood pressure changes in premature babies. Premature babies born before 32 weeks gestation or less than three pounds are at risk for IVH, which most often occurs in the first five days of life. Some bleeds may be minor and have no significant long term consequences. Severe bleeds can be potentially fatal or have significant neurologic effects.

Intussusception. When a piece of intestine telescopes upon itself creating an intestinal obstruction. The most common time this occurs is between six and 18 months of age. Symptoms include intermittent abdominal pain with pulling up of the legs. Vomiting, and poop that looks like "currant jelly" also occur. This is an emergency. Diagnosis (and treatment) can be done with a special radiological study.

Jaundice. Yellowing of the skin and the whites of the eyes due to a collection of body garbage called bilirubin. The newborn period is a unique time in life that causes a "normal" jaundice. Outside of the newborn period, jaundice is NOT normal. It requires a thorough medical evaluation to look for the cause.

Kawasaki Disease. An illness that causes the body's blood vessels to swell (vasculitis). The cause is unknown. Occurs mostly in children under two years of age. Symptoms include: fever for five or more days straight, rash on the palms and soles, peeling skin on the fingertips, pink eye, bright red lips/tongue, swollen lymph nodes in the neck, general body rash, and irritable mood. The most severe complication is swelling of the arteries that supply the heart (coronary artery aneurysm). This disease is one of the reasons that doctors want to see a child who has had a fever for five consecutive days or more.

Kernicterus. A serious consequence of jaundice. Bilirubin collects in the brain, causing permanent damage.

Labial adhesion. A condition where the labia minora (smaller lips) of the vaginal opening get stuck together. This happens in little girls because they do not make estrogen hormone yet (pre-puberty). The amount of tissue that is stuck can vary. The problem is that the urethra (opening for the bladder) is located beneath the labia. If the lips are almost completely fused shut, estrogen cream (RX) is applied so that the urine can flow out more easily. Once the labia are unstuck, it is prudent to put Vaseline on the area at diaper changes to prevent them from re-sticking. All girls outgrow this condition once they hit puberty.

Laryngomalacia. A floppy airway. Some babies are born with relaxed throat tissue. When they breathe in, they make a high pitched squeaky noise (**stridor**). Babies outgrow this condition, often by age one. These babies get evaluated by an ear, nose, and throat specialist just to confirm the diagnosis. It does not affect their breathing and no treatment is needed.

Leukemia. Abnormal production of body's blood cells which then leads to failure of the bone marrow to produce normal blood cells necessary for body functioning. Symptoms include: fever, fatigue, paleness of the skin, excessive bruising, **petechiae**, and joint pain.

Macrocephaly. Official term to describe a big head. Most of the time, a child's big head is due to his genes (i.e. someone else in the family has a big head). But, if the head size percentile is enlarging or if there are other concerning symptoms, a doctor may evaluate the head with an imaging study to rule out **hydrocephalus** or a **brain tumor**.

Malabsorption. When the intestine is not performing its job of digesting food. The result is a watery, foul smelling diarrhea. Some causes of chronic malabsorption are **celiac disease** and **cystic fibrosis**. This deserves to be checked out.

Malrotation. A congenital abnormality in the development of the intestines. The abnormal position creates a problem with blood flow to the intestines as well as potential for obstruction of food transit. Newborns with this problem have vomiting, constipation, and abdominal pain. Treatment is surgical.

Masturbation. A normal behavior of exploring one's sexual organs. Both boys and girls do it.

Meconium. The first poop a newborn passes. Black, tarry, sticky. Some babies will pass this first poop before birth during a stressful labor. If the meconium is seen prior to birth, a baby will have his nose, mouth, and throat suctioned at delivery to prevent passage of this stuff into the lungs (called **meconium aspiration syndrome**).

Meconium ileus. A failure of the newborn's poop (**meconium**) to pass because of abnormally thick intestinal secretions. This condition is associated with **cystic fibrosis**.

Meconium plug. A delay in passing of the newborn's first poop (**meconium**). This usually responds to rectal stimulation (e.g. taking a rectal temperature).

Meningitis. Inflammation of the tissues that line the brain and the spinal cord. This can be caused by a virus, bacteria, or by tuberculosis. Symptoms include: headache, vomiting, TRUE IRRITABILITY (i.e. inconsolable), bulging fontanelle (soft spot), fever, neck stiffness, seizures, **petechiae**. This is a medical emergency.

Metabolic disorder. A broad term that describes disorders in breaking down foods (see metabolic storage disease below). These disorders are different than endocrine disorders, which involve abnormal levels of body hormones (e.g. thyroid disease, diabetes, adrenal disease).

Metabolic Storage Disease (Inborn Errors of Metabolism). A group of diseases that all cause an inability to break down certain food products. As a result, byproducts of metabolism accumulate. In some of these disorders this accumulation goes to body parts (liver, heart, brain, kidney, eye) causing permanent damage or even death. The more common storage diseases are tested for on the state metabolic screens (**PKU, galactosemia**).

Microcephaly. The technical term for a small head. Head size is often hereditary. Families with small heads have small headed babies. However, if a child's head size percentile is plateauing or decreasing, an imaging study may be done to look for **craniosynostosis**.

Milk protein allergy. Milk contains protein, sugar, and fat. Some babies (about 2%) have an allergy to the protein component that causes inflammation and irritation of the intestine lining. This leads to diarrhea that can be mixed with blood or mucous. A significant percentage of

babies who are allergic to milk protein are also allergic to soy protein. The good news—most kids outgrow this problem.

Milia. A normal newborn rash on the nose that look like pinpoint white dots. These go away on their own.

Miliaria. A normal newborn rash that looks like prickly heat. This goes away on its own.

Mongolian Spots. A bruise like discoloration found on the buttocks of darker pigmented newborns. These spots fade over several years. No treatment is needed.

Murmur. (see heart murmur)

Nasolacrimal Duct Obstruction (blocked tear duct). Babies have narrow tear ducts that lead out to the corner of the eyes. Occasionally, the tube gets clogged. Tears, which are usually watery, get thick from being backed up. The result—goopy fluid that comes out of the eyes. This can happen intermittently for the first year of life. You can help open up the duct by massaging gently just below the corner of the eye near the nose. I usually refer patients to an eye doctor if this is happening beyond a year of age. The difference between blocked tear ducts and pink eye (infection) is that the eye is not red or irritated.

Natal Teeth. Every once in a blue moon, a baby is born with a tooth. These usually fall out spontaneously and the real baby teeth come in at the normal time, between 6-12 months.

Nevus Flammeus (Stork bite, angel kiss). These are newborn birthmarks located at the nape of the neck, eyelids, and forehead. They are bright pink in color. The marks on the face fade over the first year of life. The marks on the neck can last forever. These marks are not associated with cancer.

Neural tube defects. A congenital abnormality of the brain/spinal cord development. Many of these disorders can be detected prenatally via an abnormal AFP test or an ultrasound. These disorders vary in severity. The most severe form is lack of brain formation (anencephaly). The least severe form is **spina bifida occulta** (see **sacral dimple**), where there is completely normal nerve function.

Neurofibromatosis (NF). A genetic disorder (gene defect) that causes tumors of the tissue covering nerves. Babies are often born without symptoms, although some will have three or more **cafe au lait spots** at birth. As a child grows, he develops numerous (more than five) cafe au lait spots and freckles in the armpit and groin areas. The tumors on the nerves grow later and can be seen as large bumps under the skin. Most of these tumors are benign (not cancerous), but can occur in dangerous places (e.g. eye, ear, brain, kidney). Children with this disorder are seen regularly by a number of doctors. FYI: The diagnosis of NF is not made on the presence of cafe au lait spots alone—this is only one of sev-

eral symptoms and signs. Most children with a few cafe au lait spots do not have NF.

Newborn acne. (see acne)

Newborn nasal congestion. All newborns have snotty noses. They will sneeze, snort, cough, and snore. This lasts for four to six weeks. If it does not interfere with feedings or sleep, do nothing. If it is causing a problem, use saline nose drops to flush the nose before feedings or bedtime.

Nursing caries. These are cavities–the result of feeding a baby during the night after his come in. If you don't wipe teeth off after a midnight snack of breast milk/formula/milk (which all contain sugar), the sugar will sit on the teeth and make a nice place for plaque and subsequent cavities.

Omphalitis. A belly button infection. The umbilical stump and skin surrounding it looks red and swollen. There is a foul odor coming from it. If this occurs in a newborn, it usually requires admission to a hospital for intravenous (IV) antibiotics.

Orbital cellulitis. A serious infection that involves the tissue surrounding the eye. It is caused by a sinus infection that spreads into the area. Symptoms include: limited eye motion, bulging of the eyeball, eyelid swelling, eye pain, and fever. This is the reason that doctors want to see children who have eyelid swelling and a fever.

Orthotic. A custom made shoe insert designed by a podiatrist to provide arch support for people who are flat-footed. The AAP does not currently recommend orthotics for babies and young children.

Otitis media. Literally, middle ear inflammation. Acute otitis media refers to an active infection that came up shortly before it is diagnosed in the office. Serous otitis media (or otitis media with effusion) refers to residual fluid that remains after the active infection is over.

Otitis externa. (Otherwise known as swimmer's ear) Literally, external ear inflammation. This is really an infection of the skin that lines the ear canal. It is caused by water that pools in the ear canal and allows germs to grow. Symptoms include pain with touching the ear itself, swelling and redness of the canal, and sometimes a fever. This is uncommon in the under one age group.

Paraphimosis. The foreskin gets stuck behind the head of the penis in an uncircumcised boy. This causes lots of swelling and pain.

Pathologic Heart Murmur. (see Heart Murmur)

Penile adhesions. The head of the penis sticks to the shaft skin. In boys who are circumcised, it is important to visualize the edge of the head at diaper changes and clean the area of any debris (smegma). If the skin starts to get stuck together, try gently pulling down at the base of the penis to separate the area.

Perforated eardrum. Occurs with severe middle ear infection. A small hole in the eardrum lets the pus drain. It is the equivalent of a pimple popping and draining. Pus and blood will be seen draining out of the ear canal.

Periodic breathing. Newborns do not breathe in a regular pattern. They breathe 30 to 60 times a minute, but very erratically. There may be a stretch of several pants in a row, then a long p-a-u-s-e, then a big breath. That is normal, as long as that pause is less than ten seconds.

Pervasive Developmental Delay (PDD). A disorder of development that falls into the category of Autism Spectrum Disorders. Children with PDD are higher functioning and capable of limited social interactions. They may also have more language skills than those who are severely affected.

Phenylketonuria (PKU). A metabolic disorder routinely tested on the state metabolic screen. It is a genetic defect in an enzyme that breaks down phenylalanine. The incidence is one in 10,000. People with this disorder need to have a special diet. See **metabolic storage disease**.

Phimosis. Inability to pull the foreskin of an uncircumcised boy's penis back. In severe cases, circumcision is necessary to fix the problem.

Phototherapy. The term used for treatment of moderate-severe jaundice (hyperbilirubinemia). A jaundiced baby is placed in a blue light source (either via "bili" blanket or bank of lights). The lights help to breakdown the bilirubin. For babies who are mildly jaundiced, we do NOT recommend placing an undressed baby near a sunny window in the house. It doesn't help and makes the baby uncomfortable.

Pneumonia. Lung inflammation caused primarily by infection. Both viruses and bacteria can cause pneumonia. The tiny air sacs (alveoli) fill up with pus and prevent air exchange. Symptoms include fever, cough, chest pain, and respiratory distress.

Polydactyly. When there are more than five fingers or toes on a hand or a foot. The extra digit can be removed.

Port wine stain. This is a large, red/purple, flat birthmark that occurs on one side of the face or limb. These do not fade over time and are mostly a cosmetic issue. If the birthmark covers the eyelid, a child is evaluated for glaucoma. Any time it occurs on the forehead or eye, a child is also evaluated for a brain abnormality (**Sturge-Weber syndrome**).

Posterior urethral valves. A congenital defect of the formation of the urethra (tube that connects the bladder to the outside). There are valves that normally push the urine (pee) outwards. In this condition, the valves push the urine backwards into the urinary tract. This is rare, and only occurs in boys.

Post-tussive emesis. The Latin words for "after-cough" vomiting. Babies and young children have overactive gag reflexes. So a forceful cough might bring up lunch. All vomiting in children is not due to an upset stomach.

Preauricular pits and tags. Minor congenital defects of the formation of the external ear. The pits are due to remnants of a cyst that occurred prior to birth. Pits are rarely associated with hearing disorders. The tags are extra pieces of skin. If severe, these can be removed for cosmetic reasons.

Pseudostrabismus. The false appearance that a child looks cross-eyed or has a lazy eye due to the child's facial structure. Babies and young children are often referred to a pediatric ophthalmologist for concerns of a lazy eye (**esotropia, amblyopia**) and are ultimately diagnosed with this benign entity. But, it is better to be on the safe side and check out any concerns.

Pustular melanosis. A normal newborn rash found in darker pigmented babies. The original rash looks like little pimples. As the lesions fade, they leave a temporary brown freckle. Some babies have hundreds of these freckles. They go away on their own.

Pyelonephritis. An infection of the kidneys. In an acute infection, a child has fever, back pain, and pain with urination. Infants under six months of age with a bladder infection routinely get admitted to the hospital because there is a greater risk of the infection extending into the kidneys.

Pyloric stenosis. A narrowing of the outlet from the stomach to the small intestine due to a congenital abnormality in the muscle (pylorus). Babies (more commonly males) will have projectile (REALLY IMPRESSIVE) vomiting at every feeding starting between two and four weeks of life. The vomiting may start out in a small way, but progressively gets worse and more projectile. Delay in seeking medical attention results in dehydration. Treatment is surgical, by making a cut in the muscle.

Refractive errors. This fancy term means that one cannot focus an image perfectly in the eye (retina). It includes near-sightedness, far-sightedness, astigmatism, and amblyopia.

Respiratory Distress. This is the term used to describe a child who is air-hungry. If a child cannot successfully get enough oxygen in with each breath, he will breathe faster, heavier, and use chest wall muscles to get as much air in as possible. This equates to a child who is panting, grunting, flaring his nostrils, and retracting (sucking in of the ribcage).

Respiratory Syncytial Virus (RSV). This is a virus that causes different symptoms depending on the age, and health status of the person. Healthy adults may have an RSV infection and feel like they have a cold. A premature baby may have complete respiratory collapse and need hospitalization. A healthy six month old may have a ton of nasal secre-

tions, wheeze, and breathe at twice his normal respiratory rate but not have any distress. RSV shows up every year between November and April in the northern hemisphere.

Retinoblastoma. A malignant tumor of the eye that occurs in babies. Fortunately, this is quite rare. This is one of the important reasons we do an eye exam in the nursery.

Retinopathy of Prematurity (ROP). Incomplete growth of blood vessels in the eyes due to premature birth. Babies born at less than 32 weeks gestation are at the greatest risk of ROP. The growth of the blood vessels need to be monitored regularly by a pediatric ophthalmologist to head off any abnormalities, such as retinal folding/detachment, or permanent vision defects.

Retractions. The term used to describe the sucking in of the ribcage when a child has **respiratory distress**. Retractions occur when the body starts using the chest wall muscles to pull more air in with each breath. With phone encounters, we will ask you to look at how your child is breathing to tell us if he has retractions.

Rickets. Malformation of growing bones in children most commonly due to Vitamin D deficiency. Vitamin D is necessary for calcium to be deposited into the bone (which makes them hard). Bones will form with a bent shape because they are softer than they should be.

Ringworm. (see fungal infections in Chapter 13, "Infections")

Rooting reflex. This is a newborn 'primitive' reflex that causes a baby to turn his head if you stroke his cheek. It is an instinctive mechanism that encourages eating. Babies lose this primitive reflex by three to six months of age.

Sacral dimple. This is a tiny divot, or dimple in the lower portion of the back. These can be associated with a minor abnormality of neural tube development called spina bifida occulta. The L5-S1 vertebrae bone is slightly abnormal but the spinal cord (nerve) is formed normally. Most babies with sacral dimples are unaffected and do not need evaluation or treatment.

Seborrhea. (Also known as dandruff, cradle cap) A skin problem that causes greasy, flaky, and sometimes red skin in areas where 'sebaceous glands' reside–typically the scalp, ears, beside the nose, eyebrows. Many babies are afflicted with this and outgrow it. Teenagers can also get seborrhea and have it for a lifetime. Treatment includes anti-dandruff shampoos, low potency steroid creams/lotions, and vegetable oil to loosen up the flakes in the scalp.

Sensory Processing Disorder. A constellation of behaviors stemming from an inability to process and adapt to stimuli of the five senses. Children with this disorder have trouble with activities of daily living and social

encounters (aversion to textured foods, dislike of socks and tags on clothing, avoidance of messy activities, avoidance of being touched...) Diagnosis occurs most frequently in pre-school or school aged children.

Serous otitis media. Fluid in the middle ear space. This fluid can be present several weeks to months after an acute infection (i.e. ACUTE otitis media). This fluid is sterile (free of bugs), but has the potential to get re-infected. Antibiotics are not usually necessary or helpful to clear the fluid.

Shoulder dystocia. This refers to a difficult delivery where the shoulders are forcefully pulled to get the baby out. This happens to a mom with a small pelvis or a big baby. Occasionally, the collar bone (clavicle) breaks during delivery. It heals nicely without any residual problems.

Sickle cell anemia. A hereditary abnormality of the red blood cell structure, causing impaired oxygen carrying capacity and increased destruction of the red blood cells.

Sinusitis. (see Chapter 13, "Infections")

Skin tags. These are tiny pieces of raised skin that can occur anywhere on the body. In the newborn, they are most frequently found in front of the ear (**preauricular tag**) or on the vagina. They are not problematic and require no intervention.

Spina Bifida. A congenital abnormality of the spinal cord development. There is a spectrum of severity of the defect. Most severe defects cause paralysis of the legs and body parts supplied by the affected nerves (bowel, bladder function). The incidence of spina bifida is decreasing as more women are taking pre-natal vitamins (folic acid) during pregnancy. See **neural tube defects.**

Stevens-Johnson Syndrome. A serious allergic reaction that can be fatal.

Strabismus. An abnormal alignment of the eyes.

Strawberry Hemangioma. A birthmark made of a collection of blood vessels. The vessels grow and enlarge for the first few years of life. So, the birthmark gets bigger. The good news–the vessels shrink up and disappear, usually by age five years. Surgery is usually not done to remove these. However, laser therapy may be helpful for lesions on the eyes, nose, or lips. Cool trend: using topical medication to shrink the blood vessels.

Stridor. A squeaky, high pitched noise with breathing in that can be heard without a stethoscope. In newborns, it is usually caused by **laryngomalacia**. In any other situation, it is a sign of respiratory distress at the level of the throat. Children with severe **croup** infection have a very swollen airway if they have stridor. If your child has stridor, call your doctor immediately.

Stork Bites. see Nevus Flammeus

Sturge Weber syndrome. A serious disorder that includes brain abnormalities in combination with a port wine stain on the face. Brain atrophy, seizures, and paralysis can occur.

Subconjunctival hemorrhage. Broken blood vessel on the surface of the eye. Most often, this occurs in a newborn after delivery. It's not serious (even though it can look worrisome to a new parent). It can take a few weeks to resolve on its own.

Supranumerary nipple (accessory nipple). These are extra, nonfunctional nipples found along the same vertical line as the nipples themselves. They are not problematic. They can be removed for cosmetic reasons.

Supraventricular Tachycardia (SVT). The heart beats at an extraordinarily faster pace (over 200 beats per minute) because a faulty electrical circuitry in the heart. The abnormality may be detected if a baby appears pale, has trouble feeding, or is extremely irritable.

Syndactyly. Two or more fingers or toes are fused either partially or fully together. The severity of the defect determines whether treatment is required.

Thrush. (see Chapter 13, Infections)

Tongue-tied (see ankyloglossia)

TORCH infections. This is an acronym for the standard tests that are done in Mom's prenatal evaluation. They include: Toxoplasmosis, Syphilis, Rubella, Cytomegalovirus (CMV), Hepatitis B, HIV, and Herpes. In certain situations, Varicella (chickenpox) and Parvovirus are also tested. If Mom has been infected, or is a carrier of the Hepatitis B virus, her baby receives not only the Hepatitis B vaccine at birth, but also a shot of medicine to prevent passage of infection.

Torticollis. Literally means, "twisted neck." When it occurs in newborns, (about 1 in 100 babies), it is called congenital torticollis. It occurs more commonly in babies who are born in breech presentation. It usually becomes noticeable by two to four weeks of age, when the baby's head appears tilted to one side. Occasionally, a knot is felt in the neck where the neck muscle is tensed and tightened. Rarely, these babies have other associated issues like hip dysplasia or strabismus. If left untreated, babies can develop asymmetry of the face and skull. Treatment includes muscle stretching exercises and encouraging the baby turn his head in the opposite direction.

Transient Tachypnea of the Newborn (TTN). A common cause of mild respiratory distress in the newborn. Fetuses swallow amniotic fluid while in the womb. When a baby is born vaginally, that fluid gets squeezed out as the baby passes through the birth canal and cries for the first time. Rarely, some of that fluid remains in babies delivered vaginally.

More commonly, babies delivered by C-section have this problem. The good news is that the babies all do just fine. They breath faster than normal and may need a little oxygen for the first hour of life.

Transitional heart murmur. The term for a benign, flow murmur heard in the first 24 hours of life. As a baby is born, the fetal heart circulation changes over to the newborn circulation. There are a series of valves that close off the fetal blood pathways and open pathways to the lungs. We often hear the turbulence of blood flow as this is happening. It's nothing to worry about. If a murmur is heard after 24 hours of life, or has a different quality or location that it is heard, your doctor will evaluate it further.

Transmitted upper airway noise. Noise that comes from the nose that is heard and felt in the lungs. When there is a moderate amount of nasal congestion (snot) in the nose, the air going through it makes a loud noise as it passes through. Since babies and young children don't know how to blow their noses, this is often a unique occurrence in this age group.

Tuberculosis. (Known as TB. Previously known as "consumption"). Infectious lung disease that causes nodules in the lungs, but can spread to the lymph nodes and brain. The scary part of the disease is that people can be infected or be "carriers" of the infection without showing symptoms. People 0with active infection classically have fever, cough, weight loss, night sweats, and blood in the mucous they cough up. Although TB is less common than it used to be, it occurs in urban populations and immigrants from Asia, Africa, and Latin America. Recommendations for TB screening (PPD) varies among communities, but most public schools no longer require routine testing for their students.

Umbilical hernia. See **hernia.** These are very common in newborns, particularly African American babies. The size of the hernia can be quite large, but the intestine almost never (I've had one patient) gets stuck (incarcerated). These are caused by weak abdominal muscles which will get stronger as the baby starts using them. Most of these hernias resolve on their own. If the hernia is still present by age two, I'll refer a child to a pediatric surgeon for repair. Old Wives Tale: You do not need to bandage the hernia or place a coin on it to make it go away. Your baby will fix the problem himself when he starts doing Ab crunches.

Undescended testes. Failure of the male sex organs to descend into the scrotum in the newborn male. (In fetal development, they grow in the pelvic area, then travel down to the scrotum.) Often, the testes will come down on their own by six months of life. If they don't, a surgical procedure is performed to affix the testes in the scrotum. Testes in the pelvis are at slightly higher risk for testicular cancer, and make it awfully difficult to perform a monthly self-testicular exam in that location.

Uric acid crystals. A waste product found in the urine. When the urine is concentrated (low water volume), the uric acid will pull itself out of the urine solution and can be found in crystal form in the diaper. It looks like

brick dust and tends to alarm parents who think it is blood. It is an indication of mild dehydration—so aggressive feeding is the only treatment.

Urinary tract infections (UTI). An infection in the urinary bladder. It is difficult to diagnose a bladder infection in babies because they do not complain that it burns when they urinate. Sometimes fever and irritability are the only symptoms. It is a good idea to obtain a urine specimen on babies who have a fever with no obvious source of infection.

Vaginal discharge. Newborn girls often have vaginal discharge due to fluctuating hormone levels. Older girls who have vaginal discharge prior to puberty need to be evaluated for infection.

Ventricular Septal Defect (VSD). The most common type of congenital heart defect (abnormal formation of the heart in the fetus). In this defect, a hole is present in either the muscle wall or tissue between the two large chambers (ventricles) of the heart. A murmur is detected due to the blood flow that crosses between the chambers. Most of these holes close on their own with no medical intervention. Children with VSD's are followed by pediatric cardiologists until the hole closes.

Vernix. A cheesy, greasy white coating found on the skin of newborns. It will wash off at your baby's first bath.

Vesicles. Pinpoint, fluid filled blisters seen classically with chickenpox, shingles, and herpes infections. In chickenpox, these lesions appear in crops over a period of a few days.

Vesicoureteral reflux (VUR). An abnormality in the urinary tract system that causes urine to track backward towards the bladder and kidneys. This urine is not sterile, thus these children are predisposed to bladder and kidney infections. VUR is classified by the severity of how extensively the urine tracks in the wrong direction. Grade 1 is mildest and Grade 5 is the most severe. Many children outgrow this disorder, but it can take several years (up to age seven). Children with severe reflux (Grades 4-5) may need surgical repair to prevent scarring and permanent kidney damage. About 70% of children with Grade 3 reflux outgrow it on their own. Virtually all children with milder forms (Grades 1-2) outgrow VUR without any intervention. There is a hereditary predisposition to this disorder.

von Willebrand Disease. A genetically inherited bleeding disorder that affects both the platelets and the blood clotting chain reaction. People with this disorder have frequent, excessive nosebleeds, easy bruising, and heavy periods.

Whooping Cough. (See pertussis in Chapter 12, "Vaccines.")

Yeast infection. (See thrush, yeast diaper rash in Chapter 13, "Infections.")

References for this section are footnoted in Appendix F, "Footnotes."

REFERENCES

RECOMMENDED READING, WEB SITES & MORE

Appendix E

Q. How do I know if a website has reliable medical information?

Here are a few thoughts:

1. Find out who has created the website. Is there contact information?
2. What is the purpose of the website?
3. Who are the experts giving the advice?
4. What references are cited? Citations should be listed from scientific journals.
5. Be suspicious of information that is opinionated or seems biased.
6. Be suspicious of products that are touted as cure-alls or miracles.

Source: ImmunizationInfo.org

Reality Check

80% of people who Google for information online do not bother to check the source of the information they are reading. Know your source. Fact check before believing everything you read!

Good books to have in the house

Alternative and Complementary Therapies

Kemper, K. *The Holistic Pediatrician*. New York: HarperCollins, 2002.

Breastfeeding

Hale, T. *Medications and Mother's Milk*. 15th Edition. Amarillo: Pharmasoft Publishing, 2012.

Huggins, K. *The Nursing Mother's Companion*. 6th edition: 25th anniversary edition. Boston: Harvard Common Press, 2010.

Child Development/Behavior

Brazelton, T. *Touchpoints*. Revised edition. Cambridge MA: DeCapo Press 2006.

Lerner, C. *Bringing Up Baby*. Washington, D.C.: Zero To Three Press, 2005.

Davis, L. *Becoming The Parent You Want to Be*. New York: Broadway Books, 1997.

Medical Information

Woolf, A. *Children's Hospital Guide to Your Child's Health and Development.* Persens 2002.

Nutrition

Swinney, B. *Baby Bites.* New York: Meadowbrook Press, 2007.

Sleep

Ferber, R. *Solve Your Child's Sleep Problems*. Completely revised and updated. New York: Fireside, 2006.

Mindell, J. *Sleeping Through the Night: How Infants, Toddlers, and Their Parents Can Get a Good Night's Sleep*. Revised Edition. New York: Harper Collins, 2005.

Weissbluth, M. *Healthy Sleep Habits, Happy Child.* New York: Fawcett Books, 2005.

Vaccinations

Offit P and Moser C. *Vaccines and Your Child. Separating Fact from Fiction.* New York: Columbia University Press, 2011.

Myers MG and Pineda D. *Do Vaccines Cause That? A Guide for Evaluating Vaccine Safety Concerns*. Galveston: I4PH, 2008.

Reliable web sites

For starters, go to our website at baby411.com for a wealth of useful information, a visual library of rashes and diseases (see Bonus Material), parent chat room, and links to reliable websites (several of which are listed below). We also suggest you sign up for our free e-newsletter for updates on infant health news.

Adoption

University of Minnesota, Adoption Clinic	peds.umn.edu/iac/
Adoption Alliance	i-a-a.org
Association for Research in International Adoption	adoption-research.org
Centers for Disease Control	cdc.gov/ncidod/dq/
U.S. Dept. of State	travel.state.gov/adopt.html

Allergies

American Academy of Allergy, Asthma, and Immunology	aaaai.org
Food Allergy Network	foodallergy.org
Allergy and Asthma Network	aanma.org
Asthma and Allergy Foundation of America	aafa.org

Alternative Therapies/Herbal remedies

National Center for Complementary and Alt. Medicine	nccam.nih.gov/
UCSF Complementary- Alt. Med	library.ucsf.edu/collres/reflinks/cam/

Breastfeeding

iBreastfeeding Bookstore	ibreastfeeding.com
Breastfeeding.com	breastfeeding.com

Cancer

National Cancer Institute	cancer.gov/cancer_information/
Johns Hopkins	hopkinscancercenter.org

Carseats

Children's Hospital of Philadelphia	chop.edu/carseat
National Highway Traffic Safety Administration	nhtsa.gov
American Academy of Pediatrics	aap.org
National Safe Kids Campaign	safekids.org

Childcare

National Association for the Education of Young Children	NAEYC.org
Child Care Aware	childcareaware.org

Child Development

Centers for Disease Control	cdc.gov/actearly
Reach Out and Read	reachoutandread.org
Zero to Three	zerotothree.org
National Institutes of Health (cerebral palsy)	ninds.nih.gov
Learning Disabilities Association of America	ldanatl.org
Easter Seals	easterseals.org

Cord blood banking

General info	parentsguidecordblood.com
National Marrow Donor	marrow.org

Diabetes

American Diabetes Association	diabetes.org
Juvenile Diabetes Research Foundation International	jdrf.org

Emergency Care

Emergency Medical Services for Children	emscmn.org

Gastrointestinal problems (stomach/intestine)

North American Society for Pediatric Gastroenterology and Nutrition	naspgn.org

General medical information

American Academy of Pediatrics	aap.org
Food and Drug Administration	fda.gov
Keep Kids Healthy	keepkidshealthy.com
Kids Health	kidshealth.org
Mayo Clinic	mayoclinic.com
National Institutes of Health	ncbi.nlm.nih.gov
Medscape	medscape.com
Parents Magazine	parents.com
Centers for Disease Control	cdc.gov

Heart defects

American Heart Association	americanheart.org
Cincinnati Children's Hospital	cincinnatichildrens.org/heartcenter/encyclopedia/

HIV in children

U.S. Dept. of Health and Human Services	aidsinfo.nih.gov

Lung Problems

American Lung Association	lungusa.org
Cystic Fibrosis Foundation	cff.org
Stanford University CF Center	cfcenter.stanford.edu
American Academy of Allergy, Asthma, and Immunology	aaaai.org

Nervous System/Seizure disorders

American Academy of Neurology	aan.com
Epilepsy Foundation	epilepsyfoundation.org

Nutrition

Centers for Disease Control	cdc.gov
American Dietetic Association	eatright.org

Sickle Cell Disease

Sickle Cell Disease Association of America, Inc.	sicklecelldisease.org

Skin Disorders

Johns Hopkins Hospital	med.jhu.edu/peds/dermatlas
National Eczema Association	nationaleczema.org

Supplemental Newborn Screening

Baylor
Baylorhealth.com/medicalspecialties/metablicdisease/newbornscreening.htm

March of Dimes	Marchofdimes.com
Mayo	mayoclinic.com
National Newborn Screen	genes-r-us.uthscsa.edu
Pediatrix	pediatrix.com
Save The Babies	savebabies.org
National Coalition for PKU	pku-allieddisorders.org

Travel Health

Centers for Disease Control	cdc.gov/travel/index.htm

Vaccinations

American Academy of Pediatrics	aap.org
World Health Organization	who.int/gpv
Immunization Action Coalition	immunize.org
National Network for immunization info	immunizationinfo.org
Vaccine Adverse Event Reporting System	fda.gov/cber/vaers/vaers.htm
Centers for Disease Control	cdc.gov/nip
Children's Hospital of Philadelphia	vaccine.chop.edu

National Organizations

**There is a support group for virtually every medical disease and syndrome. The organizations below should be able to link you to a specific organization to meet your particular needs.*

American Academy of Pediatrics, 141 Northwest Point Blvd., Elk Grove Village, IL 60007. Phone: (847) 434-4000; Web: aap.org

Centers for Disease Control and Prevention, 1600 Clifton Road, Atlanta, GA 30333. Phone: (800) 311-3435; Web: cdc.gov

Easter Seals, 230 West Monroe St., Suite 1800, Chicago, IL 60606 Phone: (800) 221-6827 x7153; Web: easter-seals.org

March of Dimes Birth Defects Foundation, 1275 Mamroneck Ave., White Plains, NY 10605 Phone: (888) 663-4637; Web: modimes.org

National Center on Birth Defects and Developmental Disabilities, 4770 Buford Highway, N.E., Atlanta, GA 30341, Phone: (770) 488-7150; Web: cdc.gov/ncbddd

ZERO to THREE: National Center for Infants, Toddlers, and Families. 2000 M Street NW, Suite 200, Washington, DC 20036, Phone: (202) 638-0851; Web: zerotothree.org

Growth Chart: Boys (Birth to 24 months)

Birth to 24 months: Boys
Length-for-age and Weight-for-age percentiles

NAME ____________________

RECORD # ____________

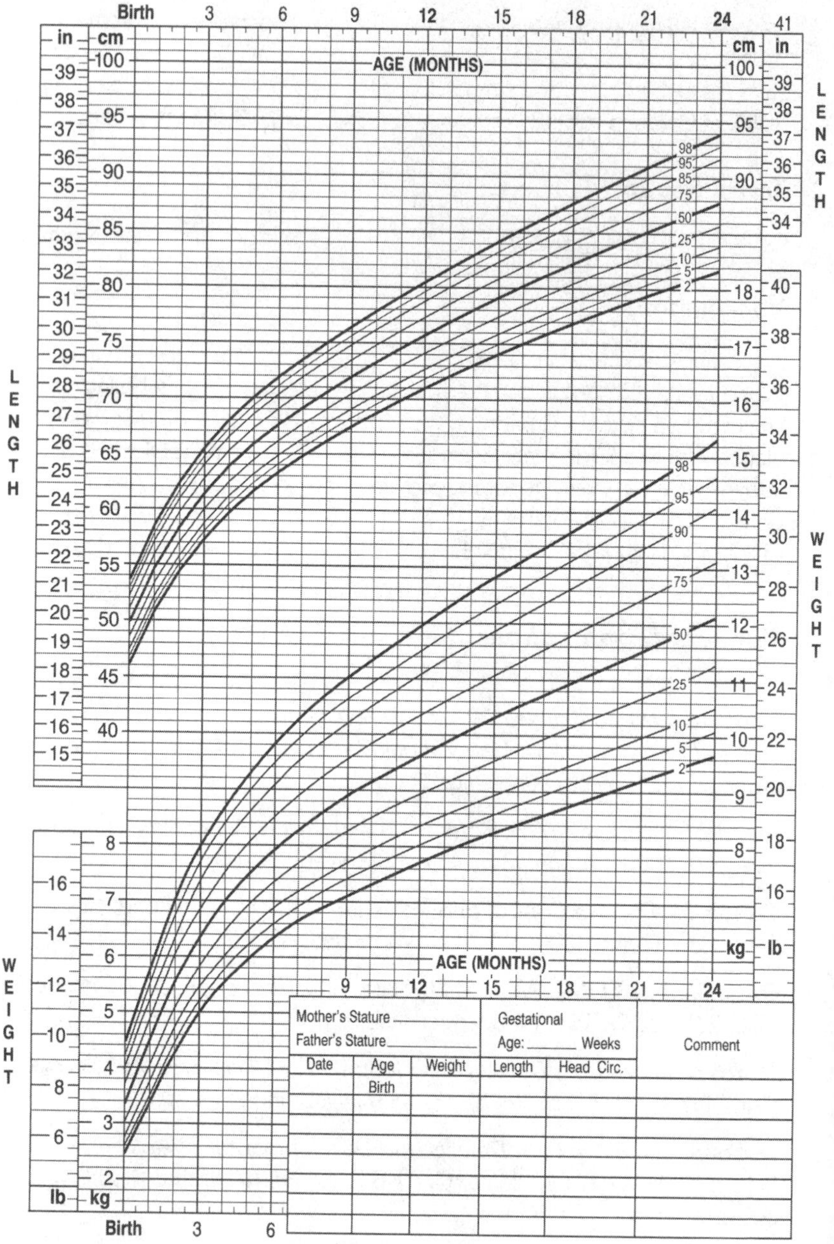

AGE (MONTHS): Birth, 3, 6, 9, 12, 15, 18, 21, 24

LENGTH (cm): 45, 50, 55, 60, 65, 70, 75, 80, 85, 90, 95, 100
LENGTH (in): 15–41

WEIGHT (kg): 2–18
WEIGHT (lb): 6–40

Percentiles: 2, 5, 10, 25, 50, 75, 90, 95, 98

Mother's Stature ______ Father's Stature ______			Gestational Age: ______ Weeks		Comment
Date	Age	Weight	Length	Head Circ.	
	Birth				

Published by the Centers for Disease Control and Prevention, November 1, 2009
SOURCE: WHO Child Growth Standards (http://www.who.int/childgrowth/en)

Growth Chart: Girls (Birth to 24 months)

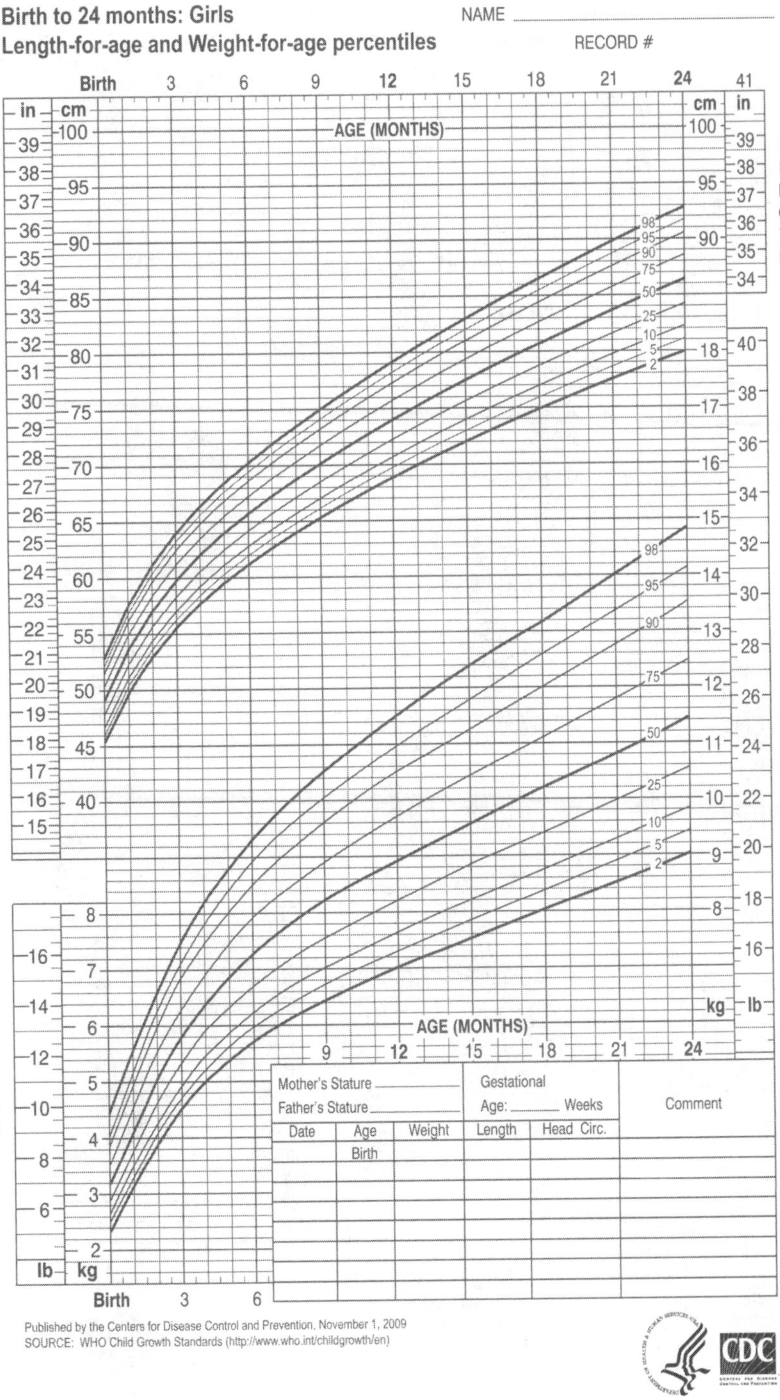

Birth to 24 months: Girls
Length-for-age and Weight-for-age percentiles

NAME ______________________

RECORD # ______

AGE (MONTHS): Birth, 3, 6, 9, 12, 15, 18, 21, 24

LENGTH (cm): 45, 50, 55, 60, 65, 70, 75, 80, 85, 90, 95, 100
LENGTH (in): 15–41

Length percentiles: 98, 95, 90, 75, 50, 25, 10, 5, 2

WEIGHT (kg): 2–18
WEIGHT (lb): 6–40

Weight percentiles: 98, 95, 90, 75, 50, 25, 10, 5, 2

Mother's Stature ______
Father's Stature ______

Gestational Age: ______ Weeks

Date	Age	Weight	Length	Head Circ.	Comment
	Birth				

Published by the Centers for Disease Control and Prevention, November 1, 2009
SOURCE: WHO Child Growth Standards (http://www.who.int/childgrowth/en)

CDC

references

Head Circumference: boys

Birth to 24 months: Boys
Head circumference-for-age and
Weight-for-length percentiles

NAME ______________

RECORD # ______________

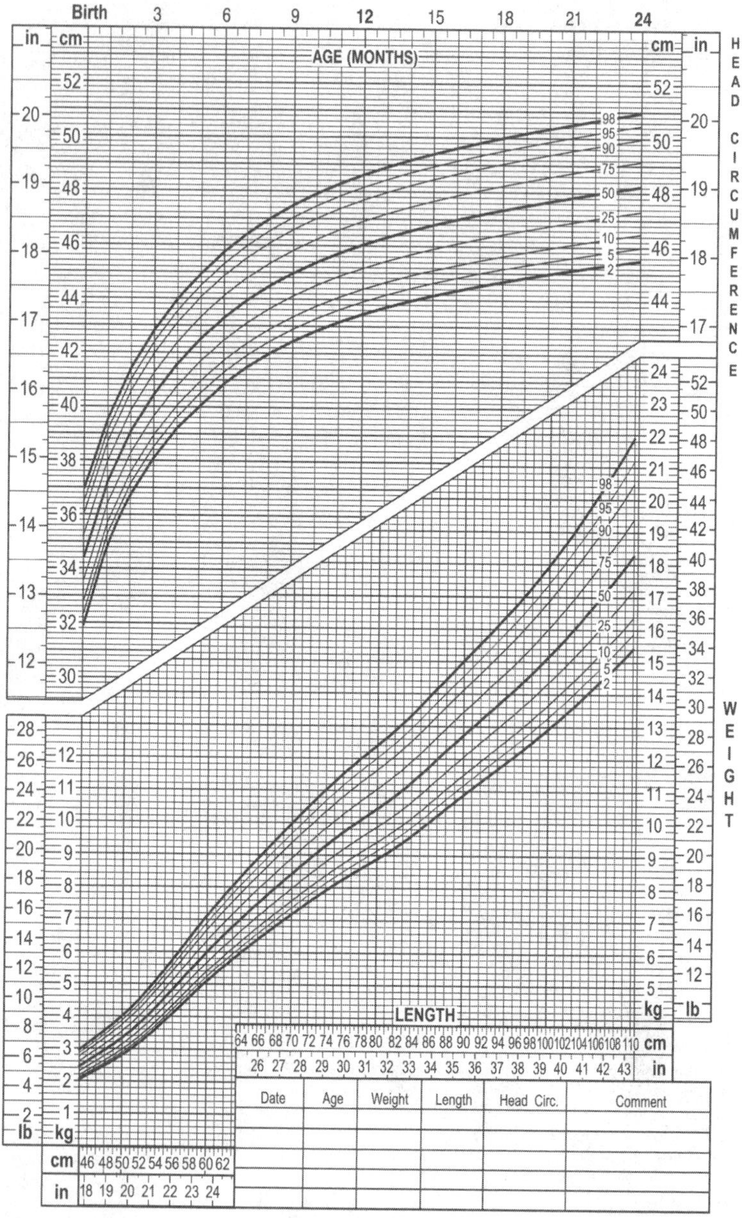

Date	Age	Weight	Length	Head Circ.	Comment

Published by the Centers for Disease Control and Prevention, November 1, 2009
SOURCE: WHO Child Growth Standards (http://www.who.int/childgrowth/en)

CDC

Head Circumference: girls

Birth to 24 months: Girls
Head circumference-for-age and
Weight-for-length percentiles

NAME ____________________

RECORD # ____________

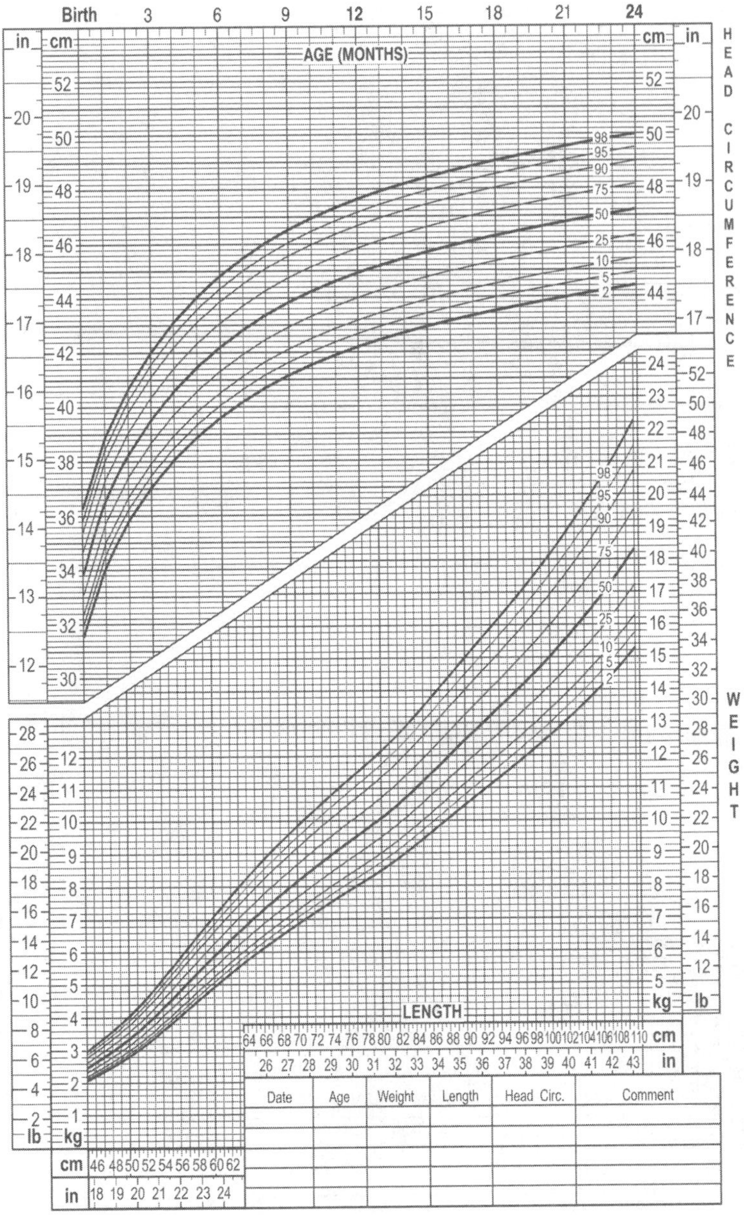

AGE (MONTHS): Birth, 3, 6, 9, 12, 15, 18, 21, 24

HEAD CIRCUMFERENCE (cm): 30, 32, 34, 36, 38, 40, 42, 44, 46, 48, 50, 52
HEAD CIRCUMFERENCE (in): 12, 13, 14, 15, 16, 17, 18, 19, 20

Percentiles: 98, 95, 90, 75, 50, 25, 10, 5, 2

WEIGHT (kg): 1–24
WEIGHT (lb): 2–52

LENGTH (cm): 46, 48, 50, 52, 54, 56, 58, 60, 62, 64, 66, 68, 70, 72, 74, 76, 78, 80, 82, 84, 86, 88, 90, 92, 94, 96, 98, 100, 102, 104, 106, 108, 110
LENGTH (in): 18, 19, 20, 21, 22, 23, 24, 26, 27, 28, 29, 30, 31, 32, 33, 34, 35, 36, 37, 38, 39, 40, 41, 42, 43

Date	Age	Weight	Length	Head Circ.	Comment

Published by the Centers for Disease Control and Prevention, November 1, 2009
SOURCE: WHO Child Growth Standards (http://www.who.int/childgrowth/en)

references

Preemie growth chart

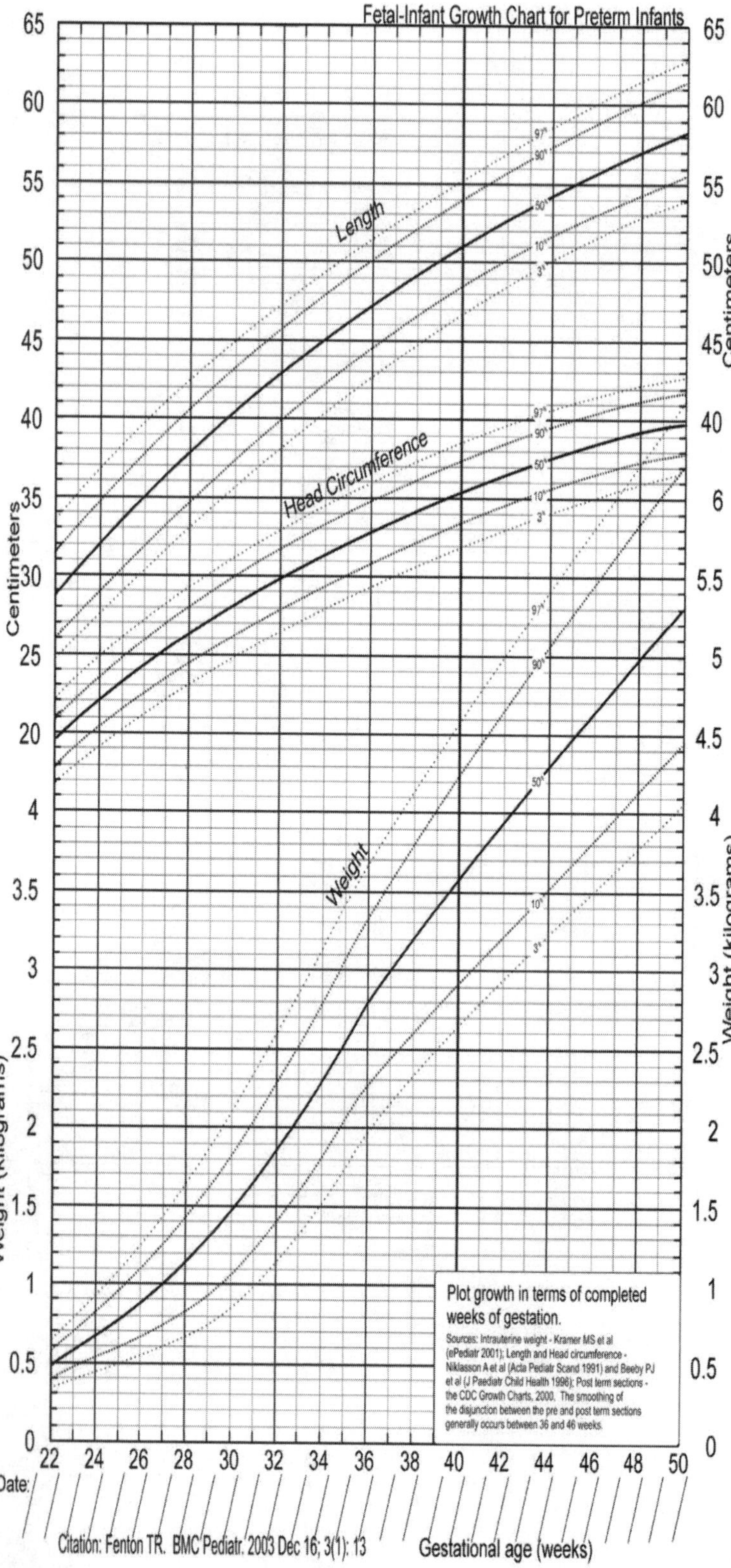
Fetal-Infant Growth Chart for Preterm Infants
Length
Head Circumference
Weight
97th
90th
50th
10th
3rd
Centimeters
Weight (kilograms)
65
60
55
50
45
40
35
30
25
20
6
5.5
5
4.5
4
3.5
3
2.5
2
1.5
1
0.5
0
22
24
26
28
30
32
34
36
38
40
42
44
46
48
50
Date:
Plot growth in terms of completed weeks of gestation.
Sources: Intrauterine weight - Kramer MS et al (ePediatr 2001); Length and Head circumference - Niklasson A et al (Acta Pediatr Scand 1991) and Beeby PJ et al (J Paediatr Child Health 1996); Post term sections - the CDC Growth Charts, 2000. The smoothing of the disjunction between the pre and post term sections generally occurs between 36 and 46 weeks.
Citation: Fenton TR. BMC Pediatr. 2003 Dec 16; 3(1): 13
Gestational age (weeks)

Footnotes
Appendix F

Chapter 1: Decisions

American Academy of Pediatrics Policy Statement: Initial medical evaluation of an adopted child. *Pediatrics* 1991; 88(3): 642-44.

American Academy of Pediatrics Section on hematology/oncology and section on allergy/immunology. Cord blood banking for potential future transplantation. *Pediatrics* 2007;119:165-170.

AAP Task Force on Circumcision: Circumcision Policy Statement. Pediatrics Vol 130 (3) Sept 2012: 585-586.

Castellsague X, et al: Male circumcision, penile human papillomavirus, and cervical cancer in female patients. *New England Journal of Medicine* 2002 Apr 11; 346 (15): 1105-12.

Celedon, et al: Day care attendance, respiratory tract illnesses, wheezing, asthma, and total serum IgE level in early childhood. *Archives of Pediatric and Adolescent Medicine* 2002; 156: 241-245.

Centers for Disease Control, Yellow Book 2010.

Collins S, etal. Effects of circumcision on male sexual function: debunking a myth? J Urol 2002 May; 167 (5): 2111-12.

Huston AC, Aronson, SR: Mothers' Time With Infant and Time in Employment as Predictors of Mother-Child Relationships and Children's Early Development. *Child Development* 2005;76 (2):467-482.

Kamper-Jorgensen M, etal. Population-based study of the impact of childcare attendance and hospitalizations for acute respiratory infections. *Pediatrics* 2006;118:1439-1446.

Kim D, etal. The effect of male circumcision on sexuality. *BJU* Int 2006 Nov 28, PMID 17155977

Martinez F. The "coming of age" of the hygiene hypothesis. Respiratory Sciences Center, University of Arizona, Respiratory Research, April 2001.

Masood S, etal. Penile sensitivity and sexual satisfaction after circumcision: are we informing men correctly? *Urol Int*. 2005:75 (1): 62-6.

Pasquini, et al: The Likelihood of Hematopoietic Stem Cell Transplantation (HCT) in the United States: Implications for Umbilical Cord Blood Storage. American Academy of Pediatrics. *Pediatrics* 1999 July; 104 (1): 116.

Quinn TC. Circumcision and HIV Transmission. *Current Op In ID* 20(1):33-38 2007

Tobian AA, etal. Male circumcision for the prevention of HSV-2 and HPV infections and syphilis. *NEJM*. 2009;360(13):1298-309.

Chapter 3: Birth Day

Abrams SA. Calcium and phosphorus requirements in newborn infants. In Rose BD (Ed), UptoDate, Waltham, MA, 2007.

American Academy of Pediatrics Clinical Report: Late Preterm Infants: a population at risk. *Pediatrics* 2007;1389-1400.

American Academy of Pediatrics Policy Statement. Newborn and Infant Hearing

Loss: Detection and Intervention. *Pediatrics* 1999; 103(2): 527-530.

Centers for Disease Control, Nov 2010. http://www.cdc.gov/mmwr/preview/mmwrhtml/rr5910a1.htm?s_cid=rr5910a1_w

Hovert DL etal. Annual summary of vital statistics: 2004. *Pediatrics* 2006 Jan;117(1):168-83

Sturgeon PE. Care of the neonatal intensive care graduate. In Basow D (Ed), *UptoDate*, Waltham, MA, 2011.

Shaheed K. Monitoring growth of preterm NICU graduates. In Basow D (Ed), UptoDate, Waltham, MA, 2011.

Chapter 4: Hygiene

American Academy of Pediatrics. Guidelines for Perinatal Care. 5th Ed. Elk Grove Village, IL: 2002

American Academy of Pediatrics Policy Statement: Oral Hygiene. *Pediatrics* 2003; 111(5): 1113-1116.

Fradin, MS: Comparative efficacy of insect repellant against mosquito bites. *New England Journal of Medicine* 2002; 347: 13-18.

Huang JT, etal. Treatment of Staphylococcus aureus colonization in atopic dermatitis decreases disease severity. *Pediatrics*. May 2009;123:e808-e814.

Palazzi DL, etal. Care of the umbilicus and management of umbilical disorders. In Rose BD (Ed), UptoDate, Waltham, MA, 2007.

Integrated Management of Pregnancy and Childbirth. Pregnancy, Childbirth, Postpartum and Newborn Care: A guide for essential practice. World Health Organization. 2nd Ed. 2006.

Wall Street Journal May 20, 2003. PD8.

Zupan J, etal. Topical umbilical cord care at birth. *Cochrane Database Syst Rev* 2004;(3):CD001057.

Chapter 5: Nutrition & Growth

American Dental Association. ADA.org, Fluoride and Infant Formula Frequently Asked Questions, indexed 3/22/07.

American Academy of Pediatrics Clinical Report. Persing J, etal. prevention and management of positional skull deformities in infants. *Pediatrics* 2003;112(1):199-202.

American Academy of Pediatrics Committee on Nutrition: Pediatric Nutrition Handbook, 6th Ed. Elk Grove Village, IL, 2009.

American Academy of Pediatrics Section on Breastfeeding. Breastfeeding and the use of human milk. *Pediatrics*. 2012;129:e827-e841

Baker RD, Greer FR, and AAP Committee on Nutrition. Diagnosis and prevention of iron deficiency and iron-deficiency anemia in infants and young children (0-3 years of age) *Pediatrics* 2010;126:1040-1050.

Behrman, RE. Editor: Nelson Essentials of Pediatrics. Philadelphia: WB Saunders, 1990.

Bernbaum JC. Primary Care of the Preterm Infant. St. Louis: Mosby,1993.

Gabbert D, etal. Adenovirus 35 and obesity in children and adolescents. *Pediatrics* 2010;126:721-726.

Gartner LM, et al: American Academy of Pediatrics. Prevention of rickets and Vitamin D deficiency. New guidelines for Vitamin D intake. *Pediatrics* 2003;111(4):908-910.

Huh SY, etal. Timing of solid food introduction and risk of obesity in preschool aged children. *Pediatrics* 2011;127:e544-e551.

Institute of Medicine, 2010 iom.edu/Reports/2010/Dietary-Reference-Intakes-for-Calcium-and-Vitamin-D.aspx

Kim J, etal. Growing up to a new standard. WHO growth charts make breastfeeding the norm. Pediatric Basics, *Journal of Pediatric Nutrition and Devel* 2007;116:16-20.

Nield LS, etal. Odd skull shapes: head's up on diagnosis and therapy. *Consultation for Pediatricians*. November 2006:701-709.

Taylor SN, etal. Vitamin D: benefits for bone, and beyond. *Contemporary Pediatrics* 2006;23(11):70-82.

Chapter 6: Liquids

American Academy of Pediatrics Committee on Nutrition: Soy protein-based formulas: recommendations for use in infant feeding. *Pediatrics* 1998;101:148-153.

American Heart Association, etal. Dietary guidelines for children and adolescents: a guide for practitioners. *Pediatrics* 2006;117(2):544-59.

Barnes GR, Lethin AN, Jackson EB, et al. Management of breastfeeding. *JAMA*.1953;151:192.

Centers for Disease Control. E. sakazakii infections associated with the use of powdered infant formula- Tennessee 2001. *MMWR* 2002;51:297-300.

Centers for Disease Control, breastfeeding statistics at cdc.gov accessed April 2011.

Chandran L. Is there a role for long-chain polyunsaturated fatty acids in infant nutrition? *Contemporary Pediatrics* 2003;20(2):107-124.

Danner SC. Breastfeeding the neurologically impaired infant. Waco, TX: *NAACOGS Clin Issu Peri Womens Health Nurs.* 1992;3(4):640-6.

Georgieff M. Taking a rational approach to the choice of formula. *Contemporary Pediatrics* 2001;18(8):112-130.

Huggins K: The Nursing Mother's Companion. Third Revised Ed. Boston: The Harvard Common Press, 1995.

Human Milk Banking Association of North America, February 2011

Lawrence, RA: Breastfeeding: A Guide for the Medical Profession, 5th ed. St. Louis: Mosby, 1999.

Montgomery-Downs HE, etal. Infant feeding methods and maternal sleep and daytime functioning. *Pediatrics* 2010 DOI: 10.1542/peds 2010-1269.

O'Connor NR, etal. Pacifiers and breastfeeding: a systematic review. *Arch Pediatr Adolesc Med* 2009;163(4):378-382.

Oddy W, etal. Breastfeeding duration and academic achievement at ten years. *Pediatrics* 2011; 127(1):e137-e145

Riordan J, Auerbach KG. Breastfeeding and Human Lactation. Sudbury: Jones and Bartlett Publishers, 1999.

Sampson, HA. Food Allergy, Part 1. Immunopathogenesis and clinical disorders. *J Allergy Clin Immunol* 1999; 103:717-28.

Schach B, etal. Colic and food allergy in the breastfed infant: is it possible for an exclusively breastfed infant to suffer from food allergy? *J Hum Lact* 2002;18(1):50-52.

Sicherer S, etal. Maternal consumption of peanut during pregnancy is associated with peanut sensitization in atopic infants. *JACI* 2010;126(6):1191-1197.

Suitor CW. Nutrition care during pregnancy and lactation: new guidelines from the IOM. *J Am Diet Assoc* 1993;93:478.

Vennemann MM, etal. Does breastfeeding reduce the risk of Sudden Infant Death Syndrome? *Pediatrics* 2009;123(3):e406-e410.

Weizman Z, etal. Effect of a probiotic infant formula on infections in child care centers: comparison of two probiotic agents. *Pediatrics* 2005;115(1):5-9.

West D. Physician's Breastfeeding Triage Tool Kit. International Lactation Consultant Association. Copyright 2006. Adapted with permission.

Chapter 7: Solids

American Academy of Pediatrics Committee on Nutrition: *Pediatric Nutrition Handbook*, 6th Ed. Elk Grove Village, IL, 2009.

Du Toit G, etal. Early consumption of peanuts in infancy is associated with a low prevalence of peanut allergy. *JACI* 2008;122(5):984-91.

Eigenmann PA, et al: Prevalence of IgE mediated food allergy among children with atopic dermatitis. *Pediatrics* 1998;101(3):e8.

Greer FR, etal. Effects on early nutritional interventions on the development of atopic disease in infants and children: the role of maternal dietary restriction, breastfeeding, timing of introduction of complementary foods, and hydrolyzed formulas. *Pediatrics* Jan 2008;121:183-191.

Hill ID. Celiac disease in children. In: UpToDate, Basow DS (Ed). UpToDate.com. Waltham, MA 2013.

Huh SY, etal. Timing of solid food introduction and risk of obesity in preschool-aged children. *Pediatrics* 2011;127:e544-e551.

NIAID. Guidelines for the diagnosis and management of food allergy in the U.S., December 2010.

Sampson HA. Food allergy. *J Allergy Clin Immunol* 2003;111(12):540-547.

Sampson HA. Food-induced anaphylaxis. In *UpToDate*, Basow, DS (Ed), UpToDate, Waltham, MA, 2011

Snell-Bergeon JK, etal. Early childhood infections and the risk of islet autoimmunity: the diabetes autoimmunity study in the young (DAISY). *Diabetes Care.* 2012 Dec;35(12):2553-8.

Wood, RA. The natural history of food allergy. *Pediatrics* 2003;111(6):1631-1637.

Chapter 8: The Other End

American Urological Association. Pediatric VUR Clinical Practice Guidelines Panel. Report on the Management of VUR in Children.1996.

American Urological Association. Management and screening of primary vesicoureteral reflux in children. 2010.

Edmunds A. Gastroesophageal reflux disease in the pediatric patient. *Therapeutic Spotlight* 2005;4-13.

Finnell SME, etal. Diagnosis and management of an initial UTI in febrile infants and young children. Pediatrics 2011;128(3):e749-770.

Friedman AL. Acute UTI. What you want to know. *Contemporary Pediatrics* 2008;25(10):68-75.

McClung HJ, et al: Constipation and dietary fiber intake in children. Pediatrics 1995;96:999-1001.

Nelson SP, etal. One-year followup of gastroesophageal reflux during infancy. *Pediatrics* 1998;102(6):e67.

Orenstein SR. Symptoms and reflux in infants: infant gastroesophageal reflux questionnaire revised (I-GERQ-R)—utility of symptom tracking and diagnosis. *Curr Gastro Rep* 2010 Dec;12(6):431-6.

van der Pol RJ, etal. Efficacy of proton-pump inhibitors in children with gastroesophageal reflux disease: a systematic review. *Pediatrics* 2011;127:925–935.

Chapter 9: Sleep

American Academy of Pediatrics, SIDS Task Force, press conference, October 10, 2005.

Coleman-Phox K etal. *Arch Ped Adol Med* 2008;162:963.

Duncan JR, etal. Brainstem serotonergic deficiency in SIDS. *JAMA* 2010;303(5):430-437.

Ferber R. *Solve Your Child's Sleep Problems*. New York: Simon & Schuster, 1985.

Kleitman N. *Sleep and Wakefulness*, 2nd Ed. Chicago: University of Chicago Press,1963.

Mindell JA, etal. Behavioral treatment of bedtime problems and night wakings in infants and young children. *Sleep* 2006;29(10):1263-1276.

Okami P, et al. Outcome correlates of parent-child bed sharing: an eighteen-year longitudinal study. *Dev and Behav Pediatrics* 2002;(23)4:244-253.

Paterson DS, etal. Multiple serotonergic brainstem abnormalities in sudden infant death syndrome. *JAMA* 2006;296(17):2124-2132.

Price AMH, etal. Five-year follow-up of harm and benefits of behavioral infant sleep intervention: randomized trial. *Pediatrics.* 130(4) 2012: p643-651.

Rao MR, etal. Long-term cognitive development in children with prolonged crying. *Arch Dis Child* 2004;89:989-992.

Stifter CA, etal. The effect of excessive crying on the development of emotion regulation. *Infancy* 2002; 3(2): 133-152.

Thach BT, etal. Deaths and injuries attributed to infant crib bumper pads. *Jnl Peds* 2007;(4)28:271-74.

Touchette E. Lecture at annual meeting of the Associated Professional Sleep Societies, 2003.

Willinger M, etal: Trends in infant bed sharing in the United States, 1993-2000: The National Infant Sleep Position study. *Arch Ped Adol Med* 2003;157(1):43-49.

Chapter 10: Development

American Academy of Pediatrics website aap.org/immunization/families/safety.html American Academy of Pediatrics, Committee on Public Education. Children, Adolescents, and television. *Pediatrics* 2001;107:423-426.

American Academy of Pediatrics. Health supervision for children with Down syndrome. *Pediatrics* 2001;107:442.

American Academy of Pediatrics. Council on Communications and Media. Policy Statement: Media use and children younger than two years. *Pediatrics*. 2011;128(5): 1040-1045.

Anderson DR, Pempek TA. Television and very young children. *American Behavioral Scientist* 2005;48(5):505-522.

Atladottir HO, etal. Autism after infection, febrile episodes, and antibiotics during pregnancy: an exploratory study. *Pediatrics*. 2012; 130(6) e1447-1454.

Brainerd, C. *Piaget's Theory of Intelligence*. Englewood, NJ: Prentice-Hall, 1978.

Brenner RA, etal. Association between swimming lessons and drowning in children: a case-controlled study. *Arch Ped Adol Med* 2009 Mar;163(3):203-10.

Chahrour M, etal. MECP2, a key contributor to neurological disease, activates and represses transcription. *Science* 2008 May 30;320(5880):1224-9.

Cheslack-Postava etal. Closely spaced pregnancies are associated with increased odds of autism in California sibling births. *Pediatrics* 2011;127(2)

Chyi LJ, etal. *J Peds* 2008;153;25-31

Croen LA, etal. Maternal and paternal age and risk of autism spectrum disorders. *Arch Ped Adol Med* 2007 Apr 161(4):334-40.

Dehaene-Lambertz G, etal. Functional organization of perisylvian activation during presentation of sentences in preverbal infants. Proceedings of the National Academy of Sciences, France, 2006. Pnas.org/ cgi/doi/10.1073/pnas. 0606302103

Fatemi SH, etal. Maternal infection leads to abnormal gene regulation and brain atrophy in mouse offspring; implications for genesis of neurodevelopmental disorders. *Schizo Res* 2008;99(1-3):56-70.

Goodwyn SW, etal. Impact of symbolic gesturing on early language development. 2000;24;81-103.

Harder AF. Learningplaceonline.com.

Jamain S, etal. Mutations of the X-linked genes encoding neuroligins NLGN3 and NLGN4 are associated with autism. *Nature Genetics* 2003;34:27-29.

Kaiser Family Foundation, 2003.

Krakowiak P, etal. Maternal metabolic conditions and risk for autism and other neurodevelopmental disorders. *Pediatrics*. 2012. 129 (5) e1221-1128.

Limperopoulos C, etal. Positive screening for autism in ex-preterm infants: prevalence and risk factors. *Pediatrics* Apr 2008; 121:758-65.

Maestro S. *Psychopathology* 1999; 32(6):292-300.

Mills JL, etal Elevated levels of growth-related hormones in autism and autism spectrum disorder. *Clinical Endocrinology* 2007;67(2):230-7.

Suren P, etal. Association between maternal use of folic acid supplements and risk of autism spectrum disorders in children. *JAMA*. 2013 Feb 13;309(6):570-7.

Vandewater EA, Bickham DS, etal. Time well spent? Relating television use to children's free-time activities. *Pediatrics* 2006:117:181-191.

Volk HE, etal. Traffic-related air pollution, particulate matter, and autism. *JAMA Psychiatry*. 2013; 70(1):71-77.

footnotes

Chapter 11: Discipline & Temperament

Harriett Lane Handbook, 2002.

High P: Data compiled at Infant Development Center, Brown Univ, 2003.

Jaafar SH, Jahanfar S, Angolkar M, Ho JJ. Pacifier use versus no pacifier use in breastfeeding term infants for increasing duration of breastfeeding. *Cochrane Database of Systematic Reviews* 2011, Issue 3. Art. No.: CD007202. DOI: 10.1002/14651858.CD007202.pub2.

Kurcinka MS. Raising your Spirited Child: A Guide for Parents Whose Child is More Intense, Sensitive, Perceptive, Persistent, Energetic. Harper, 1998.

Perry R, et al. Nutritional supplements and other complementary medicines for infantile colic: a systematic review. Pediatrics, April 2011. 127:720-733. Robertson J, etal. The Harriett Lane Handbook. A Manual for Pediatric House Officers. 17th Ed. Philadelphia: Mosby, 2005.

Savino F, etal. Lactobacillus reuteri vs. simethicone in the treatment of infantile colic: a prospective randomized study. *Pediatrics* 2007;119:e124-130.

Thomas A, Chess S. *Temperament and Development.* New York: Brunner/Mazel 1977.

Viggiano D. *Arch Dis Child* 2004;89:1121-1123.

Chapter 12: Vaccinations

American Academy of Pediatrics Technical Report: Mercury in the environment: implications for pediatricians. *Pediatrics* 2001; 108 (1): 197-205.

Centers for Disease Control website at cdc.gov/vaccines/pubs/pinkbook/ pink-appendx.htm#appg Accessed on March 8, 2009.

Centers for Disease Control website at cdc.gov/mmwr/preview/mmwrhtml/ mm57e625a1.htm. Accessed May 25, 2009.

Communicable Disease Surveillance Center, London, 2007.

Dept of Health and Human Services, Agency for Toxic Substances and Disease Registry, Tox FAQ's for Aluminum, Sept 2008.

Dept of Health and Human Services, Agency for Toxic Substances and Disease Registry, Tox FAQ's for Formaldehyde, June 1999.

DeStefano F, etal. Increasing exposure to antibody-stimulating proteins and polysaccharides in vaccines is no associated with risk of autism. *Journal of Pediatrics* 2013. DOI 10.1016/j.jpeds.2013.02.001

Eick AA. Maternal influenza vaccination and effect on influenza virus in young infants. *Arch Ped Adol Med* 2011 Feb;165(2):104-11.

EPA. Mercury study report to Congress: Vol 4: An assessment of exposure to mercury in the US; 1997. www.epa.gov/mercury.

Fenn EA: Biological warfare in eighteenth century North America: beyond Jeffrey Amherst. *Journal of American History* 2000; (86) 4: 1552-1580.

Johns Hopkins Hospital, Bloomberg School of Public Health, Institute for Vaccine Safety. Vaccinesafety.edu/cc-exem.htm.

Mitkus RJ, etal. Updated aluminum pharmacokinetics following infant exposures through diet and vaccination. *Vaccine* 2011;29:9538-9543.

Nelson K. *Pediatrics* 2003;111(3):674-678.

Newsweek at newsweek.com/id/185853

O'Brien MA, etal. Parental refusal of pertussis vaccination is associated with an increased risk of pertussis infection in children. *Pediatrics* 2009;123(6).

Offit P. Addressing parents' concerns: Do multiple vaccines overwhelm or weaken the infants' immune system? *Pediatrics* 2002;109:124.

Offit P. *Pediatrics* 2003;112(6):1394-1401.

Omer SB, etal. Geographic clustering of non-medical exemptions to school immunization requirements and associations with geographic clustering of pertussis. *Am J Epidemiology* 2008;168(12)1389-96.

Omer SB, etal. Vaccine refusal, mandatory immunization, and the risks of vaccine preventable disease. *NEJM* 2009;360(19):1981-8.

Pickering LK, editor. *Red Book: 2006 Report of the Committee of Infectious Diseases.* 27th ed. Elk Grove Village, IL: American Academy of Pediatrics, 2006.

Reis EC, et al: Taking the sting out of shots: control of vaccination-associated pain and adverse reactions. *Pediatric Annals* 1998;27(6):375-386.

Schechter R, etal. Continuing increases in autism reported to California's developmental services system: mercury in retrograde. *Arch Gen Psychiatry* 2008;65(1):19-24.

Schuval S. Avoiding allergic reactions to childhood vaccines (and what to do when they occur). *Contemporary Pediatrics* 2003; 20(4): 29-53.

Smith M, etal. On time vaccine receipt in the first year does not adversely affect neuropsychological outcomes. *Pediatrics* 2010;125:1134-1141.

Thompson WW, etal. Early thimerosal exposure and neuropsychological outcomes at 7 to 10 years. *NEJM* 2007;357:1281-1292.

UCLA website at library.ucla.edu/libraries/biomed/smallpox/

Vaccine Education Center, Children's Hospital of Philadelphia. Parent PACK Newsletter, June 2008.

Wakefield A.J, et al: Ileal-lymphoid-nodular hyperplasia, non-specific colitis, and pervasive developmental disorder in children. *Lancet* 1998;351:637-641.

Zeiger RS. Current issues with influenza vaccine in egg allergy. *Journal Allergy Clin Immunol* 2002;110:834.

Chapter 13: Infections

Baker RB. Is ear pulling associated with ear infection? *Pediatrics* 1992;90:1006-7.

Centers for Disease Control website at cdc.gov, accessed March 1, 2007.

Chai G, etal. Trends in outpatient prescription drug utilization in U.S. children 2002-2010. *Pediatrics* 2012;130:23-31.

Donowitz L. Infection control in the office: keeping germs at bay. *Contemporary Pediatrics* 2000;17(9):47.

Dowell SF. Seasonal variations in host susceptibility and cycles of certain infectious diseases. *Emerg Infect Dis* 2001;7(3):369-74.

Hoberman A, etal. Treatment of acute otitis media in children under two years of age. *NEJM* 2011. 364(2):105-115.

Leader S, etal. RSV coded hospitalizations, 1997-1999. Ped Inf Dz J. 2002:21:629.

Mangione-Smith RM, et al. The relationship between perceived parental expectations and pediatrician antimicrobial prescribing behavior. *Pediatrics* 1999;103:711-718.

MMWR March 4, 2011 Vol 60(3)

Peter G. Bacterial resistance in office practice: the need for judicious antimicrobial therapy. Lecture at 25th Annual Pediatric Postgraduate Symposium, Houston, 2003.

Pickering LK, editor. *Red Book: 2006 Report of the Committee of Infectious Diseases*, 27th ed. Elk Grove Village IL: American Academy of Pediatrics, 2006.

Post JC, et al: Is pacifier use a risk factor for otitis media? *Lancet* 2001;357:823-4.

Rosenfeld RM, etal: Clinical efficacy of antimicrobial drugs for acute otitis media: meta-analysis of 5400 children from thirty-three randomized trials. *Journal of Pediatrics* 1994;124:355-67.

Chapter 14: Diseases

Allmers H, etal. Acetaminophen use: a risk for asthma? *Curr All Asthma Rep* 2009;9(2):164-7.

Bakkeheim E, etal. Paracetamol in early infancy: the risk of childhood allergy and asthma. *Acta Paediatrica* 2011;100(1):90-96

Barrow Neurological Institute, St Joseph's Hospital and Medical Center, Phoenix AZ and Cranial Technologies, Phoenix AZ. 2008.

Beasley R, etal. Association between paracetamol use in infancy and childhood, and risk of asthma, rhinoconjunctivitis, and eczema in children aged 6-7 years: analysis from Phase Three of the ISAAC programme. *Lancet* 2008;372(9643):1039-48.

Behrman, RE. Editor: *Nelson Essentials of Pediatrics*. Philadelphia: WB Saunders, 1990.

Expert Panel Report II: *Guidelines of the Diagnosis and Management of Asthma*. 1997.

Fleisher G, Ludwig S, editors: *Pediatric Emergency Medicine*, 3rd Ed. Baltimore: Williams and Wilkins, 1993.

National Institutes of Health website at nhlbi.nih.gov/guidelines/asthma/

Ownby, D. et al: Exposure to dogs and cats in the first year of life and risk of allergic sensitization at six or seven years of age. *JAMA* 2002;288(8):963-972.

Persky V, etal. Prenatal exposure to acetaminophen and respiratory symptoms in the first year of life. *Ann Allergy Asthma Immun* 2008;101(3):271-8.

Snell-Bergeon JK, etal. Early childhood infections and the risk of islet autoimmunity: the diabetes autoimmunity study in the young (DAISY). *Diabetes Care*. 2012 Dec;35(12):2553-8.

Stein RT. Early-life viral bronchiolitis in the causal pathway of childhood asthma: is the evidence there yet? *Am J Respir Crit Care Med* 2008;178(11):1097-8.

Stellwagen L, etal. Look for the "stuck baby" to identify congenital torticollis.

Contemporary Pediatrics May 2004;21:55.

Chapter 15: Environmental Health

American Academy of Pediatrics Committee on Environmental Health: *Pediatric Environmental Health, 2nd ed.* Elk Grove Village, IL: American Academy of Pediatrics, 2003.

American Academy of Pediatrics Committee on Nutrition: *Pediatric Nutrition Handbook*, 6th Ed. Elk Grove Village, IL, 2009.

Canfield RL, etal. Intellectual impairment in children with blood lead concentrations less than 10 mcg/dl. *NEJM* 2003 Apr 17;348(16):1517-26.

Centers for Disease Control at cdc.gov/nceh/clusters/fallon/organophosfaq.htm.

Centers for Disease Control accessed April 8, 2013. atsdr.cdc.gov/toxfaqs/TF.asp?id=19&tid=3

Center for Science in the Public Interest at cspinet.org/reports/chemcuisine.htm.

Council on Environmental Health. American Academy of Pediatrics. Policy Statement Chemical-Management Policy: Prioritizing Children's Health. *Pediatrics* 2011;127:983-990.

Food and Drug Administration at FDA.gov accessed May 25, 2009.

Forman J, Silverstein J, AAP Committee on Nutrition, AAP Council on Environmental Health. Organic foods: environmental advantages and disadvantages. *Pediatrics* 2012;130:e1406.

Goldman LR. Chemicals and children's environment: what we don't know about risks. *Environ Health Perspect* 1998;106(suppl 3):875-880.

National Institutes of Health. Niehs.nih.gov/emfrapid/booklet/home.htm.

Sherburn RE, Jenkins RO. Used cot mattresses as potential reservoirs of bacterial infection: nutrient availability within polyurethane foam. *J Appl Microbiol* 2008 Feb;104(2):526-33.

Tran TT, et al: Effect of high dietary manganese intake of neonatal rats on tissue mineral accumulation, striatal dopamine levels, and neurodevelopmental status. *Neurotoxicology* 2002;23:635-643.

Wall St. Journal, June 24, 2003 p. D4.

Chapter 16: First Aid

American Academy of Pediatrics: The management of acute gastroenteritis in young children. *Pediatrics* 1996; 97(3):424-35.

Crocetti M. Fever phobia revisited: have parental misconceptions about fever changed in 20 years? *Pediatrics* 2001;107(6):1241-6.

Fleisher, G., Ludwig, S, editors. *Pediatric Emergency Medicine*, 3rd Ed. Baltimore: Williams and Wilkins, 1993.

Gunn VL, Nechyba C, editors. *The Harriet Lane Handbook: A Manual for Pediatric House Officers*, 16th ed. Philadelphia: Mosby, 2002.

Appendix A: Medications

American Academy of Pediatrics Committee on Nutrition. *Pediatric Nutrition Handbook*, 4th ed. Elk Grove, IL: American Academy of Pediatrics, 1998.

Hale T. Medications and Mother's Milk. *A Manual of Lactational Pharmacology*, 12th ed. Amarillo: Pharmasoft Publishing, 2006.

Murphy JL. editor: *Prescribing Reference for Pediatricians: Spring-Summer 2007*. New York: Prescribing Reference, Inc., 2007.

Shared PJ, etal. The effect of inhaled steroids on the linear growth of children with asthma: A meta-analysis. *Pediatrics* 2000;106(1):E8.

Appendix B: Alternative Medicines

Barrett BP, et al: Treatment of the common cold with unrefined Echinacea. A randomized, double blind, placebo-controlled trial. *Annals of Int Medicine* 2002;137(12):939-46.

Das SK, et al. Deglycyrrhizinated liquorice in aphthous ulcers. *J Assoc Physicians*

India 1989;37(10):647.
Eeles R: The effect of menthol on nasal resistance to airflow. *J Laryng Otol* 1983;97:705-9.
Fetrow CW, etal. Professional's Handbook of Complementary and Alternative Medicines, 3rd Ed. Philadelphia: Lippincott, Williams and Wilkins, 2004.
Fox N. Effect of camphor, eucalyptol, and menthol on the vascular state of the mucous membrane. *Arch Oto HNS* 1027(6):112-122.
Gardiner P. Longwood Herbal Task Force website:www.mcp.edu/herbal/
Gilroy CM, etal. Echinacea and truth in labeling. *Archives of Internal Medicine* 2003;163:699-704.
Hederos C, Berg, A. Epogram evening primrose oil treatment in atopic dermatitis and asthma. *Arch Dz in Childhood* 1996;75:494-7.
Horrobin DF. Essential fatty acid metabolism and its modification in atopic eczema. *Am Jnl Clin Nutrition* 2000;71(supp):367s-372.
Kemper, KJ: *The Holistic Pediatrician. A pediatrician's comprehensive guide to safe and effective therapies for the 25 most common ailments of infants, children, and adolescents*, 2nd ed. New York: HarperCollins, 2002.
Kopp MV, etal. Randomized, double-blind, placebo-controlled trial of probiotics for primary prevention: no clinical effects of Lactobacillus GG supplementation. *Pediatrics* 2008;121:e850-6.
Land M. Probiotics, hype or helpful? *Contemporary Pediatrics* 2008;(25)12:34-42.
Moneret-Vautrin DA, etal. Probiotics may be unsafe in infants allergic to cow's milk. *Allergy* 2006;61:507-8.
Mowrey DB. Motion sickness, ginger, and psychophysics. *Lancet* 1982;91:655-7.
National Institutes of Health. National Library of Medicine, Medline Plus. nlm.nih.gov/medlineplus accessed April 26, 2013.
National Public Radio. Politics and lobbying in the US nutritional and dietary supplements industry. National Public Radio, All Things Considered, June 23, 2003.
Paul IM, etal. Vapor rub, petrolatum, and no treatment for children with nocturnal cough and cold symptoms. Pediatrics. 2010;126:1092-99.
Perry R, etal. Nutritional supplements and other complementary medicines for colic: a systematic review. *Pediatrics* 2011;127:720-733.
Rodriguez-Bigas M. A comparative evaluation of aloe vera in the management of burn wounds in guinea pigs. *Plastic Reconst Surg* 1988;81:386-9.
Schmid R, et al. Comparison of seven commonly used agents for prophylaxis of seasickness. *Jnl Travel Med* 1994;1;203-6.
Singh M, etal. Zinc for the common cold. Cochrane Database Review. 2011. Issue 2.
Teelucksingh S. Potentiation of hydrocortisone activity in skin by glycyrrhetinic acid. *Lancet* 1990;335 (8697):1060-3.
Weizman Z, et al. Efficacy of herbal tea preparation in infantile colic. *Journal of Pediatrics*1993;122:650-2.

Appendix C: Lab Tests

Gunn VL, Nechyba C, editors: *The Harriet Lane Handbook: A Manual for Pediatric House Officers*,16th ed. Philadelphia:Mosby,2002.
Loeb S, editor: *Clinical Laboratory Tests: Values and Implications*. Springhouse, Pennsylvania: Spring House,1991.

footnotes

Appendix D: Glossary

Behrman RE, Kliegman R. *Nelson Essentials of Pediatrics*. Philadelphia: W.B.Saunders, 1990.
Cloherty JP, Stark AR. *Manual of Neonatal Care*, 3e. Boston: Little Brown, 1992.
Shelov, SP. *Your Baby's First Year.* New York: Bantam, 1998.
Urdang Associates. *The Bantam Medical Dictionary*. New York: Bantam, 1981.

INDEX

AAP. *See* American Academy of Pediatrics
AARP, 14
Abdomen, 47; acute, 201, 418, 515; CT/MRI for, 508; ultrasounds for, 507; x-rays for, 507
Abdominal pain, 321, 417-418; home remedies for, 502; questions about, 418; red flags with, 418
ABO incompatibility. *See* Coombs test
Abscesses: brain, 365; cultures for, 514
Acetaminophen, 87, 153, 307, 309, 373, 415, 441, 442, 443, 469, 475, 478; dehydration and, 445; dosing, 446, 447; ibuprofen and, 445; suppositories, 446
Acholic stool, 193; described, 515
Acid: levels, 197; suffering from, 195
Acid reflux (GER), 117, 132, 194, 222, 226, 373, 428; colic and, 196; congestion and, 429; diagnosing, 197, 198; sleeping through night and, 243-244; symptoms of, 200; teething and, 86; treating, 196-197; worrying about, 195
Acidophilus, 139
Acne, 49, 80, 515
Acrocyanosis, 47; described, 516
Activity, 53, 108, 275, 278; low-energy, 273-274; physical, 105
Acupuncture, 495
Acute life threatening event (ALTE), 428; described, 515
Acute otitis media, 361-362; described, 515
ADA. *See* American Dental Association
Adair, Steven, 88
ADD. *See* Attention Deficit Disorder
Additives, 391, 393-397; described, 329
Adenovirus, 369
ADHD, 393
Adjusted age, 61, 90, 98
Adjuvants, described, 329
Adoption: breastfeeding and, 148-149; considering, 33-34; websites on, 540
Adrenal gland insufficiency, 36, 50
Adult Onset Diabetes, 385
Adventures in the Life of Baby NGL, quote from, 245
Adverse reactions, 305, 310
Advil, 87, 415, 445, 446
Advisory Committee on Immunization Practices (ACIP), 307, 310
Affordable Care Act, 142
Agency for Toxic Substances and Disease Registry, mercury and, 327
Agenesis of the corpus callosum, 260
AIDS, 345
Air hungry, 372, 430, 427; described, 426, 516
Airway, checking, 428-429
Alcohol, breastfeeding and, 147
Aliphatic hydrocarbons, 392
All-inactivated vaccination series (IPV), 36, 307, 315, 326, 333
Allergic reactions, 181, 182, 418-420, 482, 483, 501; local, 438; questions about, 419; red flags with, 419
Allergies, 158, 372, 373, 407, 438; breastfeeding and, 178; cats and, 387; drug, 306, 310, 311, 386, 419, 420, 450, 451; eczema and, 180; egg, 178, 306; food, 7, 145, 147, 157, 168, 170, 172, 177, 178, 179, 180, 181, 182, 184, 193, 255, 310, 381, 385, 386, 387, 420, 423, 432, 450, 454; formula, 159; history of, 7, 386; metal, 85, 454; milk protein, 144-145, 156-157, 172, 173, 178, 179, 180, 182, 196, 287, 422, 501, 529-530; outgrowing, 178, 184; peanut, 147, 178, 180, 181; perennial, 386, 387; preventing, 181, 387; ragweed, 386; rashes and, 451; runny nose and, 386, 387; seasonal, 375, 381, 385, 386, 438; soy protein, 157, 179; websites on, 540

Allergy Asthma Technology Ltd., 387
ALTE. *See* Acute life threatening event
Alternative/complementary therapies, 11, 13, 495, 497, 539; study of, 499; websites on, 540
Aluminum, 329; autism and, 332; vaccines and, 332, 333
Alvarado, L., 33
Alzheimer's Disease, aluminum and, 332
Ambecides, 484
Ambiguous genitalia, 48; described, 516
Amblyopia, 61, 264, 371; described, 516
Ameda Purely Yours, 127
American Academy of Family Physicians (AAFP), 307, 310
American Academy of Otolaryngology Head and Neck Surgery, 362
American Academy of Pediatric Dentistry, 88
American Academy of Pediatrics (AAP), xv, xvii, 23, 34, 35, 45, 103, 120, 171, 271, 310, 332, 474, 488; ADD and, 393; address/phone number for, 543; autism and, 255, 258; bed sharing and, 220, 221; brain damage and, 54; breastfeeding and, 115, 118, 154; car seats and, 57, 58; chickenpox and, 319; circumcision and, 16; dental visits and, 88; DHA supplements and, 146; diarrhea and, 435; ear infections and, 363, 364; family beds and, 220, 222; feeding schedules and, 99; food and, 172, 180; growth charts and, 90; hearing screen and, 36; immunization schedule from, 320; iron and, 101; LPI discharge and, 60; media and, 275-276; milk and, 167; *On Becoming Babywise* and, 237; orthotics and, 382; pacifiers and, 285; policy statement of, 37; room sharing and, 220, 221; SIDS and, 216, 218, 220; sleep positioners and, 218; soy formula and, 158; sunblock and, 81; swimming and, 276; television and, 273; thermometers and, 446; ultimatum by, 389-390; vaccinations and, 307; vision screen and, 372; Vitamin D and, 100; VUR and, 204; walkers and, 267; weaning and, 152
American Association of Blood Banks (AABB), 23
American Association of Poison Control Centers, web site of, 273
American College of Obstetricians and Gynecologists (ACOG), 16
American Dental Association (ADA), 162; fluoride and, 103-104, 474
American Heart Association, milk and, 167
American Red Cross, 276, 277; infant scale from, 151
American Sensors, 407
American Urology Association, 16, 204
Amniocentesis, 43
Amniotic fluid, 78, 79
Amoxicillin, 346, 365, 366
Anal atresia, 47
Anal tears/fissures, 422, 423; described, 516
Anaphylactic reaction, 177, 178, 181, 309, 419; described, 516
Anderson, Kelly, 25-26
Anemia, 50, 101, 183, 332, 535; chronic, 378; described, 377, 516;iron-deficiency, 99, 102, 378, 379, 484; testing, 34
Anesthesia, 198, 370
Aneurysm, 331
Ankyloglossia, 45, 134, 137; described, 516
Anomaly, described, 516
Antacids, 479-480
Anti-fungals, using, 77
Anti-inflammatories, 490
Anti-microbials, 345
Anti-vaccine movement, 301, 306, 314, 323, 324
Antibiotic creams, 138, 490, 491
Antibiotics, 51, 139, 203, 304, 306, 320, 341, 362, 391, 423, 432, 441, 482-483; abuse of, 346-347; bacterial infections and, 345; broad-spectrum, 346, 365; drops/ointments, 50, 363, 425, 476, 478; ear infections and, 361, 364-365, 476; generic form of, 467; health issues and, 396; infections and, 366; leftover,

index

468-469; limiting, 363, 395; oral, 363, 438; prescribing, 346, 414-415; probiotics and, 500; requiring, 364; resistance to, 345-348; too many, 367-368; using, 204, 346, 347, 348, 368
Antibodies, 114, 141, 353
Antifungal creams, 140, 483, 490, 491
Antihelminthics, 483-484
Antihistamines, 340, 370, 380, 420, 473, 489, 490; hives and, 451
Antiseptics, 76
Antivirals, 484
Anxiety, 120, 133, 247, 280, 294
Apgar test, described, 53
Apnea, 46, 219, 431; described, 517; questions about, 428
Apnea of Prematurity (AOP), 59, 61
Appendicitis, 417; described, 517
AppleCare, 276
Appointments, 10, 41, 42; arriving for, 38-39; problem-focused, 38; scheduling, 9, 13, 38, 39-40, 414
Arachidonic Acid (ARA), 114, 160; described, 159
Areola, 124, 136, 137, 143
Arms: broken, 463; examining, 48-49
Arsenic, 172-173, 391, 392, 496; cancer and, 396; rice cereal and, 396-397
Artificial sweeteners, 184, 398
Asbestos, 406-407
Ascorbic acid, 399
ASD. *See* Autism spectrum disorders
Asner, Ed: quote of, 169
Asperger's syndrome, 253; described, 517
Association for Children with Down Syndrome, 259
Association of Women's Health Obstetric and Neonatal Nurses, 78
Asthma, 114, 311, 321, 323, 341, 385, 392, 427, 431; air quality and, 407; described, 372, 517; diagnosing, 375, 386; eczema and, 375, 381; factors causing, 373; intermittent, 374; medications for, 485-486, 487; mild persistent, 374; moderate persistent, 374; outgrowing, 375; preventing, 374; severe persistent, 374; symptoms of, 407; treating, 374
Athlete's foot, 77, 358, 491
Atopy, 375, 381; described, 517
Atresia, described, 517
Attachment parenting, 221-222, 231, 236; described, 5
Attachment Parenting International, 221
Attention Deficit Disorder (ADD), 327, 399; described, 282
Au pairs, 33; described, 29; finding, 29-30
Auditory processing disorder, 247
AuPairAmerica.com, 33
Authoritarian parenting, described, 5
Autism Science Foundation, 324
Autism screen, 36, 252; described, 37
Autism spectrum disorders (ASD), xvi-xvii, 61, 253-260, 393; aluminum and, 332; BMI and, 257, 258; brain growth and, 256-257; communication and, 255; described, 253, 254, 517; developmental milestones and, 255; diagnosis of, 254, 255, 256; environmental triggers for, 257; genetics and, 256; HFCS and, 398; intervention with, 254; language and, 256, 325; mercury and, 325, 328, 398; MMR and, 323-325; nutrition and, 258; prematurity and, 257; rates of, 323; red flags for, 254; risk of, 258, 331; social skills and, 254, 256; vaccines and, 254, 256, 257, 323-325, 331
Autism Toolkit, 255
Autoimmune diseases, 101, 385
Autonomy vs. doubt, 18 months to three years, 262
Autosomal dominant, 377; described, 517
Autosomal recessive, 377; described, 517-518
Azithromycin, 346
AZT, 339

Baby Bjorn, 264
Baby blues, 68, 69
Baby Book, The (Sears), 233, 234, 236
Baby Connect, 71, 120
Baby food, 169, 186, 396; making, 175, 397; organic, 176-177, 302, 396
Babysitters, 3, 27, 33
Back, hair on, 80-81
"Back to Sleep" Campaign, 216, 267

Bacteria, 51, 85, 139, 202, 286, 303, 315, 335, 337, 354, 356, 361, 369, 370, 401, 432, 438, 451; antibiotic-resistant, 396; described, 343-345; drug-resistant, 345-346, 365, 368, 414; formula and, 163; good, 343; gut, 343; infections and, 343, 344-345, 369; intestinal, 343; killing, 304, 366; mouth, 343; nostril, 343; penicillin and, 346; skin, 343; vaginal, 343; viruses and, 343, 344
Bacterial enteritis, 201
Bacterial infections, 321, 342, 354-358, 423, 426, 441, 443, 490, 505, 506; antibiotics and, 345; diagnosing, 346; medications for, 482-483; secondary, 343-344, 348, 354; signs of, 339; untreated, 365; viruses and, 344
Bacterial meningitis, 320, 356
BAER. *See* Brainstem Audio Evoked Response
Balanitis, 15; described, 518
Barenaked Ladies, quote from, 209
Barium swallow/Upper GI, 197, 508
Barking, 427, 428, 431
Barnes, Sarah, 260
Barracuda, described, 124-125
Bassinets, sleeping in, 213-214, 222, 243
Baths, 205, 284; dry skin and, 81; feedback on, 78; first, 78, 79; sponge, 78, 79
BBQ, 408; burns from, 424-425; cancer and, 399
Bed sharing, 222; avoiding, 220, 221
Bedding, 217-218; SIDS and, 216, 217, 220
Bedtime, 240; routines for, 232; scheduled, 223, 224-225
Bedwetting, 232
Behavior, 25, 38, 124-125, 240, 279, 291; aggressive, 280; attention-seeking, 293; atypical, 256; breastfeeding and, 124-125; changing, 291, 295, 332; colic and, 196; heredity vs. environment and, 282; problems, 10, 238, 260, 262, 291, 294; sleep and, 233; tips and tricks for, 294-296; unusual, 254
Bell, Edward, 468
Belladonna, 475
Belly button, caring for, 75, 76, 77
Benadryl, 152, 296, 415, 419, 420, 451, 474
Beta Strep test, significance of, 51
Bile, vomiting, 200, 435, 437
Bili blanket/bed, 57
Bilirubin, 55, 56, 57, 69, 127, 175, 318, 509
Biopsies, 198
Birth control, breastfeeding and, 114-115
Birth order, personality traits and, 6
Birth plan, 51-52
Birth weight, 120, 122, 164; loss of, 52, 117, 120; low, 23, 70
Birthmarks, 48, 49
Bisphenol-A (BPA), 391; avoiding, 164, 176; banning, 401, 402; sources of, 401-402
Bites, 420, 438, 456
Biting, 280; discipline for, 295-296
Bladder infections, 15, 85, 204, 369, 436, 467, 482, 506; diagnosing, 203; preventing, 202; treating, 356; untreated, 203. *See also* Urinary tract infection
Bladders, 48, 343; abnormal, 204; full, 418
Blankets, 220, 230, 290
Bleeding, 18, 202, 459; concerns about, 420-424; controlling, 456, 457; head, 460; lower GI, 422; persistent, 422; postpartum, 127; questions about, 420-421; uncontrollable, 420; upper GI, 421, 422
Blindness, 289
Blisters, 425
Blood, 54, 377-379; in diapers, 202; in diarrhea, 432; loss of, 457; in pee, 202; samples, 385; with vomiting, 201, 421, 422, 436, 437
Blood clots, 50, 53
Blood count, 34, 378; down syndrome and, 259
Blood culture, 51, 509, 514
Blood disorders, 19, 450, 475
Blood in stool, 43, 177, 179, 189, 193, 321, 422, 423, 506; described, 518
Blood infections, 51, 59, 204, 320
Blood pressure, 36, 60, 114, 127, 440, 449
Blood sugar, 52, 60, 126, 385, 509

index

Blood tests, 19, 25, 36, 37, 51, 378, 509-512
Blood types, 50, 56, 506, 509-510
Blood vessels, broken, 45
Blue Baby Syndrome, 397
Body Mass Index (BMI), 36, 37, 90, 385; autism and, 257, 258; described, 36; overeating/obesity and, 105-109
Bone marrow, 20, 21, 379; suppression, 339, 420
Bone scan, using, 508
Bones, 382-384; broken, 459, 462, 463
Books, 278; alternative therapies, 539; behavior, 539; breastfeeding, 140, 539; childcare, 43; development, 539; medical information, 540; parenting, 43; picture, 272; sleep, 231, 540; vaccination, 540

BOTOX injections, 384
Bottles, 153, 185; glass, 141; introducing, 142-143; plastic, 141, 401; recommended, 163-164; sterilizing, 163
Botulism, 180, 184
Bouncer seats, 289
Bovine growth hormone (RBGH), 168, 395, 397
Bowel obstruction, 321, 325
Bowleggedness, 265, 382
Boy parts, 387; caring for, 83-85
BPA. *See* Bisphenol-A
Braces, 286, 382
Brain, 92, 265; activity, 210; weight of, 91; workings of, 245
Brain damage, 54, 127, 289, 440, 448
Brain development, 91, 93, 114; autism and, 256-257; mercury and, 400; problems with, 256-257, 260, 394; stages of, 261
Brain disorder, degenerative, 306

Brainstem Audio Evoked Response (BAER), 36, 45; described, 518
Branchial cleft cyst, 46; described, 518
BRAT diet, 435
Brazelton, T. Berry, 277
Breast infections, 138, 139
Breast milk, 57, 67, 79, 102, 112, 115, 123, 132, 139, 144, 148, 155, 166, 172, 173, 182, 186, 221, 288, 378, 422, 448; alcohol and, 147; aluminum in, 333; antibodies in, 114; buying, 149; calories from, 95, 96; colors of, 141; contaminants in, 393-394; dehydration and, 434; digesting, 145, 188; enzymes in, 151; expressing, 98, 116, 126, 128, 133, 135, 140-143, 149, 150, 151, 152, 196; feeding, 108, 143, 188; fiber and, 191; and formula compared, 160; freezing, 140, 141, 142; fresh, 133, 141, 142; mature, 126, 127, 191; nutrition from, 100, 170, 171; overabundance of, 134-135; poop and, 188, 189; prebiotics in, 162; preemies and, 63; producing, 34, 54, 117, 120, 121, 122-123, 128, 129, 134, 143, 148-149, 150, 151, 153; pros/cons of, 113; sour tasting, 147; storing, 140-141; substitutes for, 153; supply of, 63, 96, 98, 116, 120, 122, 126, 127, 133, 134, 140, 141, 142, 154; thickening, 196
Breast reduction, problems from, 143-144
Breast shells, 119, 136
Breastfeeding, xiv, 5, 41, 44, 52, 54, 66, 90, 96, 100, 108, 113, 126, 128, 136, 137, 139, 195, 202, 211, 214, 223, 236, 286, 378, 421; birth to 2 weeks, 153; 2 weeks to 2 months, 154; 2 to 4 months, 154; 4 to 6 months, 154; 6 to 9 months, 154; 9 to 12 months, 155; adoptions and, 148-149; advantages of, 114; alcohol and, 147; anxiety about, 120, 128; benefits of, 115, 157; birth control and, 114-115; breast cancer and, 152; calories from, 146; categories of, 471; co-sleeping and, 222; cold medications and, 490; continuing, 65, 145, 153; diet and, 144, 147; difficulties with, 116, 117, 118; drug abuse and, 471; exercise and, 147; exhaustion from, 132; fevers and, 148; fish and, 400; fluoride and, 104, 474; food allergies and, 147, 178; formula and, 155; frequency of, 118, 120, 121; gas and, 206; herbal remedies and, 472; infant behaviors for, 124-125; iron and, 101, 484; as learned process,

115-116; length of, 115, 120, 122; LPI and, 60; medications and, 132, 471-472; moms and, 143-148; motivation for, 285; multiples and, 149; nighttime, 88; pacifiers and, 128-129; pain with, 128; poop and, 67, 123, 191; preemies and, 63, 64, 102, 149-150; problems with, 130-131, 140, 149; science of, 117; SIDS and, 114; sleep and, 129, 228, 230; starting, 118-122; stopping, 115, 152, 153, 155; successful, 78, 125, 150, 221; technique for, 119-120; teething and, 153; tips on, 118, 237; troubleshooting, 128, 133-134; vomiting and, 436; websites on, 541; yeast infection and, 86
Breastfeeding Committee (AAP), 171
Breasts: large, 143; massaging, 135; small, 143
Breath-holding spells, 295, 377; described, 518
Breathing, 44, 313; environmental hazards and, 390; fast, 427; labored, 52, 419, 425, 426, 428, 430, 431, 442; periodic, 46, 65, 428, 532; problems with, 195, 419, 425-429, 431, 450, 455, 487; rapid/shallow, 431, 449; red flags with, 65, 428; stopping, 199
Breech position, 384; described, 518
Brick dust, 54, 202
Brochopulmonary dysplasia (BPD), described, 519
Bronchiolitis (RSV), 62, 338, 339, 369, 372, 373, 426, 428, 429, 430, 506; described, 519; preventing, 488; rapid antigen assay for, 514; treating, 349
Bronchitis, 426; described, 519
Bronchodilator, 374
Bronchopulmonary dysplasia (BPD), 62
Brown, Ari, xiv, xv, xvi, xvii, 8, 118, 367, 429
Bruises, 49, 69, 462, 463; head, 44; large, 459, 460; treating, 459, 502
Bruising, 459, 460; concerns about, 420-424; questions about, 420-421
Bubble baths, avoiding, 380
Bucknam method, 236-237
Bulb syringes, 66, 421, 422, 429
Burnett, Carol: quote of, 43
Burns, 424-425
Burping, 151, 187, 188, 205
Burrito Wrap, 68, 218, 219, 283
Butler, Ginny, 333

C-Reactive Protein (CRP), 510
C-sections, 44, 68, 92, 123
Café au lait spots, 49; described, 519
Caffeine, 144, 340, 486
Calcium, 63, 97, 102, 109-111, 161, 162, 167, 172, 379; iron and, 485; required, 109-110
Calendula, using, 109, 167, 496-497
Calories, 173, 186; catch-up growth and, 171; intake of, 63, 70, 99; needed, 94-97, 146; preemies and, 95
Campaign for Safe Cosmetics, 404
Camphor, 341, 499
Campylobacter infection, 432
Cancer, 101, 391, 393, 399, 405, 407; arsenic and, 396; artificial sweeteners and, 398; BBQ and, 399; bladder, 398; brain, 405; breast, 114, 152, 401; cervical, 15; endometrial, 114; fluoride and, 475; liver, 318; ovarian, 114; penile, 15; skin, 81; testicular, 392; websites on, 541
CAP-RAST test, described, 182
Capillary refill, dehydration and, 433
Car seats, 116, 281, 430; head control and, 271; infant, 58, 64, 213, 219; preemies and, 64; sleeping in, 213, 219, 224, 284, 341; using, 57-58, 60, 64; websites on, 541
Carbon monoxide, 391, 407, 408
Careers, 117; family and, 26-28
Caries, 87, 88, 230, 286; described, 531
Carotinemia, 175; described, 519
Carpeting, 404-405
Carvalho Fisheries, 400, 409
Casein, 156, 158, 181
Castor oil packs, 138
CAT scans, head injuries and, 460
Cataracts, 44, 487; described, 519
Cats, allergies and, 386, 387
CBC. *See* Complete Blood Count
CDC. *See* Centers for Disease Control and Prevention
Celiac disease, 183, 432; described,

519; down syndrome and, 259
Cellulitis, treating, 354-355
Center care, 30, 31, 33
Center for Evaluation of Risks to Human Reproduction, 393
Centers for Disease Control and Prevention (CDC), 34, 109, 162, 303, 323, 332; address/phone number for, 543; autism and, 253, 258; chickenpox and, 319; flu vaccine and, 321; growth charts and, 90; immunization schedule from, 312, 316; pesticides and, 405; rotavirus and, 325; rubella and, 317; triclosan and, 336; vaccinations and, 307, 309, 310, 330
Cephalhematoma, 44, 56, 92; described, 519
Cereals, xiii, 191; fiber in, 192; fortified, 111, 173. *See also* Rice cereal
Cerebral palsy, 48; described, 519-520
Cetaphil, 79, 380
CF. *See* Cystic Fibrosis
Chemicals, 389, 449; exposure to, 406; industrial, 391, 392
Chemotherapy, 345
Chest: CT/MRI for, 508; examining, 46; rattling, 341, 428; x-rays for, 507
Chickenpox, 301, 304, 306, 308, 309, 316, 333, 338, 339, 340, 347, 369, 478; described, 318-319, 452-453; treating, 352-353
Chickenpox vaccine, 319, 455
Chiggers, 359
Child (magazine), 234
Child Development (journal), quality time and, 30
Childbirth: classes, 78; exhaustion from, 117, 128; recovery from, 116
Childcare, 33, 242, 296, 441; careers and, 24, 26; cost of, 26, 29; ear infections and, 368; feedback on, 32; options for, 3, 4, 24, 28-31; red flags with, 32; returning to, 347; selecting, 24-25; types of, 25; websites on, 541
Children's Health Insurance Program (CHIP), 40
Children's Hospital of Philadelphia, 58, 333
Choanal atresia, 45; described, 520
Choking, 195, 219, 427; emergencies with, 428-429
Cholesterol, 37, 102, 512
Cholesterol screen, 36; described, 37
Chorioamnionitis, 51
Chromosomes, 511; defects, 255, 256
Circadian rhythm, 210-211
Circulation, examining, 46-47
Circumcision, xiii, 4, 14-18, 387; arguments for/against, 6, 14, 15, 16; caring for, 17-18, 83; HIV and, 16, 17
Clavicle fracture, 46; described, 520
Cleaning products, 277, 404, 410
Cleft lip/palate, 45, 362; described, 520
Clostridium botulinum spores, 184
Clothes, 64, 75, 76, 94
Club foot, 49; described, 520
CMV, 257, 339
Co-sleeping, 213, 214, 220, 221, 231, 236; breastfeeding and, 222
Coagulation studies, 511
Coarctation of aorta, 46; described, 520
Cochrane Reviews, 496
Cognitive development, 247, 261, 264; 4 to 6 months, 266; 6 to 9 months, 268
Cold and flu season, 312, 322; infection control during, 368; returned calls and, 414
Cold sores, 350
Colic, 158, 161, 195, 280, 282, 283, 284, 287-290, 500, 501; acid reflux and, 196; alternative therapies for, 288; behavior and, 196; gas and, 206; gripe water and, 288; home remedies for, 502; probiotics and, 288; treatments for, 287, 288
Colitis: antibiotic-induced, 423, 516; *C. difficile,* 197, 423, 432, 483
Colostrum, 67, 117, 120, 123, 125, 128, 144; described, 119, 520
Comfort objects, 230, 290
Common colds, 41, 309, 321, 338, 340-343, 347, 361, 369, 373, 425, 429, 430, 435, 439; ear infections and, 362; length of, 340; sinus infections and, 342; treating, 341; vaccinations and, 307
Communication, 248, 249; 2 weeks, 250; 2 months, 250; 4 months,

250; 6 months, 251; 1 year, 252; achieving, 249; autism and, 255; barriers to, 270; non-verbal, 269, 271
Community programs, 276
Complete Blood Count (CBC), 51, 510
Comprehension, 1 year, 252
Computerized Tomography (CT), 460, 505, 508
Comvax, 316
Concrete operational development, 7 to 11 years, 262
Concussion, 459, 460
Conductive hearing loss, 366; described, 520
Congenital, described, 520
Congenital Adrenal Hyperplasia, described, 521
Congenital nevus, 49; described, 521
Congestion, 429-431; acid reflux and, 429; nasal, 65, 66, 153, 429, 430; relieving, 489
Conjunctivitis, 478; bacterial, 347, 355, 438; described, 521; viral, 351
Consciousness, loss of, 459, 460, 463
Constipation, 10, 67, 189, 283, 417, 418, 422, 423; described, 521; formula and, 190; medications for, 480; relieving, 190-191; rice cereal and, 191
Consumer Product Safety Commission (CPSC), 278, 402; lead toys and, 403; sleep positioners and, 218; toy safety and, 273
Consumer Reports, 82, 407
Contact dermatitis, 419
Containers: glass, 410; porcelain, 410; plastic, 402, 409; steel, 402, 410
Contaminants, 393-397, 401
Cookbooks, baby food, 175
Cooking, double/weekend, 27
Coombs test, 50, 56, 511
Copper chromium arsenate (CCA), 392
Cord blood, 257; banking, 4, 19, 20-24; using, 20, 21, 22; websites on, 541
Cord Blood Registry (CBR), 22
Corneal abrasions, 438, 439, 461, 478
Coughing, 41, 203, 315, 337, 338, 340, 341, 347, 416, 425, 428, 429-431, 436, 438, 442; chronic, 200, 314, 427, 431; forceful, 435; nighttime, 430; productive, 431; questions about, 431
Council on Environmental Health (AAP), 390
Cowpox, 301, 303
Coxsackievirus, 338, 369; described, 452-453; treating, 350
CPR, 276, 415, 429, 456; course/taking, 185, 273; preemies and, 64
CPSC. *See* Consumer Product Safety Commission
Cradle cap, 75, 80; home remedies for, 502
Cradle hold, described, 123
Craniosynostosis, 44, 91, 93; described, 522
Creams, 16, 80, 84, 138, 380, 381, 388, 483, 490, 491, 492, 493, 494
Creamy Vaseline, 380
Cribs, 5, 217, 221, 242, 243
Cross cradle, described, 123
Croup, 338, 347, 369, 426; described, 427; home remedies for, 502; treating, 349
CRP. *See* C-Reactive Protein
Cry management approach, 282, 283
Crying, 282, 283, 284, 310, 429
Crying it out, 226, 238, 239-240
Cryobanks International, 22
Cryogenic techniques, 23
CSF. *See* Spinal fluid tests
CT. *See* Computerized Tomography
Culture plate, 345
Culturelle (Lactobacillus GG), 500
Cups, drinking from, 167
Cushingoid features, 487
Cystic Fibrosis (CF), 19, 47, 375, 513; described, 522;

Dactylitis, 378
Dairy, 145, 174; alternative to, 167; diarrhea and, 434; eliminating, 178, 195, 197; organic, 394, 395, 396, 397; pasteurized, 356; requirements, 97, 110; servings of, 112; unpasteurized, 424
Day-Night Reversal, 211, 214
Daycare, 24, 32; behavior at, 296; cost of, 29; in-home, 30, 33; infections and, 362, 423; naps and, 242; sickness and, 31, 32
DDH. *See* Hip dysplasia
Decongestants, 296, 340, 370, 469, 489

index

DEET, 82, 83, 353, 392
Dehydration, 44, 57, 60, 89, 91, 126, 202, 320, 442, 478; acetaminophen and, 445; diarrhea and, 433; LPI and, 59; preventing, 434; signs of, 201, 433; vomiting and, 433, 434, 435, 437
Deliveries, 3, 54; C-section, 44, 68, 92, 123; full-term, 51; preterm, 58; traumatic, 56
Dental care, 36, 75, 88, 286; preemies and, 63
Denver Developmental Checklist, 248, 249, 268
Depression, 41, 332; postpartum, 68, 69
Detergents, 80; dry skin and, 81
Development, 25, 35, 226, 238, 277, 279, 289-290, 291; concerns about, 247, 253; described, 246; LPI and, 60, 61; theories about, 263; websites on, 541
Development Dysplasia of the Hip. *See* Hip dysplasia
Developmental assessment, 61, 64, 260
Developmental checklists, 248, 249, 250-252, 268; preemies and, 260
Developmental delays, 185, 238, 245, 249, 256, 259; global, 253; isolated, 252-253; risk of, 260
Developmental differences, 258-259
Developmental issues, 323, 393; early intervention with, 247
Developmental milestones, 34, 194, 246, 260, 323; birth to 2 months, 263-265; 2 to 4 months, 265; 4 to 6 months, 266-268; 6 to 9 months, 268-270; 9 to 12 months, 270-271, 272; achieving, 246, 247; adjusted age for, 248; autism and, 255; checklist for, 248-249; failing, 252-253; sleep, 222
Developmental screen, 36, 37
Developmental specialists, 249, 259; autism and, 258, 323
Developmental stimulation, 269-270; critical, 277-278; providing, 264, 265-266; television and, 274
Developmental therapy, 61
Dextromethorphan, 489
DHA. *See* Docosahexaenoic acid
Diabetes, 36, 52, 114, 118, 183, 321, 323; preventing, 385; solid food and, 170; Type 1: 384, 385; Type 2: 110, 384, 398; websites on, 541
Diaper bags, 26, 281
Diaper rash, xiv, 75, 422, 423, 454, 455; home remedies for, 502; treating, 77; yeast, 41, 86, 358, 369, 452-453, 491
Diaper rash creams, 490, 494
Diaper wipes, 17, 76
Diapers, xiii, 79, 194; blood in, 202; changing, 70, 187, 191, 203, 281, 283, 383; checking, 213; chlorine-free, 407; cleaning up, 76; urine in, 434; wet, 202, 433
Diarrhea, 86, 144, 159, 177, 178, 182, 183, 188, 189, 201, 203, 316, 320, 339, 347, 360, 417, 418, 431-435, 436, 437, 442, 483, 500, 501; blood in, 423, 432; chronic, 432; described, 522; dehydration and, 433; explosive, 423, 433; fat and, 434; fiber and, 434; grape jelly, 432; home remedies for, 502; juice and, 166, 432; mucous in, 432; persistent, 432, 434; questions about, 432; vomiting and, 202, 432, 433; watery, 433
Diet, 96, 179; breastfeeding and, 144, 147; carbohydrate, 435; elimination, 182; healthy, 106, 108, 385; high-fat, 167; restrictions on, 133, 144; toddler, 112; vegetarian/vegan, 172
Difficult child, described, 280
Digestive aids, 145
Digoxin, 496
Diphenhydramine, 152, 296, 415, 419, 420, 451, 474
Diphtheria, 304, 308; described, 313
Discipline, 3; effective, 291, 293; negative forms of, 5; non-physical forms of, 5; planting seeds of, 290-292, 294; teachers and, 31; temperament and, 279; travel and, 296
Diseases, 62, 312-313, 331; common, 388; exposure to, 307; hormones and, 396; preventing, 302; rates of, 392; vaccine-preventable, 305, 333
Dislocations, 384, 463
DMSA Scan, 203, 509

Docosahexaenoic acid (DHA), 102, 102-103, 114, 146, 160; described, 159
Donne, John: quote of, 299
Down syndrome, 183, 258-259
Dream feeds, 225-227
Drooling, 86, 449
Droppers, using, 445, 446
DTaP vaccine, 36, 307, 309, 326; aluminum in, 333; described, 313-314
DTP vaccine, 313
Ducts: infected, 152; plugged, 119, 131, 134, 138-139, 152, 437-438; tear, 45, 437-438
Duodenal atresia, 47; described, 522
Dyes, avoiding, 380
Dyslexia, 393

E. coli, 202, 343, 355, 369; outbreak of, 356, 424
Ear drops, 41, 476, 476-477
Ear infections, 41, 66, 153, 320, 321, 344, 345, 346, 351, 361-368, 369, 430, 436, 438, 443, 476, 482, 506; antibiotics and, 361, 364-365; bath water and, 363-364; childcare and, 368; complications from, 363; diagnosing, 364, 366-367; facts about, 361; home remedies for, 503; number of, 367, 368; pacifiers and, 286, 362, 368; preventing, 368, 370; risk factors for, 362; signs of, 365; swimmer's ear and, 361-362; too many, 367-368; travel and, 296
Ear/Nose/Throat (ENT) specialists, 61, 367, 370, 477
Ear piercing, 85
Ear treatment, guidelines for, 363
Eardrums, 45, 66, 361, 364, 368, 370, 461; perforated, 362, 363, 365, 367, 532
Early Childhood Intervention (ECI), 64, 259, 260
Early Head Start, 254
Ears, 461; described, 361; examining, 45, 366; hair on, 80-81; pulling on, 365
Earth's Best, 156, 161
Easter Seals, 260; address/phone number for, 543
Easy child, described, 280
Eating, 199, 283; breast milk production and, 134; ebbs/flows in, 106-107; habits, 184; screen time and, 275; sleeping and, 226, 229
EBV. *See* Epstein-Barr Virus titers
Echinacea, 496, 497
Echocardiogram, 375-376
ECI. *See* Early Childhood Intervention
Eco hazards, 389, 408-410
Eczema, 182, 197, 337, 385, 386, 419, 450, 454, 493, 500; allergies and, 180; asthma and, 375, 381; chronic, 81; described, 380, 522; home remedies for, 503; managing, 380, 381; severe, 381
Egocentric, 261, 294; described, 522
Elastogel, 121, 138
Electrocardiogram (EKG), 375
Electrolytes, 437
Electromagnetic fields (EMFs), 391, 408
Elimination, 65, 67-68
Elimination Communication (EC), 194
Elimination table, 72 (fig.)
Emergencies, 41, 441, 442; baby sitters for, 27; choking, 428-429; pediatricians and, 12, 13, 414, 417; websites for, 541
Emesis, described, 522
EMLA, 307
Emollients, 381, 493
Emotional growth, 260, 262-263, 289, 290
Emotional health, 41, 239, 280
Enamel hypoplasia, 63; described, 522
Encephalitis, 306, 309, 316, 319, 350; described, 522
Endocrine, 384-385; disruptors, 391
Endoscopy, 198, 384
Enfamil, 157; AR, 161, 196; Gentlease, 158; Infant formula, 160; NEWBORN, 159-160, 162; Premium, 156, 162; Prosobee, 156; Puramino, 157
Engorgement, 116, 121, 134, 135; described, 119, 522; problems with, 130; surviving, 140
Enterobacter sakazakii, 162
Enterocolitis, 158
Enteropathy, 158
Enteroviruses, 338
Environmental health, 255, 388, 390, 391, 397
Environmental Health and Toxicology, 410

Environmental Protection Agency (EPA), 327, 379, 405
Environmental Working Group, 257, 394
Epidemics, 334, 427; immunization rates and, 308; preventing, 302; vaccinations and, 303; viral, 338
Epinephrine injectable pen (Epi-Pen), 181
Epispadias, 48; described, 523
Epstein-Barr virus (EBV), 339, 512
Epstein's pearls, 45; described, 523
Erb's palsy, 49; described, 523
Erikson, Erik, 262
Eruption Hematoma, 87; described, 523
Erythema infectosum, 353
Erythema multiforme, 419, 451
Erythema toxicum, 49; described, 523
Erythrocyte Sedimentation Rate (ESR), 511
Esophageal pH probe, 197
Esophagitis, 194, 422; described, 523
Esophagus, 194, 195, 197, 198, 200; bleeding in, 201
Estrogen, 387, 393
Estrogen cream, 388
Ethylmercury, 327, 328
Eucerin cream, 380
Eustachian tubes, 343, 361, 362, 368, 370
Evening primrose oil, using, 497-498
Examinations, first, 43-44
Excited Ineffective, described, 125
Exhaustion, 132, 139; breastfeeding and, 128
Expectorants, 489
Exposures, limiting, 393, 395, 400, 402, 405
Expressing, 98, 126, 128, 133, 135, 140, 141-142, 149, 150, 151, 152, 196
Expressive language, 246-247
Expressive language delays, 253, 366; described, 523
External otitis, described, 363
Extremities: CT/MRI for, 508; examining, 48-49; x-rays for, 507
Eye drops, 438, 439, 477
Eye exams, 61; preemies and, 64
Eye infections, 339, 355, 369
Eye styes, home remedies for, 503
Eyelids: redness, 439; swollen, 438, 439
Eyes, 371-372; crossed, 264; examining, 44-45; foreign bodies in, 439; goopy, 430, 437-438, 439; problems with, 437-439; red, 439
Ezzo method, 236-237

FAAP, described, 37
Failure to thrive, 99, 183, 222, 378, 506; described, 523
Fakes, Dennis: quote of, 279
Falling asleep, 229, 232, 235, 242, 282; help with, 222, 223, 224, 239; on own, 225, 226, 227, 228, 230, 231, 239, 240; problems with, 283
Family beds, 302; advantages of, 221; disadvantages of, 220, 221-222; SIDS and, 220, 221-222; solitary sleep and, 221-222; SUID and, 221-222
Family caretakers, described, 28
Family Medical Leave Act (FMLA), 27
Fat necrosis, 309; described, 523
Fats, 112, 148; calories from, 167; diarrhea and, 434, 435
FDA. *See* Food and Drug Administration
Febrile seizures, 447, 448, 455, 456, 478
Feedback, xv; on baths, 78; on childcare, 32; on obesity, 106-107; on overweight, 106-107; on poisons, 450; on rashes, 454; on teething, 87
Feeding patterns, 5, 98, 117, 154; poor, 99; time for, 164
Feeding schedules, 63, 97-98, 237
Feeding table, 72 (fig.)
Feedings, 65, 175, 185, 200; adjusting, 151; cluster, 97, 154, 211; daytime, 150, 165; on demand, 97; distractions during, 153; hunger and, 226; logs, 70; LPI and, 60; missed, 139; morning, 237; night, 88, 108, 133, 154, 221, 222, 229, 230, 231, 236, 280; parameters for, 226; poop and, 190; preemies and, 98; red flags with, 67; refusing, 199; sleep and, 66, 211, 223, 225-227, 230, 232; volume for, 165
Feet: controlling, 246; turned-in, 382
Feingold Hypothesis, 399
Ferber, Richard, 229, 232, 233, 238
Ferber Method, 231; described, 232,

235; pros/cons of, 232
Fevers, 52, 86, 283, 310, 321, 340, 342, 343, 418, 421, 423, 427, 428, 429, 430, 431, 432, 436, 438, 439-456, 457, 458; brain damage and, 448; breastfeeding and, 148; defining, 439; infections and, 440, 443; length of, 344; misconceptions about, 440, 443; persistent, 442, 447, 506; questions about, 448; rashes and, 443, 455; red flags with, 70, 71, 448; seizures and, 447-448; teething and, 87, 448; treating, 440, 444, 445; vomiting and, 201, 449
Fiber, 109-111, 173, 192-193, 422; diarrhea and, 434, 435; dietary, 191-192; foods with, 192-193; gas and, 206
Fields, Alan, xiv
Fields, Ben, 31, 181
Fields, Denise, xiv, xv, xvi
Fifth disease, 347, 353, 369
Filters, 104, 166, 401, 474
Fine motor development, 246, 248, 249; birth to 6 months, 278; 2 to 4 months, 265; 4 to 6 months, 266, 267; 6 to 9 months, 268, 269; 6 to 12 months, 278; 9 to 12 months, 270, 272
Fingernails, 463
First Aid, 358; kits/contents of, 415
First days, changes during, 53-58
First, Lewis, 156
Fish, 144, 186; avoiding, 400, 409; breastfeeding and, 400; risky, 400, 409; safe, 400
Fish oil supplements, 102-103, 146, 159
Flame retardants, 391, 403, 406
Flaring (nostrils), 65, 426, 427, 431; described, 523
Flat angiomata, 49; described, 523
Flat feet, 382
Flat heads, 91, 219-220; tummy time and, 92-94
Flavorings, medication, 468
Flora, normal, 343
Florastor (Saccaromyces), 500
Flu vaccine, 62, 64, 306, 378
Fluids, 433; accumulation of, 365; environmental hazards and, 390; loss of, 385; need for, 146
Fluoride, 88, 163, 401; breastfeeding and, 474; cancer and, 475; formula and, 474; overuse of, 475; safety with, 475; supplements, 103-104, 166, 474-475; tooth decay and, 103; water and, 166
Fluoride supplements, 103-104, 166, 474-475
Fluorosis, 103
FMLA. *See* Family Medical Leave Act
Folic acid deficiency, autism and, 258
Fomites, 336; described, 523
Fontanelle, 44, 91, 92, 201; bulging, 460; described, 524; dehydration and, 433
Food: brain, 114; canned, 409; choking hazards with, 184; complementary, 96, 115, 152, 171; eliminating, 117, 381; environmental hazards and, 390; finger, 170, 184-185; first, 172, 173; fussiness and, 146; gassy, 146; grilled, 399; guidelines for, 111-112; healthy, 107; hidden sources of, 179; introducing, 173; iron from, 101, 102; lifestyle and, 177; offering, 96, 106; organic, 394-397; pollutants in, 391; pre-chewing, 176; preemies and, 171; processed, 179; pureed, 176; regulating, 112; solid, 96, 97, 99, 101, 102, 108, 112, 154, 155, 165, 169, 170, 171, 173, 175, 176, 182, 185, 193, 436; stage 1: 169, 172, 173, 174, 177, 184, 186, 191; stage 2: 169-170, 174, 177, 184; stage 3: 170, 174, 177, 184; vomiting and, 436
Food Allergy Network, 179, 182
Food and Drug Administration (FDA), 197, 323, 396, 430, 469, 470, 496; BPA and, 401, 402; cough and cold medications and, 340, 488; fish warnings from, 146; flu vaccine and, 322; food coloring and, 399; herbal remedies and, 495; mercury and, 186, 327; probiotics and, 501; rotavirus vaccine and, 320, 325; steroid creams and, 492; teething tablets and, 87, 475; thimerosal and, 326; vaccinations and, 305, 309, 310; website of, 494; Zantac and, 479-480
Food challenge, described, 182

index

Food coloring, 194, 399
Food poisoning, 347, 369, 422, 424, 432, 436; treating, 355-356. *See also* Gastroenteritis
Football hold, 66, 143, 150; described, 123
Foremilk, 148, 189; described, 119, 524
Foreskin, 14, 84, 85
Formal operational development, 12 to adulthood, 262
Formaldehyde, 392, 403-404; vaccines and, 329, 404
Formula, 5, 57, 97, 98, 100, 102, 112, 114, 152, 168, 171, 172, 173, 186, 288, 448; birth to 2 weeks, 164; 2 weeks to 2 months, 165; 2 to 4 months, 165; 4 to 6 months, 165; 6 to 9 months, 165; 9 to 12 months, 165; ADD and, 393; aluminum in, 333; bacteria in, 163; brands, 156, 158; and breast milk compared, 160; breastfeeding and, 155; calories from, 95, 96; casein protein, 157; commercial, 153, 157; constipation and, 190; cow's milk, 33, 158-159, 160, 161, 287, 333; dehydration and, 434; feeding, 54, 108, 144, 155-157, 164-165, 189, 196; fluoride and, 104, 474; gourmet, 159-162; high-calorie, 64, 161; iron-containing, 101, 156, 160, 378; lactose-free, 159; liquid-concentrate, 104, 162, 163, 166, 401; nutrition from, 117, 170; organic, 161, 394, 396; poop and, 67, 189; powder, 104, 162, 166, 402; with prebiotics, 162; preemies and, 63, 161; preparing, 99, 157, 163, 165; with probiotics, 161; pros/cons of, 113; ready-to-feed, 162, 163, 166, 401; soy, 156, 158-159, 160, 333, 393; supplementing with, 56-57, 125, 132, 148, 149; switching, 195; thickened, 164, 196; toddler, 162; vomiting and, 436
Foundation for the Accreditation of Cellular Therapy, 23
Four Cs, avoiding, 106-107
Fragile X Syndrome, 255, 256
Frenulectomy, 137; described, 524
Frenulum, 45; described, 524
Fruit, 107, 174; fiber from, 110, 192; introducing, 175; organic, 177, 396; pesticides and, 394; scrubbing, 409; servings of, 111-112
Fungal infections, 358-360
Fungus, 358, 369, 451, 514
Fussiness, 146, 157, 195, 199, 343, 430, 439

Gagging, 195, 219
Gagnon, Tricia, 26
Galactosemia, 36, 50, 158; described, 524
Galbreath, Laurie, 27
Gas, 17, 157, 178, 195, 205-206, 283, 417; breastfeeding and, 206; colic and, 206; described, 188; fiber and, 206; home remedies for, 502; medications for, 481; reducing, 287
Gastritis, 422
Gastroenteritis, 189, 201, 422, 423, 432, 436; described, 524
Gastroesophageal reflux (GER), 99, 117, 151, 194, 219, 282, 428, 436, 479-480; described, 524;

formula for, 161; LPI and, 62; questionnaire for, 199

Gastroesophageal reflux disease (GERD), 165, 194, 197, 283, 287, 373; diagnosing, 200; hiccups and, 205; suffering from, 195-196; symptoms of, 199; treating, 195
Gastrointestinal problems, 287; LPI and, 59, 62; websites on, 541
Gatorade, 201, 437, 481
GBS. *See* Group B strep
Gene therapy, 255, 256
Genetic disorders, 22, 183, 385
Genital mutilation, 16
Genitals, 16, 85, 387-388; examining, 47-48; playing with, 294-295; sticking, 387-388
GER. *See* Gastroesophageal reflux
Gerber Good Start, 156; Gentle Plus, 158; Protect, 161; Soothe, 161; Soy Plus, 156
GERD. *See* Gastroesophageal reflux disease
German measles, described, 317, 452-453
Germs, 65, 138, 176, 300, 304, 335; exposure to, 306, 387; fear of,

65; good, 434, 500; super, 336
Gestational age, 120
Giardia, 347, 360, 369, 432, 484
Ginger, using, 498
Gingivostomatitis, 350; described, 525
Girl parts, 387-388; caring for, 85
Glands, swollen, 342
Glaucoma, described, 525
Glucose, 509
Gluten, 183
Glycerine bullet, 190-191
Gourmet, described, 125
Grains, 174; fiber in, 192; servings of, 111
Grandparents: breastfeeding and, 117-118; childcare and, 29
Grimace, 53
Gripe water, 206, 288
Gross motor development: birth to 4 months, 265; 4 to 6 months, 266, 267; 6 to 9 months, 268, 269; 6 to 12 months, 278; 9 to 12 months, 270, 272; delays in, 253; described, 246, 248
Group A strep, 345, 365, 369, 469
Group B strep (GBS), 51, 343, 357, 369, 441
Growth, 35, 238, 277, 394; catch-up, 62, 90, 98, 171; down syndrome and, 259; first-year, 90-91; hormones and, 396; infant, 89-92; LPI and, 59, 62; nutrition and, 89; preemies and, 90; spurts, 91, 96, 97, 98
Growth charts, 89, 90, 99; boys/birth to 24 months, 554; girls/birth to 24 months, 545; preemie, 62, 548
Growth plates, 462
Growth spurts, 91, 96, 97, 98
Grunting Baby Syndrome, 189
Gums, 46; throbbing, 86
Gunter, Jennifer, 61
Gut absorption, environmental hazards and, 390
Gut instinct, going with, xviii, 14
Guthrie, Robert: PKU and, 18
Gymboree, 28, 276

Haemophilus Influenza, 365, 369, 378
Haemophilus Influenza A, 339, 348
Haemophilus Influenza B (HIB), 36, 307, 326, 339, 348; cases of, 304; described, 315-316
Haemophilus Influenza B (HIB) vaccine, 316; aluminum in, 333
Haemophilus Influenza non-typable, 365, 438
Hair: on back, 80-81; in unwanted places, 80-81
Hale, Thomas, 132
Hand/foot/mouth diseases, 336, 338, 347, 369; treating, 350
Hand sanitizers, 76, 336, 337
Hand washing, 65, 336
Happiest Baby on the Block (Karp), 289
Hay fever, 372, 381, 386
Head: bleeding from, 460; CT/MRI for, 508; holding up, 93; shape of, 44, 92; ultrasounds for, 507
Head circumference, 546, 547
Head control, 246; car seats and, 271; concerns about, 264
Head injuries, 428, 436, 455, 456, 459-460, 461, 463; handling, 459; seizures and, 460; vomiting and, 437
Head lice, 347, 360, 492
Head size, 91, 258
Head Start, 254
Headaches, 10, 321, 343, 459
Health, xvi, 35, 389, 407; concerns about, 392; environmental hazards and, 390; sleep and, 132
Health care, 40-41; tracking system, 42, 311
Healthy Sleep Habits, Happy Child (Weissbluth), 233
Hearing, 34, 263; damage, 363; language development and, 45; loss, 61, 365, 366, 520; tests, 36, 45, 61
Hearing screen, 36; down syndrome and, 259
Heart, 134, 375-376; abnormalities, 44; examining, 46-47; ultrasounds for, 507
Heart disease, 102, 114, 321; congenital, 46, 488, 521; fiber and, 110
Heart enlargement, 19
Heart failure, congestive, 47, 521
Heart murmurs, 506; described, 375-376, 525; innocent, 376; transitional, 46, 537
Heart problems, 376; down syndrome and, 259; websites on, 542
Heart rate, 44, 53, 213, 440; average,

416; LPI and, 60
Heartburn, 98, 165, 196, 198, 200, 243, 282, 283, 287, 435; formula for, 161
Height, predicting, 91
Heimlich maneuver, 273, 428
Helmets, 91, 93; penile, 84
Hematocrit, 510; described, 36
Hemoglobin, 377, 379, 510
Hemolytic Uremic Syndrome (HUS), 355, 424; described, 525
Hemophilia, 420; described, 525
Hemorrhagic disease of the newborn, 50; described, 525
Hemphill, Jim, 260
Hemphill, Meredith, 260
Henoch-Schonlein Purpura, 420; described, 525
Hepatitis A, 304, 305, 340; described, 317; screening for, 34
Hepatitis A vaccine, 317; aluminum in, 333
Hepatitis B, 148, 304, 307, 316, 326, 340; cases of, 305; described, 317-318; risk factors for, 318; screening for, 34
Hepatitis B vaccine, 53, 62, 318; aluminum in, 333
Hepatitis C, screening for, 34
Herbal remedies, 288, 469; breastfeeding and, 472; described, 540; drug interactions with, 497; safety with, 495
Herbal supplements, 134, 495
Herbs: precautions with, 496-499; uses for, 496-499
Heredity vs. environment, behavior and, 282
Hernia, 47, 417; described, 525
Herpes, 15, 336, 339, 352, 369; genital, 454; rashes, 454
Herpes stomatitis, 347, 350, 369
Herpetic whitlow, described, 452-453
Heterocyclic amines (HCA), 399
HIB. *See* Haemophilus Influenza B
Hiccups, 199, 205; described, 188
High fructose corn syrup (HFCS), autism and, 398
High-maintenance, 281, 283
Hill, Linda, 118
Hindmilk, 148, 151, 189; described, 119, 526
Hip dysplasia (DDH), 49, 384, 522; described, 526
HIPAA, 42
Hips: testing, 384; ultrasounds for, 507
Hirschsprung's disease, 47; described, 526
Histamines, 177, 178, 197, 420, 489; described, 526
HIV, 149, 336, 339; circumcision and, 16, 17; reduced risk of, 15; screening test for, 34; websites on, 542
Hives, 419, 451, 454, 455
Holistic Pediatrician, The (Kemper), 501
Homeopathic Pharmacopeia of the United States (HPUS), 501
Homeopathy, 495, 501
Honey, 184, 190
Hormones, 3, 54, 68, 69, 71, 116, 202, 258, 391, 395; abnormalities, 19; bovine growth, 168; changes in, 450; levels, 49, 439; rashes and, 454; stress, 238
Hospitalization, 11-12, 60
Household items, 449, 502-503
Household Products Database, 410
Housekeepers, hiring, 33
HPUS. *See* Homeopathic Pharmacopeia of the United States
HPV. *See* Human Papilloma Virus
HSV Type 1, treating, 350
HSV Type 2, treating, 350, 352
Huggins, Kathleen, 140
Human Milk Banking Association of North America, 149
Human Papilloma Virus (HPV), described, 15, 340, 526
Human Papilloma Virus (HPV) vaccine, 15
Hume, Mary C., 301
Humidifiers, 341, 342, 503
Hunger, 112, 226
HUS. *See* Hemolytic Uremic Syndrome
Hydrocele, 47; described, 526
Hydrocephalus, 91, 201; described, 526
Hydronephrosis, 204
Hygiene, 15, 32, 202, 387
Hygiene products, 449; formaldehyde and, 403-404
Hyland's Teething Tablets, 475
Hyperthermia, 440, 445
Hyphema, 461
Hypoglycemia, 126

Hypospadias, 47-49; described, 526
Hypothyroidism, 36, 50, 99; described, 526

IBD. *See* Inflammatory Bowel Disease
Ibuprofen, 87, 415, 442, 443, 475, 478, 479; acetaminophen and, 445; breastfeeding pain and, 135; dosing, 446, 447
Identity vs. role confusion, 12 to 18 years, 263
Idiopathic Thrombocytopenic Purpura (ITP), 420, 451; described, 526-527
Illnesses, 28, 337-338; chronic, 311, 375, 501; respiratory, 348; sleep patterns and, 231, 232; smiling and, 345; viral, 336
Imaging studies, 507-509
Immune compromise, 304, 306, 318, 319, 343
Immune responses, 306, 338
Immune system, 306, 345, 348, 441, 454; vaccines and, 302, 303
Immuneglobulin shots, 318
Immunization Action Coalition, 333
Immunization rates, 303, 308, 311, 314, 316
Immunization schedule, 36, 312, 333
Immunizations. *See* Vaccinations
Imperforate Anus, described, 527
Impetigo, 347, 354-355; described, 452-453
Inborn Errors of Metabolism, 18-19; described, 529
Independence, 6, 247, 277, 291, 294
Industry vs. inferiority, 6 to 12 years, 262
Infant Formula Act (1986), 157, 158
Infant Swimming Resource (ISR), 277
Infections, 36, 44, 64, 91, 347, 365, 372, 388, 428, 438; active, 342; antibiotics and, 366; bacteria and, 43, 131, 134, 138, 343, 344-345, 369; bladder, 148; breast, 138, 139; breast milk and, 114; common, 335; controlling, 31, 368; daycare and, 423; exposure to, 32; fever and, 440, 443; localized, 344; persistent, 346, 358; rashes and, 451; respiratory, 31; risk of, 456; serious, 312; source of, 441, 448; symptoms of, 140, 440; viruses and, 31, 108, 338, 369; womb, 148; wound, 457; yeast, 77, 85-86, 131, 134, 139, 483
Infectious diseases, xvii, 300, 307, 331, 335; LPI and, 59, 62
Inflammatory Bowel Disease (IBD), 114, 432; described, 527
Influenza, 257, 304, 309, 339, 347, 369, 425, 426, 429, 431, 442, 478; described, 321-322; length of, 340; rapid antigen assay for, 514; treating, 348; wintertime and, 338
Influenza vaccine, 321-322
Ingestions, 449-450, 455, 456
Initiative vs. guilt, 3 to 6 years, 262
Injuries, 428; accidental, 459-463; back, 461; body, 459; bone, 462, 463; body, 459; eye, 461, 463; finger, 463; mouth, 461; neck, 461, 463; nose, 461; questions about, 459; skin, 459; spine, 463; stitches and, 456; toe, 463; tongue, 457; tooth, 462. *See also* Head injuries
Insect repellants, 82-83, 405; DEET, 353; neurotoxic effects of, 83; Picardin-based, 353
Instincts, 4, 28
Institute of Medicine (IOM), 144, 305, 325
Insulin, 385
Insurance, 8, 11, 37, 39, 45, 57, 142, 157; bringing information about, 38; circumcision and, 17; nebulizers and, 374; questions about, 13
Intellectual development, 251, 252, 259, 260; age for achieving, 249; milestones of, 247; theory of, 261
International Committee on Taxonomy of Viruses, 336
International Lactation Consultant Association (ILCA), 285
International Pediatric Sleep Education Task Force, 227
Internet, 27, 41, 149
Intestinal infections, 159, 432
Intestinal obstruction, 417, 423, 436; described, 527
Intestinal problems, 179, 500
Intestines, 191, 193
Intoeing, 382
Intraventricular hemorrhage (IVH), 61; described, 527

Intussusception, 189, 193, 321, 417, 423; described, 527
IOM. *See* Institute of Medicine
IQ tests, 269, 396
Iron, 102, 109-111, 155, 172, 173; breastfeeding and, 484; calcium and, 485; vitamin C and, 111, 485
Iron deficiency, 101, 377
Iron-replacement therapy, 378, 485
Iron supplements, 64, 102, 378, 379, 485; taking, 101-102
Irritation, 81, 392, 438, 448, 459
Isomil DF formula, using, 434
ITP. *See* Idiopathic Thrombocytopenic Purpura
IVH. *See* Intraventricular hemorrhage
iVillage, 330

Jaundice, 49, 50, 52, 54, 69, 70, 120, 175, 506; abnormal, 55, 56; described, 527-528; developing, 59; LPI and, 60; physiologic, 126; red flags with, 55; risk for, 56 (fig.); significant, 126-127; treating, 56-57
Jenner, Edward, 301
Jerked elbow, 463
Jock itch, 77, 358, 491
Journal of Allergy and Clinical Immunology, 180
Juice, 109, 114, 167; diarrhea and, 166, 432; serving, 105, 166; unpasturized, 424

Kaopectate, 435
Karo cocktail, using, 190
Karp, Harvey, 289
Karyotyping, 255
Kawasaki Disease (KD), 404-405; described, 452-453, 528
Kernicterus, 54, 56, 127; described, 528
Kidney disease, 99
Kidney infections, 203, 436, 441, 506
Kidneys, 36, 384; examining, 48; malformation of, 47; ultrasounds for, 203, 507
King of the Sea, 400, 409
Knee control, 246
Knock-kneed, 382
Krum, MK, 26, 32
Kunik, Randy, 285

La Leche League, 140
Lab work, 43, 344, 505, 509-514
Labia, 48, 85, 203, 387
Labial adhesions, 48, 387-388; described, 528
Lactation consultants (LC), 57, 118, 136, 144, 149, 151, 164; advice from, 68; appointments with, 121; insurance and, 142; pacifiers and, 285
Lactobacillus, 139, 343
Lactobacillus acidophilus, 500, 501
Lactobacillus bulgaricus, 500
Lactobacillus GG, 500
Lactobacillus reuteri, 161, 288, 500, 501
Lactobacillus rhamnosus, 500, 501
Lactose, 158, 159, 160
Lactose intolerance, 159, 178; diarrhea and, 434; temporary, 432
Lancet (journal), 399
Language, 246, 261, 262, 263, 264, 274, 293, 400; 2 weeks, 250; 2 months, 250; 2 to 4 months, 265; 4 months, 250; 4 to 6 months, 266, 267; 6 months, 251; 6 to 9 months, 268, 269-270; 9 to 12 months, 271, 272; 1 year, 252; autism and, 256, 325; delays, 253, 255; expressive, 253; multiple, 271; normal, 368; sign, 269; understanding, 269
Language development, 248, 366; age for achieving, 249; hearing and, 45; milestones of, 246-247; research in, 256
Lankey, Lori, 27
Lanolin, 77, 119, 121
Lansinoh, 119, 121, 137
Large muscle development: 2 weeks, 250; 2 months, 250; 4 months, 250; 6 months, 250; 9 months, 251; 1 year, 251
Laryngomalacia, 46; described, 528
Latch, 115, 117, 121, 135, 149, 150; problems with, 60, 124, 136, 139
Late Preterm Infants (LPI), 55, 58, 126, 150, 260; discharge of, 60; looking out for, 59
Lawrence, Ruth, 147
Lazy eye, 37
LC. *See* Lactation consultants
Lead, 391, 392, 496; exposure to, 379, 393, 403
Lead poisoning, 379, 403
Lead screen, 36, 255; described, 37

"Learn the Signs, Act Early" (CDC), 253
Learning, 260, 275; described, 261-262; impairment, 332
Legs: bearing weight on, 264-265; examining, 48-49; misshapen, 382; uneven, 384
Legumes, 174; fiber in, 193
"Let Cry" Plan, 233
Let down, described, 119
Lethargy, 201, 310, 420, 432, 448, 449, 459; dehydration and, 433
Leukemia, 21, 392, 405, 408, 420, 451, 505; described, 528
Levalbuterol, 486
Lice, 369; treating, 359-360
Licorice, using, 498
Lifestyle, 108, 236-237
Lifetime burden, 391, 392
Limping, 384, 462
Lipids, 512; described, 159
Lips, 85; dehydration and, 433; swelling, 454
Little Gym, 276
Liver failure, 435, 478
Liver function tests, 511
Lockjaw, 313
Lotions, 79, 80
Lotrimin AF, 77
Lower esophageal sphincter, 194
Lower respiratory infection, 426
LPI. *See* Late Preterm Infants
Lung disease, chronic, 62, 488
Lung infections, 341, 354, 369, 375
Lung problems, 44; websites on, 542
Lungs, 372-375, 426
Lyme Disease, 82; described, 452-453
Lymph nodes, 342; CT/MRI for, 508
Lymphocytes, 339, 510
Lymphoma, 21

Macrocephaly, 91; described, 528
Mad Hatter's Disease, 327, 328
Madaras, Area, 27
Magnetic Resonance Imaging (MRI), 508
Malabsorption, 99, 193; described, 528
Malrotation, 47; described, 529
March of Dimes Birth Defects Foundation, address/phone number for, 543
Mason, Jackie: quote of, 413
Massages, infant, 206, 284, 288, 290
Mastectomy, 129
Mastitis, 131, 134, 139, 148
Masturbation, 14, 294-295; described, 529
Maternity leave, 143, 148
Mattresses: bacteria and, 406; co-sleeper, 220; conventional, 405-406; crib, 405-406; fitting, 221; greenguard, 406; hand-me-down, 406; organic, 218, 406; SIDS and, 216, 218, 406
Mature milk, described, 119
"Maybe Cry" Plan, 233
McCarthy, Jenny, 255, 302
Measles, 309, 317, 324, 326, 340, 455; cases of, 304; described, 316, 452-453; outbreaks of, 303, 308
Meat, 112, 172, 174; antibiotic-free, 396; iron-fortified, 173; organic, 396; processed, 400
Meconium, 47, 52, 53-54, 67, 123, 188, 193, 422; black, 68; described, 529
Meconium plug, 47, 189; described, 529
Medela "Pump In Style," 127
Media, 273, 275; vaccines and, 325
Medicaid, 40
Medical information: books on, 540; websites on, 542
Medical issues, xiv, 6, 7, 38, 41-42, 99, 283, 311, 371, 413
MedicAlert bracelets, 179
Medication index, 472-473
Medications, 70, 197, 243, 431; allergic reactions to, 450, 482, 483; allergy, 41, 473-474; alternative, 161, 503; anti-diarrhea, 435; anti-inflammatory, 381; anti-viral, 339; asthma, 41, 311, 372, 485-486, 487; bacterial infection, 482-483; blood pressure, 449; brand-name, 40, 467; breast-feeding and, 132, 147, 471-472; colic, 481; control, 485-486; cough and cold, 340, 341, 429, 430, 488-490; dental, 474-475; diarrhea, 480; dosing, 446, 447, 470; ear, 476-477; eye problem, 478; fever, 71, 440, 442, 443, 445, 447, 448, 469, 478-479; flavorings for, 468; gastrointestinal, 479-481; generic, 40, 469, 470; GERD, 198, 479-480; giardia, 484; heart, 449; hives and, 451; infection, 482-484; leftover, 468-

index

469; mouth, 474-475; nutrition, 484-485; oral, 140; OTC, 467, 470, 483, 490; pain, 18, 123, 475, 478-479; pinworm, 483-484; pregnancy and, 471-472; prescription, 40, 467, 468, 470; questions about, 415; rescue, 485, 486; respiratory problem, 485-490; safety with, 277; saving money on, 40; steroid, 381, 427, 487, 490, 492-493, 496; syrup, 446; teething, 87, 475-476; travel and, 296; unknown risk with, 471; viral infections and, 348; vomiting and, 467, 481

Medications and Mother's Milk (Hale), 132

Medicine bullets, 446

Melatonin, 210-211

Memory problems, 332, 400

Meningitis, 51, 91, 203, 301, 315, 320, 365, 369, 420, 436, 441, 451, 455; described, 452-453, 529; treating, 356; types of, 334

Meningitis Angels, 334

Menstrual cycles, 202, 397

Mental health, 132, 137, 390

Mental retardation, 19, 256

Mercury, 186, 496; autism and, 325, 328, 398; brain development and, 400; controversy over, 325-331; exposure to, 327, 328, 400; fish and, 327, 400

Metabolic disorders, 20, 99, 255, 388, 436, 455; described, 529; testing for, 19

Metabolic panels, 505, 509, 510

Metabolic screen, 4, 18-20, 34; described, 36

Metabolic Storage Disease, 47; described, 529

Metabolism, 19, 509; problems with, 385, 428

Methemoglobinemia, 397, 475

Methicillin Resistant Staph Aureus (MRSA), 354-355, 369

Methylmercury, 144, 327, 328, 391, 392, 400, 409

Metric system, common conversions for, 94

Microcephaly, 91; described, 529

Middle ear infections, 362, 364, 365, 366, 368

Midwest Acid Reflux Children's Institute, 198

Milestones. *See* Developmental milestones

Milia, 49; described, 530

Miliaria, 49; described, 530

Milk: antibiotics and, 395; calories from, 167; coconut, 179; cow's, 96, 114, 144, 145, 153, 155, 156, 158, 167, 378, 390, 395, 397, 422; goat's, 153, 179; intolerance, 283; nutrients in, 168; organic, 168, 390, 394, 395, 396, 397; rice, 153, 168, 173; servings of, 112; skim, 168; soy, 153, 168; unpasteurized, 168; whole, 102, 153, 168

Milk banks, 149

Milk fortifiers, using, 64

Milley, Frankie, 334

Milley, Ryan, 334

Mindell, 233, 238

Mindell Method, pros/cons of, 234

Miscarriages, 317

Mites, 369, 386, 387, 451; facts on, 359; treating for, 359

Mitochondrial disorders, 331

MMR, 304, 306, 309, 316, 317, 455; autism and, 323-325

Moeller, E., 26

Moisturizers, 79, 81, 380

Molluscum contagiosum, described, 452-453

"Mommy and Me" program, 276

Mom's Day Out program, 27

Mongolian Spots, 49; described, 530

Monilial dermatitis, 491

Monitors, 226, 238, 430

Mono, 339

Monospot/EBV titers, 511, 514

Montagu, Lady Mary Wortly, 301

Mora, Debby, 27

Moraxella, 365

More Milk Plus, 134

Moser, C., 333

Mother's Milk banks, 149

Motor development, 263, 291, 294; 2 to 4 months, 265

Motrin, 87, 135, 415, 442, 443, 445, 446, 469

Mouth: dehydration and, 433; examining, 45; white-coated, 85

Mouth burns, 449

Mouth care, 85-88

Mouth infections, viral, 369

Mouth problem, 137

Mouthwash, antifungal, 140
MRI. *See* Magnetic Resonance Imaging
MRSA. *See* Methicillin Resistant Staph Aureus
MSNBC, xvii
Mucous, 66, 189, 338, 341; clearing, 429; in diarrhea, 432; in poop, 177, 179, 193, 423, 432
Multiple sclerosis, 323
Multiples: breastfeeding and, 149; sleep and, 215, 243; sleeping through night and, 239, 243; strollers and, 284; toys and, 272
Multivitamins, 64, 102, 484, 485
Mumps, 304, 326, 340; described, 316-317
Muscles, 210, 246, 382-384
Mutations, 391
My Breast Friend, 124
Mylicon drops, using, 195, 206

Nails, clipping, 75
Nannies: described, 29; finding, 29-30, 70; sharing, 33
Naps, 213, 229, 233, 237, 293; afternoon, 241, 242; daycare and, 242; length of, 241-242; opportunities for, 68; rituals for, 232; sacrificing, 242; scheduling, 223, 224-225, 241-242
Narcotics, 123
Nasal congestion, 65, 66, 153, 429; newborn, 45, 531; questions about, 430
Nasal discharge, 340, 422, 430
Nasal sprays, xvi, 489
Nash, Ogden: quote of, 335
Nasolacrimal Duct Obstruction, 45, 438; described, 530
Natal Teeth, 46; described, 530
National Adoption Information Clearinghouse, 34
National Allergy Supply, Inc., 387
National Association for the Education of Young Children (NAEYC), 30
National Asthma Education and Prevention Program, 374
National Cancer Institute, 398
National Center for Complementary and Alternative Medicine, 495, 496, 501
National Center on Birth Defects and Developmental Disabilities, address/phone number for, 543
National Donor Program, 22
National Highway Transportation Safety Administration (NHTSA), 58
National Immunization Program (NIP), 310, 332
National Institute of Allergy and Infectious Diseases, 171, 180
National Institutes of Health (NIH), 495, 501; alternative remedies and, 499; HCAs and, 399; Vitamin D and, 100
National Lead Information Center (NLIC), 379
National Library of Medicine, 404, 410
National Marrow Donor, website of, 21
National Newborn Screening and Genetic Resources Center, 19
National Poison Control Center, 415
National Sleep Foundation, infants/sleep and, 244
National Toxicology Program, 402
National Transportation Safety Board, 296
National Vaccine Program Office, aluminum and, 332
Nebulizers, 41, 374, 486
Neck: examining, 46; rotation, 383; stretching exercises, 93; x-rays for, 507
Neck/spine disability screen, down syndrome and, 259
Neonatal intensive care unit (NICU), 58, 62, 63, 64, 95
Nervous system, 48, 212; websites on, 542
Nestle, formula and, 156
Neural tube defects, 48; described, 530
Neurodevelopmental disabilities, 393
Neurofibromatosis (NF), described, 530-531
Neurological maturity, 59, 64, 214
Neurological problems, 134, 238; LPI and, 59, 61
Neutrophils (PMNs), 344, 510
Nevus Flammeus, 49; described, 530
New England Journal of Medicine (NEJM), xvi, 15, 147, 364
Newborn hold, described, 66
Newborn screening, websites on, 543

Nichols, Jill, 329
Nicotine, breast milk and, 146
NICU. *See* Neonatal intensive care unit
Night feeders, 229, 236
Night terrors, 232
Nipple bacterial infections, 131, 134, 138
Nipple confusion, 164
Nipple enlargement, 48
Nipple pain, 130, 134, 136
Nipple shields, 119, 121, 128, 150; using, 136, 137
Nipples: Avent, 164; burning, 139-140; cracked/bleeding, 120, 137, 138, 139, 201, 421, 422; cross-cut, 164; flat, 119, 136; healing, 121, 128, 138; inverted, 119, 136; large, 143; lipstick, 136; normal, 136; recommended, 163-164; sore, 120, 137-138, 287; washing, 140
Nitrates, 397-398, 399
Nitrites, 397, 399
No Cry Sleep Solution, The (Pantley), 233, 236
Nose: breathing through, 430; congested, 429; examining, 45
Nose drops, 421; saline, 40, 65, 341, 429
Nosebleeds, 420, 421, 422, 461, 463
Novovirus, treating, 351-352
Numbing drops, 87, 477
Nurse practitioners (NPs), described, 42
Nursemaid's elbow, 463
Nursing Mother's Companion, The (Huggins), 140
Nutrition, xvi, 52, 109, 112, 113, 126, 129, 169, 171, 188, 230; autism and, 258; deficiency, 162; growth and, 89; information on, 107; liquid, 97, 169, 185, 186; LPI and, 59, 62; medications for, 484-485; milestones for, 34; needs for, 94-97; perfect, 159; poor, 379; solid, 97, 170, 186; sources of, 96, 155; websites on, 542
Nutrition Committee (AAP), 102, 162, 171, 172

Obesity, 36, 114, 167, 397; autism and, 258; avoiding, 105, 108, 385; BMI and, 105-109; feedback on, 106-107; rise in, 108-109; solid food and, 170; viral infections and, 108
Object permanence, 261
Obstetricians: circumcision and, 16-17; pediatricians and, 6
Odors, 388, 449
Office staff, meeting, 38, 39, 41-42
Offit, Paul, 324, 333
Ointments, 50, 363, 425, 478, 494
Omega-3 fatty acids, 102, 146, 160, 400
Omnibus Autism Proceedings, 331
Omphalitis, 69, 77; described, 531
On Becoming Babywise (Ezzo and Bucknam), 233, 236-237
1% Hydrocortisone cream, 80, 380
Ophthalmologists, 61, 372
Oppenheimer Toy Portfolio, 272, 276
Oral exploration, 390
Oral motor development, 170, 171; 4 to 6 months, 266; 6 to 9 months, 268; 9 to 12 months, 270; milestones of, 246
Orbital cellulitis, 438; described, 531
Organic, 177, 395-396; described, 176
Orthodontic problems, pacifiers and, 285, 286
Orthotics, 382; described, 531
Osteomalacia, 332
Osteopathic medicine (D.O.), 42
Osteopenia, 487
Osteoporosis, 114
Otitis externa, 362, 476; described, 531
Otitis media, described, 531
Otoscopes, 364
Over The Counter (OTC), 470, 483, 490
Overdosing, avoiding, 446
Overeating, BMI and, 105-109
Overproduction, 130, 134-135
Overtired children, 225, 233, 283
Overweight, 36, 109; feedback on, 106-107

PABA, 82
Pacifiers, 88, 115, 213; avoiding, 232; braces and, 286; breastfeeding and, 128-129; debate over, 228, 284-287; dental issues and, 286; ear infections and, 286, 362, 368; falling asleep and, 228;

getting rid of, 225, 228, 285; Nuk style, 285; orthodontic problems and, 286, 287; SIDS and, 127, 129, 217, 220, 285; sleep and, 229, 230, 234; Soothie, 129, 137, 287; sterilizing, 140; using, 228, 230, 284-285, 286-287
Pain, 309, 311, 418; breastfeeding, 128; chronic, 417; nipple, 130, 134, 136
Palmer, Julie DeCamp, 106
Panting, 427, 431
Pantley method, 233; pros/cons of, 236
Parainfluenza, 338
Paraphimosis, 15, 85; described, 531
Parasites, 303, 360, 369, 423, 432; intestinal, 34
Parent at home, described, 28
Parent directed feedings (PDF), 237
Parenthood, quote from, 187
Parenting, xiii, xvii-xviii, 289; styles, 4-6, 29, 71, 221, 234; vaccinations and, 302
Parent's Choice, 161; Gentle, 158
ParentsGuideCordBlood.com, 21, 23
Parvovirus, 353, 369; described, 452-453
Pasteur, Louis, 356
Pasteurization, 156, 356, 397, 424
PCBs. *See* Polychlorinated biphenyls
PCV 13: 320
PDD. *See* Pervasive Developmental Disorders
PE tubes. *See* Pressure equalization tubes
Peanut challenge test, 181
Pedialyte, 40, 201, 434, 436, 437
Pediasure, 168
Pediatricians, xv, 35, 38, 96; adoption and, 34; calling, 12-13, 413, 414; confiding in, 41; emergencies and, 12, 13, 414; hospital-based, 12, 44; on-call, 12, 413-414; parents and, 11, 13, 14; questions for, 7-8, 13; selecting, 6-14; tests and, 505-506
Pediatrics, xvi, 8, 13, 469
Pediatrics (journal), 490
Pediatrix, 307, 326
Pediculocides, 492
Pee, 71, 188, 202-204, 388; blood in, 202; red, 194
Pelvic: CT/MRI for, 508; pressure on, 53; ultrasounds for, 507
Penicillin, 320, 346, 482, 496; allergies to, 386
Penile adhesions, 16, 84, 85, 387; described, 531
Penis, 14, 47, 48, 203; caring for, 17-18, 83-84; circumcised, 83-84, 387; hidden, 16; uncircumcised, 84-85
Pentacel, 307
Peppermint, 341, 498
Pepto-Bismol, 193, 435
Perchlorate, exposure to, 393-394
Perforated eardrum, 362, 363, 367; described, 532
Perfumes, avoiding, 80, 380
Periodontal disease, down syndrome and, 259
Permissive parenting, described, 5
Personality, 246, 249; 2 to 4 months, 265; 4 to 6 months, 268; 6 to 9 months, 270; 9 to 12 months, 270; temperament and, 282
Pertussis, 304, 308, 314, 426; described, 313
Pervasive Developmental Disorder, Not Otherwise Specified (PDD-NOS), 253
Pervasive Developmental Disorders (PDD), 185, 253; described, 532
Pesticides, 176, 392, 405, 409; avoiding, 395; organophosphate, 391; residue from, 396; sensitivity to, 394
Petechiae, 355, 420, 442, 451, 455, 506
Petroleum jelly, 17-18, 77, 80, 83, 388, 422
Phenylketonuria (PKU), 18, 34, 36, 50; described, 532
Phenylketonuria (PKU)/newborn screen, 49-50
Phimosis, 85; described, 532
Phone calls, 413, 417; handling, 12-13
Phototherapy, 57; described, 532
Phthalates, 391, 402-403, 406
Physical therapists, 93, 259; help from, 383-384
Physician assistants (PAs), 42
Phytoestrogens, 391, 393
Piaget, Jean, 261
Pigeon toed, 382
Pigmentation, concerns about, 82
Pillows: nursing, 124, 143; sleeping with, 243

index

Pilot lights, checking, 408
Pincer grasp, 184, 268
Pink eye, 347, 351, 365, 437-438, 478; treating, 355
Pinworms, 347, 360, 369; medications for, 483-484
Pityriasis rosea, described, 452-453
PKU. *See* Phenylketonuria
Plagiocephaly, 93
Plastics, harmful, 402-403
Platelet count, 420, 510
Play, independent/solo, 274, 275
Plugged ducts, 134, 138-139, 152; described, 119; problems with, 131
PMNs. *See* Neutrophils
Pneumonia, 51, 316, 319, 320, 321, 344, 426, 441, 443, 482, 506; catching, 65-66; described, 532; treating, 354
Pneumonia vaccine, 378
Poison Control, calling, 273, 449, 450
Poison ivy, 420, 450
Poisons, 343, 388, 449-450, 455, 456; feedback on, 450; ingestion of, 422; questions about, 450
Poling, Hannah, 331
Polio, 304, 306, 310, 340; described, 314-315
Polio vaccine, 315
Pollens, 386
Pollutants, 389, 391; environmental, 407, 408; exposure to, 390, 393, 394
Polycarbonate, 401, 402
Polychlorinated biphenyls (PCBs), 327, 391, 392, 400
Polycyclic aromatic hydrocarbons (PAH), 399
Polydactyly, 49; described, 532
Polyethylene, 141, 330
Polypropylene, 141
Polyurethane foam, 406
Polyvinyl chloride, 403, 406
Poop, 60, 187, 337, 338, 343, 417, 443; black, 68, 379; black tar, 53-54, 67, 123, 188, 189, 193; blood in, 177, 179, 193, 321, 422, 423, 432, 506; blue, 194; breast milk and, 188, 189; breastfeeding and, 67, 123, 191; changes in, 55, 127; clay/white, 193; color of, 67, 188; consistency of, 190; explosive, 433; formula and, 67, 189; grape jelly, 193, 321, 423, 432; green, 188, 189; mucous in, 177, 179, 193, 423, 432; newborn, 121, 188-191; normal, 197; red, 194; solid, 191, 193, 422; texture of, 67, 188; watery, 432; worrisome, 189, 193
Port wine stains, 49; described, 532
Positional plagiocephaly, 91, 219-220, 264
Positioning, 115, 121, 150, 151; horizontal, 164; poor, 136; tips on, 124
Positive parenting, described, 5
Post-tussive emesis, 435; described, 533
Posterior urethral valves, 48; described, 532
PPD, 37, 513
PPIs. *See* Proton pump inhibitors
Pre-operational development, 2 to 7 years, 262
Preauricular pits and tags, 45; described, 533
Prebiotics, 162; described, 500; probiotics and, 499-501
Preemie Primer, The (Gunter), 61
Preemies: breastfeeding and, 102, 125-126, 149-150; calories and, 95; catch-up growth and, 90; developmental checklist for, 260; feedings and, 98; food and, 171; formula for, 161; primer on, 58-64; sleep and, 243; soy formula and, 158
Preemies: The Essential Guide for Parents of Premature Babies (Linden), 61
Pregnancy, 51, 71; medications and, 471-472
Prematurity, 120, 257
Prenatal care, 51, 99
Prenatal consultations: described, 6-8; questions for, 7
Prenatal vitamins, 100, 132, 258, 449
Preschools, 24, 31
Prescriptions, 40, 467, 468; finishing, 469; reading, 470
Preservatives, 328, 399, 400; described, 329; vaccine, 326, 329
Pressure equalization (PE) tubes, 41, 366, 368, 476, 477; described, 370
Prevnar, 304, 305, 320, 346, 365,

378; aluminum in, 333
Primary care provider, described, 41-42
Probiotics, 139, 434; antibiotics and, 500; colic and, 288; formula with, 161; prebiotics and, 499-501; refrigerating, 500
Procrastinator, described, 125
Progressive waiting, 25, 231, 232; described, 235; rapid extinction and, 235, 238
Protein, 148, 161; abnormal, 377; casein, 157; comfort, 158; cow's milk, 144, 145, 159; defective, 256; milk, 144-145, 156-157, 158, 172, 173, 178, 179, 180, 182, 196, 287, 422, 501, 529-530; servings of, 112; soy, 157, 179
Protein hydrolysate, 160
Proton pump inhibitors (PPIs), 197, 480
Prune juice cocktail, 190
Pseudoephedrine, 152, 489, 490
Pseudostrabismus, 372; described, 533
Psychiatric diagnostic bible (DSM-5), 253
Puberty, 397, 401
Pulse, 44, 53, 440; taking, 415-416
Pumping, 116, 117, 118, 126, 129, 133, 134, 135, 138, 139, 140, 142, 148, 152
Pumps, 133, 142; cleaning, 141; electric, 127; high-grade, 127, 134, 150; rental, 127, 150
Pus, 69, 361, 362, 363, 364, 366, 367, 456, 457, 458
Pustular melanosis, 49; described, 533
Pyelonephritis, 48; described, 533
Pyloric sphincter, 200
Pyloric stenosis, 195, 200, 417, 436; described, 533

Quality time, working parents and, 30
Quarantines, 312

Rabies, 306
Radiation, ionizing, 391
Radon, 391, 405
Ragweed, 386
Raising Arizona, quote from, 75
Rapid antigen assays, 514
Rapid extinction, 225, 233; progressive waiting and, 235, 238
Rapid Eye Movement (REM), 210
Rash-o-rama, 41, 358
Rashes, 69, 76, 177, 309, 347, 358, 380, 420, 438, 454-455; allergies and, 419, 451, 454; causes of, 450; common, 41, 452-453; diaper, 41, 75, 77, 86, 454, 455, 491, 502; fever and, 443, 455; herpes, 454; hormones and, 454; infections and, 451, 454; newborn, 450, 454; pimply, 454; questions about, 450-451; scaly, 454; severe, 77; viruses and, 347, 352-353, 369; worrisome, 451
RAST testing, 182
RBGH. *See* Bovine growth hormone
Reach Out and Read, 266
Reactive airway disease, 373
Reading, 260, 266; language and, 264
Receptive language skills, 246, 268, 271
Red blood cells, 378; abnormal, 377; destruction of, 379; nitrites and, 397
Reflexes, 263, 288, 460
Reflux, 161, 200
Refractive errors, 37, 61; described, 533
Registered nurse (R.N.), described, 42
Regularity, 281
Regurgitation, 194-201
Rehydration, 434, 437, 481
REM. *See* Rapid Eye Movement
Remedies, 499; herbal, 288, 469, 472, 495, 497, 540; home, 481, 502-503; homeopathic, 501
Repellants, citronella-based, 82
Reproductive system, 391, 392
Residuals, described, 329
Respiratory distress, 46, 200, 425-429; described, 533; questions about, 427
Respiratory rate, 44, 53, 440; average, 416; elevated, 426, 431; LPI and, 60
Respiratory Syncytial Virus (RSV), 62, 349; described, 533-534
Respiratory system: LPI and, 59, 61-62; understanding, 425
Rester, described, 125
Reticulocyte count, 512
Retinoblastoma, 44; described, 534
Retinopathy of Prematurity (ROP), 61; described, 534

Retractions, 46, 426, 431; described, 534
Rett Syndrome, 256
Reye's syndrome, 435, 478
Rheumatoid arthritis, 114
Rhinoviruses, 338, 340, 341, 369, 373
Rhus dermatitis, 420
Rice cereal, 95, 98, 170, 212; arsenic in, 172-173, 396-397; calories in, 175; constipation and, 191; fiber and, 173; sleep and, 212
Rickets, 100; described, 534; Vitamin D and, 101
Ringworm, 347, 369, 454, 491; contagiousness of, 359; described, 358, 452-453; treating, 358
R.N. *See* Registered nurse
Robeez, 273
Robert's American Gourmet, snacks from, 107
Rocking, 213, 214, 223, 224, 283-284
Rocky Mountain Spotted Fever, 451; described, 452-453
Rolling, 266-267
Room sharing, 54, 220, 221
Rooting reflex, described, 534
Roseola, 352, 369, 442-443; described, 452-453
Ross, T., 33
Rotavirus, 304, 305, 338, 339, 340, 500; described, 320-321, 325; rapid antigen assay for, 514; treating, 351
Rotavirus vaccine, 320-321
Routines, 5, 28, 37, 105, 232, 261; importance of, 26. *See also* Sleep routines
RSV. *See* Bronchiolitis; Respiratory Syncytial Virus
Rubella, 257, 304, 326, 340; described, 317
Runny nose, 86, 203, 341, 347, 351, 416, 438, 439, 442; allergies and, 386, 387; teething and, 87

Saccaromyces sp., 500
Sacral dimple, 48; described, 534
Safety, xvii, 267, 291, 459, 460; furniture, 277; preemies and, 64; tips for, 277; toy, 273
Safety gates, 242, 277
Saline nose drops, 40, 65, 66, 341, 429
Salmonella, 355, 369, 423-424, 432
Salves, 494
Sandboxes, fibers in, 406-407
Sarcomas, 405
Scabicides, 490, 492
Scabies, 347, 359, 369, 492; described, 452-453
Scarlet fever, described, 452-453
Science, 11; showing, xvi-xvii, 176-177, 503
Screen time, limiting, 274, 275
Screening tests, 34, 35, 36-37, 42, 50, 372, 377; routine, 36; state-mandated, 19-20
Scrotum, 47, 418
Sears, Bob, 233, 330
Sears method, 234; pros/cons of, 236
Seborrhea, 80; described, 534-535
Seinfeld, Jerry: quote of, 35
Seizure disorders, 455, 456; websites on, 542
Seizures, 310, 455-456, 459; fever and, 309, 447-448; head injuries and, 460; questions about, 456
Sensitivity plates, 345
Sensorimotor development, 264; birth to 1 month, 261; birth to 2 years, 261; 1 to 4 months, 261; 4 to 8 months, 261; 8 to 12 months, 261; 12 to 18 months, 261; 18 to 24 months, 261
Sensory Processing Disorder, 185; described, 534-535
Separation anxiety, 268, 280, 291, 294
Sepsis, 59, 320, 441
Septal hematoma, 461
Serotonin, 217
Serous otitis media, 366; described, 535
Serving sizes, 105, 109, 186
Severe Combined Immune Deficiency (SCID), 321
Sexually transmitted diseases, 15
Shaking, avoiding, 289
Shampoo, 79, 80; formaldehyde and, 403-404
Shannon, Michael, 410
Shigella, 355, 432
Shingles, 319, 339; described, 452-453
Shoes: buying, 272-273; corrective, 382
Shopper's Guide to Pesticides, 394
Shoulder dystocia, 46; described, 535
Shoulder support, 246
Shoulders, examining, 46

Sick child policies, 30, 31
Sick leave policy, knowing, 27
Sick visits, 9, 11, 42; appointments for, 38, 40; well-child visits and, 10, 39
Sickle cell anemia, 50; described, 535
Sickle cell disease, 34, 36, 377-378; websites on, 542
Side-lying, 151; described, 123
SIDS. *See* Sudden infant death syndrome
Silber, Seth, 87
Silverstone, Alicia, 176
Simethicone drops, 195, 206, 288
Similac, 196; Advance Early Shield, 162; Advance Organic, 161; Alimentum, 157; Early Shield Advance, 156; Expert Care for Diarrhea, 159; Soy, 156; for Spit-Up, 161; Total Comfort, 158
Simply Thick, 151
Singer, Alison, 324
Sinus: CT/MRI for, 508; x-rays for, 508
Sinus infections, 320, 321, 340, 343, 348, 354, 369, 431, 438, 443, 482, 506; common colds and, 342
Sippy cups, tooth decay and, 167
Six Commandments for Balancing Work & Baby, 25-26
Skills: cognitive, 264; coordination, 170; language, 246-247, 253, 271, 272, 293, 368; motor, 170, 171, 248, 249, 263, 291, 294; muscle, 246; parenting, 289; personality, 246, 265; problem solving, 247, 271, 275, 276; self-soothing, 213, 226; social, 246, 247, 253, 254, 256, 264, 265, 274
Skin, 65, 69, 380-381, 459; antibacterial soap and, 337; dry, 81, 201; examining, 49; irritation, 76, 77; red flags with, 70; scaly, 80, 380; sensitive, 454; yellow, 49
Skin disorders, 81; websites on, 542
Skin infections, 369, 425, 482, 506; treating, 354-355
Skin products, 451, 490
Skin stickers, 444
Skin tags, 45; described, 535
Skin tests, 182, 513
Skin turgor, dehydration and, 433
Skull, 91, 93; fracture, 460; malleable, 92; x-rays for, 508
Slapped cheek, 353, 369
Sleep, 5, 55, 65, 68, 121, 154; adult, 211; behavior and, 233; beyond first year, 242-243; breast milk production and, 134; breastfeeding and, 129, 228, 230; car seats and, 213, 219, 224; down syndrome and, 259; feedings and, 66, 211, 223, 226, 229, 230, 232; multiples and, 215, 243; newborn, 211; non-REM, 210; pacifiers and, 229, 230, 234; physical/mental health and, 132; preemies and, 63, 243; red flags with, 69; REM, 210; requirements for, 214; routines for, 5; safety with, 216-221, 221-222; science of, 206, 207-211; SIDS and, 215; special situations with, 243-244; on stomach, 215, 217; tips for, 213
Sleep associations, 223, 232, 236
Sleep crutches, 224, 232, 234, 285
Sleep cycles, 210, 224
Sleep deprivation, 132, 209, 236, 430
Sleep disruption, 86, 225, 227, 229, 231, 232, 236, 238, 240, 416
Sleep habits, 209, 234; bad, 215, 233; setting up, 222-223; undoing bad, 227-228, 230-231, 232
Sleep patterns, 98, 229; feedings and, 225-227; illnesses and, 231, 232; teething and, 231, 232; travel and, 231, 232
Sleep position, 93; SIDS and, 215, 216, 217, 218, 219, 220
Sleep problems, 38, 69, 227, 238, 280, 430; intervention in, 241; long-term, 222; newborn, 211-215; preventing, 232; solving, 227-228, 230-231
Sleep routines, 88, 154, 228, 232, 234, 244; birth to 2 months, 214; 2 to 4 months, 214-215, 222-223, 225; 4 to 5 months, 224-227; 4 to 6 months, 215; 6 to 12 months, 215; changes in, 214-215; consistency with, 222, 224, 225, 232, 240, 241; erratic, 211; establishing, 212, 213, 221-222, 225; healthy, 215, 235; mistakes with, 229; multiples and, 243; newborns and, 210; normal, 212, 231; promoting, 236

Sleep Safety Tips, 129
Sleep Tight, 289
Sleep training, 5, 226, 227, 232, 234, 239; approaches to, 236; problems with, 238
Sleep walking, 232
Sleeping through night, xvii, 98, 225-227, 228, 231, 237; age at, 240; expecting, 212; GERD and, 243-244; multiples and, 239, 243; solid food and, 170
Sleeping Through the Night (Mindell), 233
SleepSack, 217
Slow to warm up child, described, 280
Small muscle development: 4 months, 250; 6 months, 251; 1 year, 252
Smallpox, 301, 303, 304, 310, 315, 340; described, 322-323; elimination of, 308
Smallpox vaccine, 323
Smegma, 16, 84
Smoking, 146, 391, 407, 410; ear infections and, 362, 368; SIDS and, 216, 217, 220
Snacks, 26, 106, 134
Sneezing, 315, 341
Snot, 66, 337, 340, 341, 370; air passing through, 426-427; green, 342, 346, 430
Soap, 79; antibacterial, 336, 337; Dove, 79, 337; moisturizing, 380
Social development, 247, 260, 262-263; 2 to 4 months, 265; 4 to 6 months, 266, 268; 6 months, 251; 6 to 9 months, 268, 270; 9 to 12 months, 270, 272; 1 year, 252
Social skills, 246, 247, 264, 274; autism and, 254, 256
Sodium nitrate, 399-400
Soft spot, 44, 91, 92, 201
Solitary sleep, 221-222; advantages/disadvantages of, 222
Solka, Shelley, 285
Solve Your Child's Sleep Problems (Ferber), 232, 233
Soothing, 116, 188, 223; self-, 26, 213-214, 225, 226, 227, 229, 232, 234, 237, 239, 240, 283, 295; temperament and, 282; tricks for, 283-284
Sore throat, 340; home remedies for, 503; virus and, 346, 351, 369
Spanking, avoiding, 292
Speech development, 285
Sphincter muscle, 195
Spina bifida, 48, 258; described, 535
Spinal fluid tests (CSF), 344, 513, 514
Spinal manipulations, 288, 495
Spine: examining, 48; ultrasounds for, 507; x-rays for, 508
Spit up, 187, 194-201, 422, 437
Spleen, 47, 378
Sputum, cultures for, 514
Staph, 343, 369; drug-resistant, 354
Stay-at-home parents, 28
Steenhagen, Deb, 32
Stem cells, 20, 21, 22
Sternocleidomastoid muscle, 382
Steroid creams, 16, 84, 381, 492
Steroids: inhaled, 374, 527; medication, 381, 427, 487, 490, 492-493, 496; topical, 381; using, 487, 492-493
Stevens-Johnson Syndrome, 419, 483; described, 535
Stimulation: developmental, 264, 265-266, 269-270, 274, 277-278; reaction to, 53; sensory, 185
Stitches, 456-458, 459; questions about, 456
Stomach acid, 196, 197
Stomach virus, 193, 338, 347, 351, 369, 432
Stomachaches, 417, 436
Stool: acholic, 193; cultures for, 34, 514; described, 187; tests, 513. *See also* Poop
Stough, Wendy, 26, 107
Strabismus, 61, 371; described, 535
Stranger anxiety, 280, 294
Strawberry Hemangioma, 49; described, 535
Strep, 319, 329, 343, 369; antibiotics for, 347; rapid antigen assay for, 514; secondary, 353. *See also* Group A strep; Group B strep
Strep pneumoniae, 334, 345, 346, 365, 369, 378; cases of, 305; described, 319-320; treating, 357-358
Strep pneumoniae vaccine, 320
Strep throat, 320, 345, 346, 365, 482
Streptomycin, 306
Stridor, 419, 427, 431; described, 535
Sturge-Weber syndrome, 49; described, 536

Subconjunctival hemorrhages, 45, 461; described, 536
Subungual hematoma, 463
Sucking, 48, 49, 129, 153, 167, 283, 284, 286, 295; sleep and, 213
Sudden infant death syndrome (SIDS), 91, 230, 267, 323, 428; bedding and, 216, 217, 220; biochemical abnormalities and, 127; breastfeeding and, 114; ethnicity and, 217; family beds and, 220, 221-222; family history and, 217; mattresses and, 216, 218, 406; pacifiers and, 127, 129, 217, 220, 285; risk of, 216, 218, 219, 220; room temperature and, 216, 220; sleep position and, 215, 216, 217, 218, 219, 220; smoking and, 216, 217, 220
Sudden Unexplained Infant Death (SUID), 220, 221-222
Sugar, 148, 288, 384, 398
Sun burns, 424-425
Sunblock, 75, 81-82, 100
Supplementation, 56-57, 100, 115, 117, 125, 128, 132, 148, 149, 150, 168, 496
Suppositories, 190-191
Supranumerary nipple, 48; described, 536
Supraventricular Tachycardia (SVT), described, 376, 536
Survival guide, two-week, 64-71
Sutures, 456-458
Swaddling, 60, 68, 213, 214, 217, 218, 219, 384
Swallowing, 123, 427
Sweat test, 513
Swelling, 342, 438, 439, 454, 459, 462
Swimmer's ear: described, 363; ear infections and, 361-362; prevention drops for, 476
Swimming classes, 276
Swine flu (H1N1), 300
Swings/seats, 223, 284
Synagis, 62, 64, 488
Syndactyly, 49; described, 536
Syphilis, 34
Syringes, medicine, 446, 468

Tachypnea of newborn, 46
Talking: boys/girls compared, 271; television and, 274
TB. *See* Tuberculosis
Tdap, 313, 314
Tea Tree oil, using, 498
Teeth: arrival of, 86, 87, 92; brushing, 88, 167, 230
Teething, 86-87, 185, 225, 476; acid reflux and, 86; breastfeeding and, 153; drool and, 86; fever and, 87, 448; runny nose and, 87; sleep patterns and, 231, 232
Teething gels, 87
Teething necklaces, 87
Teething tablets, homeopathic, 87
Television, 273-275; food and, 105; talking and, 274
Temper tantrums, 292, 294
Temperament: discipline and, 279; learning, 280, 281; personality and, 282; soothing and, 282
Temperature, 44, 78; clothes and, 76; LPI and, 60; protocol for, 441; rectal, 441, 444-446; taking, 71, 415, 440, 443-444, 448
Temporal artery scanners, 444
Terrible Twos, 292
Testicular, ultrasounds for, 507
Tests, 37, 50, 249; government-subsidized, 19; infant development, 159; parents and, 505; pediatricians and, 505-506
Tetanus, 304, 308; described, 313
Tetanus and diphtheria booster (Td), 314, 457
Tetracycline, 469
Texture aversion, described, 185
Texture complexity, 67, 170, 188
Thermometers: digital, 444-445, 446; ear, 71, 444; oral, 444, 446; rectal, 190, 443, 444-445, 446
Thickeners, 151
Thimerosal, 322, 332; controversy over, 325-331
Thompson, Judithe A.: quote of, 113
Throat, 46, 362; cultures for, 514
Throat infections, 313, 369
Thrush, 85-86, 139, 369; contagiousness of, 359; described, 358; treating, 358
Thumb sucking, 286, 295
Thyroid, 34, 391, 512
Thyroid screening, down syndrome and, 259
Tinea capitis, 491
Tinea corporis, 491

Tinea cruris, 491
Tinea pedis, 491
Toes, 463; controlling, 246
Toilet training, 194
Tongue thrusting, 137
Tongue-tie, 45, 134, 137, 516
Tonsil viruses, 350, 369
Tonsils, 351
Tooth decay, 88; fluoride and, 103; sippy cups and, 167
Tooth gels, fluoride-free, 88
Toothpaste, fluoride, 88, 475
Topical numbing products, 475
Torch infections, 51; described, 536
Torticollis, 46, 92-94, 382-384; described, 536
Touchpoints (Brazelton), 277
Toxic Substance Control Act, 389-390
Toxic Toy Scare, 37, 403
Toxins, xvii, 37, 257, 304, 343, 389, 392, 393, 401, 403; avoiding, 400; ingestion of, 422; vulnerability to, 390
Toys, 272, 276, 438; appropriate, 278; favorite, 289-290; lead in, 403; plastic, 403; safety with, 273, 277
Trachea, 426
Transient lactase deficiency, 158
Transient Tachypnea of the Newborn (TTN), 52; described, 536-537
Transitional objects, 230, 289-290
Transmitted upper airway noise, 426; described, 537
Trauma, 428, 438, 458-463; questions about, 459
Travel: discipline and, 296; medication and, 296; sleep patterns and, 231, 232
Travel health, websites on, 543
Trial of Infant Response to Diphenhydramine (TIRED), 474
Trichomonas, 15
Truman, Harry S.: quote of, 245
Trust vs. mistrust, birth to 18 months, 262
TTN. *See* Transient Tachypnea of the Newborn
Tuberculosis (TB), 36-37, 304, 431; described, 537; screening for, 34
Tucker Sling, 196, 219
Tummy time, 217, 264, 383; flat heads and, 92-94
Tumors: abdominal, 47, 511; brain, 91, 201, 372, 436, 518; eye, 44
Twain, Mark: quote of, 89
Two-stop rule, 27
Tylenol, 87, 307, 309, 373, 415, 441, 442, 443, 469; giving, 445, 447; overdosing, 446

Ulcers, 422
Ultimate Crib Sheet, 406
Ultrasounds, 43, 49, 204, 375-376, 384, 507
Umbilical cord, 22, 24, 47, 69; caring for, 76, 77, 78
Undescended testes, 47; described, 537
Unilateral laterothoracic exanthem, described, 452-453
Upper respiratory infections (URI), 341, 346, 361, 369, 372, 386, 425-426, 430; antibiotics for, 347; ear infections and, 362; home remedies for, 502
Urethra, 48, 85, 202, 203, 343, 387
Urgent care centers, 9, 41
URI. *See* Upper respiratory infections
Uric acid crystals, 54, 202; described, 537-538
Urinalysis, 36, 512-513
Urinary tract infections (UTI), 15, 48, 85, 343, 441, 482; described, 538; treating, 204, 356
Urination, 202, 432, 436; dehydration and, 433; excessive, 385; pain with, 418
Urine, 85, 202-204, 344, 384, 385; cloudy, 203; cultures for, 514; described, 187-188; flow, 203, 204; foul smelling, 203
Urine tests, 512-513
U.S. Department of Health and Human Services, 142, 310
U.S. News and World Report, overweight children and, 108-109
USA Today, xvii
USDA, organic and, 176, 396
Uterus abnormalities, 383
UTI. *See* Urinary tract infections
UVA/UVB, 82, 100

Vaccination Revealed (Butler), 333
Vaccinations, 34, 35, 36, 300-301, 313, 455, 457, 458; colds and, 307; delaying, 302, 306, 330, 331; easing pain with, 307; hospital, 53; inactivated, 303, 304, 308-309; life expectancy and,

300; live attenuated, 303, 304, 309; LPI and, 62; number of, 305, 306; opting out of, 302, 307-308, 331; record of, 311; schedules for, 306, 312, 330, 331; side effects of, 308-309, 445; spacing out, 333; successful, 323; viral infections and, 340; websites on, 543; well-child visits and, 38
Vaccine Adverse Event Reporting System (VAERS), 309-310, 323, 325
Vaccine Education Center, 333
Vaccine Injury Compensation Program (VICP), 310
Vaccines, xiii, 13, 305, 306; aluminum and, 332, 333; anti-freeze and, 330; autism and, 254, 256, 257, 323-325, 331; combining, 307; communities and, 300; controversies over, 299, 301, 302, 310, 323-331; described, 303; effectiveness of, 304; formaldehyde and, 329, 404; immune responses to, 306; information about, 332-333; optional, 311; politics and, 300; preservatives in, 326, 329; questions about, 303-312, 330; safety with, 306, 325; shortage of, 331-332; specifics of, 312-313; success of, 300, 301; testing, 305; work of, 334
Vaccines and Your Child. Separating fact from Fiction (Offit and Moser), 333
Vaccines For Children (VFC), 40
VAERS. *See* Vaccine Adverse Event Reporting System
Vaginal discharge, 48, 202; described, 538
Vapo-rubs, 341, 499
Vaporizers, 342, 374
Varicella, 304, 305, 309, 338, 369; described, 318-319; treating, 352-353
Varicella vaccine, 319
Varicella-Zoster virus, 352
Vaseline, 83, 388, 422, 445, 499
VCUG. *See* Voiding Cystourethrogram
Vegetables, 107, 166, 174, 397; fiber in, 193; introducing, 175; organic, 177, 396; pesticides and, 394, 395; scrubbing, 409; servings of, 111-112
Ventricular Septal Defect (VSD), 376; described, 538
Vernix, 78; described, 538
Very low birth weight (VLBW), 63
Vesicles, 352; described, 538
Vesicoureteral reflux (VUR), 48, 203, 356; described, 538; treating, 204
VICP. *See* Vaccine Injury Compensation Program
Viral exanthems, 369; described, 352-353
Viral gastroenteritis, 417, 431-432, 436; treating, 351-352
Viral infections, 31, 338-339, 369, 420, 426, 435, 440, 442, 443; bacteria and, 343-344; described, 348-353; exposure to, 337; killing, 304; obesity and, 108; preventing, 340; vaccinations and, 340
Viral titers, 512
Viruses, 303, 335, 339, 340, 356, 370, 425, 438, 450, 514; bacteria and, 343, 344; cold, 64, 341, 343; described, 336; epidemic of, 338; gastrointestinal, 351-352, 369; infections and, 338, 369; monster, 31-32; mouth, 350; rashes and, 352-353, 369; sore throat and, 346
Vision, 34, 263; defects in, 93; development of, 114, 265
Vision screen, 36, 37, 259, 372
Vital signs, 44, 60, 440; taking, 415-416
Vitamin A, 144, 166, 167, 175
Vitamin B12: 172, 377
Vitamin C, 166, 167, 379; iron and, 111, 485
Vitamin D, 100, 110, 155, 160, 165, 171, 172, 484-485; rickets and, 101
Vitamin E, 167
Vitamin K, 50
Vitamins, 88, 100-104, 141, 172, 175, 484-485; preemies and, 63; iron in, 378; prenatal, 100, 132, 258, 449
Vocabulary, 265, 271, 272
Voiding Cystourethrogram (VCUG), 203, 204, 509
Volatile Organic Compounds (VOCs), 392, 404

index

Vomiting, 67, 177, 183, 194-201, 219, 273, 320, 347, 416, 417, 418, 423, 427, 431, 435-437, 442, 446, 459, 460, 463, 506; blood with, 201, 421, 422, 436, 437; coffee ground, 201, 421, 422, 437; dehydration and, 433, 434, 435, 437; diarrhea and, 202, 432, 433; fever and, 201, 449; green, 436; head injuries and, 437; home remedies for, 481, 502; medications and, 467, 481; mucous with, 421; persistent, 201, 436, 437; projectile, 195, 418, 422, 436; questions about, 421, 436; yellow, 436

Von Lengerke, S., 106

Von Willebrand disease, 420; described, 538

VUR. *See* Vesicoureteral reflux

Waiting rooms, 9, 13, 38, 308

Wakenings: night, 223, 225, 228, 232, 280; partial, 210, 229

Wal-Mart, 151, 155, 156, 158, 164, 389, 397; formula from, 161

Walkers, 267, 460

Walking, 269, 272, 284, 382

Warts, home remedies for, 503

Water, 114, 390, 391, 398, 410; bottled, 104, 163, 166; drinking, 165-166; filtered, 166, 401; fluoride and, 103, 104, 166

WBC. *See* White blood cell count

Weaning, 139, 152-153

Websites, 21, 275, 494, 539; reliable, 410, 540-543

Weight, 44, 106, 151, 257

Weight gain, 67, 90, 94, 98, 153

Weight loss, 94, 99, 126, 385; dehydration and, 433

Weight percentile, 107

Weight Watcher, 107

Weissbluth, Marc, 233, 234, 239

Weissbluth theory, 233-234; pros/cons of, 234

Well-child visits, 20, 106, 311; arriving early for, 39; sick visits and, 10, 39; standard, 35-36; vaccinations and, 38

West, Mae: quote of, 3

West Nile Virus (WNV), 82, 353

Wheezing, 180, 182, 195, 200, 372, 373, 375, 407, 426, 427, 428, 506

Whey, 158, 181

Which Toys for Which Child: A Consumer's Guide for Selecting Suitable Toys, Ages Birth Through Five (CPSC), 278

White blood cell count (WBC), 339, 344, 510

White, E., 33

WHO. *See* World Health Organization

Whooping cough, xvii, 301, 304, 308, 426, 427, 428, 431; described, 313; immunity to, 314; outbreaks of, 303, 314; threat from, 312. *See also* Pertussis

Williams, Bern: quote of, 371

Womanly Art of Breastfeeding, The (La Leche League), 140

Womb infection, 51

World Health Organization (WHO), 78, 322; aluminum and, 332; circumcision and, 16; growth charts from, 90, 99; smallpox and, 301, 323

Wounds: cleaning/caring for, 456; closing, 458; infected, 457; puncture, 456

Wright, Karen L., 376

Wrists, broken, 463

X-rays, 354, 461, 462, 507-508

Yeast diaper rash, 41, 86, 369, 491; contagiousness of, 359; described, 358, 452-453

Yeast infections, 77, 85-86, 134, 139, 483; breastfeeding and, 86; problems with, 131

Yellow fever vaccine, 306

Yersina infection, 432

YMCA, daycare and, 32

Zantac, 95, 479-480

ZERO to THREE: National Center for Infants, Toddlers, and Families, address/phone number for, 543

Zinc, 109-111, 172, 499

Zwiener, R. Jeff, 194

COME VISIT US AT BABY411.COM!

WHAT'S ONLINE?

- Rash-o-rama! Check out pictures of common rashes, birth marks and more. Click on BONUS.
- THE LATEST NEWS on medical research for babies on the BLOG.
- MESSAGE BOARDS with in-depth discussions of hot-button parenting topics.
- Sign up for a FREE E-NEWSLETTER!
- Read all the 411 books on your iPad, mobile device & desktop.

How to reach the authors:

- Email: authors@baby411.com
- Follow us on Twitter @baby411
- Like us on Facebook.com/Expecting411

More books by the Fields:

- Baby Bargains: Secrets to saving 20% to 50% on baby gear! See it at BabyBargains.com